Rational Suicide, Irrational Laws

American Psychology-Law Society Series

Rational Suicide, Irrational Laws

*Examining Current Approaches to Suicide
in Policy and Law*

Susan Stefan

OXFORD
UNIVERSITY PRESS

OXFORD
UNIVERSITY PRESS

Oxford University Press is a department of the University of Oxford. It furthers
the University's objective of excellence in research, scholarship, and education
by publishing worldwide. Oxford is a registered trade mark of Oxford University
Press in the UK and certain other countries.

Published in the United States of America by Oxford University Press
198 Madison Avenue, New York, NY 10016, United States of America.

© Oxford University Press 2016

First Edition published in 2016

Cataloging-in-Publication data is on file at the Library of Congress
ISBN 978-0-19-998119-9

9 8 7 6 5 4 3 2 1

Printed by Webcom, Canada

Estragon: I can't go on like this.

Vladimir: That's what you think.
　　　　　　　　　　　　—Samuel Becket (*Waiting for Godot*, 1954)

To my mother, Gabrielle Stefan (June 13, 1917–August 20, 2006):

I told you that I could not live without you, and I was right.

For more than three thousand days now, I have been unable to live without you.

To my husband Wes, my best friend Jamie, and my sister Didi:

In the darkness, you have always been the lights along the shore.

And to all the people reading this who cannot go on living, and do,

Especially to the people kind enough to share their stories with me:

I hope that this book does you the justice you deserve. I am glad you are still here.

Contents

Series Foreword

This book series is sponsored by the American Psychology-Law Society (APLS). APLS is an interdisciplinary organization devoted to scholarship, practice, and public service in psychology and law. Its goals include advancing the contributions of psychology to the understanding of law and legal institutions through basic and applied research; promoting the education of psychologists in matters of law and the education of legal personnel in matters of psychology; and informing the psychological and legal communities and the general public of current research, educational, and service activities in the field of psychology and law. APLS membership includes psychologists from the academic, research, and clinical practice communities as well as members of the legal community. Research and practice is represented in both the civil and criminal legal arenas. APLS has chosen Oxford University Press as a strategic partner because of its commitment to scholarship, quality, and the international dissemination of ideas. These strengths will help APLS reach its goal of educating the psychology and legal professions and the general public about important developments in psychology and law. The focus of the book series reflects the diversity of the field of psychology and law, as we publish books on a broad range of topics.

In the latest book in the series, *Rational Suicide, Irrational Laws*, Susan Stefan, a legal scholar, takes the approach of an investigative journalist and interviews individuals who had attempted suicide in order to reflect on and represent various views with respect to the issues of suicide and attempted suicide. Stefan's approach was not one of research per se; that is, she did not survey and interview individuals with the objective of representing these data as contributing to generalizable knowledge but, rather, with the intent of bringing to life the voices of those who had been affected by the very issues that Stefan addresses in this book. The purpose of this book, as Stefan writes in her introduction, is to examine and evaluate many of the legal doctrines and policy decisions across the varied areas where law and policy must respond to suicide and attempted suicide and to attempt to suggest a more consistent and helpful approach to these issues. Indeed, Stefan has done just that. Over the course of ten chapters, Stefan brings to life the legal and policy implications of various topics related to suicide and assisted suicide, including: the law of competence; the right to die, involuntary commitment, and the Constitution; assisted suicide in the United States; international perspectives on assisted suicide and euthanasia; assisted suicide and the medical profession; mental health professionals and suicide; types of suicide; discrimination on the basis of suicidality; policy and legal barriers to suicide prevention and treatment; and assisted suicide among those with psychiatric diagnoses. Stefan also includes model statutes with respect to civil commitment and provider immunity as well as for assisted suicide.

Rational Suicide, Irrational Laws presents a comprehensive and detailed analysis of these issues in a readable and relatable way, highlighted by and punctuated throughout with interviews of those who have been affected by these issues. Scholars, researchers, policymakers, and practitioners will undoubtedly find that this book has the potential to help shape the future of interactions with policy and the legal system.

Patricia A. Zapf
Series Editor

Acknowledgments

There are so many people who made this book possible. Lisa Daniels, Wes Daniels, Adrienne Stefan, and Collette Hanna put in hours of mind-numbing drudgery so that I could literally continue writing this book to the last minute. Research assistance beyond my wildest dreams was provided by that peerless researcher and poet, *Jonathan Ezekiel* (this is the closest my publisher can get to printing your name in neon). Thank you also for research assistance by another superb poet, Laura Ziegler, and by Pam Lucken and Rayni Rabinowitz at the University of Miami. The University of Miami faculty and staff were immensely supportive.

I greatly benefited from the comments and insight of Chelsea Andrus, Cara Anna, Dr. Paul Appelbaum, Dr. Michael Allen, Michael Allen, Esq. (yes, there are two of them); Clyde Bergstresser, Esq., Dr. Jon Berlin, Karen Bower, Martha Brock, Ira Burnim, Lisa Cappocia, Beckie Child, Prof. Mary Coombs, "Colleen," Dr. Glenn Currier, Katie Daniels, Laura Delano, Anne DiNoto, the Disability Rights Bar Association list serve, Sean Donovan, Dr. John Draper, Dr. Joel Dvoskin, Nick Dukehart, Dr. Robert Factor, Wyatt Ferrera, Bob Fleischner, Jenn Haussler Garing, Beth Harris, Leah Harris, Jenn Hurtado, Lynn Legere, Dr. Chuck Lidz, Cathy Levin, Gail M., Jennifer Mathis, Stephen McCrea, "Mark McPherson," Richard McKeon, Steve Miccio, Justin Mikel, Mark Nelson, Dr. Tony Ng, Carolyn Noble, Pam Nolan, Christine O'Hagan, Dr. Mark Pearlmutter, Jane Pearson, Steve Periard, Dr. Seth Powsner, Anne Rider, Josh Sebastian, Michelle Sese-Khalid, Cheryl Sharp, Skip Simpson, Esq., Cate Solomon, Dese'Rae Stage, Carrie Stoker, Mary Elizabeth Van Pelt,

Carli Whitchurch, Lex Wortley, Laura Ziegler, the many people who wanted to remain anonymous, even in the acknowledgments, and the few who were lost to follow-up.

Thank you to the 244 people who responded to the survey. I tried to listen very carefully to what each of you had to say.

My editors at Oxford University Press, Sarah Harrington and Andrea Zekus, held my hand, responded promptly to my emails, and were everything editors should be. I am deeply grateful to them.

Introduction: The Message from the Front Lines

I would not tell anyone else that he or she should choose death with dignity. My question is: Who has the right to tell me that I don't deserve this choice?

—Brittany Maynard

It's not a psychiatric illness to take a look at your life and think this is never going to get better.

—"Kara"

What is scary is the level of distress. I felt very trapped, not so much that I wanted to die, as that I didn't want to live the life that I was living, and I just wanted a way out.

—Leah Harris

What we did is not against the law, and all our rights are taken away from us, we have fewer rights than prisoners.

—Josh Sebastian

Suicide. Is it a public health scourge or a basic civil right? Should it always be prevented, with state intervention if necessary, as Justice Antonin Scalia and many mental health professionals believe? Is it a fundamental right that the state cannot interfere with, as the American Civil Liberties Union (ACLU) and Dr. Thomas Szasz believe? The rest of us struggle in the murky middle, gray areas and inconsistent and contradictory reactions. And our policies and laws reflect this: they are inconsistent and contradictory. The purpose of this book is to examine and evaluate many of the legal doctrines and policy decisions across the varied areas where law and policy must respond to suicide and attempted suicide, and try to suggest an approach that will be more consistent and helpful to us all.

Each year, the Gallup poll asks Americans whether suicide is morally acceptable. An overwhelming number say no. They are asked in the same poll whether physician-assisted suicide is morally acceptable. It's been divided at a close 50-50 for almost a decade.[1] Over the years, physicians have also been asked their opinions about suicide and physician-assisted suicide.[2] Every year, conferences and colloquia are held to discuss new treatments and screening tools for suicidal people and trends in suicide prevention.

Until very recently, no one has asked people who have attempted suicide for their opinions about much of anything. This is beginning to change. In 2014, the American Association of Suicidology for the first time added a new section specifically for suicide attempt survivors, and its annual conference featured a panel of people who had attempted suicide.[3] This was spurred in large part by the efforts of talented and courageous people such as Cara Anna,[4] Dese'Rae Stage,[5] Will Hall,[6] and Leah Harris.[7] In July 2014, the National Alliance for Suicide Prevention published the first guide to suicide prevention by people who had attempted suicide.[8]

Attending to the perspectives and opinions of people who have attempted suicide is still so new that its very nomenclature is in dispute. For years, "suicide survivors" was the term designating the family and loved ones of people who had ended their lives,[9] rather than people who had survived suicide

[1] See Chapter 3.
[2] See Chapters 3 and 5.
[3] This presentation can be accessed on YouTube.
[4] Cara Anna, *What Happens Now?* ATTEMPT SURVIVORS.COM BLOG, Jan. 5, 2015, www.attemptsurvivors.com.
[5] Associated Press, *Collection of Photos and Survival Stories of Attempted Suicides Curated by Brooklyn Photographer Offer Hope and Insight*, DAILY NEWS, Apr. 14, 2013, http://www.nydailynews.com/life-style/health/suicide-survivors-speak-prevention-efforts-article-1.1316461.
[6] Will Hall, *Living with Suicidal Feelings*, BEYOND MEDS: ALTERNATIVES TO PSYCHIATRY, Apr. 24, 2013, www.beyondmeds.com/2013/4/24/living-with-suicidal-feelings.
[7] Leah Harris, *Twenty Years Since My Last Suicide Attempt: Reflections*, MAD IN AMERICA, Oct. 7, 2013, www.madinamerica.com/2013/10/twenty-years-last-suicide-attempt-reflections/.
[8] NATIONAL ACTION ALLIANCE FOR SUICIDE PREVENTION: SUICIDE ATTEMPT SURVIVORS TASK FORCE, THE WAY FORWARD: PATHWAYS TO HOPE, RECOVERY, AND WELLNESS WITH INSIGHTS FROM LIVED EXPERIENCE (2014), http://actionallianceforsuicideprevention.org/sites/actionallianceforsuicideprevention.org/files/The-Way-Forward-Final-2014-07-01.pdf.
[9] GEORGE HOWE COLT, THE ENIGMA OF SUICIDE (1991).

attempts. Those latter survivors were pretty much erased by the stigma and shame of having attempted suicide. Now sometimes people who have attempted suicide are called "suicide attempt survivors," and people whose loved ones have committed suicide are called "loss survivors." Battles over language are a staple of suicide law and policy, from the insistence on "aid in dying" to designate assisted suicide to controversy over the term "parasuicide" to designate nonsuicidal self-injury.[10]

People who have attempted suicide have only recently begun to talk about it. As Eileen MacNamara, columnist for the *Boston Globe*, wrote, "Suicide remains the sorrow that still struggles to speak its name."[11] But they have so much to offer us. When I write books, I have always thought that the first order of business is to consult the people who are primarily affected by the policies and laws I am discussing, especially when the policies and laws are ostensibly intended to benefit them. So I read as many online stories from suicidal people as I could find—and there are many.[12] I created an online survey for people who had attempted suicide and was surprised when hundreds of people responded.[13] And I had in-depth interviews with almost a hundred people who had made serious suicide attempts.

I also think it's important to talk to people who have to implement policies and laws on the front lines, in order to chart the deep and painful chasm between the intent underlying policies and laws and how they actually play out in practice. So I interviewed not only people who had survived suicide attempts but people whose loved ones had killed themselves, emergency department physicians, emergency medical technicians (EMTs) and paramedics, civil rights and malpractice attorneys, psychiatrists, psychologists,

---

[10] Proponents of physician-assisted suicide bitterly oppose the inclusion of the word "suicide" in describing the proposals they favor. People who self-injure strongly reject the term "parasuicide" to describe what they do, since they have no desire to commit suicide, but rather to stay alive. Since I think the word suicide refers to a person intentionally taking affirmative steps that will inevitably end his or her own life, I support the term "assisted suicide" and oppose the term "parasuicide."

[11] The quotation is from 2007, quoted in MASSACHUSETTS COALITION FOR SUICIDE PREVENTION, MASSACHUSETTS STRATEGIC PLAN FOR SUICIDE PREVENTION PLAN (2009), http://www.mass.gov/eohhs/docs/dph/com-health/injury/suicide-strategic-plan.pdf.

[12] See notes 3–6; see also *Talking with Janice Sorenson*, TALKING ABOUT SUICIDE, Nov. 5, 2012, http://talkingaboutsuicide.com/2012/11/05/talking-with-janice-sorensen/; *More from Canada, Part 2: Listening to Wendy Matthews*, TALKING ABOUT SUICIDE, Oct. 22, 2012, www.talkingaboutsuicide.com/2012/10/22/more-from-Canada-part-2-listening-to-Wendy-Matthews/; Laura Delano, *On the Urge to Take My Life, and My Decision to Take It Back from the "Mental Health" System Instead*, MAD IN AMERICA, Sept. 9, 2013, www.madinamerica.com/2013/09/urge-take-life-decision-take-back-mental-health-system-instead/.

[13] The survey and its results are available in Appendix B.

nurses, peer counselors, and social workers. My interviews with people about their professional experiences almost invariably were diverted by stories about mothers, fathers, sisters, brothers, school friends, roommates, and work colleagues who had killed themselves.

I also read about and, in some cases, interviewed, a sample of the interesting intersection: people who have attempted suicide and who are now implementing programs, policies, and laws relating to suicide prevention and treatment. Marsha Linehan, who developed dialectic behavior therapy, the most successful treatment approach for suicidality to date, was herself suicidal.[14] So was Kay Redfield Jamison, the best-selling author and expert on bipolar disorder.[15] So—by definition—are the people who run peer groups and crisis centers for people who are suicidal.

I make no claim that my surveys or interviews are scientific or random; as is always the case with surveys and interviews, only the people who want to respond do so. The survey was anonymous and did not ask for age, gender, or ethnicity. I did make a concerted effort to interview men who had attempted suicide; perhaps tellingly, two-thirds of the people who were lost to follow-up when I sought permission to use quotations from their interviews were men. The voices of the people I interviewed will be heard throughout this book, but I wanted to begin with the news they bring from their own experiences. Suicide survivors have all sorts of different perspectives, of course, and the very differences in their stories serves as a caution to those who would generalize about suicide. Marsha Linehan and Kay Redfield Jamison drew extremely different conclusions from their experiences. But they shared one thing in common: fear and shame at disclosing their histories,[16] requiring decades of professional success and acceptance to even contemplate the possibility.

I learned from my survey and interviews that people want to talk— desperately want to be heard—but are still afraid to do so publicly. More than half of my interviewees requested that I use pseudonyms when quoting them, especially among the younger people. And they have so much to tell us. We will hear their different stories throughout this book, but I will begin with the aggregate: the results of the survey.

Two hundred and forty people who had attempted suicide responded to the survey. Just under 40% had attempted suicide only once. Forty-five percent had attempted suicide between two and five times and 18% had attempted suicide more than five times. For the purposes of the survey,

---

14 Benedict Carey, *Expert on Mental Illness Reveals Her Own Fight*, N. Y. TIMES, June 23, 2011, http://www.nytimes.com/2011/06/23/health/23lives. html?pagewanted=all&_r=0.

15 KAY REDFIELD JAMISON, NIGHT FALLS FAST (paperback, 2000).

16 "I cannot die a coward," said Linehan, see note 13. Jamison writes, "I have had many concerns about writing a book that so explicitly describes my own attacks of mania, depression, and psychosis," AN UNQUIET MIND (1997).

I asked them to answer questions about their first suicide attempt. Sixteen percent of them wished they had succeeded that first time, and about 37% were glad they failed. The highest response—just under 50%—were ambivalent, unsure about whether they were glad to have survived.

When asked to choose among three popular explanations for suicide: "powerless or hopelessness of changing circumstances," "despair or feeling of meaninglessness," and "sadness or grief at loss or anticipated loss," more than half picked "powerlessness or hopelessness" as their first choice.[17] This would suggest that policies to prevent suicide and help people who are suicidal should focus on supporting and increasing feelings of power, agency, control, and hope. By the same token, policies and laws that add to feelings of powerlessness and hopelessness may deepen and exacerbate suicidality over the long term.

After their first suicide attempt, 50% of my respondents were hospitalized on a psychiatric unit (27.5% involuntarily and the rest voluntarily) and 50% were not. I asked the people who were hospitalized to list which treatments were helpful, providing the choices of therapy, medication, the hospitalization itself, or "other." People choosing "other" were given the opportunity to explain their answer. Almost 50% of the respondents, who had been specifically guided by the question to focus on helpful aspects of their hospitalization, checked "other" to tell me in no uncertain terms that nothing about the hospitalization helped at all, and to detail all the damage that hospitalization created in their lives. For some people, it was the conditions of the hospital. One person said she wanted policymakers to know:

> Don't underestimate the importance of clean, well-maintained,
> well-lit facilities in the healing process. Leave me in a dark, moldy,
> filthy shithole with crumbling walls for two weeks and I'm not
> going to stop feeling like shit.[18]

For others, it was the treatment they received, especially seclusion: "People need human contact after an attempt; isolation on suicide watch makes things worse;"[19] "after my suicide attempt I was locked in a quiet room . . . not allowed to bathe or brush my teeth. I was also not allowed to have my eyeglasses."[20] For some people, the entire idea that they should be hospitalized with people who were mentally ill just because they had attempted suicide did not make sense:

> It is not helpful to be in a mental ward with seriously mentally
> ill patients or drug addicts after a suicide attempt. I know we get

---

[17] Grief at loss or anticipated loss was the first choice of barely 10% of respondents. This is interesting when compared to a survey of people who used May House, a voluntary homelike residence in England for people who were suicidal, where "grief" was highest on the list of reasons for being suicidal.

[18] Survey No. 223.

[19] Survey No. 236.

[20] Survey No. 193.

locked up for our own safety, but being in such a sterile and noisy
environment does not make any of us feel better about our place in
life and basically we all do our best to get out as fast as possible. The
others I have met in mental wards that are suicide attempters have
been professionals, nurses and of course, drug addicts—but most
of us tried to end our lives because of the overwhelming despair
and hurts and wounding of living in this world, not because we are
crazy, but because of our awareness of life traumas.

But the rejection of hospitalization included people who believed that the
cause of their suicidality was a biological illness. Even people who believe
that they have a mental illness, and who credit medications for keeping their
suicidality at bay, felt fundamentally alienated in a hospital filled with people
whose problems, they felt, bore no resemblance to their own.

Some people did think the hospitalization itself had helped, and in a few
of my interviews, some people said it helped a lot. But they were in the minority, and they were all people who had hospitalized themselves voluntarily.
Ironically, when people *sought* hospitalization, many reported a difficult time
being admitted:

I know of at least one psych hospital that will not admit anyone
not willing or able to express a very firm and detailed plan to act.
In my own case, being turned away when I approached this facility
BEFORE I went so far as to settle on a plan furthered my frustration
with carrying on and led me to attempt again in private. Only after
again failing in my desire to die was I admitted.[21]

Other people who thought hospitalization might be helpful were frustrated
with the short-term nature of hospitalization and lack of in-depth treatment.

Paradoxically, people also couldn't get help in the community. One person reported that "I was kicked out of an outpatient program for being suicidal,"[22] another that the $40 copayment for each therapy session put therapy
out of reach,[23] and many people reported that they couldn't get help at all
until and unless they were deep in suicidal crisis:

Access to continued treatment is so important. I'm barely keeping
my rent paid and don't have the money for extravagant psychiatrist
copays (which are considered specialist treatment) upfront every
2–4 weeks. . . It can be attractive to do something drastic because
you know you'll either get help or you won't have to worry about it
anymore.[24]

---

[21] Survey No. 227.
[22] Survey No. 179.
[23] Survey No. 193.
[24] Survey No. 102.

Thus, our policies and practices regarding suicide create an irrational incentive structure where people understand they have to attempt suicide to get help, help which is of questionable utility, while community-based approaches that are less expensive and work are underfunded. We have a system that doesn't work for anyone—neither the people who are supposed to be providing help, nor the people who are supposed to be receiving it.

Mental health professionals in my interviews also sounded powerless and hopeless: asked to do the impossible with ever-dwindling resources, profoundly anxious about liability, genuinely baffled about how to help some of their patients, plagued by insurance demands and paperwork. I was told by a hospital social worker that staff members focused on stabilization rather than suicidality because insurance-authorized hospital stays were so short that hospital staff figured patients would do the long-term work on suicidality in the community. A few weeks later a community mental health professional told me that the authorized fifty-minute appointments every two weeks were nowhere near enough to provide the intensive help that suicidal people needed; that was what hospitalization was for.

Thus, in our current system, some people who are actually suicidal lie to avoid hospitalization; some people who are not suicidal lie to access hospital beds, but almost no one gets help specifically targeted at suicidality. Some clinicians who determine a person does not need hospitalization admit the person anyway to avoid potential liability, and some clinicians who determine hospitalization would be appropriate don't admit the person because there are insufficient inpatient beds available. And there is no solid basis in research or in the reports of people who have attempted suicide to think that hospitalization helps most people very much or at all.[25]

We have some idea what helps, and so do the people who answered my survey: community public health support programs, such as those used by the Air Force,[26] dialectical behavior therapy,[27] and peer supports.[28] Many survey respondents and interviewees mentioned spiritual faith, meditation, and other forms of mindfulness. I suspect personal care assistants (PCAs) would help too.[29] So we do have some idea what works, but little concerted effort is made to ensure that suicidal people can actually have access to these less expensive and less traumatic community resources.

And even those programs don't begin to tackle the upstream problem: what caused the person to become so miserable in the first place? It is

---

[25] See Chapters 2, 6, and 9.
[26] See Chapter 8.
[27] See Chapter 9.
[28] See Chapter 9.
[29] See Chapter 10.

this upstream landscape that is missing from the downstream emergency department or crisis evaluation, as one of my survey respondents noted:

> Urbanization and the accompanying break-down of community that causes social isolation is a major contributor to mental health problems. Mental health professionals encounter people in a moment of crisis; the person may have no way to explain what's going on with them and the professionals have no way to judge accurately what's going on. Many people lack problem solving skills and survival skills and have been under great stress in a near crisis state for a long time, perhaps since childhood. Building healthy communities would be a pro-active way to prevent these problems from developing into grave crises.[30]

This comment resonated with me as I conducted my in-depth interviews. Although every person I interviewed had a unique story to tell, the most striking impression that emerged from my interviews was a sense of two very different groups of suicidal people. One group had histories of extremely traumatic childhoods, filled with violence, abuse, chaos, and often unfathomable cruelty. Many of those people began wishing they were dead when they were very, very young. They had multiple suicide attempts and lives filled with loss:

> My mother certainly must have known I was using drugs because I was using her drugs. She had speed. She had five kids and I took her drugs. The school people had to know because I passed out on the way to school. In true addict style, I took two while I was sitting in the guidance counselor's office. . . . I was born of incest . . . I was the reminder every time my mother looked at me of what had happened . . . She couldn't stand me. I knew I was the problem and if I wasn't there, her life would be better. When *Roe v. Wade* got passed, she said, "I am so glad that got passed, I went to get an abortion with you, I am so glad it's legal, because I was so scared I couldn't go through with it, what do you want for dinner tonight?" My grandmother said, "I remember the day you were born, it was the worst day of my life." My grandfather sexually abused me. The first time I tried to kill myself, I was eight years old.[31]

Another woman told me:

> I was violently sexually abused by a neighbor who was also a law enforcement officer. When I say violent, I mean just that,

---

[30] Survey No. 216.
[31] Interview with Lynn Legere (Dec. 16, 2013).

not fondling, not just sex, gun held to my head, ages 4–8,
burned, whipped, handcuffed, real sadistic stuff that kind of
murders innocence very early on. Because the neighbor was law
enforcement, I didn't report.[32]

Nevertheless, these people hung on stubbornly through miserable lives, grasping at the tiniest straws of kindness and hope, and showed an empathy and depth that humbled me. Many became human service workers: peer counselors, therapists, and social workers, or advocates for others who were vulnerable and needed protection. For some of the people who came from the greatest abyss of misery, faith and spirituality almost literally raised them from the dead.

The other group had relatively intact and supportive families, who provided at least some financial, emotional, and practical support. These were the kinds of families that kept people alive, even when they were hesitating on the brink of suicide:

[One] morning I couldn't sleep and at 5:30 I wandered out on
the unit and [an older male patient] was reading the Bible. He
was there because he was suicidal. He had no prior mental health
problems but his adult daughter had killed herself five years ago
and since then he's been struggling with depression. I have this
crazy soft spot for my dad, I love my dad, and that made it real
to me, what it would do to my parents. I was so stuck in my head
and the cognitive disorder that in reality people would be better
off without me and it would affect them but not that much and in
any event I wouldn't be here to deal with it. But after that I couldn't
consider suicide to be a valid option, because I love my dad too
much.[33]

These families were not unproblematic. Many of my interviewees felt driven to be perfect—straight A, hyperaccomplished people who never felt good enough on the inside. Their suicidality often emerged around the time they started applying to college, in college, or in the context of jobs or marriages where they felt they were failures. While the people with trauma histories often had concurrent substance abuse, the people in this group were more likely to struggle with eating disorders.

For many people who didn't have histories of childhood trauma, and whose suicidality emerged later in life, suicidal feelings were alien and frightening, and were more often identified as part of an illness, to which they readily looked to mental health professionals for help. For people with trauma histories, whose families frequently included suicides, the thought of death and

---

[32] Interview with Jenn Hurtado (Dec. 16, 2013).
[33] Interview with Carli Whitchurch (Apr. 18, 2014).

suicide was pretty much a constant from childhood on, and sometimes felt comforting: a potential escape route from an unbearable life. Rather than feeling threatened by suicidal feelings, many regarded suicide as an option that gave them the strength to make it through another day. Of course, even people with supportive parents can have trauma histories. One woman told me that

> I was diagnosed with PTSD. . . when I was 14, years ago, my 19 year old neighbor shot himself in the head after I threatened to tell his parents and my parents that he had been sexually abusing me since I was six. I am not sure they knew he was abusing me. I was walking back to my house I heard the gun go off. I didn't realize that had an effect on me until after therapy.[34]

The people with extensive childhood histories of trauma generally were damaged rather than helped by the current mental health framework, with its omnipresent shadow of involuntary detention, restraint, and seclusion, and diagnoses that don't begin to helpfully describe what these people have been through. As one respondent said, "The suicide attempt is not the crisis in one's life. There are precipitating events that lead up to it that are the crisis."[35] This is a core and crucial insight, which should inform policy;[36] it already informs some of the most successful treatment approaches, including those that centrally focus on narrative.[37]

And certainly, the mental health framework itself is only one way of conceptualizing responses to suicide, and a relatively modern one at that. It is considered a reform from the times when suicide was a sin or a crime. For some, including a number of my survey respondents, the decision to end one's life, like decisions to refuse treatment or decisions about reproduction, is a civil right, a fundamental liberty interest, a personal, intimate, and private decision that belongs to the person alone, which should not be the subject of state intervention.[38]

The increasing number of states and countries around the world enacting physician-assisted suicide laws also operate on the assumption that at least some people who want to control the timing of their deaths are behaving understandably and should be supported in their wishes. Some of the people I interviewed and who responded to the survey had been in enormous emotional pain and suicidal for a long, long time, and nothing had ever helped them. Just what are our rights over our bodies, over treatment refusal, over how long we live with relentless pain? Is suicide, like abortion

---

[34] Interview with Christine O'Hagan (Nov. 21, 2013).
[35] Survey No. 66.
[36] See Chapter 9 for an explanation of why this is so difficult.
[37] See KONRAD A. MICHEL & DAVID A. JOBES, EDS. BUILDING A THERAPEUTIC ALLIANCE WITH THE SUICIDAL PATIENT (2011).
[38] Survey Nos. 203 & 120.

and homosexuality, a moral and social issue that ultimately boils down to individual rights? A plurality of my survey respondents supported extending assisted suicide to people with emotional problems.

Certainly, it's no good to say people should be prevented from killing themselves at all costs, because "all costs" is precisely what our society is unwilling to pay to prevent suicide, from gun control to easy access to effective community support. Is it unconstitutional to exclude a deeply suffering person from assisted suicide if society is unwilling to provide the means to alleviate that suffering? At least one Supreme Court justice suggested this might be the case.[39] Is it hypocrisy to exclude people from assisted suicide in a country that has made clear that suicide prevention is a low priority, where even basic healthcare is a matter of titanic political and judicial controversy? Or is assisted suicide just an easy out for a society that owes its citizens a lot more than abandonment disguised as autonomy?

These are extraordinarily difficult questions of law and social policy, which will be addressed in this book. My great ambition was to develop a "unified field theory" that encompassed suicide in this country—both the kind we want to assist and the kind we want to prevent. But these questions are only the beginning of the situations in which law and policy must respond to issues involving suicide. Most people are at least familiar in passing with legal issues such as whether people should have a constitutional right to die, or whether a psychiatrist should be liable if his or her patient commits suicide. But there are many other questions: Is firing an employee for attempting suicide disability discrimination? Can a college exclude a student who attempted suicide from returning to its dorms? Are the police ever responsible in a case of "suicide by cop," and if so, when? Do the operators of the Golden Gate Bridge have a legal responsibility to put up barriers to prevent people from jumping off? Is the survivor of a suicide pact criminally responsible for assisting a suicide? Should the do not resuscitate (DNR) order of a person who attempted to kill himself be honored? Should a person who attempted suicide lose her parental rights?

All of these are issues that arise in law and policy every day, and which have been answered in conflicting ways over time, by different courts in different states, and sometimes by different courts in the same state. Many of them have implications for people who have attempted suicide and who are trying to get on with their lives. Some of my interviewees had questions for me about their legal rights, laws they found confusing, situations that seemed wrong: After I tell my university health service staff members in confidence that I am suicidal, can they really send uniformed security to escort me out of my dorm and forbid me from coming back? Does being picked up by the police for being suicidal really mean I will have a police record? Was the hospital staff member telling the truth when she said, "You have to take medicine or your insurance won't pay for the stay"?

---

[39] See Chapter 2.

This book is an attempt to survey law and policy about suicide generally, and especially law and policy relating to medical and mental health professionals, assisted suicide, discrimination, and what works to help people. There are certain major subjects I do not cover in the book. Suicide in jails and prisons is an incredibly important topic. I could not readily interview people who had attempted suicide in prison and jails to hear their stories, and I try not to write about subjects unless I have talked to and surveyed the people affected by the laws and policies I am discussing. I am not confident I could do justice to this topic and have omitted it.[40]

In my survey, I asked, "If you could tell suicide prevention policymakers and mental health professionals three things, what would they be?" There was one message that was by far the most common. Sometimes it was delivered concisely. "Listen," said Wyatt Ferrara, his message echoed by many people who longed to share what they had learned at such cost: "Listen to we who have traveled that path and lived to talk about what helped."[41] "DON'T put someone in a ward full of other people in emotional distress, treat them as if they are annoying and difficult, and pump them full of drugs. LISTEN for God's sake."[42] "Don't come from a place of preventing—come from a place of connecting . . . Most importantly be present and LISTEN."[43] "Listen, listen, listen. Listen with your whole being."[44] "Be kind. Be understanding. Listen with your heart."[45]

In writing this book, I have tried to fulfill the trust that people placed in me by telling me their stories. Obviously, my opinions are my own, and my mistakes even more so. There is something cloying about calling people inspirational, but I was humbled by my conversations with many of my interviewees. I have tried very hard not to let my affection and admiration for the many people who spoke to me, and my fear and grief for several people who had vanished by the time I asked for permission to use quotes from their interviews, affect my analysis of these issues. But, to everyone who spoke to me: even talking to you for an hour or an hour and a half made me so glad you were alive. So, all of you who spoke to me, it was an honor, and, even when your stories haunted me, I learned a lot. Thank you.

---

[40] But see Lindsay M. Hayes & National Institute of Corrections, Prison Suicide: An Overview and Guide to Prevention (2012); and, more generally Thomas J. Fagan & Robert K. Ax, eds., Correctional Mental Health Handbook (2002), and Terry Kupers, Prison Madness: The Mental Health Crisis Behind Bars and What We Must Do About It (1999).

[41] Survey No. 237.

[42] Survey No. 40.

[43] Survey No. 75.

[44] Survey No. 93.

[45] Survey No. 209.

Rational Suicide, Irrational Laws

1

"Sane" and "Insane" Suicide: The Law of Competence

"Any human being has the potential to become suicidal—the problem doesn't lie in the person's brain."

—Laura Delano, interviewee

Introduction: The Case of Josh Sebastian

Most of us don't want to die. Some of us do. This book is about how our policy and law respond to people who want to die, especially those who try to kill themselves. This chapter concerns the distinction between people who are incompetent or lack capacity, and those who do have competence or capacity. This is a crucial first inquiry, because people who lack capacity in our society lose the right to make decisions, as a matter of law, including decisions about their own bodies and lives. "Thus, competence and liberty are inextricably interwoven."[1]

The first and most important distinction all societies have made throughout time in responding to people who attempted suicide was to differentiate between people who were responsible, competent, sane, rational (or whatever words were in vogue at the time), and those who, depending on the era, were "furiously mad," not responsible, incompetent, insane, lacking capacity, or irrational.[2]

---

[1] George J. Annas & Joan E. Densberger, *Competence to Refuse Medical Treatment: Autonomy vs. Paternalism*, 15 TOL. L. REV. 561 (1984).

[2] I do not mean to suggest that all these terms are completely synonymous: competence, properly understood, involves primarily cognitive abilities, whereas insanity has sometimes involved volitional abilities. Some have argued for "affective incompetence," a minority position that I address later in this chapter.

For most of the history of Western civilization, the first group has been understood to constitute, by far, the vast majority of people who contemplate, attempt, and complete suicide. They have been treated as despicable, criminals, heretics, and cowards, but they have not been treated as lacking capacity or moral agency. Only in the last century have some mental health professionals attempted to draw all suicidal people into their diagnostic embrace, insisting that suicidality is usually the product of mental illness and (less frequently) equating suicidality with lack of capacity. Of course, the more that mental health professionals insist that suicidality is the result of mental illness that they can treat, or that it reflects incompetence or incapacity, the more they create social expectations and corresponding legal responsibilities relating to their suicidal patients that they cannot meet and should not bear.

There is an alternative model, and the story of Josh Sebastian embodies it.

In the summer of 2012, a medical ethics committee sat around a table in Wisconsin. The committee members included several psychiatrists and other physicians, nurses, social workers, and (of course) legal counsel to the committee, a health lawyer. For a third of the meeting, they permitted the patient they were discussing, Josh Sebastian, to address them.

Josh Sebastian was a 44-year-old man who was consistently and determinedly suicidal. He had been hospitalized six months earlier, after barely surviving an extremely serious suicide attempt. He had shot himself in the abdomen, fracturing his spine. He had planned this attempt in minute detail, including ensuring that his body would not be discovered by people to whom it would cause pain and distress.

After medical treatment and surgery for his injuries, Mr. Sebastian was committed involuntarily to a psychiatric institution. This did not mean that he was not legally competent. Wisconsin law explicitly insists that people who are committed to a mental institution retain their competence. Most people who are involuntarily civilly committed *are* competent. The relevant standard for involuntary civil commitment in Wisconsin requires a person to be "mentally ill," "a proper subject for treatment," and "dangerous."[3] Each of these terms is specifically defined through statutes, regulations, and case law, which we will discuss later.

Mr. Sebastian's six-month inpatient commitment was about to expire. Although he had received various medications and therapies, he remained determined to kill himself. By itself, this was not unusual—psychiatric hospitalization often has no effect on a patient's suicidality, and sometimes makes it worse.[4] But Josh Sebastian refused to engage in the time-honored

---

[3] WISC. STAT. § 51.20(1).

[4] JOEL PARIS, HALF IN LOVE WITH DEATH: MANAGING THE CHRONICALLY SUICIDAL PATIENT (2006); DAVID DAWSON & HARRIET MACMILLAN, RELATIONSHIP MANAGEMENT OF THE BORDERLINE PATIENT: FROM UNDERSTANDING TO TREATMENT (1993); DOUG JACOBS ET AL., PRACTICE GUIDELINES FOR THE ASSESSMENT AND TREATMENT OF PATIENTS WITH SUICIDAL IDEATION (American Psychiatric Association 2003).

pretextual rituals (recognized as such by both patients and mental health professionals) of earnestly denying that he had any intent to kill himself and signing whatever contracts for safety his keepers required as the price of his freedom. He said, calmly and bluntly, that he still very much wanted to die.

The question before the ethics committee was whether the hospital should petition to continue his involuntary commitment. Sebastian was clearly and explicitly dangerous to himself, but the psychiatrists who had been treating him had the honesty to acknowledge that they doubted that he was mentally ill as defined by the statute and regulations. Even if he was mentally ill, they were even more dubious that he was a proper subject for treatment under the statute.

The Wisconsin involuntary commitment statute defines "mental illness" as "a substantial disorder of thought, mood, perception, orientation, or memory which grossly impairs judgment, behavior, capacity to recognize reality, or ability to meet the ordinary demands of life, but does not include alcoholism."[5] Mr. Sebastian was certainly not psychotic. He gave a lucid and articulate account of why he wanted to kill himself, a desire that had persisted for many years despite many efforts at treatment.

The fact that his suicidality had persisted for more than twenty years despite many efforts at treatment particularly troubled committee members, because of the law's requirement that Mr. Sebastian be a "proper subject for treatment."[6] Court cases have defined this term to mean that treatment must be "likely to improve or control the symptoms" of the individual with mental illness. If treatment is unlikely to help, then involuntary detention amounts to custodial control, which the legislature decided was not a sufficient reason to involuntarily detain a person for the rest of his life. If there was no available effective treatment, in other words, simply keeping a person alive is an insufficient reason for involuntary commitment.

Josh Sebastian had tried many avenues of treatment for years, to no avail. The committee felt that personal therapy around issues of abandonment might have helped if he had been motivated, but he didn't want to talk about abandonment. Sebastian's therapist suggested cognitive behavioral therapy (CBT), a therapy oriented to solving problems in the present, but Sebastian didn't want to solve his problems. He no longer hoped or even wanted to get

[5] WISC. STAT. § 51.01(13)(b) (2013).
[6] Other states have similar requirements, including Arizona, Connecticut, Missouri, Ohio, South Dakota, and Utah: ARIZ. REV. STAT. § 36-501-32(c); CONN. GEN. STAT. ANN. § 17a-495(a) ("hospital treatment is necessary and available"); MO. ANN. STAT. § 632.350(5) (a condition of commitment is that "a program appropriate to handle the respondent's condition has agreed to accept him"); OHIO REV. CODE ANN. § 5122.01(B)(4) ("would benefit from treatment in a hospital for his mental illness"); S.D. CODIFIED LAWS § 27A-1-2(3) ("the individual needs and is likely to benefit from treatment"); UTAH CODE ANN. § 62A-15-631(10)(e) ("the local mental health authority can provide the individual with treatment that is adequate and appropriate to his conditions and needs").

better. He just wanted to be dead. Many mental health professionals might argue that Mr. Sebastian needed medication to help with these motivational issues, but he had conscientiously tried every medication that had ever been suggested to him. None of them helped. As one person present at the committee meeting said,

> He doesn't want his life to have any meaning. Is that part of his illness? Maybe, but the treatment that would lead to recovery from his illness has to be both voluntary and participatory. There are different models of treatment—one is a more mechanical model. You drop your car off at the garage and say "fix it"— surgery is a little like that. Psychiatric treatment involves a model of collaborative engagement, which is different—we're going to collaborate and I am going to be your advocate . . . I need your active participation in this process. In [Sebastian's] case, medication did not work. In some cases it would. Psychotherapy might help, but he doesn't want it. Could someone have seduced him into life? Maybe, but we can't force him to be motivated for treatment.[7]

The deliberations of the Ethics Committee were unusual in the case of a consistently suicidal man who had just spent six months in a psychiatric facility. They took the commitment law seriously, including the requirements that in order to detain Sebastian involuntarily, he had to be mentally ill and they had to be able to offer him genuine benefit. They took Sebastian seriously and respected his account of his own life. It helped that Sebastian was articulate, intellectual, and middle class. It helped even more that he had been an uncomplaining and compliant patient for his six-month commitment. When he addressed the committee, he did so calmly and eloquently. Neither voluntary nor involuntary treatment had budged Sebastian's determination to end his life. Unlike some, his close brush with death had not altered its allure.

Sebastian also achieved a remarkable feat. The committee member I interviewed added, "He presented a very compelling case for not wanting to live." What could that be, I wondered? How could an otherwise physically healthy person (except for the spinal issues connected with his suicide attempt) make a compelling case for not wanting to live? We are accustomed to thinking of people with compelling reasons for not wanting to live as those in the last stages of terminal cancer, or who have amyotrophic lateral sclerosis (ALS; also called *Lou Gehrig's disease*). In those cases, the actual decision as to whether to live or die has effectively been wrested from an individual. The person is more like a captured resistance fighter, doomed to torture and execution by the enemy. We condone taking the cyanide pill as

---

[7] This is from an interview with a member of the Ethics Committee. (This interview was conducted with explicit written consent from Sebastian, the subject of the Ethics Committee review.)

a final act of autonomy and defiance by someone who otherwise would have embraced life. In the same way, we generally assume that people who want to die because of psychiatric or emotional conditions are essentially defectors, quislings whose desire to die constitutes a kind of betrayal of the rest of us, their comrades in the struggle against the troubles life brings.

I was especially curious as to what kind of person could make a compelling case for "suicide" to a mental health professional, because that is a profession often inclined to obstruct suicide at all costs. Did Sebastian have the psychological equivalent of the torment of brain cancer or ALS? Or is a psychiatric presentation of this kind of pain and misery completely different?

I decided to try to speak to Sebastian myself. He proved to be gracious and willing to talk to me. And the conversation with him was quite unlike most of the other people I interviewed for this book who had made serious suicide attempts. I expected an individual wracked by torments of untreatable psychiatric disability, or sucked under by the thick dark muck of depression. Instead I spoke to a person who was simply profoundly tired of living and indifferent to hope. He agreed that he was depressed:

> My depression stems from the fact that I really don't want to be
> here. I can laugh and joke and have a good time, but it's mostly a
> façade, a way to dissociate myself from who I am, which is a person
> who doesn't really want to be here.

His previous attempts at voluntary treatment—therapy and medication—hadn't helped. Being involuntarily hospitalized was even less helpful:

> When I woke up, I couldn't believe I was alive. They sent me to the
> psych ward, where I had no rights at all. It felt as though I broke
> the law, no outside contact, my friends couldn't visit me, the
> environment itself is not conducive for any therapeutic effects. You're
> put in a place with a lot of different people with a lot of different
> issues. It was awful, people are screaming; staff have no idea how to
> help people with mental illnesses. For me to see how staff members
> treat other individuals was horrific in and of itself. I was treated like
> a child. I wasn't treated as bad as others because I was more lucid.
> I understood where I was at, I didn't really say much when I was
> there, I was quiet and peaceful so no one had to interact with me.

Sebastian seemed much less emotional than other suicidal individuals I interviewed for this book. At least his tone of voice (what psychiatrists would call his "affect") was far more muted. His account of his own emotions seemed disconnected from them. He described his pain in a dispassionate way. Yet he also described himself (as the committee member had not) as very angry:

> From the very earliest of when I was a child, when I was very
> young, I was very angry and I wanted to end my own life. A lot of

people I know who have been truly suicidal, we are very angry, but we don't take it out on others. I don't want others to feel my pain. I know the pain that I go through every day and I don't want my anger to affect anyone else. I am angry at a lot of the circumstances that I was put in as a child and I am angry that I let those circumstances define me, and I am angry that I am angry. I am angry that I haven't fulfilled my potential, I am angry that I haven't killed myself; I have been a failure at suicide.

But he didn't sound angry at all. He just sounded very tired.

Sebastian couldn't remember ever being more than fleetingly happy. He had gone to college, gotten a job, been briefly married, and then in a long-term relationship for more than seven years. He had been employed, taking care of men with mental disabilities. Nothing seemed to give his life purpose or meaning. Mr. Sebastian felt that there was no meaning to his life. He had gained an education and employment, had been involved in relationships, tried therapy and medication, and had read a lot of books. Nothing worked. He believed that he had tried everything to ameliorate his condition. He excelled at caring for the mentally disabled men in his charge. He had developed relationships with them and with their parents. He had made a lot of different efforts for a long time in many ways to find meaning and purpose in life, and he was done with it. He was tired.

Mr. Sebastian's account would have been familiar to the Greeks and Romans, and to the early Christian church, but it is a foreign story in modern America. Emile Durkheim, the first great scholar of suicide, might have classified Mr. Sebastian as prone to "egoistic" suicide, when an individual feels his life is meaningless or purposeless.[8] The early church would have called it "acedia" or despair, a condition that modern folk often confuse with depression, but is actually quite different from it.[9] The Puritans would have considered Sebastian's despair and hopelessness simply his cross to bear, and any attempt to avoid it through suicide would be the gravest of sins, an affront to God. Throughout hundreds and even thousands of years, Mr. Sebastian's condition would have been instantly recognizable, and throughout history, it would have been clearly distinguished from insanity, mental illness, or madness. Although all societies at all times have recognized that suicide in a minority of cases results from "madness," "furious madness," or "insanity," only in our most recent history would Mr. Sebastian have been grouped together with people suffering from madness simply because he wanted to commit suicide.

---

[8] EMILE DURKHEIM, SUICIDE (Routledge Classics, 2d ed. 2002) (1897). Durkheim posited four different kinds of suicide: egoistic, altruistic, fatalistic, and anomic. See more on this in Chapter 7.

[9] See KATHLEEN NORRIS, ACEDIA AND ME: A MARRIAGE, MONKS, AND A WRITER'S LIFE (2010) for an extensive exploration of the difference between acedia and depression.

No one on the committee doubted that Mr. Sebastian was competent. How could they? They had engaged in an extended discussion with him about his situation and his perspective. I have talked to this man: he is intelligent, thoughtful, and reflective. The question never arose. The committee did debate whether Sebastian could ethically be committed involuntarily under the statute and concluded that Mr. Sebastian was probably not mentally ill as defined by the Wisconsin commitment law. He certainly was not a fit subject for treatment. No one held out much hope that treatment would alleviate his condition after twenty years of trying.

Nevertheless, in a spirit of caution, the committee proposed a compromise to Sebastian: the hospital would forego its right to petition for a one-year involuntary commitment, if he agreed to an extension of his commitment for six months in the community. He would be free to live in the community, under court order to try one more round of therapy and one more round of medication. If it didn't work, no matter how suicidal he was, there would be no further petitions for commitment, and Mr. Sebastian would be free to do as he pleased. Sebastian completed the six months (he ceased the therapy early). Nothing helped. He was freed of all legal supervision and constraint, able to commit suicide as he chose. As of this writing, he is still alive.

Many would disagree with the committee's compromise proposal. Some ex-patient activists (and Josh Sebastian himself) contend that the state should never have had power over him in the first place. Some mental health professionals argue that his bald statement of continued suicidality was an obvious sign of depression and a cry for help, and he should remain involuntarily institutionalized as long as he remained (at least outwardly) suicidal.

However, the research and interviews I conducted for this book suggest that the committee's approach was legally required, ethically sound, and clinically astute. Mr. Sebastian obviously had not been and was unlikely to be helped by an involuntary, coercive approach. Maybe nothing will ever be able to help him, as he asserts. Maybe there is hope he cannot as yet discern. What is clearly true is that coercive and involuntary approaches are not only futile, but actually harmful to any small chance remaining for him. Mr. Sebastian could not be bullied into living. What the Ethics Committee proposed was to continue the conversation, to continue the engagement in this most profound discussion, while explicitly acknowledging that the ultimate choice would be up to Sebastian.

Of course the Ethics Committee could not have known that Mr. Sebastian would live, or how long. They took a risk. One of the central themes of this book is that good patient care, adherence to the requirements of law, and effective suicide prevention requires more risk-taking by mental health professionals than is currently the norm. This may seem paradoxical. I hope to show that recognizing the autonomy and responsibility of individuals such as Josh Sebastian and seeking to help them rather than control them will both save more lives and add to the quality of the lives that are saved.

Sharing risk with people suffering so much that they want to end their lives is only possible with competent people. No one can (or should try) to share risk with someone who is extremely intoxicated or floridly psychotic. No one can (or should) share risk with a child ("mature minors" present a more complicated issue). No one can (or should) try to share risk with a person suffering from delirium or dementia.

Yet many mental health professionals equate suicidality itself with incompetence.[10] The rest of this chapter will be devoted to the argument that this is a mistaken and harmful view, and that the vast majority of suicidal people are, in fact, competent.[11] In addition, the majority of people who have diagnoses of mental illness and are suicidal are also competent, whether they are suicidal because they are terminally ill or because they are in chronic and untreatable psychic pain, or because, like Sebastian, they are profoundly exhausted with the unrewarding task of trying to live.

To concede that suicidal people are competent does not, of course, answer the question of whether, how, and when the State ought to prevent these people from committing suicide, any more than it was the complete answer to the Ethics Committee's discussion about Josh Sebastian. The State has been constraining competent people's choices about suicide for more than a thousand years. Historically, both suicide and suicide attempts were criminalized. These days, attempted suicide often leads to voluntary or involuntary commitment to a psychiatric hospital. As Wisconsin and many other states explicitly provide, being committable is not, however, the same as being incompetent to make healthcare decisions.[12] Whether, when, and how

---

[10] J. Spike, *Physician's Responsibilities in the Case of Suicidal Patients: Three Case Studies*, 9 J. Clin. Ethics 311 (1998); State v. C.R., 173 P.3d 836, 837–838 (Or. App. 2007) (psychiatrist in civil commitment hearing testified, "Her denial and pleasant manner make it difficult to say she is psychotic, but in my judgment, suicidal thinking is psychotic"). In Sebastian's case, more sophisticated proponents of this theory might argue that he had *affective incompetence*, in which cognitive skills are unimpaired, but the individual's mood disorder renders the individual (according to these professionals) incompetent to make decisions. I address this argument later in the chapter.

[11] Competence is a legal construct; it is often used interchangeably with the clinical concept of lack of capacity. Paul Appelbaum, *Assessment of Patients' Competence to Consent to Treatment*, 357 New Eng. J. Med. 1834 (2007); National Bioethics Advisory Commission, Research Involving Persons with Mental Disorders that may Affect Decisionmaking Capacity, ch.1 n.4 (1998). My argument applies to both the legal framework, which is more fixed and rigid, and the clinical construct, which is more fluid and dynamic.

[12] For example, Alaska, Myers v. Alaska Psychiatric Institute, 138 P.3d 238, 242–43 (Alaska 2006); California Welfare and Institutions Code § 5325.1 and Riese v. St. Mary's Hospital, 271 Cal. Rptr. 199, 206 (Cal. App. 1987); Florida, § 394.459(1) and (3); Minnesota, Jarvis v. Levine, 418 N.W.2d 139 (Minn. 1988); New York, M.H.L. § 29.03 and Rivers v. Katz, 67 N.Y.S.2d 485, 493–94 (1986).

the State can or should prevent competent people from committing suicide, when they should be strong-armed rather than seduced into life, is the topic of Chapter 2. Chapters 3 and 4 will look at assisted suicide laws and policies in the United States and around the world, and examine how very different frameworks operate and the results they produce. Chapters 5 and 6 will look at the powerful role played by medical and mental health professionals as gatekeepers of suicide in this country, and propose changes to reduce the burdens and distortions that law places on doctor–patient relationships in the context of suicide.

My argument in this chapter is relatively simple: the very small minority of truly incompetent people who try to kill themselves ought to be prevented from doing so. But the vast majority of people who are thinking about suicide, attempting suicide, and committing suicide are nowhere close to incompetent under our current legal standards. The best clinical and sociological research supports this assertion, and the law insists on it. Treating suicidal people as per se incompetent makes bad law and interferes with good clinical practice. Treating people as incompetent shuts down conversation at the very point when conversation is most needed. The intent to commit suicide, or a suicide attempt, does not, standing alone, constitute incompetence. The determination that a patient is competent is not the conversation: it is the threshold determination that precedes the conversation.

The fact that suicidal people are competent does not mean that they cannot be prevented from trying to commit suicide. But if you can hold a conversation with an adult about his or her desire to commit suicide, if you can have a discussion, if you think the person may be persuadable and would not question this person's consent if he or she decided to try treatment, then the individual is competent to make the decision to end his or her life.[13] I understand that many clinically depressed people fit this standard; I agree with the research that shows depression generally does not rob people of capacity.[14] A determination of competence does not depend on whether suicide would be a grievous and tragic error. Specific standards of competence to end one's life will be discussed in more detail toward the end of this chapter.

The law is on my side. The law assumes that individuals can be competent and suicidal across a wide range of situations. Four states have legalized assisted suicide, underscoring the default assumption that terminally ill people who want to end their lives are presumed competent unless determined

---

[13] Although competence varies from context to context, people who are not competent to decide to kill themselves may well not be competent in other contexts. See, e.g., *In re* A.M. 332 P.3d 263 (Mont. 2014) (man who consumed all his medications in an attempt at "rebirth" did not competently waive his right to civil commitment hearing).

[14] I disagree with the theory of affective incompetence, which will be discussed later in the chapter.

otherwise.[15] But there is more: we permit competent suicidal death row prisoners to abandon appeals that might well save their lives and will certainly delay their deaths.[16] Insurance law contains hundreds, if not thousands, of decisions, including many Supreme Court decisions,[17] distinguishing "sane" suicides from "insane" suicides for purposes of life insurance.[18]

Understanding that some people can competently consider suicide and/ or attempt to kill themselves has a number of consequences. First of all, it preserves the integrity of the concept of competence, which is about the process of decision making rather than the decision made.[19] Second, it accurately reflects the thoughtful and reflective struggles and pain of millions of people throughout history, including Nobel Prize winners[20] and feminist icons,[21]

---

[15] The process and results of these efforts are discussed at length in Chapter 3.

[16] See discussion at pp. 20–21 infra.

[17] See, e.g., Life Ins. Co. v. Terry, 82 U.S. 580, 15 Wall 580 (1872) (exclusion of suicide from life insurance policy only applies when person takes his life while in possession of his faculties); Knights Templar and Masons Life Ins. Co. v. Jarman, 187 U.S. 197 (1902) ("suicide is not used in its technical and legal sense of self-destruction by a sane person, but according to its popular meaning of death by one's own hand, irrespective of the mental condition of the person committing the act"); Ritter v. Mutual Life Ins. Co., 169 U.S. 139, 154 (1898) (life insurance policy that paid if someone committed suicide while of sound mind would be against public policy and sound morality)

[18] Although *insane* is different from *incompetent* in criminal law, for purposes of deciding whether a person should be held responsible for his or her suicide in the context of insurance law, the definitions of insane and incompetent are similar, see, e.g., Robert I. Simon, James L. Levenson, & Daniel W. Shuman, *On Sound and Unsound Mind: The Role of Suicide in Tort and Insurance Litigation*, 33 J. AM. ACAD. PSYCHIATRY L. 176 (June 2005) (analyzing "sane/insane" and "sound/unsound mind" for insurance purposes in terms of capacity).

[19] See Chapter 2.

[20] Christian de Duve, Belgian Nobel Prize winner in Medicine, used assisted suicide to die; see, Denise Gellene, *Christian De Duve, 95, Dies; Nobel-Winning Biochemist*, N. Y. TIMES, May 6, 2013. Although the only Nobel Prize winner to use assisted suicide, he was hardly the only Nobel Prize winner to commit suicide, and not just the usual suspects, the Literature Prize winners (Ernest Hemingway in 1961 and Yasunari Kawabata in 1968), but many scientists, such as Emil Fischer, who won for chemistry in 1902 and killed himself in 1910; Hans Fischer (no relation), who won in 1930 and killed himself in 1945; and Percy Bridgman, who won the Nobel Prize in physics in 1946 and shot himself in 1961.

[21] Charlotte Perkins Gilman, see infra at 57; Virginia Woolf is probably the best-known feminist suicide (Virginia Woolf's Suicide Note, *Woolf, Creativity, and Madness: From Freud to fMRI*, www.smith.edu/woolf/suicidewithtranscript. php) but, more to the point, Caroline Heilbrun, in October 2003, see Vannessa Grigoriadis, *A Death of One's Own*, N. Y. MAG., Dec. 8, 2003, http://nymag.com/ nymetro/news/people/n_9589/. I say "more to the point" because Gilman was

philosophers,[22] and the hundreds of people I interviewed for this book. Third, the kinds of risk-sharing with suicidal patients I propose in this book can only be contemplated with competent people.

It is important to define some of the terms I will use throughout this book: *Competence* is a word that appears in statutes, regulations, and case law. Under our law, people who lack competence must have a guardian or guardian ad litem appointed to make legally binding decisions on their behalf, or, more recently, assistance and support in making decisions. *Capacity* is a medical term more often used to relate to a person's ability to make medical decisions at the moment of assessment. Some of the best scholars on competence and capacity use the terms interchangeably, especially in healthcare scholarship.

The Development of Concepts of Competence in Different Areas of the Law

The law presumes that all adults are competent.[23] Competence obviously means very different things in different contexts: competence to handle one's assets may be very different from competence to vote.[24] In this chapter, we will focus on competence to make decisions to die or hasten one's death, to exercise control over the timing and manner of one's death: in other words, competence to commit suicide. There is no current legal test for competence to commit suicide,[25] although there are proposals discussed later in this

---

mortally ill with cancer, and Woolf had well-known emotional problems, but Heilbrun, by all accounts, just decided it was the right time.

[22] Albert Camus and Bertrand Russell are only the most recent philosophers to wrestle with the problem of suicide, see ALBERT CAMUS, THE MYTH OF SISYPHUS (Justin O'Brien trans., Vintage 1955) and Peter Hanks, *What Made Russell Feel Ready for Suicide?* OUP Blog, June 7, 2015, at blog.oup.com/2015/06/bertrand-russell-suicide/

[23] See, e.g., National Conference of Commissioners on Uniform State Laws, Uniform Health-Care Decisions Act, Section 11(b) (1994). The law also presumes that virtually all people younger than certain arbitrary ages are not competent. It is important to discuss children and suicidality: virtually all of the dozens of people who have attempted suicide that I interviewed began contemplating suicide as children, including Josh Sebastian. A substantial number of the people I interviewed made their first suicide attempt as children. In many cases adults never knew or thought it was an accident. I take it as an article of faith that children should be prevented from committing suicide, although how to go about this may generate some controversy and will be discussed in Chapter 7.

[24] M. D. Green's famous article about the chaos of law governing wills and contracts also makes the point that competence is interpreted differently even in the same legal contexts, M. D. Green, *Proof of Mental Incompetence and the Unexpressed Major Premise*, 53 YALE L.J. 271 (1944).

[25] JAMES L. WERTH JR., RATIONAL SUICIDE? IMPLICATIONS FOR MENTAL HEALTH PROFESSIONALS (1996); Darien S. Fenn & Linda Ganzini, *Attitudes of Oregon*

chapter and plenty of standards for competence to make a decision that will inevitably lead to one's death.

The law deals with suicide in a multitude of areas. Cases vary from whether an ex-husband breached his child-support contract by committing suicide (he did not)[26] to whether a newspaper's false report that a man died by suicide is slander (it isn't because you can't slander dead people)[27] to whether a person who died by self-strangulation he engaged in for autoerotic purposes committed suicide (he didn't because he did not intend to die)[28] and whether the military may order a soldier accused of a crime into pretrial confinement solely for the purpose of preventing him from committing suicide (it can't).[29] Other interesting questions include whether a personal property gift made contingent on suicide is enforceable (sometimes yes, sometimes no).[30] Can suicide be considered an act of negligence?[31] Most cases involving suicide, however, also involve competence, and fall in one of six major areas: criminal law, tort law, insurance law, wills and probate, constitutional law, and healthcare law.

Three things are clear from hundreds of years and thousands of legal opinions about suicide. First, the law is internally contradictory and conflicting about suicide, in theory and in practice. Across areas of law, and within them, inconsistencies occur well beyond the normal, expected variations in any area of law. For example, for many years, suicide was decriminalized in many states, which continued to criminalize attempted suicide, even though throughout most of the law, it is impossible to criminalize attempting to do something that is not itself criminal. Children who would not be permitted under state law to make their own healthcare decisions have been held in tort cases to have made an independent and voluntary decision to kill themselves,[32] and in constitutional law cases to have the right to refuse life-saving treatment. People who literally murder their spouses, children, or parents are acquitted if those family members are suffering from a (sometimes not so) terminal illness or disability. Jurors have, for hundreds of years, consistently ignored instructions about the law in many cases involving suicide.

The second fact is that amid all these confusions, one clear and basic consistency does emerge. The law has always assumed that people are legally

---

Psychologists Toward Physician-Assisted Suicide and the Oregon Death with Dignity Act, 30 PROF. PSYCHOL. RES. PRAC. 235 (1999).

[26] Wilmington Trust Co. v. Clark, 424 A.2d 744 (Md. 1981).

[27] Lee v. Weston, 402 N.E.2d 23 (Ind. App. 1980).

[28] Padfield v. AIG, 290 F.3d 1121 (5th Cir. 2002).

[29] U.S. v. Doane, 54 M.J. 978 (A.F. Ct. Crim. App. 2001).

[30] For *a lot* of information about this topic, see Adam J. McLeod, *A Gift Worth Dying For?: Debating the Volitional Nature of Suicide in the Law of Personal Property*, 45 IDAHO L. REV. 93 (2008).

[31] Yes, but I think that's a mistaken formulation of law, see Chapter 6.

[32] Logarta v. Gustafson, 998 F.Supp. 998 (E.D. Wisc. 1998).

responsible for their suicides and suicide attempts, and the burden of proof lies with those who claim that a person who committed suicide was not responsible, competent, or sane. The name of this exception has varied over time, and across different areas of law, but the fundamental truth—that the vast majority of suicidal people are competent in the eyes of the law—has never changed. Attempting or completing suicide has never, in and of itself, been sufficient in any branch of law to determine that an individual was incompetent or lacked capacity.

Finally, for most of history, the determination of whether someone was sane or of sound mind at the time of suicide or a suicide attempt, has been a question of fact entrusted to laypeople without the need for assistance from experts. With the rise of insurance and worker's compensation, which took place concurrently with the rise and professionalization of the fields of both law and mental health, these questions, while remaining questions of fact for the jury to decide, were increasingly considered complex subjects that jurors or judges could not decide without expert opinions by physicians and psychiatrists. Yet the culture, assumptions, and standards of medicine and mental health, in those days as in the present, were often far removed from the culture, values, and standards of law. This is hardly breaking news, but it has major implications for the social, legal, and policy treatment of suicide.

The Capacity to Choose Suicide and the Criminal Law

The law has always started with the assumption that suicidal people are competent, in the sense of being responsible for their actions. This stems from the fact that, until quite recently, suicide was a crime. In Western culture, the perception that suicide was a sin began with the writings of Augustine (prior to Augustine, suicide was sometimes celebrated by Christians, especially the suicides of women to preserve their chastity). With the intertwining of church and state, suicide also became a crime across Europe, known as *felo de se* or self-murder. In 967, King Edgar of England decreed that all the worldly goods and possessions of a person who committed suicide must be forfeit to the crown (as well as forfeiture of a Christian burial, and burial at a crossroads with a stake through the body).[33]

Suicide was considered the worst of all crimes because, as the famed legal commentator Blackstone wrote, quoting a 1562 case, "the suicide is guilty of a double offense; one spiritual, in invading the prerogative of the Almighty and rushing into His immediate presence uncalled for, the other temporal, against the King, who hath an interest in the preservation of his subjects."[34]

---

[33] HOWARD KUSHNER, AMERICAN SUICIDE 17–18 (1991).
[34] Hales v. Petit, 1 Plowden 253, 75 Eng. Rep. 387 (Q.B. 1562); WILLIAM BLACKSTONE, COMMENTARIES, ch.14, p.189 (8th ed. 1778).

As a crime, suicide was tried in a court, to a jury, and the elements of the crime had to be proven. One of the necessary elements of the crime (in addition to being an adult) was that a person must be of "sound mind."[35] In fact, according to the English commentator Matthew Hale, suicide by definition required the individual to be *compos mentis*.[36] If a person killed himself or herself in the throes of madness, it was *not* suicide or *felo de se*; it was neither a crime nor a sin.[37] Thus, if a person who killed himself or herself was found by the jury to be insane, the family got to keep the individual's land and goods. Whether or not the person who killed himself or herself had an unsound mind was not considered a medical issue in any way and no expert testimony was required. But suicide while of unsound mind was initially understood to be a rare case, an exception to the rule of sane suicides. Suicide was not necessarily associated with madness any more than we currently associate murder with madness just because we have an insanity defense.

Because the penalty for suicide was total forfeiture of goods and properties, it is not surprising that juries, who generally knew the families, stretched circumstances very far to find that suicide was the result of insanity. Thus began, more than five hundred years ago, a long tradition of juries ignoring, nullifying, and distorting the law relating to suicide and assisted suicide because it simply made no sense to them. As we will see, that tradition continues to this day.

Jurors who decided whether someone was sane or insane at the time of suicide were not given definitions or much in the way of jury instructions. They listened to family and friends and neighbors and drew their own conclusions. But scholars, including legal scholars, had definitions: Robert Burton, author of *The Anatomy of Melancholy* argued that "such as are mad" "know not what they do, deprived of reason."[38] Because suicide was a crime— the murder of self—the standard for insanity that excused the offense was sometimes seen as the same standard as that which excused murder: the individual "did not know the nature and quality of the act, or does not know the act was wrong."[39]

Ultimately, the standard did not matter. The willingness of jurors to find that a person who committed suicide was insane became such a problem that Blackstone complained that juries carried the excuse to an extreme, finding

---

[35] WILLIAM BLACKSTONE, 4 COMMENTARIES ON THE LAWS OF ENGLAND 195 (5th ed. 1836).

[36] MATTHEW HALE, PLEAS OF THE CROWN, i, 411 (1800).

[37] As Blackstone wrote, "The party must be of years of discretion, and in his senses, else it is no crime." ROBERT MALCOLM KERR, THE STUDENT'S BLACKSTONE 485 (1877).

[38] ROBERT BURTON, ANATOMY OF MELANCHOLY 2784 (1621) (page number in the Google Books edition, https://books.google.com/books?id=-wEvBwAAQBAJ& printsec=frontcover#v=onepage&q&f=false.

[39] M'Naghten's Case, 8 Eng. Rep. 718 (H.L. 1843).

that "the very act of suicide is evidence of insanity; as if every man who acted contrary to reason, had no reason at all." He flatly rejected this theory: "The law rationally judges that every melancholy or hypochondriac fit does not deprive one of the capacity of discerning right and wrong." He worried that "the same argument would prove every other criminal *non compos,* as well as the self-murderer."[40]

The insanity defense for suicide (or self-murder, as it was then called) in fact preceded and perhaps led to the use of the insanity defense for murder. And just as in modern times, when a claim of not guilty by reason of insanity is often met with skepticism, the attribution of suicide to mental illness was regarded by many as an outrageous manipulation of the law.

These English customs, practices, attitudes, and laws came to America with European settlers. The Puritans, in particular, were vehemently against suicide. Increase Mather preached a scathing and widely republished sermon about suicide: *A Call to the Tempted: A Sermon on the Horrid Crime of Self-Murder.*[41] In America, however, juries and others continued to stretch circumstances to find that a person—especially a prominent person—had committed suicide while insane. When he was drafting statutes for Virginia to decriminalize suicide, Thomas Jefferson pointed to the prevalent practice of jury nullification when the crime of suicide was prosecuted: "That men in general too disapprove of this severity [of forfeiture as a sanction for suicide] is apparent from the constant practice of juries finding the suicide in a state of insanity; because they have no other way of saving the forfeiture."[42] Some states in the new United States of America began decriminalizing suicide around the time of the Revolution. Others continued to consider it a crime, while removing forfeiture as a punishment.

The dichotomy between suicide as either a crime or the behavior of a madman became quite awkward in England in 1822 when the distinguished Foreign Secretary and member of the aristocracy, Viscount Castlereagh, slit his throat. If he were deemed a felon, he could not be buried in Westminster Abbey. The alternative that would permit his burial in Westminster required accepting that Great Britain had a madman running its foreign affairs. The jury neatly solved this dilemma by finding that he had been temporarily insane at the time of his suicide, and he was buried at Westminster Abbey. As in almost all findings that temporary insanity excuses a criminal act, there was a furious public backlash. Lord Byron noted sarcastically that

[40] *Id.* at 27.
[41] Although the entire text of the sermon has not survived, fragments of it are reprinted in Increase Mather, *A Call to the Tempted: A Sermon on the Horrid Crime of Self Murder* (Ann Arbor, MI: Text Creation Partnership) available at http://quod.lib.umich.edu/e/evans/N02155.0001.001/1:2?rgn=div1;view=fulltext
[42] Thomas Jefferson, Plan Agreed Upon by the Committee of Revisors at Fredericksburg, 13 January 1777, *in* 2 PAPERS OF THOMAS JEFFERSON 325, quoted in KUSHNER, AMERICAN SUICIDE, n.33, p.30.

Of the manner of his death little need be said, except that if a poor radical had cut his throat, he would have been buried in a cross-road, with the usual appurtenances of the stake and mallet. But the minister was an elegant lunatic—a sentimental suicide—he merely cut the "carotid artery," (blessings on their learning!) and lo! The pageant, and the Abbey! and "the syllables of dolour yelled forth" by the newspapers—and the harangue of the Coroner in the eulogy over the bleeding body of the deceased—(an Anthony worthy of such a Caesar)—and the nauseous and atrocious cant of a degraded crew of conspirators against all that is sincere and honourable. In his death he was necessarily one of two things by the law—a felon or a madman—and in either case no great subject for panegyric.[43]

The public controversy surrounding the verdict after Castlereagh's death had its effect. The inequality castigated by Byron was ended, not by toughening up the enforcement of the law as would be likely in modern times, but by abandoning the practice of burying suicides at public crossroads. The following year saw the last example of that practice, and in 1824 it was prohibited by law.[44] Confiscation of the goods of a suicide was not formally outlawed until 1870. Attempted suicide continued to be punished in England: In 1860 a man who had attempted to cut his throat was treated until he recovered and then hanged.[45] The wound in his throat reopened, and "they bound up his neck below his wound until he died."[46] Suicide was finally decriminalized in England in 1961.

In the United States, forfeiture was also abolished long before suicide was decriminalized; as the U.S. Supreme Court said, "it shows gross moral turpitude in a sane person."[47] As the New Jersey Supreme Court pointed out, "suicide is none the less criminal because no punishment can be inflicted. It may not be indictable because the dead cannot be indicted. If one kills another and then kills himself, is he any the less a murderer because he can't be punished?"[48] Some states that had decriminalized suicide continued to treat attempted suicide as a crime.[49] This led to court holdings that appeared to defy logic even as they tried to faithfully follow the law:

---

[43] George Gordon, Lord Byron, Don Juan, Preface to Cantos VI–VIII, (1837), available online at http://www.online-literature.com/byron/don-juan/6/

[44] In 1824, the English Parliament's ban on the practice of burying suicides by the highway with a stake driven through the individual's heart was codified in law. The law also authorized church burial, although without religious rites and only between 9 p.m. and midnight. 4 Geo IV c. 52, s.1.

[45] J. D. DROGE & A. J. TABOR, A NOBLE DEATH: SUICIDE AND MARTYRDOM AMONG CHRISTIANS AND JEWS IN ANTIQUITY 7 (1992).

[46] Id.

[47] Travelers' Ins. Co. v. McConkey, 127 U.S. 661, 667 (1888).

[48] State v. Carney, 55 A. 45 (N.J. Sup. Ct. 1903).

[49] Royal Circle v. Achterrath, 204 Ill. 549, 565–66 (1903).

[An] attempt to commit crime imports a purpose not fully
accomplished to commit it. It is the attempt to commit suicide that
is the crime, while the taking of one's own life is no violation of the
criminal law . . . While the attempt to commit suicide is a crime,
the accomplishment of the purpose to do so is not.[50]

Several decades later another court held that "though suicide itself is not
punishable in this state because we have no forfeiture, the attempt to commit
suicide is punishable."[51] The criminalization of attempted suicide waned at
the dawn of the twentieth century. In 1906, the highest court in Maine, noting that attempted suicide was still a crime in New York, North Dakota, and
South Dakota, held that it was not a crime in Maine.[52] In 1902, prosecutors
in New York City attempted to criminally charge twenty-one people who had
attempted suicide, and in the first half of 1903, they attempted to charge nine
people who had attempted suicide.[53] Grand juries refused to return indict-
ments in any one of these cases, showing the disinclination of juries to follow
laws that make no sense to them.[54]

In England, matters were different. Both suicide and attempted suicide
were officially crimes, but successful suicides were often deemed "insane,"
while an unsuccessful suicide was punished as a crime. This understanding
was so common that it featured in Agatha Christie's 1944 detective novel,
Toward Zero. The novel opens as a man whose attempt to kill himself by
jumping off a cliff has been thwarted by landing in a tree lies in a hospital bed
and thinks to himself:

And now where was he? Lying ridiculously in a hospital bed with
a broken shoulder and with the prospect of being hauled up in a
police court for the crime of trying to take his own life.
Curse it, it was his *own* life, wasn't it?
And if he had succeeded in the job, they would have buried him
piously as of unsound mind!
Unsound mind, indeed! He'd never been saner! And to commit
suicide was the most logical and sensible thing that could be done
by a man in his position.
. . . And now here he was in a ridiculous plight. He would
shortly be admonished by a sanctimonious magistrate for doing

---

[50] Darrow v. Family Fund Soc'y, 22 N.E. 1093 (N.Y. 1889).
[51] State v. LaFayette, 188 A. 918 (County Ct. N.J. 1937) (but dismissing the case
because the court imposing the sentence did not have the authority to do so
under law).
[52] May v. Pennell, 101 Me. 516 (1906).
[53] Wilbur Larremore, *Suicide and the Law*, 17 Harv. L. Rev. 331 (1903–1904).
[54] *Id.* Prof. Larremore, the law professor reporting these facts, concluded that this
outcome was "entirely satisfactory."

the common-sense thing with a commodity which belonged to him and to him only—his life.[55]

Thus, even while suicide remained a crime in the laws of England for almost two more decades after the novel was published, the pressures of social opinion had effectively decriminalized it by 1944. But, as Christie makes clear, decriminalization was not a result of England's changing values about a person's autonomy or right to commit suicide or (as in the case of homosexuality or use of marijuana in the United States) the consequence of social normalization of the conduct. Rather, successful suicides were chalked up to insanity or incompetence. Yet, as underscored by Christie's satirical comment on the subject, English society did not really believe that suicidal people were actually insane or incompetent: unsuccessful suicide attempts were punished and continued to be punished by a week to a month in prison or a fine as late as 1959.[56]

Social values shape laws about suicide, and in turn values are shaped by law. Thus, many states in the South took much longer to decriminalize suicide than those in the North; indeed some Southern states still regard suicide as a common law crime. The North Carolina Supreme Court held that a man could be criminally prosecuted for attempted suicide in 1961,[57] the same year that Great Britain decriminalized suicide. As late as 1992, the Supreme Court of Virginia reviewed a claim for psychiatric malpractice that had been dismissed by the trial court on the grounds that suicide was immoral and criminal, and therefore the widow should not profit from her husband's immoral and criminal act.[58] The Virginia Supreme Court upheld the finding that, as a matter of common law, suicide still was a crime in Virginia, but found that in order to be a crime, the suicide must be committed by a person of sound mind. The case was reversed because the husband had been of unsound mind at the time of his suicide. As I write this, the efforts of Senator Adam Ebbin and Delegate Rob Krupicka to decriminalize suicide in Virginia have failed; a Facebook petition to support this decriminalization aiming for

[55] AGATHA CHRISTIE, TOWARD ZERO (1944).

[56] Gerry Holt, *When Suicide Was Illegal* (BBC News, Aug. 3, 2011), http://www.bbc.com/news/magazine-14374296. Christie herself makes clear her own opinion about suicide: not that it is a crime or a sign of insanity, but that it is a mistake, because we do not know what the future will hold. Thus, the failed suicide in *Toward Zero* ends the book by saving a woman from suicide.

[57] State v. Willis, 255 NC 473, 477–78, 121 S.E.2d 854 (1961) (holding that suicide was a crime that could not be punished, but attempted suicide could be punished by fine and imprisonment). North Carolina decriminalized suicide by statute in 1973, N.C. CODE § 14-17.1, c. 1205 (1973).

[58] Wackwitz v. Roy, 418 S.E.2d 861 (Va. 1992). The Virginia Supreme Court found that suicide was a common law crime in Virginia, but held that, because "suicide" required a rational mind, and Wackwitz had not been rational at the time of his suicide, he had not committed a crime. This will be discussed later in this chapter.

1000 supporters received barely half this amount. As of 2015, suicide is still a crime in Virginia.

In 1996, the highest court in Mississippi rejected a jury instruction on accident when the defendant claimed that he had accidentally shot his ex-wife while he was trying to commit suicide, because the defense of accident cannot be used when the defendant is engaged in an unlawful act, and attempting suicide is an unlawful act.[59] Two years later, a federal court recognized that suicide was still a crime in Mississippi.[60] In the military, deliberate self-injury, including attempting suicide, is still a crime under some circumstances.[61]

Social values also dictate the distinction between sane and insane suicide. In the last hundred years, many courts have tried to define the distinction between sane and insane in cases of suicide where the determination was related to suicide as a crime. No one ever really believes that all suicides are the result of mental illness. We have always had beliefs that some suicides are rational or even admirable (they are often called something other than suicide). Both the Church and State endorsed suicide by saints and martyrs, including by women to preserve their chastity. These kinds of suicides were, as a court in New Jersey in 1901 put it

> . . . ethically defensible. Else, how could a man "lay down his life
> for his friend?" Suicide may be self-sacrifice, as when a woman
> slays herself to save her honor.[62] Sometimes self-destruction,
> humanly speaking, is excusable, as where a man curtails by weeks
> or months the agony of an incurable disease.[63]

The categories of suicide generally believed to be rational are a window into culture as much as its causes. They tell us about the lives we believe are not worth living: people in comas or vegetative states; people who are

---

[59] Nicholson *ex rel.* Gollott v. State, 672 So.2d 744, 753 (Miss. 1996) (noting that even if it could not hold attempted suicide was an unlawful act, his "display of a pistol, and his heated request for Diane to shoot him, after his repeated threats against Diane" violated the law prohibiting assault.

[60] Shamburger v. Grand Casino of Miss. Inc. 84 F.Supp.2d 794 (S.D. Miss. 1998) (finding that casino could not be legally responsible for suicide when decedent was not acting under irresistible impulse).

[61] United States v. Caldwell, 72 M.J. 137 (C.A.A.F. 2013).

[62] That is, commits suicide to avoid being raped. This was sufficiently common that a court ruled (over two dissents) that a man could be convicted of murder for the suicide of a woman he had raped, since it was foreseeable that she would be so distracted with "pain and shame" as to react this way to his assault, Stephenson v. State, 179 N.E. 633 (1932).

[63] Campbell v. Supreme Conclave Improved Order Heptasophs, 49 A. 550, 553 (N.J. App. 1901). I am deeply grateful that this case is actually relevant, since its magnificent name would have forced me to come up with some reason to cite it.

at death's door and in a great deal of pain; people whose independence and autonomy are compromised, and people with chronic, incurable, but nonterminal disabilities. Recently, a young man who was just married and whose wife was expecting their first child fell out of a tree while hunting and was told he would be paralyzed for life. He asked that his life support be disconnected because life was not worth living as a paralyzed individual. This decision, considered competent, was honored.[64]

In an extensive and thoughtful article on the subject, Professors Simon, Levenson, and Shuman suggest using the state's applicable standard for insanity: "if suicide is criminalized, criminal responsibility criteria should apply to the determination of unsound mind in criminalized suicide cases, as it would to other criminal offenses."[65]

Those criteria generally revolve around the ability to understand and appreciate the nature and wrongfulness of the act. Simon, Levenson, and Shuman summarize that "unless a suicide is impulsive, the result of confusion or severe intoxication, or the result of a miscalculation, a patient's suicide is usually a conscious choice to end intolerable mental pain or circumstances."[66] In other words, the individual who commits suicide is usually competent or sane under the law.

This is certainly true in the case of many suicidal death row inmates who choose to withdraw appeals of their death sentences. Between 1976 and 2003, 106 of 885 people executed in this country were so-called volunteers, inmates who waived the appeals process. They did this because they wanted and intended to die, and their actions hastened their deaths by years or even decades, and also made them inevitable;[67] waiving appeal of a death sentence is thus a suicidal act. The law currently permits death row inmates to waive appeals if they have a "rational and factual understanding of the consequences of their decision," and if that decision is "knowing, intelligent, and voluntary."[68] Courts have repeatedly found that this standard is met in cases where the inmate is explicitly, overtly suicidal. Gary Gilmore, unwilling to wait for the firing squad, made a suicide attempt six days after withdrawing

---

[64] Steve Almasy & Michael Martinez, *Paralyzed after Fall from Tree, Indiana Deer Hunter Opts to End Life* (CNN, Nov. 7, 2013), www.cnn.com./2013/11/06/us/ paralyzed-Indiana-deer-hunter-ends-life.

[65] Simon et al., *supra* note 18, at 1179.

[66] *Id.*

[67] John H. Blume, *Killing the Willing: "Volunteers," Suicide and Competency*, 103 MICH. L. REV. 939, 940 (2005).

[68] Interestingly, inmates only have the right to waive discretionary death penalty appeals; no matter how competent or knowing or intelligent, courts have held that inmates cannot waive mandatory appeals of their own death sentences. For an exhaustive review of the topic, see Anthony Casey, *Maintaining the Integrity of Death: An Argument for Restricting a Defendant's Right to Volunteer for Execution at Certain Stages in Capital Proceedings*, 30 AM. J. CRIM. LAW 75 (2002).

his appeal. David Martin Long attempted suicide the day before his execution. In both cases the men were given emergency medical treatment; Long was revived from a coma and flown back for his execution the next evening.[69] The fact that the death row inmates are suicidal, mentally ill, brain damaged, or intellectually disabled,[70] does not preclude them from being found competent to waive their appeals.[71] The reasons for waiver vary. Many of them are, like Josh Sebastian, just "tired."[72] Many cite the miserable, hellish conditions of death row. Some actually feel remorseful. Judges, lawyers, and advocates who oppose their right to waive their appeals frequently characterize the process as state-assisted suicide, which should not be granted regardless of the competence of the individual.[73] Reasonable people can debate about this: The only point I want to make here is that the U.S. Supreme Court, understanding that some of these people are suicidal, still rules that they are competent if they have a rational and factual understanding of the consequences of their decisions.[74] Under the law, suicidal people are usually competent, and death row inmates are no exception.

Furthermore, people who are charged with crimes for behavior associated with directly following suicide attempts rarely, if ever, succeed in claims that they had even "diminished" capacity at the time of the offense, let alone being found incompetent or insane.[75]

There are other issues related to criminal law and suicide, but these will be dealt with in a later chapter. Our task here is to examine how the law divides incompetent, irrational, insane suicides from those deemed to be the acts of rational and sane people. The reader may well argue that criminal law is sui generis in that it must begin with the assumption of agency and responsibility for one's actions, or else the entire foundation of the enterprise is threatened. Fair enough: we will proceed to look at other areas of the law—insurance, torts, and healthcare—for which this is not necessarily true.

---

[69] *Id.* at 952–53, n.67. This also happened in 1995, when Robert Brecheen overdosed on sedatives, was revived, and then executed by lethal injection. Associated Press, *Killer Who Took Overdose Is Revived, Then Executed*, SYRACUSE HERALD J., Aug. 11, 1995, p. A-9.

[70] Joey Miller was found competent to waive his appeals despite having "mental retardation and brain damage." Casey, *supra* note 66, at 977, n.160.

[71] Even innocent people on death row sometimes want to forego their appeals. See Blume, *supra* note 65, at n.63.

[72] *Id.* at 939.

[73] Lehnard v. Wolff, 444 U.S. 807, 815 (1979) (Marshall, J., dissenting); Kathleen Johnson, *The Death Row Right to Die: Suicide or Intimate Decision?* 54 S. CA. L. REV. 575, 592 (1981).

[74] Some mental health professionals have argued that these inmates are "affectively incompetent." See p. 51.

[75] State v. Pagano, 23 Conn. App. 447 (Conn. App. 1990) (man tries to kill himself and shortly thereafter assaults a police officer; court holds defendant produced *no* evidence that he lacked capacity).

Tort Law, Suicide, and the Chain of Causation

Tort law is the law that permits compensation for personal injury or death when caused by the negligence or intentional act of an individual who owed a duty to the plaintiff. Tort law also clearly distinguishes between competent people who commit suicide and those who could not be considered responsible for their actions.

Initially, tort law relied on criminal law in barring recovery in tort for the estate of someone who committed suicide. Courts held that because it was against public policy to profit from a crime, a tort recovery when a person died by suicide was impossible. This was the holding of a Virginia court as late as 1992.[76] In these cases, tort law borrowed the criminal law's formulation of insane as essentially about recognition and appreciation of the nature of the act. Under this formulation, tort recovery was possible if an individual was insane and thus not responsible for his or her death.

However, as states decriminalized suicide, tort doctrine evolved greater, rather than lesser, bars to recovery of damages when a case involved suicide. Although suicide was not criminal, if it was intentional, it broke the chain of causation between the defendant's negligence and the plaintiff's death. The cause of death was an individual's own intentional act, so that the negligent defendant could not be said to have caused the person's death. Although criminal law absolved a person who committed suicide while insane, tort law insisted that even insane people could break the chain of causation as long as the individual had the requisite intention, i.e., knew the purpose and physical effect of his or her act.

The test to preclude recovery was often formulated as "the voluntary, wilful act of suicide resulting from a moderately intelligent power of choice," even when that "choice is the product of a disordered mind."[77] Courts underscored this latter point using a variety of colorful language: recovery was barred if an individual took his or her own life, even when the individual had a "morbid mind 'unable to tolerate the pain, inconvenience and humiliation' of its particular condition."[78]

---

[76] The Virginia Supreme Court allowed the suit to go forward on the grounds that the decedent had been insane at the time of the suicide, and therefore not a criminal. It upheld the designation of suicide as a crime, *Wackwitz*, supra note 58. See also Hill v. Nicodemus, 755 F.Supp. 692, 693 (W.D. Va. 1991) (suicide illegal and immoral act in Virginia and even if decedent did not have a full appreciation of the injury she would incur from her actions, her estate still cannot recover); Williamson v. Virginia Beach, 786 F.Supp. 1238 (E.D. Va. 1992); Estate of Eavey v. J. Jagan Reddy & Assoc., 27 Va. Cir. 73 (Va. 11th Jud. Circ. Jan. 22, 1992); Mea v. Spiegel, 44 Va. Cir. 122 (Va. Cir. Ct. 4th JC Dec. 4, 1997).

[77] Daniels v. New York, etc. Railroad, 183 Mass. 393, 67 N.E. 424, 426 (1903); Barber v. Indus. Comm'n, 241 Wisc. 462, 6 N.W.2d 199 (Wisc. 1942); Scoggins v. Wal-Mart Stories, Inc., 560 N.W.2d 564, 568 (Iowa 1997).

[78] *Logarta, supra* note 32, at 1005 (citations omitted).

There are only two exceptions to this rule: when the defendant has a special, often custodial, relationship with the plaintiff, or when the defendant's negligent or criminal conduct actually caused the suicide by "creat[ing] in the deceased an uncontrollable impulse, frenzy or rage, during which he commits suicide without conscious volition to produce death."[79] It is interesting that while minors are often considered not competent to make healthcare choices, a minor who commits suicide breaks the chain of causation even when the suicide would not have happened absent the actions of defendant. In *Logarta v. Gustafson*, sixteen-year-old Ronald Logarta bought a loaded gun from his sixteen-year-old friend for $5 and a credit card.[80] His friend knew that Logarta was contemplating suicide, and left him in a cornfield with the guns, "asking only that Ronald think about what he was doing." The friend returned an hour later to the cornfield, found Logarta bleeding, and told Logarta's father that his son was injured and bleeding in the cornfield. Logarta's father ran to the cornfield in time to see his son die. Logarta's parents sued the friend's parents, who owned the guns. The court held that "some moral obligations do not translate easily into legal obligations." The friend's parents had no special duty to protect Logarta, who acted not from "uncontrollable impulse or frenzy or delirium" but from "a moderately intelligent power of choice."[81] The same logic has been used to shield schools from liability for the suicide of students.

Testamentary Capacity and Suicide

For many years, wealthy people have committed suicide and disappointed would-be heirs have contested wills that omitted them on the grounds that the testator was not competent at the time the will was executed (competence at the time of death doesn't matter in these cases). As in other areas of the law, the courts have made clear that there is a vast, vast amount of room for what they variously call eccentricities, idiosyncrasies, and peculiarities before an individual would reach actual testamentary incapacity. The evidence adduced to demonstrate the incompetence of a man who worked as a senior secretary for the California Supreme Court for fifty years before he committed suicide was that (1) he was building an airplane in his attic; (2) he said there was a tunnel to Lake Merced on his property; (3) he kept loaded guns around his house; (4) he considered his property very valuable; (5) he thought he could get bargains at delinquent tax sales (this was during the Great Depression); (6) he claimed to have supernatural powers; (7) he failed to recognize friends and acquaintances; (8) he was cruel to dumb animals;

---

[79] *Id.* See also Victor E. Schwartz, *Civil Liability for Causing Suicide: A Synthesis of Law and Psychiatry*, 24 VAND. L. REV. 217 (1971).

[80] *Logarta, supra* note 32, at 1000.

[81] *Id.* at 1006.

and (9) he thought there was a valuable water supply on his property.[82] No one even mentioned the fact that he had committed suicide as a factor in determining his testamentary competence. The jury decided that the testator was incompetent and the court overrode that finding. This was appealed to the Supreme Court, which was in a difficult position: it could hardly acknowledge that it had employed an outright incompetent for years, and the entire Court couldn't recuse itself. The Court upheld the finding that the testator was competent, citing a past decision of its own (which in turn incorporated a New Jersey court decision) and summarized the law as follows:

> The abstract opinion of any witness, medical or of any other profession, is not of any importance. No judicial tribunal would be justified in deciding against the capacity of a testator upon the mere opinion of witnesses, however numerous or respectable. A man may be of unsound mind and his whole neighborhood may declare him so. But whether that unsoundness amounts to incapacity for the discharge of the important duty of making final disposal of his property, is a question which the court must determine upon its own responsibility.[83]

By 1952, the California Supreme Court was willing to acknowledge that committing suicide was "relevant" to the question of sanity, but "standing alone it is insufficient to show an insanity so complete as to destroy testamentary capacity."[84] This rule of law—that attempting or committing suicide is not sufficient to destroy the presumption of testamentary capacity—is universal in the courts,[85] and has not changed with time. What has changed is that earlier courts never bothered with any kind of psychiatric or medical testimony on testamentary competence, even when the testator had committed suicide, while now mental health professionals abound as witnesses in these kinds of cases.

There are two ways in which a person can lack testamentary capacity.[86] The first is a broad incapacity, an inability to understand the nature of one's property (or "bounty," under older legal language) and the "natural objects of

---

[82] Estate of Finkler, 3 Cal.2d 584 (Ca. 1935). Although it is not mentioned in the case, there may be a connection in Finkler's mind between beliefs 2, 4, and 9.

[83] *Id.* at 594.

[84] Estate of Lingenfelter, 38 Cal.2d 571, 581 (Ca. 1952). This was followed in a case where the decedent had made multiple suicide attempts, was addicted to barbiturates, and was frequently hospitalized, Estate of Ross, 204 Cal. App. 2d 82 (Cal. App. 1962).

[85] *In re* Butler, 2012 NY Slip Op 51324 (N.Y. Surrogate's Court, Monroe Cty, July 19, 2012); Hodges v. Genzone, 724 So.2d 521 (Ala. App. 1998), aff'd 724 So.2d 524 (Ala. 1998); Breeden v. Stone, 992 P.2d 1167 (Colo. 2000).

[86] *Breeden v. Stone* contains an excellent explanation of, and distinction between, these two different forms of testamentary incapacity.

one's bounty" (generally family members) and the ability to dispose of one's property according to some plan. This does not mean the "natural objects of one's bounty" could not be disinherited, only that a person had to understand who might be expected to inherit. Even if the person understood all these things, if he or she had a fixed delusion or hallucination that affected one of these understandings, that could also result in a finding of lack of testamentary capacity.

Thus, family members who had repeatedly tried to involuntarily commit a suicidal woman "for her own good" claimed she suffered from a fixed delusion when she disinherited them, because "she could not rationally turn against her brothers and sisters who only tried to help her."[87] The trial court agreed, but the appellate court reversed. The court said,

> We believe Mrs. Bonjean's resentment of her family's attempt to force her commitment provides a rational explanation for their disinheritance . . . We find that the facts which fostered Mrs. Bonjean's hostility toward her sisters and brother have a rational basis. The hostility is not the product of a "perverted imagination." [citation omitted] Mrs. Bonjean's hostility toward her family can be rationally explained as deriving from a threat to her personal liberty associated with those same family members.[88]

Not only is the will of a person who commits suicide virtually always held to be valid, and the decedent found to be competent, but the suicide note itself has been upheld as a holographic will (even in one case where parts of the note were illegible because they were "soiled" with the blood of the testator).[89]

Worker's Compensation Law and Suicide

Worker's compensation provides income to workers whose injuries or deaths are caused by their employment. Traditionally, it barred recovery for deaths resulting from "the deliberate intention of the workman himself to produce such . . . death."[90] Thus, a suicide while sane precluded compensation for the worker's widow and family. Conversely, suicide while insane meant that a widow could receive a pension. As in the criminal law, insane was defined more and more broadly over the years, finally including "irresistible impulse, delirium caused by injury, pain from the injury or by the use of medication

---

[87] *In re* Estate of Bonjean, 90 Ill. App. 3d 582, 413 N.E.2d 205 (Ill. App. 1980).
[88] *Id.* at 586.
[89] A holographic will is "a will entirely handwritten, dated and signed by the testator (the person making the will), but not signed by required witnesses" (Holographic Will, TheFreeDictionary.com, http://legal-dictionary.thefree-dictionary.com/holographic+will); *In re* Marion R. Craig Trust, Nos. 307618, 307684 (Mich. App. Apr. 23, 2013).
[90] Schwab v. Dept. of Labor and Industry, 76 Wash. 2nd 784, 787 (1969).

employed in the treatment of the injury or as an uncontrollable impulse with no direction of the mind."[91]

This was interpreted, in a standard adopted from tort law, to mean "a voluntary wilful choice determined by a moderately intelligent mental power which knows the purpose and physical effect of the suicidal act."[92] Workers might commit suicide years after their injuries,[93] and their widows might be initially denied compensation, but jurors repeatedly found in favor of the widows. In an interesting reversal of modern-day efforts of assisted suicide advocates to distance themselves from the term suicide, the very word suicide was only applied to competent and rational people:

> The evidence was all but conclusive that defendant was insane; and, from the testimony given by the medical experts, it was shown that his state of mind was that of a child. If his mind was in the condition showed by the evidence, it is, of course, apparent that he could not commit suicide, as that term is usually used to indicate the action of a person who is able to weigh and appreciate the thing about to be done...[94]

Sane and Insane Suicides and Insurance Law

Criminal law goes back many centuries. Insurance law, which is easily the area of law that has been most preoccupied with suicide in the United States, goes back barely 150 years. Insurance law contains the kinds of arguments about terminology that make laypeople hate lawyers: Is "shall die by his own hand" the same as "suicide"?[95] Its focus on parsing the distinction between sane and insane suicides was the subject of a number of U.S. Supreme Court and lower court decisions. The ultimate failure to define the distinction between sane and insane, a line acknowledged by the Supreme Court to be "shadowy,"[96] led to the introduction into life insurance policies of language excluding recovery whether the individual was "sane or insane," generally

---

[91]   Gotterdam v. Dept. of Labor and Industry, 185 Wash. 628, 632 (1936).
[92]   Schofield v. White, 250 Iowa 571 (1959); Trombley v. Coldwater State Home and Training School, 366 Mich. 649 (1962); Globe Security Systems v. WCAB, 518 Pa. 544 (1988); Friedeman v. State, 215 Neb. 413 (1983).
[93]   Gotterdam v. Dept. of Labor and Industry, n. 91 at628(1936) (after injury, worker becomes addicted to morphine and kills himself four years later; verdict for widow).
[94]   Hepner v. Department of Labor and Industry, 141 Wash. 55, 59 (1926).
[95]   Life Ins. Co. v. Terry, 15 Wall. 580, 21 L. Ed 236 (1872) ("die by his own hand" refers to the crime of suicide and therefore is not applicable to insane persons); Bigelow v. Berkshire Life Ins. Co. 93 U.S. 284 (1876) ("shall die by his own hand" and "suicide" mean the same thing).
[96]   *Bigelow, supra* note 95.

accepted as precluding any inquiry into the mental state of a person who committed suicide.

But even with this language, the estates of some people who killed themselves were allowed to recover, and it is instructive to look at the various tiers of sanity or competence as defined in these cases.

A sane suicide, as compared to an insane suicide, is "the voluntary act of an accountable moral agent."[97] An insane suicide, however, is "conscious of the physical nature, although not of the criminality, of the act, he could take his own life with a settled purpose to do so."[98] Or, to put it another way, if an insurance policy excluded the words "suicide, sane or insane," the estate of a person could not collect if the individual "was conscious of the physical nature of his act and intended by it to cause his death, although, at the time, he was incapable of judging between right and wrong, and of understanding the moral consequences of what he was doing."[99]

From this language, it seems obvious that the self-inflicted death of an individual so psychotic that he believed he could fly, or that he was incapable of dying, would not even fall under the word suicide as understood by the Supreme Court at that time. Thus, although an insane man was "unconscious of the great crime he was committing" because "[h]is darkened mind did not enable him to see or appreciate the moral character of his act," he still "knew he was taking his own life and showed sufficient intelligence to employ a loaded pistol to accomplish his purpose."[100]

Throughout the years and in many cases, the Supreme Court and other courts gave examples of the kinds of motivations a sane suicide would have: "anger, pride, jealousy, or a desire to escape from the ills of life,"[101] the desire to discharge one's debts,[102] humiliation at being arrested,[103] or in the case of a woman, the need to preserve her chastity.[104]

One principle is extremely clear from the insurance cases: sane people commit suicide. In fact, at the turn of the century, the legal rule was that a person who committed suicide was sane until proven otherwise.[105] In another case, the court approvingly quoted a jury instruction that "the presumption of sanity is not overthrown by the act of committing suicide. Suicide may be used as evidence of insanity, but standing alone it is not

---

[97] *Id.* at 286.
[98] *Id.* at 287.
[99] *Id.*
[100] *Id.*
[101] *Ritter, supra* note 17.
[102] *Id.* at 146.
[103] *Campbell, supra* note 63 (finding that insurance company was not liable where Dr. Campbell was sane when he committed suicide: "Dr. Campbell doubtless took his life through overwhelming chagrin due to arrest on a criminal charge.").
[104] Stephenson v. State, note 62.
[105] Royal Circle v. Achterrath, 204 Ill. 544, 558 (Ill. 1903).

enough to establish it."[106] This principle has been repeated over and over again[107] and remains good law today.

Healthcare, Competency, and Suicide

The most commonly invoked analogue to competence to commit suicide is competence to refuse healthcare, or nutrition and hydration, which will inevitably lead to death. I left this subject to the last for a number of reasons.

First, it is by far the most recent development in the law. A person's right to refuse life-saving treatment was by no means accepted in the 1960s, especially if she was the mother of children. This was initially true even when people refused treatment because their faith demanded it.[108] Doctors who were asked to discontinue life support refused on the grounds that it would violate the most basic tenets of the medical profession, using much the same language that they now use in opposing assisted suicide.[109] In addition, some argued that they would be held liable for withdrawing life support from their patients, since they had a duty to their patients to keep them alive (see Tort Law, *supra* at 22). As we will see in the next chapter, even when doctors in the 1970s specifically disclaimed any concern about legal liability for honoring treatment refusals, the courts didn't believe them.[110]

It was only beginning in the early 1980s and 1990s when doctors had been reassured by a number of court cases and the passage of immunizing legislation[111] that they could not be successfully prosecuted or sued that the right to refuse life-sustaining treatment of a competent person began to be more or less universally respected. Until that time, there had been no need to define competence to refuse life-saving treatment, because patients neither enjoyed nor exercised those rights.[112] Yet today, one of the most fundamental and universally cited tenets of both law and medicine is that all competent individuals have the right to "decide all aspects of [their own] health care in

---

[106] *Ritter, supra* note 17, at 147–48.

[107] Strasberg v. Equitable Life Assurance Soc., 281 App. Div. 9, 13 (N.Y. App. 1952) ("Insanity cannot be presumed from the mere fact of suicide for experience has shown that self-destruction is often perpetrated by the sane.").

[108] *In re* Application of the President and Directors of Georgetown College, 331 F.2d 1000 (D.C. Cir. 1964).

[109] JILL LEPORE, THE MANSION OF HAPPINESS: A HISTORY OF LIFE AND DEATH (2012) quotes from a copy of the transcript of the Karen Ann Quinlan trial. The doctors argued that withdrawing life support would set them down the road to the medical atrocities of the Nazi era. This is not as fanciful as it might seem: many disability rights activists oppose assisted suicide for the same reason.

[110] See discussion of Quinlan and other cases in Chapter 2.

[111] The Patient Self-Determination Act of 1990, P.L. 101-508, both immunized doctors who followed advance directives and penalized doctors who did not.

[112] See JAY KATZ, THE SILENT WORLD OF DOCTOR AND PATIENT (paperback 2002).

all circumstances, including the right to decline health care or to direct that health care be discontinued, even if death ensues."[113]

The principle that competent patients can make their own healthcare decisions, even unto death, is fundamental to our jurisprudence and social policy, and is essentially uncontested by the legal or medical professions. However, in practice, there has been continued and consistent resistance from the medical and especially the mental health profession to patients choosing death under circumstances that these professionals consider inappropriate. This has led to theories and practices that vastly and improperly expand the concept of incompetence when it comes to decisions about dying.

Let's look at the law first. While there never has been uniform agreement on a definition or measure of competence to make healthcare decisions, most state laws share many common elements. The closest thing to a universal standard in this country is the Uniform Health-Care Decisions Act, which defines capacity as "an individual's ability to understand the significant benefits, risks and alternatives to proposed health care and to make and communicate a health care decision."[114] The Mental Capacity Act, passed by Parliament in England in 2005, finds that "a person is unable to make a decision for himself if he is unable

(a) To understand the information relevant to a decision
To retain that information
To use or weigh that information as part of the process of making a decision, or
To communicate his decision (whether by talking, sign language, or any other means).[115]

There is certainly no specific definition of competence to commit suicide, or standards to follow, even in states with assisted suicide laws.[116] It's not clear

---

[113] National Conference of Commissioners on Uniform State Laws, Uniform Health-Care Decisions Act, Prefatory Note, p. 1 (1994) (adopted in five states). Shine v. Vega, 429 Mass. 456 (1999).

[114] National Conference of Commissioners on Uniform State Laws, Uniform Health-Care Decisions Act, § 1, (3) (approved by American Bar Association 1994), see n.107.

[115] Mental Capacity Act (2005), § 3(1).

[116] The Center for Ethics in Healthcare, Oregon Health and Science University, The Oregon Death with Dignity Act: A Guidebook for Health Care Professionals (current ed. 2008), http://www.ohsu.edu/xd/education/continuing-education/center-for-ethics/ethics-outreach/upload/Oregon-Death-with-Dignity-Act-Guidebook.pdf Darien S. Fenn and Linda Ganzini, "Attitudes of Oregon Psychologists Toward Physician-Assisted Suicide and the Oregon Death with Dignity Act," 30 *Professional Psychology: Research and Practice* 235 (1999); Matthew Hotopf, William Lee, & Annabel Price, *Assisted Suicide: Why Psychiatrists Should Engage in the Debate*, 198 BR. J. PSYCHIATRY 83 (2011).

that we need a different definition of competence from the standards cited earlier. But because competent patients are understood to have complete rights of decision about matters relating to their health, the medical and mental health professions have often, as a practical matter, expanded the concept of incompetence when the patient's decision is one with which they disagree.

First, at the crudest and least sophisticated level, the question of competence in the healthcare arena generally arises only when the patient disagrees with the recommendation of the medical or mental health professional. I once served as a healthcare proxy for a hospitalized woman with serious health problems. I received a frantic telephone message to call the hospital immediately: they needed me to act as her healthcare proxy because she had decided she wanted her ventilator disconnected. When I called back, the doctor told me (using these words), "Oh, it's all right. She's regained her competence," by which he meant she had changed her mind about the ventilator. Competence in practice for some medical and mental health professionals is simply a proxy for agreeing with the doctor's view.[117]

These assumptions of competence also operate when obviously incompetent people passively comply with recommended treatment.[118] It is an open secret that incompetent assenters to treatment proliferate in the medical and mental health system. In one of the rare decisions exposing and rejecting this practice, the Supreme Court decided that failure to protect the rights of incompetent assenters can constitute a violation of their constitutional rights to due process if they are deemed to assent to commitment and medication.[119] The practice of not questioning incompetent assent to recommended treatments, however, remains widespread.[120]

Few medical and mental health professionals would actually articulate a belief that a patient who disagreed with them was automatically incompetent.[121]

---

[117] In the Elizabeth Bouvia case, the chief of psychiatry at Riverside Hospital testified that Ms. Bouvia's decision to refuse food was the result of "impairment." When asked whether if she changed her mind and decided to eat, that decision would be "a competent health care decision on her part," he answered, "I think it would be." Transcript, at 590, quoted in George Annas, n. 1 p. 571. Another doctor in the case testified "When a patient agrees with me, the patient is rational. When an eighty-year-old lady refuses to have a massive resection of her bowel for widespread cancer, then I send her to a psychiatrist because she is not agreeing with me, so she is irrational." *Id.*

[118] Zinermon v. Burch, 494 U.S. 113, 110 S. Ct. 975 (1990).

[119] *Id.*

[120] Renee Sorrentino, *Performing Capacity Evaluations: What's Expected for Your Consult*, 13 Current Psychiatry 41 (2014); James L. Bernat, Ethical Issues in Neurology (1994) 28 (doctors only question the competence of patients who disagree with their treatment plans).

[121] Hotopf et al., *supra* note 112 ("Clearly it would be wrong to state that someone, by virtue of making a decision of which others disapprove, automatically lacks capacity").

There is, however, a distinguishable viewpoint that deserves more examination than the naked paternalism that simply equates disagreement with the doctor as incompetence or *lack of insight*. This is the view that suicidality itself (rather than simply disagreement with any treatment recommendation by a mental health professional) is always or almost always a symptom of treatable mental illness that by its very nature robs its sufferers of an understanding of the nature of their suffering.

Thus, a substantial number of mental health professionals believe that the desire to end one's life is itself the product of incompetence under any circumstances: that there can be no such thing as a competent desire to die.[122] Many psychiatrists think *anyone* who wants to end his or her life is by definition mentally ill or lacking capacity, or both.[123] This view extends even to people with terminal illness contemplating assisted suicide who (it is asserted) are only suicidal because they are suffering from depression, an illness separate and distinct from whatever terminal illness they happen to have. "Psychiatrists [insist] that suicidality [even among terminally medically ill patients] is treatable, preventable, and certainly a sign of psychiatric disorder."[124] An amicus brief to the Supreme Court when it was considering the right to assisted suicide asserted that "most cancer patients now committing suicide have discernible psychiatric illness . . ."[125] Even when terminally ill people do not have depression, other amicus briefs submitted to the Court argued that the competence of people with agonizingly painful terminal illnesses is questionable, "since patients tend to lose competence as illness becomes more severe."[126] This is a neat argument: the more severely people are suffering, the more incompetent their resulting desire to die. These arguments never consider that if terminal illness causes incompetence, the decision (or acquiescence) to live through excruciating suffering might also reflect an incompetent decision. "Psychiatric response [to proposals to legalize assisted suicide] has been almost uniformly critical of the rationality of suicide."[127] In

---

[122] This is somewhat different from a belief that a desire to die is always caused by a treatable mental illness, although the distinctions blur in practice. In the law, the distinction between a belief that suicidality is always an indication of incompetence, and suicidality is always an indication of treatable mental illness, would be manifested by the remedy: the appointment of a substitute decisionmaker in the former instance and involuntary civil commitment in the latter case.

[123] WERTH, *supra* note 25.

[124] Thomas S. Zaubler & Mark D. Sullivan, *Psychiatry and Physician-Assisted Suicide*, 19 CONSULTATION-LIAISON PSYCHIATRY 413, 415 (1996).

[125] *Id.* at 22, quoting William Brietbart et al., *Neuropsychiatric Syndromes and Psychological Symptoms in Patients with Advanced Cancer*, 10 J. PAIN SYMPTOM MGMT. 131–41 (1995).

[126] Richard G. Coleson, *The Glucksberg and Quill Amicus Curiae Briefs: Verbatim Arguments Opposing Assisted Suicide*, 13 Iss. L. MED. 3, 21 (1997). I take up the "right to die" in detail in Chapter 2.

[127] Zaubler & Sullivan, *supra* note 124, at 413.

this view, *all* suicides are the result of "curable medical disorders . . . Such an approach denies that there is any moral agency attached to the act."[128] Suicide, in this perspective, "is a symptom of psychopathology."[129]

Yet another view, held by many physicians as well as mental health professionals, is that *terminally ill* people may be competent in choosing to end their lives, because such a decision makes sense to the rest of us and they are not forfeiting much in the way of the amount or quality of the life left to them. However, otherwise medically healthy people must be incompetent if they choose to end their lives, especially if they have a diagnosis of psychiatric disability. It does not matter if this psychiatric disability is chronic, refractory, and extraordinarily painful. For example, in one survey, 72% of geriatric psychiatrists said they would counsel a competent patient with severe depression refractory to all treatments against suicide, whereas only 32% would counsel a competent patient terminally ill with pancreatic cancer against suicide.[130] And yet, mental health professionals acknowledge that there are some—as many as a third of all patients—for whom no treatment works (or works long-term). For these people, their mental and emotional pain can be truly agonizing, robbing them of their sense of self and autonomy and independence as surely as many terminal illnesses. As Anita Darcel Taylor, a person diagnosed with bipolar disorder, wrote:

> If there is a rational thought in choosing suicide, it is that the sufferer hasn't the strength to live through the agony again, much in the way that a cancer patient may not be able to withstand another bout of chemotherapy. Mental anguish can be as unruly as any terminal illness . . . I am saying to you that manic depression has the power to deplete one of a life worth living, a substantive, independent, emotionally healthy, companionable, intelligent adult life.
>
> I say this and yet I make repeated trips to the hospital. A good hospital can bring near-instant, if temporary, relief . . . But no amount of medication, therapy, or good intentions can undo the permanent damage of the disease . . . I have no grand wish for death. I do not view suicide as a desire to end life or a dramatic way to go down in flames . . . When I have lost enough of myself to this disease as to become unrecognizable even to me, I will stop. I will go no further. This, I tell myself, is my earned choice.[131]

---

[128] KEVIN YUILL, ASSISTED SUICIDE: THE LIBERAL, HUMANIST CASE AGAINST LEGALIZATION 96–97 (2013).

[129] Y. Conwell & and E. D. Caine, Rational Suicide and the Right to Die: Reality and Myth, 325 NEW ENG. J. MED. 1100 (1991).

[130] Zaubler & Sullivan, *supra* note 124, at 419.

[131] Anita Darcel Taylor, *By My Own Hand*, BELLEVUE LITERARY REV., 117–21 (2006).

Ms. Taylor's thoughts of suicide are not symptoms of her condition, manifesting during an episode; they are a thoughtful *reaction* to the reality and chronicity of her condition. Ms. Taylor, like Josh Sebastian, has reflected on suicide in a thoughtful way for many years, voluntarily sought and received available treatment, and has come to a position that no honest evaluator could call incompetent. Many courts considering malpractice cases against mental health professionals for the suicides of their patients have expressly and explicitly held that suicidal people can be, and often are, competent.[132] In Chapter 2, I will discuss whether the State should prevent Ms. Taylor from ending her life; the only argument I want to make here is that Ms. Taylor is competent by any honest measure, legal or medical.

To consider Ms. Taylor incompetent to decide to end her life would involve one of three approaches, which have been consistently rejected by law and medicine: (1) determining competence by outcome, that is, by the chosen outcome rather than by evaluating the process of decision making; (2) assuming Ms. Taylor's decision was not competent because she had a diagnosis of bipolar disorder; or (3) Ms. Taylor suffers from so-called affective incompetence—while appearing cognitively able to reason, her depressed mood makes her weigh her options irrationally. While this last approach is ostensibly based on the process of decision making rather than the decision made or the diagnosis of the decision-maker, it is simply is a more elegant way of combining the first two objections, both of which have been discredited by substantial research. I will take each of these in turn.

Outcome-based Determinations of Incompetence

Under this model, a person making a "decision that reflects values not widely held or that rejects conventional wisdom about proper health care is found to be incapacitated."[133] Competence assessment according to outcome has been rejected consistently by the law and by health and ethics commissions,[134] and by the most respected members of the medical and psychiatric professions, yet it still occurs.[135] The best-known proponent of values-based judgments of competence is Charland, who supports the proposition that a person could be

---

[132] Farwell v. Un, 902 F.2d 282, 288 (4th Cir. 1990) (experts in the case agreed that the man who committed suicide was competent); Brandvain v. Ridgeview Institute, 372 S.E.2d 265, 188 Ga. App.106, 119 (Ga. App. 1988) (finding that some suicides can be rational).

[133] PRESIDENT'S COMMISSION FOR THE STUDY OF ETHICAL PROBLEMS IN MEDICINE AND BIOMEDICAL AND BEHAVIORAL SCIENCES, MAKING HEALTH CARE DECISIONS 170 (vol. 1, 1982).

[134] *Id.* at pp. 60–62, 170.

[135] Harold I. Schwartz, *Determining Resuscitation Status: A Survey of Medical Professionals*, 8 GEN. HOSP. PSYCHIATRY 198 (May 1986) (several physicians expressed disbelief that any competent person would refuse resuscitation).

considered incompetent because his or her values are unreasonable, regardless of ability to reason, appreciate, understand, and communicate.[136]

This view has been rightly rejected by principal scholars of competence, especially those with an understanding of the law.[137] The most fundamental principle of competence law is that incompetence describes an inability to engage in a mental process, not a socially disfavored decision. The law does not judge competency according to the choice made by the patient, but according to the patient's appreciation of his or her circumstances, the ability to understand, manipulate, and weigh information, and to communicate a decision. Adult patients are permitted to refuse life-saving treatment for any condition, regardless of its cause, how easy it would be to save their lives, or the fact that doctors disagree with the patient's decision.

Nevertheless, the assertion that all choices to die are caused by mental illness and should be treated as incompetent is completely unsupported by history and research. It is not much more than an interesting window into our current culture. These days, we increasingly attribute suicide to mental illness. In 1840, Forbes Winslow, a surgeon, wrote that the increase of suicide in that day was caused by the appearance of "socialism."[138] There was, he noted, a sudden increase in suicides following the publication of Thomas Paine's *The Age of Reason*.[139] Not unaware of the complexity of the phenomenon, however, he went on to cite other causative factors such as "atmospherical moisture"[140] and, a long-time favorite, "masturbation."[141] Lest we be too ready to mock Mr. Winslow as a creature of his time, we should remember that President Dwight Eisenhower attributed the high rate of suicide in Sweden to "too much social welfare."[142]

---

[136] L. C. E. Charland, *Mental Competence and Value: The Problem of Normativity in the Assessment of Decisionmaking Capacity*, 8 PSYCHIATRY PSYCHOL. L. 135 (2001).

[137] Paul S. Appelbaum & Charles W. Lidz, *Re-Evaluating the Therapeutic Misconception: A Response to Miller and Joffe*, 16 KENNEDY INST. ETHICS J. 367 (2006).

[138] Forbes Winslow, The Anatomy of Suicide 83 (1840). This book, which serves as an excellent reminder of the degree to which "clinical" assessments of suicide arise from social values and assumptions, can be read on the internet at https://books.google.com/books?hl=en&lr=&id=a3dCAAAAIAAJ&oi=fnd&pg=PA1&dq=Forbes+Winslow+suicide+socialism&ots=IlFBSghBV2&sig=VqyZi14tu60aGQ_nMtdSfFhoPVE#v=onepage&q=Forbes%20Winslow%20suicide%20socialism&f=false

[139] *Id.* at 88–89.

[140] *Id.* at 113.

[141] Not referred to as such, but as "the secret vice," *Id.* at p. 136.

[142] Bobby Allyn, "Everyone Thinks Sweden Has a Sky-High Suicide Rate—It Doesn't," New York Magazine, May 20, 2014, http://nymag.com/scienceofus/2014/05/sweden-to-world-were-not-suicidal.html# (attributing the common misconception that Sweden has a high suicide rate to Dwight Eisenhower's 1960

The argument that anyone who chooses to end his or her life is per se incompetent or mentally ill is an assertion that anyone who seriously struggles with the question of whether life is worth living is sick. The transformation of Camus' famous proposition[143] into a symptom of mental illness dates back at least as far as 1979, when psychiatrists proposed a diagnosis of "existential despair."[144] This would certainly fit Josh Sebastian, and he would (I believe correctly) indignantly reject it as a diagnostic category. First, to turn existential despair into a psychiatric diagnosis is to demean a fundamental aspect of the human condition as pathology. Second, it's not so clear that mental health professionals are particularly well equipped to answer these questions. Even many of the proponents of the diagnosis of existential despair recognized that psychiatric treatment does not help existential despair, but that didn't stop them.[145]

Presumed Incompetence Because a Person Has a Diagnosis of Mental Illness

The law assumes all individuals' competence to make health care decisions. Many state laws also contain an explicit statement that mental illness should not be equated with lack of competence. In addition, state laws or regulations often explicitly provide that institutionalization does not rob a person of the legal right to make his or her own treatment decisions, including the decision to refuse treatment.

A number of courts have honored these laws. In fact, the first case I could find that used the phrase "right to die" involved an institutionalized woman with breast cancer who was found competent to refuse treatment for her cancer.[146] Maida Yetter, who had been institutionalized at Allentown State Hospital for over a year at the time of the hearing, had a discharge from her breast. The hospital wished to perform a diagnostic biopsy. Mrs. Yetter refused this surgical procedure. The court, describing her as "alert, interested,

---

speech blaming Sweden's embrace of socialist policies as triggering "sin, nudity, drunkenness and suicide.")

[143] "There is but one truly serious philosophical problem and that is suicide. Judging whether life is or is not worth living amounts to answering the fundamental question of philosophy." CAMUS, *supra* note 22, at 3.

[144] D. A. Schwartz, D. E. Hinn, & P. E. Slawson, *Treatment of the Suicidal Character,* 28 AM. J. PSYCHOTHERAPY 194 (1979).

[145] *Id.* Dr. John Maltsberger, a noted expert on suicide, disagreed with this conclusion, asserting that "patients such as these, if they live and are patiently supported in a not too intrusive psychotherapy, sometimes slowly develop more interest in living, often after forming an attachment to the therapist." John Maltsberger, *Calculated Risks in the Treatment of Suicidal Patients,* 57 PSYCHIATRY 199, 202, n.6 (1994).

[146] *In re* Maida Yetter, 62 Pa. D.&C.2d 619, Pa. Dist. & Cnty. Dec LEXIS 223, (1973)

and obviously meticulous about her personal appearance," quoted her as saying she was afraid of surgery, that the best course was to leave her body alone, and that performance of the biopsy might hasten the spread of the disease and do further harm. She believed that an aunt had died as a result of such a procedure (the aunt did have the procedure, but died fifteen years later of unrelated causes). The court found that Mrs. Yetter was competent to refuse the biopsy even if it led to her death, because "in our opinion, the right of privacy includes a right to die with which the State should not interfere if there are no minor or unborn children and no clear and present danger to health, welfare and morals." The court rejected her brother's petition to be appointed her guardian in order to consent to the surgery. Maida Yetter died five years later at the age of sixty-five.[147]

Nancy Milton was an institutionalized woman with uterine cancer.[148] She was hospitalized because she had an unshakable delusion that she was married to Rev. Leroy Jenkins, a well-known faith healer and evangelist, who she believed had cured her of blindness (her doctors called it hysterical blindness). Her doctor wanted her to have radiation, transfusions, and possibly surgery. He conceded that even with the treatment there was a less than 50% chance that she would be cancer-free for five years or more. He thought treatment would prolong her life. Ms. Milton, on the other hand, however, believed that she would be cured through faith healing. Her doctor acknowledged that Ms. Milton's belief in "spiritual healing is the prime thing in [the] appellant's life and she believes that it would be almost a sin to try anything else"[149] and that (other than thinking she was Rev. Jenkins' wife) she was "pretty much intact."[150] The Ohio Supreme Court upheld Ms. Milton's refusal of cancer treatment as a protection of her constitutional right to religious freedom. While conceding that "extending constitutional protection to a belief in spiritual healing can be very troubling to those who do not share these beliefs,[151] [t]here is a dichotomy between modern medicine which is scientific and based upon provable theories and religion which is *inherently* mystical, intangible, and a matter of individual faith."[152]

Laws that strongly protect the assumption that all adults are competent to refuse treatment, including life-sustaining treatment, even laws and cases that preserve those rights for individuals who are mentally ill, institutionalized, or both, often exist alongside a parallel legal universe with distinctively inferior rights and protections when it comes to refusing psychiatric

---

[147] www.ancientfaces.com/person/maida-yetter/22993060. This records the death of a woman named Maida Yetter, whose birthdate coincides with that of the Maida Yetter in the case and whose last known address is Allentown, Pennsylvania.

[148] *In re* Milton, 29 Ohio St.3rd 20, n.2 (1987).

[149] *Id.* at 23, n. 6.

[150] *Id.* at 23.

[151] *Id.* at 24–25.

[152] *Id.* at 24.

treatments. For example, the same state often has a health care proxy law for all of its citizens, and a separate health care proxy law with reduced rights for people with psychiatric disabilities to refuse psychiatric medications.[153] Other states provide greater protections for prisoners who refuse psychiatric medications than individuals in psychiatric institutions, or with psychiatric diagnoses, refusing the same medications. These disparities are occasionally challenged as discriminatory. Sometimes these challenges are successful,[154] and sometimes not.[155]

The paradox of granting all citizens the right to refuse health care treatment, while making it easier to force psychiatric medications on unwilling patients, occasionally creates dissonances that starkly highlight the discrepancies in these rights. The Kerrie Wooltorton case in England is one of the best known of these cases: Ms. Wooltorton took a fatal dose of antifreeze, and then, not wishing to die alone and in pain, took an ambulance to the hospital where she refused life-saving treatment.[156] Although the much laxer provisions of the mental health law would have permitted psychiatric medications to be forced on her, they explicitly did not permit forced medical treatment. The law protecting people's right to refuse medical treatment was much stronger, and her doctors determined she was competent under that law to refuse treatment. The hospital honored her decision to refuse treatment and provided palliative care until she died, several days later, a decision later upheld by the Coroner.

When people who have attempted suicide or their families attempt to refuse medical treatment necessary to save their lives, doctors (especially in the emergency department) tend to viscerally reject any possibility that the refusal may be competent. This belief is so strong that some doctors have suggested that a patient who is terminally ill and attempts suicide may be competent to refuse life-saving treatment of the terminal illness, while *simultaneously* being incompetent to refuse treatment related to the suicide attempt.[157] Some doctors refuse to withdraw life support after a suicide

[153] Robert D. Fleischner, *Advance Directives for Mental Health Care: An Analysis of State Statutes*, 4 PSYCHOL. PUB. POL'Y L. 788 (1998).

[154] Hargrave v. Vermont, 340 F.3d 27 (2nd Cir. 2003).

[155] DRNJ v. Velez, 974 F.Supp.2d 705 (D.N.J. 2013) (distinguishing *Hargrave* because no individualized determination was made regarding dangerousness prior to suspension of the individual's advance directive).

[156] This case is discussed in detail in Chapter 5 at pp. 247–251.

[157] See Chapter 5 for a more complete discussion. T. C. Bania, R. Lee, & M. Clark, *Ethics Seminars: Health Care Proxies and Suicidal Patients*, 10 ACAD. EMERGENCY MED. 65 (Jan. 2003), see also Ruth Townsend, *Treatment after Suicide by Townsend and Eburn*, HEALTH, LAW, ETHICS AND HUMAN RIGHTS (Aug. 5, 2013), http://healthlawethics.wordpress.com/2013/05/08/treatment-after-suicide-by-townsend-and-eburn (last visited Mar. 17, 2014).

attempt under medical circumstances where they would otherwise have withdrawn life support.[158]

I want to be clear that I am not arguing that all people diagnosed with psychiatric conditions are in fact competent to make health care decisions. There are some conditions that often result in lack of competence: delirium, dementia, certain psychoses, and intoxication. This does not mean that people with these conditions are never competent, but they are less likely to be competent when they are behaving suicidally. In my interviews, one woman with schizophrenia recognized that her suicidality was not competent and welcomed compassionate, respectful intervention:

> My suicide attempt was caused by voices making irrational statements not based in fact ... [The voices] are very loud and very constant, they overwhelm my defenses. They interfere with my sleep. I try to kill myself partly to shut them up and partly because they say the future will be so bad. They overwhelm my understanding that they are not real. They seem entirely real. Their arguments are convoluted, but I can't take them on very effectively because I am just hearing them and hearing them and hearing them and there is no time to stop and evaluate. I have to evaluate all the time. I need the time between each voice arriving to muster my arguments against them so they don't overwhelm my rationality ... the voices tell me to kill myself, that all my friends hate me, my therapist has terminated me, I am going to be homeless, they make me sad and miserable and they independently tell me to commit suicide. When the voices are that bad, I have to be in a safe place ... No one can reach me.[159]

But when this woman is psychotic, it doesn't take a sophisticated evaluation to discern it. Incompetence is generally obvious: delirium, intoxication, and psychoses generally do not take extensive training to recognize. One respected ethicist asserts that any layperson can determine whether a person is incompetent,[160] and I agree.

---

[158] Samuel Brown et al., *Withdrawal of Non-Futile Life Support After Attempted Suicide*, 13 Am. J. Bioethics, 1, 6 (2013).

[159] Interview with S.M., Feb. 23, 2014.

[160] Annas & Densberger, *supra* note 1 at 584. Some psychiatric sources disagree, advancing "affective incompetence" as a subtle form of incompetence created by mood disorders rather than distortions in cognition see p. 51, *infra*, the generally accepted cause of incompetence.

Problems in Competence and Suicide: Anorexia

People with anorexia do not want to die in the sense that the anorexia itself is not a conscious expression or unconscious form of suicidality.[161] What many people with anorexia want to do is to feel in control of their lives, to be perfect, and to live their lives in congruence with an identity that makes sense to them even though in some cases it may eventually kill them.[162] However, society, the people who love them, and the mental health profession recoil from and repudiate their behaviors and identities as disordered and dangerous, call their efforts to control their eating symptoms of mental illness, and often force people with anorexia into involuntary detention and forcible, intrusive treatment.[163] Some mental health professionals have barely controlled hostility toward people with anorexia. One of the women I interviewed spoke movingly about how staff treated a woman with anorexia who was an inpatient with her:

> Some mental health professionals pick and choose what they want to pathologize and what they don't. Annie was in treatment with

---

[161] Philip C. Hebert & Michael A. Weingarten, *The Ethics of Forcefeeding in Anorexia Nervosa*, 144 CAN. MED. J. 141, 143 (1991); Dr. Alan Apter, *Why Is the Suicide Rate So High for Anorexia? How the Eating Disorder Takes Over a Patient's Life*, Child Mind Institute, www.childmind.org/en/posts/ask-an-expert/2010-11-14-why-suicide-rate-so-high-anorexia; see also Margery Gans & William B. Gunn Jr., *End-Stage Anorexia: Criteria for Competence to Refuse Treatment, in* APPLIED ETHICS IN MENTAL HEALTH CARE: AN INTERDISCIPLINARY READER 94–95 (Dominic Sisti, Arthur L. Caplan, Hila Rimon-Greenspan, & Paul S. Appelbaum eds., 2013).Thus, the proposal to hold websites, which encourage and advise anorexics on how to lose weight, liable for assisting suicide, see Annika K. Martin, *Stick a Toothbrush Down Your Throat: An Analysis of the Potential Liability of Pro-Eating Disorder Websites*, 14 TEX. J. WOMEN & L. 151, 165 (2005) would likely fail.

[162] HILDE BRUCH, THE GOLDEN CAGE: THE ENIGMA OF ANOREXIA NERVOSA (1978). Jacinta Tan, Tony Hope, Anne Stewart, & Raymond Fitzgerald, *Competence to Make Treatment Decisions in Anorexia Nervosa: Thinking Processes and Values*, 13 PHILOS. PSYCH. PSYCHO 267 (2006); Heather Draper, *Anorexia Nervosa and Respecting a Refusal of Life-Prolonging Therapy: A Limited Justification*, 14 BIOETHICS 120 (2000); Rebecca Dresser, *Feeding the Hunger Artists: Legal Issues in Treating Anorexia Nervosa*, 1984 WISC. L. REV. 297; Emma Rich, *Anorexic (Dis)connection: Managing Anorexia as an Illness and Identity*, 28 SOCIOL. HEALTH ILLN. 284 (2006); J. Patching & J. Lawler, *Understanding Women's Experiences of Developing an Eating Disorder and Recovering: A Life History Approach*, 16 NURS. INQ. 10 (2009).

[163] In addition to therapy, people with anorexia "normally receive some form of involuntary feeding," sometimes dozens or even a hundred times, Hebert & Weingarten, *supra* note 148, at n.137 (noting that the woman in their case study had spent most of eight years in a hospital, much of the time in restraints and with a gastroscopy tube).

me . . . and she had what they would call "severe and enduring anorexia nervosa." She voluntarily checked herself into treatment. She would whip her tube out in the middle of the night, and then go to the nurse's station and say, I did it again. There was little recognition of how hard she's trying, she's not trying the way they want her to try, so she's treatment resistant. She made no effort to check herself out, how can you say she's resistant? She's just having a harder time than the other people. If you do something they like, it's like, she has insight into her illness. It's more about doing what they want than accurately describing that person's behavior and motivation. I do feel that labels are used to enforce compliance with whatever course the MH [mental health] professional has decided is right.[164]

These conflicts with family and mental health professionals, as well as the intrusive and aversive treatments, may (or may not) be what leads to people with anorexia having one of the highest suicide rates of any diagnosed mental disorder,[165] assuming it is a mental disorder.[166] As Dr. Alan Apter perceptively noted:

I think another way of understanding what drives an anorexic to kill herself is that it really becomes an ideology, a belief that she's committed to. In order to be thin, she's prepared to *do anything*.
I often use this example from my own culture. If you ask the religious Jew to eat pork, as the only alternative to dying, he may well choose to die. And I think it's very similar with anorexics. They may feel that what they want to be, *need* to be, society's just not going to let them be. And so eventually they are in this

---

[164] Interview with Kara, email confirmation Jan. 13, 2015.

[165] Everyone agrees that this statement is true, although the suicide rates attributed to anorexia vary considerably, generally between 6% and 20%, see, e.g., Gans & Gunn, *supra* note 148.

[166] Dresser, *supra* note 162, at 328–29, argued that "imposing the medical model upon the events comprising an episode of anorexia is only one of several ways to give meaning to these events." More recently, scholars such as Joan Jacobs Brumberg and Bradley A. Areheart have continued to argue that "eating disorders appear ultimately to be cultural productions, no matter what biological mechanisms they provoke," Joan Jacobs Brumberg, *From Psychiatric Syndrome to Communicable Disease: The Case of Anorexia Nervosa, in* FRAMING DISEASE: STUDIES IN CULTURAL HISTORY 149 (Charles E. Rosenberg & Janet Golden eds., 1997) and that any condition such as anorexia, which is limited to a particular time in history and a particular society and within that society, a particular socioeconomic level cannot be seen solely as either a disease or an illness, Bradley A. Areheart, *Disability Trouble*, 29 YALE L. POL'Y REV. 347 (2011).

impossible situation—everyone around them is against them—and they end up killing themselves.[167]

On the other hand, perhaps the suicide rate among people with anorexia is exceptionally high because it is hard, if not impossible,[168] to cure anorexia, and the virtually inevitable accompanying medical problems can be severe and debilitating.[169] It wouldn't be easy to conduct controlled research in an ethical way on this question of why there is such a high suicide rate among people with anorexia, so professionals continue to speculate.

The fact that our legal framework of competence is permeated with social values and assumptions is particularly obvious in the case of anorexia. People with anorexia are often highly intelligent and can understand and reason very well.[170] A woman with anorexia who is perfectly capable of understanding that if she doesn't eat she will die, and prefers death to being fat, can engage in all the understanding and reasoning required by legal standards for competence. Women with anorexia pass the standard MacArthur Competence Assessment Tool for Treatment (MacCAT-T) test of competence—considered the current gold standard for formal assessment of competence in clinical psychiatry,[171] with flying colors.[172] Their competence scores bear no relationship to the severity of their condition or their body mass index. Young women interviewed about anorexia reiterated that it was fundamental to their identity:

Q: What does your anorexia nervosa mean to you?
A: As I said before, it's quite a lot. It feels like my identity now, and it feels like, I suppose I worry that people don't know, they don't know the real me. (Participant A)
Q: Let's say . . . someone said they could wave a magic wand and there wouldn't be anorexia any more.
A: I couldn't.

---

[167] Apter, *supra* note 161; see also Ganns & Gunn, *supra* note 161, at 94–95, n.151.
[168] Rosalyn Griffiths & Janice Russell, *Compulsory Treatment of Anorexia Nervosa Patients, in* TREATING EATING DISORDERS: ETHICAL, LEGAL AND PERSONAL ISSUES (Walter Vandereycken & Pierre J. V. Beaumont eds., 1998).
[169] These include mitral valve prolapse from wasted cardiac muscle, brachycardia, and extreme fatigue, Ellen S. Rome & Seth Ammerman, *Medical Complications of Eating Disorders: An Update*, 33 J. ADOLESCENT HEALTH 418 (2003).
[170] Jacinta Tan, Tony Hope, & Anne Stewart, *Competence to Refuse Treatment in Anorexia Nervosa*, 26 INT'L J. L. PSYCHIATRY 697, 698 (2003).
[171] T. Grisso, P. Appelbaum, & C. Hill-Fotouhi, *The MacCAT-T: A Tool to Assess Patients' Capacities to Make Treatment Decisions*, 48 PSYCHIATRIC SERVICES 1415 (1997). Even its critics admit its preeminence in the field, T. M. Breden & J. Vollmann, *The Cognitive Based Approach of Capacity Assessment in Psychiatry: A Philosophical Critique of the MacCAT-t*, 12 HEALTH CARE ANAL. 273 (2004).
[172] Tan et al., *supra* note 162.

Q: You couldn't.
A: It's just a part of me now.
Q: Right. So it feels like you'd be losing a part of you.
A: Because it was my identity. (Participant I)[173]

We don't like the results of their reasoning process, but legal decisions about capacity are based on the process of understanding the options and the ability to reason about them, and not the outcome, even if we think the person's decision is mistaken or irrational. As Apter asks, is the anorexic's decision different from that of an Orthodox Jew who would rather die than eat pork (or a Jehovah's Witness who would rather die than accept a blood transfusion)? Religious beliefs are privileged irrationality in our society, because religious identities are supported in our society. I am not arguing that religion is (necessarily) a self-destructive identity, or that we should support self-destructive identities, or even that people with anorexia should never be involuntarily treated, only that a diagnosis of anorexia does not mean an individual is per se incompetent to make treatment decisions. Psychotherapy is one of the few treatment modalities that has been shown to help people with anorexia, and people have to be competent to engage in continuing psychotherapy.

Again, competence does not mean that the woman with anorexia is free to starve herself. The State can, as a separate matter, take the position that its compelling interest in life trumps a competent individual's right to make decisions about his or her body. Competence is unrelated to commitability. This proposition is discussed fully in the next chapter.

Arguments that anorexia equates with incompetence must deal with the clear and obvious ability of many individuals with anorexia to understand and reason and decide. Proponents of the per se incompetence argument contend that people with anorexia are "incompetent in the narrow area of self-nutrition"[174] or that they are "subtly incompetent."[175] While a person who refused to believe that she might eventually die as a result of her failure to ingest sufficient calories would be incompetent, a person who understands and accepts that death may be the consequence of her conduct and her treatment refusal, and who consistently refuses treatment because she prefers to die than be repeatedly hospitalized and force-fed--treatment involving a life that still revolves endlessly around her eating, just one where she has lost all control, is probably a competent person.

Just because anorexia itself is not a sublimated drive toward suicide does not mean that people with anorexia might not want to refuse the treatment—medical or force-feeding—necessary to keep them alive. How are we to assess

---

173 *Id.*
174 Tom Gutheil & Harold Bursztajn, *Clinicians' Guidelines for Assessing and Presenting Subtle Forms of Patient Incompetence in Legal Settings*, 143 Am. J. Psychiatry 1020 (1986).
175 P. Lewis, *Feeding Anorexics Who Refuse Food*, 7 Med. L. Rev. 21 (1999).

the competence of a woman with long-standing anorexia to refuse treatment for the medical conditions resulting from her anorexia, or for the anorexia itself? This issue has been raised a number of times, and been answered differently in different places.

One of the most thoughtful and interesting answers describes a case involving a woman the authors call Mrs. Black, who was forty-four, married, with two children, and had a twenty-five-year history of unsuccessful treatment for anorexia.[176] The only times that she ate normally was during her two pregnancies, the last having been eighteen years earlier. Her husband was her guardian. In 1998, after being involuntarily and voluntarily hospitalized, in any number of treatment programs (including specialized treatment programs for eating disorders) without remission, endured one full year with a gastrostomy tube, having all her teeth replaced with dentures, because of damage from repeated vomiting, on life support twice the previous year, she decided she wanted to refuse all further treatment for both her numerous medical conditions and her anorexia. Her physician placed her in hospice care, where she was content. Her husband sought a psychiatric consultation about her competence to make this decision. After interviewing Mrs. Black and her family, including her mother and children, and her treaters, the authors concluded that she was competent to refuse treatment, based on a number of factors: her long and chronic illness, her poor quality of life,[177] irreversible medical complications, the failure of multiple treatments and interventions, the support of her family, and the consistency of both her noncompliance with treatment and her wishes to refuse it over time.

These factors sound a lot like what a court might consider in deciding whether Mrs. Black's liberty interest in treatment refusal outweighed the state's compelling interest in preserving life. On the other hand, they bear very little on her competence to refuse medical treatment. Under our legal framework for competence, a competent person can refuse treatment whether or not her illness is long and chronic, whether or not treatment is futile, and regardless of the wishes of her family. But our legal framework, of course, assumes (as it must, to be of any utility at all) that competence is objective and determinable, as opposed to a malleable cultural construct reflecting choices and values that are comprehensible to the majority of people, or (perhaps more ominously) comprehensible to the elite entrusted with determining competence, be they medical or mental health professionals or judges. There are certainly a number of voices across time and many disciplines arguing that decisions about competence simply reflect the values of the decisionmaker.[178] So even this thoughtful piece about Mrs. Black boils

---

[176] See Gans and Gunn, n. 161.

[177] *Id.* Her quality of life was poor "both subjectively and objectively," write the authors, with "subjective" representing the patient's point of view and "objectively" representing her treaters,' family, and the authors' perspective.

[178] Milton D. Green, *Proof of Mental Incompetency and the Unexpressed Major Premise*, 53 YALE L.J. 271 (1944) (testamentary capacity); Blume, *supra* note 67

down to "Does this decision make sense to us in the context of this woman's life?" rather than "Is she able to understand her situation, weigh her options, and make and communicate a decision, and is that decision voluntary and uncoerced?"[179]

There are some scholars who argue that a decision to die is final and unusual enough that heightened standards for competence should be applied, including whether the decision is "well considered and consistent with their stable and enduring desires."[180] I agree that there should be heightened standards around a decision to die, but deeply and profoundly disagree that these should be accomplished by requiring a higher bar for competence. The presumption of competence should be overcome only if the individual is a minor or by evidence of psychosis or intoxication so obvious that a layperson would recognize it. To me, the rule of thumb is: Would this person's consent to treatment be accepted without hesitation? If so, the person is competent. There are other ways to create barriers to suicide, and they will be discussed in Chapter 5. Competence is too slippery and value-laden a concept, and the finding of incompetence too great an annihilation of an individual's agency, to locate the necessary discretion for individual decision making in competence doctrine.

The degree to which the decision-maker's values control the outcome of competence evaluations is clearly seen in *In the Matter of E,* the British analog to Mrs. Black case.[181] Ms. E., who was 32, had signed two separate advance directives indicating she did not want to be kept alive. Her doctors believed she was competent to execute those directives. She then asked for her feeding tubes to be removed. Ms. E., like Mrs. Black, had received extensive treatment for many years, including months in specialized treatment facilities. In both cases, their treaters had decided to end efforts at treatment: Ms. E. was in a community hospital, receiving palliative care; Mrs. Black was in hospice. As in Mrs. Black's case, the family supported Ms. E.'s decision. As Ms E.'s death became imminent, the local authority (perhaps motivated by liability concerns as well as concern for Ms E.) asked a court to decide whether Ms E. was competent to refuse food and hydration. Note

---

(competence to waive appeal of death penalty); Michael L. Perlin, *Everything's A Little Upside Down, As a Matter of Fact the Wheels Have Stopped: The Fraudulence of the Incompetency Evaluation Process,* 4 Hous. J. Health L. Pol'y 239 (2004) (incompetence to stand trial).

[179] Because her husband was her guardian, technically the answer to that question was already "no" and the findings of the professionals who conducted this extensive and thorough evaluation completely undermine the validity of Black's guardianship.

[180] Sascha Callahan & Christopher Ryan, *Refusing Medical Treatment After Attempted Suicide: Rethinking Capacity and Coercive Treatment in Light of the Kerrie Wooltorton Case,* 18 J. L. Med. 811 (2011).

[181] In the Matter of E., [2012] EWHC 1639 (COP).

that the entire point of advance directives is to create a legal mechanism to ensure that if the person is deemed incompetent, the individual's wishes *will* be honored.

The judge avoided the competence–advance directive conundrum by finding that anorexia rendered Ms E. incompetent to decide *or* to execute advance directives, even though (in order to have the advance directive respected) she had gained enough weight to be at almost normal weight when she executed the second advance directive. The judge acknowledged that "Ms. E has been described as an intelligent and charming person … who does not seek death but above all does not want to eat or be fed. She sees her life as pointless and wants to be able to make her own choices, realizing that refusal to eat must lead to death."[182] Although physicians who had treated Ms E. for years testified that she was competent, the judge instead credited the testimony of a court-appointed doctor, who had never spoken to the patient except when she was sedated and at death's door. Dr. Glover, the court-appointed expert, equated severe anorexia with lack of capacity, so he performed virtually no analysis of Ms. E.'s capacity. The judge admitted that "a person with severe anorexia may be in a Catch 22 position regarding capacity: namely, by deciding not to eat she proves that she lacks capacity to decide at all,"[183] and he quoted her parents' bitter response to Dr. Glover's opinion:

> It seems strange to us that the only people who don't seem to have the right to die when there is no further appropriate treatment available are those with an eating disorder. This is based on the assumption that they can never have capacity around any issues connected to food. There is a logic to this, but not from the perspective of the sufferer who is not extended the same rights as any other person.[184]

The judge understood that force-feeding was "not merely bodily intrusion of the most intrusive kind, but the overbearing of E's will in a way that she experiences as abusive,"[185] and that the treatment being proposed was at least one full year of force-feeding with E. in physical restraint or sedation, as well as potentially being placed on a ventilator to move her, because her medical condition was so fragile, all of which she violently opposed.

Nevertheless, despite the fact that Ms. E. had *at most* a 20% chance of recovery[186] and would have to spend at least a year restrained and force-fed, and despite the fact that the people who knew her best and loved her most opposed these actions, the judge ordered these enormous bodily intrusions

---

[182] *Id.* at Paragraph 5.
[183] *Id.* at Paragraph 53.
[184] *Id.* at Paragraph 52.
[185] *Id.* at Paragraph 131.
[186] *Id.* at Paragraph 72.

because, like Judge Wright in the *Georgetown*[187] case, this judge valued life over autonomy. In a particularly treacly and patronizing line, he wrote, "Ms. E is a special person whose life is of value. She doesn't see it that way now but she may in the future."[188] The judge described his decision as "intuitive," which is a kind word for the forcible imposition of his values onto and inside the body of a fragile and suffering woman. My guess is that if Ms. E. had decided to accept treatment, the judge would have had no trouble finding her competent.[189]

Proposed Standards for Competence to End One's Life

A number of authors and authorities have suggested a standard for evaluating the capacity of an individual to decide to end his or her own life. As I said at the beginning of this chapter, competence is only the beginning of an inquiry about when and whether suicide should be restricted, but it is always, in law and medicine, the crucial first step.

Proposed Standards for Terminally Ill Individuals Contemplating Assisted Suicide

One of the best and clearest of the general resources in the area of assisted suicide, *The Oregon Death with Dignity Act: A Guidebook for Healthcare Professionals*,[190] is almost comically deficient in its guidance about the standard in determining competence to make the decision to use physician-assisted suicide. This may be due in part to the wording of Oregon's statute itself, which requires the prescribing physician to both ensure that (1) the patient has capacity and (2) to ensure that he or she is not suffering from impaired judgment caused by a psychiatric or psychological disorder or depression. It is unclear whether the latter criterion is simply a rephrasing of the capacity inquiry. It seems unlikely that legislators intended to exclude a larger number of people than those lacking capacity, singling out only those whose impaired judgment was caused by a psychiatric disability,

---

[187] See n. 27, *supra*.

[188] In the Matter of E., note 181 at paragraph 137.

[189] In the Matter of E does not necessarily represent English law in the matter, which is wildly conflicting, see B v. Croydon Health Authority, [1995] 2 WLR 1994 (upholding the right to refuse nutrition and hydration of a woman with anorexia).

[190] Oregon Health and Science University, Center for Ethics in Health Care, *The Oregon Death with Dignity Act: A Guidebook for Health Care Professionals*, see note 116. The Internet edition of the *Guidebook* contains no page numbers, so I will refer to Chapters and Section headings to identify source material.

since this kind of reasoning has been found to violate the Americans with Disabilities Act.[191]

The *Guidebook* advises the physician to fulfill his or her first duty to determine capacity according to accepted legal standards of capacity: the patient has the ability to make and communicate health care decisions. In determining whether the patient has impaired judgment caused by a psychiatric disability, however, the *Guidebook* strongly recommends that all patients be screened with the Patient Health Questionnaire-9 (PHQ- 9), which is used to determine whether an individual has depression.[192] A manifestly sillier instrument could not possibly be imagined in the context of a terminally ill person, probably on heavy pain medication. Its questions include whether in the last two weeks, the person has been

Sleeping too much
Feeling tired or lacking energy
Having poor appetite
Having trouble concentrating
Moving so slowly that other people notice[193]

The crowning absurdity of using this instrument to measure impaired judgment in a person wanting to use assisted suicide is the question, "In the last two weeks have you thought that you would be better off dead?"[194]

The instrument itself instructs that "Diagnoses of Major Depressive Disorder or other Depressive Disorder require ruling out ... a physical disorder, medication or other drug as the biological cause of the depressive symptoms."[195] This eminently sensible instruction, if followed, probably makes the PHQ-9 useless in assessing almost all terminally ill people. As the *Guidebook* itself notes, "What appear to be depressive vegetative symptoms such as weight loss and lack of energy may be due to the underlying disease in terminal ill patients."[196]

If, on the basis of the PHQ-9, which is certain to screen in almost all end-stage terminally ill patients, the physician decides to refer the patient to a mental health professional, the *Guidebook* literally assumes that each

[191] Doe v. Rowe, 156 F.Supp.2d 35 (D. Me. 2001) (precluding only those whose lack of capacity was caused by mental illness from voting, while permitting all others without capacity to vote, violated the Americans with Disabilities Act); *Hargrave, supra* note 154.
[192] *Guidebook,* at n. 189, Recommendation 9.1.
[193] The Patient Health Questionnaire 9's questions can be found at http://phqscreeners.com/pdfs/02_phq-9/english.pdf.
[194] *Id.* (Question 9).
[195] See http://www.integration.samhsa.gov/images/res/PHQ%20-%20Questions.pdf for instructions on how to use and interpret PHQ-9, including ensuring that physical and medication-related causes for the responses are ruled out.
[196] *Guidebook,* Chapter 9, "Mental Disorders that May Influence Decisionmaking."

mental health professional will be flying by the seat of his or her pants: "Once a patient is referred for a mental health evaluation, the attending physician may write a prescription for a lethal dose of medication only if the mental health professional can state that *within his/her standards*, the patient meets the criteria of the Oregon Death with Dignity Act)."[197] There is explicitly no uniform standard to be used: "[t]he consulting mental health professional should feel free to communicate to the attending physician the standard he/she used for capacity and his/her degree of confidence regarding the determination of capacity."[198]

In addition, in contravention of virtually all the research on people with depression, the *Guidebook* seems to accept the opinion of 58% of 290 U.S. forensic psychiatrists that "the presence of a major depressive disorder should result in an *automatic* finding of incompetence for the purposes of obtaining assisted suicide."[199] Every major respectable piece of research on competence has underscored that many, if not most, people with diagnoses of major depression are competent to make health care decisions. The State may well want to prohibit persons who have treatable conditions from killing themselves, and it certainly has the power to do so. That is different from asserting that those persons are not competent. Because most people with major depression retain the capacity to make health care decisions, any such blanket policy would constitute discrimination on the basis of disability (in addition to being clinically inappropriate and insufficiently individualized).

The *Guidebook* does counsel that "the mental health professional is obligated to maximize the patient's ability to perform well on the examination,"[200] and that "most patients will qualify for the Oregon Act."[201] The *Guidebook* authors also felt it prudent to emphasize that refusal of mental health treatment is not a sufficient basis to refuse the prescription of a lethal dose of medication. This is indeed prudent, since the psychiatric literature contains a number of articles about mental health treatment, including medications, in the last few weeks of an individual's life.

Another author argued that the test for competence to request assisted suicide should require that patients be able to demonstrate an ability to understand detailed information about their illness and the consequences of treatment or withdrawal of treatment intended to cause death.[202] It is not

---

[197] *Id.*
[198] *Guidebook,* Chapter 9, "The Evaluation Process."
[199] *Guidebook,* Chapter 9, "The Evaluation Process," referring to L. Ganzini, G.B. Leong, D.S. Fenn, et al, "Evaluation of Competence to Consent to Assisted Suicide: Views of Forensic Psychiatrists," 157 Am.J.Psychiatry 595 (2000).
[200] *Guidebook,* Chapter 9, "The Evaluation Process."
[201] *Id.*
[202] C. Stewart, C. Peisah, & B. Draper, *A Test for Mental Capacity to Request Assisted Suicide,* 37 J. MED. ETHICS 1, 34–39 (2010), http://www.jme.bmj.com/content/early/2010/11/21/jme.2010.037564.full (accessed Dec. 14, 2010).

clear whether the authors believe that patients should demonstrate that they have actually understood this information, but in practical terms, an ability to understand would presumably be best demonstrated by actual understanding. The authors also say that "the decision should be consistent over time with past expressed wishes and beliefs."[203]

Proposed Standards for People Refusing Treatment That Will Lead to Death

Having an untreatable terminal illness is different from dying because of refusing treatment that could save your life. This latter scenario is more akin to the Jehovah's Witness cases of decades ago. In those days, when our society was wrestling with the difference between protected treatment refusals leading to certain death and prohibited suicide, one author, worrying that terminally ill people should not be permitted to commit suicide, proposed the following standard of competence for treatment refusal leading to certain death, one that set a far higher bar than standard competence evaluations:

(1) Whether the patient's refusal is a reflective, settled decision, consistent with the patient's general way of life or religious or philosophical convictions; or alternatively, a hasty decision made in reaction to a sudden personal catastrophe, temporary severe depression, or a mental impairment due to pain, disease, or the side effects of medication.

(2) Whether the patient's probable future life will be so diminished in quality that a reasonable person could conclude that it is not worth living; or alternatively, the patient's life could be valuable and fulfilling, thus raising doubt about whether the patient appreciates the prospects she is renouncing.[204]

Later, in a thoughtful book devoted entirely to the subject of rational suicide by people with psychiatric disabilities, Dr. James Werth and his research colleagues proposed the following standard, which included a component evaluating competence:

1. The person considering suicide has an unremitting "hopeless" condition. "Hopeless" conditions include but are not necessarily limited to, terminal illnesses, severe physical and/or psychological pain, physically or mentally debilitating and/or deteriorating conditions, or quality of life no longer acceptable to the individual.

2. The person makes the decision as a free choice (i.e. not pressured by others to choose suicide).

---

[203] *Id.*

[204] Martha Mathews, *Suicidal Competence and the Patient's Right to Refuse Lifesaving Treatment*, 75 CAL. L. REV. 707, 754 (1987).

3. The person has engaged in a sound decision-making process. This process should include the following:

   a. Consultation with a mental health professional who can make an assessment of mental competence (which would include the absence of treatable major depression)
   b. Nonimpulsive consideration of all alternatives
   c. Consideration of the congruence of the act with one's personal values
   d. Consideration of the impact on significant others
   e. Consultation with objective others (e.g. medical and religious professionals) and with significant others[205]

These criteria were sent to ethicists, mental health professionals (including suicidologists), and attorneys for comment. Some respondents would have included a specific time period to wait. Others were interested in how these requirements would be verified.[206]

While I think these standards are a helpful starting point for discussion, as stated earlier, a diagnosis of major depression should not absolutely preclude a finding of competence. I also find it amusing that even a person as thoughtful and sensitive as Dr. Werth obviously is would describe "medical and religious professionals" as "objective others."[207] Talking about being suicidal is good, as long as it is not punished by involuntary detention, commitment, and treatment—one of the surest ways of shutting down the communication that is so vital to keeping someone alive.

Conclusion

Suicide is no more caused by a lack of capacity or mental illness than crime is caused by a lack of capacity or mental illness. It is undeniably true that a small minority of people are found to be either insane at the time a crime was committed or incompetent to stand trial. However, that is no reason to run the entire criminal justice system as though mental illness caused all crime or all criminals lacked responsibility or capacity.[208] It is also undeniably true that a small minority of people kill themselves while they are psychotic or otherwise clearly incompetent (extreme intoxication or inebriation probably accounts for a high proportion of both crimes and suicides while incompetent). But that is no reason to make suicide policy and laws as though they were merely a subset of the mental health system.

---

[205] WERTH, *supra* note 25, at 62, tbl.5.1.
[206] *Id.* at 67–68.
[207] *Id.*
[208] Although this was a fashionable belief for some time, see LADY BARBARA WOOTTEN, CRIME AND THE CRIMINAL LAW (London, Stevens and Sons 1963).

I have attempted to demonstrate several propositions in this chapter. First, people can competently decide to take their own lives, even though some people who try to kill themselves are not competent. Second, the former category—people who are competent to make this decision—is vastly larger than the latter. People who are not competent to make this decision include minors below some arbitrary age,[209] people who are currently intoxicated, and people who are psychotic or in a state of delirium or extreme mania. Third, people with most psychiatric disabilities will generally be legally competent to make the decision to end their lives, and any efforts to prevent them from doing so should not center around expanding the definition of incompetence. The idea that being suicidal is itself an indication of incompetence is absurd, and subject to so many counterexamples that it hardly merits discussion. The idea that incompetence should be expanded from a cognitive model to include affective incompetence—that a person's mood can distort his or her thinking so seriously as to constitute incompetence—is more intellectually interesting, but ultimately fails because it is a clever proxy for outcome-based competence determinations. The theory only applies to people who refuse treatment, or waive appeals of death sentences. People who seek treatment can never, by definition, be affectively incompetent to consent to it.

For doctors to determine that someone lacks capacity, or courts to find someone legally incompetent, is an extremely serious act and should be undertaken with hesitation and caution. A person who is suicidal is already in doubt about his or her value in the world, already feels powerless to transform or transcend life's burdens. To declare this person incompetent is to confirm these feelings, to officially endorse the individual's hopeless state. A finding of lack of capacity or incompetence completely erases the individual as a legally and medically respected decision-maker. It is exactly the opposite policy from what we should pursue: engaging a suicidal person in an earnest and respectful conversation about why he or she wants to die. Expanding the definition of incompetence as a utilitarian means of preventing suicide or controlling the actions of a suicidal person is dangerous and unnecessary social policy.

I have emphasized that this argument is very limited. It would not preclude a society from banning or criminalizing suicide, attempted suicide, or assisted suicide. In fact, my assumptions about competence would be a prerequisite for such policies. Nor does it preclude involuntary commitment for suicidality, which will be addressed in the next chapter.

---

[209] Although minors can now avail themselves of assisted suicide in Belgium, see Chapter 4.

2

The Right to Die, Involuntary Commitment, and the Constitution

"Scarcely any political question arises in the United States that is not resolved, sooner or later, into a judicial question."

—Alexis de Tocqueville[1]

... this summer
I have conversed with death every minute
and found out I have the talent
to submit, to leave, even to flee,
and, in this, there's nothing exceptional
about me. Why, the sidewalks around Farber
are populated with so many about to die,
many of great courage and grim humor and great shuffle
getting ready, as they can, to go,
...
I am among them.
They are mine, and I am theirs.
Our motto: Fight to live; prepare to go.

—Liam Rector, "Our Summer"[2]

---

[1] ALEXIS DE TOCQUEVILLE, DEMOCRACY IN AMERICA 74 (Signet Classic 1956) (1835).

[2] The poet Liam Rector had undergone heart surgery and had colon cancer when he killed himself on Aug. 15, 2007, at the age of 57. Margalit Fox, *Liam Rector, a Poet and Educator, Dies*, N. Y. TIMES, Aug. 17, 2007, http://www.nytimes.com/2007/08/17/arts/17rector.html. *Our Summer* copyright © 2006 by the University of Chicago. Reprinted from LIAM RECTOR, THE EXECUTIVE DIRECTOR OF THE FALLEN WORLD (University of Chicago Press 2006) with permission of University of Chicago Press. All rights reserved.

Introduction

In Chapter 1, I argued that most people who want to die are competent to make the decision in the sense of understanding and appreciating the nature and consequences of their actions. Even opponents of assisted suicide tend to acknowledge that people who are suicidal are, for the most part, competent under current standards of capacity.[3] In addition, both the law and mental health research confirm that most people with psychiatric diagnoses are competent to make health care decisions. I argued in the first chapter that this includes competence to make decisions about suicide, whether the people with psychiatric diagnoses are terminally ill or not.

The fact that the government can and should prevent people who lack competence from killing themselves does not necessarily mean the converse: that government can and should permit people who are competent to commit suicide. Most women are competent to decide to have abortions, or clitoridectomies, but that competence alone has never translated into the right to have an abortion[4] or a clitoridectomy.[5] Whether the government can prohibit us from killing ourselves is a matter of constitutional and statutory law that is quite separate from issues of competence.

This chapter looks at whether there is or should be a constitutional right to die, and to what extent that right should apply to someone who is suicidal. It will also look at whether and to what extent the right to die intersects with the constitutionality of involuntarily detaining and committing a suicidal individual *because* he or she is suicidal. Both of these questions have historically been intertwined with the right to refuse treatment, which has been acknowledged to be a constitutional right[6] for the last twenty-five years.

One reason that prompted me to write this book in the first place was that no one seemed to think it was unusual to have a robust national discussion about whether there was a constitutional right to die from which people with psychiatric disabilities were explicitly excluded by universal consensus without any discussion. Indeed, the possibility that assisted suicide might be used by people with psychiatric conditions was one of the principal arguments against it, and accepted by a court as sufficiently persuasive to strike

---

[3] Herbert Hendin, *Seduced by Death: Doctors, Patients, and the Dutch Cure*, 10 Issues L. Med. 123, 164 (1994) (Hendin says that "the acceptance of euthanasia for psychiatric patients who are suicidal. . .seems the inevitable consequence of allowing such criteria as 'competence' and 'intolerable suffering' to determine the outcome rather than sound clinical judgment.").

[4] States are increasingly enacting restrictions on abortions, Heather D. Boonstra & Elizabeth Nash, *A Surge of State Abortion Restrictions Puts Providers—And the Women They Serve—in the Crosshairs*, 17 Guttmacher Pol'y Rev. 1 (Winter 2014), www.guttmacher.org/pubs/gpr/17/1/gpr170109.html.

[5] Federal law criminalizes the performance of clitoridectomies, 18 U.S.C. § 116.

[6] A right riddled with exceptions, see pp. 86–90 *infra*.

down a ballot initiative approved by a majority of the citizens of Oregon.[7] There is currently no clearcut constitutional right to die; whether there should be such a right takes up the first part of this chapter. I will argue that if such a right exists, or is found to exist in the future, people with psychiatric diagnoses cannot be excluded from it solely on the basis of their diagnoses, nor can any limitations or contingencies exclude people with psychiatric diagnoses as a class.

Even if there is no constitutional right to suicide, that does not automatically permit the State to deprive people of their right to liberty for being suicidal by involuntarily committing them. Because the right to liberty is a fundamental right, the State must show that this involuntary confinement is narrowly tailored to meet compelling state interests. In the second part of the chapter, I argue that it is far from clear that the State can constitutionally involuntarily confine people who have articulated suicidal thoughts or threatened suicide.

The History of the Right to Die

The notion of the right to die seems paradoxical.[8] Death seems to be the ultimate in nondiscrimination: whether you are asserting a right to it or running from it as hard as you can does not really matter in the end. In the context of suicide, many people's reaction might be, "Why do you need a right? Who's stopping you?" There are actually a number of serious answers to this question.

One answer, as thousands of people in emergency departments and psychiatric wards at this very moment will tell you, is that the State *does* intervene to stop people from killing themselves every day. As befits an act that is still a crime in some states, the State's intervention often first takes the form of the arrival of the police. Hotline operators call the police,[9] therapists who are worried about liability call the police, family members

---

[7] Lee v. Oregon, 891 F.Supp. 1429 (D. Ore. 1995), *vacated and remanded* 107 F.3d 1382 (9th Cir.), *cert. den. sub. nom.* Lee v. Harcleroad, 522 U.S. 997 (1997).

[8] I am not the first person to note the anomalous nature of demanding death as a legal right, see Donald Beschle, *Autonomous Decisionmaking and Social Choice: Examining 'the Right to Die,'* 77 Ky. L.J. 319 (1988).

[9] This is done if the person is considered at imminent risk of suicide. Emergency services are called, whether the caller requests it or not, and often these *emergency services* include police. This process of involuntary detention of people who called a hotline for help is called "initiating active rescue," see John Draper, Gillian Murphy, Eduardo Vega, David W. Covington, & Richard McKeon, *Helping Callers to the National Suicide Prevention Hotline Who Are at Imminent Risk of Suicide: The Importance of Active Engagement, Active Rescue, and Collaboration between Crisis and Emergency Services*, SUICIDE & LIFE-THREATENING BEHAV. 1, 5 (2014).

call the police,[10] bystanders call the police. The curious and anomalous role of the police as our default first responders to hundreds of thousands of desolate, despairing, depressed, hopeless, or psychotic people is discussed in Chapter 7. Individuals who are suicidal also often call 911—a number which, of course, often goes straight to the police.

The police come to the home. Sometimes they assess the situation and go away. Sometimes injury and death result almost immediately. Often, the suicidal person is handcuffed[11]—standard protocol for anyone riding in the back of a police vehicle—and taken to an emergency department. Sometimes an ambulance is called and the person in despair is strapped to a gurney and immobilized, and taken to a hospital whether he or she wants to go or not.

Police in all states can temporarily detain an individual they suspect of being mentally ill and suicidal, just long enough to transport the individual to a hospital or emergency department. Any lengthier detention must pass through a medical or mental health professional gatekeeper, who is given this power by the State. A few suicidal people who are involuntarily detained are extremely grateful, many others are angry, and a not insubstantial number are very badly damaged by the experience. The people in the latter categories often conclude that next time, they will not reach out for help, because reaching out for help leads to the enormous helplessness and humiliation of the police car, the handcuffs, the emergency department, and the hospital ward. The next time, they will not fail.

But one thing is clear, which is the answer to "Who is stopping you from killing yourself?" The government is, acting through the police, the ambulance, the emergency department, mental health professionals, the courts, and the entire apparatus of involuntary detention and treatment in this country.

---

[10] There are literally hundreds of examples in case law of family members calling police for help with a suicidal family member and later suing after the police arrived and killed the family member, see Chapter 8, pp. 362–363, notes 232–236, *infra*.

[11] This handcuffing, allegedly for protection, has not prevented a number of people from shooting themselves in the back of police cars, see *Police: Handcuffed High School Student Shoots Self in Back of Car* (NBC News, Dec. 5, 2012), http://usnews.nbcnews.com/_news/2012/12/05 and *Shooting Death of Man in Patrol Car Ruled a Suicide*, (NBC News, Aug. 20, 2012), http://usnews.nbcnews.com/_news/2012/08/20 and Carl Dix, *Not Again! North Carolina Cops Claim Handcuffed Teen Committed Suicide*, Revolution Newspaper, Jan. 27, 2014, http://revcom.us/a/328/north-carolina-cops-claim-handcuffed-teen-committed-suicide-en.html and Daniel Bethencourt, *One Year Later: Victor White's Family Says They Have Yet to Hear Account of Son's Death in Backseat of Police Unit; Coroner: Man Shot Himself While Cuffed*, The Advocate, March 4, 2015, http://theadvocate.com/news/11760842-123/story.html. Note that these stories are all about different people. It was a huge victory in Vermont when the state passed a statute prohibiting the automatic handcuffing of suicidal and depressed minors by police taking them for psychiatric care.

There is a second answer about the perceived need for a right to die. People do not want to die alone, but they hesitate to place their families and friends at very real risk of criminal prosecution. These worries are not groundless. In a number of cases, a family member's assistance—or even that individual's failure to prevent—a suicide leads to criminal prosecution.[12] Family members' accounts and the bitter words of suicide notes[13] reflect that, although people are free to kill themselves, their inability to do it either openly or painlessly sometimes results in gruesome or lonely deaths. This is essentially a plea for social recognition or validation of the notion of rational suicide, so that it can take place painlessly and without subterfuge or shame. Virtually all of the individuals I interviewed attempted suicide secretly, and most felt that there were very few, if any, people they could talk to honestly about their desire to die (including their therapists—perhaps especially their therapists).

Third, many people's ideas about the right to die include assistance from physicians.[14] To die painlessly, they believe they need the assistance of a physician to determine what kind of drugs and what dosage will accomplish their goal. This is not necessarily true: many of my interviewees combed the Internet for this information and got it quite easily. It is the goal of several organizations, including the Hemlock Society, Exit and its offshoots, and Dignitas in Switzerland, to enable this information to be shared with all who seek it.[15] I believe that involving medical professionals directly in assisting intentional deaths is not necessarily a good idea.[16]

This chapter examines whether a competent individual should have a right to die, and if so, what that means and under what circumstances. It will examine whether the right to die is, as some claim, inextricably intertwined with the right to refuse treatment. Finally, we will look at whether involuntary detention and commitment to a psychiatric facility of a person who is suicidal violates the Constitution.

---

[12] In one highly publicized case, a nurse named Barbara Mancini was arrested for attempting to assist her father to commit suicide, see Chris Kelly, *Prosecuting Woman in Dad's Death Is Wrong Choice*, TIMES-TRIBUNE, Aug. 25, 2013, http://m.thetimes-tribune.com/opinion/editorials-columns/christopher-j-kelly/chris-kelly-prosecuting-woman-in-dad-s-death-is-wrong-choice-1.1541398 (on Feb. 11, 2014, a judge dismissed the case); Frank Bruni, *Fatal Mercies*, N. Y. TIMES, Aug. 10, 2013, http://www.nytimes.com/2013/08/11/opinion/sunday/bruni-fatal-mercies.html?_r=0; Daniel C. Maguire, *Death, Legal and Illegal*, ATLANTIC MONTHLY, Feb. 1974.

[13] SHERWIN NULAND, HOW WE DIE: REFLECTIONS ON LIFE'S FINAL CHAPTER 152 (1995) (quoting the suicide note of Percy Bridgman, a Nobel Prize winner in the final stages of cancer, who shot himself, "It is not decent for Society to make a man do this to himself. Probably, this is the last day I will be able to do it myself").

[14] See Chapter 5.

[15] This is discussed in Chapter 4.

[16] See Chapter 5.

The right to die was first conceptualized as a moral right, a human right, before being specifically framed as a legal right. The first mention that I could find of the concept of the right to die was in the suicide note of Charlotte Perkins Gilman, a well-known feminist who killed herself in 1935 after being diagnosed with terminal breast cancer. In a note that reflects many women's values, she wrote:

> No grief, pain, misfortune or "broken heart" is excuse for cutting off one's life while power of service remains. When all usefulness is over, when one is assured of unavoidable and imminent death, it is the simplest of human rights to choose a quick and easy death in place of a slow and horrible one. I have chosen chloroform over cancer.[17]

This statement associating life with "usefulness" was not simply a statement of personal choice: it was a statement of social policy that explains why many advocates with severe physical disabilities passionately oppose the right to die. Gilman's suicide was the final embodiment of a personal philosophy that lamented "the dragging weight of the grossly unfit"[18] in society and supported mercy killing of severely handicapped individuals.

Shortly after Gilman's death, the minister Charles Francis Potter founded the National Society for the Legalization of Euthanasia. *Time* magazine covered the story, noting that the Society was organized because Potter "and a sizable group of other notable men believe so strongly in the right of an incurably diseased individual to have his life terminated gently."[19] Thus, the first notions of the right to die were associated with terminal illness, the medical profession, and having your death administered to you by someone else: euthanasia. However, they did not spring from any principles of individual autonomy and choice: Supporters of euthanasia often also supported mercy killing of severely handicapped disabled people, who were lumped together with the terminally ill as socially useless and drags on society.

This association of euthanasia and eugenics did not generate a great deal of opposition—in fact, public opinion was swinging in favor of mercy killing of disabled individuals[20]—until the horrific experiments and mass murder of people with disabilities in Nazi Germany.[21] When the United States and British Euthanasia Societies tried unsuccessfully to get euthanasia included as

---

[17] Judith Nies, Nine Women: Portraits from the American Radical Tradition 145 (1977).

[18] Carl E. Schneider, *The Road to* Glucksberg, *in* Law at the End of Life 20 (Carl E. Schneider ed., 2000).

[19] *Potter and Euthanasia*, Time, Jan. 31, 1938, www.time.com.

[20] Ian Dowbiggin, A Concise History of Euthanasia: Life, Death, God and Medicine, 2007 at p. 89.

[21] Indeed, when Karen Ann Quinlan's case was argued in New Jersey, the doctors who refused to disconnect her life support invoked Nazi Germany to explain their refusal to obey the family's wishes.

a human right by the United Nations in 1950, this history haunted them, and the effort failed.

Any aspiration to rehabilitate the euthanasia movement from its early unfortunate alliance with eugenics failed when philosopher and theologian Joseph Fletcher emerged as a primary spokesperson for euthanasia and the right to die in the 1950s. Fletcher wrote several articles in pastoral journals with "Right to Die" in their titles. These received some attention, but nothing like the attention accorded his coauthored piece, "The Right to Die," published in the *Atlantic Monthly* in 1968. In this article, Fletcher asserted that parents had no reason to feel guilty if they "put away" their children with Down's Syndrome, either in an institution or "in a more responsible lethal sense" because "[t]rue guilt arises only from an offense against a person, and a Down's is not a person."[22]

This statement was not taken out of context. Nor was it Fletcher's only assertion that people with mental disabilities do not deserve to live. He also wrote that anyone with an IQ below 40 was "probably not a person."[23] The history of the right to die and euthanasia movement, especially the writings and statements of Joseph Fletcher, go a long way to explain why some disability rights activists are so worried about the right to die. Disability activists distrust the right to die because they cannot take for granted the recognition of their right to *live*. And the social devaluation of disabled lives is real: to date, the only U.S. court cases recognizing the right to die for an individual who neither terminally ill nor in a vegetative state have involved people with severe physical disabilities.[24] Newspaper articles repeatedly underscore the assumption that people who want to die because they have severe physical disabilities are behaving rationally, even in the absence of any kind of terminal illness.[25]

The Right to Die: Evolution in the Courts

The vulnerability of disabled people is frequently asserted as an interest of the State in litigation opposing the right to die. The legal debate of the last

---

[22] Bernard Bard & Joseph Fletcher, *The Right to Die*, ATLANTIC MONTHLY 59–64 (Apr. 1968). While Bernard Bard was a coauthor of this article, Fletcher by that point was so well known for advocating this point of view that it is often attributed to him alone.

[23] He also wrote in an article entitled *Indicators of Humanhood: A Tentative Profile of Man*, HASTINGS CENTER REP. 2 (1972) that anyone with an IQ below 40 was probably not a person.

[24] McKay v. Bergstedt, 801 P.2d 619 (Nev. 1990); Bouvia v. Superior Court, 225 Cal. Rptr. 297 (Cal. App. 1986). See fuller discussion *infra* at pp. 65–70 and Chapter 10.

[25] Steve Almasy & Michael Martinez, *Paralyzed after Fall from Tree, Indiana Deer Hunter Opts to End Life* (CNN, Nov. 7, 2013), www.cnn.com./2013/11/06/us/paralyzed-Indiana-deer-hunter-ends-life.

fifty years centers around whether the states' prohibition of assisted suicide infringes on substantive due process rights, including the right to privacy, of U.S. citizens. The idea of framing dying as a legal right asserted against the State and litigated in court is particularly American. These court cases are simply a typically American way of carrying on a social dialogue about competing values of autonomy, community, and the role of the State as intruder or protector. In the 1970s and 1980s, judges embraced the role of moderator of this discussion. In more recent times, judges have become uneasy with this role, and have often (but not always) kicked it back to state legislatures. In the case of assisted suicide, physicians and mental health professionals are crucial parties to the debate. They don't necessarily have to be: in some ways, it is a historical and jurisprudential accident that they are.

We take for granted that medical professionals are part of the assisted-suicide debate because litigation on the right to die has always been intertwined with the medical profession, but that is an artifact of how the debate arose historically. Medical associations have been among the chief opponents of the right to die, even while a substantial proportion of doctors admit to having assisted patients to die. Doctors have also been some of the right to die's most celebrated and vilified proponents, from Dr. Jack Kevorkian to Dr. Timothy Quill.[26] Physicians' involvement has been taken for granted because assisted suicide cases evolved legally out of the right to refuse treatment, but, as we will see in Chapter 4, there are assisted suicide regimes that do not involve doctors at all.

The right to die has essentially had four phases: (1) prior to the *Quinlan* decision in 1976; (2) from *Quinlan* to the end of the 1980s and the *Bouvia* case; (3) from *Cruzan* and the appearance of Kevorkian in 1990 to the Supreme Court decisions in *Washington v. Glucksberg* and *Vacco v. Quill* in 1997; and (4) from those latter decisions to the present day.

The First Right-to-Die Cases: 1962–1976

The right to die began its jurisprudential history in the United States as the right to refuse medical treatment necessary to maintain life—almost always blood transfusions—for religious reasons.[27] These early cases used terms similar to *the right to die* (e.g., a New Jersey Supreme Court noted that "[i]t

---

[26] Doctors were the only plaintiffs in the two assisted-suicide cases to be heard by the Supreme Court because the terminally ill patients who had been plaintiffs died long before even the lower court rendered a decision. The legal process takes so long that this is not uncommon, see Susan Stefan, *Dead Serious About Plaintiffs*, 85 A.B.A. J. 104 (Jan. 1999), and it is particularly common in right-to-die cases except when the plaintiff is in a vegetative state.

[27] Erickson v. Dilgard, 44 Misc. 2d. 22 (N.Y. Sup. Ct., Nassau Cty 1962); John F. Kennedy Memorial Hosp. v. Heston, 58 N.J. 576, 279 A.2d 670 (N.J. 1971); Application of the Directors of Georgetown College, 331 F.2d 1000 (D.C. Cir. 1964).

seems correct to say that there is no constitutional right to choose to die."[28]) and cited to law review articles that used the phrase explicitly. In these cases, the constitutional right claimed by the plaintiffs was the first amendment right of the patient to the free exercise of his or her religion, rather than the later assertion of the constitutional right to privacy.

There are two striking characteristics about these early cases. First, the cases clearly associated refusing life-saving treatment with suicide, even when the patient did not actually want to die but was simply following the tenets of his or her religion. Second, the early cases recognized third parties as having interests equal to and overriding any constitutional rights the individual patient might have. These third parties included minor children (the first description of the patient in these court cases virtually always included his or her parental status). More surprisingly, health care professionals were also deemed to have equivalent interests.[29] The degree of deference accorded to the medical profession in these early cases is astonishing by today's standards. Also foreign to our modern thinking was the assumption that once a patient sought healthcare of any kind, he or she was essentially estopped from refusing any treatment the doctors deemed necessary, as it was "unfair" to doctors to accept some forms of treatment and not others.

Although many judges acknowledged that these patients were not suicidal, in general the physicians and hospitals involved considered any refusal of life-saving treatment tantamount to suicide.[30] Courts in these early cases discussed the suicide issue extensively, and several seemed to indicate their agreement with the argument of the hospitals:

> Appellant suggests there is a difference between passively
> submitting to death [by refusing blood] and actively seeking it. The
> distinction may be merely verbal, as it would be if an adult sought
> death by starvation instead of a drug. If the State may interrupt one
> mode of self-destruction, it may with equal authority interfere with
> the other. It is arguably different when an individual, overtaken by
> illness, decides to let it run a fatal course. But unless the medical

---

[28] Heston v. John F. Kennedy Memorial Hosp., 58 N.J. 576, 580 (1971).

[29] There were a few exceptions to this, *Erickson v. Dilgard*, 44 Misc.2d at 27; *In re Estate of Brooks*, 205 N.E.2d 435 (Ill. 1965).

[30] Erickson v. Dilgard, 252 N.Y.S2d 705 (N.Y. App. 1962) (patient's refusal of blood transfusion must be respected even though hospital characterized it as "tantamount to suicide"); United States v. George, 239 F.Supp. 752 (D. Conn. 1965) ("psychiatric reports indicated the patient showed a lack of concern for life and a somewhat fatalistic attitude about his condition was described as 'a variant of suicide'"); *Heston v. John F. Kennedy Memorial Hosp.; Application of the Directors of Geo. Coll.* There appear to be no cases involving Christian Scientists, perhaps because they do not show up at hospitals requesting some form of treatment but not others; Christian Science cases involving failure to obtain medical treatment usually show up as criminal cases involving the failure to obtain medical treatment for children.

option itself is laden with the risk of death or of serious infirmity,
the State's interest in sustaining life in such circumstances is hardly
distinguishable from its interest in the case of suicide.[31]

The courts noted whether or not the patient was competent,[32] and in one
famous case that determination proved decisive,[33] but for the most part, competence was necessary but rarely sufficient to sustain a refusal of treatment.
More important to the courts was the fact that the patient did not object
to blood transfusions, as long as the transfusions were court ordered and
received without consent.

One court, acknowledging that the patient had constitutional rights to
freedom of religion, held explicitly that the doctors' consciences and professional oaths trumped those rights. Doctors' consciences and professional
oaths have no explicit source of protection in the Constitution, but for the
first fifteen years of litigation in these cases, the burdens placed on doctors
and hospitals in caring for a patient refusing treatment was a powerful and
often deciding factor in the cases.

The Courts Assert Jurisdiction: *Quinlan* to *Bouvia*

It did not take long for treatment refusal cases to extend beyond the
Watchtower.[34] The case that is best known for beginning the legal conversation about the right to die is *In re Quinlan.*[35] As most readers know, Joseph
Quinlan wanted to disconnect the life support that sustained the existence
of his daughter Karen Ann, who was in a vegetative state. Quinlan was
described by the New Jersey Supreme Court as "debilitated,"[36] "moribund,"[37]
"profoundly damaged,"[38] and "hopelessly damaged." *Quinlan* also initially
involved a religious claim, because Karen Ann Quinlan's family were devout
Catholics.[39] Indeed, the New Jersey Bishop's Conference was allowed to submit an amicus brief,[40] which the New Jersey Supreme Court emphasized was
relevant only to understanding the principles that guided Quinlan's father.[41]
The Catholic amicus brief supported Quinlan's actions, bringing the first
wide publicity to the principle of double effect, which holds that an action

---

[31] *Heston v. John Kennedy Memorial Hosp.* at 582. The same court would go on five
years later to decide *In re* Quinlan, 70 N.J. 10 (1976).

[32] *United States v. George, supra* n. 30.

[33] *Application of the Directors of Geo. C.* at n.30.

[34] *The Watchtower* is the official monthly publication of the Jehovah's Witnesses.

[35] 70 N.J. 10 (1976).

[36] *Id.* at 18, 26.

[37] *Id.*

[38] *Id.* at 38.

[39] *Id.* at 35–36. Quinlan lost this claim. *Id.* at 36–37.

[40] *Id.* at 30–31.

[41] *Id.* at 30.

done for a proper purpose (such as oversedation with morphine to control pain), even with the knowledge that it will cause death, does not constitute euthanasia because death is not the primary purpose of the action. Nor did Catholic theology require "extraordinary means," such as a ventilator, to be used to keep a patient alive, as had happened to many brain-dead patients.

But Karen Ann Quinlan was not brain dead, she was alive in all senses of the word,[42] and her doctors absolutely refused to disconnect her life support. They demurred to any suggestion that they were motivated in any way by fear of civil and criminal liability (a denial to which the New Jersey Supreme Court reacted with hearty and rather tactless skepticism).[43] Instead, they declared their unwillingness to emulate the Nazi doctors who had killed hundreds of thousands of disabled individuals.[44] The trial court ruled against Joseph Quinlan, essentially finding that it had no jurisdiction in this area because it was entirely the province of the medical profession:

> The nature, extent, and duration of care by societal standards is the responsibility of the physician. The morality and conscience of our society places this responsibility in the hands of the physician. What justification is there to remove it from the control of the medical profession and place it in the hands of the courts?[45]

The answer to this latter question was not long in coming. The New Jersey Supreme Court, in a long, thoughtful, and extraordinary decision, acknowledged that "such notions of the distribution of responsibility" (i.e., that these decisions belonged to the medical profession) were "heretofore generally entertained," but that determinations as to human values and rights "must, in the ultimate, be responsive not only to the concepts of medicine but also to the common moral judgment of the community at large."[46] Modern readers will be surprised to discover that determination of the common moral judgment and its implementation was deemed to be a nondelegable duty of the courts, but the New Jersey Supreme Court was prepared to do its duty, however difficult and complex it might be.

In response to the trial court's position that medical decisions and medical care must be left up to the doctors, the New Jersey Supreme Court noted

---

[42] *Id.* at 20.

[43] Because the County Prosecutor and State Attorney General had notified the court that they would consider the acceleration of Karen Quinlan's death to be a crime, the court had some reason to question the doctors' professed lack of concern about liability, *id.* at 51.

[44] *In re* Quinlan at 51. See also Jill Lepore, *The Politics of Death*, NEW YORKER, Nov. 30, 2009, http://www.newyorker.com/magazine/2009/11/30/the-politics-of-death and Lepore's chapter about the *Quinlan* case in THE MANSION OF HAPPINESS: A HISTORY OF LIFE AND DEATH (2012).

[45] *In re* Quinlan, 137 N.J. Super.227, 259 (1975).

[46] *In re* Quinlan, 70 N.J. 10, 44 (1976).

that "courts in the exercise of their parens patriae authority to protect those under disability have sometimes implemented medical decisions and authorized their carrying out under the doctrine of substituted judgment."[47] This sufficed for the case at hand, since Karen Ann Quinlan was doubtless under disability, but did not address what might happen when people who wished to disconnect their life support were perfectly competent. The Supreme Court addressed in minute detail the liability concerns that the doctors and hospital adamantly denied, advising the creation of hospital ethics committees to help doctors in these situations. Furthermore, the court asserted that it could not be a crime to exercise a constitutional right, and that termination of life support by a doctor therefore could not be a crime: "there is a real and in this case determinative distinction between the unlawful taking of the life of another and the ending of artificial life-support systems as a matter of self-determination."[48]

Thus, while "the trial court was correct in its summary of the situation existing when it made its ruling"[49] that decisions to disconnect life support were the sole province of medicine, times were changing. Joseph Quinlan had raised three separate constitutional claims, on behalf of himself and his daughter: the right to freedom of religion, the right to be free from cruel and unusual punishment, and the right to privacy. The court quickly disposed of the first two[50] and found that Quinlan himself had no constitutional right to assert any claim in his own right as a father.

However, he could assert his daughter's right to privacy. The right to privacy, which had begun its ambiguous life in the penumbras of the Bill of Rights[51] was very much a live topic in 1976, three years after it had been used to uphold a woman's right to terminate her pregnancy in *Roe v. Wade*. The right to privacy, as explicated by the New Jersey Supreme Court, supported "a patient's decision to decline medical treatment under certain circumstances."[52]

Standing against this right was "the right of the physician to administer medical treatment according to his best judgment" (the court does not

---

[47] *Id.* at 44. The court pointed to two cases to support this assertion, one of which involved the donation of a kidney by a man with mental retardation to his brother, and by an infant to her identical twin. The court did not advert to the most famous court decision implementing a medical decision, Buck v. Bell, 274 U.S. 200 (1927) in which the Supreme Court authorized the involuntary sterilization of an allegedly mentally retarded woman with the infamous remark that "three generations of imbeciles are enough." *Id.* at 207. Later scholarship proved that Carrie Buck was not retarded, PAUL LOMBARDO, THREE GENERATIONS, NO IMBECILES (2009).

[48] *Quinlan*, note 35, at 52.

[49] *Id.* at 45.

[50] *Id.* 35–39.

[51] Griswold v. Connecticut, 381 U.S. 479, 484 (1965).

[52] *In re* Quinlan, 70 N.J. 10, 40 (1976).

tell us the source of the physician's right in this regard). The New Jersey Supreme Court acknowledged that defendants had asserted that permitting Quinlan to discontinue life support "unwarrantably offends prevailing medical standards."[53]

It is worth noting how wrong all of the medical experts were about Karen Ann Quinlan's condition. They said she needed a respirator to live;[54] she did not. They said she would die within six months to a year, even on the respirator;[55] she lived for ten more years off the respirator, although still in a vegetative state. These issues have echoed in modern assisted-suicide data, where people whose life expectancies were determined by physicians to be less than six months (and who *want* to die—that's how we have their data) are still alive one, two, and sometimes even three years later.

Thus, *Quinlan* provided a constitutional rationale for cases that would become known as "right-to-die" cases, despite the *Quinlan* court's own explicit rejection of that concept:

> Judicial refusals to order life-saving treatment in the face of
> contrary claims of bodily self-determination or free religious
> exercise are too often cited in support of a pre-conceived 'right
> to die,' even though the patients, wanting to live, have claimed
> no such right. Conversely, the assertion of a religious or other
> objection to life-saving treatment is at times condemned as
> attempted suicide even though suicide means something quite
> different in the law.[56]

Quinlan is truly a watershed case: the unquestionable transformation of a paradigm from a private matter controlled by medicine to a legal rights matter in which the final decision-maker was the State, in the form of both the courts and the legislature.[57] The next seven years saw an explosion in the number of cases involving "the right to die"[58] in the sense of the right to refuse life-sustaining measures, as well as state statutes embodying these court decisions. In addition to the constitutional right to privacy, courts found support for their decisions in the common law doctrine that an unconsented touching constituted battery, so that doctors and hospitals could not

---

[53] *Id.* at 42.

[54] *In re* Quinlan, 70 N.J. 10, 25 (1976).

[55] *Id.* at 26.

[56] *Quinlan, id.* at 46, citing Robert M. Byrn, *Compulsory Lifesaving Treatment for the Competent Adult*, 44 FORDHAM L. REV. 1 (1975–1976).

[57] This is not to say that the medical profession did not fight back vigorously at this loss of power, see, e.g., Arnold S. Relman, *The Saikewicz Decision: Judges As Physicians*, 298 NEW ENG. J. MED. 508 (Mar. 2, 1978), in which the editor of the *New England Journal of Medicine* invited judges to take tours of hospitals.

[58] Superintendent of Belchertown State Hosp. v. Saikewicz, 317 N.E. 2d 417 (Mass. 1977); *In re* Colyer, 660 P.2d 738 (Wash. 1983).

treat competent patients without their consent. Some of these cases involved competent individuals; others involved noncompetent individuals, including individuals in vegetative states. Some involved ventilators; others involved artificial nutrition and hydration, which courts generally did not differentiate from medical treatment. But all of them involved people who, if not at death's door, were certainly in the neighborhood: people who would die without mechanical life support.[59]

In 1983, the first case reached the courts involving a person who specifically wanted to die rather than live, who was not on any kind of life support, and who was in no danger of dying anytime soon. This individual actually wanted to commit suicide rather than refusing treatment as a religious obligation or as resignation to a hastening and inevitable end. Her name was Elizabeth Bouvia.

Elizabeth Bouvia was twenty-six years old and had cerebral palsy, a condition which had caused her to be almost quadriplegic. She used a wheelchair and experienced constant pain from spasticity, as well as arthritis. At twenty-six, she could use her right hand, and she could feed herself. Assuming she received needed assistance in activities of daily living, experts testified she could expect to live for another fifteen or twenty years.[60] But she didn't want to live. She had been institutionalized at the age of ten when her divorced mother remarried. After eight years of institutionalization, she left, went to college, got a degree in social work, got married, and entered a master's program in social work. Then her social work program told her she would never get a job because of her disability, refused to advocate for her, and her husband left her.

On September 8, 1982, her father, with whom she had been living, drove her to the emergency department of Riverside Hospital, where she stated that she wanted to die by starving herself to death. She asked to be admitted to the psychiatric unit because "it was the only place you can get admitted to a hospital by just talking."[61] Rather like Kerrie Wooltorton, she asked the hospital to relieve her pain and assist her with her daily living requirements until she died. Unlike Wooltorton, she had not taken any steps to put the dying

---

[59] Bartling v. Superior Court, 163 Cal. App. 3d 186 (1984) and Satz v. Perlmutter, 322 So.2d 160 (Fla. App. 1978).

[60] Bouvia v. Riverside Hosp., No. 159780 (Super. Ct. Riverside) (complaint filed Dec. 16, 1983). The decision of the court in *Elizabeth Bouvia v. County of Riverside* is reproduced in full at 1 Issues L. & Med. 485 (1985–1986). [Hereinafter, citations to this case will be referred to as *Bouvia 1* and will be to the pages in the journal.] As usual the experts were wrong. According to Dr. Tia Powell, Bouvia was still alive in 2012, Tia Powell, *Honoring the Wishes of Patients When Death Is Inevitable*, THE DOCTOR'S TABLET BLOG (Oct. 9, 2012), http://blogs.einstein. yu.edu/honoring-the-wishes-of-patients-when-death-is-inevitable/.

[61] Judith Cummings, *Judge Prepares to Rule on Death Plea*, N. Y. TIMES, Dec. 13, 1983, www.nytimes.com/1983/12/13/us/judge-prepares-to-rule-on-death-plea.html.

process in motion,[62] with a swift end in sight. Rather, Bouvia's plan of starvation involved weeks and maybe months.

Of course, Elizabeth Bouvia could not have picked a worse place to announce a desire to commit suicide—let alone ask for support and assistance—than an inpatient psychiatric ward.[63] After she went to court, the head of psychiatry announced that even if she won, he would defy any court order to let her die. In addition, as the hospital pointed out in its court filings, it had quite a few patients who were suicidal, and staff who were trying to change those patients' minds and it would be "demoralizing" for staff to assist one patient's suicide while involuntarily treating others. Even today, people who believe in the right to suicide, assisted or otherwise, probably would not go so far as to insist that this right be honored in a psychiatric ward. But—irony of ironies—although there was nothing acutely medically wrong with Bouvia, as a suicidal person, the psychiatric ward could not discharge her either.

Ms. Bouvia brought a lawsuit asking the court to prohibit Riverside Hospital from force-feeding her *and* to prohibit it from discharging her *and* to prohibit it from transferring her *and* to require the hospital to administer pain medication and hygienic care until her death occurred.[64] As the court summarized, "the essence of Plaintiff's claim is that she has the right to determine when and how her life shall end and that society has the obligation to honor and to assist her in achieving that individual right."[65] Ms. Bouvia's case provoked enormous national and individual responses:

> Disabled individuals held vigils at hospitals to convince her to change her mind. Bouvia's estranged husband hitchhiked to Riverside from Iowa, retained lawyers, and asked to be named her legal guardian ... Richard Nixon sent a letter encouraging Bouvia to 'keep fighting.' ... A meeting with President Ronald Reagan was discussed. Two neurosurgeons offered free surgery to help her gain the use of her arms. A convicted felon offered to shoot her.[66]

And this was all before social media and the Internet.

Her estranged husband was allowed to intervene in the case, arguing that Bouvia was either mentally incompetent or her judgment was impaired, and that she was being "set upon" by the American Civil Liberties Union (ACLU) and euthanasia societies (all contentions that the court found to be

---

[62] As far as I can tell from intensive research, she had not even stopped eating while she was at her father's house.

[63] Which is not to say that the medical nonpsychiatric staff were sympathetic. The Deputy Chief of Medicine at the hospital called Bouvia's claims "diabolical."

[64] The court's decision in *Bouvia 1* is reproduced in full at 485–86, see n. 60.

[65] *Id.* at 486.

[66] Robert Sternbrook & Bernard Lo, *The Case of Elizabeth Bouvia: Starvation, Suicide, or Problem Patient?* 146 ARCH. INTERNAL MED. 161 (1986).

without merit).[67] He asked the court to order a psychiatric evaluation for his wife in November. The judge refused. His wife, who did not view these efforts as gestures of reconciliation from a husband who had previously abandoned her, initiated divorce proceedings while simultaneously litigating her right to die.

Bouvia's case caught the attention of disability rights activists, who feared that the public was being given an erroneous impression that disabled people lived such miserable, worthless lives that suicide was a rational option. Many disabled people sought to meet Elizabeth Bouvia and change her mind. One activist, Wesley Sutton, had cerebral palsy himself. He held a thirteen-night vigil at Riverside, hoping fruitlessly to get a chance to talk to her. He did take the opportunity to speak to the press. He said he thought he knew what she was going through, noting that when Bouvia had been far more able-bodied than she was now, she had tried to kill herself three times, unsuccessfully. "When it came right down to it, he said, she would not end up killing herself. He'd bet on that, he said."[68] An organization called Advocacy for Developmental Disabilities was permitted to intervene in the case, arguing that granting Bouvia's petition would be terrible for disabled people everywhere, and that she was not really seeking her right to privacy or self-determination, but her death.[69] The organization did not acknowledge that these two goals might overlap or coincide.

As the judge noted, exactly what Bouvia was trying to do by bringing her case was a matter of great contention throughout the proceeding. "Elizabeth Bouvia's decision to end her life has been called

1. The right of self-determination
2. The right of privacy
3. The right to determine the quality of one's life
4. The right to control one's own life and body
5. The right to be let alone
6. The right to be protected from forced feeding
7. The right to determine one's own future
8. The right to escape a useless body
9. Freedom of choice
10. The acceptance of death
11. Self-starvation

---

[67] *Bouvia 1*, at 486, 488.

[68] Mary Johnson, *Right to Life, Fight to Die: The Elizabeth Bouvia Saga*, ELECTRIC EDGE (web edition of THE RAGGED EDGE), Jan./Feb. 1997, http://www.ragged-edge-mag.com/archive/bouvia.htm.

[69] *Bouvia 1* at 486. As a legal matter, granting this organization status as a party (as opposed to permitting an amicus brief) is an extreme stretch of the definition of a party with standing in the issue of whether Bouvia should or should not be forced to accept involuntary nutrition and hydration.

12. Self-destruction
13. Suicide
14. Voluntary euthanasia, and finally
15. The right to die with dignity"[70]

The court found that Bouvia was rational, competent, and understood the consequences of her proposed course of action.[71] The court found as a fact that "despite displaying certain effects of depression (or dysthymic disorder) she was, at the time she filed the action, free from any acute mental or physical disorder that would require care or treatment in any service at Riverside General Hospital." The court found that she was not making the decision because of a failed marriage, lack of employment, or termination of education, but rather "because of the nature and extent of her physical disability and her dependence on others to maintain her person in all areas of physical activity."[72]

Nevertheless, the court denied Bouvia's request to prohibit Riverside Hospital from force-feeding her. Although the outcome does not surprise us today, the rationale given by the court in 1983 probably does: although the strongest argument was the State interest in preservation of life,

> the next in order of importance in this case are the interests of
> third parties. In the instant matter the third parties include other
> patients in the hospital, other persons similarly situated who suffer
> from chronic disabling diseases and health care professionals
> employed at Riverside Hospital who would have to assist in
> Bouvia's demise.

These third party interests, including the interests of other people with cerebral palsy and other disabling conditions, were more important than society's interest in the prevention of suicide, which was also recited by the court as a factor in its decision. Finally, the fourth interest, "maintenance of the integrity of the medical profession," was an interest so strong that "the established ethics of the medical profession clearly outweigh and overcome Bouvia's own right of self-determination."[73] Thus, presumably the interests of the third parties also outweighed and overcame Bouvia's right of self-determination. The decision contained no citation to case law whatsoever.

In the aftermath of the decision, several people offered to permit Bouvia to stay at their houses to die, including a feminist festival promoter.[74] Bouvia

---

[70] *Bouvia 1* at 488–89.
[71] *Bouvia 1* at 487–88.
[72] *Id.* at 488.
[73] *Bouvia 1* at 490.
[74] *Bouvia Rejects Feminist's Haven*, LAKELAND LEDGER, Jan. 1, 1984, www.news. google.com/newspapers?nid=1346&dat=19840101&id=btwvAAAAIBAJ&sjid= bfsDAAAAIBAJ&pg=4047,40069.

initially appealed the decision, but then withdrew her appeal.[75] Apparently, she experienced some form of epiphany at a hotel in Mexico and decided to live.[76] Her friends removed her from Riverside and tried to find a place for her. Her physical condition deteriorated and ultimately she wound up in a bed at another public hospital, High Desert Hospital. While at Riverside she could feed herself and ambulate in a wheelchair, but by the time she was at High Desert, she spent most of her days in bed, spoon-fed. Even with a morphine drip permanently implanted in her chest, she still had nausea, and often stopped eating when she felt she would vomit. At a point when her weight reached about 65 pounds, the hospital (apparently without going to court, and against her will expressed both orally and in writing) inserted a nasal gastric tube.

Bouvia went to court again. This time, she disclaimed any suicidal intent; she did not actually want to starve herself to death, she said, but she was entitled to refuse invasive treatment, as long as she was aware of the probable consequences. She again lost at the initial level. The trial court, echoing the Association for Developmental Disabilities in 1983, found that she was "trying to commit suicide with the state's help rather than a bona fide exercise of her right to refuse treatment."[77] This time Bouvia did pursue an appeal, and, in 1986, in an opinion as laden with legal precedent as the previous opinion had lacked it, she won the right to have the nasal gastric tube removed.[78] As to the argument that she wanted to commit suicide, the Court of Appeals ruled that "no evidence supports this conclusion."[79] In any event, the court added, in another watershed moment in this jurisprudence, her motivations in making treatment decisions were irrelevant to her right to refuse treatment: [T]he trial court seriously erred by basing its decision on the 'motives' behind Elizabeth Bouvia's decision to exercise her rights. If a right exists, it matters not what "motivates" its exercise.[80] Even if motivation were relevant, the court went on, Bouvia's situation was not suicide, nor were her physicians being asked to assist her to commit suicide:

> It is not necessary to here define or dwell at length upon what
> constitutes suicide. Our Supreme Court dealt with the matter in
> the case of *In re Joseph G.* (1983) 34 Cal.3d 429 [194 Cal. Rptr. 163,
> 667 P.2d 1176, 40 A.L.R. 4th 690], wherein, declaring that the state

---

[75] *Bouvia v. Superior Court*, 179 Cal. App. 3d 1127, 1136 (1986) [hereinafter *Bouvia 2*].

[76] "After several months of expressing her desire to starve to death, Bouvia recently agreed to resume eating." *End of Starvation Effort Is Reported*, N.Y. TIMES, Apr. 27, 1984, § 1, at 7, col. 1.

[77] *Bouvia 2*.

[78] *Bouvia 2*.

[79] *Id.* at 1135.

[80] *Id.* at 1144.

has an interest in preserving and recognizing the sanctity of life, it observed that it is a crime to aid in suicide. But it is significant that the instances and the means there discussed all involved affirmative, assertive, proximate, direct conduct such as furnishing a gun, poison, knife, or other instrumentality or usable means by which another could physically and immediately inflict some death-producing injury upon himself. Such situations are far different than the mere presence of a doctor during the exercise of his patient's constitutional rights.[81]

Thus, in 1983, when Ms. Bouvia was able to feed herself but announced her intention to forego food, a court authorized forcible and involuntary insertion of a nasal gastric tube to feed her against her will. In 1986, when she could no longer feed herself but had to be fed by a tube, a court found that she had a right to refuse this treatment, and exercising that right did not amount to suicide. Thus does socially repugnant suicide turn into the right to refuse treatment: it's simply the process of the person becoming more disabled. Ms. Bouvia's motivations were the same in both cases; the means of keeping her alive identical. The differences in her two situations would be described differently by different people. Disability rights activists might point out that Ms. Bouvia was more disabled in 1986 than in 1983. Others might say the right to refuse intrusive treatment was immediately at issue in 1986, and only prospective in 1983, or that the courts were different.

What is clear is that the tenor of the judiciary's opinion had changed remarkably, as it did between the trial and appellate levels in *Quinlan*. Although the opinion cited to case law in California and across the country to support its holding, it was obvious that the judges were also deeply emotionally involved in the decision. The last line of Judge Compton's concurring opinion declares, "If there is ever a time when we ought to be able to 'get the government off our backs,' it is when we face death—by choice or otherwise."[82] Would he have felt the same way and written the same words if Elizabeth Bouvia had been a thirty-one-year-old woman with a master's in social work who was not disabled? What if Elizabeth Bouvia had had a psychiatric diagnosis? What if Elizabeth Bouvia had been a man—would the trial court have decided differently?[83]

---

[81] *Id*. at 1145.

[82] *Id*. at 1148 (Compton, J., concurring).

[83] Steven H. Miles & Allison August, *Courts, Gender and "The Right to Die,"* 18 L. MED. & HEALTH CARE 1-2, 85–95 (Spring-Summer, 1990). (These authors studied cases in which incompetent people were on life support and their doctors and families believed they would want to be disconnected. Judges agreed with the men in 75% of cases and with women in 14.3% of cases. The language judges used in the cases involving the men conceptualized the life support as assaultive and the men as rational in their supposed preference, while women were seen as needing protection from neglect and any preference for death as emotional and irrational).

As is so often the case when suicidal people are told that they retain the option of suicide and will not be constrained or restrained or detained or involuntarily prevented from carrying out their plans, Elizabeth Bouvia did not implement her right to starve herself to death. Like Mr. Sebastian, like 50% of the people who obtain lethal prescriptions in Oregon, like the best-selling author Andrew Solomon[84] and numerous others, she clung to her option to die and stayed alive.[85] Ironically, her attorney and friend, Richard Scott, who was also a doctor and cofounder of the Hemlock Society, killed himself in 1992. As is the case with many people who are truly determined to kill themselves, he shot himself, apparently without consulting or forewarning Elizabeth Bouvia, who was still alive, or anyone else.[86] His wife noted that he had long battled depression.

The *Bouvia* case inspired many scholarly articles and comments, with everyone reflecting their own perspective: Bouvia as "problem patient,"[87] Bouvia as "courageous lady,"[88] and Bouvia as a depressed woman who "hated her disabled self."[89] Many disabled people believed that Bouvia would have been glad to live in a society which honored her social work degree and gave her options other than complete dependence and a hospital bed.

After Bouvia won her case, a few other disabled but nonterminal individuals won right-to-die cases, but they were being kept alive by machines.[90] The only nonterminally ill individuals who have prevailed at the appellate level in cases involving the right to die are (1) individuals in comas or vegetative

---

[84] Andrew Solomon, The Noonday Demon: An Atlas of Depression (2001).

[85] A work of fiction based on a version of this phenomenon is Paulo Coelho, Veronika Decides to Die (1998), in which the heroine tries to commit suicide, wakes up in the hospital, and is told she has only a few months to live, which creates in her the desire to live.

[86] Beverly Beyette, *The Reluctant Survivor: 9 Years After Helping Her Fight for the Right to Die, Elizabeth Bouvia's Lawyer and Confidante Killed Himself— Leaving Her Shaken and Living the Life She Dreaded*, L. A. Times, Sept. 13, 1992, www. http://articles.latimes.com/1992-09-13/news/vw-1154_1_elizabeth-bouvia. Nancy Cruzan's father also committed suicide six years after her death, *Joe Cruzan, 62, Whose Four-Year Battle to Stop Life...* Baltimore Sun, Aug. 20, 1996, http://articles.baltimoresun.com/1996-08-20/news/1996233107_1_ nancy-cruzan-heart-attack-died-of-kidney.

[87] Sternbrook & Lo, *supra* note 66.

[88] William Dann, *A Tribute to a Courageous Lady*, Lawrence J. World, Jan. 5, 1984, http://news.google.com/newspapers?nid=2199&dat=19840105&id=Caoy AAAAIBAJ&sjid=i-gFAAAAIBAJ&pg=5124,946891 (political advertisement paid for by William Dann).

[89] Johnson, *supra* note 68.

[90] In the Matter of Hector O. Rodas, Case No. 86-PR-139 (Colo. Dist. Ct. Mesa Cty Apr. 3, 1987). This opinion is summarized in Ross v. Hilltop Hosp., 676 F.Supp. 1528, 1531–33 (D. Colo. 1987); McKay v. Bergstedt, 801 P.2d 617 (Nev. 1990); State v. McAfee, 259 Ga. 579 (1989).

states who have others making the request on their behalf; and (2) competent physically disabled people who are dependent on machines or artificial nutrition and hydration. These individuals' wish to be dead is understandable to society in a way that people with unmanageable grief or untreatable emotional suffering is not. As Woody Allen noted,

> I feel that life is divided into the horrible and the miserable. That's the two categories. The horrible are like, I don't know, terminal cases, you know, and blind people, crippled. I don't know how they get through life. It's amazing to me. And the miserable is everyone else. So you should be thankful that you're miserable, because that's very lucky, to be miserable.[91]

This is something that people who are desperate and suicidal have heard over and over again, from many people: you're very lucky. It doesn't help.

The Heyday of the Right to Die: *Cruzan* and *Kevorkian* to *Glucksberg*

Shortly after *Bouvia* was decided, the right of a nonterminally ill person to choose to end his or her life leapt into the headlines again with the advent of Dr. Jack Kevorkian, who roamed the land between 1990 and 1998. The year of Dr. Kevorkian's first assisted suicide—1990—was also the year that the Supreme Court decided its first right-to-die case. The time period between 1990 and 1997 was the closest that the United States ever came to finding a constitutional right to assisted suicide, and ended in 1997 with the Supreme Court deciding unanimously that no such right exists.

Between 1988 and 1997, a few courts did find a due process right to commit suicide, and the academic and popular literature devoted thousands of pages to analyzing the issue from philosophical, legal, ethical, medical, and myriad other perspectives. After Dr. Kevorkian's first assisted suicide in Michigan, the legislature passed a statute criminalizing such activity. Three separate lower courts in Michigan found the statute unconstitutional; one of them held that "when a person's quality of life is significantly impaired by a medical condition and the medical condition is extremely unlikely to improve, and that person's decision to commit suicide is a reasonable response to the condition causing the quality of life to be significantly impaired, and the decision to end one's life is freely made without undue influence, such a person has a constitutionally protected right to commit suicide."[92] These three cases were swiftly reversed by the Michigan Court of Appeals.[93] The Michigan Supreme Court, which by then had Kevorkian-related cases

---

[91] *Annie Hall* (1977) United Artists.

[92] These cases were consolidated on appeal in a single case, Hobbins v. Attorney General, 518 N.W.2d 487 (Mich. App. 1994).

[93] *Id.*

littering its docket, further consolidated these three cases with three other cases.[94] After disposing of some procedural wrangles,[95] the court held that there was a difference between the constitutional right to refuse treatment, even when that refusal inevitably led to death, and a constitutional right to suicide. The court's holding on suicide as a fundamental right essentially reads like a synopsis of the Supreme Court's decision in *Glucksberg* three years later, focusing on our history of rejecting and criminalizing suicide as a rationale and completely avoiding the repeated invitation of right-to-die advocates to analogize this right to abortion, which had also been criminalized until it was enshrined as a constitutional right.[96] Finally, clearing out the rest of the *Kevorkian* docket, the court revisited and overruled *People v. Roberts*, a venerable case well-known to law students holding that assisting a suicide constituted murder.[97]

The three lower courts in Michigan had relied on the holding of a federal court in Washington that there was a constitutional right to die,[98] a finding initially reversed by the Ninth Circuit[99] but upheld on reconsideration *en banc*[100] by the Ninth Circuit.[101] On the East Coast, the Second Circuit held that criminalizing assisted suicide violated the Constitution's guarantee of equal protection because competent terminally ill patients on life support could choose to end their lives, while similarly situated terminally ill patients not on life support could not decide to do so.[102]

The judges in these cases believed they were taking their lead from the U.S. Supreme Court, which decided its first right-to-die case in 1990.[103] The situation in *Cruzan v. Missouri* was similar to the situation in *Quinlan*—a young woman in a vegetative state whose family wanted to disconnect her from life support,[104] but the Court approached the case in a different way

---

[94] Kevorkian v. Michigan, 527 N.W.2d 714 (Mich. 1994).

[95] *Id.* at 719–24 (the statute was challenged on the grounds that its purpose changed as it wended its way through the Legislature, and that it embraced multiple objects; the court rejected both challenges).

[96] *Id.*

[97] See Chapter 8 for a fuller discussion of People v. Roberts.

[98] Compassion in Dying v. State, 850 F.Supp. 1454 (W.D. Wash. 1994).

[99] 49 F.3d 586 (9th Cir. 1995).

[100] Usually appellate cases are decided by a panel of three judges. When an extraordinarily important issue is presented, all judges on the circuit can decide to rehear and redecide the case. Because the Ninth Circuit, which includes California, Oregon, Washington, Alaska, and Hawaii, is so large, eleven judges of the circuit can rehear the case and issue a decision *en banc*.

[101] Compassion in Dying v. Washington,79 F.3d 790 (9th Cir. 1996).

[102] Quill v. Vacco, 80 F.3d 716 (2nd Cir. 1996).

[103] The Court itself characterized the decision in this way, 497 U.S. 261, 277 (1990).

[104] Although in Nancy Cruzan's case, the life support was nutrition and hydration, so there was no chance she could remain alive, as Quinlan did after her respirator was disconnected.

and reached different conclusions. Justice Rehnquist noted that while state court decisions could look to common law and their own constitutions in deciding these cases, the U.S. Supreme Court must limit its search to the U.S. Constitution. Perhaps not surprisingly, Chief Justice Rehnquist rejected the privacy right relied on in *Quinlan:* not only was it associated with the toxic controversy around abortion and *Roe v. Wade,* but also because he disliked locating constitutional rights in the "emanations" and elusive "penumbras"[105] of the Bill of Rights, where the right to privacy had initially been discovered by Justice Douglas. However, the Court did find that "the principle that a competent person has a constitutionally protected liberty interest in refusing unwanted medical treatment may be inferred from our prior decisions."[106] A "liberty interest" is not as potent as a "fundamental right" and it must be weighed against a state's countervailing interests.

Also unlike *Quinlan,* the Court in *Cruzan* differentiated between decisions made by an individual and those made on the individual's behalf by surrogates. Thus, the majority of the Court upheld Missouri's requirement that a third party seeking to disconnect life support must prove that this reflected the true desires of a person now in a vegetative state by clear and convincing evidence.

The Court was quite divided in its response to Nancy Cruzan's situation: five of the Justices wrote separate opinions. Although many courts, including the courts in both *Quinlan* and *Bouvia,* hastened to draw a distinction between deaths occurring from refusal of treatment and suicide,[107] Justice Antonin Scalia would have none of it. He called the distinction "irrelevant," "specious," and (a particularly derogatory term in this context) "nice."[108] He argued that there was no distinction between starving one's self to death and putting a gun to one's head, and if distinctions should be made, they should be made between "those forms of inaction that consist of abstaining from 'ordinary' care and those that consist of abstaining from 'excessive' or 'heroic' actions."[109] Making this kind of distinction, he believed,

---

[105] See Griswold v. Connecticut, 381 U.S. 479, 484 (1965) (after reviewing a number of cases which appeared to expand on a basic right—freedom of speech, or freedom of association—in order to ensure protection of that right, Justice Douglas summed these up as standing for the proposition that "The foregoing cases suggest that specific guarantees in the Bill of Rights have penumbras, formed by emanations from those rights that help give them life and substance." This may be the single sentence in a Supreme Court opinion most loathed by conservative jurists and scholars.

[106] *Id.* at 278.

[107] *Bouvia 2.*

[108] Cruzan v. Missouri, 497 U.S. 261, 298 (1990) (Scalia, J., concurring).

[109] *Id.* at p. 296. This, of course, mirrors Catholic doctrine, see pp. 61–62 *supra,* although Justice Scalia did not say so.

should be left up to legislatures rather than the courts. He asserted that refusal of treatment, when such refusal was certain to result in death, was essentially identical to the right to commit suicide,[110] and that States had the right to "apply physical force to prevent" people from committing suicide,[111] including refusing treatment when that refusal would cause the patient to die. Justice Scalia also expressed skepticism that any right to die could be limited to those who were terminally ill or in a vegetative state; if Nancy Cruzan had this right under those circumstances, she would have it under any circumstances. But, he emphasized, she didn't did not have this right at all. From Justice Scalia's point of view, the only substantive due process rights protected by the Constitution were those that were firmly rooted in our nation's history and traditions, and what he characterized as "the right to suicide"[112] could hardly be described in those terms.

After the Supreme Court ruled in June 1990, the Cruzans went back to court to present evidence that would meet the standard of clear and convincing evidence. Missouri, having won the legal issue, withdrew from the case in September. With essentially no opposition, the court ruled that the Cruzans had met their burden, and on December 14, Nancy Cruzan's feeding tube was withdrawn. This did not take place without considerable opposition: seven separate petitions were filed with the court to resume feeding Ms. Cruzan, and on December 18, nineteen people entered the hospital and tried to reattach the feeding tube. They were arrested and on December 26, 1990, Nancy Cruzan died.[113] At her burial, her father said, "I would prefer to have my daughter back and let someone else be this trailblazer."[114] Three years later, he hanged himself.[115]

It was not only Dr. Kevorkian, a pathologist of dubious credentials and uncertain motivations, who gained publicity by his active involvement in helping patients die. In 1991, the year after *Cruzan* was decided, Dr. Timothy Quill published an article in the *New England Journal of Medicine* about his thoughtful and difficult decision to assist a terminally ill patient of his named Diane to kill herself after she received a diagnosis of acute leukemia. Dr. Quill

---

[110] *Cruzan v. Missouri* at 294 (U.S. law has always accorded the State the power to prevent, by force if necessary, suicide—including suicide by refusing to take appropriate measures necessary to preserve one's life). See Alan Stone, *The Right to Die: New Problems for Law and Medicine and Psychiatry*, 37 Emory L.J. 627 (1988).

[111] Cruzan v. Missouri, 497 U.S. at 298 (Scalia, J. concurring).

[112] *Id.* at 295.

[113] Tamar Lewin, *Nancy Cruzan Dies, Outlived by a Debate Over the Right to Die*, N. Y. Times, Dec. 27, 1990, p. A-1.

[114] Scott Canon, *Father's Empathy Recalled: Joe Cruzan, Who Fought for Daughter's Right to Die, Committed Suicide*, Kansas City Star, Aug. 19, 1996, p. A-1. Lester Cruzan was known as "Joe" to his family and friends.

[115] Eric Pace, *Lester Cruzan is Dead at 62; Fought to Let His Daughter Die*, N. Y. Times, Aug. 19, 1996. p. B-12.

provided Diane with prescriptions for medication he knew she would use to kill herself. Critics of Dr. Quill made much of the fact that she was a recovered alcoholic who had suffered from depression. Whatever one might think of Dr. Quill's ultimate decision, it was crystal clear that he knew his patient very well, and was by far in the best position to assess her competency and clarity of thought in wanting to die. It was evident from his account that what motivated Diane was what turns out to motivate most people who choose assisted suicide:[116] a desire to be in control of the circumstances of her life and death.[117]

After the publication of the article in *New England Journal of Medicine*, the New York authorities attempted to criminally indict Dr. Quill, but the jury refused to return the indictment. Within five years, Quill was the named plaintiff in one of a pair of cases asserting the constitutional right to assisted suicide in the United States Supreme Court.

These companion cases were *Compassion in Dying v. Washington*[118] and *Quill v. Vacco.*[119] The Ninth Circuit in *Compassion in Dying* (decided by the Supreme Court under the name *Washington v. Glucksberg*) had found that the substantive due process clause created a liberty interest in determining the time and manner of one's death, and that the State of Washington could not vindicate its own legitimate interests in protecting life and preventing suicide by criminalizing the conduct of physicians who supplied terminally ill people with prescriptions for medications to end their lives.[120]

Although ostensibly more cautious and less polemical than the appellate court opinion in *Bouvia*, the *Glucksberg en banc* opinion in many ways laid a jurisprudential foundation to support *Bouvia*'s conclusion. Finding that individuals have a protected liberty interest in determining the time and manner of their death, the court found that this interest could be outweighed by the state interest in preventing suicide if the reason for the suicide was "any problem, physical or psychological, that could be significantly ameliorated."[121] Phrasing the state's interest in this way, rather than in the language of terminal illness that the plaintiffs had themselves advocated, encompassed cases such as those of Karen Ann Quinlan and Nancy Cruzan, who were not terminally ill and whose right to die had been upheld by the courts. It also might be seen as encompassing Elizabeth Bouvia's circumstances, depending on how those circumstances are described.

Analogizing the right to die to the abortion right, the court noted that the "outcome of the balancing differs as a person's physical or medical condition

---

[116] See Chapter 3, p. 148.
[117] This motivation was criticized as pathological by many psychiatrists; see Chapter 5, pp. 228–230.
[118] 79 F.3d 790 (9th Cir. 1996) (*en banc*).
[119] 80 F.3d 716 (2nd Cir. 1996).
[120] *Compassion in Dying*, n. 118, at 793-794.
[121] *Id.* at 820.

deteriorates,"[122] just as a woman's right to an abortion weakened the later in the pregnancy she sought to assert it. The situations were also similar as a practical matter: whether or not the practice was legalized, people in need used it anyway. The court noted that doctors had been quietly and privately helping people to die for decades, regardless of their official position. Judge Reinhardt was skeptical of the medical profession's opposition to the right to die: the American Medical Association had also opposed the right to abortion on the basis of the Hippocratic oath twenty years previously, he noted, but once legalized, doctors had learned to accept abortions. Nor did he accept the argument that doctors could respect a patient's right to refuse treatment, but could not actively promote death: pulling the plug on a respirator was just as active as writing a prescription, if not more so, since the patient had to fill the prescription and take the drugs and was thus more in control of the dying process than when a respirator was disconnected.

The Ninth Circuit *en banc* majority recognized the argument about the historical criminalization of suicide and rebutted it, not only by pointing to societies where suicide was accepted and even admired, but by pointing to numerous constitutional rights recognized by the Supreme Court that had a long past history of criminalization, for example, interracial marriage and abortion. Rather than simply looking to history, the majority opinion asserted that constitutional rights were those that were necessary to the "concept of ordered liberty."[123] In any event, Judge Reinhardt wrote, prefiguring today's heated debates about terminology, he wasn't even sure that the kind of conduct being discussed could be considered "suicide."[124]

The Ninth Circuit's interpretation of due process rights would have also supported the right to assisted suicide for people in chronic and incurable pain, even if not terminally ill, because of its language linking the state's interest in preventing suicide due to "a problem which can be significantly ameliorated." It seems that it might have eventually supported a right to suicide for an individual such as Joshua Sebastian, who had wanted to kill himself for decades, faithfully tried treatment and had treatment forced on him, and had never changed his mind about wanting to die. It would not have supported a right for Kerrie Wooltorton on the facts available to us, competent though she might have been, because there was no indication that her suicidality might not have been significantly ameliorated.

In *Quill v. Vacco*, the Second Circuit upheld assisted suicide not as a matter of due process, but on Equal Protection grounds. The court found no distinction between assisting suicide and other life-shortening treatments, such as aggressive pain medication with opioids, or withdrawing life-sustaining treatment.[125]

---

[122] *Id.* at 800.
[123] Poe v. Ullman, 367 U.S. 497 (1961).
[124] Compassion in Dying, n. 118 at 802 and 824.
[125] Quill v. Vacco, 80 F.3d 716, 731 (2nd Cir. 1996).

The Supreme Court Rejection of *Glucksberg* and *Vacco*

The Supreme Court reversed both *Compassion in Dying* and *Quill v. Vacco* unanimously.[126] Justice Rehnquist's short, curt opinion reversing *Quill* is almost angry. Assisted suicide, Justice Rehnquist asserts, is fundamentally different from refusal of life-saving treatment or aggressive pain medication. In assisted suicide, the patient and doctor *intend* to cause the patient's death; a patient refusing treatment wants to live, but "free of unwanted technology, surgery or drugs."[127] When treating pain aggressively, the physician understands that the patient will die more quickly, but his purpose or intent is "only to ease the patient's pain."[128] The Court illustrates this point with an analogy that paints the physician in a heroic light: General Eisenhower at Normandy knew American soldiers would die on D-Day, but that was not what he intended.[129] In assisted suicide, the physician's prescription of lethal medication *causes* the death; refusal of treatment simply permits the underlying disease to take its course.

In some ways, this is pretty disingenuous. Most people who request assisted suicide also want to live. They want to live very much. But knowing they can't live much longer, they would prefer not to live with amyotrophic lateral sclerosis (ALS) or cancer destroying all that makes life meaningful or even endurable. They probably have much more in common with people who request that their life-support machines be disconnected than Justice Rehnquist says they do. Furthermore, they share the motivation of most people who attempt suicide: to end a life that is no longer worthwhile under circumstances that at least appear to the individual to be immutable and inescapable.

As to causation, Nancy Cruzan was not killed by her underlying condition, except insofar as her underlying condition precluded her from feeding and hydrating herself. She died because she was denied food and water and could not ingest them herself, in common with many patients fed by J-tubes, G-tubes, and other artificial means.

The Court's decision in *Washington v. Glucksberg* was longer and less angry, but equally easy to summarize: assisted suicide is suicide, and we are not going to find a fundamental right to do something that we have historically criminalized and condemned. Unlike Judge Reinhardt, the Justices had no difficulty calling the conduct in question "suicide." In my opinion they are correct: taking steps to intentionally end one's life is, in fact, suicide. If people

---

[126] Vacco v. Quill, 521 U.S. 793 (1997) and Washington v. Glucksberg, 521 U.S. 702 (1997). As in *Cruzan*, some concurrences could be characterized as dissents.

[127] Vacco v. Quill, 521 U.S. 793, 802 (1997) (quoting Matter of Conroy, 98 N.J. 321, 351 (1985)).

[128] Id. at 802. Again, the Catholic doctrine of double effect, see pp. 61–62, supra.

[129] *Vacco v. Quill* at 803 (citing Judge Kleinfeld's dissent in *Compassion in Dying v. Washington,* 79 F.3d 790, 858 (9th Cir. 1996).

have very good reasons to do it, and we want to support them, we can say suicide is acceptable under some circumstances, rather than trying to argue that what we consider acceptable suicide isn't actually suicide at all, which is verbal legerdemain that doesn't help further understanding of a complex moral and jurisprudential problem. If we want to destigmatize suicide, this certainly isn't the way to go about it.

The Ninth Circuit opinion's repeated analogies to abortion probably did not help its argument. The Supreme Court might as well have had a one-sentence opinion in *Glucksberg*: "We got ahead of the country on the abortion issue and created a political firestorm, and now we're stuck with it because three Justices believe that precedents should be honored,[130] but we are not going to make the same mistake twice on a hot-button issue with precisely the same deeply felt divisions as abortion."

When *Roe v. Wade* was decided in 1973, twenty states had legalized abortion under some (admittedly often narrow) circumstances; when the Court was considering assisted suicide, only Oregon had legalized it, and at the time the Supreme Court was considering assisted suicide, Oregon's assisted-suicide operation had been stopped before it ever got started by a lower federal court.[131] This ruling was vacated by the Ninth Circuit a month after oral argument in the assisted-suicide cases.[132] So at the time the Court was being asked to find a constitutional right to physician-assisted suicide, it existed (legally) nowhere in the United States.

Thus, perhaps it was unsurprising that the *Glucksberg* decision invoked the long tradition of historical opposition to suicide, which avoided the Ninth Circuit's argument that sometimes history was wrong, and that in any event what was being protected by the decision was not suicide. But the Supreme Court might just as well have written, "Fool me once, shame on you; fool me twice, shame on me." This time, on this hot-button issue, the Court would permit the states to develop different approaches before it ruled; as in the case of gay marriage, the Court wanted to see how states dealt with the issue rather than the more painful and controversial leadership it had assumed with its jurisprudence on abortion.

The concurrences emphasized that some right to die might exist if a person was in pain that could not be controlled, or if the State prohibited access to pain medication. But until such a case was brought to its attention, the Court was content to permit the so-called laboratory of the states to explore the right to die.

---

[130] Planned Parenthood of Southeastern Pa. v. Casey, 505 U.S. 883 (1992) (the three-justice concurrence of Justices O'Connor, Souter, and Kennedy asserting that while they did not necessarily support the concept of a constitutional right to abortion, the requirements of *stare decisis*, i.e., the need to be able to count on settled law, drove them to uphold abortion rights in the wake of *Roe v. Wade*).

[131] Lee v. State, 891 F.Supp. 1429, 1438–39 (D. Ore. 1995).

[132] Lee v. Oregon, 107 F.3d 1382 (9th Cir. 1997).

Although *Glucksberg* was technically unanimous, the concurrences all seemed bent on softening and moderating Justice Rehnquist's majority opinion. Most of the concurring Justices underscored that this was a facial challenge to the Washington statute, meaning that the parties challenging the statute had to prove it was unconstitutional under *all* circumstances. The concurring Justices made clear that they might respond more sympathetically to an "as applied" challenge—a challenge by an individual in particular circumstances. For example, Justices O'Connor and Breyer made clear that they joined the opinion because they believed that adequate alleviation of pain was available to people who were terminally ill; otherwise, they might have decided differently. Justice Stevens analogized the decision to upholding the death penalty against a challenge that it was unconstitutional in all circumstances, while continuing to find that in certain cases—executing people with mental retardation, or minors—it constituted cruel and unusual punishment violating the Constitution.

Justice Rehnquist, in his turn, attempted to undermine and limit the concurring Justices' attempts to undermine and limit his majority opinion. He conceded that "our opinion does not absolutely foreclose a more particularized challenge" but notes that "given our holding that the Due Process Clause of the fourteenth amendment does not provide heightened protection to the asserted liberty interest in ending one's life with a physician's assistance, such a claim would have to be quite different from the ones advanced by respondents here."[133]

The concurrences' invitation of "as applied" challenges to assisted suicide statutes is, in any event, a little disingenuous. Unlike people on Death Row, terminally ill people do not have time to wait for the ponderous processes of law to unfold.[134] Indeed, *Glucksberg* began as a case with three terminally ill patients and their doctors; by the time it reached the Supreme Court, only the doctors were left alive. Almost all of the terminally ill plaintiffs we will read about in the coming chapters are dead by the time the court decides their cases.[135] The

---

[133] Glucksberg, n. 126, at 735.

[134] An outstanding article, by James Coleman about the attempt by lawyers at Wilmer, Cutler, and Pickering to get a court to give Ted Bundy's appeals a fair hearing, called the process, which took just under three years, *Litigating at the Speed of Light* 16 LITIGATION 14 (1990). The title is accurate as to the dizzying speed of the appellate process in Bundy's case. Even though death penalty cases are unique in usually taking a decade or more, three years would be a very brisk pace for a civil case to be filed, taken through the appellate process, and decided by the Supreme Court. Dying people rarely have that long. None of the terminally ill plaintiffs in either the Quill or Glucksberg cases even lived to read the circuit court decisions in their cases, let alone the Supreme Court case.

[135] See, e.g., the *Alda Gross* case before the European Court of Human Rights, the *Nicklinson* case in the United Kingdom, and the *Carter* case in Canada, discussed in Chapter 4.

plaintiff in the New Mexico case only outlived her case because when she filed the case she was in remission. [136]

Justice Stevens' and Justice Souter's concurrences are interesting, because both are more thoughtful struggles with the issues than the majority opinion, and because they point in such different directions.[137] Justice Stevens' concurrence reads more like a dissent: his opening salvo is to assert "there is also room for further debate about the limits the Constitution places on the power of States to punish the practice" of physician-assisted suicide.[138] Both Justice Stevens and Justice O'Connor explicitly agree that the individual's right to autonomy does not extend to a constitutional right to end his or her life at will. Justice Stevens invokes John Donne ("no man is an island") and sketches a poignant and moving tableau to support his point:

> The State has an interest in preserving and fostering the benefits that every human being may provide to the community—a community that thrives on the exchange of ideas, expressions of affection, shared memories, and humorous incidents, as well as on the material contributions that its members create and support. The value to others of a person's life is far too precious to allow the individual to claim a constitutional entitlement to complete autonomy in making a decision to end that life.[139]

This vision resonates with my own personal life. On the other hand, it also immediately calls to mind my clients who lived under bridges, in filthy and unsafe so-called assisted living, in wards where the screaming alternated with the endless blaring of television while staff sheltered behind the nurse's station. If personal autonomy is going to be limited in the name of the value that others place on an individual's life, it would be nice, to paraphrase Barney Frank, if that valuation showed up some time prior to the exact moment that the individual decides to commit suicide.[140] Justice Stevens' vision is a lot like that of the book *Stay,*[141] which eloquently reminds people of the damage their suicide will cause to their friends and family.

But the fact is, a lot of people feel alone and are alone. People who are suicidal either fundamentally believe their deaths would relieve rather than grieve the people in their lives, or they are correct in perceiving themselves

---

[136] See Chapter 3 for an extensive discussion of this case.

[137] Stevens' concurrence begins at p. 738; Souter's concurrence begins at 752.

[138] Glucksberg, n. 126, at 738.

[139] *Id.* at 749.

[140] Barney Frank, former Congressman from Massachusetts, was famous for saying that Republicans think life begins at conception and ends at birth. Charles Pierce, *To Be Frank*, Boston Globe Mag., Oct. 2, 2005, http://www.boston.com/news/globe/magazine/articles/2005/10/02/to_be_frank/?page=4.

[141] Jennifer Michael Hecht, Stay: A History of Suicide and the Philosophies Against It (2013).

as essentially alone in the world. There may be reasons to permit the State to override individual autonomy in matters of suicide, but "the value to others of a person's life" isn't one of them. To accept it would further devalue the lives of people whose circumstances proclaim the utter indifference of others: people in institutions who have never received a single visitor, people who live in cardboard boxes. Life may be made worth living because of our connections with others, but the law's insistence that each life has intrinsic value cannot depend on whether others value it, or are even aware of it.

Nevertheless, Justice Stevens' concurrence also captures a truth for which there are (as yet) no real jurisprudential terms: that the right to end one's life on one's own terms comes from something deeper than the right to refuse treatment, deeper even than the common law, and is best understood as the ultimate embodiment of the agency that expresses our essential humanity, the inalienable right we struggle to capture with the word *dignity*.

Justice Souter's concurrence probably comes the closest to my own views about the matter, and also (for people interested in this) is prefaced by an outstanding summary of the history of due process jurisprudence. Reduced to lay terms, Justice Souter's concurrence says that the argument, on the one hand, that people have a right to choose to die and, on the other, that the State has a compelling interest in preventing them from killing themselves are simply two conflicting moral positions. But the State's argument that people who actually don't want to die might get caught up in a program of physician-assisted suicide is one where both sides agree on the morality: no one wants this. The two sides just disagree on the degree to which State legalization of assisted suicide creates or elevates that risk. And when it comes right down to it, Justice Souter just doesn't trust the doctors to not "assist" too much. It's not that there are Dr. Mengeles lurking across the land, so much as misguided compassion and desire to relieve suffering that he fears will lead to assisting people who lack competence, or even euthanasia:

> The State claims interests in protecting patients from mistakenly and involuntarily deciding to end their lives, and in guarding against both voluntary and involuntary euthanasia. . . . Voluntary and involuntary euthanasia may result once doctors are authorized to prescribe lethal medication in the first instance, for they might find it pointless to distinguish between patients who administer their own fatal drugs and those who wish not to, and their compassion for those who suffer may obscure the distinction between those who ask for death and those who may be unable to request it. The argument is that a progression would occur, obscuring the line between the ill and the dying, and between the responsible and the unduly influenced, until ultimately doctors and perhaps others would abuse a limited freedom to aid suicides by yielding to the impulse to end another's suffering under conditions going beyond the narrow limits the respondents propose. The State

thus argues, essentially, that respondents' claim is not as narrow as it sounds, simply because no recognition of the interest they assert could be limited to vindicating those interests and affecting no others.

> . . . this difficulty [in assessing the 'knowing and responsible mind'] could become the greater by combining with another fact within the realm of plausibility, that physicians simply would not be assiduous to preserve the line. They have compassion, and those who would be willing to assist in suicide at all might be the most susceptible to the wishes of a patient, whether the patient were technically quite responsible or not. Physicians, and their hospitals, have their own financial incentives, too, in this new age of managed care. Whether acting from compassion or under some other influence, a physician who would provide a drug for a patient to administer might well go the further step of administering the drug himself; so, the barrier between assisted suicide and euthanasia could become porous, and the line between voluntary and involuntary euthanasia as well.[citation omitted] The case for the slippery slope is fairly made out here, not because recognizing one due process right would leave a court with no principled basis to avoid recognizing another, but because there is a plausible case that the right claimed would not be readily containable by reference to facts about the mind that are matters of difficult judgment, or by gatekeepers who are subject to temptation, noble or not.[142]

This argument is similar (but not identical) to the contention of Lord Justice Sumption in a case before the highest court in the United Kingdom. Justice Sumption asserts that "[t]he different legal treatment of the person who wishes to commit suicide and the person who is willing to assist him is not arbitrary."[143] He points out that the nature of the decision to commit suicide is inescapably different from the nature of the decision to assist, which does not depend on "an overpowering negative impulse arising from perceived incapacity, failure or pain." Basically, suicide is a self-limiting proposition, whereas assistance (as George Exoo, Dr. Jack Kevorkian, and Dr. Lawrence Egbert[144] have amply demonstrated) can be extended dozens if not hundreds of times.

Euthanasia is even less self-limiting than assisted suicide. Justice Souter (inevitably) turns to the example of the Netherlands.[145] He says that courts

---

[142] Glucksberg, n. 126 at 782, 783, 784, 785.

[143] R (Application of Nicklinson and another) v. Minister of Justice, [2014] ¶ 214 (Sumption, J.)

[144] See Chapter 10.

[145] See Chapter 4 for a detailed analysis of why the Netherlands is the eternal bogey state of those who oppose assisted suicide, rather than Belgium or Switzerland, whose regimes are arguably far more liberal and less well regulated.

are the wrong place to decide this issue—quite a departure from the opinion in *Quinlan*—and that it is the wrong time to decide it.[146] This issue needs time to ripen in state legislatures across the country, so that the Court may profit from that experience.

The message of *Glucksberg*, as a political rather than jurisprudential matter, was clear: if there was no right to physician-assisted suicide because there was a historical tradition of prohibiting suicide, the answer was to rename physician-assisted suicide, and its advocates went to work on this immediately. All future state ballots and legislative initiatives referred to the proposal as "aid in dying"[147] or "death with dignity" or—excluding the death language altogether—"end-of-life options."[148] Meanwhile, proponents of assisted suicide are also joining to medicalize it as another treatment at the end of life, including excoriating media who would describe the legislative proposals and ballot initiatives using the term suicide.[149]

Modern Day Law: What the Future Portends

Most lay people would not initially understand the close kinship and association shared by abortion and physician-assisted suicide as a matter of constitutional law. Both involve struggles between the concept of individual autonomy and social values; both practices have a history of criminalization and shame. When *Glucksberg* was decided, they also had in common the assumption that the involvement of a physician was necessary to give the right any meaning. As Justice Souter wrote in 1997,

> Without physician assistance in abortion, the woman's right
> would have too often amounted to a nothing more than a right
> to self-mutilation, and without a physician's assistance in the
> suicide of the dying, the patient's right will often be confined to
> crude methods of causing death, most shocking and painful to the
> decedent's survivors.[150]

---

[146] Justice Souter's opinion in *Glucksberg* should be read side by side with his concurrence in *Casey* to get a full understanding of his position on how the passage of time and the reliance of the citizenry affects the decisions of the Supreme Court.

[147] A bill introduced into the Connecticut Legislature in 2015 was entitled, "An Act Providing a Medical Option of Compassionate Aid in Dying for Terminally Ill Adults" (Conn. Gen. Assembly, S.B. 668, 2015), which pretty much covers the waterfront in terms of the buzzwords, http://www.cga.ct.gov/asp/cgabillstatus/cgabillstatus.asp?selBillType=Bill&bill_num=SB668&which_year=2015.

[148] In 2015, S.B. 128, the "End of Life Option Act" was introduced in the California Legislature, http://www.leginfo.ca.gov/pub/15-16/bill/sen/sb_0101-0150/sb_128_bill_20150120_introduced.html.

[149] Press Release, End of Life Choices New York, Disability Rights Legal Center, Aid in Dying Language Matters; see Chapter 6.

[150] Glucksberg, n. 126 at 778.

But in this as in so many things, technology's advances were unanticipated. In the twenty-first century, abortion is in the process of demedicalization, as a combination of the development of pills that can cause an abortion, and the ability to procure such pills through the Internet.[151] Thus, countries (or states in the United States) where abortions are difficult or impossible now cannot prevent abortions as long as people have access to the Internet and a place to pick up their mail. The combination of the availability of pills, the ubiquity of the Internet, and the fact that abortion is constitutionally protected in some parts of the world, means that women can distance themselves from the medical framework that once provided needed legitimacy for the effort to legalize abortion. Demedicalizing abortion is an explicit goal of feminists who work on making these pills available to women where abortions are illegal.[152] But this is just starting to happen, almost forty-five years after *Roe v. Wade*.

At the same time, proponents of physician-assisted suicide are trying more and more to portray it (at least at the end of life) as another form of medical treatment.[153] This is probably an essential step in legalization and destigmatization of assisted suicide. Attempts to demedicalize assisted suicide—by groups such as the Final Exit Network—have been met with swift criminal reprisals in states where prosecutors have long turned a blind eye to doctors who help their patients to die.[154] Suicide assisted by doctors will have to be discussed, legalized, and socially accepted to a far greater degree before it is possible to distance assisted suicide from a medical framework.

This is a path familiar to proponents of legalization of marijuana who, like proponents of suicide, have found society far more willing to change its mind about practices that have been criminalized and characterized as socially deviant when those practices become prescribed and overseen by the medical profession.[155] In all three cases, which involve issues that go to

---

[151] Emily Bazelon, *The Dawn of the Post-Clinic Abortion*, N. Y. TIMES MAG., Aug. 30, 2014, http://www.nytimes.com/2014/08/31/magazine/the-dawn-of-the-post-clinic-abortion.html. These pills still have to be prescribed by a doctor, but not necessarily a doctor in the woman's home country.

[152] *Id.*

[153] See Chapter 6, "Mental Health Professionals and Suicide."

[154] See Chapter 10.

[155] Medical marijuana use dates back to 1976, *see* United States v. Randall, 104 Daily Wash. L. Rptr 2249 (D.C. Super. Ct. Nov. 24, 1976), *available at* http://www.drugpolicy.org/docUploads/randall.pdf. Following the court's refusal to criminalize the use of marijuana by a man with glaucoma, the federal government operated a program at the University of Mississippi to dispense medical marijuana to sick individuals, but the George H. W. Bush administration ended it and only a few people still receive it. However, states passed medical marijuana bills well before voter initiatives legalizing recreational marijuana passed in Colorado and Washington in 2014.

the very heart of social values and principles, obtaining the blessing and involvement of the medical profession may only be a stage in a journey whose goal is complete individual autonomy to make these decisions. Just as Justice Blackmun's narrative of abortion as a shared decision resulting from joint and intimate discussions between a woman and her physician does not reflect many women's experiences of abortion, Justice Stevens' lionization of the medical profession as providing a "ministry" at the end of life[156] probably doesn't square with many peoples' experience with doctors either.

Presently, it is safe to say that there is a constitutional right to refuse treatment, with glaring exceptions that will be considered in the next section. The only potential constitutional right to die, or, as they now say, to choose the time and manner of your death, is either by refusing to eat or drink[157] or by turning off the machine that is keeping you alive, and both these circumstances are subject to exceptions in law and in practice.

The Supreme Court did leave open the option for states to experiment with assisted suicide. To refuse to declare a national, federally guaranteed right to assisted suicide is very different from prohibiting it. So far no state court has reached this conclusion based on state constitutions.[158]However, we will see in Chapter 3 that the Supreme Court held true to its promise to permit states to be laboratories of change.

Who's Missing from this Picture? Exceptions and Exclusions in Constitutional Rights to Make Decisions about One's Body

Prisoners

Although there is a constitutional right to refuse treatment and generally control your body, that right is not absolute. Nowhere is that more clear than in the case of people with psychiatric diagnoses, prisoners, and the particular circle of hell where those two categories overlap. *Cruzan*'s announcement that a competent individual has a liberty interest in refusing unwanted medical treatment was handed down the same year as *Washington v. Harper*,[159] which overrode a competent prisoner's right to refuse psychotropic medication in non-life-threatening situations as less important than the State's interest in a safe prison environment. The Supreme Court did devise certain substantive due process protections,

---

[156] *Id.* at 748.
[157] See a detailed discussion of this in Chapter 7.
[158] The *Baxter* court in Montana strongly hinted they would find such a right if they were forced to do so, but adroitly sidestepped the question, see Chapter 3.
[159] 494 U.S. 210 (1990).

ostensibly to protect the prisoner: forced medication could only be imposed on prisoners who, as a result of mental illness, were dangerous to themselves or others.[160] However, the Court undermined any meaning those substantive protections might have by imposing "procedural protections" ensuring that prison officials would decide whether the substantive standard was met.[161] The prisoner has no right to a lawyer or legal assistance in this hearing, although there is a right for a prison employee to help the prisoner present his or her case.

It is not only dangerous prison inmates who lose the right to refuse treatment. While courts were approving the disconnection of nasal gastric tubes from people who would otherwise live for many years, citing the major bodily intrusion of these tubes, they were also approving involuntary and forcible use of nasal gastric tubes to force-feed nondangerous prisoners who had made obviously competent decisions to stop eating.[162] And although kidney dialysis is even more intrusive than nasal gastric tubes, the Iowa Supreme Court upheld an order authorizing a jail to forcibly subject an inmate to dialysis.[163] Those cases were justified by the courts, as in *Harper,* in part by the need to keep order in jails and prisons, although it is not clear why all hell would break lose in the cellblocks if an inmate died in a prison hospital after refusing dialysis.

Not all courts denied prisoners the right to refuse treatment.[164] The California Supreme Court held that a quadriplegic prisoner could refuse life-sustaining treatment. Interestingly, the court specifically noted its agreement with these lines from *McKay v. Bergstedt,* a right to die case involving a person with quadriplegia:

> If a competent adult is beset with an irreversible condition such
> as quadriplegia, where life must be sustained artificially and
> under circumstances of total dependence, the adult's attitude or
> motive [in wanting to refuse life-sustaining treatment] may be
> presumed not to be suicidal.[165]

This description of the emptiness of life with quadriplegia would be news to many, including Stephen Hawking and the late Ed Roberts, who directed

---

[160] *Id.* at 227.

[161] *Id.* at 222, 226.

[162] *In re* Caulk, 125 N.H. 226 (1984); Von Holden v. Chapman, 87 A.D. 66 (N.Y. 1982) (the request to refuse food and water was made by Mark Chapman, who killed John Lennon); McNabb v. Dep't of Corr., 180 P.3d 1257 (Wash. 2008); Illinois Dept. of Corr. v. Millard, 782 N.E.2d 966 (Ill. App. 2003); State *ex. rel.* White v. Narick, 170 W.Va. 195 (1982).

[163] Polk County Sheriff v. Iowa District Court, 594 N.W.2d 421 (Iowa 1999).

[164] See Zant v. Prevatte, 248 Ga. 832 (1982).

[165] Thor v. Superior Court, 855 P.2d 375, 5 Cal.4th 725, 742 (1993).

the California Department of Vocational Rehabilitation, among thousands of others.[166]

Psychiatric Patients

The two major justifications that courts have used to deny prisoners the right to refuse treatment were 1) the need to maintain order in prisons, and 2) that the right to refuse treatment has never included the right to commit suicide.[167] Neither of these justifications apply to cases approving involuntary nasal gastric tubes to administer medication to competent and unwilling psychiatric patients whose refusal placed them in no danger of dying or even serious injury.[168] The World Medical Association and Amnesty International have called forced nasal gastric tubes in the context of force-feeding torture, and asserted that doctors should never do this.[169] And yet institutionalized psychiatric patients who are not in any serious danger of dying have been subjected to forcible nasal gastric tubes to receive medications for non-life-threatening illnesses.

In fact, the very fact that a patient's condition was *not* life-threatening was used as a rationale to support involuntary injection of antibiotics into a refusing and competent psychiatric patient. The court held that "overwhelming public policy considerations" trumped any right an individual might have to refuse treatment, finding that psychiatric patients' rights to court hearings before involuntary treatment applied only to "extraordinary" forms of treatment:

> Simply stated, court authorization should not be required in order for a mental hospital to treat a patient with antibiotics, debridement (removal of devitalized tissue) and dressing changes. Overwhelming public policy considerations make it imperative that mental hospitals *not* be required to go to court in order to perform routine, accepted, non-major medical treatment which poses no significant risk, discomfort, or trauma to the patient.[170]

Imagine if people who did not have psychiatric diagnoses were informed that they had no say over routine treatment decisions, and if they disagreed with the decisions of their medical professionals, they could be held down

[166] For a longer discussion at the dismay of many people with serious physical disabilities over courts' empathy with the desire of a physically disabled person to end his or her life, see Chapter 10.

[167] *McNabb v. Dep't of Corr, supra* at n. 162.

[168] *In re* Mary Ann D. 179 A.D.2d 724 (N.Y. App. Sup. Ct. 1992) (nasal gastric administration of lithium to patient deemed incompetent); Matter of Martin, 527 N.W.2d 170 (Minn. App. 1995).

[169] See Chapter 6.

[170] *In re* Salisbury, 524 N.Y.S.2d 352 (1988).

and forcibly injected with antibiotics or restrained for painful tissue debridement and dressing changes. The legal basis for this does not rest only on the fact that the plaintiff was institutionalized. It is not at all clear that the Court would honor a competent person's refusal of treatment even outside institutional settings, *if* the competent individual was refusing treatment for a suicide attempt,[171] refusing to ingest food because of anorexia,[172] or just refusing psychotropic medication because the side effects were unbearable.[173]

Courts have protected the right to make decisions about medical treatment and one's own body even unto death for people who do not have psychiatric disabilities. But while courts, scholars, and ethicists were declaiming the autonomy, dignity, and right of self-determination of medical patients, the identical courts, scholars, and ethicists were stumbling over each other to assure their readers that they weren't referring to *psychiatric* patients. In fact, the difficulty of ensuring that individuals with psychiatric disabilities did not avail themselves of the right to die was repeatedly cited as a reason to prohibit physician-assisted suicide, even by authors who are otherwise sympathetic to assisted suicide.[174] It is axiomatic that those sympathetic to a right to commit suicide consistently and explicitly exclude people with diagnoses of mental illness.[175] Even Dr. Jack Kevorkian, on trial for assisting a woman to die who had attempted suicide in the past, stoutly denied that the woman had any psychiatric problems, implicitly acknowledging he would never have helped her if he thought she did.

Not surprisingly, the difficulty of line-drawing to exclude people with psychiatric disabilities from the right to control the time and manner of their

---

[171] Justice Scalia's concurrence in *Cruzan* makes it abundantly clear that he does not believe that individuals retain a right to refuse treatment necessary to save their lives after suicide attempts, *Cruzan v. Missouri* at 293–300.

[172] The majority in *Cruzan* noted that a liberty interest in refusing treatment did not mean that a state was "required to remain neutral in the face of an informed and voluntary decision by a physically able adult to starve to death." *Cruzan v. Missouri* at 280.Although I have been unable to find reported cases in the United States, the U.S. medical literature acknowledges that force-feeding is a common response to serious anorexia. English law has several cases on force-feeding women with severe anorexia, which have been decided both ways, see Chap. 1 at pp. 44–46.

[173] United States v. Charters, 863 F.2d 302 (4th Cir. 1988) (*en banc*) ("the patient's competence to make an informed judgment in this matter is properly treated as simply another factor in the ultimate medical decision to administer the medication involuntarily").

[174] David A. Pratt, *Too Many Physicians: Physician-Assisted Suicide after Glucksberg/Quill*, 9 ALB. L.J. SCI. &.TECH. 161, 203 (1999) ("if assisted suicide is legalized, many requests based on mental illness are likely to be granted").

[175] Phyllis Coleman & Ronald Shellow, *Suicide: Unpredictable and Unavoidable: Proposed Guidelines Provide Rational Test for Physician's Liability*, 71 NEB. L. REV. 641, 647 (1992).

death is underscored by both commentators[176] and courts.[177] They paint a picture of people with psychiatric disabilities as being so cunningly talented at
dissembling and concealing their conditions that even experienced clinicians
mistake them for people who could safely be allowed to exercise their right to
die. It is commonly asserted that most physicians and medical practitioners
are too unsophisticated and ill-trained to be able to screen out people whose
depression should preclude them from any right to die. No one in the United
States questions the underlying assumption that people with psychiatric disabilities should be precluded from assisted suicide.

How could it be that 1988 through 1997 were the years when the legal
right of a citizen to commit suicide were most ardently advocated, when
Congress passed a law requiring hospitals to ensure that patients were
informed about advance directives and had those advance directive honored;[178] when two federal appellate courts held that terminally ill people had
a right to physician assistance to end their lives, yet virtually no one ever seriously discussed whether these rights of privacy and autonomy should extend
to people with psychiatric disabilities?[179]

Many reasons might be offered to answer this question. Let us consider
all of them in turn.

The first argument is that the right to die should not apply to people with
psychiatric disabilities because those conditions are assumed to be treatable and curable. This argument generally includes some vague reference to
medications. Technically, states adopting assisted suicide require a terminal
illness, although as we will see in the next chapter, what constitutes a terminal illness is being stretched quite far. If, as in the European countries that
permit assisted suicide (and as in the case of some people with physical disabilities being kept alive by machinery in this country), a chronic, incurable,
and extremely painful condition is all that is required, then some people with
psychiatric disabilities should be part of the conversation. Although up to a

---

[176] Bioethics Professors Supporting Petitioners, Washington v. Glucksberg, 1996
WL 656345 (citing the case of an unsuccessfully treated alcoholic who has lost
everything, and asking, "Why does the court think that it or the state can determine that this person's very real, ongoing and life long suffering and humiliation do not meet the constitutional requirements for assisted suicide, but that a
cancer patient's suffering at the end of life does? No constitutional principle can
distinguish these two cases").

[177] Krischer v. McIver, 697 So.2d 97 (Fla. 1997); Sampson v. State, 31 P.2d 88
(Alaska 2001).

[178] Patient Self-Determination Act, 42 U.S.C.A. § 1395 cc(f), § 1396 a(w).

[179] Exceptions include THOMAS SZASZ, FATAL FREEDOM: THE ETHICS AND POLITICS
OF SUICIDE (1999); Diane Kjervik, The Psychotherapist's Duty to Act Reasonably
to Prevent Suicide: A Proposal to Allow Rational Suicide, 2 BEHAV. SCI. & L.
207 (1984); JAMES WORTH, RATIONAL SUICIDE? IMPLICATIONS FOR MENTAL
HEALTH PROFESSIONALS (1996).

third of people with psychiatric disabilities do get better whether they take medications or not, another third have intractable or refractory conditions not responsive to medication or treatment. These conditions cause unbearable anguish and pain that for many people is worse than any physical pain they have suffered. The reader should be clear: not all mental illness can be ameliorated or reduced, and its manifestations can be experienced as torture. The general public doesn't really understand how terrible this emotional pain can be. Recent brain studies have shown that the parts of the brain that are associated with suicidality are the same parts affected when people are raped or experience combat trauma, and not the same as those related to physical pain.

Second, one of the most prevalent stereotypes and misconceptions, held by doctors as well as laypeople, is that people with psychiatric disabilities lack competence or capacity to make decisions, especially the decision to end their lives. This is such a crucial issue that I devoted the entire first chapter to refuting it.

Third, to the extent that people with psychiatric disabilities are found in institutions, prisons, or jails, their rights, including the right to refuse treatment, are often subsumed in courts' sympathy with State actors responsible for administering the institution. But that does not explain the widespread exclusion of people with psychiatric disabilities from assisted suicide ballot initiatives, from state statutes on advance directives, and innumerable other rights taken for granted by much of the citizenry.

However, there is one explanation that I find both compelling and rarely articulated, because it is so deeply embedded in social assumption and jurisprudence. The extraordinary deference displayed by courts to the judgment of medical professionals over the autonomy rights of patients prior to the *Quinlan* case continues, virtually undisturbed, in courts' attitudes toward the judgment of mental health professionals.[180] The early courts' tendency to consider that a patient's right to refuse treatment was a medical decision virtually outside of the jurisdiction of the courts corresponds to consistent Supreme Court holdings, doctrine, and dicta, that issues which might be considered to involve privacy and liberty (bodily restraint, involuntary commitment, involuntary treatment) are complicated and uncertain medical judgments outside the competency of courts, which should not interfere with the operations of mental health professionals and administrators.[181] The Court displays the kind of unquestioning deference and faith in the beneficence and objectivity of the medical profession that characterized courts'

---

[180] See Susan Stefan, *Leaving Civil Rights to the "Experts": From Deference to Abdication Under the Professional Judgment Standard*, 102 YALE L.J. 639 (1992).

[181] See Youngberg v. Romeo, 457 U.S. 307, 322–23 (1982); Parham v. J.R., 442 U.S. 584, 609 (1979); Addington v. Texas, 441 U.S. 418, 430 (1979); Heller v. Doe, 509 U.S. 312, 329 (1993).

rulings on medical patients' right to refuse treatment before *Quinlan* and *Bouvia*. As the Supreme Court said in *Washington v. Harper*, "the fact that the medication must first be prescribed by a psychiatrist, and then approved by a reviewing psychiatrist, ensures that the treatment in question will be ordered only if it is in the prisoner's medical interests, given the legitimate needs of his confinement."[182] The Court knows very well that many prisons and jails are havens for unlicensed psychiatrists[183] fleeing discipline in other states,[184] when there are psychiatrists present at all.[185] The dockets of courts across the United States groan with the weight of litigation reflecting the indifference and hostility of overworked, underpaid, and inadequately monitored medical providers in jail and prison settings.[186] Only in the Court's decisions does the ideal of attentive and disinterested mental health professionals in the correctional system hold sway, and even there it is beginning to crack.[187]

The Court's formulation that an institutionalized mentally disabled person's constitutional rights are protected as long as professional judgment was followed in his or her care operates as the sole protection against intrusive and unwanted treatment (a "negative" right or right to be left alone) in a number of courts.[188] Of course, applying the professional judgment standard to the cases of Jehovah's Witnesses, Karen Ann Quinlan, Nancy Cruzan,

---

[182] Washington v. Harper, 494 U.S. 210, 222 (1990).

[183] Paul von Zielbauer, *In City's Jails, Missed Signals Open Way to Season of Suicides*, N. Y. Times, Feb. 28, 2005, http://www.nytimes.com/2005/02/28/nyregion/28jail.html?pagewanted=4&_r=0 (the New York prison system kept ten unlicensed psychiatrists even after they failed state medical tests; at Rikers Island alone, one psychiatrist had license revoked for forging his diploma from a Mexican medical school; another doctor in had lost license in New Jersey for being "danger to the public"; yet another was criminally convicted of "selling blood in a scheme to charge the state for bogus tests");

[184] *Id.*

[185] The Iowa correctional system has three psychiatrists for a prison population of 8000, of whom 1800–2000 have mental illness; Arkansas has four. For a detailed explanation of underfunding and poor conditions leading to inadequate care and high turnover in virtually all the states, see generally, Human Rights Watch, *Ill-Equipped: U.S. Prisons and Offenders with Mental Illness* (Sept. 2003), http://www.hrw.org/reports/2003/usa1003/index.htm.

[186] Means v. Cullen, 297 F.Supp.2d 1148 (W.D. Wisc. 2003) (nurse did not depart from standards of care when she told suicidal inmate that no one would care if he died).

[187] See Brown v. Plata, 563 U.S. __, 131 S.Ct. 1910, 1924 (2011)(upholding a court order requiring California to discharge inmates until prison was reduced to 137% of its capacity, noting that "suicidal inmates may be held for prolonged periods in telephone-booth sized cages without toilets" and "wait times for mental health care range as high as twelve months").

[188] *United States v. Charters*; Jurasek v. Utah State Hosp., 158 F.3d 506 (10th Cir. 1998); White v. Napoleon v. White, 897 F.2d 103 (3rd Cir. 1990) (prisoner).

Elizabeth Bouvia, and countless others would have meant that plaintiffs lost in each and every one of these cases. Modern courts would never do that in the case of medical patients, because they recognize the primacy of constitutional rights and the need for courts to be the final arbiters of those rights— just so long as the plaintiff isn't a psychiatric patient.

Because the courts insisted that competent individuals had the constitutional right to make the final decisions about medical treatment, the medical profession slowly but surely came around to embrace the concept. After *Quinlan* and *Bouvia* and the publications of the President's Commission for the Study of Ethical Problems in Medicine and Biomedical and Behavioral Research,[189] after Jay Katz's highly influential *The Silent World of Doctor and Patient*,[190] after the Patient Self-Determination Act was passed in 1990, and with medical ethics emerging as a respected specialty, the medical establishment finally accepted the rights of its patients to be more involved with decision-making about their medical treatment, including refusing life-saving treatments.

Meanwhile, the psychiatric establishment, under no similar pressure from the courts, maintained an entrenched hostility to patients' rights to autonomy. For example, while the *Journal of the American Medical Association* published "It's Over, Debbie," and the *New England Journal of Medicine* published Dr. Quill's account of helping his patient Diane to die, the *Bulletin of the American Academy of Psychiatry and Law* published " 'Rotting with Their Rights On': Constitutional Theory and Drug Refusal by Psychiatric Patients," by two noted psychiatrists.[191]

Thus, because in this country the right to assisted suicide developed as a legal and civil right to privacy asserted against the State, people with psychiatric disabilities have been excluded from it. Historically, Roman, Greek, and (more recently) European support for assisted suicide as good social policy specifically envisioned that people with disabilities would be part of the population using it.[192] Situating the right as one relating to autonomy of a person's decision-making about his or her own body and life excludes people with psychiatric disabilities, who have always suffered from social misconceptions about their inability to make decisions and lack of insight, especially decisions associated with medical and psychiatric treatment, and even more particularly decisions concerning how and when to die.

---

[189] Established by Congress in 1978, this highly influential body published a number of reports that are cited to this day, including DEFINING DEATH (1981), MAKING HEALTH CARE DECISIONS (1982) and DECIDING TO FOREGO LIFE-SUSTAINING TREATMENT (1983).

[190] JAY KATZ, THE SILENT WORLD OF DOCTOR AND PATIENT (1984).

[191] Paul Appelbaum & Thomas Gutheil, 7 BULL. AM. ACAD. PSYCHIATRY & L. 306 (1979).

[192] Remnants of this historical legacy, including the eugenics movement, are, in fact, one of the principal reasons that many in the disability community are vocally and passionately opposed to assisted suicide.

All states have a legal mechanism, guardianship, which is used to divest a person deemed to be incompetent of his or her presumptive right to make certain (or all) life decisions. Many people with psychiatric disabilities are subject to guardianship. Many states that give their citizens rights to control their health care when incompetent through advance directives have separate (and unequal) advance directive statutes for people with psychiatric disabilities.

The perception that people with psychiatric disabilities have impaired decision-making, combined with the perception that they are frequently suicidal, and the courts' deference to mental health professionals whose devotion to principles of patient autonomy is shaky at best, form the basis for the universal consensus in the United States that people with psychiatric disabilities are not, and can never be, appropriate candidates for any right to die. Even Dr. Kevorkian, who was willing to help a woman with acute pelvic pain die,[193] steered clear of people with psychiatric disabilities who wanted to die, whether they had painful illnesses or not. It is no coincidence that people with psychiatric disabilities have been excluded from state physician-assisted suicide initiatives in the United States. As we will see in Chapter 3, these initiatives have been explicitly marketed as excluding people with depression and other psychiatric disabilities, and would never have passed absent those exclusions.

Thus, the exclusion of people with psychiatric disabilities from discussions about the right to die springs from the same set of cultural and legal assumptions that dilutes their right to refuse treatment: doubts about competence, social mythology that most or all mental illness can be cured, and a lingering distaste and misunderstanding of the degree of pain involved in psychiatric disability. But most of all, I think, it stems from the unique powers (and liabilities) assigned to mental health professionals by the legal system. Both these powers and the liabilities associated with them undermine the abilities of mental health professionals to actually help suicidal people, as I will try to show in Chapter 6.

The Constitutionality of Involuntary Commitment for Suicidality

It should be crystal clear that even if there is no affirmative constitutional right to assistance in dying, that does not mean that the State acts constitutionally if it deprives an individual of liberty for extended periods because he or she articulated suicidal thoughts or even made suicidal threats. Here is one imperfect analogy: the State need not fund or assist any woman to have an

---

[193] Marjorie Wantz was alleged to be a person suffering from a psychiatric disability, but Dr. Kevorkian always stoutly denied this, implicitly asserting he would not help someone with a psychiatric disability die.

abortion,[194] but it may not constitutionally pass a law imprisoning a woman for having an abortion. The State can spend taxpayer money to discourage people from having abortions, but it cannot involuntarily detain them to prevent them from having abortions.

It is possible in our legal system for individuals to have no constitutional right to either commit suicide or to have assistance in dying at the time and manner of their choice, while having a constitutional right to be free of involuntary commitment and involuntary treatment for suicidal ideation or talking about suicide, or even threatening suicide.

The interesting jurisprudential anomaly is that the discussion of limitations on the State's ability to involuntarily commit and treat people for being suicidal has always taken place in the context of the fundamental right to liberty, while right-to-die cases grew out of privacy doctrine. The former should result in better outcomes, since the right is more firmly grounded in historical tradition, and more clearly subject to strict scrutiny analysis, but it hasn't worked out that way at all.

To briefly summarize the fundamental right to liberty (supposedly) enjoyed by all adults in our country: any federal or state law that completely takes away an individual's fundamental right to liberty is subject to strict scrutiny. That means the courts will look very carefully at such laws to ensure that the State's interest is compelling, and that the law has been narrowly tailored to serve that interest.[195]

As early as 1972, four years before *Quinlan*, the Supreme Court held that a state cannot involuntarily detain or institutionalize individuals unless "the nature and duration of the confinement bear some reasonable relationship to the purpose of confinement."[196] Three years later, in *O'Connor v. Donaldson*, the Court confirmed that all people—even mentally ill people—who were capable of living safely in freedom, by themselves or with the help of willing friends and family, could not be involuntarily committed.[197] Only people with mental illness causing them to be dangerous to themselves or others can be involuntarily committed.[198] Involuntary civil commitment thus requires two basic prongs: mental illness, and dangerousness that cannot be mitigated by available community resources.

I propose that involuntary civil commitment of an individual on the basis of suicidal ideation ("I wish I were dead" or "I think about suicide") violates many *existing* state commitment statutes and the court decisions

---

[194] Maher v. Roe, 432 U.S. 464 (1977) (states need not fund abortion as part of Medicaid); Harris v. McRae, 448 U.S. 297 (1980) (federal government need not fund abortion).

[195] United States v. Salerno, 481 U.S. 739 (1987); Foucha v. Louisiana, 504 U.S. 71 (1992).

[196] *Jackson v. Indiana*, 406 U.S. 715 (1972); *Foucha v. Louisiana*.

[197] O'Connor v. Donaldson, 422 U.S. 563 (1975).

[198] *Id.*

interpreting them. Thus, involuntary commitment for suicidal ideation is clearly unconstitutional under current law. I also argue that, while many state statutes and the court decisions interpreting them currently explicitly permit civil commitment of people with mental illness whose dangerousness to themselves is manifested solely by threats of suicide, these laws are also unconstitutional. That is because threats of suicide are insufficiently probative of the actual propensity to commit suicide, or the likelihood that the person will make a seriously life-threatening attempt. In addition, there is insufficient evidence that hospitalizing a person reduces his or her chances of suicide; some experts in the field, and one interpretation of the available research, suggests that involuntary hospitalization may actually increase the likelihood of suicide after discharge. The constitutional mandate that deprivations of liberty must be narrowly tailored to accomplish state goals is not met, because there is insufficient support for a causal connection between suicidal threats and suicide, and insufficient support for the proposition that involuntary hospitalization serves the compelling state interest of preventing suicide. Thus, total deprivation of liberty on the basis of suicidal threat cannot survive strict scrutiny. There are three prongs to my argument.

First, some people who talk about and threaten suicide are not mentally ill at all under the meaning of Supreme Court doctrine. "Mental illness" for the purpose of justifying involuntary commitment is a legal rather than clinical term,[199] defined with at least some clarity by the Supreme Court. There are a substantial number of people whose suicidality is not caused by the kind of mental illness required by Supreme Court precedent in order to justify involuntary commitment. These include people who might be diagnosed with adjustment disorder, dysthymia, personality disorders, and many people with depression, such as Josh Sebastian from Chapter 1. People with bipolar disorder who, like Anita Darcel Taylor, have contemplated suicide over a long period of time as their condition becomes less and less responsive to treatment, also do not have the kind of mental illness the Supreme Court requires to justify involuntary commitment.

Second, even for people who do have a mental illness that meets the Supreme Court definition, involuntary commitment solely on the basis of danger to self from suicidality and suicidal threats bears an insufficiently reasonable relationship to the (concededly compelling) state purpose of preserving life because it is impossible to predict which one-half of 1% of the millions of people thinking about suicide, talking about suicide, and threatening suicide will actually die by suicide.

Third, even if it were possible to unerringly predict which people would actually make a serious suicide attempt, there really is no evidentiary basis to support the contention that involuntary hospitalization serves the compelling state interest of preserving life, and it may actually undermine that interest.

---

[199] Kansas v. Hendricks, 521 U.S. 346, 359–60 (1997); Kansas v. Crane, 534 U.S. 407, 413–14 (2002).

This is a limited argument against involuntary commitment. I acknowledge that the law supports a brief involuntary detention (72 hours) of people to assess their competence, allow them to detox from drugs and alcohol, check for medical causes of being suicidal, and even to restrain completely competent, but impulsive, attempters. People who hear command hallucinations to kill themselves or who are intoxicated or who are younger than eighteen, or who are suffering from delirium or extreme mania are not competent to make decisions to end their lives. Under parens patriae doctrine, which protects people who lack capacity from the consequences of their actions, it is constitutional to subject people who truly lack capacity to involuntary detention and even commitment if they are imminently suicidal.[200] But—and this is crucial to my point—in almost all of these cases, the person will be committable as gravely disabled, that is, unable to meet his or her basic needs for food and shelter.[201] My proposal would not interfere with standard civil commitment law in the case of either grave disability or people who were dangerous to others.

Current statutory law in most states precludes the involuntary commitment of hundreds of thousands of people who have done no more than talk about suicide, that is, people who say they want to be dead, or wish they were dead, or even people who are seriously considering suicide. This is so-called suicidal ideation, and millions of people have it. As a separate matter, I also propose that even people who threaten suicide may not be constitutionally committable. Most of these people are committable under state statutes today, but that is because no serious effort has been made to inform the court of the state of the research and argue that such commitments are constitutionally deficient.

People who are suicidal need so much to be able to speak freely, and those who can help them need to be able to hear them and talk to them and stay with them through their struggles. I propose that there should be a line drawn between clearly dangerous suicidal conduct,[202] including dangerous attempts[203] and talking about one's feelings. To be able to talk freely about one's feelings without fear of involuntary detention and treatment would help patients, and to declare involuntary commitment for suicidality unconstitutional absent lack of capacity or an actual dangerous attempt would free mental health professionals to listen without fear of liability. I also propose, in Chapter 6, that any legislation repealing involuntary commitment for

---

[200] See Chapter 1. An incompetent individual cannot be involuntarily detained indefinitely, *Jackson v. Indiana*. The law requires appointment of a guardian or the making of substituted judgment decisions for a person who is incompetent.

[201] Some people attempt or succeed in gouging out their eyes or mutilating their genitals, Waldrop v. Evans, 871 F.2d 1030 (11th Cir. 1989). These people desperately need help and protection.

[202] Some self-injury, such as cutting, is known to not be an attempt to kill one's self and would not be counted in this category.

[203] This would not include conduct mischaracterized as "suicide attempts," such as scratching one's forearms with a safety pin or paper clip, pulling at scabs, J. J. Muehlenkamp & P. M. Gutierrez, *Risk for Suicide Attempts Among Adolescents Who Engage in Non-Suicidal Self-Injury*, 11 ARCH. SUICIDE RES. 69 (2007).

talking about or threatening suicide be combined with legislation granting immunity from negligence liability for mental health providers treating individuals in the community who commit suicide, as long as the mental health providers did not behave intentionally or recklessly.[204]

As we have seen, the State certainly has compelling interests in preserving life, preventing suicide, and protecting incompetents. The State can act in furtherance of those interests, even to the point of deprivation of liberty, but the deprivation of liberty must be narrowly tailored to further those interests. Several implicit assumptions underlie the premise that involuntary detention of people with suicidal ideation or suicidal threats furthers the State interest in preserving life, preventing suicide, and protecting people who are incompetent. Perhaps the benefit of involuntary detention seems obvious: if people say they are thinking about suicide, doesn't extended involuntary hospitalization under 24 hour observation at the very least prevent them from killing themselves? The reality is far from simple.

I would like in particular to challenge three assumptions in the involuntary commitment of people who talk about or threaten suicide:

1. Suicidality is not automatically or necessarily a manifestation of mental illness as defined by the Supreme Court. Supreme Court precedent categorically prohibits involuntary detention unless both mental illness and dangerousness to others can be shown.[205]
2. People who talk about suicide or threaten suicide are insufficiently dangerous to themselves to further the State purpose of preventing suicide without an unacceptably high number of false positives. The fact that someone articulates suicidal thoughts or even threatens to commit suicide has virtually no predictive value that the individual will attempt or complete suicide in the near future. The false positive rate is too great to justify the drastic step of total deprivation of liberty. In legal terms, the deprivation of liberty is not narrowly tailored to advance the compelling state interest of preventing suicide; thus, the commitment statute is fatally overbroad.
3. The nature and duration of extended involuntary commitment does not bear a reasonable relationship to the state purpose of decreasing suicide rates. It may even, with certain populations, increase the risk of suicide. There is no evidentiary basis for the proposition that involuntary hospitalization reduces the suicide rate at all.

Let us take each of my contentions in turn.

---

[204] An example of intentional behavior would be to assist a suicide in a state where this was a criminal offense; an example of reckless behavior would be to sleep with the patient or the patient's spouse. See Chapter 6 for more details.
[205] If the person has committed a crime and is pleading not guilty by reason of insanity, the dangerousness can be inferred, but not otherwise, Jones v. United States, 463 U.S. 354 (1983); *Foucha v. Louisiana* at n. 195.

Many People Who Talk About, Threaten, or Attempt Suicide Are Not Mentally Ill as Defined by the Supreme Court

The State cannot involuntarily commit a person unless he or she is mentally ill, and, as a result of that mental illness, dangerous to himself or herself or others. As both courts and clinicians recognize, "mental illness" for the purposes of supporting total deprivation of liberty is a legal term, not a clinical one.[206] The first part of this section argues that many people who talk about suicide or threaten it are not mentally ill in the sense required by the Supreme Court to justify involuntary commitment. The second part argues that many people who are suicidal are not even mentally ill in the sense recognized by clinicians (unless the clinician believes that suicidality, by itself, is a sign of underlying mental illness, which makes the whole thing a self-proving tautology not open to debate).

The Supreme Court has made clear that an individual cannot be subject to involuntary civil commitment unless that person is *both* mentally ill and, *as a result* of the mental illness, dangerous to himself or herself or others, and unable to live safely in the community, even with the help of willing friends and family.[207] In some states, such as Wisconsin, the person must also be able to benefit from treatment in order to justify commitment. In other states, the treatment the person needs to ameliorate or mitigate his or her mental illness must be shown to be available.

In *Foucha v. Louisiana*,[208] the Court made it clear that a person cannot be involuntarily committed on the grounds of dangerousness alone, but must also be mentally ill. Thus, under *Foucha*, a person who is suicidal but does not meet the Court's definition of mental illness cannot be civilly committed on the basis of dangerousness to self alone. In the *Foucha* case, Louisiana conceded that antisocial personality was not a mental illness, so the Court did not focus on the precise meaning of mental illness that was required in order to subject an individual to involuntary commitment.

However, since *Foucha* the Supreme Court has fleshed out the meaning of mental illness for purposes of civil commitment, and it's certainly not adjustment disorder or dysthymia. The meaning of mental illness was the focus of two cases, *Kansas v. Hendricks* and *Kansas v. Crane*. In *Hendricks*, a case involving civil commitment of a pedophile, the Supreme Court (once

---

[206] Robert Simon, *Introduction in* DIAGNOSTIC AND STATISTICAL MANUAL OF MENTAL DISORDERS (5th ed., American Psychiatric Association 2013); in fact, courts have accepted "mental illness" diagnoses that are not only controversial but discredited, *McGee v. Bartow*, 593 F.3d 556 (7th Cir. 2010).

[207] *O'Connor v. Donaldson; Addington v. Texas* (burden of proof required that individual is mentally ill and dangerous is clear and convincing evidence); *Foucha v. Louisiana* (person who is no longer mentally ill cannot be subject to involuntary commitment even if he is still dangerous); Kansas v. Hendricks, 521 U.S. 346 (1997); *Kansas v. Crane*.

[208] 504 U.S. 71 (1992).

again)[209] ignored the brief of the American Psychiatric Association, which asserted that sexual psychopathy was not a mental illness.[210] Nevertheless, the Court held that civil commitment was possible if a person had "a mental abnormality or personality disorder that makes it difficult, if not impossible, for the person to control his dangerous behavior."[211] Another part of the opinion defined the "mental illness" requirement as "a volitional impairment rendering them dangerous beyond their control."[212]

This definition was supplemented, if not elaborated,[213] in *Kansas v. Crane*, another case involving the commitment of a sexual offender. In this case, Crane was not a diagnosed pedophile. Like Foucha, he had antisocial personality disorder, but he also "suffer[ed] from exhibitionism."[214] The Court in *Crane* revisited its definition of mental illness from *Hendricks*, and held that the Constitution did not require that the inability to control behavior be "absolute," just "a special and serious lack of ability to control behavior."[215] This requirement was necessary in order to distinguish committable people from run-of-the-mill criminals who also find it difficult to control their behavior. This is a high bar: the Court emphasized that the disorder or mental abnormality must be characterized by a *serious* difficulty in controlling behavior, which could have "volitional, emotional [or] cognitive" roots. [216]

The decision in *Crane* opens the door pretty wide for civil commitment of people who try to kill themselves because of mental conditions such as psychoses or mania or intoxication, and perhaps even people with brain injuries, strokes, and intellectual disabilities. It raises extremely interesting and complex conceptual questions about dissociative identity disorder and eating disorders. But, for honest clinicians who take the requirements of law seriously, it slams the door shut on many personality disorders (what used to be called "Axis II conditions"),[217] such as borderline personality

---

[209] See Chapter 6.

[210] Amicus brief of the American Psychiatric Association, *Kansas v. Hendricks*, on file with author.

[211] *Kansas v. Hendricks* at 358.

[212] *Kansas v. Hendricks*.

[213] "I suspect that the reason the Court avoids any elaboration is that elaboration which passes the laugh test is impossible," Justice Scalia wrote in dissent, 534 U.S. 407, 423 (2002).

[214] *Id.* at 410.

[215] *Id.* at 413.

[216] The Supreme Court has upheld involuntary commitment for individuals who are dangerous because of their developmental disability, although many states have abolished such commitments.

[217] Until the introduction in 2013 of the American Psychiatric Association's *Diagnostic and Statistical Manual of Mental Disorders* (DSM-5), the American Psychiatric Association suggested that diagnoses be made along five axes, with the first axis consisting of serious mental illnesses, such as thought or mood disorders, and the second axis consisting of personality disorders. Axis III involved concurrent medical issues, Axis IV concerned ongoing social problems, and Axis V

disorders,[218] antisocial personality disorder,[219] almost all depressions, and many other conditions listed in the fifth edition of the American Psychiatric Association's *Diagnostic and Statistical Manual of Mental Disorders* (DSM-5).

Therefore, according to the Supreme Court, the legal term "mental illness" under the Constitution is limited to circumstances when a psychiatric disorder renders it impossible or very seriously difficult for the individual to control his or her behavior, in the same way that someone who is psychotic or manic or has a brain injury or pedophilia has serious difficulties controlling his or her behavior. A person such as Josh Sebastian, who can negotiate and fulfill an agreement not to attempt suicide for six months, actually does not have a mental illness under the Supreme Court's definition of the term at all.

I would like to go further and argue that many suicidal people are not seriously mentally ill (being suicidal makes a person an obvious candidate for adjustment disorder, or perhaps dysthymia, but I am talking about the diagnostic categories that exist for purposes beyond insurance reimbursement). One of the most persistent myths about suicide is that people who commit suicide are mentally ill, and therefore, by extension, people who talk about suicide, threaten suicide, and attempt suicide are mentally ill. The most famous, most often quoted, and most questionable statistic is that 90% of people who commit suicide have some form of mental illness.

This is based on bad science, and the best researchers and most famous suicidologists acknowledge it.[220] The 90% figure is based on so-called psychological autopsies—*after the fact* reconstructions of a person's mental state through interviews with family and friends, who are now understandably viewing every statement, behavior, and attitude through a lens that will provide its own new meaning to them all. In these studies, many of the suicides deemed to be post facto mentally ill had not been diagnosed as mentally ill, treated for mental illness, or even perceived as mentally ill while they were alive. The diagnoses are discovered postmortem by researchers who, like experts testifying in death penalty cases, did not interview the person and could not pick him or her out of a lineup. It is certainly true that some genuine psychiatric conditions go

---

asked for an estimate of the individual's current functioning in a global, or comprehensive, sense.

[218] People with disabling obsessive-compulsive disorder may meet the Court's definition of mental illness; the question would be whether such individuals were dangerous to themselves or others.

[219] In *Foucha v. Louisiana*, the State conceded that antisocial personality was not a mental illness, see 504 U.S. 71, 75.

[220] See, e.g., Edwin Shneidman, at text and notes 201–202, *infra*; Michael Phillips, *Rethinking the Role of Mental Illness in Suicide*, 167 Am. J. Psychiatry 731 (2010); H. Hjelmeland, G. Dieserud, K. Dyregrov, B. L. Knizek, & A. A. Leenaars, *Psychological Autopsy Studies as Diagnostic Tools: Are They Methodologically Flawed?* 36 Death Stud. 7, 605–26 (2012), doi:10.1080/07481187.2011.584015; Said Shahtamasebi, *Suicide Research: Problems with Interpreting Results*, 5 British Journal of Medicine and Medical Research 1147 (2014); Saxby Pridmore, *Why Suicide Eradication Is Hardly Possible*, 1 Dynamics Hum. Health 4, art. 24 (2014).

undiagnosed and untreated, but, as discussed next, even prospective attempts to identify people who will kill themselves from pools of already-diagnosed, already-hospitalized people uniformly fail, while the vast majority of people who commit suicide continue to be apparently functional, occupied, even cheerful, until the final weeks, days, or even moments.

The degree to which mental illness is superimposed on suicidality after the fact is illustrated by a Harvard study in which doctors were given edited case histories of suicides and asked them whether the individuals were mentally ill. Only the fact that the person had committed suicide was omitted. The doctors diagnosed mental illness in only 22% of the group if they were not told that the patients had committed suicide; when the single fact was added that the individual had committed suicide, the doctors diagnosed 90% of the patients as mentally ill.[221]

Some statistics are true but subject to misinterpretation. For example, it is true that compared to the general population, people with certain psychiatric diagnoses are more likely to kill themselves than people without those diagnoses.[222] This is true. It is also true of many people with medical illnesses: cancer,[223] epilepsy,[224] chronic obstructive pulmonary disorder,[225] attention deficit hyperactivity disorder,[226] and asthma.[227] It may just be more stressful to live

---

[221] HERBERT HENDIN, SUICIDE IN AMERICA 189–90 (1982).

[222] PsychCentral.com, www.psychcentral.com.

[223] The suicide risk in individuals with cancer is between two and ten times as high as that of the general population, National Cancer Institute, *Depression: Suicide Risk in Cancer Patients*, DEPRESSION—FOR HEALTH PROFESSIONALS (PDQ') (last updated Aug. 28, 2014), http://www.cancer.gov/cancertopics/pdq/supportivecare/depression/HealthProfessional/page4.

[224] Jana E. Jones, Bruce P. Hermann, John J. Barry, Frank G. Gilliam, et al, "Rates and Risk Factors for Suicide, Suicidal Ideation and Suicide Attempts in Chronic Epilepsy," 4 Epilepsy & Behavior 31 (2003). More recently, a comprehensive Danish study confirmed that while psychiatric comorbidity raised the risk, people with epilepsy have considerably higher suicide rates than the general population, especially shortly after diagnosis, Jakob Christensen, Mogens Vestergaard, Preben Bo Mortensen, "Epilepsy and Risk of Suicide: A Population-Based Case-Control Study," 6 The Lancet Neurology 693 (2007).

[225] Renee D. Goodwin, *Is COPD Associated with Suicidal Behavior?* 45 J. PSYCHIATRIC RES. 1269 (Sept. 2011); R. T. Webb, E. Kontopantelis, T. Doran, F. Qin, et al., *Suicide Risk in Primary Care Patients with Major Physical Diseases: A Case Control Study*, 69 ARCH. GEN. PSYCHIATRY 256 (2012) (finding association between elevated suicide risk and chronic obstructive pulmonary disease [COPD], osteoporosis, coronary heart disease, and stroke, with all explained by depression except men with osteoporosis; suicide risk of two to three times the general population in women with cancer and heart disease not explained after adjusting for depression).

[226] People diagnosed with this condition have three to six times the number of suicides of the general population, Blanks v. Fluor Corp., (Mo. App. Sept. 16, 2014).

[227] Benjamin Druss & Harold Pincus, *Suicidal Ideation and Suicide Attempts in General Medical Illness*, 160 ARCH. INTERNAL MED. 322 (2000) (finding increase

with these conditions than to live in good health. It may have something to do with the dispiriting and socially stigmatizing impact of those diagnoses. It may be an effect of the conditions themselves or the medications that people take for them. What it does *not* mean is that the vast majority of people who commit suicide have epilepsy, or cancer, or depression. Nor does it mean that the majority of people with these diagnoses commit suicide.

The iconic Dr. Edwin Shneidman, who founded the field of suicidology and who developed the entire concept of psychological autopsies on which the 90% figure is based, flatly rejected the equation of suicidality with mental illness.[228] As he wrote in a letter to the *New England Journal of Medicine*, disagreeing strongly with the proposition that "the crux of suicide prevention lies in the diagnosis (and treatment) of affective disorders":

> I do not believe this is necessarily so. Forty years of practice and research as a suicidologist have led me to believe that the assessment and treatment of suicidal persons is best conceptualized not in terms of psychiatric nosologic categories (such as one finds in the *Diagnostic and Statistical Manual*), but rather in terms of psychological pain and thresholds for enduring that pain.
>
> Some suicidal persons have psychiatric disorders. Many suicidal persons are depressed. Most depressed patients are not suicidal. (One can live a long, unhappy life with depression.) But it is undeniable that all persons—100 percent—who commit suicide are perturbed and experiencing unbearable psychological pain. The problem of suicide should be addressed directly, phenomenologically, without the intervention of the often obfuscating variable of psychiatric disorder.
>
> In human beings pain is ubiquitous, but suffering is optional, within the constraints of a person's personality. Just as it is important to distinguish between the treatment of physical pain and the treatment of suffering, so there are also important differences between the diagnosis of depression and the assessment of psychological pain. A focus on mental illness is often misleading. Physicians and other health professionals need the courage and wisdom to work on a person's suffering

---

in risk for people with medical illnesses, and greater increase in people with two or more medical illnesses, and finding that cancer and asthma carried the highest increased risk).

[228] Edwin Shneidman, *Letter to the Editor: Rational Suicide and Psychiatric Disorder*, 326 NEW ENG. J. MED. 889 (1992), *available at* www.nejm.org/doi/full/10.1056/NEJM199203263261311; SARA K. GOLDSMITH, RISK FACTORS FOR SUICIDE: SUMMARY OF A WORKSHOP 16 (National Academies Press 2001) ("Dr. Shneidman expressed his opposition to medicalization of suicide, which he sees as an essentially human condition. He spoke of suicide not as a disease...[it] does overlap at times with mental illness").

at the phenomenological level and to explore such questions as
"How do you hurt?" and "How may I help you?" They should
then do whatever is necessary, using a wide variety of legitimate
tactics, including medication, to reduce that person's self-
destructive impulses. Diagnosis should be adjunctive to a larger
understanding of the person's pain-in-life.[229]

Most of the time, suicide is far more complicated than being the final
fatal symptom of a treatable condition. "The majority of individuals who
commit suicide do not have a diagnosable mental illness. They are people
just like you and I who at a particular time are feeling isolated, desperately
unhappy and alone. Suicidal thoughts and actions may be the result of life's
stresses and losses that the individual feels they just can't cope with."[230]
"Suicides are attempted and completed by a broad range of people, from persons who appear to present no evidence of mental illness to those who are
severely handicapped by their issues. What is most apparent about suicidal
persons is unhappiness, a quality of life issue that is not necessarily equated
with mental illness."[231]

So while it is absolutely true that *some* people who attempt suicide or
articulate thoughts of suicide have psychiatric disabilities, and of this group,
sometimes suicidality is a symptom of those disabilities, it is not automatically true that all people who attempt suicide or talk about it have psychiatric
disabilities. The suicidality does not permit automatic assumption of mental
illness, as many people seem to believe. What the real research shows is that,
at the very most, 50% of people who are suicidal have a psychiatric disability,
and that is likely to be a very high estimate.

One reason—not the only reason—why involuntary psychiatric hospitalization doesn't help and actually hurts suicidal people in the long
run is that a significant percentage of people who are suicidal—even
those who attempt and commit suicide—are not mentally ill. Of more
than 200 people I surveyed who had made serious suicide attempts, only
half of them had been hospitalized, and of those, less than a third felt that
the hospitalization helped them. Many people I interviewed expressed a
sense that the people on the psychiatric unit did not have the same kinds
of problems that they did, and found the environment chaotic and unre-
sponsive to their needs.

---

[229] Shneidman, *supra* note 228.

[230] MARGARET APPLEBY & MARGARET CONDONIS, HEARING THE CRY: SUICIDE
PREVENTION (1990).

[231] DAVID MACE, VIRIAM KHALSA, JOHN CRUMLEY, & JOHN AARONS, "IN HARM'S
WAY: A PRIMER IN DETENTION SUICIDE PREVENTION: THE LANE COUNTY
MODEL 91, www.sprc.org/sites/sprc.org/files/library/LaneCoJuvJust.pdf.

Many People Who Talk About or Threaten Are Not Dangerous as Defined by the Supreme Court

It Is Impermissibly Overbroad to Involuntarily Confine People Who Talk About or Threaten Suicide

To involuntarily commit an individual, he or she has to be dangerous as a result of mental illness to himself or herself or others, or (in some states) gravely disabled, that is, unable to meet his or her basic survival needs in the community, and without sufficient assistance from friends or family to do so.

All states have commitment statutes that further elaborate on the term *dangerous*. In many states the "dangerousness" must be "imminent":[232] the evidence must reflect a "substantial risk of imminent harm;"[233] the dangerousness has to be "imminent" or "serious;" in others, there must be a "recent attempt or threat"[234] or an "overt act" manifesting the dangerousness.[235] In Wisconsin, where Josh Sebastian lives, dangerousness is defined as "a substantial probability of physical harm . . . as manifested by evidence of recent threats of or attempts at suicide or serious bodily harm."[236] A suicide attempt, especially a serious suicide attempt, is sufficient to meet the requirements of substantial risk, imminence, and overt action *if* the person is still suicidal. A number of my interviewees were relieved that they had survived, and no longer presented a risk of dangerousness to self.[237] What counts for civil commitment purposes is the individual's present mental state and what it augurs about his or her immediate conduct if released into the community.[238]

These commitment statutes have also been interpreted by the state courts, which have applied them in specific cases that illustrate their meaning. This is an important inquiry because judges or "jurors are asked in these difficult cases to determine whether clear and convincing evidence supports a finding of dangerousness, knowing they should neither wrongly deprive a person of liberty nor fail to authorize intervention before a dangerous person harms himself."[239] The cases permit the courts to apply the statute in a number of different individual situations.

Although each state has different statutes and different case law, some principles appear established. First, the danger to self must be proven by the State to result from the mental illness. Thus, a woman who twice got out of a car driven by her mother in dangerous traffic situations was taking

---

[232] Haw. Rev. Stat. 334-60.2; Va. Code Ann. 37.2-808.

[233] Ga. Code Ann. 37-3-1.

[234] Minn. Stat. § 253B.02(13)(a)(3).

[235] Not all states require "overt acts," see *In re* L.R. 497 A.2d 753, 755–57 (Vt. 1985).

[236] Wis. Stat. § 51.20(1)(a)2.a.

[237] A substantial number were angry with themselves for failing and still determinedly suicidal.

[238] M. L. v. Meridian Services, 956 N.E.2d 752 (Ind. App. 2011).

[239] *In re* Michael H., 2014 WL 127 (2014).

dangerous risks, but it was because she wanted to get away from her mother, which (the court implies) any of us might want to do. The court found that the State had not shown that the "conduct which was predictive of future dangerousness would not occur but for the individual's mental illness."[240] This requirement was necessary, or else people with psychiatric disabilities could be civilly committed any time they engaged in any risk-taking behavior. The rest of us have the right to make reckless choices without sacrificing our liberty, and so should people with psychiatric disabilities.[241]

The mere apprehension that a person may commit suicide is insufficient for commitment. Rather, the State must establish through evidence that it is highly probable that an allegedly mentally ill person will attempt to commit suicide in the near future as a result of the person's mental disorder.[242] It is not sufficient to be thinking about dying. Involuntary commitment for "suicidal ideation," in the absence of any other indicators of imminent dangerousness, is simply such a common phenomenon that it is far too tenuously connected to the likelihood of a suicide attempt, let alone to suicide itself. Conservatively, 17,000 of every 100,000 people have suicidal ideation; 11 of every 100,000 people actually commit suicide. In Oregon, "an expressed desire to die, by itself, is not sufficient"[243] to support involuntary commitment. The American Psychiatric Association's Task Force on Psychiatric Emergency Services, as well as other resources and guidelines, advise that people with "thoughts of death, but who do not have a plan, intent, or behavior" should not be hospitalized.[244] Nevertheless, they often are, especially when they present to emergency departments.

Thinking about suicide and dying (*suicidal ideation*) is different from threatening suicide, although each is, for very different reasons, not particularly likely to lead to attempts at suicide or suicide itself. Thinking about suicide is a solitary pursuit; threatening suicide is an interaction with another person. Many states permit involuntary commitment for a *threat* to commit suicide, although there is thoughtful disagreement among the states as to what conduct is necessary to constitute evidence of a committable threat.[245]

---

[240] Commitment of J.B. v. Midtown Mental Health Clinic, 581 N.E.2d 448 (Ind. App. 1991).

[241] *Id.*

[242] State v. R.E., 273 P.3d 341 (Ore. App. 2012).

[243] State v. M.S., 42 P.3d 374 (Ore. App. 2002); State v. N.A.P., 173 P.3d 1251 (Ore. App. 2007).

[244] DOUGLAS JACOBS, A RESOURCE GUIDE FOR IMPLEMENTING THE JOINT COMMISSION ON ACCREDITATION OF HEALTHCARE ORGANIZATIONS (JCAHO) 2007 PATIENT SAFETY GOALS ON SUICIDE (SCREENING FOR MENTAL HEALTH [SMH] 2007) *available at* www.MentalHealthScreening.org or by calling 781-239-0071.

[245] Compare In re Vencil, 2015 Pa.Super 157 (2015)(carefully parsing evidence in the record to conclude that references to suicidal thoughts were to past thoughts rather than present thoughts) with In re SL, 339 P.3d 73 (Mont. 2014) (finding

However, it is not necessary to show that the person has a plan to commit suicide to justify involuntary commitment, at least not in Wisconsin.[246]

Many of the published cases reflect situations where an involuntary civil commitment was clearly both constitutional and warranted: a suicide attempt by drinking rubbing alcohol on the same day (although this did not support forced treatment because "there was no evidence, let alone clear and convincing evidence, that Celexa and Neurontin would be of substantial benefit in treating M.L.'s mental illnesses, and not just controlling his behavior, and that the probable benefits of the treatment outweighed the risk of harm to, and personal concerns of, M.L.")[247] What is clear is that, according to research and statistics, simply wishing you were dead, talking about killing yourself, or even threatening suicide in a generalized way, is not grounds for anyone to make a reliable prediction that you will kill yourself or attempt to kill yourself any time soon.

It Is Impossible to Predict on an Individual Basis Who Will Attempt or Commit Suicide[248]

Edwin Shneidman, the acknowledged dean of suicidology, says that people who are planning suicide often give hints to others.[249] He also says, on the same page, that some people planning suicide give no indication whatsoever that they are suicidal.[250] My own anecdotal experience, those of most of the

that a series of past suicide attempts as ways to get out of untenable situations were sufficient to constitute a "present indication of probable physical injury which is likely to occur at any moment or in the immediate future").

[246] *In re* Michael H. *supra* at note 239.

[247] M.L. v. Meridian Services, 956 NE2d 752 (Ind. App. 2011).

[248] J. M. Bolton, R. Spiwak, & J. Sareen, *Predicting Suicide Attempts with the SAD PERSONS Scale: A Longitudinal Analysis*, 73 J. CLIN. PSYCHIATRY 6, e735–e741 (June 2012) (Neither SAD PERSONS nor Modified SAD PERSONS [MSPS] scale are effective tools to measure suicide risk); M. A. Oquendo, D. Currier, & J. J. Mann, *Prospective Studies of Suicidal Behavior in Major Depressive and Bipolar Disorders: What Is the Evidence for Predictive Risk Factors?* 114 ACTA PSYCHIATRICA SCAND. 3, 151–58 (2006) (Although groups at risk can be identified, the prediction of suicide in individuals is difficult because individual risk factors account for only a small proportion of the variance in risk and lack sufficient specificity, leading to high rates of false positives); L. Ronquillo, A. Minassian, G. M. Vilke, & M. P. Wilson, *Literature-Based Recommendations for Suicide Assessments in the Emergency Department: A Review*, 43 J. EMERG. MED.5, 836–42 (2012) (while it is impossible to tell who is at highest risk of committing suicide with a short assessment, it may be possible to tell who is at the lowest risk, permitting discharge); ROBERT I. SIMON, PREVENTING PATIENT SUICIDE: CLINICAL ASSESSMENT AND MANAGEMENT (2011) ("No risk factors identify imminence of suicide. It is imperative for the clinician to assess, treat and manage acute high-risk factors that are driving a suicidal crisis rather than attempt the impossible task of predicting when or whether a patient will commit suicide.").

[249] Edwin S. Shneidman, The Suicidal Mind 56 (1996).

[250] *Id.*

people I interviewed, and abundant case law, is that many people who kill themselves often plan their suicides carefully and conceal those plans with great success from the people who know them best, including friends and family.[251] The people I interviewed were unanimous in saying that the more determined they were to kill themselves, the more they concealed their intentions from the people in their lives.

Although many things seem obvious in retrospect, the successful suicide of a friend,[252] client, relative,[253] employee,[254] student,[255] or celebrity[256] often takes us completely by surprise. We are shocked, in a visceral way, by the suicide of someone we know, even someone with a long-time psychiatric disability. Sometimes this is because suicidal people don't talk to even their closest friends. Stephen Fry, the British actor, likened suicidality to "an unsightly genital wart you would only want professional medical consultants to see."[257]

But we are also shocked if someone with known depression or difficulties commits suicide. That is not surprising either. There are so many thousands of people who talk about suicide for every person who dies by suicide—there are hundreds and hundreds of people who attempt suicide for every person who dies—that this surprise is actually, eminently rational.

---

[251] Interview with Dr. Charles Lidz, July 23, 2012; interview with Beckie Child, Sept. 30, 2012; interview with Robert Elmer, Dec. 20, 2012; John Bateson, The Final Leap: Suicide on the Golden Gate Bridge (2012).

[252] Solomon's *To an Aesthete Dying Young: In Memoriam T.R.K.* is one of the more beautiful elegies to a friend who died of suicide that captures very well the hints and behaviors that only assume prophetic significance in hindsight, and the guilt of close friends for having missed what they imagine to be the true meaning of various events, Andrew Solomon, ANDREWSOLOMON.COM (July 2010), http://andrewsolomon.com/articles/to-an-aesthete-dying-young/. I would argue that the meaning of events is not concrete but fluid with different interpretations being placed on the same events depending on the frame through which a person sees and remembers those events.

[253] Pete Croatto, *A Year Later, Trying to Comprehend a Young Player's Suicide*, N. Y. TIMES, Sports Section, p. 5, Oct. 26, 2014 (star hockey player with possible concussion-related issues jumps off George Washington Bridge; parents, girlfriend, friends "unaware that [he] was hurting"); Erin Schwantner, *I Was an Accomplice to My Brother's Suicide* (CNN, May 3, 2014), http://www.cnn.com/2014/05/03/health/suicide-erin-schwantner-irpt/index.html ("'Funny, happy people do not kill themselves. It doesn't make sense.' That's usually what people say...I know, because I used to say these things about my brother Evan.")

[254] Elmer, *supra* note 251.

[255] LINDA MABRY, FALLING UP TO GRACE (2013).

[256] It is not only Robin Williams; Stephen Fry, the British actor, spoke publicly about a serious suicide attempt that left him with four broken ribs, see *Stephen Fry: I Tried to Kill Myself Last Year*, CHORTLE, June 5, 2013, www.chortle.co.uk/news/2013/06/05/18030/stephen_fry:_i_tried_to_kill_myself_last_year

[257] *Stephen Fry*, supra note 256.

The research literature confirms people's anecdotal experience. There is not now, and never has been, a reliable way to predict who will commit suicide, even among groups of psychiatric inpatients, people with depression, or other high risk groups.[258]

There are many reasons for this. Psychiatric and statistical experts agree that a valid predictive instrument is hard to develop for a number of reasons. First, as noted above, suicide is extremely rare, statistically speaking.[259] Second, many of the factors associated with suicide—alcohol or substance abuse, for example—tend to be very common. Nevertheless, the hunt for the holy grail—a short set of questions whose answers reliably predict suicide—continues, and continues to receive funding of millions of dollars.

Most Screening Instruments Do Not Work and May Be Counterproductive

It is absolutely true that there are risk factors for suicide, and that in large population studies, these risk factors correlate with heightened risk for suicide. But there is no evidence that any single risk factor or combination of risk factors, assuming people told the truth about them, has anything like the kind of predictive strength needed for a "clear and convincing" standard of involuntary commitment. While "[m]uch research has attempted to develop quantitative methods to identify patients at high risk for suicide, there is no single universally accepted scoring system, as existing scoring systems are not sensitive enough to predict which patients will eventually complete suicide."[260]

---

[258] A. D. Pokorny, *Prediction of Suicide in Psychiatric Patients: Report of a Prospective Study*, 40 ARCH. GEN. PSYCHIATRY 249 (1983); A. D. Pokorny, *Suicide Prediction Revisited*, 23 SUICIDE & LIFE-THREATENING BEHAV. 1 (1993); Jan Fawcett, *Time-Related Predictors of Suicide in Major Affective Disorders*, 147 AM. J. PSYCHIATRY 1189, 1189 (1990); Robert I. Simon, *Imminent Suicide: The Illusion of Short-Term Prediction*, 36 SUICIDE & LIFE-THREATENING BEHAV. 296 (2006); Paul H. Soloff & Laurel Chiappetta, *Prospective Predictors of Suicidal Behavior in Borderline Personality Disorder at 6-Year Follow-up*, 169 AM. J. PSYCHIATRY 5, 484–90 (2012), *available at* http://ajp.psychiatryonline.org/doi/full/10.1176/appi.ajp.2011.11091378.

[259] "In contrast to contemporaneous assessments, the evaluation of a person's future mental state and consequent behaviors is fraught with particular difficulty, especially when the outcome being predicted occurs at a relatively low frequency." PAUL APPELBAUM, JUDGE'S GUIDE TO MENTAL HEALTH EVIDENCE IN REFERENCE MANUAL ON SCIENTIFIC EVIDENCE 818 (3d ed, National Academy of Science 2011); see generally, NATE SILVER, THE SIGNAL AND THE NOISE: WHY MOST PREDICTIONS FAIL BUT SOME DON'T (2012) and NASSIM NICHOLAS TALEB, THE BLACK SWAN: THE IMPACT OF THE HIGHLY IMPROBABLE (2007) for highly readable accounts of the difficulty in predicting events that occur rarely.

[260] Ronquillo et al., *supra* note 248, at 838–39.

Shneidman, as well as the many people I interviewed for this book, would say that the entire search for some kind of instrument with scripted questions misses the point of what suicidal people need most, which is a deep and personal attention to their individualized suffering and anguish. The inevitable use of rote questions ("Do you have a plan? Do you have the means to carry out the plan?") alienates suicidal people and convinces them that the questioner does not care about them as people, only as risks to be quantified. They confirm that if they have made up their minds to kill themselves they are going to lie when answering questions, whether in the emergency department or on a hospital ward:

> The most counterproductive part of our mental health laws—
> permitting the use of force when people are experiencing that level
> of stress—tells people that their feelings are not okay. If someone is
> feeling like killing themselves, the current solution is to lock them
> up for a couple of days and think that's going to solve the problem.
> I can't imagine there is anyone who has reached the point of being
> suicidal and was able to "recover" and "get back to normal" with
> a few days of hospitalization. Everyone I know who tried to kill
> themselves and was hospitalized basically lied their way out and
> then tried to kill themselves again—everyone I know lied their
> way out. The advice I got from friends was to suck it up, say what
> you need to say, lie your way out and then do whatever you want.
> I don't think that system is conducive to healing people, it's a
> system that teaches people to say what professionals want to hear.
> This environment is about risk assessment and preventing any risk
> and they're not even doing that well.[261]

The system of asking questions not only results in false negatives, it also results in false positives.[262] As one of my interviewees said:

> We need better mental health systems to take care of people in a
> fuller way, in order to get admitted you shouldn't have to try to
> kill yourself . . . this guy says to me I can't get help. I said tell them
> you have a plan, tell them you tried to kill yourself—how else is he
> going to get in there? People who need help shouldn't have to try to
> lie about being suicidal.[263]

Basically, our current laws—civil commitment laws, liability laws, and insurance laws—and policies have created a system. Providers navigate the liability and civil commitment system, and the reality that they are overloaded with people waiting for help, by asking rote questions that do not have anything to

---

[261] Interview with "Colleen" (pseudonym).
[262] See Chapter 7, "Contingent Suicidality" at pp. 335–338.
[263] Interview with Anonymous.

do with an individual person's misery and desperation and desolation. Often, lack of funding and fear of liability if a person is discharge results in suicidal people being parked in sterile cubicles with a person watching them for many hours, sometimes days, and occasionally weeks. Patients navigate this system by lying, either pretending to feel better than they do, or worse, depending on their perception of their needs. Sometimes they are so frustrated and angry by this system that they act impulsively and get put in restraints. Everyone knows how to navigate the system, but deprivations of liberty through the operation of the system cannot be said to be narrowly tailored to meet compelling state interests in preserving life.

Talking About or Threatening Suicide Does Not Predict Suicide with Sufficient Accuracy to Justify Involuntary Commitment

The proportion of people who take their lives, as compared to those who think about and talk about suicide, is simply so miniscule as to suggest that the former cannot serve as any kind of predictor for the latter. The Centers for Disease Control and Prevention conducted what was by far the largest sample of the population subject to study on this issue, and it found that 8.3 million people had seriously thought about committing suicide in the same year that 37,500 people committed suicide. In other words, if everyone who thought about committing suicide was hospitalized in order to prevent suicide, you would have a false positive rate of between 99.5% and 99.7%.[264] In the case of young women, and especially young minority women, the false positive rate would be even higher. The rate of adults thinking about suicide in any given year is 3700/100,000.[265] One-third of those people come up with a plan (1000/100,000) and half of those make an attempt (500/100,000). But fewer than 10% of people who make a suicide attempt die by suicide, and making an attempt does not predict successful suicide.

In Massachusetts, for example, there were 75,000 admissions to psychiatric hospitals in 2012. Of these, 45,000 were involuntary admissions under the state's involuntary commitment laws.[266] Not all were for suicidality, but because so few involuntary commitments are grounded in danger to others, it is safe to assume that a substantial proportion of these involuntary admissions were because of predictions that the individual would attempt

---

[264] Douglas Jacobs, supra n. 244, citing Crosby (1999). Using the same method with 2011 data from the Centers for Disease Control and Prevention, the figure is just over 99.5%.

[265] A. E. Crosby, B. Han, L. A. Ortega, S. E. Parks, J. Gfroerer, *Suicidal Thoughts and Behaviors Among Adults ≥18 Years—United States, 2008–2009*, 60 MORBIDITY & MORTALITY WKLY. REP. SURVEILLANCE SUMMARIES 13, 1–22 (Oct. 21, 2011), 60-SS13, http://origin.glb.cdc.gov/mmwr/preview/mmwrhtml/ss6013a1.htm?s_cid

[266] Personal Communication from Mark Larsen, Committee for Public Counsel Services, Mental Health Division.

suicide. That year, 4258 people visited the emergency department because of self-inflicted injuries,[267] and 624 people killed themselves.[268] Thus, even using ballpark estimates of the proportion of people involuntarily detained for suicidality compared to the number of suicides, the rate of false negatives for involuntary commitment must be extraordinarily high. Furthermore, as the next section argues, it is not at all clear that the people being detained are the ones at greatest risk of dying.

Challenging Predictions of Suicide: *Daubert* and Current Court Decisions
Regarding Prediction of Harm

The case law and the research[269] are repetitive to the point of monotony that mental health professionals cannot predict suicide. Yet at the same time, most state civil commitment statutes permit involuntary civil commitment—for up to five years in some states[270]—if someone is mentally ill and dangerous to self. My argument is that no expert can validly predict which people who talk about suicide and threaten suicide will ultimately be dangerous to themselves, and statistically, the former is insufficiently predictive of the latter to serve as a basis for complete loss of liberty. Yet clinicians regularly involuntarily commit individuals who have not even threatened to commit suicide but simply have suicidal ideation (i.e., they think about suicide and dying).[271]

If suicide cannot be predicted, why do mental health professionals testify in court that an individual should be committed because of suicidality? There are many reasons for this.

The first is that some individual mental health professionals have spent decades making a living off predictions that the American Psychiatric Association has long maintained are invalid and untrustworthy. The best known of these is the prediction that a specific individual will commit murder or violent crimes in the future.[272] People have been executed based on testimony by experts who never met them or spoken to them that they were

[267] Massachusetts Executive Office of Health and Human Services (EOHHS), Department of Public Health, Injury Surveillance Program, *Suicide and Self-Inflicted Injuries in Massachusetts: Data Summary* (these figures are for FY 2012). http://www.mass.gov/eohhs/docs/dph/injury-surveillance/suicide/suicide-update-winter-2015.pdf

[268] *Id.*

[269] Simon, *supra* note 258.

[270] N.H.Rev.Stat.Ann. 135C:46 (2014).

[271] Rodriguez v. City of New York. 72 F.3d 1051, 1054 (2nd Cir. 1995).

[272] Barefoot v. Estelle, 463 U.S. 880, 896 (1983); Estelle v. Smith, 451 U.S. 454 (1981). Beyond this, the Washington State Supreme Court rejected the Washington Psychiatric Association's position that there was no basis for psychiatric testimony that any particular mental disorder predisposed an individual to rape, *In re* Young, 122 Wash.2d 1, 55 (1993)(*en banc*).

dangerous and could not be rehabilitated. People are literally sentenced to die on the basis of predictions about their behavior by a psychiatrist who could not pick them out of a lineup. [273] This behavior is unethical,[274] but legal.[275] The American Psychological Association implored the Supreme Court in a case called *Coble* to at least review a case that held that admittedly unreliable psychiatric expert testimony used to sentence a man to death *must always*, as a matter of law, be admitted into evidence. The Texas court based its holding on the Supreme Court's decision in *Barefoot v. Estelle*, which found that because lay testimony on dangerousness could be admitted, even unreliable psychiatric testimony could be admitted, leaving the (often inept and inexperienced, if not outright drunk[276]) lawyers for the defendant to sort out the credibility issues on cross-examination. Thus, the Texas court in *Coble* held that psychiatric testimony, no matter how unreliable, on the issue of future dangerousness could *never* be excluded. The Supreme Court refused to even review the *Coble* decision.[277]

Courts want expertise because they want to be able to have "objective" grounds for executing and involuntarily detaining people, and individual mental health professionals, however unethical, are willing to provide the testimony. Ordinary evidentiary protections, such as reliability and peer support for methodology, have been discarded; the Supreme Court has ruled that experts, such as mental health professionals, do not need to have *any* evidentiary basis beyond their own training and experience.[278] Nor is

---

[273] Tigner v. Cockrell, 264 F.3d 521 (5th Cir. 2001); Flores v. Johnson, 210 F.3d 456 (5th Cir. 2000).

[274] American Psychiatric Association brief in *Barefoot v. Estelle*, cited in *Flores v. Johnson* id at n. 274.

[275] *Barefoot v. Estelle* at n. 272.

[276] People v. Harrison (1989) (affirming murder conviction of man whose lawyer drank in the morning, during court recesses, and in the evening, and who on the second day of trial was arrested for drunk driving with a blood alcohol content of 0.27 when the legal limit was 0.08); People v. Badia, 159 A.2d 577 (N.Y. App. 1990) (upholding the conviction of a man whose lawyer was high on heroin and cocaine throughout the trial; shortly after the trial the lawyer was convicted for conspiracy to distribute narcotics); Frye v. Lee, 235 F.3d 897 (4th Cir. 2000); Gardner v. Dixon, 1992 U.S.App.LEXIS 28147 (4th Cir. 1992); Haney v. State, 603 So.2d 412 (Ala. 1992) (affirming the murder conviction of a woman whose attorney showed up to trial so drunk that the judge threw him out of court and sent him to dry out in the drunk tank); White v. State, 664 So.2d 242 (Fla.1995) (affirming the murder conviction of a man whose lawyer's behavior was so problematic that the judge ordered the prosecutor to check the attorney's breath before trial started each morning); Holsey, executed despite the fact that his attorney admitted to drinking a quart of vodka every night during trial).

[277] Coble v. Texas, cert. den. 131 S.Ct. 1330 (2011); See Brief of the American Psychological Association. http://www.apa.org/about/offices/ogc/amicus/coble.pdf

[278] Kumho Tire v. Carmichael, 526 U.S. 137 (1999).

there any requirement that their testimony meet any scientific standard of reliability.[279]

The courts, from the lower courts all the way up to the Supreme Court, have been crystal clear about this. The Supreme Court repeatedly asserts that psychiatric diagnosis is imprecise[280] and that psychiatric prediction is completely unreliable, no better than a layperson's prediction or tossing a coin. But, the courts assert quite unashamedly, without this testimony, how else are we going to commit people, either civilly or as sexual predators?[281]

Some courts acknowledge that psychiatric prediction is unreliable and assert that civil commitment is a legal, not a medical decision. Ironically, these pronouncements generally come in decisions to involuntarily commit an individual when mental health professionals testify in favor of release, asserting that the individual is not dangerous.[282] When one conservative federal judge had the courage to write a detailed opinion explaining why psychiatric testimony should be inadmissible in proceedings to sentence a man to death,[283] he was excoriated by some legal scholars.[284] For people who wish to explore this issue further, Judge Garza's opinion is definitely worth reading as a clear, cogent explanation of why psychiatric testimony about future violence is too unreliable to even be admitted in court. Judge Garza succinctly characterized this kind of evidence as "subjective testimony without any scientific validity by one who holds a medical degree."[285]

When it comes to psychiatric testimony in civil commitment cases, the courts have resembled Alvy in Woody Allen's *Annie Hall*: "[T]his guy goes to a psychiatrist and says, "Doc, my brother's crazy; he thinks he's a chicken." And the doctor says, "Well, why don't you turn him in?" The guy says, "I would, but I need the eggs."[286]

The courts need the eggs of psychiatric testimony because they want to be able to incarcerate certain groups of people on the grounds of future dangerousness, and our constitutional principles generally prohibits preventive detention. The state's interests in saving someone from self-harm, while

---

[279] *Barefoot v. Estelle* at n. 272.

[280] *O'Connor v. Donaldson* at n. 197; *Addington v. Texas* at n. 181.

[281] *In re* Harris, 98 Wash.2d 276, 280 (1982) ("Petitioner's argument would eviscerate the entire law of involuntary commitment as well as render dubious the numerous other areas where psychiatry and the law intersect. There is no question the prediction of dangerousness has its attendant problems . . . But we are not prepared to abandon the possibility of conforming the law of involuntary civil commitment to the requirements of the constitution."); *In re* Young *supra* at n. 272. See generally, Alexander Scherr, *Daubert and Danger: The Fit of Expert Predictions in Civil Commitment*, 55 HASTINGS L.J. (Jan. 2003).

[282] Scherr, *supra* note 282; see also *McGee v. Bartow*, at n. 206.

[283] *Flores v. Johnson* at 464–70 (Garza, J. specially concurring).

[284] Scherr, *supra* note 282.

[285] Flores v. Johnson, 210 F.3d 456, 458 (2000) (Garza, J. specially concurring).

[286] *Annie Hall, supra* note 88.

strong, are not even as strong as its interests in protecting the public, and predictions of suicide are even less reliable than predictions of dangerousness to others.

In contrast to individual testimony that has not and cannot be shown to be reliable, massive epidemiological studies over many years reflect that the vast, vast majority of people who think about dying, and even those who threaten to commit suicide, are not dangerous to themselves. Statistically, you'd be better off involuntarily committing people who are alcoholics or substance abusers, because their risk of suicide is greater than people who say they are thinking about suicide. Yet we correctly recognize that there are so many alcoholics and substance abusers who do not commit suicide that using this as a basis of commitment to prevent suicide would not serve the State interest in preventing suicide. As an actuarial matter, we would be on sounder ground to involuntarily commit impulsive substance abusers to prevent suicide than when we involuntarily commit people who think about, talk about, or threaten suicide.

If you think about it long enough, any argument in favor of committing people who talk about or threaten suicide has its basis in the powerful stigma against discussing these feelings in our society. Because of the stigma, the hundreds of thousands of people who are feeling suicidal don't talk about it, and when they do, deeply uncomfortable family and friends, afraid to say the wrong thing, turn to "expert" help. The experts, afraid of being sued, or of a tragic outcome, use their powers of involuntary treatment.

All of this used to be equally true when terminally ill people wanted to die. They were afraid to express their feelings, and if they did, the experts refused to permit them to implement their desires. Now children are encouraged to have end-of-life discussions with their parents. It may very well be that someone who articulates suicidal thoughts is asking for help; it is probably not so true that he or she is asking for the police to show up, or an ambulance to the noisy and crowded emergency department for a series of formulaic questions ("Do you have a plan?") and involuntary detention for hours, if not days or weeks.

People Who Talk About or Threaten Suicide Are Demographically Different from People Who Complete Suicide

The kinds of people who attempt, threaten, or think about suicide are different in all kinds of ways from the kinds of people who are successful: "it is important to realize that, despite some overlap, suicide attempters and completers show demographic, personality, and clinical differences."[287] As most people know, successful attempters are white, middle-aged and older males;

---

[287] K. R. Conner & P. R. Duberstein, *Predisposing and Precipitating Factors for Suicide Among Alcoholics: Empirical Review and Conceptual Integration*, 28 ALCOHOL CLIN. EXP. RES 5(Suppl), 6S–17S (2004).

threateners are younger white females with personality disorders who have been described as "chronically suicidal."[288]

This truth is best illustrated by the following statistics: the ratio of successful suicides versus attempts for individuals older than sixty-five is 1 in 4;[289] the ratio of successful suicides versus attempts in individuals aged fifteen to twenty-four is about 1.5/1000.[290] Another way to illustrate this is to look at suicides in Wyoming, the state with the highest suicide rate in the country: 40% of all suicides in Wyoming are committed by men aged fifty-five or older. [291]

The fact is that, demographically, people who talk about suicide and even attempt suicide look very different from people who succeed in committing suicide. Great writers and observers of the human condition from William Shakespeare[292] to Edward Arlington Robinson[293] to Robertson Davies have all commented on the fact that the people who talk about suicide—"unpack their hearts with words" are less likely to kill themselves, while the suicides are the "quiet ones, who can't find the words to fit their misery."[294]

Hamlet notwithstanding, people who talk about suicide are much more apt to be women, especially younger women; when they attempt suicide, they use pills and are often rescued. People who commit suicide are much more likely to be men, especially older white men, using guns. Elderly suicide attempters look very much like elderly suicide completers—they are medically ill, plan their suicides carefully, and use guns. They don't look very much like people aged sixteen to fifty-nine who attempt suicide.[295] They also don't talk nearly as much about suicide as their younger counterparts.[296] Many have never had either mental health diagnoses or treatment (although that doesn't prevent the final indignity of being diagnosed postmortem with mental illness by researchers who never knew them while they were alive).[297]

---

[288] JOEL PARIS, HALF IN LOVE WITH DEATH: MANAGING THE CHRONICALLY SUICIDAL PATIENT (2007), see ch.7.

[289] H. Friedman & R. Kohn, Mortality in the Suicidal Population, 38 SUICIDE & LIFE-THREATENING BEHAV. 287 (2008).

[290] S. K. GOLDSMITH, T. C. PELLMAR, A. M. KLEINMAN, W. E. BUNNEY, EDS. REDUCING SUICIDE: A NATIONAL IMPERATIVE (2002).

[291] WYOMING DEPARTMENT OF HEALTH, PREVENTING SUICIDE IN WYOMING: 2014–2016 STATE SUICIDE PREVENTION PLAN, 4 (July 2014), http://www.sprc.org/sites/sprc.org/files/WDH%20Suicide%20Prevention%202014-2016%20FINAL.pdf.

[292] WILLIAM SHAKESPEARE, HAMLET (1603).

[293] Edward Arlington Robinson, Richard Cory in CHILDREN OF THE NIGHT (1897).

[294] ROBERTSON DAVIES, LEAVEN OF MALICE 176 (1954).

[295] Robert L. Frierson, Suicide Attempts by the Old and Very Old, 152 ARCH. INTERNAL MED. 141 (1991).

[296] Susanne S. Carney, Charles L. Rich, Patricia A. Burke, et al., Suicide Over Sixty: The San Diego Study, 42 J. AM. GERIATRICS SOC'Y 174 (1994).

[297] S. L. Horton-Deutsch, D. C. Clarl, et al. Chronic Dyspnea and Suicide in Elderly Men, 43 PSYCHIATRIC SERVICES 1198 (1992) (describing elderly men who committed suicide as "fiercely independent," as though that were a bad thing).

In Massachusetts, the suicide rate among men forty-five to fifty-four was 22.9/100,000. The suicide rate among Hispanic females was 0.8/100,000.[298]

This leads to an interesting phenomenon: people who get involuntarily detained, involuntarily committed, and involuntarily treated for being suicidal are largely nonelderly women, who are statistically quite unlikely to commit suicide, but far more likely to talk about feeling suicidal or threaten suicide to mental health professionals, or to make attempts that are called cries for help because of the nature or context of the attempt. Clinicians who specialize in the treatment of chronically suicidal women, who are often labeled with the diagnosis of borderline personality disorder, generally argue that involuntary hospitalization is not helpful to them and is often harmful.[299] It is likely that mental health professionals involuntarily commit and treat people, not because they are truly likely to kill themselves, but because those are the people who are in front of them threatening suicide. It certainly seems to be the case that often, despite all the involuntary detentions and treatment, people who talk about being suicidal keep feeling suicidal, sometimes more suicidal (although some are more circumspect about talking about their feelings after experiencing involuntary detention and treatment). Maybe elderly white males are not being involuntarily detained because society simply does not care enough to prevent the suicides of elderly people. It is obvious from states that have legalized assisted suicide that suicide by older, medically ill people just does not seem crazy to us. In addition, many suicidal men do not want help, do not ask for help, and never come to the attention of anyone with the power to commit them.

However, my interviews and my thirty years of experience representing people with psychiatric diagnoses, many of whom talked about suicide, all point toward one answer. The mental health system involuntarily commits and involuntarily treats people who talk about being suicidal, and who make nonfatal and sometimes not-even-very-serious attempts. Many of my women clients talked about committing suicide literally for decades, and some of these women were involuntarily committed dozens and sometimes hundreds of times as a result. On the other hand, my clients who actually killed themselves—both male and female—never gave me or anyone else the slightest inkling about what they were going to do. For at least a few, their life situations seemed to be improving.

---

[298] Massachusetts Executive Office of Health and Human Services, Department of Public Health, Injury Surveillance Program, "Suicide and Self Inflicted Injuries in Massachusetts: Data Summary" (Winter 2015) http://www.mass.gov/eohhs/docs/dph/injury-surveillance/suicide/suicide-update-winter-2015.pdf

[299] PETER DAWSON & HARRIET MACMILLAN, RELATIONSHIP MANAGEMENT OF THE BORDERLINE PATIENT: FROM UNDERSTANDING TO TREATMENT (1993); PARIS, *supra* note 262; Joel Paris, *Managing Suicidality in Patients with Borderline Personality Disorder*, PSYCHIATRIC TIMES, July 1, 2006, http://www.psychiatrictimes.com/articles/managing-suicidality-patients-borderline-personality-disorder.

There are even two substantial categories of people recognized by research and practice who claim to be suicidal but whose chances of actually killing themselves are extremely low: people who are contingently suicidal and people who are chronically suicidal. These categories are discussed in more detail in Chapter 7, but together they comprise a substantial number of suicidal patients seen by mental health professionals, and they are defined by their propensity to threaten suicide but not actually kill themselves. They are described as being "personality-disordered" rather than "depressed,"[300] and whether they should be diagnosed or not, plenty of suicidal people have confirmed that they are suicidal for years—even decades—without ever making a single attempt.[301]

I think people who talk about suicide because they are in unbearable pain and don't know what to do are being subjected to involuntary detention and involuntary treatment which, for the most part, doesn't help them, while people who are determined to kill themselves go on killing themselves, and that is why the suicide rate has not changed despite the expenditure of billions of dollars on suicide prevention by federal, state, and private sources.

There is so little (if any) evidence that involuntary detention for any extended period of time reduces suicide that a total deprivation of liberty to provide treatment to cure or treat suicidality raises serious constitutional issues.

The search for the holy grail of predictive instruments has been going on for the past sixty years and continues to be funded, but the basic answer is these instruments don't work very well. While "[m]uch research has attempted to develop quantitative methods to identify patients at high risk for suicide, there is no single universally accepted scoring system, as existing scoring systems are not sensitive enough to predict which patients will eventually complete suicide."[302] Every honest expert will tell you that the best that a clinician of integrity can do is discuss possibilities and probabilities that a person will commit suicide, and most people who know someone who has killed himself or herself will tell you that they were blindsided. In Oregon, courts agree: the prediction of a mental health professional that an individual is suicidal in the absence of specific supporting conduct is insufficient to support involuntary commitment,[303] as is a stated desire to die,[304] and a history of suicide attempts.[305]

---

[300] Paris, *supra* note 288.

[301] Interview with Cheryl Sharp (Dec. 6, 2013).

[302] Ronquillo et al., *supra* note 248, at 838–39.

[303] State v. C.R., 173 P.3d 836 (Ore. App. 2007); State v. N.A.P., 173 P.3d 1251 (Ore. 2007).

[304] *In re* R.E., 273 P.3d 341(Ore. App. 2012); State v. M.S.,180 Ore. App. 255, 258, 42 P.3d 374 (Ore. App. 2002) (during prehearing hospitalization, individual shouted, "God take my life, I don't care anymore" insufficient to sustain involuntary commitment).

[305] State v. D.P. 144 P.3d 1044 (Ore. App. 2006); State v. D.A.H., 250 P.3d 423 (Ore. App. 2011); In the Matter of Lott, 122 P.3d 97 (Ore. App. 2005).

There are many reasons for this. Psychiatric and statistical experts agree that a valid predictive instrument is hard to develop for a number of reasons. First, suicide is extremely rare, statistically speaking.[306] Second, the risk factors associated with suicide—alcohol or substance abuse, for example—tend to be very common. There are many, many more people who abuse alcohol and substances than people who commit or even attempt suicide. This is especially true of people talking about being suicidal, which is not even listed as a risk factor for suicide on most lists of this kind.

In any event, most instruments depend on self-report; most people with experience in this area, including the people I interviewed who had made serious suicide attempts, confirm that when they were most seriously suicidal, they would lie in response to questions about their suicidality. These are not lies that are easily caught; people who are seriously suicidal can be extremely skilled at concealing their intent from families and friends, let alone total strangers.

So we are left with clinical judgment, which in the hands of a few skilled professionals can be enormously effective,[307] but in the hands of most others is little better than chance at predicting people who will attempt suicide.[308]

Involuntary Psychiatric Detention Increases the Risk of Suicide For Many People

Involuntary psychiatric detention increases rather than decreases the risk of suicide for many people, while evidence-based treatments that actually reduce suicidality are all community-based.[309] The Constitution requires that any complete deprivation of liberty be "narrowly tailored to achieve the State's compelling interest."[310] Obviously a deprivation of liberty that in many instances does not achieve the State's interest, and in some cases defeats it, does not survive this test. It is not at all clear that involuntary hospitalization prevents rather than increases the likelihood of suicide, especially in the long term. For some people, it is absolutely true that hospitalization is helpful,

---

[306] "In contrast to contemporaneous assessments, the evaluation of a person's future mental state and consequent behaviors is fraught with particular difficulty, especially when the outcome being predicted occurs at a relatively low frequency." APPELBAUM, *supra* note 259; SILVER, *supra* note 259.

[307] See Jon Berlin, *Advanced Interviewing Techniques for Psychiatric Patients in the Emergency Department, in* BEHAVIORAL EMERGENCIES FOR THE EMERGENCY PHYSICIAN 25 (Leslie Zun ed., 2013); Avram Fishkind, *Agitation II: De-Escalation of the Aggressive Patient and Avoiding Coercion, in* EMERGENCY PSYCHIATRY: PRINCIPLES AND PRACTICE 125 (Rachel S. Glick, J. S. Berlin, Avram Fishkind, & Scott Zeller eds., 2008).

[308] See CHRISTOPHER SLOBOGIN, PROVING THE UNPROVABLE (2006).

[309] See Chapter 9 for a comprehensive discussion of these treatments.

[310] Shelton v. Tucker, 364 U.S. 479, 488 (1960).

reducing the chances of suicide in the short term. The more successful the hospitalization, in some ways, the more likely that the transition back into the environment that created the context for suicidality will be difficult. That is why many experts caution against hospitalizing people with "chronic suicidality"[311]—it doesn't help and only becomes a revolving cycle that prevents them from becoming engaged in their lives.

But there are a lot of other people for whom involuntary hospitalization will increase suicidality. For someone who feels desolate, isolated, and lonely, strict confinement, loss of privacy and control over one's life, isolation from peers, loved ones and pets, and removal from all the small joys of life does not seem like the best solution.

It is not only that hospitalization is ineffective, but that in some cases it is extremely damaging: several of my interviewees were sexually assaulted in the hospital. For others, watching other patients being held down and forcibly medicated is very upsetting. Many respectable, mainstream mental health professionals believe that involuntary institutionalization can be a traumatizing experience that increases the likelihood of suicide in the long run, especially with certain kinds of patients: those whose need for control is a profound and fundamental part of their identity, such as people diagnosed with borderline personality disorder.[312]

The need for control often arises from childhood trauma, where the individual was powerless to prevent abuse and violence. Many people who are suicidal were traumatized as children, where they were powerless to control what was happening to them. Issues of control become supremely important, and involuntary commitment and treatment can be experienced as extremely damaging.

Other people feel hopeless and helpless, and being involuntarily committed communicates that other people share this perspective: they cannot be trusted to take care of themselves, they must be under complete and total supervision. In many of my interviews, and in the case law, one theme recurred: people who did not seek help when they were suicidal because they were afraid of being sent to the hospital, or people who attempted suicide when they thought they were about to be sent to the hospital.[313] The people I interviewed survived; the people in the cases, for the most part, did not.

---

[311] See Chapter 7 for a comprehensive discussion of chronic suicidality.

[312] See David Dawson and Harriet MacMillan, Relationship Management of the Borderline Patient: From Understanding to Treatment (Brunner/Mazel 1993).Joel Paris, Half in Love with Death (paperback 2007).

[313] Mahoney v. Allegheny College, No. AD 892-2003 (Pa. Ct. C.P., Dec. 22, 2005), http://www.bsk.com/site/files/Mahoney_v._Allegheny_College.pdf (student did not seek help when he was feeling worst because he was "fearful of being returned to 'that terrible mental ward' which he described as a traumatic experience for him"); Hobart v. Shin, 705 N.E.2d 907, 910 (Ill. 1998) ("Her mother urged her to contact her doctors, but she refused because she did not want to

Even if all we cared about was short-term elimination of the risk of suicide, hospitalization can't accomplish that either. Like prisons and jails, mental institutions and hospitals cannot completely prevent suicide.[314] The methods that they use to try to prevent suicide—seclusion, restraint, and one to one observation—are the ultimate loss of control for patients whose great need is for hope, mastery, and to see themselves as agents in their own lives.

In sum, I think the Constitution permits involuntary detention (the usual three-day detention that precedes most involuntary commitments) for imminent suicidality. This detention is permissible for a range of reasons: the person may be truly incompetent (very psychotic or intoxicated); the person may have medical issues that are causing apparently suicidal behavior, especially in older people, younger people, and people who are suddenly and uncharacteristically suicidal; the person may need a short-term detox, either from alcohol or substances or from an escalated and unbearable emotional situation. Sometimes, in some places with some people, the person may actually get help in those three days. But after three days, for the most part, people who are competent and sober need to be discharged unless they meet extremely narrow criteria outlined by the United States Supreme Court.

To justify longer term involuntary civil commitment, the Constitution requires the State to prove, by clear and convincing evidence,[315] three things: that that this individual is very likely to commit suicide in the very near future, *and* that the person's suicidality is caused by a mental disorder that creates a very serious difficulty for the person to control his or her suicidality,[316] and that hospitalization would provide effective treatment for the mental disorder, and that this treatment would be ineffective in the community.

This is a difficult, but not impossible, standard to meet, and I think the Constitution requires it. It would stop people from being diagnosed just

---

be hospitalized again"); Martin v. Smith, 438 SE2d 318 (W.Va. 1993) (man shot himself on a pass home because he did not want to be transferred to state hospital); Wackwitz v. Roy, 418 S.E.2d 861, 862 (Va. 1992) (man slashed his wrist because he had been told he was going to be sent to a psychiatric institution for thirty years, and he would rather be dead).

[314] Between 5% and 10% of all suicides take place in hospitals, see Chapters 6 and 7 and D.A. Schwartz, D.E.Flinn, & P.F.Slawson, *Suicide in the Psychiatric Hospital*, 132 AM. J. PSYCHIATRY 150 (1975). The numerous malpractice cases brought on behalf of people who committed suicide while under the supervision and custody of psychiatric facilities attest to this, see, e.g., Shelton v. Arkansas Dep't of Human Services, 677 F.3d 837 (8th Cir. 2012); Carrington v. Methodist Medical Center, 740 So.2d 827 (Miss. 1999); State Hosp. v. Wood, 823 So.2d 598 (Miss. App. 2002); Graham v. Northwestern Memorial Hosp., 965 N.E.2d 611 (Ill. App. 2012); Terrell State Hosp. v. Ashworth, 794 S.W.2d 937 (Tx. App. 1990); Dunson v. Stricklin, 1998 U.S. Dist. LEXIS 11082 (S.D. Ala. July 7, 1998).

[315] *Addington v. Texas*, 441 U.S. 418 (1979).

[316] *Kansas v. Crane*, 534 U.S. 407 (2002).

because they were suicidal; it would stop people from being committed whose suicidality was the result of reflection, choice, and assessment of their lives, and most of all, it would (I hope) force states to acknowledge that involuntary treatment does little or nothing to reduce suicide or depression or the human misery and loneliness and hopelessness and longing for meaning that are hallmarks of suicidality. There is no research evidence that involuntary hospitalization reduces suicide. The State might present evidence of expert opinion, based on their own experience, but it could not point to a single study that hospitalization was an effective treatment for suicidality.

Conclusion

When we look at the case law about rights and people's decisions about dying, several things stand out in striking ways.

First, we are much more likely to assume today that a competent person's decisions about dying rightfully belong to that person alone, and that autonomy and choice are crucial and fundamental values to be protected, particularly in the arena of final choices. But it wasn't always this way. When courts began to consider people's decision-making about their bodies, the first assumption was that this was a medical area in which courts should not be involved at all. Even when they did get involved, courts often found that families had competing rights, which trumped a person's decision if he or she had small children. Courts found that doctors and the medical profession had competing rights, which could also trump someone's right to decide what happened to his or her own body. When a disabled person, such as Elizabeth Bouvia, asserted her right to die, the court that heard her case considered that other disabled people who might be harmed by finding that she had a right to die not only deserved to be heard as witnesses, but should be granted intervention as parties to the case. This would never, ever happen today.

But the march of progress toward individual autonomy left people with psychiatric disabilities behind, not only as a matter of social practice but as a matter of jurisprudence. Because their rights to make their own decisions about their bodies were litigated primarily in institutional settings, the State's interests were correspondingly greater, and different standards were developed to govern those decisions.

They were also assumed, because of discriminatory attitudes and overgeneralizations, to be incompetent to make their own decisions about treatment. For everyone else, wanting to die raised profound questions of privacy and the limits of State intervention. For people with psychiatric disabilities, wanting to die was just a symptom to be cured. For everyone else, the right to die and assisted suicide were live moral issues to be debated and discussed. For people with psychiatric disabilities, the only question was how to screen the ones who wanted to die into hospitals—involuntarily if necessary—and how best to provide "interventions." There certainly was never any thought that the debate about assisted suicide applied to them, except insofar as the difficulty in screening them out was used as an argument against assisted suicide.

Nevertheless, several states enacted assisted suicide regimes, and the existence of people with psychiatric disabilities forced some questions in the practical operations of such programs. What happens if a person is certified as meeting the requirements of assisted suicide and then is institutionalized for depression? What happens if a competent terminally ill person who is not part of the assisted suicide program attempts suicide? What happens when federal and state laws conflict, or the laws of one state conflict with those of another? These questions will be answered in the next chapter. Still others— "Should emergency medical technicians honor the do not resuscitate (DNR) order of a suicidal person?" and "What are the rules for disconnecting life support in the case of the suicide attempt of a person with terminal illness?"— will be answered in Chapter 6.

This chapter builds on the previous chapter to conclude that competent people with psychiatric disabilities cannot constitutionally be subjected to involuntary civil commitment for thinking about suicide, talking about suicide, threatening suicide—in other words, for their words rather than their conduct. The connection between talking about suicide and committing suicide is just too tenuous, and the benefits of involuntary hospitalization too uncertain, to justify complete restriction of an individual's liberty. I acknowledge that a brief (72 hour) involuntary detention to determine if a person is competent, and to deter the most impulsive people, is constitutional, but beyond that, "harm to self" commitments are justified, if at all, based only on specific conduct. We need to free people to talk about their distress and desire to be dead if we are going to help them at all. At the same time, I suggest in Chapter 6 that mental health professionals be relieved of liability for the suicides of their outpatients absent intentional or reckless malfeasance, to enable them to listen more freely.

3

Assisted Suicide in the States

Introduction: The Case of *Gonzales v. Oregon*

The Supreme Court relied on the historical record in *Washington v. Glucksberg* to find that there was no constitutional right to physician-assisted suicide or physician aid in dying. Suicide has been historically criminalized, not permitted, by the states, and if there was going to be any change, the Justices wrote, it should take place in the "laboratory of the states."[1] Almost ten years later, they kept faith with the concept that the states should be free to experiment with this complex and difficult issue by rejecting the federal government's attempt to use federal law to thwart Oregon's Death with Dignity Act.[2]

The Bush administration argued in *Gonzales v. Oregon* that prescribing the drugs necessary for assisted suicide was not a "legitimate medical practice,"[3] and that Oregon physicians who did so were violating the 1970 Controlled Substances Act.[4] This federal legislation, which divided potentially dangerous drugs into categories called "Schedules,"[5] was meant to thwart physicians who prescribed drugs to people who abused prescription medication. If a physician violates the Controlled Substances Act, he or she loses the federal registration required to lawfully prescribe Schedule II drugs.

---

[1] Washington v. Glucksberg, 521 U.S. 702, 737 (1997) (O'Connor, J., concurring).

[2] Gonzales v. Oregon, 546 U.S. 243 (2006)

[3] *Id.* at 249.

[4] *Id.*

[5] *Id.* at 250. The drug used at the time to cause death in Oregon, pentobarbital, is a Schedule II drug. Schedule II drugs are the most heavily regulated drugs for which prescriptions may be written, and physicians must obtain licenses to do so. Schedule I drugs such as heroin, mescaline, and psilocybin may not be prescribed. Pentobarbital's close chemical relative phenobarbital is a Schedule IV drug, which is used to treat epilepsy.

At issue in the case was Oregon's power to declare that physician-assisted suicide was a "legitimate medical practice." This went to the very heart of the state experimentation that the Court had commended as the best way to engage in the "earnest and profound debate about the morality, legality, and practicality of physician-assisted suicide" in *Glucksberg*.[6]

The *Gonzales* decision was close. By a 5-4 majority, the Court held that, as a statutory matter, the Controlled Substances Act was meant to combat drug abuse, and that physician-assisted suicide was not contemplated in the drafting and passage of the Act. It found that Oregon had the final authority to regulate medical practice in its state, and that the U.S. Attorney General's institutional lack of expertise in medical matters fatally undermined his attempt to regulate the area. The Attorney General argued that this was a legal and not a medical matter. The Court, however, pointed out that assisted suicide was still a crime in Oregon, and was legal only when practiced by licensed physicians under a number of conditions, including that the patient must be terminally ill. Therefore, the use of these drugs was a medical, rather than legal, matter, and the U.S. Attorney General was invading a standard state prerogative when he tried to use his federal powers to essentially redraft Oregon's definition of the crime of assisted suicide.

This decision, casting the question as one of states' rights, would not have been so surprising had it not been for the Court's decision seven months previously in in the legally similar (some would say close to identical) case of *Gonzales v. Raich*.[7] In that case, the Court upheld the federal government's power to criminally prosecute users of medical marijuana in California under the Controlled Substances Act, even though California had legalized medical marijuana. In both cases, the States had taken a practice that is generally illegal and carved out an exception in a very specific, medically supervised context. The Court's two decisions looked inconsistent and contradictory.

For fans of legal reasoning, the distinction the Court majority made between the two cases was that in the assisted suicide case, the Court was reviewing the Attorney General's interpretation of a federal statute (the Controlled Substances Act), whereas in the medical marijuana case, the question was whether the Commerce Clause of the Constitution gave Congress the power to prohibit the use of medical marijuana through the Controlled Substances Act.

Justice Thomas didn't buy this distinction for a minute. He had dissented in *Raich* (i.e., he would have supported California's right to legalize medical marijuana) because the federal government's powers are limited under the Constitution. But if *Raich* had been correctly decided, according to Thomas, then the Court must necessarily have upheld the federal government's interpretation of the Controlled Substances Act, since the federal government

---

[6] *Washington v. Glucksberg* at 735, quoted in *Gonzales v. Oregon* at 249.
[7] 545 U.S. 1 (2005).

certainly had greater power to interpret its own statutes than it had to limit actions of the states under the Constitution. Thus, *Raich* should have predetermined the result in *Gonzales v. Oregon*, according to Thomas. But it didn't.

Gonzales was crucial to the slow but steady acceptance by the states of the Court's invitation in *Glucksberg* to serve as a laboratory for social change. At the time, Oregon was the only state that had legalized assisted suicide. One more vote from the Supreme Court, and assisted suicide would have been impossible in Oregon and foreclosed anywhere else.

In the ten years since *Gonzales,* four more states (Washington, Montana, Vermont, and California) have legalized assisted suicide, which is 10% of all the states in the union. Some states adopted assisted suicide through legislation; others through citizen ballot initiatives, and still others by way of the courts. This chapter examines how these states came to legalize assisted suicide, the legal ramifications of permitting assisted suicide, and what the experience of these laboratories has to tell the rest of us.

When Gatekeepers Collide: The Story of Michael Freeland

Let us begin with the story of Michael Freeland. After his mother committed suicide when he was 21, Mr. Freeland struggled with depression. He made several suicide attempts, and had been hospitalized in a psychiatric facility. His last psychiatric hospitalization was in January 2002. Before he returned home, local authorities entered his house and removed thirty-two guns and thousands of rounds of ammunition.[8] By that point, however, Mr. Freeland, who had been diagnosed with terminal lung cancer in late 2000, had also accumulated a cache of lethal drugs, which he had obtained legally under Oregon's Death with Dignity Act in early 2001. When the guns (which he apparently also owned legally) were removed, the drugs, which were also discovered, were left in place because he had obtained them through the Death with Dignity statute. Around that time, a judge had declared Mr. Freeland incompetent and appointed a temporary guardian for a month. The guardianship lapsed before anyone could figure out what to do about the drugs.

We know all of this because right after his cancer diagnosis, Mr. Freeland, in search of a doctor to prescribe him lethal medication, mistakenly called an *anti*-assisted-suicide group (Physicians for Compassionate Care) instead of a *pro*-assisted-suicide group (Compassion in Dying[9]). A social worker and her

---

[8] John Schwartz, *Opponents of Oregon Suicide Law Say Depressed Man Was Wrongly Given Drugs*, N. Y. TIMES, May 7, 2004, www.nytimes.com/2004/05/07/national/07SUIC.html.

[9] Known since its merger with the Hemlock Society in 2007 as Compassion & Choices.

physician husband at Physicians for Compassionate Care tried to talk him out of suicide, and ended up befriending him.[10] However, he subsequently called the right number and was seen by Dr. Peter Reagan, who interviewed him, found him competent, and provided the prescription. Although people are only supposed to receive the prescriptions if they have six months to live, Dr. Reagan offered to renew Mr. Freeland's prescription if he lasted longer than six months.

Mr. Freeland entered hospice, then stopped hospice services because he felt they were trying to give him morphine when he didn't need it. When his pain returned, he called his friends at Physicians for Compassionate Care, who took steps to ensure alleviation of his pain. In fact, Mr. Freeland, who had lethal doses of drugs available to him for nearly two years, never used them. He died of lung cancer on December 5, 2002.

Physicians for Compassionate Care apparently sought and received permission from Mr. Freeland to release and publicize his records after his death. They publicized his story through a piece in the *American Journal of Psychiatry*.[11] As opponents of assisted suicide, they asserted that a depressed man with a history of suicide attempts sneaked through the screening mechanisms for assisted suicide, and claimed that his story showed the perils of the project and the inadequacy of screening. Advocates for assisted suicide, on the other hand, embraced Mr. Freeland as a success story: Dr. Reagan's judgment that Mr. Freeland was not suicidally depressed was vindicated by the fact that he did not take his lethal dose of medication rashly and impulsively (or at all).

As I write this, the Oregon Department of Health's website contains a page explaining to people how they can avail themselves of assisted suicide. A different page on the same website declares that Oregon has prioritized suicide prevention as part of its state policy. If two people in Oregon on the same day each take the same quantity of the same prescription pills, each with the identical intention of ending his or her life, and they are discovered to have done so, one will be taken by ambulance to an emergency department and may have his or her stomach pumped or be involuntarily committed to a psychiatric ward. The other will not only be permitted to die but the death that he or she caused and intended won't even be recorded as suicide. The only difference is that in one case a doctor ratified the decision and in the other case, the doctor did not. The degree of significance to attribute to the doctor's ratification is a question that is not often raised.

I know what you're thinking: the major difference is that one person is terminally ill. But a terminally ill person who hoards pills to commit suicide,

---

[10] N. Gregory Hamilton & Catherine A. Hamilton, *Competing Paradigms of Response to Assisted Suicide Requests in Oregon*, 162 Am. J. Psychiatry 1060, 1062 (2005).

[11] *Id.*

and takes them without the blessing of a medical professional, is also going to be taken by ambulance to a hospital and treated for the suicide attempt, even against his or her will.[12] On the other hand, as we have seen with Michael Freeland, an allegedly suicidal man who gets the blessing of the assisted-suicide program will be permitted to keep lethal medication even as firearms are removed by the dozen from his house.

As I discussed in Chapter 1, some medical professionals believe that a terminally ill individual who attempts suicide is incompetent to refuse treatment aimed at counteracting the suicide attempt, while simultaneously being competent to refuse treatment for the terminal illness. Perhaps this should not be surprising: it's only been about thirty years that terminally ill people have even had the right to refuse treatment for the condition that makes them terminally ill (see Chapter 2). Now they can ask for medicine to commit suicide and receive it, at least in five states. The experience in these states is both reassuring and cautionary, but it tells us very little about what will happen now that a huge state with urban centers numbering in the millions— California —has legalized assisted suicide.

Overview of States Where Assisted Suicide Is Legal

Oregon and Washington legalized physician-assisted suicide through voter referenda in 1994[13] and 2009,[14] respectively. On May 20, 2013, Vermont became the first state to pass a statute legalizing physician-assisted suicide. Montana is widely believed to have legalized physician-assisted suicide through its 2009 Supreme Court decision, *Baxter v. State*, which held that under certain circumstances, physicians charged criminally or civilly with assisting a terminally ill mentally competent patient's death could offer the defense that the patient consented and, more importantly,[15] that application

---

[12] Cathleen F. Crowley, *Terminally-Ill Cancer Patient Revived After Suicide Attempt*, TIMES UNION, Sept. 25, 2011, http://blog.timesunion.com/healthcare/ terminally-ill-cancer-patient-revived-after-suicide-attempt/2874/; MARGARET M. BARRON, CASE STUDY: A TERMINALLY ILL SUICIDE PATIENT IN THE ED, CATHOLIC HEALTH ASSOCIATION OF THE UNITED STATES (2011), https://www. chausa.org/docs/default-source/general-files/case-study---a-terminally-ill-suicide-attempt-patient-in-the-ed-pdf.pdf?sfvrsn=0.

[13] Oregon's Ballot Initiative was stayed because of court action, see pp. 142–143, *infra*. Later the legislature attempted to repeal the ballot initiative through another ballot initiative. When voters rejected this in 1997, Oregon began implementing its assisted-suicide program, see *infra*.

[14] Washington tried, and failed, to pass a ballot initiative in 1991.

[15] More important in the sense that in assisted suicide prosecutions, the consent of the person committing suicide is presumed; in the absence of patient consent, the charge would not be "assisting suicide" but murder.

of the consent defense in such a case would not necessarily be a violation of public policy.[16] Recently, an appellate court in New Mexico rejected a state constitutional right to assisted suicide; that decision is currently pending in the New Mexico Supreme Court, which will likely decide the issue as this book goes to press.

In a less publicized decision, the Georgia Supreme Court struck down the law that criminalized assisted suicide on First Amendment grounds because the act of promoting suicide was an element of the crime.[17] Because the crime of assisting suicide was inextricably intertwined with the criminalizing the action of an individual "publicly advertis[ing], offer[ing] or hold[ing] . . . out as offering that he or she will intentionally and actively assist another person in the commission of suicide and commits any overt act to further that purpose," the court held that the entire statute must be struck down.[18] However, the Georgia Supreme Court made it clear that this was a First Amendment decision, and that the *act* of assisting suicide itself could still be criminalized if the legislature saw fit to do so.[19] Less than three months later, the Georgia legislature hastened to enact legislation banning assisted suicide.[20]

---

[16] Baxter v. Montana, 354 Mont. 254 (2009). Although many other courts have considered arguments that physician assisted suicide is a right protected by the state constitution, all other state supreme courts considering the issue have rejected the argument, preferring to leave it to the legislative process (Alaska, Krischer v. McIver, 697 So.2d 97 (Fla. 1997) (upholding state legislative prohibition on assisted suicide against constitutional challenge). This approach has also been adopted by lower courts that considered the issue, Blick v. Office of the Div. of Crim. Justice, 2010 Conn. Super. LEXIS 1412 (Ct. Super. June 2, 2010). Federal courts have taken a more divided approach. Several federal courts have held that there is a right to assisted suicide, but the Supreme Court reversed these decisions (see Chapter 2). Other courts have refused to consider challenges to assisted suicide statutes in the absence of criminal prosecution, concluding that the issue was not ripe for resolution, Cooley v. Granholm, 291 F.3d 880 (6th Cir. 2002).

[17] This case and others like it is discussed in detail in Chapter 7.

[18] Final Exit Network v. State, 290 So.2d 508 (Ga. 2012). In 1994, the Georgia legislature passed a law criminalizing publicly advertising, offering, or holding oneself out as offering to intentionally and actively assist another person commit suicide, combined with any overt act to further the purpose of intentionally and actively assisting another person to commit suicide. Ga. Code Ann.§ 16-5-5(b). The first time prosecutors attempted to enforce this statute, sixteen years later, it was successfully challenged and struck down by the Georgia Supreme Court as being a content-based restriction on speech in violation of both the state and federal constitutions. *Final Exit Network v. State.*

[19] The Minnesota Supreme Court also invalidated a conviction for assisted suicide based on First Amendment grounds, finding the statute's prohibition against advising or encouraging suicide too broad, but upholding the part of the law that criminalized actually assisting the suicide, State v. Melchert-Dinkel, 844 N.W.2d 13 (Minn. 2014). This decision is discussed in detail in Chapter 7.

[20] H.B. 1114, enacted as O.C.G.A. §16-5-5 (2015).

It is no surprise that Georgia acted so briskly to renew its ban on assisted suicide. Even the states that permit physician-assisted suicide[21] both civilly commit suicidal people and criminalize assisted suicide by anyone other than a physician. Unlike some countries in Europe,[22] where family and friends can, under some circumstances, assist someone to commit suicide and where the law explicitly frowns on physician involvement in suicide,[23] in the United States, only doctors can legally assist suicides. Even though other professionals have authority to prescribe medications in states such as Oregon, only doctors can prescribe lethal medications under Oregon's Death with Dignity Act.[24] But this is not because in the United States we have supreme trust in our doctors. Unlike some European countries permitting physician involvement in suicide,[25] the five states permitting physician-assisted suicide absolutely prohibit euthanasia: the physician is prohibited from administering the deadly dose.

Oregon's law is the oldest in the country. It was passed in 1994, but was not implemented until 1997.[26] Most state initiatives since then have been patterned on Oregon's law as a model. When Vermont was considering an assisted suicide initiative of its own, it commissioned a study of outcomes in Oregon.[27] Other versions of a model assisted suicide law have been offered,[28] but most states prefer to pattern their proposals on Oregon's program.

Voters and citizens in many states have attempted to legalize assisted suicide for decades. From the first ballot initiative in California in 1988 to the most recent initiatives in Massachusetts,[29] from the first legislative proposal

---

[21] MCA 45-5-10 (2013).

[22] As in Great Britain and Switzerland, see Chapter 4.

[23] As in Great Britain, see Chapter 4.

[24] For example, nurse practitioners can prescribe medication in Oregon, but cannot prescribe under the Death with Dignity Act, OREGON STATE BOARD OF NURSING, PRESCRIPTIVE AUTHORITY IN OREGON: FOR ADVANCED PRACTICE NURSES (2013), www. Oregon.gov/OSBN/pdfs/publications/prescriptive_booklet.pdf.

[25] See Chapter 4.

[26] Initially, the initiative was blocked by the federal court in Lee v. Oregon, 891 F.Supp. 1429 (D. Ore. 1995). This is discussed more fully below.

[27] ROBIN LUNGE, MARIA ROYLE, & MICHAEL SLATER, OREGON'S DEATH WITH DIGNITY LAW AND EUTHANASIA IN THE NETHERLANDS: FACTUAL DISPUTES (Vermont Legislative Council 2004), *available at* www.leg.state.vt.us/reports/04death/death_with_dignity_report.htm.

[28] C.H. Baron, Clyde Bergstresser, D.W. Brock, G.F. Cole, *et. al.* "Model State Statute to Authorize and Regulate Physician-Assisted Suicide," 33 Harv. J. Legis. 1 (1996). This model is broader than the Oregon model in that it permits assisted suicide in the case of incurable conditions where the competent individual experienced intractable and unbearable suffering, *id.* at 11-12; it imposed more conditions than the Oregon model in that it required mental health assessments of all individuals seeking assisted suicide. *Id.* at 16.

[29] After Question 2, a ballot initiative, failed in 2012, bills to legalize assisted suicide failed in the Massachusetts Legislature. The most recent bill, House 1991,

in Ohio in 1906 to the most recent legislation passed in California, from the earliest court cases in Michigan, Florida, and Alaska to more recent ones in Connecticut and California, almost all have failed. Between 1991 and 2011, twenty-five states introduced 122 legislative proposals to legalize assisted suicide.[30] Since 2011, two states have legalized assisted suicide: Vermont in 2013 and California in 2015.

Parsing the historical record of attempts to pass assisted suicide ballot initiatives and laws over the years paints a fascinating picture of American values and assumptions. Understanding the assisted suicide debate requires understanding the conflicted American attitude toward both suicide and physicians, as well as recognizing the fundamental power of language and how it has been deployed in this debate.

American Attitudes Toward Suicide, Physician-Assisted Suicide and Euthanasia: The Importance of Language

Basically, Americans deeply disapprove of suicide, except when they empathize with the reasons behind it. When ending one's life is understandable, we call it by some other name than suicide. One proponent in England rejected the word because "suicide is an irrational thing, whereas I think that for some people asking for an assisted death is a very rational thing."[31] One of the drafters of the Oregon Death with Dignity statute rejected the term because "if a person's death is imminent and inevitable, calling it suicide is a grave disservice. 'Would we say the people who jumped from the World Trade Center were committing suicide?' she asks. 'I wouldn't, because the fire was in their face and they chose a different kind of death.'"[32]

If people who jumped from the World Trade Center were not committing suicide, it's not because they chose a different kind of death. The people who jumped from the World Trade Center might have been desperately seizing an infinitesimal chance of survival. The crux of suicide is the desire that

---

was introduced into the Massachusetts Legislature on January 15, 2015. An emotional hearing was held on this bill on October 27, 2015, http://newbostonpost. com/2015/10/27/assisted-suicide-bill-draws-heartfelt-testimony-pro-and-con/

[30] See PATIENT RIGHTS COUNCIL, ATTEMPTS TO LEGALIZE EUTHANASIA/ASSISTED SUICIDE IN THE UNITED STATES (2011), www.patientsrightscouncil.org/site/wp-content/uploads/2011/03/201103_Attempts_to_Legalize_Assisted_Suicide.pdf.

[31] *Discworld's Terry Pratchett on Death and Deciding* (NPR, Aug. 11, 2011) www.npr.org/2011/08/11/139262401/discworlds-terry-pratchett-on-death-and-deciding?ps=rs.

[32] Julie Sabatier, *Assisted Suicide Advocate Uses Law to End His Life* (NPR, Mar. 12, 2012), http://www.npr.org/2012/03/12/148459270/assisted-suicide-   advocate-uses-law-to-end-his-life.

one's actions or omissions lead to one's death.[33] That's why physician assisted suicide is clearly suicide. The person may prefer to live without a terminal illness and great suffering, but if the person chooses death over his or her current, actual life situation, the person is committing suicide.

These linguistic issues matter a great deal, as we shall see later in this chapter. Plaintiffs in recent cases have argued that they have a state constitutional right to physician aid in dying precisely because it is not suicide,[34] a strategy born of the U.S. Supreme Court's decision in *Washington v. Glucksberg*.[35] Suicide, from the point of view of Americans, is a rejection of the blessings and opportunities of life, and they disapprove of it. Thus, polls show strong opposition in the U.S. to suicide, mixed support for physician-assisted suicide, and strong support for both assisted suicide and euthanasia when neither the words "suicide" or "euthanasia" are used.

Americans understand suicide in the case of people who are suffering from a terminal illness at the end of life or when people are elderly and facing deterioration, or when they are adults of any age with a severe physical disability, especially those who are permanently dependent on mechanical assistance to stay alive. This latter kind of understanding makes some disabled Americans very, very nervous.

Because all of these understandable reasons relate to the depredations on quality of life and autonomy caused by medical conditions (unlike understandable, "rational" suicides of the past, which involved financial reversals and loss of honor due to rape, criminal accusations, or shameful failures[36]), Americans want physician ratification of life-ending decisions.

---

[33] Obviously, people may be indifferent to their survival, or conflicted about it, and flirt with death, or find comfort in the idea of death, or change their minds from week to week or even day to day about their own intentions and desires. But, as the World Health Organization says, the definition of suicide is "as an act deliberately initiated and performed by a person in the full knowledge or expectation of its fatal outcome." *Suicide, in* OECD FACTBOOK 2013: ECONOMIC, ENVIRONMENTAL AND SOCIAL STATISTICS (Organisation for Economic Cooperation and Development, Jan. 9, 2013, www.oecd-ilibrary.org/sites/factbook-2013-en/12/01/03/index.html/ . Physician-assisted suicide surely fits this definition of suicide.

[34] Morris et al v. Brandenburg, No. D-202-CV 2012-02909 (Dist. Ct. Bernalillo Cty Jan. 13, 2014). See also Erik Eckholm, *New Mexico Judge Affirms Right to "Aid in Dying,"* N. Y. TIMES, Jan. 13, 2014, www.nytimes.com/2014/01/14/us/new-mexico-judge-affirms-right-to-aid-in-dying.html?_r=0.

[35] See Chapter 2 for an extensive discussion of this case.

[36] When a bridge collapsed in 1876 in Ashtabula, Ohio, sending a train into a ravine and killing 92, the bridge's chief engineer committed suicide, even though the bridge's failure implicated Amasa Stone, the railroad manager who had ignored the engineer's urgings to use a shorter span. Seven years later, several steel mills owned by Stone failed, and he in turn committed suicide, leaving his fortune to his wife and two daughters, one of whom was married to John Hay. *Amasa Stone, in* ENCYCLOPEDIA OF CLEVELAND HISTORY, http://ech.cwru.edu/ech-cgi/article.pl?id=SA8. A famous case, appearing in many criminal law textbooks,

Physician-assisted suicide tells Americans that a doctor has concluded that both the individual and his or her decision to end life are rational.

Physicians themselves generally support assisted suicide in some individual cases at their own individual discretion, but are resistant to formalizing or legalizing assisted suicide.[37] In every ballot initiative or case of proposed legislation except in Oregon and California, the state medical society has vigorously opposed physician-assisted suicide, even while many individual physicians in the state acknowledge having participated or assisted their patients to die on an individual basis.

But as we saw in the last chapter, the majority opinion in the medical and psychiatric professions does not necessarily rule. Just as some psychiatrists are perfectly happy to predict future dangerousness when the American Psychiatric Association asserts that there is no evidentiary support for such predictions, a small group of physicians who ardently favor assisted suicide can (and do) essentially operate the assisted suicide program in any state that passes such legislation. I am not suggesting that physicians who participate in assisted suicide programs are fraudulent in the same way as psychiatrists who predict future dangerousness in death penalty cases without seeing the inmate. I am only saying that in both these situations, a small minority of the medical profession is all that is needed to keep a controversial social practice flourishing.

There can be no doubt that Americans viscerally disapprove of suicide. The Gallup poll has been conducting an annual poll on American Values and Beliefs since 2001. In that poll, Americans are asked whether a number of practices are "morally acceptable." According to this poll, the vast majority of Americans have always found suicide to be morally unacceptable. The most recent poll results, in 2014, showed 81% of Americans felt that suicide was not morally acceptable.[38] For the last twelve years, the number of Americans who think "suicide" is morally acceptable has ranged between 12% and 19%. In 2014, suicide was barely more acceptable than "polygamy" (86% disapproved) and "cloning humans" (87%).[39] It is this stigma and disapproval that

---

Stephenson v. State, involves the second-degree murder conviction of a man who abducted and raped a woman who subsequently committed suicide. Rape victims are still thirteen times more likely to attempt suicide than people who have not been raped, Dean G. Kilpatrick, *The Mental Health Impact of Rape*, MEDICAL UNIVERSITY OF SOUTH CAROLINA, NATIONAL VIOLENCE AGAINST WOMEN PREVENTION RESEARCH CENTER (2000), https://mainweb-v.musc.edu/vawprevention/research/mentalimpact.shtml.

[37] See Chapter 5 for detailed discussion of physicians and their attitudes and practices relating to assisted suicide.

[38] Rebecca Riffkin, *New Record Highs in Moral Acceptability*, May 30, 2014, www.gallup.com/poll//170789/new-record-highs-moral-acceptability.aspx (last visited July 1, 2014).

[39] *Id.* For the record, the activity most widely believed to be morally unacceptable was "married men and women having an affair," which 93% of respondents considered morally unacceptable.

advocates of physician-assisted suicide seek to avoid when they seek to use other terms, such as "death with dignity," and "aid in dying," and it is one of the reasons why all assisted suicide legislative and ballot proposals insist that a physician-assisted death cannot be recorded as a "suicide" on the death certificate.[40]

The moral acceptability of physician-assisted suicide and euthanasia is a much closer call, with 51% of Americans finding it morally acceptable in 2014. This very close margin led Gallup to call physician-assisted suicide the moral issue on which Americans are most divided in 2011,[41] and in 2014 it remained one of the two most contentious moral issues in American society (abortion is the other).[42] What is the difference between "suicide," which is so stigmatized that supporters of physician-assisted suicide don't even want to use the word "suicide" in describing their proposals, and "physician-assisted suicide," which is currently legal in five states? Clearly, the difference between "suicide" and "physician-assisted suicide" lies in the modifier: "physician-assisted." Having a physician approve of your plans to end your life to the extent of giving you a helping hand is worth about a 30% lift in moral approval.

If you add to this by taking out the stigmatized word "suicide," you can get a 70% approval rating in the polls for euthanasia, which is the percentage of Americans responding favorably to the question, "When a person has a disease that cannot be cured, do you think doctors should be allowed to end the patient's life by some painless means if the patient and his or her family request it?" These numbers drop substantially—to 56%—if essentially the same question is asked using the word "suicide": "When a person has a disease that cannot be cured and is in severe pain, do you think doctors should or should not be allowed by law to assist the patient to commit suicide if the patient requests it?"[43] Some might conclude that these poll results demonstrate that the American people support euthanasia more than they support assisted suicide. I conclude that they show that the American people reflexively oppose anything with the word "suicide" in it.

But our distaste for suicide is ameliorated to a great degree if a physician is introduced into the equation, because we believe that "physician assistance" serves as a proxy for the existence of certain greatly limiting factors—terminal illness, great suffering—associated with physician-assisted suicide. On a deeper level, however, I would argue that physician assistance

---

[40] The other reason for the death certificate provisions is to enable survivors to collect life insurance proceeds, as well as ensuring that doctors will not be prosecuted for assisting a suicide.

[41] http://www.gallup.com/poll/147842/doctor-assisted-suicide-moral-issue-dividing-americans.aspx (2011).

[42] Riffkin, *supra* note 38.

[43] Gallup Poll, May 31, 2007. http://www.gallup.com/poll/27727/public-divided-over-moral-acceptability-doctorassisted-suicide.aspx

is most important as a proxy for competence or the "rationality" of the individual committing suicide: if it's okay with the physicians, it must be rational and understandable. In effect, we trust physicians to share our general moral disapproval of suicide; the physician serves as the cultural gatekeeper for acceptable suicide.

But the moral transformation is even greater than simply an assurance of rationality. People who avail themselves of physician-assisted suicide, which involves painless ingestion of pills, are routinely described as "courageous,"[44] whereas people who hang or shoot themselves (which can be much more painful forms of death and certainly require more of the individual involved) are often called "cowards."[45] In fact, a Fox news commentator briefly generated a firestorm of public rage by calling Robin Williams, who hanged himself, a coward.[46] No one called Brittany Maynard (the young woman who used assisted suicide to end her life after a diagnosis of terminal brain cancer) a coward—quite the opposite.

Physicians serving as the gatekeepers of assisted suicide would have been unthinkable fifty years ago. This situation is only possible because of the decades of court cases described in Chapter 2. Without them, few doctors would have been willing to assist suicide because of both ethical and liability concerns. Although nothing about the phrasing of the Gallup poll's question precludes it, there is also an absolute cultural understanding in the United States that the "incurable disease" in the question about euthanasia is not a mental illness and that the physician assisting a suicide is not a psychiatrist. Psychiatrists are physicians, but in the United States, psychiatrist-assisted suicide is unthinkable (although certainly not in Europe, as we will see in Chapter 4). In the United States, the professional culture for physicians has evolved to the point where physicians are permitted to acknowledge to their patients that they have hopeless conditions that can no longer be treated (or cannot be treated without enormous suffering). This only happened recently: as we saw in Chapter 2, for most of history a doctor generally did not tell patients that their conditions were hopeless or that they were going to die. U.S. physicians can help their patients die without being accused of failure or murder, although most physician-assisted suicide in this country is done quietly and unofficially.

---

[44] *In re* New York City Asbestos Litigation, Lori Konopka-Sauer et al. v. Colgate-Palmolive, 32 Misc. 3d 161, 921 N.Y.S.2d 466, 471 (N.Y. Sup. Ct. N.Y. Cty 2011).

[45] This attitude dates back thousands of years: Plato, Aristotle, and Plutarch all condemned suicide as cowardly, see Alan H. Marks, *Historical Suicide*, *in* HANDBOOK OF DEATH AND DYING 310 (Clifton Bryant, ed. Sage 2003). These philosophers compared suicide to a soldier abandoning his post in battle.

[46] Elias Isquith, *Fox News' Shep Smith: Robin Williams Was "Such a Coward,"* SALON, Aug. 12, 2014, http://www.salon.com/2014/08/12/fox_news_shep_smith_robin_williams_was_such_a_coward/. Smith later apologized for his remarks.

The culture in which psychiatrists operate is far different. Although some psychiatric patients used to be called "chronic" and the "back wards" of hospitals were reserved for "incurable" patients, the currently favored recovery model posits that anyone can recover from a mental illness. It is very difficult to imagine a psychiatrist saying to a patient that his or her condition is hopeless. In fact, patients who are not helped by treatment are called "treatment-resistant" and "refractory," as though it was their fault. Some psychiatrists who wish to avoid chronically and unremittingly suicidal patients tell them their conditions are too "complex" for that particular psychiatrist's skills to manage, but implicitly, there is a better equipped mental health professional waiting in the wings who *can* help. But assisting or even understanding and supporting a patient's suicide? This is not in the realm of possibility for psychiatrists, even psychiatrists whose patients are suffering a terminal medical illness. Physicians can, under assisted suicide programs, support patients and their families to achieve the patient's stated desire to die. A psychiatrist, being a physician, could theoretically fulfill this role, but in fact, under the Oregon and other models, psychiatrists and other mental health professionals lurk in the background as a potential veto, the only individuals in the entire framework with the power to defeat the will of the patient, his or her family, and two physicians. Mental health professionals are theoretically the final gatekeepers of assisted suicide, and they are known to oppose suicide. It is no wonder that the physicians involved in assisted suicide, who by definition support the concept, rarely refer their patients for mental health evaluation. The structure is troubling on both ends: the physicians involved, often members of Compassion & Choices, have one agenda that may cloud their judgment, and the psychiatrists, on the other end of the spectrum, have a professional perspective that may equally bias them in the opposite direction. The individual patient, whose autonomy is supposedly so crucial to assisted suicide, is pretty much at the mercy of the doctors, the very situation assisted suicide is supposed to alleviate.

Americans' comfort level with physician-assisted suicide is striking. It reflects an abstract faith in a physician's objectivity to make doctors the gatekeepers for assisted suicide. This trust does not change even when people are confronted with physicians who operate beyond the fringes of professional ethics. Dr. Jack Kevorkian never lost the support of a majority of Americans, even after he lost his medical license. This public support continued after his criminal conviction for murdering a patient.[47]

Even so, there is a very clear limit on Americans' trust of physicians, and it is strikingly different from the attitude of many Europeans.[48] Americans will not countenance a formal, legalized program of euthanasia, where a

---

[47] In 1999, 55% of Americans thought Kevorkian should not be imprisoned; eight years later, 53% still supported him, Associated Press, *Americans Still Split on Doctor-Assisted Suicide*, May 29, 2007, www.nbcnews.com/id/18923323/ns/health-health_care/Americans-still-split-doctor-assisted-suicide.

[48] See Chapter 4.

doctor injects a patient with drugs to end his or her life. Many Europeans prefer this method because it is believed to be safer, more effective, and less prone to abuse.[49] As the next section illustrates, assisted suicide initiatives got nowhere in the United States until euthanasia was dropped as an option.

History of Assisted Suicide and Euthanasia Initiatives

From the 1870s until the 1990s

For well over 150 years, all efforts and discussion around legalizing physician-assisted suicide involved euthanasia. The advent of anaesthesia suggested to Samuel Williams in the 1870s that a combination of ether and morphine could be used to painlessly end the life of patients who were mortally ill and suffering.[50] For many years, euthanasia was the exclusive focus of proponents of assisted suicide, perhaps because a person ending his or her own life— suicide—was so stigmatized. The first attempt to legalize euthanasia was in Ohio in 1906. There was also a great debate in Iowa in 1906 about assisted suicide. The legislature rejected the Ohio bill.

In 1909, the territory of Hawaii passed a statute providing that "nothing shall forbid any person from giving or furnishing any remedial agent or measure" to be given to patients when so requested by or on behalf of the affected person if they are certified in writing to be "hopeless and beyond recovery."[51] Although sometimes cited as an assisted suicide statute, the Attorney General of Hawaii issued an opinion in 2011 that in fact this legislation was intended to provide legal immunity to healers providing novel or herbal treatments to the incurably ill, including in particular people with leprosy on the island of Molokai.[52]

In 1915, a doctor's acknowledgment that he had permitted a deformed baby to die—the famous "Black Stork" case—was nationally publicized and debated; the doctor's actions were generally regarded with revulsion. Nevertheless, as is common in economic hard times, the euthanasia debate revived considerably during the world Depression. In 1936 and 1937, bills

---

[49] *Id.*

[50] Ezekiel Emmanuel, *Whose Right to Die?* 279 ATLANTIC MONTHLY 73 (Mar. 1997); MICHAEL MANNING, EUTHANASIA AND PHYSICIAN-ASSISTED SUICIDE: KILLING OR CARING? (1988).

[51] HAW. REV. STAT. § 453-1.

[52] *See,* Letter from Heidi M. Rian, Deputy Attorney General, State of Hawaii, to Hon. Joshua Booth Green, M.D., Senator, Third District, Hawaii (Dec. 8, 2011), http://choiceisanillusion.files.wordpress.com/2011/12/ag_opinion_as_not_legal.pdf. (Attorney General's opinion regarding Hawaii Statute § 453-1, stating that the statute does not authorize physicians to assist terminally ill patients with dying).

legalizing euthanasia were introduced into the national legislative bodies of England and the United States, the latter by Senator John Comstock.[53] In 1939, the Euthanasia Society drafted a "painless killing" law, which was described by the *New York Times* under the headline " 'Mercy Death' Law Proposed in State."[54] Prefiguring later debates about language, the Euthanasia Society took exception to the use of the words "killing" and "death" as too "sinister" and suggested that euthanasia should be described as a "merciful release."[55]

Although Dr. Joseph Fletcher publicized the right to die in the 1960s, and Senator Frank Church held hearings on "Death with Dignity,"[56] the first attempt to legalize assisted suicide in modern times was the "Humane and Dignified Death Act," introduced as a citizen's ballot initiative in California in 1988, which would have legalized euthanasia and assisted suicide under the name, "aid-in-dying." This failed to gain enough signatures to be placed on the California ballot, perhaps in part because "aid in dying" in combination with euthanasia apparently had unfortunate connotations for many voters.[57] The euthanasia initiative was not helped by the infamous "It's Over, Debbie" article published the same year in the *Journal of the American Medical Association* by an anonymous gynecology resident who took it upon himself to give a fatal dose of morphine to a twenty-year-old woman dying of ovarian cancer whom he had never previously met because she had looked at him and said, "Let's get this over with."[58] He reported doing this without taking the precaution of checking with her to make sure they were both on the same page about her desires and intentions. Even the most ardent advocates of euthanasia were shocked by "It's Over Debbie."[59]

---

[53] Bryan Hilliard, *The Moral and Legal Status of Physician-Assisted Death: Quality of Life and the Patient-Physician Relationship*, 18 ISSUES IN INTEGRATIVE STUDIES 45, 50 (2000). http://www.oakland.edu/upload/docs/AIS/Issues%20 in%20Interdisciplinary%20Studies/2000%20Volume%2018/06_Vol_18_pp_ 45_63_The_Moral_and_Legal_Status_of_Physician-Assisted_Death_Quality_ Of_Life_and_the_Patient-Physician_Relationship_(Bryan_Hilliard).pdf

[54] *Mercy Death' Law Proposed in State*, N. Y. TIMES, Jan. 27, 1939, at 21.

[55] Letter to the Editor from Charles E. Nixdorff, Treasurer of the Euthanasia Society, *Explaining Euthanasia*, N. Y. TIMES, Jan. 30, 1939, at 12.

[56] *Death with Dignity: An Inquiry into Related Public Issues. Hearings before the Special Commission on Aging*, U.S. Senate, 92nd Cong. 2d Sess. Part 2. Aug. 8, 1972; IAN DOWBIGGAN, A MERCIFUL END: THE EUTHANASIA MOVEMENT IN AMERICA (2003).

[57] R. L. Marker & W. J. Smith, *The Art of Verbal Engineering*, 35 DUQ. L. REV. 1, 81–107 (1996).

[58] *It's Over, Debbie*, 759 J. AM. MED. ASSOC. 272 (1988).

[59] Isabel Wilkerson, "Essay on Mercy Killing Reflects Conflicts on Ethics for Physicians and Journalists," New York Times, Feb. 23, 1988, http://www. nytimes.com/1988/02/23/us/essay-mercy-killing-reflects-conflict-ethics-for-physicians-journalists.html?pagewanted=all

In 1991, Washington's Initiative 119, which would also have permitted euthanasia, was defeated. Backers of the initiative acknowledged that its opponents used the potential for euthanasia to help defeat it. Karen Cooper, the I-119 Initiative campaign director, admitted that initiative proponents knowingly obscured the part of the initiative that included lethal injections by physicians.[60] She concluded that this strategy was a mistake, and others agreed: "including injections in the proposed laws and calling them 'aid in dying' gave salience to opposition arguments that proponents were attempting to put one over the electorate."[61] An advertisement in Washington, for example, featured a middle-aged nurse speaking directly to the camera: "I'm a hospice nurse . . . Initiative 119 would let doctors kill my patients."[62] Another ad was even more blunt: "No special qualifications are required: Your eye doctor could kill you."[63]

Other opponents of the Washington initiative warned of the potentials of coercion of vulnerable populations: "There are no rules against coercion, i.e., nothing to prevent 'selling the idea' to the aged, the poor, and the homeless;" and "There are no reporting requirements: No record keeping required."[64] These ads reflected a number of specific concerns about the Washington initiative: it did not define the type of physician who could provide assisted suicide, there was no requirement for psychological evaluations, and there was no specified waiting period between the time the patient asks for assistance and their actual death.[65] According to Derek Humphry, the famed founder of the Hemlock Society, Washington's initiative failed because:

> [The campaigners] made the tactical mistake of painting their law with a broad brush, intending to sit down with the medical and legal profession after victory to hammer out the detailed guidelines under which euthanasia could be carried out. But the

---

[60] D. Hillyard & J. Dombrink, Dying Right: The Death with Dignity Movement (2001).

[61] Id. See also Mark O'Keefe, Assisted-Suicide Measure Survives Heavy Opposition, Oregonian (Portland), Nov. 10, 1994 ("In California, the 'chilling television commercial image of a hypodermic needle and the words 'death by mistake' struck fear into voters.").

[62] T. Egan, Washington Voters Weigh Aid of Doctors in Suicide, N. Y. Times, Oct. 14, 1991, http://www.nytimes.com/1991/10/14/us/washington-voters-weigh-aid-of-doctors-in-suicide.html?pagewanted=all&src=pm.

[63] R. Carson, Washington's I-119, 22 Hastings Center Rep. 2, 7–9 (1992).

[64] D. W. Cox, Hemlock's Cup: The Struggle for Death with Dignity 167–68 (1993).

[65] N. J. Crutchfield, To Succeed or Not to Succeed: How Do Political Influences, Culture, and Demographics of a State Affect the Passing of Physician Assisted Suicide Initiatives? (Dec. 19, 2008) (unpublished Ph.D. dissertation, Auburn University).

public did not want euthanasia laws on the books without built-in safeguards—a sign of the general distrust of the medical and legal professions.[66]

It is also worth noting that the Washington vote on Initiative 119 took place shortly after Dr. Jack Kevorkian enabled the suicides of two women with nonterminal illnesses. Marjory Wantz and Sherry Miller died together on October 23, 1991. They were the second and third individuals to use Kevorkian's services.[67]

The following year, California advocates of assisted suicide tried again with Proposition 161 ("Death with Dignity Act"), permitting "aid-in-dying," which similarly would have permitted either euthanasia or assisted suicide, and qualified for the ballot. Despite early polling showing the measure was supported by 68% of the electorate, it ultimately failed, when voters rejected it by 54% to 46%.[68] This is a common sequence in assisted suicide ballot measures: strong early approval from the public, which wanes in the face of vigorous campaigns by religious organizations, disability organizations, and organized medicine.

The disconnect between poll results and the failure of assisted suicide ballot and statutory proposals may be attributable to the fact that the medical profession can influence one kind of poll—voting on a ballot—far more than it can influence the results in the polls taken by Gallup. The medical profession's influence on public policy relating to end-of-life decisions has been crucial.[69] Assisted suicide would not have been possible without medical support for treatment refusal at the end of life, and treatment refusal at the end of life would not have gained the wide consensus of support it enjoys without concrete reassurances from state legislatures and courts that medical professionals would not be civilly or criminally liable for honoring treatment refusals leading to death. It is no accident that the first approval of assisted suicide in the United States came in a state whose medical society did not opposed assisted suicide. Let us turn now to the story of assisted suicide in Oregon and what it has to tell us.

---

[66] Cox, *supra* note 64.

[67] *Kevorkian Going to Trial Fourth Time for Suicides*, N. Y. TIMES, Mar. 31, 1996, http://www.nytimes.com/1996/03/31/us/kevorkian-going-on-trial-for-4th-time-in-suicides.html. Wantz had chronic pain, which medical treatment had been unable to address. Ms. Miller had multiple sclerosis.

[68] DARYL J. MILLER, LEGAL KILLING: THE IMMINENT LEGALIZATION OF A PHYSICIAN'S AFFIRMATIVE AID-IN-DYING, 34 Santa Clara Law Rev. 663, 682 (1994).

[69] See Chapter 5.

Assisted Suicide in Oregon

The Legal and Political History of Ballot Measure 16

Following the failed attempts in Washington and California in 1988, 1991, and 1992, the Euthanasia Research and Guidance Organization (ERGO) commissioned a poll in 1993 to determine whether "euphemisms allow people to come to grips with brutal facts which, stated another way, would be repugnant to them."[70] The poll's purpose was to determine how legal reformers could best word a referendum question on assisted suicide in order to secure majority support.[71]

The poll indicated that the greatest number of respondents (65%) would favor a law using the terminology "to die with dignity."[72] Oregon reformers therefore used what Marker and Smith refer to as "the art of verbal engineering."[73] The authors of the proposed bill focused on each word used within the statute. "Aid-in-dying" was eliminated from the title of the proposed statute, the definition section, all subheadings, and the body of the measure. Phrases such as "death with dignity," "to die a dignified death," and "humane and dignified" were added. Additionally, the first five drafts contained the term "informed consent," a medical term meaning that the patient is fully informed prior to consenting to surgery or treatment, which his or her doctor has recommended. But proponents realized that the term could become questionable because it sounded as though the patient was consenting to a proposal or recommendation by the doctor to terminate his or her life, and a new term, "informed decision," was used instead.

They also looked at substantive problems that had blocked the passage of earlier initiatives. They drafted their referendum to contain a number of procedural protections missing from earlier proposals. Most of all, they remembered the opposition ads reminding voters that euthanasia meant "your doctor could kill you."[74] Early drafts of the Oregon bill (then titled, "A Bill for an Act Relating to the Rights of Patients Who Are Terminally Ill to Receive Aid-in-Dying") enabled doctors to directly end the lives of patients by lethal injection. This provision was removed[75] as the bill's supporters decided to focus on a theme of patient autonomy. The final draft provided that a doctor could write a prescription for a patient "for medication to end his or her life in a humane and dignified manner."[76] The theme of autonomy downplayed

---

[70] Marker & Smith, *supra* note 57.

[71] N. Maghami, *Universal Hemlock Care: America's Suicide Lobby*, CRC Capital Research Center (Sept. 1, 2009), http://www.capitalresearch.org/2009/09/universal-hemlock-care-americas-suicide-lobby/.

[72] *Id.*

[73] Marker & Smith, *supra* note 57.

[74] *Id.*

[75] *Id.*

[76] *See* Or. Stat. §§ 127.810–127.855. The statute references "dignified" at least eight times in the existing statutory provisions.

the role of physicians in assisting suicide and used language reminiscent of abortion rights debate. As one ad asserted:

> This is my body. I don't need you. I don't need government. I don't
> need any church playing politics with my choices, with my life.
> If I'm terminally ill, I will decide how and when and in what way
> I will end my life.[77]

Perhaps most importantly, the medical community in Oregon did not oppose Ballot Measure 16. Nor was the disability community highly visible. "[A]ctive public opposition came primarily through religious organizations arguing for the sanctity of life."[78] Even so, the margin of victory was relatively narrow: Ballot Measure 16 passed by a margin of 51% to 49% in 1994.

The case of *Lee v. Oregon* stayed the implementation of the law.[79] At the time the district court decided *Lee*, a Ninth Circuit panel had already decided *Compassion in Dying v. State of Washington*, upholding Washington's right to criminalize assisted suicide against a constitutional challenge.[80] Significantly, the crux of the plaintiff's successful challenge to the Oregon ballot initiative in *Lee* was that it unconstitutionally deprived terminally ill people in Oregon of the law's protections against committing suicide that nonterminally ill people enjoyed. These "protections" included involuntary detention and involuntary civil commitment.[81] As the court noted:

> It is "rational" to conclude that competent terminally ill persons
> may not want protection from their suicidal impulses . . .
> The problem is that the procedures designed to differentiate
> between the competent and incompetent are not sufficient . . .
> It is undisputed that one of the factors that motivates suicide is
> depression. Suicide requests may represent a plea for help by a
> distraught person in physical and emotional pain . . . Seriously ill
> people commonly suffer feelings of alienation, guilt, and feelings of
> unworthiness.[82]

The court concluded that the failure to provide for independent evaluation of people seeking assisted suicide by mental health professionals, the brevity of the fifteen-day waiting period, the lack of independent oversight by a court such as in civil commitment, and the immunization from liability for

---

77 Marker & Smith, *supra* note 57.
78 Gloria L. Krahn, *Reflections on the Debate on Disability and Aid in Dying*, 3 DISABILITY & HEALTH J. 51, 52 (2010).
79 *Lee v. Oregon*, 891 F.Supp. 1429 (D.Ore. 1995) *vacated and remanded*, 107 F.3d 1382 (9th Cir.), *cert den. sub. Nom. Lee v. Harcleroad*, 522 U.S. 927 (1997).
80 49 F.3d 586 (1995), *rev'd* 79 F.3d 790 (9th Cir.1996) (en banc), *rev'd sub nom Washington v. Glucksberg*, discussed at length in Chapter 2.
81 *Lee v. Oregon*, n. 79 at 1436 and 1438.
82 *Id.* at 1434.

any physician who acted in good faith, violated the Equal Protection rights of people with terminal illnesses, who were given less protection against abuse or error than people who wished to die who were not terminally ill.[83] The court found that there was no rational reason for differentiating between terminally ill and nonterminally ill people in protection against suicide.

In 1997, the Ninth Circuit overruled the district court in *Lee* on procedural grounds, finding that the plaintiffs did not have standing because the injury they claimed—the possibility that the law might result in availing themselves of assisted suicide while they were incompetent to do so—was too speculative.[84] For a plaintiff to have standing to litigate an issue in court, he or she must point to a real and immediate injury caused by the challenged action. The single patient-plaintiff had progressive muscular dystrophy and had been suicidal in the past. The Ninth Circuit found that in order to suffer the injury she claimed that the ballot measure would inflict on her, she would have to (1) become incompetent; (2) become suicidal; (3) not be recognized as incompetent by either the attending or consulting physician when she requested the medication; (4) not be recognized as incompetent by witnesses to her written request, and on and on: a host of contingencies. This lack of immediate concrete injury also doomed the efforts of doctors and nursing homes to represent their terminally ill patients, as well as the class action plaintiffs had sought to bring.

This decision may not have come as a complete surprise, since the Ninth Circuit had, in the meantime, decided to rehear the *Compassion in Dying* case involving the State of Washington with a much larger number of judges participating in the decision.[85] The new decision had reversed the panel, found Washington's prohibition on assisted suicide unconstitutional, and went out of its way to criticize the district court's decision in *Lee*. The Ninth Circuit's reversal on procedural rather than substantive grounds was a canny political move: the Supreme Court refused to review *Lee*, and the court challenge to the ballot measure was over.

The Oregon legislature then passed a bill that created another ballot measure to permit Oregon voters to rescind Measure 16. However, the voters of Oregon decisively rejected this opportunity, by a vote of 60-40, a much

---

[83] *Id.* at 1435–37.

[84] *Lee v. State of Oregon*, 107 F.3d 1382 (9th Cir.), cert. den. 1997.

[85] This is known as rehearing en banc. Federal courts of appeal generally decide cases with a panel of three judges. If a case is sufficiently important, all the judges in the circuit may be asked to vote on whether to rehear it with a larger number of judges. If a majority of the circuit's judges agree, the case is reheard by all of the circuit's judges, except in the Ninth Circuit, which just has too many appellate court judges, and which limits en banc panels to eleven judges, Circuit Rule 35–3 Limited En Banc Court (2015), http://cdn.ca9.uscourts.gov/datastore/uploads/rules/rules.htm#pID0E0TJ0HA.

stronger endorsement than the 1994 vote. In 1997, assisted suicide finally became available to the citizens of Oregon.

In 1999, the legislature added several amendments to the original initiative, which will be discussed in the following section.

The Framework of the Oregon Assisted-Suicide Program

To request a prescription for lethal medication, an individual must be at least eighteen years old, a resident of Oregon, and diagnosed with a terminal illness that a doctor judges will cause death in six months or less. The individual must be capable of making an informed decision (judgment not impaired by depression or other mental disorder).[86] Additionally, the patient must make two oral requests to his or her doctor, separated by at least fifteen days; the patient must provide a written request to his or her physician, signed in the presence of two witnesses. The prescribing physician and a consulting physician must confirm the diagnosis, prognosis, and the patient's capacity to make an informed decision. If either physician believes the patient's judgment is impaired by a psychiatric or psychological disorder, the patient must be referred for a psychological examination. In addition, the prescribing physician must inform the patient of feasible alternatives to assisted suicide, including comfort care, hospice care, and pain control; and must request, but may not require, the patient to notify his or her next of kin of the prescription request.[87]

In 1999, the Oregon legislature added several provisions to the law. Most importantly for this book, the general provision that a physician cannot prescribe life-ending medication to a person whose psychiatric or psychological disorder impaired his or her judgment was amended to explicitly include "depression" as a cause of impaired judgment. The 1999 amendments also added a requirement that the physician must report to the Department of Human Services (DHS) all prescriptions for lethal medications within seven working days of prescribing the medication.[88] Reporting is not required if patients begin the request process but never receive a prescription. Finally, the amendments added a requirement that pharmacists must be informed of the prescribed medication's ultimate use. More specifically, the attending physician, with the patient's written consent, must (1) contact a pharmacist and inform the pharmacist of the prescription and (2) deliver the written prescription personally or by mail to the pharmacist, who will dispense the medications to either the patient, the attending physician, or an expressly identified agent of the patient.[89] Physicians who act in good faith, as well as

---

[86] *See* OR. STAT. § 127.805.

[87] *See* OR. STAT. §§ 127.810, 127.815, 127.820, 127.825, 127.830, 127.835, 127.840, 127.845, 127.850.

[88] OR. STAT. § 127.855, 127.865.

[89] *Id. See also* Oregon's Administrative Rules, OAR 333-009-0010(3): "To comply with OR. REV. STAT. 127.865(1)(b), within 10 calendar days of dispensing medication pursuant to the Death with Dignity Act, the dispensing health care

their patients, are protected from criminal prosecution if they adhere to the requirements of the Act.[90]

Implementation of the Oregon Assisted Suicide Program

The first legal assisted suicides in Oregon generated some media attention.[91] The Hemlock Society helped an individual with cancer obtain and fill a lethal prescription shortly after the ballot measure took effect. She waited several months to use the prescription. Her family did not want her death publicized. The second individual, who also had cancer, made a tape two days before her death,[92] which was played at a press conference held by Compassion in Dying after her death. On the tape, she says, "I'm looking forward to it, because, being I was always active, I cannot possibly see myself living out two more months like this."[93] She was in her mid-eighties, in hospice, and both her doctor and a second doctor had refused her request for assisted suicide. The second doctor thought she was depressed. Her husband called Compassion in Dying, whose medical director, Dr. Peter Goodwin,[94] spoke to the woman at length, as well as to the second physician. Goodwin said she felt powerless and frustrated, but was not depressed, and he referred her to a physician. This physician, in turn, referred her to a specialist (presumably an oncologist) and a psychiatrist. Each determined that she met the prerequisites for assisted suicide under the law. The physician was interviewed on public radio, and stated that he had difficulty finding a pharmacist who would fill the prescription, but eventually succeeded, and was present with the patient's family when she died.[95]

---

provider shall file a copy of the 'Pharmacy Dispensing Record Form' prescribed by the Authority with the State Registrar, Center for Health Statistics, 800 NE Oregon St., Suite 205, Portland, OR 97232 or by facsimile to (971) 673–1201."

[90] Or. Stat. §127.885; *see also* Oregon DHS, Office of Disease Prevention and Epidemiology, Eighth Annual Report on Oregon's Death with Dignity Act 7–8 (Mar. 9, 2006).

[91] Erin Hoover & Gail K. Hill, *Two Die Using Suicide Law*, Oregonian, Mar. 26, 1998, at A-1; Erin Hoover, *Two Deaths Add New Angle to Debate*, Oregonian, Mar. 27, 1998; Diane M. Gianelli, *Praise, Criticism Follow Oregon's First Reported Assisted Suicides*, Am. Med. News, Apr. 13, 1998.

[92] *Law Mixes Private Deaths, Public Policy*, Oregonian, Mar. 29, 1998.

[93] *Id.*

[94] Eight years later, Goodwin would be diagnosed with corticobasal ganglionic degeneration, a rare brain disorder. Fourteen years later he would avail himself of the law he had championed to end his life. *Peter Goodwin Dies at 83, Aided by Death with Dignity Law He Championed* (CBS News, Mar. 14, 2012), http://www.cbsnews.com/news/peter-goodwin-dies-at-83-aided-by-death-with-dignity-act-he-championed/.

[95] Kathleen Foley and Herbert Hendin, "The Oregon Experiment," in Kathleen Foley and Herbert Hendin, eds., The Case Against Assisted Suicide: For the Right to End of Life Care 147 (2002).

Between 1997, when the law took effect, and 2013, 1173 people received prescriptions for lethal medication in Oregon.[96] Of these, 752 died from ingesting the medication. In 2006, only about one in ten people who obtained lethal prescriptions ever filled them.[97] Over the life of the program, only about half of people who initiate the process and obtain prescriptions use them, and most do not do so right away. It may be that the security of having the pills available is what people want most, as people who are despairing hang on to the option of suicide as a way to get them through difficult times.[98]

Keeping these records on a year-to-year basis is tricky, because sometimes people who received the drugs on the basis that they had six months to live ingested them one and even two years later.[99] For example, although the median length of time between making the request for the medication and dying was 47 days, the range was 15 to 1009 days (or two weeks to just under three years).

Examining the reports released by the Oregon Department of Health over the years is an interesting study in the routinization of physician-assisted suicide. The first few years of reports were filled with data about every conceivable concern: the specialty of the prescribing doctor, his or her years in practice, the type of drugs used, the functional status of the patient, and many other items of information. The first year, 27% of people who requested lethal medications were referred for psychological evaluation.[100] By 2014, the seventeenth year, the report is no longer headed by the great seal of Oregon, the amount of text has been reduced by about 90%; the data collected has also been pared way down, and only 2.9% of the patients are referred for psychiatric evaluation.[101]

The median age of all persons who have used physician-assisted suicide is seventy-one, with a range of twenty-five to ninety-six. Over the years, the

---

[96] OREGON DEPARTMENT OF HEALTH, OREGON'S DEATH WITH DIGNITY ACT—2013, http://public.health.oregon.gov/ProviderPartnerResources/EvaluationResearch/ DeathwithDignityAct/Documents/year16.pdf.

[97] DAVID JEFFREY, A TALE OF TWO CITIES (2006), http://www.pccef.org/articles/ PCCEF_June07_posting.pdf.

[98] ANDREW SOLOMON, THE NOONDAY DEMON (paperback ed. 2007); Interview with C.L.

[99] In 2013, eight of the seventy-one patients who died by ingesting medication prescribed under the Death with Dignity Act had received their prescriptions in 2011 or 2012.

[100] OREGON DEPARTMENT OF HEALTH, DIVISION OF PUBLIC HEALTH, OREGON'S DEATH WITH DIGNITY ACT: THE FIRST YEAR'S EXPERIENCE (Feb. 18 1999), https:// public.health.oregon.gov/ProviderPartnerResources/EvaluationResearch/ DeathwithDignityAct/Documents/year1.pdf.

[101] OREGON DEPARTMENT OF HEALTH, DIVISION OF PUBLIC HEALTH, OREGON'S DEATH WITH DIGNITY ACT—2014, https://public.health.oregon.gov/ ProviderPartnerResources/EvaluationResearch/DeathwithDignityAct/ Documents/year17.pdf.

vast majority of people availing themselves of assisted suicide have had cancer (78%); the next largest category, amyotrophic lateral sclerosis (ALS), constituted 8.3% of the total. However, over the years, the underlying "terminal" illness has also been characterized as "benign or uncertain neoplasms"(i.e., tumors that were not cancerous at all), viral hepatitis, and diabetes mellitus. Forty-seven people, or 5.5% of the total, have been referred for psychiatric evaluation, a number that has fluctuated over the years.[102] In 2007, not a single patient was referred for evaluation, a statistic that was found to be "concerning."[103] Since then, several people a year have been referred for evaluation. Physicians are occasionally reported for disciplinary action for "incorrect" or "incomplete" forms, including consent forms.[104]

A study by Dr. Linda Ganzini and her colleagues of fifty-eight Oregonians who had requested aid in dying is very frequently cited by opponents of assisted suicide, because three of the people who ingested lethal medication were found to be suffering from depression.[105] However, the study's methodology and findings are complex and interesting enough to warrant closer examination. First, all fifty-eight participants in the study—terminally ill Oregonians who had expressed an interest in assisted suicide—were competent to engage in the study and not cognitively impaired. Of the fifty-eight people who had asked about assisted suicide, eighteen—less than a third—ultimately received a prescription for lethal medication.[106]

In addition, although the researchers tried their best to be objective in diagnosing depression, they made various questionable methodological decisions, for example, attributing physical symptoms, such as fatigue or weight loss, to depression rather than to the terminal illness.[107] They measured depression by using the Hospital Anxiety and Depression scale and a structured interview. Despite the fact that these measures of depression differed starkly in their outcomes (eight out of fifty-eight subjects were depressed on the Hospital Anxiety and Depression scale, while twelve—but not necessarily the same

---

[102] *Id.*

[103] Robert Steinbrook, *Perspective: Physician-Assisted Death: From Oregon to Washington State*, 359 NEW ENG. J. MED. 2513 (Dec. 11, 2008).

[104] See OREGON DEPARTMENT OF HEALTH, *supra* note 95 and OREGON DEPARTMENT OF HEALTH, DIVISION OF PUBLIC HEALTH, OREGON'S DEATH WITH DIGNITY ACT—2008, https://public.health.oregon.gov/ProviderPartnerResources/EvaluationResearch/DeathwithDignityAct/Documents/year11.pdf

[105] Ganzini, Goy, & Dobscha, *Prevalence of Depression and Anxiety in Patients Requesting Physicians' Aid in Dying: A Cross Sectional Survey*, 337 BRIT. MED. J. (2008) at 1682.

[106] *Id.*

[107] The researchers said they did this because "when moderate thresholds were used for mood criteria, presence or absence of physical symptoms no longer influenced categorization of depression." This might be a reason to exclude consideration of these physical symptoms, rather than including them.

people-- were diagnosed as depressed as a result of the clinical interview), the researchers *combined* the results of the two scales so that anyone who had been considered depressed under either method was counted as depressed. This resulted in the maximum number of people deemed depressed: fifteen of the fifty-eight people requesting assistance in suicide. The vast majority of these fifteen people (80%) did *not* ultimately ask for lethal prescriptions. Of the eighteen people who received prescriptions, only three of them were from the group of fifteen people originally diagnosed as depressed by the researchers. Of these eighteen people, only nine ingested the medications: the three people diagnosed as depressed were among the nine.

Because there were only three people, the authors were able to describe them quite fully. One of them was an old man with cancer who had met the Hospital Anxiety and Depression scale for depression, but had not been considered depressed by the clinician who had conducted the structured interview. The second patient, a middle-aged woman with cancer, was considered depressed by the clinical interviewer but not on the Hospital scale. But the third patient, an elderly woman, had the most telling result of all. She qualified as depressed by the interview, but not the Hospital scale, asked for and received psychiatric treatment, including medication, and was documented by a psychiatrist to have her depression in remission. She then took her lethal prescription.

A number of studies have been done of Oregonians contemplating and completing assisted suicide. All the studies agree that most of the people who choose to die this way are white and well-educated and choose to die because of their loss of autonomy, loss of dignity, and inability to engage in activities that make life enjoyable.[108] Pain, an issue made much of before the courts, doesn't even make the top five reasons.

In some ways one of the most troubling aspects of the Oregon physician-assisted suicide law is that, the majority of the time, the physician who assists the patient to obtain a prescription for lethal medication is not actually the patient's own physician.[109] Although the Death with Dignity Act requires by

---

[108] OREGON DEPARTMENT OF HEALTH, *supra* note 91. These reasons were cited by 91.4%, 80.9%, and 88.9% respectively.

[109] David Jeffrey, *Physician Assisted Suicide vs. Palliative Care: A Tale of Two Cities*, PHYSICIANS FOR COMPASSIONATE CARE EDUCATION FOUNDATION (posted June 2007), http://www.pccef.org/articles/PCCEF_June07_posting.pdf ("most commonly their own doctor will not agree but refers the patient to a hospice program. The hospice doctors do not sign lethal prescriptions but may refer the patient to another doctor who is willing to do so or patients contact the organization Compassion & Choices Oregon which has a list of doctors who are willing to carry out PAS.") Although Jeffrey is an outspoken opponent of physician-assisted suicide, the data appears to confirm his claim. For example, in 2004, there were 9382 doctors practicing in Oregon Public Citizen, *Oregon's Increased Number of Doctors: Government Data Refutes Medical Lobby Claims* (Aug. 2004), http://

its terms that the prescribing physician be the "attending physician," defined by statute as "the physician who has primary responsibility for the care of the patient and treatment of the patient's terminal disease,"[110] most of the time, the patient gets the prescription from a completely different doctor, generally someone referred to the patient by Compassion in Dying. A majority of the time, patients have to ask more than one doctor before finding one who is willing to prescribe the medication.[111] Although most doctors who were involved in physician-assisted suicide provided only one patient with prescriptions, in 2014, one doctor wrote twelve prescriptions.[112] In one hospice where twenty-eight patients had used assisted suicide, twenty-three of them had used the same doctor.[113]

Over the course of the Oregon experience, the median length of time the doctor has known the patient for whom he or she is prescribing fatal medication is 13 weeks, but the range is from zero weeks to 1905 weeks.[114] If the public is under the impression that physicians as a profession are acting as gatekeepers for assisted suicide, or that the patients' own doctors are performing this function, the public is mistaken. Whether this is good policy or not is unclear,[115] but, as with prescription of addictive painkillers such as OxyContin and predictions of future dangerousness used to justify capital punishment, it only takes a few doctors to make a program viable.

Oregon healthcare professionals have the benefit of a thoughtful manual prepared by the Oregon Health & Science University (OHSU) providing guidance on the Death with Dignity program.[116] Although it does have one

---

www.citizen.org/documents/ACF8DE.pdf. In 2004, forty doctors wrote sixty prescriptions for lethal medications, with one physician writing seven prescriptions and one writing four prescriptions, DEPARTMENT OF HUMAN SERVICES, OFFICE OF DISEASE PREVENTION AND EPIDEMIOLOGY, SEVENTH ANNUAL REPORT ON OREGON'S DEATH WITH DIGNITY ACT (Mar. 10, 2005), https://public.health.oregon.gov/ProviderPartnerResources/EvaluationResearch/DeathwithDignityAct/Documents/year7.pdf. I discuss this concern at greater length in Chapter 5, including my own recommendation that prescriptions of lethal medication be limited to health care professionals with a history of treating the patient.

[110] O.R.S. 127.800 §.1.01(2).

[111] OREGON HEALTH & SCIENCE UNIVERSITY (OHSU), THE OREGON DEATH WITH DIGNITY ACT: A GUIDEBOOK FOR HEALTHCARE PROFESSIONALS, 49. (2008).

[112] OREGON DEPARTMENT OF HEALTH, *supra* note 96.

[113] Jeffrey, *supra* note 109.

[114] OHSU, *supra* note 111.

[115] I take the position in Chapter 5 that it is not.

[116] Developed by the Task Force to Improve the Care of Terminally Ill Oregonians, *The Oregon Death with Dignity Act: A Guidebook for Health Care Professionals* (last updated 2008) is a thorough, fifteen chapter handbook that is remarkably balanced and informative. http://www.ohsu.edu/xd/education/continuing-education/center-for-ethics/ethics-outreach/upload/Oregon-Death-with-Dignity-Act-Guidebook.pdf

serious problem in its recommendations regarding assessing competence,[117] overall it represents a thorough discussion of issues likely to be faced by health professionals who are asked to dispense medications intended to cause death, including the nuts and bolts of implementation, rules and forms, legal issues, financial issues, and the inevitable emotional impact on the provider.

Because the OHSU guidance is intended for healthcare professionals, its chapter on legal issues focuses on those legal issues of greatest interest and relevance to healthcare professionals, primarily issues of liability and competence assessment. But in fact, as a state with a major policy that runs completely counter to federal policy,[118] there have been a number of interesting legal issues arising out of Oregon's adoption of the Death with Dignity program.

Legal Issues Arising Out of Assisted Suicide in Oregon

Conflicts with Federal Law

The same year that assisted suicide was finally implemented in Oregon, Congress passed the Assisted Suicide Funding Restriction Act of 1997[119] "to continue current Federal policy by providing explicitly that federal funds may not be used to pay for items and services (including assistance) the purpose of which is to cause (or assist in causing) the suicide, euthanasia, or mercy killing of any individual."[120] This law effectively prohibited Oregon from using federal Medicaid funds or Medicare funds to help pay for assisted suicide, as well as precluding any federal veteran's facilities in Oregon from participating in the assisted suicide program. Nothing about the ballot initiative or subsequent legislative action required that state funding cover the expenses of assisted suicide. Nevertheless, in 1998, Oregon decided to cover physician assisted suicide under Medicaid, paying all the costs out of the Oregon treasury.

This creates some ticklish issues. Under federal Medicaid law, Oregon Medicaid officials must inform recipients of Medicaid when they may be eligible for services covered under the Medicaid program. Therefore, when Oregon's Medicaid program declined to cover certain cancer treatments that it deemed too experimental, Oregon's Medicaid officials duly informed the recipients—Barbara Wagner, who had lung cancer, and Randy Stroup, who had prostate cancer, that although the cancer treatment they sought could

---

[117] As discussed in Chapter 1, it suggests use of an instrument measuring depression that is not particularly useful in the context of a person dying of a debilitating disease, see pp. 46–48.

[118] Other examples of this include states that have legalized marijuana use, and, until recently, states that have legalized gay marriage.

[119] 42 USC § 14401.

[120] 42 U.S.C. § 14401(b).

not be covered, medications for assisted suicide would in fact be covered.[121] This created a firestorm of protest, because in the United States, unlike the Netherlands and Belgium, assisted suicide is not seen as a form of medical treatment, at least not yet.[122]

Section 1553 of the Affordable Care Act protects health care providers and institutions from punishment or discrimination if they refuse to provide assisted suicide services. It does not by its terms preclude the states from using federal Medicaid money to provide those services, because other federal laws already contain this prohibition.

Conflicts with Laws in Other States

The best illustration of the arcana of suicide law arises in a case involving the question of which state's law should apply to a wrongful death suit. This is literally a million dollar question, because some states (like Oregon) have caps on recovery for wrongful death, and others (like New York) do not. An Oregon woman who contracted mesothelioma, and tried to manage her disease with yoga and other holistic approaches,[123] found (perhaps unsurprisingly) that her efforts were to no avail. In intense pain from advanced stages of the disease, she chose to use assisted suicide.[124] However, her mesothelioma had been caused by exposure to asbestos in New York, and because New York does not cap damages, her estate sought to have New York law apply to her wrongful death claim. The judge was convinced for other reasons that Oregon law should prevail, but also pointed out that physician-assisted suicide was a crime in New York, and that her deliberate suicide might constitute an intervening cause of death precluding any recovery at all under New York law, so her estate might be better off applying Oregon law after all.[125]

Insurance Law

The Oregon law mandates that assisted suicide will not be treated as suicide for purposes of issuing death certificates or life insurance. Theoretically, a person could buy a life insurance policy and then avail himself of assisted suicide, leaving his family with a big payout. Insurance companies aren't worried. In the first place, few people use assisted suicide in Oregon. In the second place, as one official said, people with terminal illnesses get turned

---

[121] Marilyn Gold, *Op-Ed: Too Many Flaws in Assisted Suicide Laws*, N. Y. TIMES, Apr. 10, 2012, http://www.nytimes.com/roomfordebate/2012/04/10/why-do-americans-balk-at-euthanasia-laws/too-many-flaws-in-assisted-suicide-laws.

[122] See Chapters 4 and 5.

[123] *Lori Konopka-Sauer* et al. *v. Colgate-Palmolive* note 44 at 161, 165.

[124] *Id.*

[125] *Id.* at 166.

down for life insurance policies in any event.[126] A person who applied for a life insurance policy knowing he or she had such an illness, who failed to disclose this fact, would invalidate the policy in any event. So there has not been any legal controversy in Oregon related to the mandate that assisted suicide should not be treated as suicide for insurance purposes.

A number of questions do remain unanswered. Although the Death with Dignity Act provides both civil and criminal immunity to a physician who acts in good faith to assist a suicide,[127] if a physician were ever to be sued for actions related to the Act, it is not clear whether malpractice insurance would cover him or her, since most insurance contracts exempt intentional acts resulting in death or injury. It is not clear how malpractice insurance carriers would interpret their responsibilities to a physician sued for, for example, assisting a person who was not an Oregon resident or who was alleged to be incompetent, or who provided mistaken information about dosages and how to take the medication.

Why Oregon?

There are a number of reasons that have been suggested for Oregon's place as the first state to adopt assisted suicide. First, the advocates who organized Oregon's initiative were not only true believers, they were sophisticated and savvy. Hawaii advocates have wanted to pass assisted suicide in Hawaii as much as those in Oregon, but they have pursued a markedly less sophisticated strategy in doing so.

Second, Oregon is one of the least religious states in the country, and opposition from religious groups has been very strong in otherwise liberal states, such as Massachusetts and Hawaii.

Third, Oregon was (until 2015) the only state where the state medical society did not take an active role in opposing assisted suicide; the Oregon Medical Society remained officially neutral.

Fourth, the governor in Oregon actively supported assisted suicide. Other governors, even those who privately supported assisted suicide such as Governor Deval Patrick in Massachusetts, remained studiedly silent during the process leading up to the vote on the ballot.

Fifth, this law can be seen as an expression of Oregon culture. David Jeffrey, a visiting palliative care specialist from the United Kingdom, quoted an American physician as saying that that the United States is "drunk on autonomy"[128] and Oregonians are even more intoxicated than most Americans.

---

[126] *Life Insurers Shrug at Assisted Suicide*, Insure.com (Apr. 20, 2004), http://www.insure.com/life-insurance/assisted-suicide.html.

[127] Or. Rev. Stat. § 127.885(5)(d)(B)(4).

[128] Jeffrey, *supra* note 97.

Other States Legalizing Assisted Suicide

The Washington State Ballot Initiative

Washington attempted to pass an assisted suicide law in 1991, Initiative 119, which would have legalized both euthanasia and physician-assisted suicide. As noted earlier, the failure of Ballot Initiative 119 proved instrumental in teaching the Oregon advocates how to draft and market their own ballot measure. Washington, however, did not succeed in passing a ballot initiative until 2008, when a campaign to pass the ballot measure (Initiative 1000) was spearheaded by former Governor Booth Gardner, who had Parkinson's disease. Although he knew he could not qualify for assisted suicide, he empathized deeply with those who wanted control over the circumstances of their deaths. Although the ballot measure was extremely controversial[129] and bitterly opposed by the Washington State Medical Association, Gardner's popularity contributed to the measure's victory in 2008, and Washington began its assisted-suicide program in 2009.

The Washington program is identical to the Oregon program. It requires a person to be a Washington resident,[130] competent,[131] voluntary, older than eighteen, and with a terminal illness and a prognosis of six months or less. Washington is the thirteenth most populated state, twice as large in population as Oregon, and well ahead of Montana, New Mexico, and Vermont. Washington has only been keeping statistics on the use of assisted suicide for five years, but they generally mirror the profile of assisted suicide users in Oregon, although as a proportion of total population, Oregonians avail themselves of prescriptions more frequently and use them less often.[132]

---

[129] Associated Press, *Washington State Battles over Vote to Allow Lethal Meds for Dying Patients*, Oct. 11, 2008; see also John Iwasaki, *"Playing God" or Dignified Death? Faith Based Groups Taking Crucial Role in Initiative Battle*, SEATTLE POST-INTELLIGENCER, Oct. 13, 2008.

[130] R.C.W. §70.245.020(1)(2014). Although a doctor who has attended many deaths acknowledges that "there are ways around that." Brian Hutchinson, "Assisted Suicide is a Soft Sell in this Affluent but Aging Washington State Community," National Post, Nov. 26, 2013, http://news.nationalpost.com/news/assisted-suicide-is-a-soft-sell-in-this-affluent-but-aging-washington-state-community

[131] R.C.W.§ 70.245.020(1)(2014) One man has already gone to prison for shooting his wife, whose brain cancer rendered her mentally incompetent and therefore ineligible to use the statute, Diana Hofley, "Bothell Man Gets 2 Years for Slaying Terminally Ill Wife". Herald Net, Feb. 1, 2013, http://www.heraldnet.com/article/20130201/NEWS01/702019906

[132] In 2013, 173 Washingtonians obtained prescriptions, and 119 are known to have used them. Another 26 people died without having used them, and the origin of death of 14 people remains unknown. Washington State Department of Health, 2013 DEATH WITH DIGNITY ACT REPORT, EXECUTIVE SUMMARY, http://www.doh.wa.gov/portals/1/Documents/Pubs/422-109-DeathWithDignityAct2013.pdf. The comparable figures for Oregon, a state with half the population of

Like Oregon, the vast majority of Washingtonians obtaining prescriptions (92%) had cancer or ALS or a similar neurodegenerative disease, almost all (97%) were white, and almost all (91%) expressed concerns about autonomy. Almost all of the 173 Washington assisted suicides (96%) took place west of the Cascades (meaning in populated urban areas such as Seattle) in 2013.

Because Washington is a much larger state, it has larger medical institutions. One of these, the Seattle Cancer Care Alliance, became the first healthcare organization to publicize its assisted-suicide protocols.[133] The Cancer Care Alliance asserts that "[p]roviding access to doctor-hastened death is an element of top-notch care for terminally ill patients ... is simply one of a full range of high-quality end-of-life options."[134] The protocols and associated discussion, published in the *New England Journal of Medicine*, "'adds to the literature that is developing a standard of care around aid in dying,'" commented an advocate for physician-assisted suicide.[135]

These protocols precluded about 40% of the 114 patients who expressed interest in physician-assisted suicide, either because they weren't sufficiently terminal or because of "mental illness or mental competence" issues. Ultimately, forty of the Cancer Care Alliance patients over two and a half years were given the lethal medication and twenty-four patients used it to hasten their deaths. These twenty-four deaths comprised 10% of assisted suicides in Washington over that time period but only 0.02% of all deaths of cancer patients at the Alliance.

Compared to physician-assisted suicides in Washington generally and in Oregon, the Cancer Care Alliance patients were far more likely to be minorities (27.5% compared to 4.8% and 2.4%, respectively), more likely to be uninsured (10% compared to 2.7% and 1.7%), and likely to have known their physicians for a longer period of time (average of thirty-three weeks compared to fourteen and twelve weeks).

Ironically, concerted efforts by European pharmaceutical companies opposed to capital punishment may have the unintended effect of making assisted suicide more difficult. The drug most commonly used in assisted suicide, pentobarbital, is also the drug most commonly used in executions in the United States. European pharmaceutical companies have blocked delivery of this drug to the United States, forcing individuals seeking assisted suicide to use Seconal, which, at $2000 a dose, is four to seven times as much

---

Washington, was 122 people receiving prescriptions and 71 known deaths, OREGON DEPARTMENT OF HEALTH, *supra* note 91.

[133] E. T. Loggers, H. Starks, M. Shannon-Dudley, A. L. Back, et al., *Implementing a Death with Dignity Program at a Comprehensive Cancer Center*, 368 NEW ENG. J. MED. 1417 (2013).

[134] Kevin B. O'Reilly, *Cancer Center Goes Public with Assisted Suicide Protocol*, AM. MED. NEWS, Apr. 22, 2013, http://www.amednews.com/article/20130422/profession/130429973/2/.

[135] *Id.*

as an appropriate dose of pentobarbital.[136] Of course, a person only needs a single dose, but Compassion in Dying has decided to subsidize the costs until different suppliers can be located.[137]

The *Baxter* Case in Montana

In contrast to Washington and Oregon, Montana provides physicians with protection from civil and criminal prosecution for assisted suicide under most circumstances through a state supreme court case, *Baxter v. State of Montana*.[138] Although the plaintiffs in *Baxter* asked the Montana Supreme Court to decide that terminally ill patients had a constitutional right to receive a prescription for lethal medication from their physicians, the court avoided the constitutional question, holding that any physician sued or prosecuted for supplying terminally ill, competent patients with lethal medication could assert a statutory defense of consent.

Even this limited holding is the broadest imprimatur provided by a state supreme court to physician-assisted suicide.[139] It is singular to Montana because it depends on a feature of state law that permits consent of the victim to be used as a defense to a criminal charge unless doing so would violate public policy. The decision is in the best tradition of antigovernment, populist Montana: It leaves the matter entirely private unless someone complains. There is no waiting period, no second physician requirement, and the Montana State Department of Health will not be compiling statistics or posting them on the Internet, as in Oregon and Washington.

Baxter was brought by four Montana physicians, Compassion & Choices,[140] and Robert Baxter, a seventy-six-year-old truck driver from Billings, Montana, who was dying of lymphocytic leukemia.[141] Baxter was receiving chemotherapy, and as a result of both the cancer and the chemo, suffered from "infections, chronic fatigue and weakness, anemia, night sweats, nausea, massively swollen glands, significant ongoing digestive problems, and generalized pain and discomfort."[142]

---

[136] Deborah Home, *'Right to Die' Drug in Short Supply* (KIRO TV, June 27, 2014), www.kirotv.com/news/news/right-die-drug-short-supply/ngTyX/.

[137] *Id.*

[138] *Baxter v. State*, 354 Mont. 234, 224 P.3d 1211 (2009).

[139] Michigan and New Mexico appellate courts found a state constitutional right to physician-assisted suicide, but the Michigan case was reversed on appeal and the New Mexico case is pending (see pp. 162–167 *infra*.). The highest courts in Florida and Alaska also refused to hold that their state constitutions provided this right.

[140] 224 P.3d 1211, 1214 (Mont. 2009). The statements of Robert Baxter in support of his claims can be viewed on the Compassion & Choices website, *available at* http://www.compassionandchoices.org/act/legal_work/baxter.

[141] Baxter died the day that the district court issued its decision recognizing that the Montana constitution protected his right to assistance in dying.

[142] *Baxter v. State*, at 1214.

Under Montana law,[143] a person who purposely or knowingly causes the death of another human being in Montana commits the offense of homicide. Conduct is deemed the cause of the person's death if the defendant's acts were committed knowingly or purposely and the death would not have occurred without them.[144] Therefore, a physician who intentionally provides a lethal prescription could be prosecuted and convicted of homicide, because the physician knows how the medication will be used, intends for its use to cause death, and without the physician's aid in prescribing the medication, the death of the patient would not have occurred in this manner.

The plaintiffs challenged the application of Montana's homicide statute to a physician providing a prescription to a terminally ill, mentally competent patient, for medication that the patient could consume to bring peaceful death if he found his dying process unbearable.[145] Plaintiffs argued that Montana citizens had a right protected by the Montana constitution's guarantees of privacy, as most plaintiffs have done since *Quinlan*. However, the Montana constitution contains another guarantee less common to other state constitutions: "The dignity of the human being is inviolable."[146] Plaintiffs argued that this provision also guaranteed their right to aid in dying. Finally they claimed that the doctrine of consent precluded criminal prosecution of a physician who helped his or her competent, voluntary patient to die.

On December 5, 2008, the district court accepted the plaintiff's constitutional arguments.[147]

The district court concluded that not permitting physician-assisted suicide would violate the patient's dignity because, "if the patient were to have no assistance from his doctor, he may be forced to kill himself sooner rather than later because of the anticipated increased disability with the progress of his disease, and the manner of the patient's death would more likely occur in a manner that violates his dignity and peace of mind, such as by gunshot or by an otherwise unpleasant method, causing undue suffering to the patient and his family."[148] The district court further held that the patient's right to die with dignity immunizes the patient's physician from prosecution under Montana's homicide statute.[149]

The district court also found that the decision implicated the state constitutional right to privacy. As with many courts, the trial court used the analogy of abortion rights to support the holding a patient may use the

---

[143] MONT. CODE ANN. § 45-5-10.

[144] MONT. CODE. ANN. § 45-2-201 provides that consent of the victim is a defense to a criminal charge unless it would violate public policy to permit such a defense.

[145] *Id.* at 1214.

[146] Mont. Constitution, Art. II, § 4 (2015).

[147] Baxter v. Mont., No. 2007-787, 2008 Mont.Dist.LEXIS 482 (Mont. 1st Jud. Dist. Dec. 5, 2008).

[148] *Id.* at *19.

[149] *Id.* at *28, 36.

assistance of a physician to obtain prescription medication in a lethal dosage.[150] Interpreting the privacy right to include the "right of each individual to make medical judgments affecting his or her bodily integrity and health in partnership with a chosen health care provider free from the interference of the government," the district court reasoned that the decision to end one's life by assisted suicide was a medical judgment, and that the decision to commit assisted suicide "certainly is one of personal autonomy and privacy."[151]

On appeal, the Montana Supreme Court avoided the constitutional questions and affirmed 5-2 on the grounds of the doctrine of consent.[152] The court held that a physician charged with homicide for assisting a terminally ill, mentally competent adult patient to die could avail himself or herself of the consent defense, and to do so would not contravene public policy as long as the physician was not directly involved in the final act. In its extended discussion of why physician-assisted suicide did not violate public policy, however, the court clearly implied that it would uphold the constitutionality of physician-assisted suicide if the issue were presented directly.

The court described the case as presenting two questions. The first was whether the consent defense would apply in the case of a physician charged with homicide for supplying a fatal prescription to his patient, and the second was whether, if such a defense were permitted, it would contravene public policy.

Only one case interpreted the long-standing consent defense: a case involving intoxication, public brawling, and endangerment to others.[153] The court held that the consent defense is "against public policy" in assault cases characterized by aggressive and combative acts that breach public peace and physically endanger others.

On the other hand, the acts of a physician supplying medicine to a terminally ill patient, and the patient's subsequent private act of taking the medication, are not comparable to violent, peace-breaching conduct. The relationship between the patient and physician is "private, civil, and compassionate" when physician and patient work together to create a means by which the patient is in control of his own mortality. Thus, the court's understanding of the patient-physician relationship forms the foundation of its conclusion that a consent defense would not violate public policy. In addition, the language of the statute creating the consent defense requires that consent is not effective if given "by a person who is legally incompetent to authorize the conduct,"[154] and not by someone who "by reason of youth, mental disease or defect, or intoxication, is unable to make a reasonable judgment as to the nature of harmfulness of the conduct."[155]

---

[150] *Id.* at* 26.

[151] *Id.* at *24.

[152] *Baxter*, 224 Pd.3d 1211, 1222 (Mont. 2009).

[153] State v. Mackrill, 345 Mont. 469 (Mont. 2008).

[154] Mont. Code Annotated § 45-2-211(2)(a)(2014).

[155] Mont. Code Annotated § 45-2-211(2)(b) (2014).

Notably, nothing about the court's logic in interpreting the consent defense limits it to terminally ill patients. However, in determining that physician aid in dying does not violate public policy, a necessary step under the consent defense, the court relied heavily on the Montana Rights of the Terminally Ill Act. This statute "very clearly provides that terminally ill patients are entitled to autonomous end-of-life decisions, even if enforcement of those decisions involves direct acts by a physician."[156] The Terminally Ill Act expressly shields physicians from civil and criminal liability for honoring these requests.[157]

Because of this provision, the court concluded that the Act reflects legislative respect for the patient's end-of-life autonomy and the physician's legal obligation to comply with the patient's declaration. Thus, *Baxter* by its terms only shields physicians, and only in "end of life" situations. Unlike other states, however, "end of life" is not limited to six months, and the statute's references to terminal illness and "death within a relatively short time"[158] gives broader temporal scope for terminally ill individuals who wish to end their lives.

Again, while the language of the consent statute might be read to permit an authorized third party to provide consent on behalf of an incapacitated person, the court's conclusion explicitly tied its finding that physician-assisted suicide was not against public policy to the requirement that "the patient—not the physician—commits the final death-causing act by self-administering a lethal dose of medication." [159]

The opinion provoked a bitter and anguished dissent from Justice Jim Rice, who underscored the difference between withdrawing treatment and the affirmative act of providing life-ending medication, which he reminded the majority was defined as an offense under criminal statutes.[160] Justice Rice, like Justice Rehnquist in *Vacco v. Quill*, felt that the physician's intent was crucial, and that this difference in intent (intending to cause the patient's death vs. intending to provide palliative treatment) was the crux of the difference between criminal and noncriminal acts.[161]

Opponents of assisted suicide in Montana have not chosen to try to limit or challenge the reach of *Baxter* in the courts: rather, they filed a bill in the legislature, which would have made statutory opposition to physician-assisted suicide crystal clear. Had that bill succeeded, the only remaining basis for physician-assisted suicide in Montana would have been state constitutional rights; the Montana Supreme Court implied that if pushed, they

---

[156] *Baxter*, n. 152, at 1216.
[157] Mont. Code Ann.§ 50-9-204.
[158] Mont. Code. Ann.§50-9-103(2).
[159] *Baxter*, 224 P.3d 1211, 1222 (Mont. 2009).
[160] *Baxter v. State*, 224 P.3d at 1233.
[161] *Id*. at 1233–34.

would find the right to physician-assisted suicide for terminally ill people in the State Constitution, as the District Court had done.[162] However, legislative efforts in Montana to repeal *Baxter* have failed so far.

The Vermont Legislation

Vermont's assisted suicide scheme also reflects the distinctive character of the state. Unlike Oregon, Washington, and Montana, Vermont enacted assisted suicide through legislation. The legislation is the kind of bizarre hybrid produced by legislative compromise. It requires Oregon and Washington style reporting and protection for three years, and after that Montana-style privacy and nonregulation.

Vermont assisted suicide advocates, such as State Senator Clare Ayer, worked hard to pass assisted suicide legislation for more than ten years. In 2012, a bill introduced by Ayer failed in the Vermont Senate. That year, Richard Mallary, a popular former Speaker of the Vermont House suffering from prostate cancer, who had publicly supported the assisted suicide bill and hoped to see it enacted, killed himself after its failure. Vermont is a small state, and Mallary's death affected many in the legislature.

Ayer's bills generally replicated the Oregon model, which was seen as having been successful. In 2004, the Counsel for the Legislature of Vermont produced a study of how assisted suicide worked in Oregon and the Netherlands in response to requests by legislators. The study was generally positive about results in Oregon but noted that Oregon had outstanding end-of-life services in place, such as hospice and palliative care, when assisted suicide was adopted, including in rural regions of Oregon. The study did not comment on whether such services were available in Vermont.

Advocates in Vermont apparently never sought to establish assisted suicide through litigation, and the state does not permit ballot measures of the type that succeeded in Oregon and Washington.[163] Ballot initiatives can only be presented to Vermont voters through a vote of the legislature, and only to amend the constitution. Thus, ballot initiatives were never an option. Jessica Itse, who worked for Compassion & Choices Vermont, said in an interview that ballot measures are up and down votes, whereas working with legislation permitted the kind of compromises that eventually succeeded in 2013. Commentators were divided on whether the legislative method is superior to ballot initiatives. John Dillon, a public radio reporter who covered the process for years, said, "It does seem easier to win a campaign in a legislature of a couple of hundred people than in a popular

---

[162] Justice Nelson, in a specially concurring opinion, wrote at length to support the conclusion that the Montana Constitution included a right to physician-assisted suicide. Id at 1223.

[163] Paula Span, *Vermont Passes Aid in Dying Measure*, N. Y. Times, May 14, 2013.

referendum."[164] However, assisted suicide was very popular in Vermont, according to polls, and, as Michael Sirotkin, a lawyer representing Patient Choices Vermont, argued, legislation "is actually a harder path, because often the public is ahead of legislators on controversial issues."[165]Legislation can also be repealed more easily than a ballot initiative. However, in Vermont, the legislation was made permanent a year ahead of the scheduled sunsetting of various provisions.[166]

In 2013, the Patient Choice and Control at the End of Life Act (Act 39) was finally passed and signed into law on May 20, 2013, by Governor Shumlin, a supporter of assisted suicide, but not without last-minute legislative drama. In the Senate, Act 39 was replaced at the last minute by a bill known as the Cummings/Galbreath amendment. The Cummings/Galbreath amendment would have substituted bare-bones physician immunity for the original bill, which essentially replicated Oregon's detailed process and protections. Some legislators supported assisted suicide but balked at the government regulation involved in the Vermont model. Others, however, supported assisted suicide only with the protections and regulation written into the original bill.

The bill finally signed into law represented the ultimate horse-trading compromise. The Oregon model of assisted suicide is adopted for the first three years, with requirements of physician reporting, second physician's confirmation, fifteen days, and other structures described in the Oregon model. After three years, these regulatory burdens would be swept away and assisted suicide becomes a matter between doctor and patient. These provisions became permanent with legislation signed in 2015. [167]Only physicians can prescribe end-of-life drugs, although other healthcare professionals have prescribing power in Vermont.[168]

The new law, like the Oregon law, provides immunity from civil and criminal prosecution, as well as licensing and disciplinary actions, to physicians for "actions performed in good faith compliance with the provisions" of the law. Like the Affordable Care Act, the law also expressly prohibits "facilities" from discriminating against physicians for participating in or

---

[164] Carey Goldberg, *How Vermont Passed Assisted Suicide (and Where Can We Go to Die?*, COMMON HEALTH: REFORM AND REALITY (WBUR, May 15, 2013), www.commonhealth.wbur.org/2013/05/assisted-suicide-vermont.

[165] Paula Span, id. at n. 165.

[166] Paris Achen, "Permanent Version of Vermont Assisted Suicide Bill Passed," Burlington Free Press, May 20, 2015, http://www.usatoday.com/story/news/nation/2015/05/20/permanent-version-of-vt-assisted-suicide-bill-signed/27675289/. The article noted that one of the first Vermonters to use the legislation was an old family friend of Governor Peter Shumlin. Her children thanked him for signing the legislation.

[167] *Id.*

[168] 18 V.S.A. Ch. 113 §5283 protects only physicians.

refusing to participate in assisted suicide.[169] The definition of "facilities" expressly includes "mental hospitals," "psychiatric facilities," and "mental health agencies." However, the facility may prohibit a physician from writing a prescription for a facility resident who wishes to use the prescription within the confines of the facility.[170]

Because of previously existing Vermont legislation requiring physicians to inform all patients at the end of life about all options available to them,[171] it appears that even physicians who do not want to participate in assisted suicide must inform their patients about its availability, and make referrals to a physician who is willing to participate in the program, or at the least to an advocacy organization which can give them further information.[172]

Unlike Washington and Oregon, Vermont has a "duty to aid" statute,[173] which requires bystanders to assist people at risk of death or serious injury if the bystander could do so without risk to himself or herself. The Vermont law expressly immunized people who are present when a person with a terminal condition takes a lethal dose of medication from "the duty to aid." Interestingly, this immunity does not depend on the person having followed any of the requirements of the Act, and therefore does not require that the person taking the lethal dose of medication do it for the purpose of ending his or her life. Presumably the requirement that the person be terminally ill will limit the potential reach of this immunity.

Unlike the Oregon legislation, the Vermont legislation also prohibits malpractice insurers from taking a physician's willingness or unwillingness to participate in assisted suicide into consideration when setting rates, and also forbids the state's licensing board from disciplining physicians who have followed the requirements of the Act.

The Vermont Secretary of Health said that he expected the process to be covered by health insurance within Vermont, but it's unclear whether he meant to indicate only that Vermont Medicaid would cover the process or whether all health insurers operating in Vermont would be required to cover the process.[174] As of March 2015, six people (out of a population of 696,000) had taken advantage of the law, to the knowledge of the authorities.[175]

---

[169] The Affordable Care Act also prohibits other providers and insurance companies from discriminating against providers unwilling to take part in assisted suicide.

[170] 18 V.S.A. Ch. 113 § 5286.

[171] 18 V.S.A. § 1871.

[172] See *Physician Assisted Death (PAD): Act 39: Patient Choice and Control at the End of Life*, VERMONT ETHICS NETWORK, http://vtethicsnetwork.org/pad.html.

[173] 12 V.S.A 519.

[174] Wilson Ring, "Vermont Legalizes Assisted Suicide," Huffington Post, May 21, 2013, http://www.huffingtonpost.com/2013/05/20/vermont-assisted-suicide_n_3309210.html

[175] Bob Kinzel, *Senate Extends Law Allowing Terminally Ill to Request Life-Ending Drugs* (VPR [News], Mar. 11, 2015), http://digital.vpr.net/post/senate-extends-law-allowing-terminally-ill-request-life-ending-drugs.

New Mexico and the *Morris* Case

A case currently pending before the New Mexico Supreme Court amply demonstrates how far advocates of physician-assisted suicide have come, and where they intend to go. The New Mexico Supreme Court heard oral argument on October 26, 2015, concerning the question of whether its citizens have a state constitutional right to assisted suicide.

The plaintiff patient, Aja Riggs, has been diagnosed with uterine cancer, but she is currently in remission. She was not terminally ill at the time the complaint was filed, but was specifically seeking "peace of mind" in knowing that she could avail herself of physician-assisted suicide "if her cancer returns."[176] Interestingly, the State never raised the question of Riggs' standing to challenge a statute that does not currently affect her, and neither did any of the judges who heard the case. Riggs is essentially asking the court for an advisory opinion should she decide at some future date to seek aid in dying. The named plaintiff, Katherine Morris, is an oncologist, as is a third plaintiff.

Acknowledging that New Mexico criminalizes assisted suicide, the complaint asserts that aid in dying, done by a physician, is not the same as the "assisted suicide" criminalized in New Mexico. "Aid in dying," the plaintiff's complaint asserts, "is a recognized term of art for the medical practice of providing a mentally competent terminally ill patient with a prescription for medication that the patient may choose to take in order to bring about a peaceful death."[177] If aid in dying were considered the same as the crime of assisted suicide, that would violate the New Mexico constitution's right to privacy, the plaintiffs claimed, pointing to the *Baxter* language.[178] Like Montana, New Mexico has a unique constitutional provision; while Montana recognized its citizens' rights to dignity, New Mexico recognizes its citizens

---

Unlike Oregon and Washington, the Vermont data is very difficult to find. The Vermont Department of Health is required to collect forms from participating physicians, but it does not publish the information. One death was reported in 2014, see *25 Surprising Physician Assisted Suicide Statistics*, HEALTHRESEARCHFUNDING.ORG, July 13, 2014, www.healthresearchfunding. org/physician-assisted-suicide-statistics/.

However, an individual's obituary mentioned that she had taken advantage of Act 39, and the *Burlington Free Press* editorial in favor of continuing reporting requirements (not that these are available anywhere on the Internet that I could find) mentioned three people who had used it. Aki Soga, *Keep Patient Choice Oversight*, BURLINGTON FREE PRESS, Feb. 1, 2015, available at http:// www.burlingtonfreepress.com/story/opinion/editorials/2015/02/01/editorial-keep-patient-choice-oversight/22597773/.

[176] *Morris et al. v. Brandenburg*, No. D-202-CV-2012-02909 (Jan. 13, 2014), ¶. 13.

[177] Plaintiff's Complaint, *Morris v. Brandenburg*, ¶ 12.

[178] As noted *supra* at note 155, they could not point to the holding in *Baxter* or any other state supreme court, as no high court has ever found any constitutional right to assisted suicide.

rights to "seek[] . . . and obtain [] safety and happiness."[179] (They don't call it the Land of Enchantment for nothing.) Plaintiffs also argued that this provision supported the right to choose the time and manner of one's death.

The trial court agreed that aid in dying was medical treatment. Its findings of fact included that "a standard of care for physician aid in dying, informed by clinical practices and authoritative literature, including Clinical Practice Guidelines, has developed."[180] Further, the court characterized aid in dying as "fall[ing] within the medical ambit of end of life choices available to a terminally ill patient."[181] However, it found that aid in dying still constituted assisted suicide under the statutory definition of assisted suicide and therefore was a felony under New Mexico law. Unlike *Baxter*, the court did not consider possible defenses, but went directly to plaintiff's constitutional challenge. The court found that there was a constitutional right under the New Mexico constitution to assisted suicide, becoming the first court since the *Glucksberg* decision to make this finding.

A deeply divided Court of Appeals reversed the district court's holding that aid in dying was a fundamental constitutional right. The two judges who so concluded both agreed with the district court's holding that the State's criminal prohibition on assisted suicide applied to aid in dying, and both relied heavily (as did the State at oral argument) on the U.S. Supreme Court's decision in *Washington v. Glucksberg*.[182] All three judges spent a great deal of time parsing the application of the Supreme Court's recent decision on gay marriage[183] (yes, gay marriage—more on that below) to assisted suicide, but differed substantially on many of the legal issues presented to them. The two basic holdings of the case are that criminalization of assisted suicide applies to physicians who provide aid in dying, and assisted suicide is not a fundamental right under the New Mexico constitution.

The Court of Appeals majority did emphatically reject—as had the District Court—plaintiffs' efforts to distinguish "aid in dying" from "suicide."[184] According to plaintiffs' witness, suicide is "a despairing, lonely experience," which shocks and alienates family members, as contrasted to aid in dying, which is done to maintain a sense of self and to maintain

---

179 New Mexico Constitution, Article II, Section 4.

180 *Morris et al. v. Brandenburg*, No. D-202-CV-2012-02909 (Jan. 13, 2014), Findings of Fact, ¶ 21.

181 *Id.* Conclusions of Law, ¶ II-N (although the court denominated its Conclusions of Law with "II," there is no "I" in the opinion).

182 *Morris v. Brandenburg*, 2015 N.M.C.A. 100 (Aug. 11, 2015), *cert. granted* Aug. 31, 2015), see especially paragraphs 30, 32, 33, 37, 58, 63, and 66. A detailed discussion of *Washington v. Glucksberg* can be found in Chapter 2.

183 Obergefell v. Hodges, 576 U.S. __, 135 S.Ct. 2584 (2015).

184 The dissent accepted this distinction (¶ 114), and went so far as to accuse the majority of "shocking disrespect for the individuals whose circumstances would bring them to seek aid in dying." *Id.*

relationships and connections.[185] The court acknowledged that these distinctions may be psychologically compelling, but found them legally irrelevant. Suicide is the taking of one's own life, whether it is done with rational consideration or impulsive wretchedness, and giving someone pills with the intention that the person will take those pills to end his or her life is assisting suicide, regardless of the reasons for the suicide.

In finding no fundamental right to assisted suicide, both judges in the majority relied heavily on the U.S. Supreme Court's holding in *Washington v. Glucksberg*, and discussed the meaning of the Supreme Court's references to *Glucksberg* in its 2015 decision finding a constitutional right for gay people to marry.[186] People who aren't lawyers may be scratching their heads—where is the association between gay marriage and assisted suicide? But *Glucksberg* actually presents a very thorny problem in constitutional jurisprudence to a holding that the U.S. Constitution protects the rights of gay people to marry. In finding no right to physician-assisted suicide in *Glucksberg*, the Supreme Court looked to the moral condemnation and criminalization of suicide throughout history as one of the basic reasons that assisted suicide could not be deemed a fundamental right. Sound familiar in the context of gay marriage?

In both gay marriage and assisted suicide, parties are seeking constitutional protection for actions that were historically abominated and are currently prohibited by law in at least some states. So when Justice Kennedy wrote his soaring and truly beautiful gay marriage decision, noting that concepts of liberty and justice change over time and the Due Process Clause interpretation must change with them, dissenting justices were quick to point to the dissonance between this language and *Glucksberg*, going so far as to say that "the majority's position requires it effectively to overrule *Glucksberg*, the leading modern case setting the bounds of due process."[187]

Justice Kennedy, who voted against assisted suicide in *Glucksberg*, took the time to specifically preclude using his decision on gay marriage to revisit assisted suicide:

> *Glucksberg* did insist that liberty under the Due Process Clause must be defined in a most circumscribed manner, with central reference to specific historical practices. Yet while that approach may have been appropriate for the asserted right there involved (physician-assisted suicide) it is inconsistent with the approach this Court has used in discussing other fundamental rights, including marriage and intimacy.[188]

---

[185] *Morris v. Brandenberg*, 2015 N.M.C.A. 100 at ¶ 7.
[186] *Obergefell v. Hodges*, 576 U.S. __, 135 S.Ct. 2584 (2015).
[187] *Obergefell v. Hodges*, 135 S.Ct. 2584, 2621 (2015) (Roberts, C.J. dissenting).
[188] *Obergefell v. Hodges*, 135 S.Ct. 2584, 2602 (2015).

This is not extraordinarily persuasive: it's different because I say so. But, even though the claims in *Morris* relied solely on the New Mexico state constitution, it is not surprising that the appellate judges in *Morris* felt that they had to grapple with the question of whether *Obergefell* had, indeed, effectively overruled *Glucksberg*.

Judges Garcia and Judge Hanisee were content to take Justice Kennedy at his word, without worrying too much about conflicting analytic frameworks; to them, Justice Kennedy had gone out of his way to specifically reaffirm the holding of *Glucksberg*,[189] a U.S. Supreme Court case specifically on point with the decision before them. Judge Vanzi, in dissent, questioned (as did the dissent in *Obergefell*) whether *Glucksberg* even remains as dispositive precedent.[190] Judge Vanzi, who is seeking appointment to the New Mexico Supreme Court,[191] filed a deeply researched and extensively argued opinion, which should save her (or favorably inclined justices) a lot of research and writing if she is chosen for the New Mexico Supreme Court.

In the opinion, she disagreed with virtually all of the legal analysis of the majority opinion. She assailed her colleagues for their mindless reliance on *Glucksberg*, inappropriately narrow reading of New Mexico's constitutional protections,[192] and failure to evaluate more carefully the purported state interests in criminalizing assisted suicide as provided by physicians to competent, terminally ill patients. In Judge Vanzi's opinion, the narrowness of the proposed right is crucial to its constitutional success.[193]

The judges in the majority, by contrast, were troubled by the *narrowness* of plaintiffs' claims.[194] By strategic necessity in assisted suicide cases, the plaintiffs must argue that assisted suicide is a tremendous benefit, desperately needed to alleviate excruciating suffering, but will apply only to the narrowest segment of society, and not be used to coerce vulnerable people into unwanted deaths. The plaintiffs' counsel in *Morris* may have erred by emphasizing to an appellate court in New Mexico how overwhelmingly white and upper middle class use of assisted suicide has turned out to be.[195] "What about everyone else in excruciating pain?" demanded the majority.[196] What about incompetent people, and people with more than six months to live? How can you argue that this is a fundamental right for all New Mexico citizens who are protected by the state constitution, but able to be utilized by

---

[189] *Morris v. Brandenburg*, ¶¶ 34–36, 58.
[190] *Id.* at ¶¶ 94–97, 100–102.
[191] Associated Press, *New Mexico Supreme Court Vacancy Attracts Eight Applicants* (KRQE News 13, Oct. 13, 2015), http://krqe.com/2015/10/13/new-mexico-supreme-court-vacancy-attracts-8-applicants/.
[192] *Morris v. Brandenburg*, ¶¶ 103–109.
[193] *Id.* at ¶¶ 127, 133.
[194] *Id.* at ¶¶ 44–47, 62, 64.
[195] *Id.* at ¶ 45.
[196] *Id.* at ¶¶ 44, 45, 64.

only the tiniest sliver of the population? Because all members of the court accepted as fact what the State, perhaps improvidently, conceded: that there are some terminally ill people whose pain cannot be controlled.[197] In addition, the majority was disturbed by the fact that immunity was extended only to physicians. What about loving family members? If aid in dying is a fundamental right, then immunity from assisting a person to exercise a fundamental right must extend to anyone who does it.[198]

Judge Garcia was open to arguments that plaintiffs might prevail in other claims, with different standards, and wanted to remand to the district court for further findings (which he surely could predict, given the tenor of the district court's decision). By contrast, Judge Hanisee firmly articulated the position of judicial restraint, which was that assisted suicide was no place for an unelected branch of government to be contradicting the legislature and striking down its statutes. Relying on both *Glucksberg* and New Mexico state law, Judge Hanisee asserted that a statute criminalizing assisted suicide would survive any level of judicial review, be it strict scrutiny, intermediate scrutiny, or rational basis scrutiny. Judge Vanzi found it unconstitutional under any of these three levels of scrutiny.

All judges of the court, and the State itself, agreed that citizens have a right to make their own end-of-life decisions and bring about their own deaths without the aid or assistance of another person.[199] Indeed, Judge Garcia hinted, patients who know they are terminally ill can stockpile morphine, and doctors can provide prescriptions for these medications, with perfect legality under current law. This showed a defect in plaintiffs' education of the judges: the kinds of drugs used for aid in dying are not the same drugs that are generally administered for pain. The kinds of drugs used for aid in dying (secobarbital in the United States and pentobarbital [Nembutal] in other countries) are not drugs used to relieve pain.[200] They are sleeping pills. Pentobarbital is the drug most commonly used to execute prisoners condemned to death and animals who are being put down. They are better for that purpose than most pain medications, especially opiates, which are relatively difficult drugs to use for purposes of suicide. Any doctor whose terminally ill patient asked him for a prescription for one of these drugs would probably at least suspect what the patient had in mind,[201] making him or her susceptible to the criminal law in New Mexico.

---

[197] *Id.* at ¶ 5.

[198] *Id.* at ¶¶ 46–47, 64.

[199] *Id.* at ¶ 28.

[200] Jennifer Fass & Andrea Fass, *Physician-Assisted Suicide: Ongoing Challenges for Pharmacists*, 68 Am. J. Health System Pharmacy 846 (2011).

[201] See Andrew Solomon's wonderful and informative piece, *A Death of One's Own*, N. Yorker, May 1995, http://andrewsolomon.com/articles/a-death-of-ones-own/ (his mother requested pills for insomnia, but refused to accept any but Seconal: "it seems likely the doctor knew why only Seconal would do.")

Judge Vanzi, in challenging the State's arguments about potential abuses of assisted suicide, made an argument that embodies one of my major concerns about the law of suicide in general, that the actions and decisions of third parties about someone else's death be differentiated from the actions and decisions of the person himself or herself about dying.[202] She noted that in cases involving terminal sedation, which is legal in New Mexico, third parties could be making decisions for the patient that did not necessarily comport with the individual's own desires.[203] I agree with her that third party decisions and actions that hasten a person's death should be subject to searching scrutiny, but not that potential abuses occurring in the present system of care necessarily constitute a valid argument for physician-assisted suicide.

The New Mexico Supreme Court heard oral argument at the end of October 2015, and will probably have decided the case by the time this book is released. The court is considered a liberal court, and California's recent passage of an assisted-suicide law may be influential.

Other States' Experiences with Assisted-Suicide Proposals

In Florida[204] and Alaska,[205] advocates of assisted suicide used the court system to argue for a constitutional right to assisted suicide. In both cases the Supreme Courts rejected the advocates' attempts, saying that an issue as contentious and divisive as assisted suicide should be resolved by the legislature. However, the experience of other state legislatures appears to indicate that this is, in many cases, an uphill battle. In California, legislative attempts to pass physician-assisted suicide failed in 1999, 2006, and 2007.

California

In the beginning, California was at the forefront of initiatives to legalize assisted suicide. In 1987, the California State Bar Conference passed Resolution No. 3-4-87 supporting physician assisted suicide. But after the failure of Proposition 161 in 1992, California fell off the radar screen as Oregon and Washington ballot initiatives took center stage. Legislative attempts to pass physician-assisted suicide came and went quietly in 1999, 2006, and 2007.

---

[202] For more discussion about my concerns that the rights of people to end their lives be clearly distinguished from the rights of anyone else to make this decision for another person, or actively implement such a decision, see Chapters 2, 4, and 7 in particular.

[203] *Morris v. Brandenburg*, note 182 at ¶ 134.

[204] Krischer v. McIver, 697 So.2d 97 (Fla. 1997).

[205] Sampson v. State, 31 P.3d 88 (Alaska 2001).

In 2015, advocates of assisted suicide roared back, combining legislative[206] and litigation[207] initiatives. The plaintiffs in one lawsuit are represented by a traditional big-name law firm,[208] showcasing the degree to which physician-assisted suicide has entered the mainstream. The case is cocounseled by Kathryn Tucker, who is cocounseling the other case filed in San Francisco Superior Court.[209] Tucker was the lawyer in *Baxter* and is counsel in *Morris*.

The language of the California complaint, like the New Mexico complaint in *Morris*, describes "aid in dying" as a "recognized medical practice"[210] with a "standard of care" and "clinical practice guidelines."[211] The lead plaintiff, Christine Donorovitch-O'Connell, is described as intolerant of morphine and unable to benefit from most common forms of pain management.[212] This is very important as a jurisprudential matter, because several justices in *Glucksberg* underscored that they might be willing to approve physician-assisted suicide if pain management was not available.[213] There are, as always, doctors named as plaintiffs in the complaint. In the California cases, they assert a claim under the First Amendment that the criminal prohibition on

---

[206] S.B. 128, introduced by Senators Lois Wolk and William Monning, essentially duplicates the Oregon and Washington programs. *California Lawmakers to Introduce New Right-to-Die Legislation*, CALIFORNIA HEALTHLINE, Jan. 21, 2015, http://www.californiahealthline.org/articles/2015/1/21/calif-lawmakers-to-introduce-new-righttodie-legislation.

[207] *Donorovitch-O'Donnell v. Harris*, No. 37-2015-00016404-CU-CR-CTL, Super. Ct., Cty of San Diego, Complaint and Request for Expedited Injunctive Relief (Super. Ct., San Diego County, May 15, 2015), https://www.compassionand-choices.org/userfiles/Complaint-CA-Lawsuit-Revised.pdf.

[208] O'Melveny and Myers is the lead law firm in *Donorovitch-O'Donnell v. Harris*, No. 37-2015-00016404-CU-CR-CTL, *id.*

[209] Brody v. Harris, Super. Ct. of the Cty and County of San Francisco, Complaint filed Feb. 11, 2015, [Disability Rights Legal Center], available at http://disability-rightslegalcenter.org/sites/www.disabilityrightslegalcenter.org/files/2015-02-11%20CA%20Aid%20in%20Dying%20Complaint.pdf.

[210] Donorovitch-O'Donnell v. Harris, Complaint, ¶ 2, [Compassion & Choices.org], https://www.compassionandchoices.org/userfiles/Complaint-CA-Lawsuit.pdf.

[211] *Id.* at ¶ 28.

[212] *Id.* at ¶ 5.

[213] *Washington v. Glucksberg*, note 1 at 736–37 (because terminally ill patients have no barrier to obtaining medication to alleviate suffering, no need to reach the question of whether a mentally competent person experiencing great suffering has a constitutionally cognizable interest in controlling the circumstances of his or her imminent death), and 745 (Stevens, J. concurring) ("Avoiding intolerable pain and the indignity of living one's final days incapacitated and in agony is certainly '[a]t the heart of [the] liberty . . . to define one's own concept of existence, of meaning, of the universe, and of the mystery of human life' [citation omitted]' ").

assisted suicide precludes them from referring their patients to doctors in another state.

The superior court judge in the *Donorovitch* case rejected the plaintiffs' constitutional claims, finding that the case required the judge to make new law. As the lowest rung in the judicial hierarchy, the judge declined to do this, indicating this was a job for higher courts or for the legislature.[214] He also joined the U.S. Supreme Court in upholding the distinction between withdrawing life support and providing the means to end life.[215] Supreme courts in other states, such as Florida,[216] Alaska,[217] and Connecticut,[218] have also rejected advocates' attempts to establish a right to aid in dying, saying that an issue as contentious and divisive as assisted suicide should be resolved by the legislature.

However, the California legislature and Governor Jerry Brown rendered court action moot when the legislature passed and Governor Brown signed legislation implementing assisted suicide in California. Thus, if the California Supreme Court hears any case, it will be one challenging assisted suicide rather than the prohibition on assisted suicide. When S.B. 128, the End of Life Option Act,[219] did not pass during the legislative session, advocates of assisted suicide reintroduced it during a special session called by Governor Jerry Brown to deal with healthcare issues. Although Governor Brown criticized the use of the special legislative session for this purpose, he had signed the first law in the country allowing terminally ill people to withdraw life-sustaining treatment in 1976, and spoke to Brittany Maynard on the telephone in her last week of life. He signed the legislation, stating,

> In the end I was left to reflect on what I would want in the face of my own death. I do not know what I would do if I were dying in prolonged and excruciating pain. I am certain, however, that it would be a comfort to be able to consider the option afforded by this bill. And I wouldn't deny that right to others.[220]

---

[214] Julie Watson, *San Diego Judge Indicates He'll Dismiss Right to Die Lawsuit by Terminally Ill Californians*, U.S. NEWS AND WORLD REPORT (online), July 24, 2015, http://www.usnews.com/news/us/articles/2015/07/24/california-judge-to-rule-on-right-to-die-lawsuit.

[215] *Id.*

[216] Krischer v. McIver, 697 So.2d 97 (Fla. 1997).

[217] Sampson v. State, 31 P.3d 88 (Alaska 2001).

[218] Blick v. Office of the Div. of Crim. Justice, No. CV-09-533392 (Ct. Sup. Ct. June 1, 2010).

[219] See California Legislative Information, *SB-128 End of Life (2015-2016)*, https://leginfo.legislature.ca.gov/faces/billVersionsCompareClient.xhtml?bill_id=201520160SB128 for the most recent version of the bill.

[220] Patrick McGreevy, *After Struggling, Jerry Brown Makes Assisted Suicide Legal*, L. A. TIMES, Oct. 5, 2015.

These are moving words, and make puzzling his rejection, a week later, of legislation that would authorize terminally ill people who had exhausted all treatment options and wanted desperately to live to have access to promising drugs and devices still under review by the Food and Drug Administration, the so-called Right to Try legislation.[221] Although Brown stated that his reason for rejecting this bill was that federal law already permitted "compassionate use" exceptions to the prohibition on access to unapproved drugs, state laws providing access to unapproved drugs for terminally ill people already exist in 24 states.[222] It may be worth noting that the medical community generally opposed the Right to Try bill.[223] Conversely, potentially powerful opposition to assisted suicide was neutralized when the California Medical Association changed its position on aid in dying from opposition to neutrality on S.B. 128 in May 2015, a huge change from past practice.[224] In addition, Senator Dianne Feinstein endorsed the bill.[225]

The new law is modeled on Oregon's assisted-suicide program, but with a number of important distinctions. It sunsets in ten years. Most important for our purposes, the provisions regarding people with psychiatric disabilities may run afoul of the Americans with Disabilities Act (ADA)'s prohibition against discrimination on the basis of disability. While previous states' enactments had carefully limited consideration to whether an individual's capacity to make decisions was impaired, the California legislation requires referral to a mental health professional if "there are indications of a mental disorder."[226] Since this section is in addition to a separate section regarding capacity, it constitutes an eligibility criterion for assisted suicide that applies only to people with mental disabilities. The ADA prohibits "eligibility criteria that screen out or tend to screen out individuals with a disability" from "fully and equally enjoying any service, activity or benefit" provided by state law.[227] This would require a court to assume that aid in dying is a benefit to terminally ill people in that it permits them autonomy (and therefore is not discrimination), as opposed to adverse treatment on the basis of disability

---

[221] Tracy Seipel, *"Right to Try" Bill; Brown Rejects Proposal to Let Terminal Patients Use Unapproved Drugs and Devices*, SAN JOSE MERCURY NEWS, Oct. 12, 2015, http://www.mercurynews.com/health/ci_28954390/right-try-bill-brown-vetoes-proposal-let-terminal?source=JBarTicker.

[222] *Id.*

[223] *Id.*

[224] Press Release, California Medical Association, *California Medical Association Removes Opposition to Aid in Dying Bill*, May 20, 2015, http://www.cmanet.org/news/press-detail?article=california-medical-association-removes.

[225] Josh Richman, *Dianne Feinstein Endorses CA. Assisted Suicide Bill*, CONTRA COSTA TIMES, Mar. 17, 2015, http://www.ibabuzz.com/politics/2015/03/17/dianne-feinstein-endorses-cas-assisted-suicide-bill/.

[226] S.B. 128 § 443.5(a)(1)(A)(ii).

[227] 28 C.F.R. 35.130(b)(8).

because it manifests society's lesser valuation of their lives. Both are probably true, but a court would have to sort through these questions.

There are several potential defenses to such a claim. Would a person's consent to the putative discrimination represented by aid in dying shield the statute? People with mental disorders are not excluded from assisted suicide unless the mental health professional determines they lack capacity,[228] but it is an extra step that is required only for people with mental disorders. Because this burden is imposed on top of the legitimate capacity inquiry (and therefore imposed unnecessarily), it may discriminate against people with psychiatric disabilities by forcing them to take an extra step to exercise their rights under the law.[229]

There are definitely good provisions in the Act. It makes starkly clear that aid in dying cannot be requested on a person's behalf by a third party, and underscores that disability is not, in and of itself, a sufficient reason for provision of a lethal prescription.

This law may well be challenged in the courts. But, as in *Lee v. Oregon*,[230] the procedural aspects of such a challenge are tricky. The concept of standing to assert a claim, which requires that the person asserting the statutory challenge be injured by the statute, makes it difficult to figure out who the potential plaintiffs might be. Opponents of the concept of assisted suicide point to the larger injury done to the social fabric and to vulnerable people, but passage by the legislature is understood to mean that the legislature weighed these factors and concluded that the benefits of aid in dying outweighed its potential risks. A person being coerced into assisted suicide is protected by the statute itself, which provides an action against such coercers. People who are seeking assistance in dying are presumably not going to challenge the statute. Physicians are protected in the statute itself from being forced to participate in assisted suicide.

Nevertheless, as noted earlier, a court may never consider the substantive issue of whether assisted suicide constitutes discrimination against people with disabilities, because the only people suffering an "actual injury" under the law—the people using assisted suicide—are unlikely to challenge the law. Disabled people have argued that assisted suicide devalues their lives, but that kind of assertion is not concrete enough to state a legal claim.

One path for opponents of assisted suicide is to go back through the legislative process, but experience in Oregon, Montana, and Vermont suggests that this will not be successful. In California, more than most states, ballot

---

[228] S.B. 128, § 443.5(a)(1)(A)(iii).
[229] See, e.g., *Ellen S. v. Florida Board of Bar Examiners*, 859 F.Supp. 1489 (S.D. Fla. 1994); *Medical Society of New Jersey v. Jacobs*, Civ.A. No. 93-3670 (W.G.B.), 1993 WL 413016 at *7 (D.N.J. Oct. 5, 1993).
[230] See Chapter 3, pp. 142–143.

initiatives of all kinds have been offered to undo unpopular legislation, but there is little to show that this legislation is unpopular.

The implementation of the End of Life Option Act will change the face of assisted-suicide policy in the United States. California has 38,802,500 people,[231] well over twice the population of all states to have approved assisted suicide so far, even if you include New Mexico.[232] Certainly California is larger than the Netherlands, Belgium, Switzerland, and Luxembourg combined.[233] In fact, California is the largest political entity ever to have passed assisted suicide.

This difference in size and population means that assisted suicide in California will look very different than it does in Vermont, Oregon, Washington, and Montana—or even the Netherlands or Belgium—where medicine is still practiced by individual doctors, where the population is primarily white, and where there are no pockets of extreme poverty to raise questions about the relationship between aid in dying and access to care.

Kaiser Permanente has more than 7,800,000 members in California,[234] more than the combined population of Vermont, Montana, New Mexico, and Oregon, and just over the population of Washington State. When the Oregon Death with Dignity Act became law, Kaiser attempted to implement its provisions while reassuring member doctors that participation was entirely voluntary.[235] If a member wished to avail himself or herself of aid in dying and his or her physician was unwilling to take part, Kaiser would check with the chief of the primary or specialty care service involved with the patient to identify another Kaiser physician who was willing to do so.[236] Kaiser set up a regional ethics service to screen requests by its members for aid in dying, including providing a consulting doctor not affiliated with Kaiser. The memorandum asked physicians to voluntarily identify themselves if they were

---

[231] United States Census Bureau, State & County QuickFacts, People QuickFacts 2014, http://quickfacts.census.gov/qfd/states/06000.html.

[232] The Census Bureau gives the following figures for 2014: Oregon 3.97 million; Washington 7,062,000; Vermont 626,562; Montana 1,024,000; and New Mexico 2,086,000.

[233] The combined populations of Belgium, the Netherlands, and Luxembourg add up to about 29 million people (as of 2013), see BeNeLux Business Council, *About Luxembourg*, BENELUXBC.COM, http://portal.beneluxbc.com/uae-and-benelux/about-luxembourg.

[234] *Fast Facts about Kaiser Permanente*, KAISER PERMANENTE (Aug. 2015), http://share.kaiserpermanente.org/article/fast-facts-about-kaiser-permanente/.

[235] Email from Janet Price to Kaiser Permanente Northwest Division, in Press Release, Oregon Death with Dignity Act: Physician Participation (Aug. 6, 2002) (for a copy of the memorandum laying out this process, see http://www.kaiserpapers.org/ass.html).

[236] *Id.*

willing to participate in aid in dying, either for their patients or for members who were not their patients.[237]

I am not suggesting in the least that there is anything wrong in complying with the law. I disagree with those who suggest that health maintenance organizations (HMOs) would aggressively pursue assisted suicide to reduce their costs.[238] But the sheer size of a number of California HMOs means that if they systematize assisted suicide, it will vastly increase the practice from today's numbers. It is not just that California has more people; while Compassion & Choices may have a list of individual doctors and a staff trying to facilitate aid in dying, HMOs are huge operations that can set up aid in dying systemically. It's been individualized in states such as Vermont and Oregon, one person at a time, and reporting is easily manageable where it is required. Systems must be created when millions of people are involved, but systemic problems are very different from individual problems. It is hard to imagine how this system can be effectively monitored by the State. These problems of size and systems issues could be a potent mix with Kaiser's well-publicized problems regarding the adequacy of its care for its suicidal members in California.[239]

I am not trying to pick on Kaiser Permanente. It is just a very large and visible proxy for one set of issues that much smaller states have not faced after they adopted assisted suicide. There are other issues unrelated to HMOs, for example, translation of the concepts of aid in dying into dozens of different languages, including American Sign Language. This is not much of an issue in Vermont, Montana, and Oregon. But it will be in California.

Finally, California is large enough that it will likely present any number of issues: Can a competent person refuse treatment for a treatable illness that will be terminal without treatment (e.g., tuberculosis, or perhaps, anorexia) and then request aid in dying? Does the answer change if the person is a Jehovah's Witness? It is certain that implementing aid in dying in California

---

[237] *Id.*

[238] See, e.g., Wesley J. Smith, *Doctors of Death: Kaiser Solicits Its Doctors to Kill,* Nat' Rev. Online, Aug. 19, 2002, reprinted by the Discovery Institute, http://www.discovery.org/a/1246.

[239] In 2013, the California Department of Managed Health Care levied a $4 million fine against Kaiser for blocking its members from timely access to mental health services, Cynthia H. Craft, "Kaiser to Pay $4 Million Fine Over Access to Mental Health Services," Sacramento Bee, Sept. 9, 2014, http://www.sacbee.com/news/local/health-and-medicine/healthy-choices/article2609176.html. Also in 2013, a class action lawsuit was filed against Kaiser by members with mental health issues, *Futterman v Kaiser Foundation Health Plan, Inc. and Does I-XX, Inclusive,* Case No. RG13 697775 (Superior Ct. Alameda Cty), which contained specific allegations that delays in treatment caused some Kaiser members to commit suicide. On Aug. 31, 2015, the judge struck some of the plaintiffs' claims and sustained others, http://www.sl-employmentlaw.com/files/order-on-demurrer.pdf.

will bring to the fore the issue of access for people with psychiatric disabilities. People with serious mental illness are massively more likely to have cancer, much less likely to get decent medical treatment, and much more likely to die of cancer. If they are denied access to aid in dying that is available to other terminally ill cancer patients, there may well be a (winning) lawsuit alleging discrimination on the basis of psychiatric disability (see Chapter 10 for an extended discussion of this issue). What about terminally ill patients in state psychiatric institutions or prisons?

There are other questions. How will California regulate the involvement of the medical profession in meeting the demand to end life in dubious cases? Already in California, doctors have been charged with murder and manslaughter for deaths associated with prescription overdoses.[240] This is a rare occurrence, but one which is associated with misuse of a medical license to inappropriately prescribe drugs.[241] It is certainly possible to differentiate between reckless overprescription of drugs that *may* lead to death and knowing prescription of drugs that *will* lead to death. But enforcement actions against medical professionals are few and far between,[242] and boards of licensing in medicine must usually wait for complaints. In any event, the bill prohibits any criminal, liability, or disciplinary action against any medical professional participating "in good faith" in accordance with the provisions of the Act. There will surely be court cases in years to come regarding the interpretation of the immunity provisions and others in the End of Life Options Act.

New York

The same double-pronged approach being pursued in California has also been launched in New York, with bills in the legislature, and yet another lawsuit with Drs. Timothy Quill, Samuel Klagsbrun, and Howard Grossman as plaintiffs[243]—grayer, with a bigger beard in the case of Quill, but still trying to

---

[240] Marisa Gerber, *Murder Trial Sends Message to Doctors: Don't get Reckless, Medical Expert Says*, L. A. TIMES, Aug. 31, 2015, http://www.latimes.com/local/lanow/la-me-ln-murder-trial-tseng-doctor-20150829-story.html; Tracey Kaplan, *Deadly Overdose: Los Gatos Doctor Prosecuted in Rare Pill Mill Case*, SAN JOSE MERCURY-NEWS, June 22, 2015.

[241] In 2002, a Florida doctor was convicted of manslaughter in the OxyContin-related death of a patient, *Florida Doctor Convicted of Manslaughter in Oxycontin Overdose Case*, CALIFORNIA HEALTHLINE, Feb. 20, 2002, http://www.californiahealthline.org/articles/2002/2/20/florida-doctor-convicted-of-manslaughter-in-oxycontin-overdose-case?view=print; doctors have also been convicted in New York.

[242] See Chapter 5 for an extensive discussion of the deficiencies in professional oversight of medical professionals.

[243] Myers et al. v. Schneiderman et al., No. 151162/2015 (N.Y. Sup. Ct. N.Y. Cty).

bring physician-assisted suicide to the State of New York. The lawsuit claims that the law criminalizing assisted suicide does not apply to "aid in dying," because "aid in dying" is not "suicide." It also revives the equal protection and due process claims of the previous lawsuit in which Quill was a plaintiff. In another echo of older times, one of the plaintiffs, Steven Goldenberg, has AIDS, a condition far less commonly seen these days in discussions of assisted suicide. The lead plaintiff, Sara Myers, has ALS. The third plaintiff, Eric Sieff, has cancer which is "potentially terminal." None of the conditions is necessarily expected to cause the plaintiff death in six months.

Although the plaintiffs do not rely on any federal rights—no one is asking the Supreme Court to reconsider *Glucksberg* or the previous *Quill*—the Attorney General of New York filed a motion to dismiss the case in April 2015, arguing that there was no reason to believe that the New York State constitution provided greater protection than the federal constitution.[244]

Three proposed New York bills called "The End of Life Options Act,"[245] (plural where the California legislation is End of Life Option Act), proposed in the New York State Senate, the Death with Dignity Act, proposed in the New York State Assembly, and the Patient Self-Determination Act, are much more similar to Oregon's current program than California S.B. 128. These bills died in the New York legislature. The court case is considered the better option by assisted-suicide advocates in New York.[246]

The same considerations discussed with relation to California apply to New York, although they might be more manageable, as they would center around the New York City area.

Hawaii

Of all the states where assisted suicide remains illegal, Hawaii has probably tried the hardest to legalize it. Hawaii has tried more often to pass assisted-suicide legislation than any other state. After all, it had been the first state (in 1993) to take gay marriage seriously. In 2002, assisted-suicide legislation very similar to the Oregon Death with Dignity Act passed the Hawaii House of Representatives and failed in the Hawaii Senate by three votes.[247]

---

[244] *Myers et al. v. Schneiderman*, Defendant's Motion to Dismiss (N.Y. Sup. Ct. N.Y. Cty Apr. 2015), http://endoflifechoicesny.org/wp-content/uploads/2015/05/2015-04-14-Mem.ofLawinSupp.ofMotiontoDismiss.pdf.

[245] New York State Senate, *Senate Bill S3685: Establishes the New York End of Life Options Act*, http://open.nysenate.gov/legislation/bill/S3685-2015.

[246] Joseph Ryder, *Dying with Dignity: A Patients* (sic) *Right to Die*, STONY BROOK PRESS, May 29, 2015, http://sbpress.com/2015/05/dying-with-dignity-a-patients-right-to-die/.

[247] Patients Rights Council, *Courts to Determine If Assisted Suicide is "Legitimate" Under Federal Law*, 16 UPDATE 024, 1 (2002), http://www.patientsrightscouncil.org/site/update024/#26 (regarding 2002 bill failure to pass).

In 2009[248] and 2011,[249] no fewer than three assisted-suicide bills were introduced in the legislature and failed to advance.

Assisted suicide has broad popular support in Hawaii. However, Josh Green, the Chairman of the Senate Health and Judiciary Committee is a doctor, and the Hawaii Medical Society firmly opposes physician-assisted suicide. Scott Foster, the communications director for a group that advocates assisted suicide, expresses concern that the majority of legislator campaign funds come from the health sector.[250] With those practices hindering progress on any death with dignity bills, Foster mentions, "there will be no resolution to one of the most important issues of our time."[251]

Finally, in 2013, assisted-suicide proponents agreed to limit their proposals to people with terminal illnesses who were older than fifty, and to have a "monitor" to protect the patient.[252] To obtain a prescription, the patient had to designate a competent adult to witness the event and complete a required form. The monitor can stop the administration of medication and get medical assistance to reverse the effect of the medication "if the monitor has reason to believe that the qualified patient has had a change of mind and is not able to effectively express or communicate the wish not to proceed."[253] Needless to say, this language is not found in any other state permitting assisted suicide. And the bill still did not pass.

Conclusion

After you clear away the smoke and bombast of the proponents and opponents of assisted suicide, a few facts remain. First, the floodgates argument was greatly exaggerated, at least as to Oregon, but that may be changing now. While there are no cars lined up at the Oregon and Washington borders, Brittany Maynard is only one of a number of people who moved to Oregon specifically to take advantage of its assisted-suicide laws. After seventeen years in Oregon and six years in Washington, assisted suicides account for a tiny minority of all deaths, and even a small minority of deaths by suicide. The increase in assisted suicides over the years doesn't even equal the increase in population. Most of the people who get prescriptions for lethal medication don't fill them, and half the people who fill them don't take them. Not even Freeland, who was depressed and suicidal enough to be committed to a psychiatric ward, used the lethal medication he had in his house for more than two years to commit suicide. There are many indications that

---

[248] 2009 Haw. H.B. 587 (N.S.); 2009 Haw. H.B. 806 (N.S.); 2009 Haw. S.B. 1159 (N.S.).

[249] 2011 Haw. S.B. 803 (N.S.).

[250] Id.

[251] Id.

[252] 2013 Haw. H.B. 606 (N.S.).

[253] Id.

these prescriptions are obtained to provide the comfort of control to people who have little of it left in their lives, just as the option of suicide has always provided the comfort of control to people who are not terminally ill, but also experience their lives as painful and powerless.

Nor are there—so far—poverty-stricken, disabled people being coerced into assisted suicide. Rather, the majority of people seem to be upper-class and upper-middle-class white people accustomed to controlling their lives, who are now controlling their deaths as well—doctors, attorneys, and well-educated professionals who are not used to waiting in misery and discomfort for anything and are certainly not going to start putting up with that at the end of their lives. Thus, so far, right now, autonomy and control rather than uncontrollable pain drive assisted suicide. Everyone acknowledges that physical pain is practically a nonissue in driving people to end their lives.

Conversely, the requirement that only people who are doomed to die in six months from a terminal illness are getting these prescriptions cannot be met and is not being met. As doctors themselves would have been the first to tell you, the assessment that people will die in six months is sophisticated guesswork. The conditions that people have are terminal in a lot of cases: cancer and ALS account for the vast majority of diagnoses of people who avail themselves of assisted suicide. And if you read the reports carefully enough, you can spot a few ringers, such as benign neoplasms. Really?

Nor are people often obtaining prescriptions from their own doctors. And while some doctors have known the individual for whom they are prescribing a fatal dose of medication for many years, a significant number of doctors met the patients for the sole purpose of examining them and providing them with a prescription for fatal medication. There is significant evidence of doctor-shopping: that is, some patients who seek prescriptions are refused by one or multiple doctors and keep asking until they find one.[254]

But there are new developments on the horizon that may change this relatively stable experience. Montana, Vermont, and Oregon are states with small populations, and not much in the way of urban megacenters. Individuals who wanted to avail themselves of assisted suicide would call up Compassion & Choices if their own doctors didn't want to help, and get an individual doctor. Organized medicine didn't touch assisted suicide—until recently.

The program of the Seattle Cancer Care Alliance is the first time a group practice has publicly announced that it offers physician-assisted suicide in its menu of treatments. This, however well-intentioned, is a game-changer, and it is an initiative that is sure to be followed if New York and California's

---

[254] This personal approach seems to work better than the approach of Ernst Haas, described in Chapter 4, who sent a mass mailing to 170 psychiatrists in Switzerland attempting to find one who would evaluate his competence and prescribe medication to allow him to die.

assisted-suicide initiatives pass. I don't think it's an accident that the Seattle Cancer Care Alliance physician-assisted suicide program has netted substantially more minorities and Medicaid participants in assisted suicide than is the case for the State of Washington as a whole. It's not that this a sinister or ominous conspiracy: it's that entitled upper middle class white people are more likely to have both the time and the experience to take the initiative to arrange for physician-assisted suicide when it is not offered by their regular physicians. When assisted suicide is offered as an option to people, rather than people having to go to some lengths to pursue it for themselves, my guess is that both a larger and a very different group of people will participate.

So looking to the Oregon experience is fine, if you're Vermont. It's not so persuasive if you are New York or California. Even proponents of assisted suicide in New York think that in one year, 200 to 300 New Yorkers will end their lives: almost half of the 700 or so Oregonians who have died in the last eighteen years.[255] Oregon, Vermont, Montana, and New Mexico represent a very small scale compared to New York and California. And when substantially sized healthcare entities begin adopting assisted suicide and framing it as a treatment option, we will be in a whole new ballgame with regard to assisted suicide, and the former analyses, arguments, and data will carry less weight in prognosticating the future.

In this environment, courts in New York and California may want to follow the lead of the courts in Florida, Alaska, and Connecticut that declined to rule on the issue. The New York and California plaintiffs do not say that they want to die now; several of them would not even meet the criteria of the legislative proposals in their own states that they be six months from death's door. As members of the Supreme Court noted in *Glucksberg*, this is the kind of issue that benefits from discussion on many fronts, not simply a few lawyers and judges.[256] Now that California has adopted physician-assisted suicide, our national experience of this mode of dying will be very different than it has been for the past twenty years.

---

[255] Dareh Gregorian, *Three Terminally Sick Patients Sue New York Over Assisted Suicide Law Against Doctors—Hoping to Follow in Brittany Maynard's Footsteps*, N. Y. DAILY NEWS, Feb. 15, 2015, http://www.nydailynews.com/new-york/3-terminally-sick-patients-sue-ny-assisted-suicide-law-article-1.2103304.

[256] Stephen R. Latham, *"Aid in Dying" in the Courts: Policy and Politics*, 45 HASTINGS CENTER REP. 3, 11–12 (May-June 2015).

4

International Perspectives on Assisted Suicide and Euthanasia

Introduction

About a million people commit suicide every year; 60% of them are from Asian countries,[1] which is roughly proportional to Asia's share of the world's population. Suicide rates in different countries are far from proportional, however; they vary wildly across the world, from 2.4 per 100,000 (Israel)[2] and 7.6 per 100,000 (Spain)[3] to 29.1 per 100,000 in South Korea to more than 100 per 100,000 in Greenland. The United States can be found comfortably in the middle of the world pack at 12.6 in 100,000.[4] While data about suicide is internally conflicting even in the United States, it is doubtful that the variation in suicide rates across the world can be entirely accounted for by poor or inaccurate recordkeeping. Nor does the availability or sophistication of mental health treatment seem to correlate with reduced suicide rates.

Rather, as Durkheim posited more than a century ago, national cultural attitudes toward suicide, including assumptions about individual autonomy

---

[1] Ah-Young Lim, Ah-Rong Lee, Ahmad Hatim, et al., *Clinical and Sociodemographic Correlates of Suicidality in Patients with Major Depressive Disorder from Six Asian Countries*, 14 BMC PSYCHIATRY 37 (2014), http://www.biomedcentral.com/1471-244X/14/37.

[2] Yaron Kelner, *Israel Records First Drop in Suicide Rates Since 2007*, YEDIOTH INTERNET, June, 29, 2014, www.ynetnews.com/articles/0,7340,L-4534971,00.html.

[3] Press Release, Instituto Nacional de Estadistica, Deaths According to Cause of Death: Year 2012, (Jan. 31, 2014), p. 7, www.ine.es/en/prensa/np830_en.pdf.

[4] See Chapter 7, see also American Foundation for the Prevention of Suicide, *Suicide Prevention Investment Needed to Reverse Trend of Increasing Suicide* (Oct. 8, 2014), https://www.afsp.org/news-events/in-the-news/suicide-prevention-investment-needed-to-reverse-trend-of-increasing-suicide.

and communitarian responsibility, seem to hold much stronger sway, and not always in the direction one might predict.[5] China, for example, is one of the very few countries in the world where more women commit suicide than men, by a factor of about three to one (in the United States, men commit suicide four times as often as women).

Attitudes and practices regarding assisted suicide also vary across the world, and seem, as in the United States, to be relatively unrelated to attitudes or practices about suicide and suicide prevention.

The differences between how suicide and assisted suicide are treated by law and policy in the United States and in the rest of the world is striking, especially the rest of the Western industrialized world. In part, this is the result of the fact that Europe, Australia, and New Zealand are far more secular societies than the United States, and that Roman Catholics and fundamentalist Protestants form one of the principal sources of opposition to assisted suicide in the United States. However, nations with strong Catholic presence, such as Belgium, also have extremely broad acceptance of assisted suicide, and predominantly Catholic Quebec just passed the first euthanasia law on the North American continent.[6]

While the United States is more religious than Europe, and thus more skeptical about assisted suicide, it is also more distrustful of government and medical expertise, and its emphasis on autonomy and civil liberties leads to a greater emphasis on the rights of people to make the decision to end their lives. Even people with psychiatric disabilities, who are usually excluded from generalizations about autonomy, are accorded (at least on paper) significant procedural and substantive rights before they are involuntarily committed for being suicidal.

Thus, in Europe, a broader population of people have access to and avail themselves of assisted suicide than in the United States, while at the same time, a broader population of people are involuntarily detained and treated for being suicidal. This is not as paradoxical as it might seem: in both situations, medical professionals are the gatekeepers of death, either to admit and facilitate or to forcibly prevent entrance. Europeans seem to trust medical professionals more than Americans do, with the result that medical professionals have more power to decide when people should and should not be allowed to kill themselves.

This European trust in the medical profession extends in some countries to giving doctors the power to do the killing themselves. In European countries where euthanasia is permitted, it is preferred over assisted suicide, where the individual makes the final decision to take the drugs. In Belgium, euthanasia was legalized before assisted suicide. In the Netherlands, a physician

---

[5] EMIL DURKHEIM, SUICIDE: A STUDY IN SOCIOLOGY 152–71 (John Spaulding trans., 1997 (Free Press 1951).
[6] See pp. 208–209, *infra*.

initiated the movement toward permitting euthanasia, and, for the most part, organized medicine approved. Finally, because all the European countries that permit assisted suicide and euthanasia do so not only for terminal conditions, but for incurable disabilities, in European countries permitting assisted suicide, people with chronic and intractable psychiatric disabilities can avail themselves of assisted suicide.

In evaluating assisted suicide in other countries, we will examine cases involving people with psychiatric disabilities, the processes used in different countries, the role of the medical and mental health professions, and the distinctions between assisted suicide and euthanasia in the policy and practices of these countries. I have divided the discussion into geographical areas of the world, and emphasized Europe because it has by far the most developed policies and law. I am not covering all of the countries in the world, or indeed in Europe, but only selected ones to give a context to the debate in the United States.

Assisted Suicide and Euthanasia in Europe

While the majority of European countries criminalize assisted suicide,[7] a number of them have permitted assisted suicide for decades. There is no consensus in Europe on assisted suicide.[8] Federations such as Germany and Switzerland have different practices from state to state and canton to canton, in the same way the United States has different practices from state to state. European practices are very different from those in this country, and from each other. As noted earlier, in countries such as the Netherlands and Belgium, euthanasia is used far more often than assisted suicide. In these countries, in sharp contrast to the United States, euthanasia is considered to provide greater protection against abuse. In Switzerland, however, euthanasia is strictly prohibited, and physicians need not be involved in assisted suicide at all. In Germany, assisted suicide is also prohibited, although physicians who take part in it are subject to far lesser penalties than others who assist suicide. In Great Britain, conversely, assisted suicide is more likely to be criminally prosecuted if the person assisting the suicide is the person's treating physician.

---

[7] Koch v. Germany, No. 497/09, Eur. Ct. H. R. 303 July 19, 2012; [2013] 56 Eur. Ct. H. R. 6 (at the time, thirty-six of forty-three member states criminalized assisted suicide; since then, France has approved legislation that permits people to be placed into "deep sleep"—essentially anaesthetized—until they die, see Angelique Chrisafis, *French Parliament Votes Through "Deep Sleep" Bill for Terminally Ill*, THE GUARDIAN, Mar. 17, 2015, http://www.theguardian.com/world/2015/mar/17/french-parliament-deep-sleep-law-terminally-ill-euthanasia.)

[8] Haas v. Switzerland, App. No. 31322/07, 53 Eur. H.R. Rep. 33 (2011) [Eur. Ct. H.R. (2011/10)], http://hudoc.echr.coe.int/sites/eng/pages/search.aspx?i=001-102940.

European countries have a much broader idea of which conditions are appropriate for assisted suicide; they include people suffering from incurable conditions causing intractable pain. Many European courts and policymakers find the U.S. approach, limiting assisted suicide to terminal illness with months to live, absurd:

> Quite apart from the notorious difficulty in assessing life expectancy even for the terminally ill, there seems to me significantly more justification in assisting people to die if they have the prospect of living for years a life that they regarded as valueless, miserable and often painful than if they have only a few months left to live.[9]

These countries also turn down as many as half the requests received for assisted suicide (no data is kept on this in the states permitting assisted suicide in the United States). Advocates of assisted suicide in the Netherlands are currently promoting assisted suicide for anyone who wants to die and is older than the age of seventy. In Belgium and in the Netherlands, minors of any age in severe, intractable, and incurable pain can already avail themselves of assisted suicide.

Most interesting for purposes of this book, the countries in Europe that permit assisted suicide consider psychiatric disabilities to be another kind of potentially painful, intractable, and incurable condition. In the United States, people with psychiatric disabilities are supposed to be rigorously screened out from assisted suicide, and the possibility that they might avail themselves of assisted suicide is one of the principal arguments against it. In Switzerland, the highest court has ruled that excluding people with psychiatric disabilities from assisted suicide programs constitutes illegal discrimination. Conversely, both Switzerland and the Netherlands do not hesitate to investigate and prosecute when it appears that people who might have been incompetent were assisted to die.

The European Court of Human Rights

Although European countries are both independent and different from each other, their common values are asserted in the European Convention on Human Rights and enforced by the European Court of Human Rights. While some human rights are absolute across all countries, others implicate cultural issues, and the court allows leeway in different national practices. This leeway is called "the margin of appreciation," and it has proved crucial to the court's handling of cases involving assisted suicide.

---

[9] R (on the Application of Nicklinson and another) v. Minister of Justice, [2014] U.K.S.C. 38, para. 122, https://www.supremecourt.uk/decided-cases/docs/uksc_2013_0235_judgment.pdf.

The European Court of Human Rights has considered five assisted suicide cases: The first involved a person with tetraplegia and was brought against Spain. It was dismissed for lack of jurisdiction because the complainant killed herself before the case was heard.[10] The next four cases represent a fascinating evolution of the legal understanding of the right to die in Europe.

In *Pretty v. the United Kingdom*,[11] a woman with motor neuron disease (degenerative and ultimately fatal) sought assurances from the government that her husband would not be prosecuted for helping her travel to Switzerland to avail herself of assisted suicide there. The U.K. Director of Public Prosecutions (DPP) refused her request, and after this action was upheld by the House of Lords, she took her case to the European Court of Human Rights. While Diane Pretty ultimately lost her case, it was important in the same way that *Quinlan* was important in the United States: It was the first time the court considered a claim relating to the right to die, and, like *Quinlan*, it permitted the court to sort through the potential legal claims individuals could make in support of that right. Ultimately, as in *Quinlan*, the court endorsed the right to privacy as the applicable claim.

Like Joseph Quinlan, Pretty brought a plethora of legal claims. Just as Quinlan had argued that keeping his daughter alive constituted cruel and unusual punishment, Pretty argued that preventing her from receiving assistance in her suicide constituted inhuman and degrading treatment under Article 3 of the European Convention on Human Rights. Although there is no margin of appreciation for claims of inhuman and degrading treatment, the court flatly rejected the argument that the United Kingdom's refusal to accede to Pretty's request that her husband not be prosecuted constituted inhuman and degrading treatment.[12] Like Quinlan, she advanced religious freedom (Article 9) and equal protection (Article 14) arguments and lost those as well.

As in *Quinlan*, the winner was the right to privacy, found in Article 8, which guarantees to each person "the right to respect for his private and family life." Article 8 forbids member states from interfering with this right, unless it is "necessary in a democratic society in the interests of national security, public safety, or the economic well-being of the country, for the prevention of disorder or crime, for the protection of health or morals, or for the protection of the rights and freedoms of others."[13] The United Kingdom

---

[10] Sanles v. Spain, App. No. 48335/99, Eur. H.R. Rep. 348 Oct. 26, 2000 [2001], http://hudoc.echr.coe.int/eng?i=001-22151.

[11] Pretty v. U.K., App. No. 2346/02, Eur. Ct. H.R. 2002, [2002] 35 Eur. H.R. Rep. 1, http://hudoc.echr.coe.int/sites/eng/pages/search.aspx?i=001-60448.

[12] *Id.* Like Justice O'Connor in the *Glucksberg* case, the Court held open the possibility that if a member state were to deny an individual suffering from a terminal illness access to pain medications or palliative care, a claim could be brought.

[13] European Court of Human Rights & Council of Europe, European Convention on Human Rights (1994), http://www.echr.coe.int/Documents/Convention_ENG.pdf.

argued that this right did not apply at all, as it pertained to how an individual lived his or her life, not the manner in which he or she departed from it. This argument was rejected by the court: "The applicant in this case is prevented by law from exercising her choice to avoid what she considers will be an undignified and distressing end to her life. The court is not prepared to exclude that this constitutes an interference with her right to respect for private life."[14] This fell short of an explicit recognition that Article 8 applied to right to die cases, but the decision made clear that if such a right existed, it would be found in Article 8.

The court went on to hold that the United Kingdom had shown that whatever interference might exist with Pretty's Article 8 rights was necessary for the protection of the rights and freedoms of others, namely vulnerable elderly and disabled people who might be injured were assisted suicide to be legal. While Pretty argued strongly that she was simply asking for an exception in her case, the court felt that it could not phrase a decision that would not create an unworkable precedent for future cases.

The *Pretty* decision set the stage for the second case, decided almost ten years later: *Haas v. Switzerland*.[15] The *Haas* case, decided in 2011, involved a man with severe bipolar disorder who, after twenty years of unsuccessful treatment, two suicide attempts, and various stays in psychiatric facilities, argued that Switzerland had an obligation to provide him with access to the drugs necessary for a painless suicide. Ernst Haas had tried to get his doctors, and other doctors, to give him a prescription for lethal drugs, but all refused, citing fear of legal prosecution if they were to give such a prescription to a person with a psychiatric disability who was not terminally ill.

Haas first appealed to the Swiss legal system, asserting that lack of clarity of Swiss law resulted in doctors' fear to provide him with the prescription. Haas's case was a landmark Swiss case: The highest court in Switzerland upheld the right of people with "incurable, permanent, severe psychological disorders" to avail themselves of assisted suicide, if it was the result of a "rational" and "well-considered" decision.[16] The court also ruled that Haas must obtain a prescription from a doctor who had conducted a "thorough psychiatric exam" to ensure that these conditions had been met.

Haas then sent a mass mailing to 170 psychiatrists in Switzerland asking them to assess his competence to commit suicide and for a prescription to enable him to do so. He made clear that he had no interest in treatment

---

[14] *Pretty v. U.K.*, App. No. 2346/02.

[15] *Haas v. Switzerland*, App. No. 31322/07.

[16] *Haas v. Switzerland*, Schweizerisches Bundesgericht [Federal Court] Nov. 3, 2006, Ruling 03.11.2006 2A.48/2006 (Switz.). Excerpts from this decision translated into English are found in para. 16 of the subsequent decision of the European Court of Human Rights, see *supra* at note 8 and are used here. All quotations to which I cite from the decision of the Swiss high court can be found in this paragraph.

for his condition; twenty years of such treatment had done him no good. All the doctors refused, either for ethical reasons, because they thought he was treatable, because they felt they lacked the skills to comply with his request, or (more coldly) because of "lack of time."

Haas took his case to the European Court of Human Rights, arguing that the requirement of obtaining a prescription from a physician interfered with his autonomy and should be waived in order for him to obtain the necessary medications. Because of *Pretty*, the sole legal claim asserted was under Article 8.

The Swiss position, somehow characteristically Swiss, was three-fold: First, there were plenty of ways for Haas to kill himself, and Switzerland was not obligated to provide him with his first-choice method. Second, the Swiss brief pointed out at length and with some indignation that Switzerland absolutely did not obstruct the opportunities of people with psychiatric disabilities to avail themselves of assisted suicide, as shown by the substantial number of people who had been assisted to commit suicide who had psychiatric disabilities. The fact of the matter, the Swiss brief asserted, was that Haas had simply written a poorly composed and unpersuasive letter to the 170 psychiatrists, in that he indicated he was unwilling to undergo therapy, and just wanted the medications to kill himself: what doctor could accede to that? It was his own fault that the doctors had turned him down.

Finally, at the end of their presentation, and rather as an afterthought, the Swiss submitted the argument that Americans would have expected all along: for people with psychiatric disabilities, unlike people with terminal illnesses, assisted suicide does not amount to a choice between a painful death and a painless death, but rather a choice of death over life. They added, almost cursorily, that for many people, suicidality is a symptom of mental illness and a cry for help, and it shouldn't be made too easy to obtain.

Like Pretty, Haas lost his case but contributed mightily to the evolution of law relating to assisted suicide. Because of his case, both Switzerland and the European Court of Human Rights recognized explicitly for the first time that Article 8 protected an individual's right to choose the time and manner of his or her death, and that it applied to people with psychiatric disabilities as well as people with terminal or degenerative medical conditions.

In deciding *Haas*, the court explicitly adverted to the paradox that drove me to consider writing this book. The court acknowledged the tension between the rights inherent in Article 8 and those in Article 2, requiring the States to protect human life: "For the Court, this latter Article obliges the national authorities to prevent an individual from taking his or her own life if the decision has not been taken freely and with full understanding of what is involved." As has been the case throughout human history, the key distinction between permissible and impermissible self-destruction is competence or capacity. Noting that the member countries had very different legal regimes concerning assisted suicide, the court concluded that countries should have a significant "margin of appreciation" or leeway in balancing the rights of competent people to choose the time and manner of their deaths, and the need to protect incompetent people from self-destruction. In Switzerland, this balance was achieved in two ways: the requirement that a physician confirm the individual's competence; and that a physician write a prescription for the lethal drugs. Recognizing the liberality of the Swiss regime, the court in effect said to Haas: if you can't get assisted suicide in Switzerland, you must *really* be an inappropriate candidate. The court even echoed the Swiss criticism of the way that Haas wrote his letter.

Having considered first the case of a woman with a painful and terminal physical condition, and then the case of a man with a long-standing severe and intractable psychiatric disorder, the court was confronted with the final, logical step in *Gross v. Switzerland*[17]: an elderly woman who saw herself growing older and more frail and wanted to die.[18] As the court put it, ". . . her life was becoming more and more monotonous. She could hardly bear her physical decline. Further, she increasingly suffered from eczema and backaches and every change in her environment terrified her."

Alda Gross was neither physically nor mentally ill; like Josh Sebastian,[19] she was just tired of being alive. Like both Sebastian and Haas, she failed in an attempt to kill herself and spent months in a psychiatric hospital. Unlike Haas, she was willing to see a psychiatrist over a long enough period of time for him to vouch for her competence. Although willing to vouch for her competence, neither he nor several other physicians were willing to prescribe the fatal medication, because the state of the law was too uncertain to guarantee them that they would not be punished in some way.

This time, the court did find a violation of Article 8, not because Switzerland necessarily owed Gross a prescription of fatal medication, or waiver of such a prescription, but because it provided insufficient guidance to doctors on the circumstances under which a doctor could prescribe medications to facilitate suicide to a competent person who was not terminally ill. The only guidance were physicians' ethics codes, which were not legally binding and in any event addressed only the situations of people who were terminally ill. Accordingly, the court ordered Switzerland to develop such guidance. Switzerland could determine for itself the content of the

---

[17] *Gross v. Switzerland*, App. No. 67810/10, Eur. Ct. H.R. (2013).

[18] In 2013, the court also decided that German courts must hear the case of a man whose paralyzed wife had asked German courts for permission to obtain a prescription to kill herself, and who traveled to Switzerland for assisted suicide after she was refused. German courts held the man had no standing to pursue her appeal, and the Court of Human Rights said he had a right to be heard by the courts (*Koch v. Germany*, No. 497/09). The case returned to Germany, where the courts dutifully granted a hearing, and reissued essentially the identical opinion (Verwaltungsgericht Köln [trial court] May 13, 2014, 7 K 254/13, http://www.justiz.nrw.de/nrwe/ovgs/vg_koeln/j2014/7_K_254_13_Urteil_20140513.html).

[19] See Chapter 1.

guidance, but doctors and people such as Gross were entitled to know where they stood.

Switzerland appealed this decision, which was supposed to have been heard by the Grand Chamber of the European Court of Human Rights in April 2014. However, in a rather bizarre turn of events, the attorneys on both sides of the case claimed to have discovered only in January 2014 that Gross had obtained a prescription for lethal medication through the Swiss group Exit and had killed herself more than two years previously on November 10, 2011. Her lawyer claimed that she had told him that hearing from him directly about the proceedings caused her stress and asked him to communicate through a pastor, which he had done. The pastor, in turn, had been bound by pastoral confidentiality to maintain Gross's secret (that she was dead), because she wanted the court to decide her case to benefit others in her situation. The Court of Human Rights huffily dismissed the entire case,[20] so the injunction on Switzerland to clarify its law is void, and Switzerland will continue with its status quo (until the next case).

In 2015, the court decided that it did not violate Article 2 (the right to life) for French doctors to disconnect life support from a man in a vegetative state whose wife supported the decision, but whose family opposed it.[21] The court also rejected an appeal by Tony Nicklinson's widow and Paul Lamb, who had lost their right-to-die cases in England for essentially procedural reasons.[22]

Switzerland

Switzerland also was one of the first countries in the world to effectively legalize assisted suicide; in 1937 it enacted a criminal code that took effect on January 1, 1942, which criminalized "inciting and assisting suicide" only where done for "selfish motives," such as financial gain.[23] Euthanasia, or, as

---

[20] Gross v. Switzerland, Eur. Ct. H.R., Grand Chamber, Sept. 30, 2014, App. No. 67810/10.

[21] Lambert & Others v. France, App. No. 46043/14, Eur. Ct. H.R. 185 (2015).

[22] See *infra* pp. 201–202. Nicklinson & Lamb v. U.K., Eur. Ct. H.R. 245 (2015). The court held that Lamb had failed to exhaust his remedies in domestic court and that Nicklinson's widow could not raise art. 8 (privacy) issues.

[23] Swiss Penal Code (SR 311.0) (1937, in force since Jan. 1, 1942) art. 115 (amended 1989, in force since 1990). There is no official English version of the Swiss criminal code. Language used here is from the written testimony of Prof. Dr. Schwarzenegger and Sarah Summers of the University of Zurich Faculty of Law, C. Schwarzenegger & S. Summers, Criminal Law and Assisted Suicide in Switzerland: Hearing with the Select Committee on the Assisted Dying for the Terminally Ill Bill, House of Lords (Feb. 3, 2005), http://www.rwi.uzh.ch/lehreforschung/alphabetisch/schwarzenegger/publikationen/assisted-suicide-Switzerland.pdf.

the English translation of the Swiss Penal Code puts it "a person who, for decent reasons, especially compassion, kills a person on the basis of his or her serious and insistent request," is a crime under Article 114, although it is not punished as severely as murder, or, for that matter, assisting someone to commit suicide for selfish motives. A doctor cannot prescribe medications unless a person is competent and needs the medications for legitimate medical reasons (e.g., relief of pain) without being in violation of civil requirements relating to narcotics and pharmaceutical products.

The Swiss government has issued guidance indicating a preference that individuals availing themselves of assisted suicide be terminally ill, chronically ill, or severely disabled, but the law does not preclude assisted suicide for anyone, and many people have been assisted to kill themselves in Switzerland who did not meet these criteria. Some people have simply been married to a person who was being assisted to commit suicide and wished to join them in death. In 2009, for example, Sir Edward Downs accompanied his terminally ill wife to Switzerland and both were assisted to die. He was not terminally ill, although he was blind and losing his hearing. Technically, anyone in Switzerland is eligible for assisted suicide: the individual need not be dying or old or even sick. One older woman was reported to have gone to Switzerland from England to die because "technology had ruined face to face relationships."[24] The highest court in Switzerland has ruled that anyone may seek assistance in suicide if he or she meets the following criteria:

1. Competence or "faculty of judgment"
2. Lack of impulsivity or "due consideration"
3. Unchanging wish to die or "persistence"
4. Not influenced by others or "autonomy"
5. By his or her own hand or "agency."[25]

The Swiss have not hesitated to criminally prosecute deaths that do not meet these criteria.

Switzerland is the only country in the world to permit nonresident-assisted suicide, and more than a thousand people from thirty-one countries have gone to Switzerland to commit suicide. Almost half are from Germany, but they hail from as far away as Zimbabwe and Morocco.[26] This has given rise to the phrase "suicide tourism"; efforts to restrict assisted suicide to Swiss

---

[24] Claire Ellicott, *Teacher Died at Dignitas Because She Couldn't Bear Modern Life: Healthy Spinster's Despair at Fast Food, Email, and Lack of Humanity*, DAILY MAIL, Apr. 6, 2014, http://www.dailymail.co.uk/news/article-2598102/They-say-adapt-die-At-age-I-adapt-Retired-teacher-89-ends-life-Swiss-euthanasia-clinic-disillusioned-modern-life.html.

[25] Exit, *Frequently Asked Questions (FAQ)*, www.exit.ch/en/faq.

[26] Saska Gauthier, Julian Mausbach, Thomas Reisch, & Christine Barsch, *Suicide Tourism: A Pilot Study on the Swiss Phenomenon*, 1 J. MED. ETHICS 3, tbl.2 (2014), *available at* doi:10.1136/medethics-2014-102091.

residents (or ban it altogether) have met with overwhelming opposition from the Swiss and have failed.[27]

Although assisted suicide has been legal for a long time in Switzerland, the country did not become well known for assisted suicide until recently, when groups such as Dignitas (founded in 1998)[28] and Exit (founded in 1982) were established to coordinate assisted suicide. Although Dignitas and Exit are the best-known groups, there are a number of other groups, each with different requirements.[29] One group, Suizidhilfe, was founded by a psychiatrist named Dr. Peter Baumann specifically because Exit was not doing enough to help people with psychiatric disabilities commit suicide.[30] Because he could not prescribe medication for this purpose under Swiss law, he provided his patients with a bag, filled with helium or nitrous oxide.[31] The Swiss authorities promptly arrested him for assisting suicide for "selfish" motives; because he did not profit from his assistance, he was charged with doing it for "egoistic" reasons. Although the initial prosecution was dismissed, when, like Dr. Jack Kevorkian, he assisted a suicide on television, he was charged again and ultimately served time in prison.[32] His group dissolved with the ebbing of his own fortunes.

The most recent assisted suicide organization, Lifecircle, has been founded to assist "underserved populations," such as couples.[33] Each organization has its own rules, within the limits of Swiss law. Thus, for example, Exit only assists Swiss residents,[34] while Dignitas believes that it would be immoral and contrary to the European Convention on Human Rights to restrict assisted suicide to Swiss residents. Dignitas offers its assistance to people with "hopeless or incurable illnesses, unbearable pain, or unendurable disabilities." In 2014, Exit expanded its services to elderly people suffering from the psychological or physical effects of old age, as long as they are competent.[35] Exit will

---

[27] *Switzerland: Zurich Votes to Keep Assisted Suicide*, BBC News, May 15, 2011, www.bbc.co.uk/news/world-europe-13405376.

[28] Dignitas [brochure], www.dignitas.ch.

[29] Gauthier et al., *supra* note 26.

[30] Guenter Lewy, Assisted Death in Europe and America: Four Regimes and Their Lessons 110 (2011).

[31] This method gained notoriety through the efforts of the Final Exit Network, see Chapters 3, 5, and 10, and (of course) does not require medical training.

[32] *Doctor Sentenced Over Assisted Suicides*, Swissinfo.ch, July 6, 2007, http://www.swissinfo.ch/eng/doctor-sentenced-over-assisted-suicides/5988876.

[33] World Federation of Right-to-Die Societies, *World Right-to-Die Newsletter* 64 (July 2014), http://www.worldrtd.net/sites/default/files/newsfiles/WF%20Newsletter-july%202014.pdf.

[34] Exit *FAQ, supra* note 25.

[35] *Exit Members Vote to Broaden Assisted Suicide Services* (SwissInfo, May 24, 2010), www.swissinfo.ch/eng/end-of-life-decisions_exit-members-vote-to-broaden-assisted-suicide-services/38653642; Maddy French, Swiss Group to Allow Assisted Suicide for the Elderly Who Are Not Terminally Ill, The Guardian,

also honor living wills from people with Alzheimer's disease and other forms of dementia, although it is not clear how that would operate in practice, as euthanasia is strictly forbidden in Switzerland. Dignitas has evolved a system to enable people who cannot swallow and arrive at the Dignitas facilities with an intravenous port to avail themselves of lethal medication intravenously as long as they can open the valve of the intravenous access tube by themselves.

How Assisted Suicide Operates in Switzerland

Although assisted suicide is theoretically available to any competent individual in Switzerland who wants to die, the vast majority of Swiss continue to stubbornly try to kill themselves on their own (Dignitas documents 66,650 failed suicide attempts in Switzerland annually). Most assisted suicides, however, are accomplished through Exit[36] or Dignitas. Dignitas asserts that for most Swiss residents, the individual's family doctor is generally willing to issue a prescription. For foreigners, Dignitas has affiliated physicians who must personally interview the individual at least twice. Exit's figures show that it receives more than 2500 annual requests for assisted suicide, approves about 880 of them, and assists in 480,[37] with 2 or 3 of these a year being people with unbearable psychiatric difficulties.[38] Exit rejects applications that do not meet its criteria (e.g., nonresident of Switzerland, and either "hopeless prognoses, unbearable symptoms, or unacceptable disabilities"[39]). Since being founded in 1998, Dignitas, a smaller operation, has assisted more than 1700 of its members to die.[40] Many of these individuals appear to be foreigners.

Both Exit and Dignitas characterize their missions as devoted to ensuring the autonomy of their members, including suicide prevention, assistance in creating living wills, and palliative care. Dignitas charges a fairly hefty fee for assisting suicide; obtaining painless death can run up quite a tab. Exit's assisted suicide services are free to members. Each organization provides assistance only to members, and membership fees for Dignitas involve a one-time payment of about US$240 and an annual fee of US$95 a year, while Exit's fees are about US$50 a year. But that is only the beginning: Dignitas

---

May 26, 2014, www.theguardian.com/society/2014/may/26/swiss-exit-assisted-suicide-not-terminally-ill.

[36] Not to be confused with Exit-International, a different organization in Switzerland founded by Rolf Sigg, which does provide assistance to nonresidents of Switzerland. This organization in turn should not be confused with Exit International, previously known as Voluntary Euthanasia Research Foundation (VERF), headed by Dr. Philip Nitschke of Australia, which was founded in 1997.

[37] *Exit at a Glance*, https://www.exit.ch/en/exit-at-a-glance.

[38] Exit FAQ, *supra* note 25.

[39] Exit *FAQ, supra* note 25.

[40] Dignitas, *How Dignitas Works*, http://www.dignitas.ch/index.php?option=com_content&view=article&id=23&Itemid=84&lang=enta.

asks for an upfront fee of US$8400 if it is not taking care of funeral and/or cremation arrangements, and US$12,600 if it is. Its brochure assures readers that it will take money through PayPal, and one can apply for a scholarship of sorts if one is of modest means, but these costs, combined with the costs of travel to Switzerland, ensure that suicide tourism is available only to those who are well off or who use most of their assets to accomplish their deaths.

Dignitas offers a transparent and detailed description of the process a person must undergo to obtain assisted suicide, from the first application with medical records, through the "provisional green light"[41] after the application is examined by an affiliated doctor, through the personal evaluation by the affiliated doctor, and his or her provision of the desired prescription to Dignitas. The individual never receives the prescription, nor does he or she take it alone. There are always at least two people from Dignitas present. In the case of Exit, there is always at least one person from that organization. Dignitas encourages early involvement and approval of family members, but if a person has no family, Dignitas will supply two companions. In any event, all assisted suicides orchestrated by Dignitas are observed by at least two Dignitas staff in order to be able to testify later, if necessary.

Assisted Suicide and People with Psychiatric Disabilities in Switzerland

Any doubt that people with psychiatric disabilities could avail themselves of assisted suicide was resolved by the highest court in Switzerland on November 3, 2006.[42] Although the name of the petitioner was anonymous, it was obviously Haas[43]and while the high court denied Haas the relief he sought—assisted suicide without having to obtain a prescription from a medical professional—it affirmed the rights of people with "permanent, incurable and severe" psychiatric disabilities who make "rational" and "well-considered" plans to avail themselves of assisted suicide. To prohibit them would be discrimination on the basis of psychiatric disability. However, the high court upheld the requirement of a psychiatric evaluation and prescription by a physician to screen out people whose suicidality is the result of "treatable psychological disturbance" and thus denied Haas the relief he sought.

Dignitas and Exit, the principal Swiss clinics, assist people with psychiatric diagnoses, or those who have spent time in psychiatric hospitals, to die if they are competent. However, the attitudes of each group toward

---

[41] Dignitas brochure, *supra* note 28.

[42] Schweizer Bundesgericht [Federal Court], Urt. V. 03. Nov. 2006, 2A.48/2006/ble.

[43] The European Court of Human Rights in its *Haas* decision referenced a decision denying Haas the relief he sought on Nov. 3, 2006, the date of the ruling on the anonymous plaintiff with bipolar disorder.

this population are substantially different. Exit's online information under-scores how rarely it assists people with psychiatric disabilities to die—only one or two every year—while Dignitas takes the position that people with incurable or unbearable psychiatric disabilities have just as much right to avail themselves of this benefit as anyone else.[44] A study of forty-three con-secutive assisted suicides in Basel between 1992 and 1997 (about 10% of all suicides) showed that six people had spent time in psychiatric clinics, and eleven of the people did not have terminal illnesses.[45]

Thus, practice had apparently sanctioned assisted suicide for people with psychiatric diagnoses for many years when the Swiss Federal Supreme Court held that people with "incurable, permanent, severe" psychiatric dis-abilities were entitled to avail themselves of assisted suicide. The court made a distinction between people with short-term and treatable conditions and people with severe, long-term mental illness who have made rational and well-considered decisions to end their own lives. This does not appear to have opened the floodgates, for a wide variety of reasons. First, there never do seem to be dammed-up floods of people anxious to commit suicide by following a set of formal procedures, wherever and whenever it is legalized. Second, ethical codes of Swiss physicians and psychiatrists remain much stricter than Swiss law, and assisted suicide in Switzerland requires a prescription from a Swiss doctor. As seen earlier in the *Gross* case, Swiss law itself is unclear, and doctors and psychiatrists remain uneasy about becoming involved with assisting people with psychiatric disabilities to kill themselves, especially since the Swiss continue to criminally prosecute when they believe a psychia-trist has assisted an incompetent patient, and these convictions are generally affirmed.[46]

In another case that put a damper on the willingness of the Swiss to extend assisted suicide in practice to people with psychiatric disabilities, a German woman who suffered from depression asked her German doctor to write a false report that she had terminal cirrhosis of the liver so that she could get needed time off from work. He did so, and she promptly took his report to Switzerland, where she persuaded Dignitas to assist her suicide. When her body was returned to Germany, an autopsy showed that she had never had any physical illness at all. Upon learning this, the doctor who had

---

[44] Imogen Foulkes, *Dignitas Boss: Healthy Should Have Right to Die* (BBC News, July 1, 2010), www.bbc.co.uk/news/10481309.

[45] Andreas Frei, et al., *Assisted Suicide as Conducted by a 'Right to Die' Society in Switzerland: A Descriptive Analysis of 43 Consecutive Cases*, 131 Swiss Med. Wkly. 375 (2001).

[46] Stijn Smet, *Haas v. Switzerland and Assisted Suicide*, Strasbourg Observers, Jan. 27, 2011, strasbourgobservers.com/2011/01/27/has-v-switzerland-and-assisted-suicide/.

assisted her in Switzerland (although not the German doctor) committed suicide himself (without assistance).[47]

Although doctors are definitely involved in assisted suicide in Switzerland, interviewing for competence and providing prescriptions, the culture around assisted suicide in Switzerland is more similar to that in the United States than the rest of Europe. Euthanasia is absolutely prohibited. The medical profession, and especially the mental health profession, has resisted assisted suicide more than in the Netherlands or Belgium; the legality of assisted suicide does not stop medical regulatory groups from adopting guidelines that limit its use. Organizations such as Exit and Dignitas are not operated by doctors. Conversely, the Swiss are powerfully invested in a culture of autonomy and self-sufficiency, and efforts made to introduce more government regulations and limitations have been blocked at the polls. The current status of the *Gross* decision of the European Court of Human Rights, requiring the Swiss to develop clearer guidelines on when assisted suicide is permissible, is unclear.

The Netherlands: Assisted Suicide and Euthanasia

The Netherlands has become almost an iconic symbol in the minds of people opposed to assisted suicide. Experience in the Netherlands was cited (and miscited) in the parties' and amicus briefs in the *Quill* and *Glucksberg* cases, as well as by the justices themselves. Assertions about the Netherlands vary from frank accusations of murder of incompetent people and unconsented euthanasia to warnings that in the Netherlands, euthanasia is a cure for depression.[48] At the very least, some, including some prominent Dutch citizens, argue that the Netherlands' experience embodies the slippery slope inherent in legalizing assisted suicide.[49] The only information the average layperson in the United States has about assisted suicide practiced internationally is probably a vague idea that elderly and vulnerable people are in peril from zealous practitioners of assisted suicide in the Netherlands.

Much of this lay recognition of assisted suicide in the Netherlands is because of the efforts of Dr. Herbert Hendin, a psychiatrist who was director

---

[47] Michael Leidig, *Dignitas Is Investigated for Helping Healthy Woman Die*, 331 BRIT. MED. J. 1160 (2005).

[48] Herbert Hendin, *Assisted Suicide, Euthanasia, and Suicide Prevention: The Implications of the Dutch Experience*, 25 SUICIDE LIFE-THREATENING BEHAV. 193 (1995).

[49] Steve Doughty, *Don't Make Our Mistake: As Assisted Suicide Bill Goes to Lords, Dutch Watchdog Who Once Backed Euthanasia Warns UK of "Slippery Slope" to Mass Deaths*, DAILY MAIL, July 9, 2014, www.dailymail.co.uk/news/article-2686711/Dont-make-mistake-as-assisted-suicide-bill-goes-Lords-Dutch-regulator-backed-euthanasia-warns-britain-mass-killing.html. This article relates Theo Boer's testimony before U.K. Parliament on Lord Falconer's 2014 bill legalizing assisted suicide.

of the American Foundation for Suicide Prevention and an ardent opponent of assisted suicide. Hendin is a thoughtful individual who has visited the Netherlands and spoken with many of the physicians who have assisted suicide there. Unlike the more standard opponents of assisted suicide, Hendin has focused on understanding why physicians might want to participate, and posits a range of possibilities from the doctor's frustration at his own powerlessness to assist his patient (assisters of suicide tend to be men, and many of the patients in publicized cases tend to be women) to the doctor's own conflicts about death.

The Netherlands may be viewed with more alarm and revulsion by Americans than Switzerland because the Netherlands offers a much more medicalized model of assisted suicide. First, euthanasia, rather than assisted suicide, is the preferred method; the Dutch believe this prevents both abuse of the process and unfortunate botches by laypersons. Second, unlike the United States and Switzerland, a substantial proportion of the medical profession has been on board with assisted suicide and involved in developing policies related to assisted suicide since the very beginning. A person can only receive euthanasia in the Netherlands from his or her treating physician. In fact, right to die advocates in the Netherlands consider that the medical profession is too complacent about its own judgments of a patient's best interests in matters of assisted suicide, and not sufficiently protective of the patient's autonomy. These concerns dovetail and are highlighted in the concerns about unconsented euthanasia, where apparently competent patients are euthanized without their consent. This is largely avoided in the United States and Switzerland by strict insistence that the patient ingest the fatal medication without assistance. The Netherlands also operates mobile units that go to people's homes to provide assisted suicide in areas where doctors are unavailable or inconvenient. These mobile units have inevitably been referred to as "death squads."[50]

Finally, the Netherlands also has a lot more data on its practices than Switzerland (or any other country in the world).[51] It is this rich volume of data that is key to both advocates and opponents of assisted suicide, who present it in the forms that best advance their particular agendas.

The Netherlands is (mistakenly) seen as having the broadest scope of assisted suicide, the very embodiment of the slippery slope.[52] The fact that right to die advocates in the Netherlands argue in favor of permitting anyone

---

[50] *Mobile Death Squads to Kill Sick and Elderly in Their Own Homes Leads to Surge in Suicide Rates in the Netherlands*, DAILY MAIL, Sept. 24, 2013, http://www.dailymail.co.uk/news/article-2430479/One-thirty-deaths-Holland-euthanasia-choosing-end-lives-cancer.html.

[51] This is acknowledged even by critics of the Netherlands, see, e.g., Herbert Hendin, *Seduced by Death: Doctors, Patients, and the Dutch Cure*, 10 ISSUES L. MED. 123, 128 (1994).

[52] *Id.* at 124.

older than seventy to avail themselves of assisted suicide, which has not yet been permitted, is cited with horror by Americans who probably don't realize that for decades now in Switzerland, literally any adult of any age could be assisted to commit suicide for any reason.

In 1973, the *Postma* case involved a physician who euthanized her mother following repeated requests by the mother. The defendant was convicted of murder but given a suspended sentence of one week in prison and one year's probation,[53] and the court set out criteria under which a doctor would not be required to keep a patient alive contrary to the patient's will. Dr. Postma founded Right to Die-NL in 1973, and by 1984, the highest court in the Netherlands reversed the conviction of a physician who assisted his patient to die, finding that the physician was untenably torn between the requirements of the law and his medical duty to relieve his patient's suffering.[54]

From 1984 to 2002, assisted suicide was generally practiced in the Netherlands, although it remained officially illegal. A series of court cases defined circumstances in which physicians would be immunized from legal action, essentially when driven by their professional responsibility to relieve the suffering of a patient for whom there was no alternative cure. As in Switzerland (and everywhere), there was a requirement that the patient's request be freely made, competent, and persistent. Unlike Switzerland, the Dutch courts required that the physician consult with a professional colleague. In 2001, the Netherlands enacted a statute, the Termination of Life on Request and Assisted Suicide Act, to legalize both euthanasia and assisted suicide.

In contrast to the requirement in the United States that a person availing himself or herself of physician-assisted suicide have capacity unimpaired by depression and be terminally ill, or Switzerland, which has only the require-ment of capacity, assisted suicide in the Netherlands encompasses people with capacity who wish to die because they have conditions that create "last-ing and unbearable suffering."[55] More than ten years ago, the highest court in

---

[53] Tony Sheldon, *Andries Postma*, 334 BRIT. MED. J. 7588 (2007), *available at* http://www.ncbi.nlm.nih.gov/pmc/articles/PMC1796690/; Ezekiel Emanuel, *Euthanasia: Historical, Ethical and Empiric Perspectives*, 154 ARCH. INTERN. MED. 1890, 1896 (1994).

[54] Euthanasia and Assisted Suicide—Euthanasia in the Netherlands, http://www.libraryindex.com/pages/573/Euthanasia-Assisted-Suicide-EUTHANASIA-IN-NETHERLANDS.html.

[55] Termination of Life on Request and Assisted Suicide (Review Procedures) Act of 2001, sec. 2(1)(b). Several translations of this law exist; this is taken from 8 EUR. J. HEALTH L. 183 (2001). This law requires the physician be satisfied that the suffering is "unbearable" and that there is no prospect of improvement. The requirement mirrors language that the individual have "lasting and unbear-able suffering"; the requirement was imposed by the Supreme Court of the Netherlands in the *Brongersma* case, upholding the conviction of Dr. Philip Sutorius for aiding an eighty-six-year-old man to die because he was "tired of life," Nederlandse Jurisprudentie 2003, no. 167.

the Netherlands held that an eighty-six-year-old man, who was neither physically nor mentally ill, but just "tired of life," was not entitled to avail himself of assisted suicide.[56] His doctor, Dr. Sutorious,[57] was thus convicted of the crime of assisted suicide, but no punishment was imposed because Sutorious, who had known his patient for a long time, was found to have acted out of concern for his patient. The Royal Dutch Medical Association subsequently set up a committee to examine "tired of life" cases.[58]

In the Netherlands, like the United States but unlike Switzerland, only doctors can assist suicide or perform euthanasia. Like Belgium (see *infra* "Belgium: Assisted Suicide and Euthanasia"), the law in the Netherlands also applies to minors between the ages of sixteen and eighteen; unlike Belgium, the Netherlands prohibits euthanasia for children younger than the age of twelve (between twelve and sixteen the child must have the parents' consent). After the age of sixteen, the minor's parents must be consulted, but ultimately, assuming the minor meets the remainder of the legal criteria, the decision is in the hands of the minor regardless of the parents' opinions.

Like Switzerland, courts in the Netherlands accept that people with psychiatric disabilities can have "lasting and unbearable suffering." The milestone case on this issue is the *Chabot* case, far better known than both *Haas* cases (the case in the highest court in Switzerland and the decision of the European Court of Human Rights). Chabot was a psychiatrist who assisted a woman to commit suicide who was suffering from unbearable grief after the death of her two sons. Although Dutch guidelines require consultation with another physician, Chabot asked seven colleagues, including two bereavement experts, the majority of whom supported his assisting the woman to commit suicide (although one bereavement expert thought she could be treated). None of these experts met with Chabot's patient. Chabot also insisted that the woman meet with him to attempt treatment. He saw her for more than thirty hours, and met her sister- and brother-in-law, who supported her desire to end her life.

The proportion of people with psychiatric disabilities who avail themselves of assisted suicide in the Netherlands is small: 13 out of 4188 deaths in 2012. More than three times as many people with dementia died through assisted suicide or euthanasia than people with psychiatric disabilities. As in Switzerland, the majority of people with psychiatric disabilities who ask for assisted suicide are rejected in the Netherlands. "Each year 300 to 500 psychiatric patients request euthanasia, and over the past 15 years, doctors

---

[56] Tony Sheldon, *Being "Tired of Life" Is Not Sufficient Grounds for Assisted Suicide*, 326 Brit. Med. J. 7380 (2003).

[57] More details on Dr. Sutorius are provided in Chapter 5.

[58] Tony Sheldon, *"Existential Suffering" Not a Justification for Euthanasia*, 323 Brit. Med. J. 7326 (2001).

have granted 77 of those requests. The majority of deaths, 42, occurred last year [in 2013]."[59]

Although many, many false assertions are made about the experience of assisted suicide and euthanasia in the Netherlands,[60] some facts seem to emerge from the data. The use of assisted suicide and euthanasia is increasing. The slippery slope argument is not completely an exaggeration. The Right to Die-NL group has recently called for the legislation to make euthanasia available to anyone older than seventy, sick or not.[61] In addition, Right to Die-NL now operates mobile euthanasia teams to help people die at home.[62]

There are about 3500 assisted suicide or euthanasia deaths a year in the Netherlands; doctors reject about two-thirds of requests. The culture in the Netherlands sees assisted suicide as a medical end-of-life decision; however, as some have pointed out, as the scope of assisted suicide extends beyond those who are terminally ill, the involvement of doctors seems less and less justified.[63]

Belgium: Assisted Suicide and Euthanasia

Belgium enacted its statute in 2002, the same year as the Netherlands. In 2012, about 1133 deaths, mostly of people with cancer, were recorded. This constituted 1% of the deaths in 2012. Interestingly, "the majority of patients mentioned they were suffering both physically and psychologically."[64] Like the Netherlands, Belgium authorizes both assisted suicide and euthanasia. Again like the Netherlands, these measures may only be performed by medical professionals. Belgium permits assisted suicide or euthanasia for anyone who can make his or her wishes clear and who is certified by a doctor

---

[59] Heather Beasley Doyle, *Right to Die: Netherlands, Belgium Ignite Global Debate on Euthanasia*, AL JAZEERA AMERICA, Mar. 4, 2014, http://america.aljazeera.com/articles/2014/3/4/right-to-die-netherlandsbelgiumigniteglobaldebateoneuthanasia.html.

[60] Perhaps the most prominent was the assertion by Rick Santorum when he was running for president in 2012 that 5% (or 10%, depending on the speech) of the Dutch population died from assisted suicide, see Michael Morse, *Santorum's Bogus Euthanasia Claims*, THE WIRE, Feb. 22., 2012, http://www.factcheck.org/2012/02/santorums-bogus-euthanasia-claims/.

[61] David Jolly, *Push for the Right to Die Grows in the Netherlands*, N. Y. TIMES, Apr. 3, 2012, www.nytimes.com/2012/04/03/health/push-for-the-right-to-die-grows-in-the-Netherlands.htm.

[62] *Id.*

[63] G. Bosshard, B. Broeckaert, D. Clark, et al., *A Role for Doctors in Assisted Dying? An Analysis of Legal Regulations and Medical Professional Positions in Six European Countries*, 34 J. MED. ETHICS 28 (2008).

[64] European Institute of Bioethics, *Euthanasia in Belgium: Ten Years On* (Apr. 2012), 3, http://www.ieb-eib.org/en/pdf/20121208-dossier-euthanasia-in-belgium-10-years.pdf.

to be in a "medically futile condition" with "suffering that is constant and unbearable" for which "medical treatment is futile and there is no possibility of improvement."[65] Unlike the United States, for whom this statistic would be unthinkable, the majority of Belgians who avail themselves of euthanasia die in hospitals.[66] In one case, Godelieva de Troyer, a woman with depression, checked herself into a Belgian hospital for the express purpose of being euthanized there.[67] In Belgium, all cases of euthanasia must be reported to a federal commission, which is charged with making sure the law is followed and turning questionable cases over to prosecutors. The cochair of this commission is Dr. Wim Distelmans, nationally and internationally famous as a zealous advocate of euthanasia. The commission has never found that a euthanasia violated the law.

Distelmans may in fact hold some kind of dubious European record for the most controversial and publicized assisted suicides. He received global attention for being the only physician willing to grant the suicide request of two healthy deaf Belgian twins who decided to seek assisted suicide after they learned that they were both going blind.[68] Although "it took them almost two years to find a medical institution to carry out the procedure," they eventually died by lethal injection. Their parents, who had objected, were ultimately persuaded by their arguments and were present at their deaths. Then, Distelmans assisted the suicide of a man whose sex change operation went wrong, leaving him with both breasts and a penis.[69] He was also the physician who euthanized de Troya without the knowledge of her son, who has filed a complaint against him, and soon after, a second complaint was lodged against him for euthanasia of another woman with depression. As noted, Distelmans also serves as the chair of the federal commission entrusted with ensuring that euthanasia in Belgium is carried out according to the law.

---

[65] Tinne Smets et al., *Legal Euthanasia in Belgium: Characteristics of All Reported Euthanasia Cases*, 47 MED. CARE 1 (Dec. 2009); Jacob M. Appel, *A Suicide Right for the Mentally Ill? A Swiss Case Opens a New Debate*, HASTINGS CENTER REPORT (May-June 2007), http://www.thehastingscenter.org/Publications/HCR/Detail.aspx?id=814.

[66] Smets et al., *supra* note 65, at 3.

[67] Margaret Wente, *Assisted Suicide: What Could Possibly Go Wrong?* GLOBE AND MAIL, Feb. 20, 2014, www.theglobeandmail.com/globe-debate/assisted-suicide-what-could-possibly-go-wrong/article16982181.

[68] Simon Tomlinson, *Deaf Belgian Twins Bought New Suits and Shoes Before Killing Themselves, Reveals Brother Who Was with Them When They Died . . . But Couldn't Talk Them Out of It*, DAILY MAIL, Jan. 15, 2013, www.dailymail.co.uk/news/article-2262630/Brother-deaf-Belgian-twins-killed-euthanasia.

[69] Bruno Waterfield, *Belgian Killed by Euthanasia after a Botched Sex Change Operation*, TELEGRAPH, Oct. 1, 2013, http://www.telegraph.co.uk/news/world-news/europe/belgium/10346616/Belgian-killed-by-euthanasia-after-a-botched-sex-change-operation.html.

Belgium also has the only Nobel Prize laureate to have died of euthanasia, Dr. Christian de Duve. Very soon after assisted suicide was legalized, Belgium's most famous novelist availed himself of the opportunity. Thus, Belgium, unlike most of the rest of the world, has famous and notable citizens using assisted suicide.

In February 2014, Belgium expanded its law to permit euthanasia for incurably ill children who were suffering unendurable pain.[70] The child's wish to die has to be verified by the parents, two doctors, and a psychiatrist. A story was recently aired on the news of a loving and educated parent having "the talk" with her child—not about sex, but about the fact that if he ever was sick and wanted to die, she would support him. This is not a discussion most Americans can imagine having in the abstract.

Although 91% of the people who avail themselves of assisted suicide have "death envisaged in the very short term" from natural causes, of the 9% who do not, the majority are people with "neuropsychiatric diseases."[71] These diseases are not, apparently, the same as psychiatric conditions: they include depression and psychoses, but also Huntington's chorea, and Alzheimer's disease.[72]

Although Belgium has not had anything like the notoriety of the Netherlands, it may be getting there. A physically healthy twenty-four-year old woman who had been institutionalized for three years because of depression and suicidality was approved for euthanasia by doctors in 2015;[73] cases like these, such as the case of the deaf twins, and the legalization of euthanasia for minors are gaining increasing notoriety for Belgium. "Euthanasia is becoming a Belgian trademark, just like waffles," lamented Carine Brochier of the European Institute of Bioethics in Brussels, who prefers that palliative care be offered.[74]

Luxembourg: Assisted Suicide and Euthanasia

Luxembourg legalized both euthanasia and assisted suicide in 2009. This legislation actually precipitated a constitutional crisis: the Grand Duke of Luxembourg refused to sign the legislation, and for the first time Luxembourg's Parliament decided that laws passed by Parliament were valid

---

[70] Dan Bilefsky, *Belgium Close to Allowing Euthanasia for Ill Minors*, N. Y. TIMES, Feb. 13, 2014.

[71] European Institute of Bioethics, *supra* note 64, at 3.

[72] *Id.*

[73] Eilish O'Gara, *Physically Healthy 24-Year-Old Granted the Right to Die in Belgium*, NEWSWEEK, June 29, 2015, http://europe.newsweek.com/healthy-24-year-old-granted-right-die-belgium-329504.

[74] Elisabeth Braw, *Should a Sick Child Be Allowed to Choose Death? Belgians Think So*, NEWSWEEK, Dec. 5, 2013, www.newsweek.com/should-sick-child-be-allowed-choose-death-belgians-think-so-223851.

without his signature.[75] Since the legalization of assisted suicide and euthanasia in 2009, very few people have used it: the number remains in the single digits.

Great Britain: Policies on Assisted Suicide and Euthanasia in Flux

In contrast to the United States, where the great momentum for physician-assisted suicide occurred in the 1990s (and perhaps because of the attention paid to the issue by Americans), in Great Britain the movement to legalize assisted suicide crested in the decade after 2000. By the end of the decade, the DPP had clarified that in most cases, relatives or others who acted from compassion in assisting a competent adult who was determined to commit suicide were unlikely to be criminally prosecuted. In contrast to the United States, in Great Britain, an individual is more likely to be prosecuted for assisting suicide if he or she is the person's treating physician.

Great Britain decriminalized suicide in 1961, but specifically retained criminal sanctions for assisting suicide. For years, the situation in Great Britain was similar to the situation in the Netherlands; until 2002, assisted suicide was technically against the law, but rarely, if ever, prosecuted. In the first decade of the twenty-first century, the subject of assisted suicide attracted a great deal of attention, beginning with Diane Pretty, whose case was eventually heard by the European Court of Human Rights.[76] She died in May 2002, a few days after losing her case.

In 2005, Lord Joffe revised and reintroduced his "Assisted Dying for the Terminally Ill" bill. Previously, the bill had included euthanasia as an option and, as in the United States, had no chance because of that. Joffe revised the bill's language to permit "an adult who has capacity and who is suffering unbearably as a result of a terminal illness to receive medical assistance to die at his own considered and persistent request."[77] The bill failed.

In 2009, Debbie Purdy brought a case similar to Pretty's case. Purdy had multiple sclerosis, and was afraid that by the time her condition had deteriorated to the point that she wanted to kill herself, she would no longer be able to do so. Her husband was willing to help her, but she did not want him to run the risk of being criminally prosecuted. So she asked the House of Lords

---

[75] Kristina Ebbott, *A 'Good Death' Defined by Law: Comparing the Legality of Aid in Dying Around the World*, 37 WM. MITCHELL L. REV. 170 (2010).

[76] Sarah Barclay, *It's Not Life, I'm Already Dead*, THE OBSERVER, May 11, 2002, http://www.theguardian.com/theobserver/2002/may/12/featuresreview.review; for a discussion of Pretty's case in the European Court of Human Rights, see p. 183, [text at notes 11–14] *supra*.

[77] D. Harris, B. Richard, & P. Khanna, *Assisted Dying: The Ongoing Debate*, 82 POSTGRAD MED. J. 479 (2006). The bill can be found at http://www.publications.parliament.uk/pa/ld200405/ldselect/ldasdy/86/8617.htm.

to reassure her that, when the time came, her husband could assist her in going to Switzerland to commit suicide through the organization Dignitas.

The House of Lords was more sympathetic to Purdy than they had been to Pretty. They noted that people had been assisting suicide for years in Great Britain without being prosecuted. More than one hundred Britons had used the services of Dignitas alone, including Daniel James, a twenty-three-year-old ex-rugby player who was quadriplegic,[78] not terminally ill. To clarify the law, the House of Lords ordered the DPP to issue a written policy explaining when someone would be prosecuted for assisting suicide, and when a person could be reassured that he or she would not be prosecuted. The DPP complied on February 25, 2010, with a document broad enough to reassure almost anyone who was contemplating assisting a suicide.[79] It listed a number of factors that the Director would consider as weighing in favor of prosecution (including that the person assisting in the suicide was the doctor of the person committing suicide, as well as the usual issues relating to age, mental capacity, profit from the person's death, etc.)[80] and issues that would weigh against prosecution (including the determination of the person to end his or her life, his or her competence, proof that the assister sought to dissuade the individual, and cooperation with police).[81]

The policy was issued amid tumultuous controversy about charges brought against Kay Gilderdale, who "assisted" her paralyzed daughter's suicide by giving her morphine, feeding her medications through her nose tube, and injecting air into her veins. Despite the fact that this was clearly *not* assisted suicide under the law, since Gilderdale actually killed her daughter, she was acquitted. Even so, the public was outraged about her prosecution.[82] The judge himself said, "I do not normally comment on the verdict of jurors, but in this case their decision, if I may say so, shows the common sense, decency, and humanity which makes jury trials so important in a case of this kind." Public sentiment ran so deeply against the prosecution of Gilderdale that some suspected that the prosecution was brought to further the DPP's hidden agenda *favoring* assisted suicide.[83]

---

[78] "Quadriplegic" means paralyzed from the chest down, including paralysis of all limbs, NEW OXFORD AMERICAN DICTIONARY (3d ed., 2010), s.v. *quadriplegic.*

[79] Director of Public Prosecutions, Policy for Prosecutors in Respect of Encouraging or Assisting Suicide (Feb. 2010, updated Oct. 2014), https://www.cps.gov.uk/publications/prosecution/assisted_suicide_policy.html.

[80] *Id.* at para. 43.

[81] *Id.* at para. 45.

[82] Jenny Booth, *DPP Defends Bringing Murder Charges Against Right-to-Die Mum Kay Gilderdale,* TIMES LONDON, Jan. 26, 2010, www.thetimes.co.uk/tto/news/uk/crime/article1877794.ece.

[83] Steve Doughty, *DPP Brought Mercy Case to Build Public Sympathy for Assisted Suicide, Say MPs,* DAILY MAIL, Jan. 27, 2010, www.dailymail.co/uk/news/article-1246367/DPP-brought-mercy-case-build-public-sympathy-for-assisted-suicide-say-MPs.html.

If the House of Lords thought that this clarification would lay the issue of assisted suicide to rest, it was deeply mistaken. In 2011, a man known only as Martin, immobilized by a stroke that made it difficult to travel to Switzerland, brought litigation claiming that he had a right to euthanasia or assisted suicide without having to travel for it.[84] The following year, Tony Nicklinson, suffering from locked-in syndrome and similarly unable to travel, also brought suit. When the High Court of Justice ruled against Nicklinson, photographs of his anguished countenance and tears went viral on the Internet. As he had threatened, immediately after the ruling, he refused all food and liquids, and died of pneumonia shortly after the ruling. A man named Paul Lamb, who could only move his right hand as a result of a car crash, joined his suit, and Lamb and Nicklinson's widow appealed the high court ruling to the U.K. Supreme Court,[85] which considered it with Martin's appeal and that of Lamb.

In a 132-page ruling, the Supreme Court affirmed the High Court's ruling, finding that absolutely prohibiting assisted suicide in all circumstances did violate the rights of British citizens, but that there were insufficient safeguards in place to protect vulnerable people if it were to simply strike down the criminal provisions. Like many recent court decisions refusing to strike down criminalization of assisted suicide, it kicked the whole issue back to Parliament,[86] in part because Parliament was once again considering a bill to legalize assisted suicide modeled on assisted suicide in the United States, that is, limited to competent individuals with six months or less to live. On September 11, 2015, Parliament decisively defeated this bill, which had generated more letters and emails to members than any other issue in the past two Parliaments.[87]

Ireland and Assisted Suicide: No Rights, No Enforcement

Ireland decriminalized suicide in 1993, much later than England.[88] In Ireland, as in England, assisted suicide is a crime, subjecting a person to

---

[84] Sarah Boseley, *Man in Assisted Suicide Case Spells Out Why He Wants to Be Helped to Die*, THE GUARDIAN, Aug. 18, 2011, www.guardian.co.uk/society/2011/aug/18/man-in-assisted-suicide-case.

[85] A little bit of clarification is in order regarding the judicial system in the United Kingdom for close readers of this chapter. Purdy's case was one of the last decided by the House of Lords, which was replaced beginning in 2009 by a Supreme Court unrelated to the House of Lords, which serves as the highest court in the United Kingdom. Thus, the progress from lowest to highest court in this case was High Court to Court of Appeal to Supreme Court. For even more details, see The Supreme Court, Courts and Tribunals Judiciary, https://www.judiciary.gov.uk/about-the-judiciary/the-justice-system/the-supreme-court/.

[86] *R (on the Application of Nicklinson)*, Ministry of Justice, U.K.S.C. 38, para. 122.

[87] John McDermott & Sarah Neville, *UK Parliament Votes Heavily Against Assisted Suicide*, FINANCIAL TIMES, Sept. 11, 2015, http://www.ft.com/cms/s/0/f791f80c-58a0-11e5-9846-de406ccb37f2.html#axzz3oZUIzt5x.

[88] Criminal Law (Suicide) Act of 1993, sec. 2(1).

fourteen years in prison if he or she "aids, abets, counsels or procures" the suicide of another.[89] Although Ireland has one of the highest suicide rates in Europe,[90] very few Irish citizens avail themselves of the services of Dignitas in Switzerland. Between the time that it was established in 1998 and 2013, only eight Irish citizens have traveled to Switzerland to die.[91]

In 2003, Ireland tried to extradite and prosecute an American Unitarian minister, George D. Exoo, for allegedly assisting in the suicide of a Rosemary Toole Gilhooly, an Irish woman who had mental health problems. Exoo instructed her on how to commit suicide with pills, a plastic bag, and helium, and traveled to Ireland with a friend (on Gilhooley's tab) to help her out.[92] According to the case filed against him, he helped her practice her suicide and was with her when she died.[93] Exoo responded that he had only been present to comfort the woman and read a few prayers.[94] Exoo managed to leave Ireland before the body was discovered.

Although he was arrested at his home in Beckley, West Virginia, a federal court there denied the request for extradition.[95] The U.S. extradition treaty with Ireland permits extradition only in cases of "dual criminality"—in other words, only if Exoo's conduct in Ireland was "substantially analogous" to federal criminal statutes, or West Virginia criminal statutes, or criminal statutes in a substantial proportion of every state. Assisting suicide is not a federal crime and is not a crime in West Virginia. After an exhaustive parsing of the laws regarding assisted suicide in every U.S. state, the court concluded that an insufficient number of U.S. state statutes were "substantially analogous" to the conduct criminalized by Ireland. Given the primacy of the First Amendment in U.S. law, which has been found to protect conduct the Irish might criminalize,[96] the court may have been correct. Conversely, the law seems to have been close enough that remanding Exoo to the tender mercies of the Irish court would also have constituted a legitimate interpretation of the language of U.S. statutes.

---

[89] *Id.* at para. 2.

[90] Eanna O Caolli, *Ireland Has "Exceptionally High Rates" of Suicide*, IRISH TIMES, Mar. 21, 2014, http://www.irishtimes.com/news/social-affairs/ireland-has- exceptionally- high-rates-of-suicide-1.1732791.

[91] *One Irish Person Used Swiss Euthanasia Clinic Last Year*, IRISH JOURNAL, Jan. 14, 2014, http://www.thejournal.ie/switzerland-assisted-suicide-irish-ireland-dignitas-1263561-Jan2014/.

[92] *In re* Extradition of Exoo, 522 F. Supp. 2d 766, 768 (S.D. W. Va. 2007).

[93] *Id.*

[94] A fuller picture of the bizarre and unsettling adventures of Exoo, suggesting considerably more involvement in Gilhooley's suicide than the federal case reports, is told at length in JON RONSON, LOST AT SEA: THE JON RONSON MYSTERIES (2013).

[95] *Extradition of Exoo*, 522 F. Supp. 2d 766.

[96] Both the Minnesota and Georgia Supreme Courts have found that a great deal of speech associated with promoting and even encouraging suicide is protected by the first amendment; see Chapter 10.

Since this time, Exoo has continued his self-proclaimed work as "midwife to the dying"[97] with no interference from U.S. courts. He even has an assistant in training, a woman who met him because she intended to commit suicide, but ended up changing her mind because she could not find anyone to take care of her pet snake.[98] The Irish Arts Council gave a grant of more than €400,000 to playwright Enda Walsh and composer Donnacha Dennehy for an opera called *Gas*, based on Gilhooley's death, performed at the 2015 Dublin Theater Festival.[99]

The most famous and most recent assisted-suicide case in Ireland involved another woman with multiple sclerosis, Marie Fleming, who, after losing in the High Court,[100] petitioned the Supreme Court of Ireland to relax its ban on assisted suicide. She was fifty-nine and had asked for permission for her partner, Tom Curran, to accompany her to Switzerland to die. Fleming challenged the ban on assisted suicide on the usual privacy grounds, but because she had lost the use of her hands, she added a claim that the ban discriminated against her on the basis of disability, because suicide was decriminalized but she would need help to commit suicide.[101] Finally, as in the *Gross* and *Koch* cases in the European Court of Human Rights, and the *Purdy* case in England, Fleming asked that Ireland promulgate more specific guidelines clarifying who would and would not be prosecuted for assisting suicide.[102]

Although the High Court judges had gone to great lengths to express sympathy for Fleming individually, praising her as "the most remarkable witness which any member of this court has been privileged to encounter,"[103] the court refused her request, asserting that it had to act on behalf of "the aged, the disabled, the poor, the unwanted, the rejected, the lonely, the impulsive, the financially compromised and emotionally vulnerable"[104] who were not before it. The High Court decision was very emotional, and focused on the message sent to the citizens of Ireland if assisted suicide were to be embraced.

---

[97] Jon Ronson, '*I Make it Look Like They Died in Their Sleep*,' THE GUARDIAN, May 12, 2008, http://www.theguardian.com/society/2008/may/12/mentalhealth.health.

[98] Jo Case, *Reverend Death: 'A Midwife to the Dying*,' WHEELER CENTRE, Nov. 5, 2012, http://www.wheelercentre.com/notes/c5e215e5d713.

[99] Eithne Shortall, *Toole Gilhooley Suicide Opera to Hit the Stage*, SUNDAY TIMES, Dec. 14, 2014, http://www.thesundaytimes.co.uk/sto/news/ireland/News/article1495920.ece?CMP=OTH-gnws-standard-2014_12_13.

[100] Fleming v. Ireland & Ors, [2013] I.E.H.C. 2 (Jan. 10, 2013).

[101] The Irish Human Rights Commission concurred with her on this claim. Fleming v. Ireland, [2013] I.E.S.C. 19, para. 44.

[102] *Fleming v. Ireland & Ors*, at n.95, at para. 3(3).

[103] *Id.* This is the third sentence of the summary of judgment delivered by P. Kearns on Jan. 10, 2013, *Fleming v. Ireland & Ors*, I.E.H.C. 2, http://www.bailii.org/ie/cases/IEHC/2013/H2.html.

[104] This quotation is from the fifth paragraph of the summary of judgment delivered by P. Kearns on Jan. 10, 2013. *Id.*

The Supreme Court was far brusquer in disposing of Fleming's claims, almost blaming her for trying to exploit the tragedy of her situation:

> 137. The Court concludes that there is no constitutional right to commit suicide or to arrange for the determination of one's life at a time of one's choosing.

> 138. Thus, the appellant has no right which may be interfered with by any disability. As there is no right to commit suicide no issues, such as discrimination, do not arise; nor do values such as dignity, equality, or any other principle under the Constitution, apply to the situation and application of the appellant, as discussed above.

> 139. The Court rejects the submission that there exists a constitutional right for a limited class of persons, which would include the appellant. While it is clear that the appellant is in a most tragic situation, the Court has to find constitutional rights anchored in the Constitution. The appellant has relied on her very distressing situation on a fact based argument that the blanket ban affects her adversely. That is not a basis upon which a constitutional right may be identified. It has not been the jurisprudence of the Constitution that rights be identified for a limited group of persons.[105]

The Irish Supreme Court, like the U.K. Supreme Court in *Nicklinson,* invited the Irish Parliament to legislate on the matter if it wished to accommodate situations such as Fleming's. Eight months later, Fleming was dead.[106]

Following the Supreme Court's rejection of Fleming's appeal, the first and only criminal charge ever brought in Ireland for assisting a suicide was brought against Gail O'Rorke (or O'Rourke),[107] a forty-two-year-old woman accused of assisting Bernadette Forde, a fifty-one-year-old suffering from multiple sclerosis, to commit suicide. O'Rorke had tried to help Forde arrange a trip to Switzerland to end her life, but the travel agent tipped off the Gardai (the Irish police), who prevented her from leaving. Forde died from an overdose of medication ordered from Mexico. O'Rorke was charged on three counts: for ordering the medication, for helping her friend prearrange her funeral, and for trying to help her make travel arrangements to

---

[105] *Fleming v. Ireland*, I.E.S.C. 19, paras. 137–39.

[106] Conor Feehan, *"Right to Die" MS Sufferer Marie Fleming Has Passed Away,* IRISH NEWS, Dec. 20, 2013, http://www.independent.ie/irish-news/right-to-die-ms-sufferer-marie-fleming-has-passed-away-29855136.html.

[107] *First Person Ever Charged with Assisting Suicide to Go on Trial Here Today,* INDEPENDENT.IE, Apr. 13, 2015, http://www.independent.ie/irish-news/courts/first-ever-person-charged-with-assisting-suicide-here-to-go-on-trial-today-31137408.html. In this news story, the text refers to the defendant as Ms. O'Rourke while the photograph is captioned "O'Rorke."

Switzerland.[108] The judge ordered the jury to find in O'Rorke's favor on the first two charges; she was tried on the third.[109] The jury's acquittal on the third count may have been influenced when the judge addressed O'Rorke as a "faithful, honest and decent woman" who faced "an immense dilemma."[110]

The Americas

Canada: The Latest Country to Legalize Assisted Suicide

In 2015, the Canadian Supreme Court upheld the right to physician-assisted suicide with barely a reference to the word *suicide* in a sixty-seven-page opinion. This decision came just over twenty years after the Supreme Court had upheld the ban on assisted suicide in a sharply divided decision,[111] and just over a year after Quebec passed a law legalizing euthanasia and assisted suicide for terminally ill individuals. The court found that the object of criminalizing assisted suicide was limited to "protect[ing] vulnerable persons from being induced to commit suicide in a moment of weakness" and explicitly rejected Canada's submission that the goal of the statute was "preservation of life."[112] The court also rejected any notion that the object of a law criminalizing assisted suicide was to prevent suicide.[113]

Both the 1994 and 2015 Supreme Court decisions originated from cases in the province of British Columbia. In the earlier case, a woman named Sue Rodriguez who had amyotrophic lateral sclerosis (ALS) sued for the right to have her doctor assist her to die. In 1994, the year after the Canadian Supreme Court rejected her claim, she was assisted to die by an anonymous physician.[114]

The 2015 case was brought by Gloria Taylor, a woman with ALS, and Lee Carter, the daughter of Kay Carter, a woman who had spinal stenosis, along with a doctor and the British Columbia Civil Liberties Association. While ALS is invariably fatal, spinal stenosis is not generally considered a terminal illness; both can be very painful and are progressively debilitating. Carter went with her family to Switzerland, where she was assisted to die in 2010.

---

[108] Dearbhail McDonald, *Assisted Suicide Trial: Gail O'Rorke (43) Found Not Guilty of Helping Friend Take Own Life*, IRISH NEWS, Apr. 28, 2015, http://www.independent.ie/irish-news/courts/assisted-suicide-trial-gail-ororke-43-found-not-guilty-of-helping-friend-take-own-life-31178920.html.

[109] *Id.*

[110] *Id.*

[111] Rodriguez v. Canada [1993] 3 S.C.R. 519, was decided 5-4.

[112] *Rodriguez*, para. 74.

[113] *Rodriguez*, para. 78.

[114] Sandra Martin, *Supreme Court to Rule Soon If Assisted Suicide Is a Human Right*, GLOBE AND MAIL, Oct. 4, 2014, http://www.theglobeandmail.com/news/national/whats-at-stake-when-assisted-suicide-case-reaches-top-court/article20926049/.

Her daughter's claim as plaintiff in the case was that she was forced to break Canada's unjust law against assisted suicide in order to help her mother die. Taylor, who could not afford to go to Switzerland, died in late 2012. In the United States, it would be unlikely that the remaining plaintiffs—the doctor, the Civil Liberties Union, and Kay Carter's daughter—would have standing to bring the case,[115] but the Canadian Supreme Court is empowered to issue advisory opinions.

In 1993, Rodriguez brought claims similar to those initially brought in the *Quinlan* and *Cruzan* cases: the privacy claim (called "security of the person" in Canada), cruel and unusual punishment, and discrimination, because able-bodied persons could end their lives, but she could not. Like the European Court of Human Rights, the Canadian Supreme Court found that Rodriguez's security rights were impaired by the criminalization of assisted suicide, but that nevertheless the state's interests in preserving life and protecting vulnerable people from abuse justified the prohibition.

In a decision that bore some resemblance to the U.S. Supreme Court's opinion in *Glucksberg*, Justice John Sopinka looked to Canadian social opinion. Just as the U.S. Supreme Court held that U.S. society had always rejected suicide, Justice Sopinka wrote that "it cannot be said to represent a consensus by Parliament or Canadians in general that the autonomy of those wishing to kill themselves is paramount to the state interest in protecting the life of its citizens."[116] Of course, one purpose of constitutional rights is to protect certain fundamental rights against majoritarian impulses. If there was a consensus in Parliament or among Canadians in general, assisted suicide would be legislated. Determining the consensus of Canadian opinion and acting on it can be described as the role of Parliament, not the courts.

It is true, however, that this was also the approach taken by judges in the United States considering whether assisted suicide was a constitutional right. There is a major strand in U.S. constitutional jurisprudence that sees concepts of due process as evolving with the development of society. Other judges, originalists such as Justice Scalia, look to the framers of the Constitution for their understanding of its meaning. To those judges who believe that constitutional principles evolve, the understanding of whether certain issues violate due process, equal protection, or guarantees against cruel and unusual punishment, such as, execution of minors or people who are mentally retarded,[117] or, more obviously, equal rights for gay people, follows in the wake of public acceptance rather than blazing the trail for it. For

---

[115] See Chapter 3, discussion of the Ninth Circuit Court's dismissal of *Lee v. Oregon* on standing grounds in a case where a plaintiff with terminal illness remained in the case. Of course standing, such as many jurisdictional and procedural issues, is readily manipulable by courts that want to duck (or to decide) a particular case.

[116] *Rodriguez v. British Columbia (AG)*, [1993] 3 S.C.R. 519.

[117] *Roper v. Simmons*, 543 U.S. 551, 607–30 (2005).

originalists such as Justice Scalia, public acceptance is not even relevant to interpretation of the Constitution.[118]

Much had changed by the time the trial court in *Carter* held that the criminalization of assisted suicide violated the plaintiffs' constitutional rights, despite the clear precedent of *Rodriguez*. Well aware of the importance of the case, the trial judge canvassed ethics, the practices in other countries, and the positions of various organizations who had been permitted to intervene as parties. The judge didn't even get to the Canadian law until paragraph 885, page 203, of a 323-page decision. Judge Smith, seizing on the language of the majority opinion in *Rodriguez*, held that the passage of time and development of the law had changed the jurisprudential landscape.[119] In addition, the judge found that the plaintiffs prevailed on grounds raised but not addressed by the Canadian Supreme Court in *Rodriguez*, that is, that not only the right to security was involved, but the right to life, because criminalization of assisted suicide drove people to end their lives earlier than they otherwise might have. It is one of the many paradoxes of suicide law that plaintiffs asserting the right to assisted suicide make that claim under the right to life. Another paradox (given the vocal opposition of many in the disability community to assisted suicide) was the trial court's finding that prohibiting assisted suicide unconstitutionally discriminated against people with physical disabilities, because it left them only starvation and dehydration as means of dying, while able-bodied people retain the full panoply of methods described by Dorothy Parker.[120]

The appellate court would have none of it. *Rodriguez* applied directly, and it was not for a lower court to reverse the Supreme Court of Canada. It reversed the trial court, paving the way for an appeal to the Canadian Supreme Court, which also heard from numerous intervenors,[121] including the Canadian Medical Association, about whether the jurisprudential landscape had changed since *Rodriguez*.

In one respect, the jurisprudential landscape had changed drastically since *Rodriguez*. As the *Carter* case worked its way through the Canadian court system, the province of Quebec was tackling the issue of assisted suicide legislatively. Like the United States, Canada has a federal form of government, with a central national government and nine provinces. Thus, in *Rodriguez*, the Supreme Court of Canada held that there was no constitutional right to assisted suicide, and that British Columbia could continue to

---

[118] Although see his opinion about execution of people with mental retardation.

[119] Carter v. Canada (AG), 2012 BCSC 886.

[120] Dorothy Parker, "Resumé" in *Enough Rope* (1926), which reads "Razors pain you/Rivers are damp/Acids stain you/and drugs cause cramp/Guns aren't lawful/Nooses give/Gas smells awful/You might as well live." http://www.poetryfoundation.org/poem/174101. The Canadian trial court did not refer to Dorothy Parker.

[121] In the United States, intervention would grant standing as a party, but apparently this is not the case in Canada.

criminalize it. But just as the *Glucksberg* holding that there was no federal constitutional right to assisted suicide did not preclude Oregon from passing its assisted suicide initiative, *Rodriguez* did not prevent other provinces from legislatively enacting assisted suicide regimes. In 2013, the province of Quebec passed the first law permitting euthanasia and assisted suicide in 2013. Véronique Hivon, the junior Minister of Health in Quebec credited with getting the legislation passed, has a distinctly different view of the issue than the plaintiffs in the *Carter* case. Perhaps naturally, given her position in the government, she views euthanasia and assisted suicide as a part of the continuum of care to be offered to terminally ill individuals; the legislation is entitled "An Act with Respect to End of Life Care."[122] Her view is similar to that embraced by the Netherlands and Belgium. The plaintiffs in the Taylor case, however, see assisted suicide as a human right springing directly from the autonomy of the individual, similar to the philosophy underlying the laws in Oregon, Washington, Montana, and Vermont.

Certainly a lot had changed since 1993. Justice Sopinka was no longer on the court, and Justice McLachlin, who had written a spirited dissent in *Rodriguez*, was now chief justice. And the opinion certainly reflected *that* change.

The Canadian Supreme Court began its decision by referring to people who are "grievously and irremediably ill," and whose condition causes them "suffering that is intolerable to the individual in the circumstances of his or her condition."[123] This clearly describes a much broader range of individuals that terminal illness, or (as in the United States) terminally ill with a life expectancy of six months or less; it also embraces the subjectivity of individual experience. This is especially true because the court explicitly states that a condition may be "irremediable" if treatments for it are "unacceptable to the individual."[124] If a Canadian citizen with a medical condition that causes great suffering wants to die ("clearly consents to termination of life"), he or she has a constitutional right to obtain assistance from a physician without that assistance being criminalized. The court also explicitly limits its holding to "physician-assisted death"; it is not at all clear how assistance from the Final Exit Network or helpful family members would be treated. Because the court places a great deal of emphasis on the ability of physicians to determine decisional capacity and informed consent,[125] assistance by others not considered equally skilled in this regard might still be constitutionally prohibited.

The Canadian Supreme Court rejected the arguments that "the right to life" was the appropriate provision to consider challenges to the prohibition on assisted suicide, but made very clear that an individual can waive his

---

[122] CQLR c. S-32.0001.

[123] Carter v. Canada (AG), SCC 5 (Feb. 6, 2015), 1 S.C.R., paras. I (1) and (4) (2015).

[124] *Id.* at para. 127.

[125] *Id.* at para. 115.

or her right to life. To hold otherwise would impose "a duty to live," rather than a right to life, and would imperil existing rights to refuse life-saving treatment.[126]

Rather than the right to life, the Canadian Supreme Court located the right to assisted suicide where it has been firmly entrenched since *Quinlan*: in the right to liberty ("the right to make fundamental personal choices free from state interference") and security (the right of "control over one's bodily integrity free from state interference"). But just as the *Glucksberg* majority foreordained the outcome by analyzing the right to physician-assisted suicide in light of the history of criminalizing suicide, the Canadian Supreme Court foreordained its own affirmation of the right to physician-assisted suicide when it decided that the only appropriate reason to criminalize assisted suicide was to "protect vulnerable people from being induced to commit suicide in a moment of weakness." The court rejected Canada's position that the goal of criminalizing assisted suicide was to preserve life, as too broad, and leading automatically to upholding the statute. It rejected the argument that the object of the statute was to prevent suicide because attempting suicide is no longer a crime. This is more than a little disingenuous: the State can discourage activities it disapproves of, including suicide, even if they are not crimes. Criminalizing assisted suicide would certainly be one way of preventing suicide: the very stories of the plaintiffs in *Carter* demonstrated the statute's value in that regard, and the court later acknowledges this.[127]

The crux of the court's position was that Canada could achieve its goal of protecting vulnerable people from being induced to commit suicide in less drastic ways than by criminalizing assisted suicide.[128] The court implicitly approved the trial court's formulation of the issues to be considered in deciding whether criminalizing assisted suicide was the least drastic way of accomplishing the State's goals:

> In the trial judge's view, an absolute prohibition would have been necessary if the evidence showed that physicians were unable to reliably assess competence, voluntariness, and non-ambivalence in patients; that physicians fail to understand or apply the informed consent requirement for medical treatment; or if the evidence from permissive jurisdictions showed abuse of patients,

---

[126] The Roman Catholic Church, which pretty much imposes a duty to live on its adherents, resolves this conundrum by recognizing that a person has a moral right to refuse extraordinary treatment which only minimally prolongs life, and to accept treatments, such as pain medication, which may shorten life as long as they are not taken with the intention to reduce a person's lifespan.

[127] *Carter v. Canada*, n.109, at paras. 99–101.

[128] *Id.* at paras. 103–104.

carelessness, callousness, or a slippery slope, leading to the casual termination of life.[129]

Canada's principal challenge to the conclusion of the trial court that it was possible to create an assisted suicide system that would acceptably minimize these risks focused on the slippery slope portion rather than the assessing competence portion of the formulation. As happened in *Lee* and in other cases, Canada's argument about the inevitability of a slippery slope pointed to cases, not only of children, but where (gasp) people with psychiatric disorders had been able to avail themselves of assisted suicide.[130] When it comes to concerns about disabled and vulnerable people, the court in *Carter* looked at the same body of evidence as the Irish High Court had looked at in *Fleming* and drew the opposite conclusion. Inevitably, the Irish High Court had canvassed the experience of the Netherlands (but also Belgium and Switzerland, to give it credit) and was concerned about the rate of "legally assisted deaths without explicit request" (LAWER), which range from 0.4% to more than 1% of all deaths.[131] Conversely, the Canadian Supreme Court dismissed the parade of horribles reflecting the overreach of assisted suicide in the Netherlands and Belgium as both "anecdotal" and as reflective more of Dutch and Belgian cultural attitudes that would not play out in the same way in Canada.[132]

At the very end of its decision, the court indicates sympathy to a "conscience clause" that would exempt physicians from having to provide assisted suicide to their patients. As I point out in the next chapter, this is easily done, because once assisted suicide is legalized, you actually only need a few doctors who are willing to implement the system for it to succeed. The court suspended its ruling for a year to give Canada and the provinces a chance to respond legislatively. The next year will see a flurry of legislation on all levels. Whether Canada and its provinces look to the U.S. model of patient autonomy reflected in *Carter* or the more deeply medicalized model on which the recent Quebec law is based will determine a great deal about end-of-life care in Canada in the years to come.

Latin America: Differing Practices

Mexico, like many (but not all) Latin American countries, is extremely conservative about end-of-life issues. Only in April 2008 did Mexican law begin to permit even the withdrawal of life-sustaining treatment from patients.

---

[129] *Id.* at para. 104, *quoting* the court at paras. 1365–66.
[130] *Id.* at paras. 111, 114.
[131] Fleming v. Ireland [2013] I.E.H.C. 2, paras. 96, 99, 101 (0.4% of all deaths in the Netherlands were LAWER in 2005; 1% in Switzerland in and 1.8% in Belgium in 2007).
[132] *Carter v. Canada*, at n.118, paras. 108, 112, 113.

This was accomplished legislatively. Yet tolerance for euthanasia appears in the strangest of places. For example, in Uruguay although a person must appear in court, yet Article 27 of the Penal Code (effective 1934) says: "The judges are authorized to forego punishment of a person whose previous life has been honorable where he commits a homicide motivated by compassion, induced by repeated requests of the victim."

In Colombia, liberalization of laws regarding euthanasia happened in the way that most lawyers seeking systems reform fear the most: an opponent of euthanasia brought a lawsuit to establish and clarify that euthanasia was illegal in Colombia, and on May 20, 1997, the Colombian Constitutional Court held that, in fact, voluntary euthanasia *was* legal for terminally ill people.[133]

Asia

Japan: A Different Cultural Approach

Someone recently wrote into "The Straight Dope" with the following question:

> Assisted suicide remains a controversial topic just about wherever
> it's brought up. But I was wondering something. How does the
> issue fare in a place like Japan? Think about it. In Japanese culture,
> as I understand it, suicide can be an honorable act. So assisted
> suicide for those in terminal pain should be a non-issue there,
> right? Yet I've never heard of Japan legalizing assisted suicide. So
> how exactly does assisted suicide fare in places where suicide is
> accepted (for various reasons) to begin with? I'm sure Japan is not
> the only place.[134]

This is a good summary of one reason I became curious about suicide policy in the United States. How is it that suicide and assisted suicide are so cabined off and isolated from each other in terms of policy? Assisted suicide advocates have relentlessly pursued this approach, seeking to distinguish themselves from the stigma of suicide by using phrases such as "aid in dying," "death with dignity," and "assisted death." And to a large extent, at least in this country, they seem to have succeeded. In Chapter 3, I hypothesized that one major for this success is that U.S. doctors are increasingly comfortable with suicide at the end of life, when a patient is terminally ill, and the U.S. public, by and large, trusts doctors to sift out rational from irrational suicides (although not to administer the final dose, as in the Netherlands and Belgium). The U.S. public (although not its mental health

---

[133] Sentencia No. C-239/97 (Corte Constitucional, May 20, 1997); see *Columbia's Top Court Legalizes Euthanasia*, ORLANDO SENTINEL, May 22, 1997, at A1.

[134] Question from Jim B., The Straight Dope: Fighting Ignorance Since 1973 (July 4, 2012), http://boards.straightdope.com/sdmb/showthread.php?t=657420.

professionals[135]) have accomplished a conceptual separation between "rational" suicide of terminally ill (and, more ominously, elderly or disabled) people, who are to be admired for their courage, and make the cover of *People* magazine,[136] and the "irrational" suicide of everyone else, with the extraordinarily misleading and incorrect statistic that 90% of people who commit suicide have some kind of mental illness.[137]

The equation of suicide and mental illness does not hold up under scrutiny, and one of the best illustrations of this is that Asian countries have much higher rates of suicide than the United States, but far lower rates of depression.[138] In Japan, suicide is both far more embedded in the culture, and far less subject to either courts or physicians. Japan, unlike Europe, the United States, and Latin America, does not have a Christian heritage with an absolute religious prohibition against suicide, and in Japan, suicide has long been culturally understood as an appropriate response to shame and dishonor. Suicide was (and remains in many ways) central to Japanese culture. The ritual of "seppuku" was assisted suicide: the nobleman initiated the act of suicide, but his loyal retainer finished him off. Family and communitarian values dominate Japan and its attitude toward suicide: honorable suicide was the appropriate response to shaming or disgracing one's family. On the other hand, Josh Sebastian's reasons would be considered "dishonorable" by the Japanese: like Aristotle, they believe that one should overcome personal difficulty or unhappiness, and not cause family the grief and turmoil associated with suicide.[139]

There are many "popular suicide spots" in Japan.[140] One of them, the Aokigahara forest, is a popular tourist destination for non-suicidal people, who take holidays to the forest to look for corpses and scavenge for their

---

[135] See Chapters 1 and 5.
[136] On Oct. 27, 2014, Brittany Maynard, who had announced that she would avail herself of assisted suicide in Oregon on Nov. 1 in order to avoid dying a painful death from brain cancer, made the cover of *People* magazine. The tone of the accompanying article was admiring of both Maynard and her family, who moved to Oregon with her. Nicole Weisenee Egan, *My Decision to Die*, PEOPLE, Oct. 17, 2014, *available at* www.peoplecom/article/terminally-ill-Brittany-Maynard-decision-to-die.
[137] This statistic is based on a retrospective study where the *researcher* combed the records of people who had already committed suicide, searching for signs of mental illness. Dr. Edwin Shneidman, who devoted his life to suicide, thought that most people who were suicidal were not mentally ill.
[138] Lim et al., *supra* note 1.
[139] Edward S. Harris, *The Moral Dimensions of Properly Evaluating and Defining Suicide*, OHIO UNIVERSITY INSTITUTE FOR APPLIED & PROFESSIONAL ETHICS (July 27, 2009), www.ohio.edu/ethics/2001-conferences/the-moral-dimensions-of-properly-evaluating-and-defining-suicide/index.html.
[140] Larissa MacFarqhar, *Last Call: A Buddhist Monk Confronts Japan's Suicide Culture*, NEW YORKER, June 24, 2013, at 56, *available at* www.newyorker.com/magazine/2013/06/24/last-call-3.

belongings.[141] The forest and other similar venues have been celebrated in Japanese fiction, nonfiction, and movies: a best-selling book on suicide in Japan called the Aokigahara forest "a perfect place to die."[142] Very much unlike the United States, there is a culture in Japan of people committing suicide in groups. These suicides are arranged on the Internet, and in some ways are the Japanese equivalent of the flash mob.

Because suicide in Japan is less medicalized, prevention efforts have been based outside its mental health system. Rather than being systemic, prevention seems to be the crusade of individuals, such as a Buddhist monk profiled in the *New Yorker*[143] or a filmmaker.[144] Systemic efforts seem woefully inadequate: one report says that people have to call suicide hotlines thirty or forty times to get through.[145]

Doctors in Japan appear to have both more power and less public trust than in the United States or Europe. As one Japanese commentator states, in translation,

> [w]e can say generally that there are careful attitudes on euthanasia in Japan. There is also a kind of distrust to medical professions in the background of this situation. Therefore many people tend to reject to establish a kind of an act or provision which makes "active euthanasia" lawful like in the Netherlands or "physician assisted suicide" like in the State of Oregon in the USA.[146]

The Japan Society for Dying with Dignity's focus is on persuading people to complete living wills and advance directives and then attempting to make sure that those documents are enforced.[147] Despite the efforts of the organization, which has a substantial membership, there is no legal right to have advance directives or living wills enforced in Japan. This is because there is no right to refuse treatment in Japan: continuation or cessation of treatment

---

[141] *Id.*

[142] Wataru Tsurumi, The Complete Manual of Suicide (1993).

[143] Ittetsu Nemota is profiled in MacFarqhar, *supra* note 142, at 56.

[144] Rene Duignan, an Irish filmmaker, set out to interview Japanese people with the goal of reducing Japanese suicides by 10,000, his 2012 documentary was very well received in Japan, see SUICIDE IN JAPAN DOCUMENTARY: SAVING 10,000: WINNING A WAR ON SUICIDE IN JAPAN (Top Documentary Films 2013), *available at* http://topdocumentaryfilms.com/saving-10000-winning-war-suicide-japan.

[145] *Id.*

[146] Katsunori Kai, *Euthanasia and Death with Dignity in Japanese Law*, 27 WASEDA BULL. COMP. L. 1 (Mar. 2009), *available at* www.waseda.jp/hiken/jp/public/bulletin/pdf/27/ronbun/A02859211-00-00270001.pdf.

[147] In 1980, a man brought a case asking the court to issue a ruling that his advance directive would be honored, and the court declined to rule, essentially invoking the doctrine that the case was not ripe for adjudication (he had not yet suffered an injury to be remedied by the court). Rihito Kimura, *Death, Dying and Advance Directives in Japan: Sociocultural and Legal Point of View, in*

is considered the doctor's decision, as it was in the United States until the *Quinlan* case. "The course of treatment is rarely influenced by the individual patient's personal preferences, or choices among possible therapies."[148] Many doctors in Japan still consider it inappropriate to even tell a competent patient that he or she is dying of cancer, and would not tell the patient prior to telling his or her family in any event. It's hard to imagine the development of a right to refuse treatment in the absence of any apparent right to informed consent, or even to a diagnosis of one's medical condition.

The first euthanasia case to be decided by a Japanese court was handed down in 1972. It involved a terminally ill father pleading with his son to kill him, and the son's compliance by giving the father milk with agriculture pesticide.[149] In Japan at the time, killing an ancestor was a particularly heinous crime, punishable by death or a lifetime of penal servitude; murder of a nonrelative, conversely, carried a sentence of as little as three years. Assisted suicide was punishable by between six months and seven years in prison. The court held that euthanasia would be acceptable if six criteria were met: imminent death, severe pain, no alternative treatment, request by the dying individual, that a physician perform the act, and that the method was ethically acceptable. Although the son was convicted (he wasn't a doctor and insecticide is not an "ethical" means of euthanasia), he was only sentenced to a year of imprisonment with three years' probation.[150] This decision, by a lower court, was the only word on euthanasia for years in Japan, and eleven years later the Japanese Supreme Court invalidated the enormous differential between punishment for killing one's ancestors and anyone else. There were four cases involving men killing severely ill wives or mothers after the Nagoya case; in each case, the man was convicted but given a minimal sentence.[151]

Cases involving euthanasia by physicians appeared for the first time in the 1990s. In the first case, the son of a man about to die implored his doctor to either "end" or "alleviate" his father's suffering (the son later denied having asked the doctor to end his father's life). The father was in a coma, and not apparently suffering at all, but was making the snoring noises common to someone in the dying process. The doctor took the father off life support, but the father kept snoring away. The son came back and said it was unbearable to hear his father's noises, and the doctor accordingly injected the father with a double dose of sedative. Nevertheless, the father continued to struggle with

ADVANCE DIRECTIVE AND SURROGATE DECISIONMAKING IN TRANSCULTURAL PERSPECTIVE (Hans Martin Sass, Robert M. Veatch, & Rihito Kimura eds., 1998), *available at* www.bioethics.jp/licht_adv8.html.

[148] Mike Hayashi & T. Kitamura, *Euthanasia Trials in Japan: Implications for Legal and Medical Practice*, 25 INT'L J. L. PSYCHIATRY 557, 567 (2002).
[149] *Id.* at 560–61.
[150] *Id.* at 561.
[151] Kimura, *supra* note 147.

his breathing, and the doctor once again injected him with a double dose of sedative. The father continued to soldier on, and the son said to the doctor (according to the doctor), "What are you doing? My father is still breathing! I want to take him home soon."[152]

After two more efforts to give the Rasputin-like father drugs that might conceivably be related to treating his condition, the doctor relented and injected the father with potassium chloride, which finally succeeded in killing him. The son then denied ever asking the doctor to end his father's life, and the doctor was convicted of murder. However, although the prosecutors asked for a sentence of three years, he was sentenced to two years of hard labor with a suspension of the sentence. This court found that euthanasia was permissible, but only if the patient himself had asked for it explicitly, was imminently terminal, was in unbearable pain, and the pain could not be alleviated by alternative means.[153]

The circumstances of the second case were similar to the first, in that a patient who was terminally ill had a breathing tube removed by a doctor (although not in compliance with any family request). This is the account of what happened next:

> Contrary to her expectations, he did not die, and was breathing with difficulty, bending backwards like a shrimp. As the doctor could not quiet such a breath, she thought it was undesirable to show the situation to the patient's relatives, among whom there were infants. She then made a nurse inject muscle-slacking drug into patient's vein and killed him.

In 2009, the Japanese Supreme Court upheld an eighteen-month suspended sentence for this doctor, who wrote a book a year later called *Was it Murder That I Committed?*[154] The doctor was investigated but not prosecuted on the grounds that it was unclear whether the muscle relaxant dosage was sufficient to kill the patient. (There seemed to be no question that the doctor intended to kill the patient rather than simply unbend him.)

One of the ways in which Japanese culture influences this debate is the importance of the opinion of the family with regard to a person's medical treatment. When a doctor was investigated for murder in connection with disconnecting the ventilators of seven terminally ill patients, his defense was that the families had consented to the procedure. He was not prosecuted.[155] Thus, while the Japanese might share American skepticism about the medical

---

[152] Kai, *supra* note 146, at 4.
[153] Kai, *supra* note 146, at 5.
[154] Jun Hongo, *Euthanasia: The Dilemma of Choice*, JAPAN TIMES, Feb. 15, 2014, http://www.japantimes.co.jp/life/2014/02/15/general/euthanasia-the-dilemma-of-choice/#.VTLEImdFBD8.
[155] *Id.*

profession, they do not at all share Americans' notions that autonomy is a cherished value for individuals, and it rests with those individuals, and not their families, to exercise.

India: Behind the Recent Decriminalization of Attempted Suicide

Attempted suicide was a crime in India until 2014.[156] This fact gained international attention, because of the case of Irom Sharmila Chanu.[157] She lives in the state of Manipur in northwestern India, where the Indian army has run roughshod over civil rights, authorized by an Indian law called the Armed Forces Special Powers Act.

In 2000, Chanu began a hunger strike to protest this law. When it looked as though she might die, she was arrested for attempting suicide and force-fed. She has pled not guilty, and never actually gone to trial. This has now been going on for fourteen years. On August 20, 2014, a court ordered her release. On August 22, when the authorities ascertained that she was going to continue her hunger strike, she was rearrested, and force-feeding recommenced. Her "internal organs are atrophied, her lips are rubber-like."[158] She began her hunger strike at the age of twenty-eight and is now forty-two. Although attempted suicide is (ironically enough) a bailable offense, Chanu has refused to sign bail bonds because she contends that this would constitute acceptance that her behavior constitutes a crime. She asserts that she is not suicidal: "I do not want to take my life but I want justice and peace." Of course, if all of us wanted justice and peace as much as Chanu, and were willing to go that far to get it, the world would be a very different place—either much more just and peaceful or almost completely depopulated, depending on your point of view.

The U.S. Department of Defense also described hunger strikers at Guantánamo Bay as "attempted suicides rather than protests, contrary to the observations of many of its own officers and medical staff that hunger strikes were indeed protests and not attempts at self-harm.[159] The role of physicians in force-feeding hunger-striking protesters who are described as "suicidal" will be examined in more detail in Chapter 5.

---

[156] *Govt Decides to Repeal Section 309 from IPC; Attempt to Suicide No Longer a Crime*, Z NEWS, Dec. 10, 2014, http://Zeenews.india.com/news/india/govt-decides-to-repeal-section-309-from-ipc-attempt-to-suicide-no-longer-a-crime_1512479.html.

[157] Priyanka Borjupari, *Suicide or Protest? Hunger Strike Rivets India*, BOSTON GLOBE, Sept. 8, 2014, at A-14.

[158] *Id.*

[159] *Executive Summary* in ETHICS ABANDONED: MEDICAL PROFESSIONALISM AND DETAINEE ABUSE IN THE WAR ON TERROR: TASK FORCE REPORT, p. xxv

Two individuals convicted of assisting a suicide and sentenced to six years in prison appealed their convictions, asserting that the provision of Indian law criminalizing assisted suicide violated the Indian Constitution.[160] The High Court held that both euthanasia and assisted suicide are illegal in India and can only be established by legislation, effectively overruling a prior lower court decision, which had struck down the criminalization of attempted suicide.[161] Later the High Court of India suggested to the Parliament that it repeal the crime of attempted suicide, because "[a] person attempts suicide in a depression, and hence he needs help rather than punishment."[162]

The court has to approve withdrawal of treatment from a person in a persistent vegetative state because:

> In our opinion, if we leave it solely to the patient's relatives or to the doctors or next friend to decide whether to withdraw the life support of an incompetent person there is always a risk in our country that this may be misused by some unscrupulous persons who wish to inherit or otherwise grab the property of the patient. Considering the low ethical levels prevailing in our society today and the rampant commercialization and corruption, we cannot rule out the possibility that unscrupulous persons with the help of some unscrupulous doctors may fabricate material to show that it is a terminal case with no chance of recovery. There are doctors and doctors. While many doctors are upright, there are others who can do anything for money (see George Bernard Shaw's play [*The Doctors Dilemma*]). The commercialization of our society has crossed all limits. Hence we have to guard against the potential of misuse (see Robin Cook's novel [*Coma*]). In our opinion, while giving great weight to the wishes of the parents, spouse, or other close relatives or next friend of the incompetent patient and also giving due weight to the opinion of the attending doctors, we cannot leave it entirely to their discretion whether to discontinue the life support or not.[163]

(Institute on Medicine as a Profession & Open Soc'y Foundations, Nov. 2013), www.imapny.org/wp-content/themes/imapny/File%20Library/Documents/IMAP-EthicsTextFinal2.pdf.

[160] Gian Kaur v. State of Punjab, 1996(2) S.C.C. 648.
[161] P. Rathinam v. Union of India, 1994(3) S.C.C. 394.
[162] Shanbaug v. Union of India, MANU/SC/0176/2011 (Supreme Court of India), at para. 100.
[163] Aruna Ramchandra Shanbaug v. Union of India & Ors, [2011(4) S.C.C. 454] (Supreme Court of India) Mar. 7, 2011; see Mark Magnier, *India's Supreme Court Lays Out Euthanasia Guidelines*, L. A. Times, Mar. 8, 2011, http://articles.latimes.com/2011/mar/08/world/la-fg-india-euthanasia-20110308.

Australia: Federalism Issues and Assisted Suicide

Australia's Northern Territory legalized assisted suicide in 1995, passing legislation entitled the Rights of the Terminally Ill Act. The legislation required the individual to be older than eighteen, of sound mind, terminally ill (although without any time limitation as to when the person will die), and experiencing pain or suffering. The person had to be seen by a doctor, who would discuss prognosis and options, including palliative care, and a psychiatrist, who would be required to determine that the person was not suffering from treatable clinical depression. As a matter of curiosity, I determined that during the time that this legislation was passed, the entire Northern Territory had four psychiatrists.[164] The same year that the Northern Territory established this law, Dr. Philip Nitschke founded Exit International (originally called the Voluntary Euthanasia Research Foundation) in Australia. Nitschke, who (like Kevorkian before him) has been called "Dr. Death," led workshops on suicide and has assisted a number of Australians to die. In 1997, the same year the U.S. Supreme Court decided *Vacco* and *Glucksberg*, the Australian Federal Parliament passed a law prohibiting euthanasia or assisted suicide in the territories (the Northern Territory has less autonomy than the six Australian states). Nevertheless, Nitschke has continued his activities. In five of the six Australian states, a conviction for assisted suicide can lead to life in prison, although in Victoria it is punished by only five years in prison.

However, in late 2014, Nitschke was stripped of his license to practice medicine. His offense was to email back and forth with a non-terminally ill forty-five-year-old man who was contemplating suicide and not attempting to stop him. This might be seen as quite ironic in light of the fact that Nitschke has been widely known to have assisted dozens, if not hundreds, of people to kill themselves since he first became active in this movement almost twenty years ago. However, this forty-five-year-old, non-terminally ill man was different from Nitschke's usual clients: he was apparently a serial killer, a fact which caught Nitschke off guard, to say the least.

As in the United States, spirited opposition to physician-assisted suicide was spearheaded by those who claimed that terminally ill people suffered from treatable depression, or "demoralization syndrome," a term coined by Australian researchers.[165]

---

[164] Australian Medical Workforce Advisory Committee, The Specialist Psychiatry Workforce in Australia: Supply, Requirements and Projections, 1999–2010 (AMWAC Report 1999.7, Nov. 1999), at 24, tbl.4, *available at* www.ahwo.gov.au/Documents/Publications/1999/The%20specialist%20 Psychiatry%20workforce%20in%20Australia.pdf.

[165] D. W. Kissane, D. M. Clarke, & A. F. Street, *Demoralization Syndrome—A Relevant Psychiatric Diagnosis in Palliative Care*, 17 J. Palliative Care 12 (2001).

Conclusion

The world offers differing models of approaches to suicide, assisted suicide, and physician-assisted suicide. Many countries outright prohibit and criminalize all three. The Netherlands and Belgium have medicalized physician-assisted suicide as another treatment option for patients in irremediable and unbearable pain. Japan has many suicides, but does not regard suicide as the right of an autonomous individual; Japan does not even provide its citizens with the right to refuse medical treatment or create advance directives, much less make decisions about the time and manner of their deaths. Germany and Great Britain place greater burdens on physicians who assist suicides than family and friends who do so. Switzerland lets virtually anyone avail themselves of assisted suicide, and does not deliver the gatekeeper function to physicians as happens in the United States.

Thus, our model is only one of many, and both our own experience[166] and the experience of other countries suggests that it cannot last as currently formulated. The boundary line of terminal illness is not one that any other country permitting assisted suicide draws; it cannot be enforced, and in any event makes no sense, as will be argued in Chapter 5. Likewise, the complete and total exclusion of people with psychiatric disabilities, whether terminally ill or suffering from chronic and incurable illness that no treatment has been able to alleviate, is also not shared by any other country permitting assisted suicide, and it cannot and should not be enforced in any regime that permits assisted suicide at all.

---

[166] See Chapter 3.

5

Assisted Suicide and the Medical Profession

"Aid in dying and assisted suicide have nothing to do with each other. One is a medical practice and the other is a felony."

—Barbara Coombs Lee
President, Compassion & Choices (2014)[1]

"Suicide is not a do-it-yourself proposition."

—Donald Westover
President, Hemlock Society[2]

"As a physician, I resent the term 'physician-assisted suicide.' I have never felt I was assisting a suicidal patient, but rather aiding a patient with his or her end of life choice."

—Dr. Peter Goodwin
Professor Emeritus
Oregon Health Sciences University

"I don't think it's suicide. I think it's a well-thought-out death wish."[3]

—Petra DeJong (supporting a "suicide pill")
Executive Director
Right to Die Netherlands

---

[1] Richard Harris, *Choosing Death: Aid in Dying Gains Support*, FORBES (July 18, 2014), http://www.forbes.com/sites/nextavenue/2014/07/18/choosing-death-aid-in-dying-gains-support/.

[2] Jeanne Grunwell, *The Cover Interview: John Westover, Hemlock President, Calls for More Control Over Death*, VILLAGE LIFE (1998), www.villagelife.org/news/archives/hemlockinterview.html.

[3] Heather Beasley Doyle, *Right to Die: Netherlands, Belgium Ignite Global Debate on Euthanasia* (AL JAZEERA AMERICA, Mar. 4, 2014), http://america.aljazeera.com/articles/2014/3/4/right-to-die-netherlandsbelgiumigniteglobaldebateoneuthanasia.html.

The Medical Profession as Gatekeepers of Suicide

There is no end to the stigma associated with the term "suicide." As we saw in the last two chapters, the only way to be suicidal without shame and condemnation is to have a doctor's stamp of approval on your desire to die. If the doctor disagrees with you, even if you are terminally ill and competent, you are liable to end up being carted off to the emergency department (ED) and revived against your wishes.[4] Doctors are the gatekeepers of suicide: a person who wants to die may get a prescription for a lethal medication, or be involuntarily committed. It's basically up to the medical profession.

Doctors do not issue the stamp of approval for suicide readily, and certainly prefer not to do so publicly. Indeed, everyone in the medical profession understands that doctors have in fact been helping people to die for decades,[5] if not centuries—they admit as much—but they'd rather do so on a case-by-case basis, privately, quietly, maintaining secrecy and deniability, than as part of a process open to public scrutiny and state regulation. Many doctors are uncomfortable with an official, state-sanctioned program that formally links doctors with providing the means of ending life to their patients, even while they concede that there may be a place for unofficial mercy. Nowhere is this better illustrated than in the fact that in 1936, King George V of England, who was terminally ill, was helped along by his doctor, Lord Dawson, in order that morning papers such as *The Times* could announce the King's death rather than the more unsavory evening newspapers.[6] Shortly after he administered

---

[4] See Cynthia M. A. Geppert, *Saving Life or Respecting Autonomy: The Ethical Dilemma of DNR Orders in Patients Who Attempt Suicide*, 7 INTERNET J. L. HEALTHCARE & ETHICS 1 (2010), http://ispub.com/IJLHE/7/1/11437; Brandon Cohen, *Should You Resuscitate a Suicide Patient?* MEDSCAPE (Oct. 8, 2013), www.medscape.com; Jane Brody, *Is Doctor-Assisted Suicide Ever an Acceptable Option?* SUN-SENTINEL, Mar. 25, 1993, http://articles.sun-sentinel.com/1993-03-25/features/9302010885_1_doctor-assisted-suicide-patient-sanctions/2.

[5] F. DAVID MARTIN, FACING DEATH: THEME AND VARIATIONS 81 (2006); J. Pugliese, *Don't Ask, Don't Tell: The Secret Practice of Physician-Assisted Suicide*, 44 HASTINGS L.J. 1291 (1991-1992); Sherwin Nuland, *How We Die*, BOSTON GLOBE, Apr. 26, 1993, at 1 (finding that one in five physicians polled had been asked to assist a suicide and 19% of those asked had done so); William Carlsen, *AIDS Patient Tells How It Works/Physician-Assisted Suicide Practiced Quietly, Especially in the Bay Area*, SFGATE, June 27, 1997 (half of the Bay Area's leading AIDS doctors provided prescriptions for lethal doses of medication), http://www.sfgate.com/news/article/AIDS-Patient-Tells-How-It-Works-2834067.php.

[6] Joseph Lelyveld, *1936 Secret Is Out: Doctor Sped George V's Death*, N. Y. TIMES, Nov. 28, 1986, http://www.nytimes.com/1986/11/28/world/1936-secret-is-out-doctor-sped-george-v-s-death.html.

a lethal dose of morphine and cocaine to the dying king, Lord Dawson testified against a bill to legalize euthanasia in England.[7]

Of course there are always individual doctors whose public willingness to help people die is either heroic or a little unsettling,[8] depending on your point of view, and then, on a different plane altogether, missionaries of death like Dr. Jack Kevorkian and George Exoo.[9] Sometimes the doctors who assist in suicides or perform euthanasia discuss their actions later, as in the cases of Drs. Timothy Quill and Katharine Morris.[10] These discussions are often poignant and personal, reminding us of the shared humanity and connection between doctors and patients. Indeed, some doctors seem drawn to sharing the end of life with their patients, not because of macabre delight but because the time is so momentous, intimate, and profound.[11]

More often, however, doctors who assist in suicide prefer to remain in the shadows, anonymous respondents to questionnaires and surveys. The most notable of the early surveys was published in the *New England Journal of Medicine* around the time of the *Vacco* and *Glucksberg* cases.[12] It was not so much the percentage of doctors who admitted having assisted suicide or engaged in euthanasia that was startling (3.3% and 4.7% of the responding doctors, respectively, with a total of 6.4% of doctors having done one or the other), as the range: the number of times an individual doctor had assisted suicide or engaged in euthanasia. Thus, the range that doctors acknowledged having assisted suicide was one to twenty-five, meaning one doctor wrote twenty-five prescriptions for fatal medications. The range for euthanasia

---

[7] *Id.*

[8] Kevin B. O'Reilly, *Five Hawaii Doctors Offer Assisted Suicide to Terminally Ill Patients*, Am. Med. News, Apr. 17, 2012, www.amednews.com/article/20120417/profession/304179996/8/; Roger S. Magnusson, *The Sanctity of Life and the Right to Die: Social and Jurisprudential Aspects of the Euthanasia Debate in Australia and the United States*, 6 Pac. Rim L. & Pol'y J. 1 (Jan. 1997) (in a letter to the premier of Victoria province, seven Australian doctors admitted to having performed euthanasia; no action was taken against them).

[9] Exoo was a self-proclaimed midwife of death profiled in Jon Ronson's Lost at Sea. Every so often the media publicizes the stories of medical professionals who seem driven to encourage people to commit suicide. Most recently, William Melchert-Dinkel, a nurse in Minnesota was convicted of assisted suicide, Steve Karnowski, *Judge Convicts Ex-Nurse of Assisting Suicide*, Boston Globe, Sept. 10, 2014, https://www.bostonglobe.com/news/nation/2014/09/09/judge-convicts-nurse-assisting-suicide/YetkeDvKNb8XPvQ8UfH5LJ/story.html.

[10] Robert Siegel, *Doctor: Helping a Patient Die Will Never Become Routine* (NPR, Nov. 3, 2014), www.npr.org/2014/11/03/361206245/doctor-helping-patient-die-will-never-become-routine.

[11] *Id.* See p. 226 *infra.*

[12] Diane E. Meier, Carol-Ann Emmons, Sylvan Wallenstein, Timothy Quill, et al., *A National Survey of Physician-Assisted Suicide and Euthanasia in the United States*, 338 New Eng. J. Med. 1193 (1998).

was 1 to 150, meaning that at least one doctor engaged in euthanasia an eye-popping 150 times.[13] A close reading of the table in which this information was presented shows that doctors reported their patients *asking* for lethal injections in a range of one to fifty per doctor. The unavoidable conclusion is that at least one doctor engaged in an ample practice of unrequested euthanasia.

The Oregon data also reflect a relatively small proportion of doctors in the state providing all the prescriptions for lethal medications,[14] although the range (one to twelve prescriptions per doctor in the latest Oregon figures[15]) is far lower than that recorded in the *New England Journal of Medicine*, probably because the latter recorded lifetime figures and the Oregon data is only for a single year. Also, these are only the physicians who operate within the Oregon system. Dr. Tom Cooper, a retired urologist in Washington State said (prior to the legalization of assisted suicide there) that when his patients' cancers metastasized, he gave them "a big bottle of Percocet," and that he "would never seek a second opinion. It's too much of a pain…. Why would I want to fill out 14 forms for the State when I can do it the way I did twenty years ago?"[16]

Although data is not systematically collected on this issue, anecdotal evidence suggests that many patients in Oregon and Washington are refused lethal prescriptions by their own doctors, or do not even ask them. They call Compassion & Choices (formerly Compassion in Dying) for referral to a physician more sympathetic to their requests. Data *is* collected on the length of the doctor–patient relationship, and every year, the low end of the range is always fifteen days—the precise minimum number of days that a patient must wait between his or her initial request and second request, the one that results in a prescription for lethal medication.

The fact of the matter is that despite the opposition of the American Medical Association,[17] almost all state medical associations,[18] and most doctors,[19] assisted-suicide programs only need a few participating

---

[13] *Id* at tbl.3.

[14] The State of Washington does not keep the range of prescriptions per doctor, which is a shame.

[15] "Eighty-three physicians wrote 155 prescriptions during 2014 (1-12 prescriptions per physician)." Oregon Public Health Division, *Oregon's Death with Dignity Act—2014*, at 3, https://public.health.oregon.gov/ProviderPartnerResources/EvaluationResearch/DeathwithDignityAct/Documents/year17.pdf.

[16] Daniel Bergner, *Death in the Family*, N. Y. TIMES MAGAZINE, Dec. 2, 2007, http://www.nytimes.com/2007/12/02/magazine/02suicide-t.html?pagewanted=7&_r=1.

[17] American Medical Association, *AMA Code of Medical Ethics: Opinion 2.211—Physician-Assisted Suicide*, June 1994, www.ama-assn.org/ama/pub/physician-resources/medical-ethics/code-medical-ethics/opinion2211.page?.

[18] Only Oregon and California's Medical Associations have remained neutral on assisted suicide.

[19] James A. Colbert, Joann Schulte, & Jonathan N. Adler, *Physician-Assisted Suicide—Polling Results*, 369 NEW ENG. J. MED. e15 (Sept. 12, 2013), http://www.

doctors to operate successfully. The experience of Oregon, Washington, the Netherlands, Belgium, and Switzerland underscores this truth. When the Cancer Care Alliance in Washington State began its assisted-suicide pilot program, only 29 of 200 doctors surveyed in a confidential internal poll were willing to participate as prescribing physicians.[20] But this "small cadre" proved to be sufficient, and as the program continued, "a few clinicians who were initially strongly opposed subsequently expressed their willingness to participate as prescribing or consulting physicians."[21] Thus do cultures change.

Physician culture has changed more readily than psychiatrist culture, for a variety of understandable reasons. When patients die of cancer, families rarely blame the oncologist. When patients commit suicide, their mental health treaters are probably filled with more guilt and self-blame than oncologists, not to mention worrying about being blamed by others.

While mental health professionals worry about liability for being unable to predict and prevent a patient's act of self-destruction, physicians' liability and disciplinary concerns for patients who refuse life-saving treatment, or even for assisting suicide, are virtually nil unless the physician does the actual killing.[22] Although national and state medical societies uniformly condemn assisted suicide in the strongest of terms, I found very few doctors who had ever been disciplined for assisting suicide.[23]

The basic culture of both physicians and psychiatrists—to oppose and defeat disease and death—was the same for a long time. There is a rich literature on the changes in physician culture over the last forty years: accepting competent patients as the final decision-maker, attending to quality rather than length of life, understanding that the goal of defeating death cannot trump every other value in medicine. These cultural changes have slowly but increasingly resulted in a significant minority of physicians (especially younger ones) accepting assisted suicide under at least some circumstances. These cultural changes have not, for the most part, influenced mental health professionals. We will examine the causes and results of this divergence in both this chapter and the next.

---

nejm.org/doi/full/10.1056/NEJMclde1310667, (67% opposed physician-assisted suicide).

[20] Elizabeth Trice Loggers et al., *Implementing a Death with Dignity Program at a Comprehensive Cancer Center*, 368 NEW ENG. J. MED. 1417 (Apr. 11, 2013).

[21] *Id.*

[22] And even then the risks are pretty minor, see Gallant v. Board of Medical Examiners, 974 P.2d 814 (Ore. App. 1999) (in the very year that Oregon first implemented assisted suicide, a doctor who euthanized his patient had his license suspended for 60 days and was required to pay the costs of the disciplinary proceeding); see also Chapter 8.

[23] See pp. 264–267, *infra.*

Understanding Why Some Doctors Participate in Assisted Suicide and Others Do Not: Clashes in Conceptions of a Physician's Role

Dr. Herbert Hendin, a psychiatrist who is adamantly opposed to assisted suicide, has done almost the only work I could find that tries to understand why some doctors participate in assisted suicide and others do not. He speculates that doctors who assist suicide feel powerless and frustrated by an incurable condition and see assisting a patient's death as a final way in which they can be professionally useful or involved, or helpful to the patient. Somewhat surprisingly, he considers this a defect, an indication of over-involvement or some form of professional grandiosity. Hendin believes that patients need doctors to be calm, comforting, reassuring, and strong rather than empathizing with, and thus encouraging, a patient's hopelessness or despair at his or her diagnosis.

Hendin interviewed Dr. Boudewijn Chabot, the psychiatrist in the famous "Netty Boomsma" case in the Netherlands, which established that assisted suicide was permissible in the case of people with psychiatric disabilities.[24] Because of this case, Dr. Chabot is probably the psychiatrist most publicly associated with euthanasia. Hendin found Chabot to be "kind, considerate, and responsive" and could understand why he had been described as "sweet and gentle." Chabot explained that promising to help a patient die if treatment did not work often helped lure the patient into life-saving treatment, and gave an example of one such patient whose treatment was successful. On the other hand, his most famous patient—Netty Boomsma—did not appear to ever seriously attempt therapy with Dr. Chabot.

Hendin also interviewed Dr. Herbert Cohen, who had performed between 50 and 100 euthanasias. One of Dr. Cohen's earliest cases was an elderly woman who had been tortured in a concentration camp. As she got older, she became increasingly unable to repress the memories of her torture. Dr. Cohen also helped numerous nonterminally ill but extremely physically disabled women to die. He noted the prevalence of women in cases that break new ground in law relating to assisted suicide and euthanasia.[25] Dr. Cohen said that he performed so many euthanasias because it brought him so close to the patient: "You become part of a family... There is a special warmth and intimacy and harmony. It is true for them as well; it improves relations among the family. My absolution is the Christmas cards I receive from relatives."[26] Dr. Cohen ceased performing euthanasias after he became exhausted, a condition finally discovered to be caused by sleep apnea, which was treated and

---

[24] See p. 196, *supra*, Chapter 4.
[25] His perception related only to Dutch cases, but as it happens, it is true across Europe and the United States as well.
[26] Herbert Hendin, *Seduced by Death: Doctors, Patients and Assisted Suicide* 67 (1998)(paperback edition).

cured. Dr. Hendin, unsolicited, offers Dr. Cohen a psychiatric interpretation that his difficulty breathing was related to his work assisting people to die, to which Dr. Cohen responds with a polite skepticism that it must be buried very deep indeed in his subconscious. Despite his cure, Dr. Cohen did not return to performing euthanasia. He told Hendin that it never became "easy" and that "The price for any dubious act is doubt. . . . I don't sleep for the week after."[27]

Reading Hendin's account of these interviews, one cannot help but feel that he and the Dutch physicians and psychiatrists he interviews are talking past each other. Each bases his actions and judgments on a completely different set of principles which they never fully articulate to each other. The Dutch doctors are basically trying to ensure that suicidal people are fully competent, as well as persistent and unswerving in their desire to die. There is some effort made to ensure that the people desiring assisted suicide or euthanasia have attempted treatment, and that it has been unsuccessful, and that further efforts would be futile. But their actions seem to spring from the conviction that a competent person with a persistent desire to die has a right to end his or her life. Hendin, on the other hand, clearly believes that it is the psychiatrist's essential job to change a person's mind about suicide, regardless of the individual's competence, or the persistence of the desire to die. He believes psychiatrists are uniquely qualified to stave off suicidality and that it is their duty to do so until the very end, standing as beacons of hope, pinpricks in the darkness by whose light their patients might steer a course away from death.

The misunderstanding between Hendin and the Dutch professionals results from two completely different ideas of the role of a medical professional. Many principled Dutch physicians have embraced the notion of assisted death and euthanasia as another form of medical treatment, just as the Cancer Care Alliance and Compassion & Choices have characterized assisted suicide in the United States. Dutch physicians have so dominated the assisted-suicide movement that nonmedical advocates complain. When Hendin was in the Netherlands, the president of the Netherlands Voluntary Euthanasia Society (who was herself a doctor and a coroner) criticized the Royal Dutch Medical Association for "wanting to medicalize euthanasia."[28] The Society and the physicians interviewed by Hendin, seeing these events as solely in the province of the doctor, strongly prefer euthanasia to assisted suicide, because euthanasia (as they told Hendin) precludes the possibility of patients botching the process.[29]

---

[27] *Id.* at 68.

[28] *Id.* at p. 71.

[29] Chabot did, however, later wrote a book on how to die by starvation and lack of hydration, BOUDEWIJN CHABOT, A HASTENED DEATH BY SELF-DENIAL OF FOOD AND DRINK (2008).

228 Rational Suicide, Irrational Laws

The Dutch focused on the patient's competence and persistence of the desire to die, and then perceived ending the life of the patient as something that needed to be done professionally and competently. Hendin, on the other hand, focused on the physician's job as cajoling and luring the patient away from death. Both see the doctors' professional responsibility as ensuring that the patient does not suffer needlessly. They just have completely different notions of how to carry out that responsibility. But ultimately, both Hendin and the Dutch physicians share a view of the death-desiring patient as the physician's responsibility, and the physician as the possessor of expertise and authority that the patient does not have.

Therefore, Hendin saves his most scathing criticism for Dr. Timothy Quill, an American doctor whose influential article about helping "Diane" to die[30] was a turning point in the U.S. debate about assisted suicide, and, more subtly, in the American understanding of the proper role of physicians in end-of-life decision-making. Coming a year after Dr. Kevorkian's first use of his contraption of death,[31] and two years after the infamous "It's Over, Debbie" article was published in the *Journal of the American Medical Association*,[32] Dr. Quill's article represented the first time an apparently reputable, responsible, and thoughtful doctor endorsed assisting suicide.[33] Dr. Quill comes across in all his writings as conscientious and caring, and he certainly knew his patient Diane for a number of years, unlike either Dr. Kevorkian or the anonymous doctor in the "Debbie" article. The *New York Times* said his "account seems to answer many of the ethical and moral objections that had been raised in previously well-publicized cases."[34] Dr. Ronald Cranford, a medical ethicist, said "People will have trouble criticizing this procedure."[35] Cranford apparently did not know psychiatrists, whose critique of Quill was forceful and fairly unified.[36]

Quill's account was of his longtime patient Diane, a woman who had successfully struggled with depression and alcoholism and had carved out a productive professional and personal life. She had been doing well for several years when she received a diagnosis of leukemia. Treatment would provide a one in four chance of long-term recovery.[37] To have the best chance at

---

Timothy Quill, *Death and Dignity—A Case of Individualized Decisionmaking*, 324 NEW ENG. J. MED. 691 (1991).

[31] See Chapter 2.

[32] See Chapter 3.

[33] Quill, *supra* note 30.

[34] Lawrence K. Altman, *Doctor Says He Gave Patient Drug to Help Her Commit Suicide*, N. Y. TIMES, Mar. 7, 1991, http://www.nytimes.com/1991/03/07/us/doctor-says-he-gave-patient-drug-to-help-her-commit-suicide.html.

[35] *Id.*

[36] See, e.g., Patricia Wesley, *Dying Safely*, 8 ISSUES L. & MED. 467 (1993).

[37] This was a higher chance of recovery than Ms. E's., who was court-ordered to be restrained or sedated and force-fed for a year, see Chapter 1, pp. 44–46.

recovery, Diane needed to start right away, and her oncologist had scheduled chemotherapy to begin that day. Far from being grateful for his efficiency, Quill reports that Diane was "enraged at his presumption that she would want treatment, and devastated by the finality of the diagnosis."[38]

Diane refused to begin immediate treatment and after discussing the issue at length with her family, a psychologist, and Quill, remained determined to refuse all treatment. She thought she would suffer unspeakably from the hospitalization, chemotherapy, bone marrow transplants, and the loss of control of her body, and considered that 25% was not good enough odds to go through with it. Quill discussed her situation at length with her and decided she had made an informed and competent decision that was right for her. So far, so good. In 1991 the right of patients to refuse life-saving treatment was well established, and there was no guarantee at all that this treatment would be life-saving: indeed, the odds were against it.

But then, things got more complicated. She asked him to give her a prescription for drugs to help her commit suicide, so that she would not die a lingering death. He explains his reaction:

> Knowing of her desire for independence and her decision to stay in control, I thought this request made perfect sense....In our discussion it became clear that fear of a lingering death would interfere with Diane's getting the most she could out of the time she had left until she found a safe way to ensure her death. I feared the effects of a violent death on her family, the consequences of an ineffective suicide that would leave her in precisely the lingering state she dreaded so much, and the possibility that a family member would be forced to assist her...[39]

Although Quill tells Diane he cannot assist her because it is against the law, he refers her to the Hemlock Society, telling her they might be "helpful." When she returns to ask him for a prescription for barbiturates, he writes it, making sure she knows the amount needed to commit suicide. At the end of the article, he concludes that he did the right thing, reflecting on Diane's promise that they will be reunited among dragons at Lake Geneva. Indeed, Diane changed Quill's life. He became one of the leading advocates of assisted suicide. His was the civilized face that agonized over the decision of a patient well known to him, as opposed to Dr. Kevorkian, the fierce and avid missionary of death.

Even Hendin concedes that Quill makes a "seemingly reasonable" case for assisting his patient to kill herself. But, as he says in a telling phrase, "It was left to psychiatrists...to challenge both Quill's role in Diane's decision and his account of their interaction, in which he appears simply as a

---

[38] See Quill, *supra* note 30, at n.15.

[39] Quill, *supra* note 30.

compassionate figure responding in a disinterested way to her needs."[40] Hendin condemns Quill because he "never questions her insistence on total control," which Hendin believes is frankly pathological:

> Quill never questions her insistence on total control, an impossible demand in the face of serious illness, or sees this as potentially an aspect of depression, not simply a reasonable response. But characteristically it is suicidal people who are most afflicted by the need to control and to make demands on life that life cannot fulfill. Determining the time, place, and circumstances of death is the most dramatic of such demands.[41]

This is curious, because determining the time, place, and circumstances of one's death is not a "demand on life that life cannot fulfill," as about 38,000 Americans a year could tell Dr. Hendin, if they were still alive to do so.[42]

Hendin is outraged that Quill referred Diane to the Hemlock Society, "implicitly, if unwittingly, giving her the message that. . . if you cannot be fully independent, you are better off dead.'" This was not at all the message Quill gave Diane—perhaps mistakenly, but very wittingly, he gave Diane the message, "This is your decision to make, and as your doctor, I will help you carry out your wishes." Maybe that's a mistake, but anyone reading Quill's article fairly would understand that his mission, as he understood it, was to help Diane implement her informed decisions, and reduce her suffering, as she understood it. This is what moves those American doctors who have embraced assisted suicide. Rather than the Dutch perspective, which simply expands the physician's expertise to include euthanasia, those American doctors who have publicly participated in assisted suicide echo Quill's message of alliance and collaboration with patients who ultimately chart their own courses. The emphasis on patient autonomy and control is much more pronounced in American doctors who endorse assisted suicide than in Dutch doctors who do so.

There is a limit to this mission—I don't think Dr. Quill would have euthanized Diane at her request—and the difficult question facing all of us,

---

[40] Herbert Hendin, "*Seduced by Death: Doctors, Patients and the Dutch Cure,*" 10 *Issues L.&Med.* 123, 126 (1994). "Left to psychiatrists," indeed, and we will later explore whether psychiatrists' almost uniform opposition to assisted suicide arises from a greater understanding of the dynamics governing the decision to terminate one's life or simply a reaction from their own experience of patient suicide as the ultimate professional failure.

[41] *Id.*

[42] Give or take however many hundreds of people who die during psychotic breaks or while heavily intoxicated or when they thought they would be found in time, and thus cannot be said to have determined the time, place and manner of their deaths.

especially doctors, is where to draw that limit. This is the question that troubles Dr. Atul Gawande:

> I fear what happens when we expand the terrain of medical practice to include actively assisting people with speeding their death. I am less worried about abuse of these powers than dependence on them. Proponents have crafted the authority to be tightly circumscribed to avoid error and misuse. . .Nonetheless, the larger culture invariably determines how such authority is employed.[43]

As is invariably the case,[44] Gawande points to the Netherlands as an example: it has expanded its euthanasia program and has been "slower than others to develop palliative care programs."[45] Gawande insists that "our ultimate goal is not a good death but a good life to the very end,"[46] and tells the story of his daughter's piano teacher, who in her initial despair following the news of her imminent death might have chosen assisted suicide had it been available, but was persuaded instead to use hospice to live out her days as she had initially thought impossible to do: continuing to give piano lessons to her beloved pupils. Like Gawande, famed palliative care pioneer Dr. Ira Byock is uneasy about the wider social implications of adopting assisted suicide: "I believe that deliberately ending the lives of ill people represents a socially erosive response to basic human needs."[47] He is also troubled by the "rebranding" of assisted suicide, calling "Orwellian" the tactic of deliberately omitting the word "suicide" while promoting a program to permit people to end their own lives.[48]

Quill, Gawande, and Byock may have subtle differences in their approach to assisted suicide and the autonomy of patients. But unlike many courts granting the right to die to nonterminally ill physically disabled people,[49] Quill's message is not, as Hendin would have it, that a fully independent life

---

[43] ATUL GAWANDE, BEING MORTAL 244 (2014).

[44] See Chapter 4 for comments on why the Netherlands' experience with euthanasia is invariably brought up in American discussions rather than, e.g., Belgium or Switzerland.

[45] *Id.* However, Oregon's palliative care programs improved after it adopted assisted suicide.

[46] *Id.*

[47] Ira Byock, *Op-Ed: We Should Think Twice about 'Death with Dignity,'* L. A. TIMES, Jan. 30, 2015, http://www.latimes.com/opinion/op-ed/la-oe-0201-byock-physician-assisted-suicide-20150201-story.html#page=1.

[48] *Id.*

[49] McKay v. Bergstedt, 801 P.2d 617 (Nev. 1990); Thor v. Superior Court (Andrews), 855 P.2d 375 (Ca. 1993) (upholding quadriplegic prisoner's right to refuse gastrostomy or gastrojejunostomy tube even though necessary to save his life); *Bouvia v. Superior Court*, see extensive discussion in Chapter 2, pp. 65–71.

is not worth living. Quill's message is that it's up to Diane to determine what kind of life is worth living. The problem with this approach (if it's a problem) is that once accepted, there is no logical reason to limit it to people with terminal illness, especially when you consider people such as Diane, with plausibly treatable terminal illness.

Hendin compares Quill's treatment of Diane to his own treatment of "Tim," who had the same disease as Diane, the same likelihood of survival, and the same initial preoccupation with suicide.[50] Hendin counseled Tim, with a very specific idea about what was best for Tim under these circumstances. This, Hendin, asserts, is the duty of the doctor at a time of shock and overwhelming grief for the patient: to guide the patient away from choosing death and to help make the patient's last days as meaningful as possible. Tim decided to accept treatment for his cancer, "complained relatively little about the unpleasant side effects,"[51] and died anyway. However, "[t]wo days before he died, Tim talked of what he would have missed without the opportunity for a loving parting."[52] Hendin does not refer to the fact that Quill's account of Diane illustrates that she, too, had a loving parting with her husband and son.

Hendin believes that doctors share with some patients the inability to tolerate situations they cannot control, and that this can

> explain both the doctor's tendency toward excessive measures
> to maintain life in the dying as well as the need to make death a
> physician's decision. By deciding when patients die, by making
> death a medical decision, the physician has the illusion of mastery
> over the disease and the accompanying feelings of helplessness.
> The physician, not the illness, is responsible for the death. Assisting
> suicide and euthanasia becomes a way of dealing with the
> frustration of being unable to cure the disease. A patient's suicidal
> feelings can evoke a similar response in psychiatrists. The threat
> of suicide can arouse both a sense of personal injury and an angry
> vulnerability in psychiatrists that makes them unable to deal with
> the illusory promise death holds for the patient.[53]

Ultimately, I think Hendin cannot forgive Quinn's implicit presumption that he is Diane's ally and collaborator, helping her implement the decisions she has made about her illness and treatment. Hendin and other physicians, in all good faith, understand the doctor–patient relationship as one in which the doctor counsels, directs, and guides the patient in the direction of life and health. The literature is replete with physicians who actually refuse patients'

---

[50] Hendin, n. 26, at pp. 31-32.
[51] Hendin, n. 40 at 128. No one knows what suffering is encapsulated in that phrase.
[52] Hendin, n. 26 at 32.
[53] Herbert Hendin, "Seduced by Death," at n.40 at p. 129.

request to cease treatment:[54] doctors' accounts of patients whose pleas to disconnect the ventilator are ignored,[55] who bargain unsuccessfully with their doctors for control over their own bodies and lives.[56] This is particularly true when patients want to do more than to cease treatment, not simply leaving the door open for death to arrive, but rather to head over to death's dwelling and invite themselves in early.

Stephen McCrea, a mental health professional who I interviewed, said that physicians' own difficulties dealing with death might land them on either side of the assisted-suicide issue:

> Both sides of the issue have people who are emotionally
> unhealthy... Doctors have their own issues that they bring to
> their profession, and these can easily influence their decisions
> beneath their own awareness. Truly professional doctors,
> whatever their views on assisted suicide, are going to understand
> that their personal beliefs and feelings and reactions are going to
> come into play when they are dealing with someone facing these
> difficulties, and they are going to have to recognize their own
> emotional reactions and learn to set those feelings aside. Doctors
> should sit down and talk to the person [who wants to die] and
> say, 'What makes you think you want to do that?' and carefully
> listen to the answer without judgment, even if it is emotionally
> difficult or painful for them. I believe that the ultimate role
> the doctor plays is determined by their openness to emotional
> experience.[57]

Thus, doctors bring to any interaction with a patient, especially one as fraught as decisions about dying, not only the culture of their profession but their own image of the role of the doctor, and how they can best fulfill that role: counseling, comforting, collaborating, enabling, or protecting the patient all potentially point in different directions as doctors stand at the gates of decisions about death.

---

[54] CHRISTOPHER HITCHENS, MORTALITY (2014); Sidney Hook, *In Defense of Voluntary Euthanasia*, *in* ARGUING EUTHANASIA: THE CONTROVERSY OVER MERCY KILLING, ASSISTED SUICIDE AND THE "RIGHT TO DIE" 237 (Jonathan Moreno ed. 1995) (Dr. Hook, a prominent philosophy professor, tells of unremitting agony in the hospital: "In one of my few lucid intervals, I asked my physician to discontinue all life-supporting services or show me how to do it. He refused my request and predicted that some day I would appreciate the unwisdom of my request." Hook survived and, although he returned to writing and research, he wrote an essay to underscore that he thought the doctor was wrong in refusing his request.)

[55] Diane Flescher, *Mr. Stone*, *in* AT THE END OF LIFE: TRUE STORIES ABOUT HOW WE DIE 119–28 (Lee Gutkind ed., 2012).

[56] Sidney Hook, see n. 54.

[57] Interview with Stephen McCrea, Aug. 26, 2014.

The Role of Patient Autonomy in Shaping Policy
Decisions About Suicide

There are two issues at the heart of any discussion of suicide, including physician-assisted suicide. The first is the appropriate role of the physician, and the second is the understanding of and value given to the principle of personal autonomy.

For years, both these questions were understood to be reserved for physicians to answer, through their organizational affiliates and licensing boards. Until the 1970s, most courts did not even recognize that they had jurisdiction over questions regarding the role of physicians in the treatment of patients, even when physicians acted in ways that impacted people's constitutional rights, because courts did not recognize that there was any intersection between medical issues and constitutional rights.

Even today, the principle that competent patients have the constitutional right to decide what intrusive medical treatments will be imposed on them is diluted by many, many formal legal exceptions. People in jail and prison custody can be and are force-fed and force-medicated,[58] and competent patients in mental hospitals in some places can have routine blood draws over their refusal.[59] Women for many years were forced to have caesarian sections that they did not want,[60] including one woman who was terminally ill with cancer and at death's door.[61] Courts approved forced sterilization of poor women and disabled women for many years[62] and unwanted medical and psychiatric treatment of inmates sentenced to death.[63] Doctors performed all of these

---

[58] Courts almost uniformly approve force-feeding of prison inmates and detainees; courts also virtually uniformly approve forced psychiatric medication, including through nasal-gastric tubes, of people in institutional settings; courts approve forced electric shock. Until very recently, courts uniformly approved forced sterilization of people with disabilities; in scattered cases, this continues today. Even noninstitutionalized people receive treatment they don't want in hospitals. See Flescher, *supra* note 50 for a tragic story of a fully competent man who consented to surgery on the express condition that he would not be placed on a ventilator, and was placed on a ventilator anyway, over his protests and the protests of his wife.

[59] Makas v. Miraglia, 2007 U.S. Dist. LEXIS 15628 (S.D.N.Y. Mar. 5, 2007), *vacated in part on other grounds*, Makas v. Miraglia, 300 F.App'x 9 (2d Cir. 2008) (summary order).

[60] Jefferson v. Griffin Spalding Hosp. County Auth., 247 Ga. 86 (1981); Women started winning these cases in the 1990s, *In re* Baby Boy Doe, 632 N.E. 2d 326 (1994), *but see* Pemberton v. Tallahassee Mem'l Reg'l Med. Ctr., 66 F. Supp. 2d 1247 (1999) (no cause of action against medical center that performed involuntary cesarian pursuant to court order).

[61] *In re* A.C. 533 A.2d 611 (1987). After initially being upheld, this decision was eventually reversed by the full court (after the baby and mother both died in the involuntary operation), *In re* A.C. 573 A.2d 1235 (D.C. App. 1990).

[62] See Susan Stefan, *Silencing the Different Voice*, 47 U. Miami L. Rev. 763 (1993).

[63] See Chapters 1 and 2.

court-approved involuntary medical intrusions on patients, and doctors continue to limit and control patients' choices and autonomy to this day,[64] including force-feeding political protesters and detainees at Guantanamo, and ignoring do not resuscitate (DNR) orders when those documents do not accord with the physician's own idea of the appropriate course of action.[65]

Thus, we are nowhere near settling the powerful and evolving debate over what constitutes the physician's proper role, the scope and limits of patient autonomy, and when the State can and should intervene on either side. Ironically, *Roe v. Wade*,[66] which was the keystone in the social and legal structure of patient autonomy, was framed as a decision protecting the patient and her doctor from interference by the State.[67] I call it "ironic" because ever since *Roe* held that a zone of privacy and autonomy existed between doctor and patient that was protected from State interference, federal and state legislatures have passed hundreds of laws regulating what doctors can and cannot do[68] and even say[69] about abortion to their patients, and courts have examined and evaluated these laws, upholding some and striking down others,[70] both protecting and limiting the medical intervention known as abortion precisely because it directly intersects with constitutional principles and values.

There are many potential roles for both physicians, patients, and the State in contemplating the legal and social issues raised by suicide, which proponents of assisted suicide are passionately advocating should also be considered a medical procedure. It is only by understanding just how contingent our current cultural and legal understandings of these roles truly are that we can contemplate the range of possibilities.

---

[64] Doctors force unwanted treatments even on other doctors, see CHARLES McKHANN, A TIME TO DIE: THE PLACE FOR PHYSICIAN ASSISTANCE 2 (1999) ("For many years after my father's death, I mulled over the irony that an intelligent, competent man, himself a physician, hospitalized in a major medical center, had absolutely no control over stopping useless treatment which everyone knew could not give him more time.").

[65] See pp. 251–257 *infra*.

[66] 410 U.S. 113 (1973).

[67] *Id.* at 163 ("This means, on the other hand, that for the period of pregnancy prior to this 'compelling' point, the attending physician, in consultation with his patient, is free to determine, without regulation by the State, that in his medical judgment, the pregnancy should be terminated. If that decision is reached, the judgment may be effectuated by an abortion free of interference by the State.")

[68] Heather D. Boonstra & Elizabeth Nash, *A Surge of State Abortion Restrictions Puts Providers—and the Women They Serve—in the Crosshairs*, 17 GUTTMACHER POL'Y REV. 1 (Winter 2014), www.guttmacher.org/pubs/gpr/17/1/gpr170109.html.

[69] Rust v. Sullivan, 500 U.S. 73 (1991).

[70] Webster v. Reproductive Health Serv., 492 U.S. 490 (1989); *Rust v. Sullivan*, at n.52; Planned Parenthood v. Casey, 505 U.S. 833 (1992).

Competing Cultural Understandings of Assisted Suicide: Medical Procedure or Patient Autonomy?

As discussed in the last two chapters, the Netherlands and Belgium have a strong culture that has incorporated assisted suicide as part of medical treatment, a position strongly endorsed by Compassion & Choices in the United States and adopted by the Cancer Care Alliance of Seattle, Washington, when it decided to offer assisted suicide as a potential treatment for its terminal cancer patients. Yet to much of the public in the United States, the notion of assisted suicide as a medical treatment is grotesque. This was reflected by public reaction when the Oregon Medicaid program, following a legal requirement that it must apprise a patient denied experimental treatment of all available Medicaid-funded alternatives, sent letters to two terminal cancer patients in Oregon explaining that Oregon's Medicaid program covered assisted suicide.[71] This caused a national uproar here in the United States, but it would have been completely unremarkable in the Netherlands.

There have been two direct results of the medicalization of assisted suicide in the Netherlands and Belgium: first, there is far more euthanasia than assisted suicide, because euthanasia is what the doctor does and assisted suicide is what the patient does. Second, I believe the expansion of the scope of euthanasia to include children (including infants) and the nonterminally ill elderly is directly due to conceptualizing it as a compassionate medical treatment. To people who understand assisted suicide and euthanasia as medical treatment, excluding infants and the elderly from relief of their suffering seems inhumane. To people who understand assisted suicide as a question of individual autonomy, the concept of infants and the very elderly exercising such "autonomy" raises understandable concerns. In the United States, which has not (yet) adopted the medical perspective, it may even carry echoes of eugenics. But these associations can evaporate over time: the physicians in *Quinlan* did not want to disconnect life support from a patient in a chronic vegetative state because that, too, reminded them of eugenics.

In Switzerland and most of the United States, support for assisted suicide is not primarily framed as one relating to providing access to medical treatment. It is seen as an issue of personal autonomy, a question of control over one's own destiny, for which a doctor is supposedly only required because of the need to ensure that the patient is competent to make decisions, and because prescriptions are key to a painless and certain death. But I think there is a powerful way in which the participation of physicians legitimizes suicide: if you really just wanted a painless death, you could legalize the activities of the Final Exit Network, with their plastic bags and helium tanks. If you want to limit assisted suicide to the terminally ill, you could (as I propose in this chapter) give competent people in hospice a card that would

---

[71] Susan Donaldson James, *Death Drugs Cause Uproar in Oregon* (ABC News, Aug. 6, 2008), http://abcnews.go.com/health/story?id=5517492.

entitle them to lethal medication without having to get a prescription from a doctor.[72]

In fact in Switzerland, physicians are much less involved in assisted suicide than in the Netherlands and Belgium. Yet there is still a role for physicians in Switzerland, as there is here in the United States. In England, the guidelines of the Public Prosecutor make it clear that a case of assisted suicide is *more* likely to be prosecuted as a crime if carried out by the individual's treating medical professionals.[73]

What is the role that physicians should play with patients who want to die? In the Netherlands and Belgium, it appears to be ascertaining that the patient's condition is chronic, incurable, and unbearably painful, assuring that the patient both voluntarily and consistently wants to die, and then providing the most painless possible death. Dr. Quill saw his role as collaborator and ally with a competent patient making a reasonable choice in choosing death over continued cancer treatments. Dr. Hendin believes that doctors should actively try to persuade patients to live. The Supreme Court has conceptualized the clear line that states can draw in criminalizing assisted suicide while protecting a patient's right to refuse treatment in terms of intention: physicians can (if the state chooses) be criminally prosecuted for affirmatively engaging in conduct with the intention of assisting the patient to die, regardless of the patients' competence, wishes, or decisions, because this is not the role of a physician. Under this view, prescribing terminal sedation satisfies the "principle of double effect" endorsed by the Roman Catholic Church: sedation given for the purpose of reducing pain but with the knowledge that it would hasten death is acceptable to the Church and ethicists alike.[74]

Assisted Suicide and the Treating Physician

Many of the doctors who support assisted suicide, at least under some circumstances, emphasize the importance of knowing the patient, and his or her values and aspirations, and having a relationship with the patient over time.[75]

---

[72] See details about this proposal, *infra* at pp. 244–46.

[73] The Crown Prosecution Service, Policy for Prosecutors in Respect of Cases of Encouraging or Assisting Suicide, 43(14), www.cps.gov.uk/publications/prosecution/. In 2014, the Public Prosecutor limited this to the individual's own treating medical professionals; prior to 2014, any time any medical professional was involved in assisting suicide it was considered a factor in favor of prosecution.

[74] Richard M. Doerflinger & Carlos F. Gomez, *Killing the Pain Not the Patient: Palliative Care vs. Assisted Suicide*, UNITED STATES CONFERENCE OF CATHOLIC BISHOPS, http://www.usccb.org/about/pro-life-activities/respect-life-program/killing-the-pain.cfm.

[75] See *Interview with Timothy Quill, M.D.* (FRONTLINE, Apr. 1996), http://www.pbs.org/wgbh/pages/frontline/kevorkian/medicine/quill1.html; GAWANDE, *supra* note 43.

To me, the most troubling aspect of assisted suicide as it is currently practiced is that a few doctors with an agenda can assist the suicide of literally hundreds of people they barely know at all. It makes me uneasy to imagine the first-ever encounter between a doctor and a patient taking place over the desire of the patient to end his or her life, with the doctor referred to the patient by an organization whose primary goal is to advance patients' ability to end their lives, sometimes within less than three weeks after the first phone call. This structure means that the doctor–patient relationship is explicitly created and solely focused on the patient's desire to die. You can be completely in favor of patient autonomy and skeptical about medical paternalism, as I am, and still be very uneasy about even characterizing this encounter as a "doctor–patient relationship." The Code of Ethics of the American Medical Association requires that

> The relationship between patient and physician is based on trust
> and gives rise to physicians' ethical obligations to place patients'
> welfare above their own self-interest and above obligations to other
> groups, and to advocate for their patients' welfare.[76]

I understand that physicians may believe there is no conflict between the patient's welfare and his or her membership in organizations such as Compassion & Choices (on the one hand) and Physicians for Compassionate Care (on the other). But I do. I think these memberships represent having already taken a side on an issue where the physician's job is to be on the patient's side. The physician is the patient's ally, collaborator, and counsel, and that requires knowing the patient, at least over some period of time.

Meeting your doctor for the first time to obtain a prescription for lethal medication is thus qualitatively and quantitatively different from the Dr. Quill–Diane story, or any situation where the physician knows the patient well, has been invested in her care, and understands her values, aspirations, and idiosyncrasies. It's not the same as being presented with a list of disabilities and complications by an already-diagnosed stranger who wants to die.

Oregon and other states that have legalized assisted suicide statutorily require that the prescribing physician be the "attending physician"—the physician treating the terminal illness.[77] This requirement is not enforced. It would be a better way of protecting vulnerable patients than playing fast and loose with competency standards, because a physician who has known the patient over time has a better understanding of whether the decision to die is consistent with a person's values over time and not the result of an impulse

---

[76] American Medical Association, AMA Code of Medical Ethics: Opinion 10.015—The Patient-Physician Relationship, Dec. 2001, http://www.ama-assn.org/ama/pub/physician-resources/medical-ethics/code-medical-ethics/opinion10015.page?.

[77] See Chapter 3.

of the moment.[78] It honors the meaning of the doctor–patient relationship. It is, like many other protective mechanisms, subject to differing interpretations and abuse. Supreme Court justices who incline toward decriminalization of physician-assisted suicide envision it as occurring under these circumstances:

> For doctors who have a long-standing relationship with their patients, who have given their patients advice about alternative treatments, who are attentive to their patients' individualized needs, and who are knowledgeable about pain symptom management and palliative care options [citation omitted], heeding a patient's desire to assist in her suicide would not serve to harm the physician-patient relationship.[79]

Any other kind of relationship risks a form of exploitation: subsuming the individual patient to a cause. It doesn't matter whether the cause is right, or will reduce suffering overall, or is good social policy. The minute that a doctor–patient relationship stops being solely about the particular patient in his or her particular circumstances, something very valuable has been lost. The legalization of physician-assisted suicide in Oregon and Washington is working slowly to change physician culture there, but from the beginning, a small cadre of physicians who were willing to prescribe fatal medications for perfect strangers ensured the program would work. As a federal constitutional matter, at least, a previously existing treatment relationship could be required, even by justices who generally support assisted suicide, to protect patients from abuse or exploitation.

Another objective and measurable protective measure is the waiting period. The fifteen-day waiting period in Oregon and Washington serves the purposed of deterring extremely impulsive decisions; doctors who know their patients would recognize impulsivity too. If the state is going to medicalize suicide (a big if), then let's authentically medicalize it by locating it within an ongoing doctor–patient relationship. Let's not simply grant any doctor the power to prescribe a dose of fatal medication to a relative stranger just because he or she has a medical license. Let it be a treating medical professional familiar with a patient over time, and with the patient's values, as Dr. Quill was with Diane, a physician who feels responsible for the patient

---

[78] Note that the requirement that a person's decision is stable over time is value neutral about what the outcome may be. Josh Sebastian, from Chapter 1, is a classic example of a competent person whose desire to die was consistent with his values over time. Kerrie Wooltorton, see *infra* at pp. 247–251 may actually be another, as she had been suicidal for years. For another example of this, see Hywote Tay & David Magnus, *Suicide and the Sufficiency of Surrogate Decisionmakers*, 13 Am. J. Bioethics 1, 1–2 (2013).

[79] *Glucksberg*, 521 .S. 702 at 748 (Stevens, J., concurring).

and the patient's care in a way that doctors referred for the purposes of writing a fatal prescription for a dying patient cannot be. As Dr. Quill's case makes clear, it was in fact the longtime treating physicians who were providing assisted suicide before it was legalized. They did so on a case-by-case basis, when they judged it was right for the patient. Yes, this gave doctors a lot of power. But so does legalizing assisted suicide.

How you feel about the fact that a small group of doctors is doing virtually all the assisted suicide prescribing obviously has a lot to do with how you feel about the underlying procedure. Whether prescriptions for fatal doses of medication resemble prescription pain medication, or medical marijuana, or providing abortions in conservative rural communities, depends on your point of view. All have two things in common: they are socially and politically controversial, and only a few doctors participate in providing them.

Banning Euthanasia: The Importance of Maintaining the "Sui" in "Suicide"

The proposal just outlined is limited to assisting suicide by prescribing medication for the patient to take. No matter how well the doctor knows the patient, I don't think the United States should follow the example of the Netherlands and Belgium and legalize active euthanasia. This policy recommendation strikes me as overdetermined: there are almost too many reasons to list.

First of all, the most potent preventer of suicide is fear—fear of dying, fear of botching it, fear of what lies beyond—and many people who want to die in the moment soldier on because they can't overcome the fears that nature and common sense have planted in their way. Making death painless is different from making it someone else's job to kill you. The former is an argument to permit assisted suicide, whether by physicians or the Final Exit Network; the latter is the risk of euthanasia. There has been talk about coercive pressure to commit suicide even with the clients of Kevorkian, Exoo, and the Final Exit Network, and they all do the last-minute, fatal actions themselves.[80] Even Brittany Maynard's death raised issues of pressure after she postponed her originally scheduled "dead"-line (as it were). In the past, even I, an attorney in the health law field, have found it difficult to disagree with or oppose my doctor.[81] A society that is worried about coercing vulnerable people to die does not want to have doctors administering lethal injections. The concerns of the disability rights community that people with disabilities will be done away with under a regime of socially approved "suicide" have historical

---

[80] Except for Kevorkian's last "client."
[81] Now I have a great primary care physician and the issue does not arise.

support in euthanasia proposals. The American Medical Association is right to counsel its doctors to refrain from participating in executions.[82] Doctors should not kill people.

I understand the argument that the distinction between active euthanasia and terminal sedation or disconnecting life support is amorphous and blurry. I disagree with Chief Justice Rehnquist in *Vacco v. Quill* that the distinction between the two is easy to make.[83] However, unlike many commentators, my disagreement doesn't nudge me in the direction of approving physician-assisted suicide; it just makes me slightly more uneasy about terminal sedation and disconnecting life support. This is because of my profound agreement with Chief Justice Rehnquist in *Cruzan* when he asserts that there is an important distinction between third parties deciding to end or ending another person's life, and a person deciding and carrying out the life-ending conduct him- or herself.[84] This perspective is shared by Lord Neuberger of the Supreme Court of the United Kingdom:

> To my mind, the difference between administering the fatal drug to a person and setting up a machine so that the person can administer the drug to himself is not merely a legal distinction. Founded as it is on personal autonomy, I consider that the distinction also sounds in morality. Indeed, authorising a third party to switch off a person's life support machine [citations omitted] seems to me, at least arguably, to be, in some respects a more drastic interference in that person's life and a more extreme moral step than authorising the third party to set up a lethal drug delivery system so that a person can, but only if he wishes, activate the system to administer a lethal drug.[85]

To me, the question of intention that weighs so heavily with Chief Justice Rehnquist is more complex than he allows. A physician providing a prescription for a fatal medication may not intend that a patient die, but rather that the patient feel secure enough to live longer. A physician increasing sedatives may intend to relieve a patient's pain, but if this goal can only be achieved by the patient's dying, who is to say what is intended? I am much more focused

---

[82] American Medical Association, AMA Code of Medical Ethics: Opinion 2.06— Capital Punishment, updated June 1994, http://www.ama-assn.org/ama/pub/physician-resources/medical-ethics/code-medical-ethics/opinion206.page. See discussion *infra*, pp. 206.

[83] *Vacco v. Quill*, 521 U.S. 793, 801–02 (1997).

[84] *Cruzan*, 497 U.S. 261, 286 (1990).

[85] R. (on the Application of Nicklinson and Another) v. Minister of Justice, [2014] U.K.S.C. 38, para. 94, https://www.supremecourt.uk/decided-cases/docs/uksc_2013_0235_judgment.pdf. See also para. 92 and Lord Wilson's concurrence with this position at para. 200.

on the concrete: who actually carries out the actions that directly result in death? As Oregon and Washington experience has shown, handing someone a prescription for a fatal dose of medication doesn't begin to predict whether the person will fill it or take it. As we know so profoundly, people may want to die, intend to die, and never act. I don't want efficient and proactive doctors showing up to erase that ambivalence.

The worries of disability rights activists are at their most warranted in these third-party scenarios, when an individual is helpless to implement any decision, whether to live or die; add to that the cadre of doctors who are willing to write prescriptions for people they barely know, and you have every reason to preclude euthanasia, and punish it criminally when it does take place. Concerns about disability discrimination are not fantastical: DNR orders continue to make their way into the medical records of patients with developmental disabilities without the individual's knowledge or consent, without any discussion, often even at the direction of the guardian or family.[86]

Ultimately, the guiding principle is this: each competent individual is the only judge of his or her quality of life, be it deciding to stay alive and endure the pain, or deciding to die.[87] But competent people change their minds too and get to places they had not imagined possible: competent or not, decisions to die should not be impulsive, and should reflect the person's authentic self over at least some period of time. As Rebecca Dresser has persuasively argued, the person who wrote the advance directive while healthy may be a very different person with different values than the person currently suffering from terminal cancer.[88]

It is because the focus must be so intensely on the individual in matters of policy and law regarding suicide that I resist the efforts of advocates of physician-assisted suicide to erase the "suicide" and amplify the "physician" aspect of the policies. "Physician aid in dying" emphasizes the physician's role, as do all of the ballot and legislative initiatives and court cases in this

---

[86] Association for Retarded Citizens of Connecticut v. Thorne, 30 F.3d 367, 368–69 (2d Cir. 1994), *cert. den.* 513 U.S. 1079 (1995) (invalidating an injunction against the Department of Health Services to implement a medical advisory plan which limited the use of DNRs for patients in Department of Mental Retardation Facilities, because DHS had been improperly joined as a defendant), *Messier v. Southbury Training School,* 1999 U.S. Dist. LEXIS 1479 (D. Ct. Jan. 5, 1999), *final decision,* 562 F.Supp. 2d 594 (D. Ct. 2008). In *Messier,* the court refused to try the claims because plaintiffs could not point to an individual with an inappropriate DNR in his or her record.

[87] Carol Gill, *Professionals, Disabilities and Assisted Suicide: An Examination of the Relevant Empirical Evidence and Reply to Batavia,* 6 PSYCHOL. PUB. POL'Y & L. 526, 528–30 (2000).

[88] Rebecca Dresser, *Pre-Commitment: A Misguided Strategy for Securing Death with Dignity,* 81 TEX. L. REV. 1823 (June 2003). See *In re* Martin, 450 Mich. 204 (1995) (man's mother admitted he said he didn't want to be kept on a machine but thought he had changed his mind).

country, which always feature physicians as coplaintiffs. It might be argued that this is logical, because they are the ones who may be subject to criminal prosecution (and because they are the only ones left alive while the long slow machinery of the law lumbers to a decision). But that logic would equally support litigation by family members who would otherwise assist a person in dying, and family members are never coplaintiffs in these cases. There has never been a case brought by a person who wanted family or nonmedical assistance such as the Final Exit Network, even though these criminal prosecutions are far more likely than any prosecution of doctors.[89]

Any general policy decisions will necessarily result in at least some cases of error; that is the inescapable nature of policy.

But how should we err? If we are going to involve doctors in suicide, I think we should err on the side of requiring doctors to be more like Dr. Quill[90] and less like Dr. Kevorkian: in it for the patient rather than the principle. Thus, in the English case of *In re* E.,[91] the longtime treating professionals who believed E. was competent and supported her desire to end treatment and die should have trumped the opinion of the court-appointed expert Dr. Glover, who didn't know E. at all, that she should be force-fed.[92] Some warn that patients with eating disorders and some suicidal patients are so difficult that doctors may be tempted to support their right to suicide for the wrong reasons.[93] I still think that the opinions of doctors who know the patient well should be given more policy weight than those who met patient for the first time at the end of a complex and harrowing journey through illness and pain.

This perspective leads to a number of policy consequences. In states where assisted suicide is legal, nurse practitioners and physician's assistants with state-granted prescription authority should be able to prescribe these medications to patients they are treating; there is nothing magic about an M.D. that makes its holder more trustworthy with life and death decisions than nurse practitioners and physician's assistants who know their own patients just as well.

In addition, if assisted suicide is permitted in a state, a person who knows that he or she may want to use it someday should find (ahead of time) a treating physician who is open to the concept. This discussion should be part and parcel of discussions about advance directives and health care proxies. While

---

[89] See Chapter 10 for discussion of the criminal prosecution of members of the Final Exit Network.

[90] At least the earlier version, Diane's doctor, as opposed to the national crusader and named plaintiff for physician-assisted suicide.

[91] See Chapter 1, pp. 44–46.

[92] See Chapter 1. Some Doctors worry that long-term caretakers may actually despise some patients with anorexia, substance abuse, or personality disorders; E. had all three.

[93] See Chapter 1.

a person may believe that he or she has time after a diagnosis of terminal illness to make this decision, in most cases, all the doctors treating the terminal illness will be new to the patient. The only doctor with continuing care responsibility—the only Quill—will be the primary care physician. At the very least, if the individual believes he or she may want to consider assisted suicide, the individual should talk this over with prospective oncologists. If there is one overriding message in this book, it's that people need to talk more about dying, and the ways they foresee it happening to them.

To the extent that advocates of physician-assisted suicide succeed in differentiating and destigmatizing it by changing its name, they will have succeeded in reframing our understanding of suicide without explicit discussion, and embedding physicians in a process that does not necessarily require them. The experiences of Switzerland and the Final Exit Network show that people can be helped to die without medicalizing the process. I think national policy discussions about whether to endorse assisted suicide need to separately parse out and evaluate the role of physicians as gatekeepers, especially physicians previously unknown to the person.

Excluding Doctors from Decisions About Suicide: A Recommended Approach

What would assisted suicide look like without the "physician" part? In the last twenty-five years, various writers and scholars, including doctors, have tried without success to come up with ways to have assisted suicide in the United States without physician involvement,[94] or with only involvement of specially trained physicians variously dubbed "thanatologists"[95] or doctors who specialize in "euthanatrics."[96] The very creepiness of these latter proposals suggests how far from medicalization of end of life suicide we are as a society in the United States, and this is all to the good, I think.

You could have assisted suicide without much physician involvement, as in Switzerland, or without the procedure being medical at all, as in the Final

---

[94] Julian J. Z. Prokopetz & Lisa Lehmann, *Redefining Physicians' Role in Assisted Dying*, 367 NEW ENG. J. MED. 97 (2012) (suggesting independent federal- or state-operated dispensation system once physician had diagnosed terminal illness and prognosis of six months); Thomas Szasz, Fatal Freedom: The Ethics and Politics of Suicide (2002) (no physician involvement in suicide at all).

[95] Jacob M. Appel, *A Suicide Right for the Mentally Ill?* 37 HASTINGS CENTER REP. 21 (2007), http://www.thehastingscenter.org/Publications/HCR/Detail.aspx?id=814.

[96] J. Donald Boudreau, *Physician-Assisted Suicide and Euthanasia: Can You Even Imagine Teaching Medical Students How to End Their Patients' Lives?* 15 PERMANENTE J. 4, 79 (2011), www.ncbi.nlm.nih.gov/pmc/articles/PMC3267569/ (this was part of an essay meant to discourage adoption of physician-assisted suicide and euthanasia by demonstrating what would follow such an adoption, including medical school education in euthanasia and the formation of a specialty in euthanasia).

Exit Network's "guides" with their helium tanks and bags.[97] But I am uneasy about assistance by strangers who don't know the individual, and for different reasons, also uneasy about assistance by family members.[98] In fact, I am uneasy about third-party involvement in suicide, period.

But that doesn't mean we should abandon the effort to conceptualize a system providing the benefit of assisted suicide—respect for patient autonomy in the final months of life, alleviating anxiety about unnecessary suffering in people who are terminally ill—without involving physicians so much as gatekeepers. Although the medicalization of assisted suicide is already deeply embedded in our culture, it need not be.

One way to do this that is receiving increasing attention is for the individual to voluntarily cease eating, or eating and drinking. This approach is discussed in detail in Chapter 7, and has the tentative support of many organizations that oppose physician assisted suicide.[99] But there are other possibilities.

The crucial characteristic of American assisted suicide in the states where it is accepted is the limitation of terminal illness (all programs of assisted suicide require that the patient be competent). Yet close examination of the reported "terminal illnesses" in the data submitted in the Oregon report reveals a few ringers,[100] and every year, a number of people who have received prescriptions of lethal medications remain alive. One way to ensure that the six-month requirement is a little less porous is to provide it only to patients who are in hospice, by means of a hospice identification card to which all hospice patients would be presumptively entitled, and which would suffice to enable an individual to request a pharmacy for the medication. The "six-month" window is an eligibility requirement for hospice services, and a patient's doctor must make the certification that a patient is terminally ill with six months or less to live to the hospice provider. Physicians do this all the time without being involved in assisted suicide. Hospice providers also do their own in-depth assessment of patients, and would be in a good position to judge whether a person was competent, especially over time. The hospice provider would not be involved at all in obtaining the lethal medication. It would simply provide the identification that the person was a hospice patient, available to anyone who was receiving hospice services. The card could only

---

[97] See Chapters 8 and 10.

[98] See Chapter 8.

[99] For an exhaustive list of organizational positions on physician-assisted suicide, see Hospice Analytics, *Hospice & Palliative Medicine Resources Opposing Physician-Assisted Suicide*, http://www.hospiceanalytics.com/hospice-care-products-and-services/oppose-pas.

[100] "Includes deaths due to benign and uncertain neoplasms"—really? Oregon Department of Public Heath, *Oregon's Death with Dignity Act—2014*, 6, n.6, https://public.health.oregon.gov/ProviderPartnerResources/EvaluationResearch/DeathwithDignityAct/Documents/year17.pdf.

be denied to an individual determined to be incompetent to make medical decisions. It is true that some hospice patients live beyond six months, but when you compare the figures of hospice patients with individuals receiving prescriptions under Oregon's Death with Dignity Act, as a proportional matter the former is a more accurate way of determining that a person is truly terminally ill.

When presented with a request for lethal medications, the pharmacist could counsel the patient as to the potential risks of taking the medication and its probable result, and require the individual to wait fifteen days to pick it up. The medications would also come with very clear and precise instructions and warnings. There are two potential issues with taking doctors out of this process: the patients would have to pay the cost of the medications, which would not be reimbursed, as they currently are by Oregon Medicaid. And the federal government, which prohibits any federal funds to be used to finance assisted suicide, and which regulates transactions involving these drugs, would have to be reassured on both counts. Currently, many patients who avail themselves of assisted suicide are already in hospice, so that should not be an issue. And presumably the kinds of regulations that safeguard opiates and medical marijuana could be written to ensure only eligible hospice patients in states that had already legalized assisted suicide could have access to lethal medications.

The access to lethal medication would probably be less subject to abuse than access to opioids, amphetamines, and medical marijuana, because the demand has got to be lower. I know that hospice providers, who are wary at best about assisted suicide, will not thank me for this proposal, but it actually emerges from my great respect for hospice providers as focused on the whole person, on a person's individuality and humanity, and respect for that person. I trust hospice providers to engage in long conversations with people about these decisions in ways that honor the individual. Hospice providers will not be writing the prescriptions, but they will be in a position of caring for the individual, who may or may not have family. I just don't want suicide to turn into a medical procedure, mediated by doctors who don't know the patient.

There are interesting parallels in this idea with the evolution of the process of abortions. Increasingly, women don't need physicians for the procedure. Up to the first two months, anyone who can get access to misoprostol doesn't need a doctor for an abortion. Both abortion and suicide used to be personal and private events, cloaked with danger and deep shame, which evolved into medical procedures for a variety of complex political and social reasons.[101] Doctors' willingness to perform abortions was a crucial step in making the procedure more socially acceptable and socially visible. Stories of botched attempts at

---

[101] Suzanne M. Alford, *Is Self-Abortion a Fundamental Right?* 52 DUKE L.J. 1011 (2003).

abortions drove some of the policy arguments in favor of making it safe and legal,[102] just as the potential consequences of botched suicide attempts have been used to support arguments for physician-assisted suicide. Abortion is currently more highly medicalized than suicide, but that may change with the advent of misoprostol. Even in states such as Oregon and Washington, which have legalized assisted suicide, most people still commit suicide without resort to "physician aid in dying,"—whether they are terminally ill nor not.[103]

Women who try to self-induce abortions, like people who tried to kill themselves, were not historically regarded as mentally ill. But when women needed help to have safe abortions, before abortions were legal, one of the only ways to accomplish this was by accepting a label of mental illness. Whether suicide should be medicalized or psychiatrized, and if so, under what circumstances, is one of the crucial components of the social and legal discussion in which we engage today.

Doctors' Duties to Patients
Who Have Attempted Suicide

The Kerrie Wooltorton Case

The question of the proper role of doctors and the incongruity between the autonomy granted to medical patients and denied to psychiatric patients were principal features of the case of Kerrie Wooltorton in England.

In 2007, Kerrie Wooltorton swallowed antifreeze and called an ambulance. This, in and of itself, is not unusual. People the world over attempt suicide, immediately regret it, and seek help to save their lives. Many of the people I interviewed did exactly the same thing.

---

[102] Waldo L. Fielding, Letter to the Editor, *Repairing the Damage, Before Roe*, N. Y. TIMES, June 3, 2008 ("The familiar symbol of illegal abortion is the infamous 'coat hanger'—which may be the symbol, but is in no way a myth. In my years in New York, several women arrived with a hanger still in place. Whoever put it in—perhaps the patient herself—found it trapped in the cervix and could not remove it. . . . However, not simply coat hangers were used. Almost any implement you can imagine had been and was used to start an abortion—darning needles, crochet hooks, cut-glass salt shakers, soda bottles, sometimes intact, sometimes with the top broken off."), see http://www.nytimes.com/2008/06/03/health/views/03essa.html?_r=0

[103] In 2003, Oregon had the fourth highest suicide rate among older adults in the country (figures that did not include assisted suicide). In 2004, 93% of older adults who committed suicide had a chronic illness. X. Shen, L. Millett, & M. Kohn, *Violent Deaths in Oregon: 2004 Oregon Dept. of Human Services, 2006, in* OREGON OLDER ADULT SUICIDE PREVENTION PLAN: A CALL TO ACTION, http://public.health.oregon.gov/PreventionWellness/SafeLiving/SuicidePrevention/Documents/plan.pdf. This plan was updated in 2011.

However, Kerrie Wooltorton did not regret her suicide attempt at all, nor did she want help saving her life. She called the ambulance not because she wanted to save her life, but because she didn't want to die alone and in pain. She had written a detailed note explaining her desire to refuse any treatment that would save her life, but asking that she be given comfort measures. This note, which she showed to everyone at Norfolk and Norwich Hospital who interviewed her, is reproduced in full as follows:

> To whom this may concern, if I come into hospital regarding taking an overdose or any attempt of my life, I would like for NO lifesaving treatment to be given. I would appreciate if you could continue to give medicines to help relieve my discomfort, painkillers, oxygen etc. I would hope these wishes will be carried out without loads of questioning. Please be assured that I am 100% aware of the consequences of this and the probable outcome of drinking anti-freeze, eg death in 95-99% of cases and if I survive then kidney failure, I understand and accept them and will take 100% responsibility for this decision. I am aware that you may think that because I call the ambulance I therefore want treatment. THIS IS NOT THE CASE! I do however want to be comfortable as nobody wants to die alone and scared and without going into details there are loads of reasons I do not want to die at home which I realise that you will not understand and I apologise for this. Please understand that I definitely don't want any form of Ventilation, resuscitation or dialysis, these are my wishes, please respect and carry them out.[104]

Upon being handed this document, Wooltorton's attending physician understandably consulted immediately with a colleague, and contacted the hospital's medical director. This gentleman even more predictably sought the advice of the hospital's lawyer, who serendipitously happened to be an authority on the newly enacted Mental Capacity Act. This Act defined competency to refuse treatment, and the hospital's obligations when a competent person refused treatment.

Wooltorton was assessed three times as her condition deteriorated, and each time she reaffirmed her desire to die. After medical and legal consultations, hospital staff concluded that Wooltorton was competent to refuse treatment. When she lapsed into unconsciousness, and therefore was by definition no longer competent, they determined that her stated desires while she was conscious controlled, as well as the letter that she carried with her. Later commentators inaccurately asserted that the letter constituted an advance

---

[104] Christopher J. Ryan & Sascha Callaghan, *Legal and Ethical Aspects of Refusing Medical Treatment After a Suicide Attempt: The Wooltorton Case in the Australian Context*, 193 MED. J. AUST. 239 (2010).

directive or advance decision under the Mental Capacity Act. Thus, the medical staff kept her at the hospital, honored her wishes to be comfortable, gave her no treatment for the antifreeze, and she died two days later.[105]

Two years later, a Norfolk County Coroner upheld the hospital's decision as correct under the circumstances. The coroner, Armstrong, conducted an inquiry and determined that there was unanimous agreement among all those who had evaluated and treated Wooltorton, as well as those who knew her, that she was competent, and therefore entitled to refuse life-saving treatment under the Mental Capacity Act. Indeed, her note tracked the requirements of the Mental Capacity Act. Health care providers reading this book may be unsurprised to learn that, despite the coroner's adjudication that the hospital had acted correctly under the law, Ms. Wooltorton's family (who had not been present when she died and indeed had been so detrimental to her well-being that she had been placed in foster care for most of her childhood) expressed plans to sue.[106]

However, Ms. Wooltorton's dubious relations were not the only ones to express dismay at the coroner's report. A firestorm of controversy erupted in England and elsewhere. The basic problem identified by many commentators was a conflict of law: the Mental Health Act, like the Wisconsin commitment law applicable to Josh Sebastian, permitted involuntary detention and forced mental health treatment of a person who was mentally ill and dangerous to herself or others. Indeed, Ms. Wooltorton had previously swallowed antifreeze and had been committed under the Mental Health Act. Like Mr. Sebastian, involuntary treatment she received had not allayed her suicidality (and may have increased it, for all we know).

The Mental Health Act provided that mental health treatment could be forced on unwilling recipients who met its requirements. On the other

---

[105] *Id.*

[106] John Bingham, Lucy Cockcroft, & Rosa Prince, *Family of "Living-Will" Girl to Sue Hospital*, Telegraph [London], Oct. 7, 2009, www.telegraph.co.uk/news/uknews/law-and-order/6252339/Family-of-living-will-girl-to-sue-hospital.html. Ms. Wooltorton's father, Colin Wooltorton, also told the *Telegraph* that the law made him "ashamed to be British," John Bingham, *Andy Burnham: Living Wills Law Could Be "Revisited" After Kerrie Wooltorton Suicide Case*, Telegraph [London], Oct. 4, 2009, www.telegraph.co.uk/news/health/news/6259181/Living-wills-law-could-be-revisited-after-Kerrie-Wooltorton-suicide-case-Andy-Burnham.html. Interestingly, she spent much of her life in foster care, not living with Colin Wooltorton or her mother. Paul Bracchi, *Special Investigation: What Kind of a Country Have We Become If Doctors and Lawyers Allow a Disturbed Young Woman to Die?* Mail Online, Oct. 9, 2009, www. Dailymail.co.uk/news/article-1219389/SPECIAL-INVESTIGATION-What-kind-country-doctors-lawyers-allow-disturbed-young-woman-die.html. In addition, Mr. Wooltorton did not make these comments when his daughter actually died, in 2007, but only two years later when the coroner's report was made public.

hand, the Mental Capacity Act of 2005 gave adults who have mental capacity the absolute right to refuse medical treatment for any reason. Saving Ms. Wooltorton's life would have required kidney dialysis to flush out the effects of the antifreeze, and she was clearly refusing that medical treatment. The Mental Health Act explicitly excludes forced medical treatment. Many media stories and even a few commentators identified her note as an advance directive or advance decision, as the documents are called in England. This was not the case, at least when she first arrived at the hospital, because she was still conscious and able to convey her wishes.

The controversy over Ms. Wooltorton's case rises directly out of the still unsettled tensions around autonomy and decision-making authority as between doctor and patient, as well as our visceral feelings about suicide and psychiatric disability. Many commentators to Internet stories about Ms. Wooltorton supported her right to commit suicide (upholding her right to autonomy) but strongly condemned her for putting the medical professionals who cared for her in such an agonizing dilemma (because of their recognized roles as people who provide needed medical treatment for curable conditions). One doctor wrote (incorrectly as a matter of law, but in a telling reflection of his concept of the physician's role): "Requiring doctors not to save a failed suicide would be in effect to force them to complete the suicide."[107] Doctors have been known to refuse to terminate life support for patients who have attempted suicide whose medical conditions would otherwise warrant termination of life support.[108] When doctors in New Hampshire refused to honor either the living will of a woman who had attempted suicide or her husband's requests to turn off her life support, her husband, filed with guilt, frustration and despair because he had called 911 and thwarted his wife's desires, fatally shot her in her hospital bed and then turned the gun on himself.[109]

It is the physician's role that distinguishes the case of Wooltorton from that of Josh Sebastian.[110] In each case, the two principal questions are whether a person with no terminal medical condition and a history of psychiatric hospitalization and previous suicide attempts is competent to make the decision to die, and to what extent (if any) law and medical ethics require health care professionals to resort to involuntary measures to thwart this decision.

But the demands on the physicians are very different in the two cases. Mr. Sebastian simply wanted to be left alone; he did not ask for anything but freedom from interference and intervention by mental health professionals.

---

[107] Thaddeus Mason Pope, *Shooting in the ICU after Hospital Refused to Follow Advanced Directive*, MEDICAL FUTILITY BLOG (Dec. 31, 2014), https://medicalfutility.blogspot.com/2014/12/shooting-in-icu-after-hospital-refused.html, (comments following the post).

[108] Samuel L. Brown, C. Gregory Elliott, & Robert Paine, *Withdrawal of Nonfutile Life Support After Attempted Suicide*, 13 AM. J. BIOETHICS 3 (2013).

[109] Pope, *supra* note 107.

[110] See Chapter 1.

Ms. Wooltorton, on the other hand, affirmatively sought care from medical professionals—palliative care—as she died from a condition they could have reversed. Was providing that care in the highest traditions of the Hippocratic Oath, refusing to abandon the patient? Or was it supporting and even colluding with suicide? Many people I have interviewed, and who commented on the Wooltorton case, expressed both support for her right to kill herself and outrage that she placed the doctors in such an uncomfortable position.

There is another distinction between the Kerrie Wooltorton case and Josh Sebastian's situation: the treating professionals who questioned the legality and clinical efficacy of recommitting Josh Sebastian had known him for six months. When Kerrie Wooltorton showed up at the ED, the doctors being asked to make momentous life and death decisions about her had no idea who she was. One reason that I support in Chapter 1 a brief hold to determine the competency of a person who wants to end his or her life is precisely because most emergency department personnel neither know the person or are in a very good position, given how emergency departments operate, to get to know the person.

But ironically, from the point of view of how the law operates, probably the most crucial distinction between Kerrie Wooltorton and Josh Sebastian is that Ms. Wooltorton had already attempted suicide, whereas the question with Mr. Sebastian turned on whether and how he could be prevented from making the attempt. Requiring a treating doctor–patient relationship or a waiting period in order for a medical professional to assist suicide still doesn't answer the question posed by the Wooltorton case, which is about refusing treatment in the aftermath of a suicide attempt rather than asking for a fatal prescription to potentially end one's life in the future. The physician's involvement is completely different: the question is not whether to collaborate in a decision to shorten life, but whether to resuscitate or involuntarily treat an individual who refuses treatment. In Wooltorton's case, the only curative treatment would have been dialysis; if she didn't want it, she might have had to be restrained. Involuntary dialysis is virtually unheard of and may be the most salient reason that Wooltorton did not receive involuntary treatment. The following section looks at legal and policy issues raised by refusal of treatment after suicide attempts.

Do Not Resuscitate Orders and Suicide Attempts

In theory, a competent patient can both make current treatment decisions and execute a document, called a "living will" or "advance directive," refusing certain treatments in the future. A patient perceived as competent can also secure from a doctor an order called a "DNR," which represents the doctor's concurrence with the patient's decision not to be resuscitated under certain circumstances. This order is prospective and authoritative.

Nevertheless, in practice these legal rights, and even the doctor's assessment and order embodied by a DNR, rarely trump another doctor's contemporaneous decision that treatment is necessary. Thus, terminally ill people with DNR orders will be resuscitated against their explicit wishes if they attempt suicide—even if they are at death's door,[111] even when their family opposes resuscitation, even in Oregon or Washington (unless their suicides have the imprimatur of the Death with Dignity program).

There is actually a fairly robust ethical and medical literature about the applicability of DNR orders to suicide attempts.[112] Most of the articles acknowledge that ED physicians have a professional inclination to resuscitate patients,[113] which is amplified when the patient has attempted suicide. Sometimes the insistence on resuscitating people with DNR orders who have attempted suicide is interpreted as resulting from the association of suicide with mental illness, but there is also a substantial amount of evidence supporting the proposition that ED doctors resuscitate because they fear liability if they do not. For example, in one survey, 92% of ED physicians reported that their decisions about whether to perform resuscitations were influenced by liability concerns.[114] Over half reported having performed CPR more than ten times in three years under circumstances they believed were completely futile simply because of fear of liability.[115]

Emergency department doctors routinely ignore DNR orders and advance directives, often on the basis of idiosyncratic intuitions that have no basis in law or ethics. In a Medscape discussion of the issue, one ED doctor

---

[111] J. Jankowski & L. Campo-Engelstein, *Suicide in the Context of Terminal Illness*, 13 AM J. BIOETHICS 3, 13 (2013).

[112] Cohen, *supra* note 4; Brown et al., *supra* note 108; Jankowski & Campo-Engelstein, supra note 111; G. F. Blackall, R. L. Volpe, & M. J. Green, *After the Suicide Attempt: Offering Patients Another Chance*, 13 AM. J. BIOETHICS 14 (2013); Geppert, *supra* note 4; Renee Cook, Philip Pan, Ross Silverman, & Stephen Soltys, *Do-Not-Resuscitate Orders in Suicidal Patients: Clinical, Legal and Ethical Dilemmas*, 51 PSYCHOSOMATICS 277 (2010); D. Sontheimer, *Suicide By Advance Directive?* 34 J. MED. ETHICS, e4 (Sept. 2008); H. Karlinsky, G. Taerk, K. Schwartz, et al., *Suicide Attempts and Resuscitation Dilemmas*, 10 GEN. HOSP. PSYCHIATRY 423 (Nov. 1988).

[113] Although some might think they also have a legal obligation under Emergency Medical Treatment and Active Labor Act (EMTALA), which requires hospital EDs to identify emergency medical conditions and stabilize them, EMTALA does not apply to patients who refuse treatment, and cases have interpreted the mandate of a patient's DNR to relieve the hospital of its obligation to provide treatment to stabilize the patient.

[114] C. A. Marco, E. S. Bessman, G. D. Kelen, *Ethical Issues of Cardiopulmonary Resuscitation: Comparison of Emergency Physician Practices from 1995 to 2007*, 16 ACAD. EMERG. MED. 3, 270–73 (Mar 2009). In a Medscape discussion of whether to resuscitate patients who had attempted suicide, even though no lawyer was present in the discussion, in the two-page summary provided by Medscape of the discussion, at least half the comments revolved around legal liability.

[115] *Id.*

said he would ignore a DNR if the cause of the life-threatening emergency was not "natural"; for example, if a person with a DNR was shot in a drive-by shooting, he would resuscitate because the resulting death would not be "natural."[116] There is no basis in the law or medical ethics for this distinction.

Another survey reported that doctors would resuscitate a patient with a DNR if the patient's life-threatening emergency was caused by medical error. This is also not a correct understanding of the nature and purpose of DNR orders, which depend on the medical techniques and devices needed (i.e., no "extraordinary means" or no ventilator or intubation) rather than what caused the need for these techniques and devices. Admittedly, following the law on DNR orders leads to unnerving situations, such as when an elderly lady's nephew attempted to smother her with a pillow in her nursing home bed; nursing home staff pulled him away, but did not resuscitate the woman because she had a DNR (a position supported by a court when her son sued them).[117]

Others have posited that patients should be resuscitated after suicide attempts because anyone who attempts suicide is by definition incompetent. First of all, that is simply not true, and neither research nor law supports the assumption.[118] A substantial number of people who commit suicide and/or make suicide attempts are terminally ill and would qualify for assisted suicide in the states where it is legal. In fact, in one survey, 58% of Oregon emergency physicians reported resuscitating terminally ill people after failed suicide attempts.[119] Second, the whole point of DNR orders is that they are made while a patient is competent and thinking calmly about treatment choices to take effect precisely when the person is not competent. Therefore, absent evidence that the DNR order is invalid because the individual completing it was incompetent at the time it was created, it must be honored. This is particularly true in the case of DNR orders, which are signed by physicians. If the doctor witnessing the DNR order saw no reason to question the patient's choice or competence, the doctor implementing the DNR order should not either.

Some authors have suggested that DNR orders should not be honored if they are part and parcel of the suicide plan.[120] It may well be true that a DNR completed right before a suicide attempt is not valid, but that would

[116] Cohen, *supra* n.4.
[117] Kay v. Fairside Riverview Hosp., 531 N.W.2d 517 (Minn. App. 1995) (the son attempted to argue that the DNR was invalid because his mother had not signed it, but the court disregarded this argument since he himself had signed it).
[118] See Chapter 1.
[119] T. A. Schmidt, A. D. Zechnich, V. P. Tilden, et al., *Oregon Emergency Physicians' Experiences with Attitudes toward and Concerns about Physician-Assisted Suicide*, 3 ACAD. EMERG. MED. 938 (1996). Ten percent of responders had treated more than five terminally ill patients who had attempted suicide.
[120] Geppert, *supra* note 4, see n.96.

be because it does not have the required physician's signature. If the document is not a DNR but a living will, in many states it still must be witnessed. Whether or not the document is valid, it is important to underscore that people who attempt suicide are not per se incompetent,[121] and taking the trouble to anticipate being found and filling out a DNR to ensure that one's suicidal intent is fulfilled is evidence of competence (planning and foresight) rather than incompetence.

Some argue that honoring the DNR order in these circumstances is assisting suicide, a criminal act in almost all states. Once again, research suggests that this is simply not true. Each state has its own statutory language forbidding assisting suicide,[122] but there are several commonalities that tend to rule out criminal liability. Generally the crime of assisted suicide requires that the accused share in the intent that suicide be committed and commit some affirmative act in furtherance of that intent: procuring and providing the means of suicide; helping the suicidal individual plan and execute the attempt; or soliciting, advising, or encouraging the act. As the Alaska Supreme Court explicitly stated, simply honoring a patient's right to refuse treatment does not fit into any understanding of the crime of assisted suicide:

> Physicians have no duty, indeed no right, to treat patients who
> voluntarily reject medical treatment. Physician omission of further
> treatment does not create liability for assisting a suicide.[123]

Finally, virtually all hospitals have created their own extralegal and possibly illegal exception to the laws of their state, in that most hospital policies simply state without providing any legal basis that DNR orders and advance directives will be considered "suspended," "rescinded," or "nonoperative" if a patient is having surgery, or even a medical procedure. Two Oregon physicians wrote that they had to work with their hospital to assure that a patient's DNR status was communicated, for example, to the radiology department, because a patient who coded while going for a computerized tomography (CT) scan was going to be resuscitated even if that patient would not have been resuscitated when he or she was on the hospital ward.

But the greatest misconception about the law is that we have one set of legal principles that govern these issues. This is a quintessential state law issue, with fifty different approaches, and a federal and state regulatory overlay that only serves to confuse matters. In addition, the issue arises in a number of

---

[121] See Chapter 1.

[122] A number of these statutes have survived various forms of constitutional challenges—Alaska: 11.141.120(a)(2), see Sampson v. State, 31 P.3d 88 (Alaska 2001) (patient with AIDS); California: Ca. Penal Code 401, *Donaldson v. Lundgren*; Colorado: 18-3-104(1)(b), Sanderson v. People, 12 P3d 851 (Colo. App. 2000) (first amendment); Connecticut; Florida, 782.08, Krischer v. McIver, 697 So.2d 97 (Fla. 1997) (patient with AIDS privacy, due process, equal protection); and Michigan.

[123] *Sampson v. State*, see n.122.

different factual scenarios. Some terminally ill people have DNR orders and try to take their own lives. Some terminally ill people with DNR orders are both terminally ill and also have a psychiatric disability. Some people obtain DNR orders right before attempting suicide in an effort to ensure that they will not be rescued if they are found while they can be revived.[124] Some people are taken to hospitals that have religious affiliations, or are being treated by physicians with strong religious beliefs.

Each of these factual differences makes a potential legal difference. Some state statutes authorizing and implementing living wills and DNR orders require that the patient be terminally ill for these documents to be effective; others require either terminal illness or some other set of discretionary conditions.[125] Some have complicated procedures that permit doctors with conscientious objections to refuse to honor DNR orders as long as they follow these procedures.[126]

So if you have a DNR in a state that mandates that your DNR be respected, except by doctors who disagree with them, you'll just have to take your chances on who's in the ED when you arrive. Most of these statutes have provisions for transfer, but generally by the time those can be invoked, you've been resuscitated. Some states don't honor DNR orders unless they are on yellow paper (you know who you are, Florida).[127]

Finally, even if you are in a state where they honor DNR orders without exception, and even if your doctor has no statutory excuse for ignoring your DNR, you may or may not have a legal remedy. Many courts have refused to recognize a tort claim for "wrongful life" or "wrongful living"[128] or "wrongful prolongation of life."[129] On the other hand, there have in fact been many lawsuits arising out of ignoring DNR orders and many of them have netted the plaintiffs substantial sums, especially when the individuals were terminally ill and simply suffered egregiously after being resuscitated.[130]

---

[124] Cook et al., *supra* note 112.

[125] Wisc. Stat. Ann. § 154.17(4) (2014) (that the resuscitation would be ineffective or would cause significant physical pain or harm outweighing the possibility that it would restore cardiac or respiratory function for an indefinite period of time).

[126] See Tex. Health & Safety Code, § 166.045 and § 166.046 (2014).

[127] Florida Department of Health, *Frequently Asked Questions about Do Not Resuscitate Orders*, Florida Health, http://www.floridahealth.gov/about-the-department-of-health/about-us/patient-rights-and-safety/do-not-resuscitate/faq-page.html.

[128] *Anderson v. St. Francis-St. George Hospital, Inc.*, 77 Ohio State 3d 82 (1996).

[129] *Estate of Taylor v. Muncie Med. Inv. LP*, 727 N.E.2d 466 (Ind.App. 2000).

[130] *Scheibel v. Morse Geriatric Center, Florida*, jury verdict for $150,000 on claims of medical negligence and breach of contract, *Nursing Home Ignores Patient's End-of-Life Directives and Wishes*, 7 Searcy Denney Scarola Barnhart & Shipley, PA of Counsel Newsletter 2, www.searcylaw.com/wp-content/uploads/2014/02/Nursing-Home-Ignores-Patient%E2%80%99s-End-of-Life-Directives-and-Wishes.pdf.

In some ways, the lower quality of life that society perceives a person to have, the greater the damage award for ignoring a DNR. Nursing home residents whose DNR orders are ignored have a good chance at high awards. In another example of irrational law, some states have implemented legislation establishing the legal right to a DNR while also providing immunity to doctors who ignore them.

This question becomes even more complicated with out-of-hospital DNR orders.[131] Many older people (including my parents when they were alive) have out-of-hospital do not resuscitate (OHDNR or OOHDNR) orders, which are advance directives and DNR orders kept in their refrigerator against a time when they might need to be consulted by emergency medical technicians (EMTs) and paramedics. Despite the fact that many states have statutorily recognized such documents, and many public health departments have protocols instructing that these DNR orders must be honored, emergency service personnel routinely ignore such documents and resuscitate patients.[132]

This is especially true of patients who have attempted suicide.[133] A number of state emergency service protocols explicitly exclude situations of homicide and suicide from the mandate to respect OOHDNRs.[134] Even in states such as Oregon, with assisted-suicide legislation and specific and recognized OOHDNR programs, EMTs are expected to resuscitate people who are terminally ill and have attempted suicide. In a discussion about this issue in *Academic Emergency Medicine*, various authors reiterated that people availing themselves of assisted suicide and their families and physicians must be counseled not to call 911 in the event of delayed death or complications, because even people who have officially availed themselves of the Death with

---

[131] Tex. Admin. Code § 157.25 (2014).

[132] Estate of Maxey v. Darden, 187 P.3d 144, 146 (Nev. 2008) (paramedics resuscitated woman after suicide attempt even though individual who was her power of attorney attempted to refuse treatment on her behalf; paramedics said "suicide attempt cancels power of attorney"); see also Anderson v. St. Francis-St. George Hosp., 671 N.E.2d 225 (Ohio 1996) (no cause of action against a hospital that revives a patient in violation of his DNR because there can be no action for wrongful life; however, damages can be recovered for any injuries caused by resuscitative efforts).

[133] Spencer A. Hall, "An Analysis of Dilemmas Posed by Prehospital DNR Orders," 15 Journal of Emergency Medicine 109 (1997); David M. Sine, "EMS, Suicide, and the Out of Hospital DNR Order," 6 Online Journal of Health Ethics 1 (2010), http://aquila.usm.edu/cgi/viewcontent.cgi?article=1062&context=ojhe

[134] This is the case in New Mexico, Texas (Tex. Admin. Code 157.25(f) ("If there are any indications of unnatural or suspicious circumstances" the patient will be resuscitated until a physician says otherwise)). In another part of the regulation that may or may not pass muster under the U.S. Constitution, pregnant women's OOHDNRs are explicitly forbidden to be honored, Tex. Admin. Code 157.25(g).

Dignity program will be resuscitated by EMTs.[135] This distinction in honoring OOHDNRs may or may not be legal. The EMT protocol cannot go farther
than the state law permits, and some protocols may conflict with state DNR
laws. The County Attorney of San Diego County has issued an opinion saying
OOHDNRs must be honored even if it appears the individual has attempted
suicide,[136] The State of New York has also instructed emergency service personnel to respect DNR orders regardless of the circumstances in which the
emergency occurs. This seems to be the most legally rational and respectable
solution, the one that does not require EMTs and paramedics to make difficult on-the-spot assessments that they should not be required to make.

Terminating Life Support After Suicide Attempts

If a DNR is not honored, a person who has attempted suicide may be kept
alive on life support. Often people who attempt suicide do not have DNR
orders. Tragically, news accounts of teen suicides often involve the parents
having to make the decision to take their child off life support.[137]

Should the fact of the suicide attempt have any bearing on the decision
about whether to withdraw life support? The *American Journal of Bioethics*
devoted an issue to consideration of the question of treatment refusal after a
suicide attempt[138] in which various authors propose a number of answers to this
question.

Drs. Brown, Elliott, and Paine propose a test in which a surrogate
requests the withdrawal of life support, the request is medically reasonable, and a reasonable passage of time (the authors suggest seventy-two
hours) is permitted. Basically, they argue that if a request for discontinua-
tion of life support would have been reasonable in the case of a person who
had not attempted suicide, then it should be honored. The authors argue

[135] Letters to the Editor regarding "Oregon emergency physicians' experiences
with, attitudes toward and concerns about physician-assisted suicide," 4 ACAD.
EMERG. MED. 926–27 (1997).
[136] Kristi Koenig & Angelo A. Salvucci, *Out-Of-Hospital Do Not Attempt
Resuscitation in the Suicidal Patient: A Special Case*, 4 ACAD. EMERG. MED.
926 (1997).
[137] Michelle Garcia, *Jadin Bell Taken Off Life Support*, THE ADVOCATE, Jan. 29, 2013,
http://www.advocate.com/society/youth/2013/01/29/teen-taken-life-support-
after-suicide-attempt (bullied gay teenager); David Knowles, *Canadian Girl, 17,
Removed from Life Support Days After Suicide Attempt, Family Says she Was
Raped by Four Boys and Relentlessly Bullied*, N. Y. DAILY NEWS, Apr. 9, 2013,
http://www.nydailynews.com/news/world/girl-dies-suicide-attempt-article-
1.1312102; *California Teen on Life Support After Anti-Gay Bullying*, LGBTQ
NATION, Sept. 26, 2010, http://www.lgbtqnation.com/2010/09/california-boy-
on-life-support-after-suicide-attempt-another-case-of-anti-gay-bullying/.
[138] 13 AMERICAN JOURNAL OF BIOETHICS 3 (2013).

strongly that issues of mental illness should be separated from withdrawal of care:

> We do not believe that the cause of the critical illness or disability should be relevant to decisionmaking about withdrawal of care. To require consideration of the source of the illness imposes an unfair burden on people with psychiatric illness. If a given degree of therapeutic burden and future disability is adequate to justify withdrawal of care in a patient without psychiatric illness, then it should be adequate to justify withdrawal in the aftermath of attempted suicide. . . . We do not believe the stigma and emotional valences of suicide have the ethical weight required to override the principle of fairness.[139]

In this formulation, an individual's psychiatric diagnosis and history is irrelevant. The authors acknowledge that some psychiatric conditions may be so longstanding and treatment refractory (like Sebastian's, assuming he even has a psychiatric condition) that withdrawal of care after a suicide attempt may be appropriate. However, the uncertainty of prognosis—people can recover from psychiatric disability—leads them to consider that a person on life support with psychiatric disabilities should not be withdrawn, even if the both the person and his or her family request it.

This proposal drew a variety of comments. Ayesha Bhavsar argues that people who attempt suicide are essentially incompetent, a serious error that is rebutted by other authors in the journal, as well as in my first chapter.[140] Taye and Magnus at the Stanford Center for Bioethics comment on the article by discussing a case that recently took place at Stanford, where a woman had attempted suicide and did not want life-sustaining care. Although she was determined incompetent, her husband, who was her Durable Power of Attorney, agreed with her request to end life-sustaining care, confirming that this was an expression of her long-term values and principles. The Department of Psychiatry, pointing out that the patient had a long history of depression, argued that her husband could not make a valid decision because he never had a chance to know her in a nondepressed state. Again, this perspective is at odds with the requirements of the law, which only permit second-guessing a legally valid surrogate's decision under extreme circumstances.

Instead of explaining that this is a legal requirement, Taye and Magnus write rather breezily that "surrogates get it wrong all the time, but no one really seems to mind or want to stop deferring to surrogate decisionmakers."[141] More seriously, as long as surrogate decision-makers focus on the

---

[139] Brown et al., *supra* note 108, at 6.

[140] Ayesha Bhavsar, *Respect and Rationality: The Challenge of Attempted Suicide*, 13 AM. J. BIOETHICS 24 (2013).

[141] Hywote Taye & David Magnus, *Suicide and the Sufficiency of Surrogate Decisionmakers*, 13 AM. J. BIOETHICS 1, 2 (2013).

long-term values of the individual, rather than the suicide attempt, the authors believe that surrogate decision-makers' end-of-life decisions should be honored, whatever they decide.[142] This is clearly correct, assuming the governing state statute permits surrogate decision-makers to refuse treatment in the circumstances.

The final and best commentator, Ben Rich, points out that any differentiation of the rights of a competent person based on a suicide attempt— including those proposed by Brown and colleagues—violates both ethics and the law. After crisply reciting both clinical research and law for the proposition that most suicidal people retain capacity, he reminds us that the health care decisions of competent people need not correspond with what medical people would recommend or consider reasonable, or else the autonomy of a competent person would lose much of its meaning. A person with current capacity, or who made an advance directive, has a right to refuse treatment, absent evidence of coercion or manipulation by others. He criticizes the "curious and potentially nefarious coupling of the suicidal impulse and act with a subsequent need for life-sustaining treatment so as to deprive these patients of a right to refuse treatment that is now a core principle of both medical ethics and medical jurisprudence."[143] This, it seems to me, is the correct position. Adding in Brown's proposed seventy-two-hour waiting period may be sensible, since many of the people that I interviewed woke up consternated and angry that their suicide attempts failed, but after a few days began to adjust to being alive. The requirement that the surrogate agrees with the withdrawal of life support makes no sense at all: A surrogate has no legal power if a patient is competent and can articulate his or her own decisions. And in what way does it make sense to ask a family member to choose to honor his or her loved one's choices when it means losing that person forever? There is enough permanent damage done to the people who remain by the suicide of a family member without implementing this portion of Brown's proposal.

The *Maxey* Case

The most important practical thing to remember is that while a competent patient's right to refuse treatment is a matter of constitutional law across the country, states may differ from one another in terms of what doctors legally can do with regard to treating a patient who is not competent. In *Estate of Maxey v. Darden*, an older woman took 200 pills in an attempt to commit

---

[142] Brown and colleagues are much more skeptical of surrogate decision-makers in the wake of a suicide attempt, and believe their decisions should be subjected to a heightened scrutiny, see n. 132. Brown et al., *supra* note 103, at n. 132.?

[143] Ben Rich, *Suicidality, Refractory Suffering and the Right to Choose Death*, 13 Am. J. Bioethics 18 (2013).

suicide.[144] Her ex-husband Theodore, who was her power of attorney and still lived with her, found her barely alive and dithered for several hours, explaining later that he knew she wanted to die and felt he should respect her wishes. Theodore finally talked it over with Avis Maxey's daughter in law, and an ambulance was called. Theodore tried to stop paramedics' efforts to resuscitate Ms. Maxey as her power of attorney, but was told, probably incorrectly, that "suicide attempt cancels power of attorney."[145] Theodore rode along to the hospital and signed a document classifying Ms. Maxey as a "Class III patient" who would receive diagnostic and comfort care, but no efforts to prolong her life.

Theodore then requested that Avis Maxey be extubated, and later that her oxygen mask be removed. The Nevada Uniform Act on the Rights of the Terminally Ill permits a competent person to refuse life-sustaining treatment, or to designate a health care proxy to carry out his or her wishes. If the patient is not competent and has no proxy, a valid surrogate decision-maker can request an attending physician to remove life support from a patient in a "terminal condition," and when that request is reduced to writing with the signature of two witnesses, it can be validly executed.

After Dr. Darden removed the ventilator and oxygen mask, Avis Maxey continued to breathe, and Dr. Darden left well enough alone. However, at 4:35 p.m., a different doctor, Dr. Mower, came on duty, and while there is no record that Theodore made any further requests, at 7:20 p.m., Dr. Mower ordered nurses to begin giving Ms. Maxey 100 mg. morphine "at short intervals" "for pain relief." Ms. Maxey was dead within half an hour. About four months later, Dr. Mower was stripped of his medical license on an emergency basis for "committing malpractice resulting in the death of his patient."[146] Less than a year later, his license was revoked.[147]

Meanwhile, Avis Maxey's family sued Darden, the hospital, and Theodore for her wrongful death. The Nevada Supreme Court held that it was not clear whether Theodore's decision was a valid surrogate decision, not because he was Avis Maxey's ex-husband,[148] but because the document he signed was witnessed only by the doctor and the law required two signatures. Furthermore, the Nevada Supreme Court rejected Dr. Darden's assertion

---

[144] *Estate of Maxey v. Darden*, at note 132.

[145] *Id.* at 146.

[146] http://medverification.nv.gov/verification/Details.aspx?agency_id=1&license_id=1338&

[147] See http://medboard.nv.gov/ and click on "Disciplinary Actions." Dr. Mower's name appears in the alphabetical list, and by clicking on his name the fact that his license was revoked on June 23, 2003, and that he was required to pay costs in the amount of $46,006.72 will appear.

[148] All parties agreed that Dr. Darden did not know Theodore was not Avis' husband and could not reasonably have been expected to find out, *Estate of Maxey v. Darden*, at 148, n.10.

that his determination that Ms. Maxey had a "terminal condition" could not be contested as a matter of law. To its credit, the court made no reference to the fact that Ms. Maxey's condition was the result of a suicide attempt.

This decision is in line with *Cruzan* and other cases that require a more searching inquiry into the decisions of third parties that a person would prefer to die. Ms. Maxey is, in this case, one step removed from Kerrie Wooltorton, who stuck to her decision to die even as it was taking effect, and was determined to be competent to do so. Wooltorton showed up prepared with an advance directive that was carefully drafted to conform to legal requirements and tailored to her individual situation. By contrast, Maxey wasn't the individual directly asking to die, didn't have an advance directive or a DNR, attempted suicide in a place where her ex-husband, still resident, would be certain to find her, and took pills. The caution exercised by courts in a case such as Mrs. Maxey's is well-founded, both as a matter of law and policy.

Force-Feeding Hunger Strikers on the Pretext of Suicidality

As we saw in the last chapter, India has been force-feeding a woman protesting the tactics of the Indian Armed Forces for fourteen years under the rationale that she is attempting suicide, until recently a crime in India. Indeed, commentators have indicated that the law criminalizing attempted suicide was not repealed for years in part to enable the Indian Government to force-feed Irom Sarmila Chanu.

But of course, it is not the Indian government that is administering intrusive and invasive nasogastric tube nutrition to Ms. Chanu against her will. It is doctors who are doing this. They are doing this in spite of the World Medical Association's strong and explicit stance against doctors force-feeding a hunger-striking patient who has made an informed refusal of food and the potential violation of the Geneva Conventions.[149] The U.S. government, through military doctors, also force-feeds detainees at Guantanamo,

---

[149] Common Article 3 of the Geneva Conventions provides that detained persons must be treated humanely at all times and cruel, inhumane, and degrading treatment is prohibited. See also World Medical Association, *WMA Declaration of Malta on Hunger Strikers* (Nov. 1991, rev. Sept. 1992 & Oct. 2006), www.wma.net/en/30publications/10policies/h31; International Committee of the Red Cross, *Hunger Strikes in Prison: The ICRC's Position*, ICRC Resource Center, Jan. 31, 2013, https://www.icrc.org/eng/resources/documents/faq/hunger-strike-icrc-position.htm; Ellen Policinski, *Guantanamo Hunger Strike: Force Feeding and Differing Interpretations of Common Article Three*, Humanity in War Blog, July 7, 2013, http://humanityinwarblog.com/2013/07/07/guantanamo-hunger-strike-force-feeding-and-differing-interpretations-of-common-article-3/#_edn36.

even though the President's Bioethics Council called it a form of torture. An American nurse who recently refused to force-feed detainees—following the ethics of his profession–was discharged, but not (as the military initially threatened) court-martialed. In 2006, more than 250 doctors signed a letter to *Lancet* condemning force-feeding of hunger-strikers and recommending that doctors who engaged in force-feeding be subject to discipline by their professional organizations.

Closer to home, as mentioned in Chapter 2, courts all over the United States have almost always upheld force-feeding of hunger-striking prison inmates[150] (one of the few exceptions, interestingly, involved a quadriplegic inmate[151]). The Dutch also have decided it is acceptable to force-feed asylum-seeking detainees, over the strong objections of the Royal Dutch Medical Society. The contrast between this decision and the Dutch attitude toward assisted suicide has been noted by more than one commentator:

> The tension, on the one hand, between an ethics of care that
> doesn't decry death, as is the case with euthanasia in the
> Netherlands and, on the other, "death as protest" indicates that
> for asylum-seekers another ethics (or lack thereof) applies. While
> voluntary death as a means to end suffering is allowed, death as a
> form of protest is not.[152]

Hunger-strikers almost never raise issues of competence. Like people with terminal illness, they don't actually want to die. (In fact, even the most forceful condemnation of force-feeding hunger-strikers strongly implies that if they *did* want to die, force-feeding them would be acceptable.) Thus, governments that force-feed these individuals often describe them as "suicidal" in order to avoid political difficulties and condemnation.[153]

Whether the individual is suicidal or not, the brutality of force-feeding cannot be gainsaid. In the case of *Rochin v. California* in 1952, the

---

[150] See cases gathered and discussed in Comm'r of Corr. v. Coleman, 38 A.3d 84 (Conn. 2012).

[151] Thor v. Superior Court, 21 Cal. Rptr. 2d 357 (Ca. 1993). The other exception is an older case from Georgia, *Zant v. Prevatte*, 286 S.E.2d 715 (1982), which held that a competent inmate without dependents could not be force-fed. In *Hill v. Dep't of Corr.*, 992 A.2d 933 (Pa. Commw. Ct. 2010), the court held that the inmate's life was not yet at risk, so that the Department of Corrections had acted too soon in force-feeding him.

[152] Patricia Schor & Egbert Alejandro Martina, *The Alien Body in the Contemporary Netherlands: Incarceration and Force-Feeding of Asylum-Seekers*, CRITICAL LEGAL THINKING, Oct. 14, 2013, www.criticallegalthinking.com/2013/10/14/alien-body-contemporary-netherlands-incarceration-force-feeding-asylum-seekers/.

[153] Aamer v. Obama, 953 F.Supp. 2d 213 (D.D.C. July 16, 2013).

U.S. Supreme Court described running a tube filled with emetics involuntarily down a man's throat into his stomach as "bound to offend even the most hardened sensibilities . . . methods too close to the rack and the screw to permit of constitutional differentiation . . . force so brutal and offensive to human dignity."[154] The process of force-feeding is identical to the process of forcing an emetic down a stomach tube. Police can't do it to criminals, but governments do it to political protesters, seekers of asylum, and people with eating disorders. All of these individuals are competent, but only the force-feeding of the first two groups causes sustained outrage.

It is clear from all of these cases that the legality of the force-feeding turns on the particular circumstance that the individual is in involuntary detention, which U.S. courts have held creates an affirmative obligation on the government to provide medical treatment to preserve the individual's life. For those in correctional detention, an interest in institutional security often trumps the inmate's acknowledged fundamental right to refuse medical treatment and be free from unwanted bodily intrusions. There have also been attempts in nursing homes to force feed competent patients who are refusing to eat.

Force-feeding a competent, nonconsenting patient who is not in government custody is an illegal battery, and should never be tolerated. It still occasionally happens in nursing homes, both through actual force-feeding and through the nonconsensual insertion of feeding tubes, although most nursing home staff recognize that this is illegal.[155] It is clear that courts have approved of force-feeding competent individuals in government custody. Nevertheless, the fact that courts have held force-feeding is legal should not stop doctors and nurses from refusing to take part in it. More broadly, it is time for the medical profession to question rather than collude in the assumption that labelling the hunger-striker "suicidal" justifies any amount of involuntary bodily violence and intrusion.

---

[154] Rochin v. California, 342 U.S. 165, 172, 174 (1952).

[155] When a nurse posed a question on the Allnurses forum about a surgeon's order to "force-feed" a competent patient, it was greeted with the unanimous and overwhelming message that this was illegal, unethical, and undignified, ceecel. dee, *Force Feed*, ALLNURSES.COM, Apr. 28, 2003, http://allnurses.com/nursing-issues-patient/-quot-force-feed-35864.html; nevertheless, involuntary feeding tube placement raises many of the same issues, see Legal Counsel for the Elderly, Nursing Home Issues, Consent to Treatment, Tube Feeding a Frequent Issue, http://www.uaelderlaw.org/nursing.html The Legal Counsel for the Elderly notes that this issue occurs particularly frequently in nursing homes in the State of Alabama.

Criminal and Licensing Consequences for Medical Participation in Assisted Suicide

Assisting suicide remains a crime in forty-six states,[156] ranging from misdemeanor to felony.[157] Although there is ample evidence that doctors and nurses assist patients to commit suicide in states where assisted suicide is not legal, they are very rarely charged with any crime, unless they actually kill the patient,[158] and often not even then.[159] Even when prosecutors bring murder charges, jurors often refuse to convict,[160] even when the facts very clearly warrant conviction.[161] When they do convict, judges hand down sentences

---

[156] The exceptions are Wyoming and Utah. Virginia retains the common law criminalization of suicide, and so presumably a person who assisted suicide would be an accomplice. This would obviate the need for any specific statute criminalizing assisted suicide. North Carolina abolished the crime of suicide in 1973 and has no law criminalizing assisted suicide. In fact, George Exoo bought land in Gastonia, North Carolina, to set up an office to assist suicide, but became embroiled in zoning issues. Lauren Bahari, *Local Hospice Weighs in on Alternatives to Assisted Suicide*, GASTON GAZETTE, Oct. 31, 2014, http://www.gastongazette.com/news/local/local-hospice-weighs-in-on-alternatives-to-assisted-suicide-1.394852.

[157] Idaho passed a statute in 2010 explicitly designating physician-assisted suicide as a felony, IDAHO STAT. 18-4017 (2014).

[158] One source reports nine cases of physicians facing murder charges for assisting a patient's suicide in the United States up to 1988, *Juries Kind to Doctors Who Assist*, CAPITAL TIMES, Mar. 17, 1992, at D1, quoted in Michael J. Roth, *A Failed Statute, Geoffrey Feiger, and the Phrenetic Physician: Physician-Assisted Suicide in Michigan and a Patient-Oriented Alternative*, 28 VALPARAISO U. L. REV. 1415 (1994).

[159] Dr. James D. Gallant killed a patient in Oregon in 1999, the year that the Death with Dignity Act took effect, and faced only mild professional discipline, see pp. 265–66 infra.

[160] See Associated Press, *Doctor Accused of Killing Dying Patient Cleared*, L. A. TIMES, June 27, 1997, http://articles.latimes.com/1997-06-27/news/mn-7335_1_doctor-kill-accused. This is true across the world: in Britain, from 1956, when a doctor named Adams was acquitted for injecting an 81-year-old patient with 2.5 grams of morphine and 2.6 grams of heroin, despite the fact that he inherited a chest containing silver and a Rolls Royce from the patient, Henry Palmer, *Dr. Adams' Trial for Murder*, CRIMINAL L. REV. 365, 367, 374 (1957).

[161] Roth, *supra* note 158, at 1432, n.106. Maguire recounts a case in 1950 where a Dr. Sander injected air into the veins of a patient whose "incessant demands" for him to kill her "wore him down"; he was acquitted by a jury that found he did not cause her death, Daniel C. Maguire, *Death, Legal and Illegal*, ATLANTIC ONLINE, Feb. 1974, www.theatlantic.com/past/docs/issues/95sep/abortion/mag.htm; see William J. Baughman et al., *Euthanasia: Criminal, Tort, Constitutional and Legislative Considerations*, 48 Notre Dame L. Rev. 1202, 1205 (1973); *State v. Montemarano* (jury acquittal of physician who killed patient who had been given two days to live); *State v. Rosier* (Michigan 1988); *State v. Egbert* (Arizona 2011) (doctor accused of fatally poisoning terminally ill patient acquitted for

that are ludicrously lenient in the context of a murder conviction.[162] As far as I can tell, Kevorkian is the only doctor who has served time in prison for killing a patient who wanted to die, and he had lost his license by then, and was not conforming to the style or demeanor expected of medical professionals in any event.

Doctors have equivalently lenient experience with medical disciplinary boards, as long as they don't seek publicity. Compare the cases of Dr. Jack Kevorkian and Dr. James Gallant. Dr. Kevorkian lost his Michigan license in 1991, after assisting in the nationally covered suicide of three people, each of whom consciously made the final movement that resulted in her death; he was charged with murder in all three deaths.[163] Dr. James Gallant, on the other hand, under pressure from a terminally ill patient's daughter, ordered the patient to receive an injection of succinylcholine with the express intention of killing her, which it did. He was investigated and had his license suspended for sixty days.[164] The district attorney decided not to file criminal

---

lack of causation, *Arizona Jury Acquits Doctor in Phoenix Woman's Suicide*, Crime Time, STAR-TELEGRAM, Apr. 22, 2011, http://blogs.star-telegram.com/crime_time/2011/04/arizona-jury-acquits-doctor-in-phoenix-womans-suicide.html#storylink=cpy. Note that Dr. Egbert was, at the time of his acquittal, under indictment by the State of Georgia for assisting suicide, *id.*

[162] When a jury found Dr. Joseph Hassmann guilty of poisoning a terminally ill patient, the judge sentenced him to two years' probation, 400 hours of community service, and a $10,000 fine. "Dr. Daniel Caraccio was brought up on murder charges for injecting a patient with a lethal dose of potassium chloride, pled guilty, and was sentenced to five years' probation." When an English jury found a doctor guilty of murdering a suffering patient by injecting her with potassium chloride (her death was recorded as being caused by bronchopneumonia) the judge gave him a suspended sentence, W. Luke Cormally et al., *The Final Autonomy*, 340 LANCET 976 (1992) (editorial).

[163] Kevorkian's medical license was suspended by Michigan in 1991 and revoked by California in 1994. Michael Granberry, *State to Revoke License of 'Dr. Death:' Euthanasia: Jack Kevorkian Gained Worldwide Note for Helping 20 People, including Costa Mesa man, End Lives*, L. A. TIMES, July 28, 1994, http://articles.latimes.com/1994-07-28/local/me-20818_1_jack-kevorkian. Other doctors have been disciplined for engaging in euthanasia.

[164] *Gallant v. Board of Medical Examiners.* He also had to pay the costs of the disciplinary proceedings. Gallant got in trouble at least twice more with the Board of Medicine, once for failing to properly file worker's compensation claims while working as the medical director of the Heart of the Valley Center in 2001 (*In re* James David Gallant, http://www.propublica.org/documents/item/12914-oregon-actions-for-james-d-gallant%0A) and once for an unspecified reason in 2014 (Oregon Medical Board, *Meeting of the Board*, Jan. 9–10, 2014, http://www.oregon.gov/omb/MeetingMinutes/January%209-10,%202014.pdf); see also Oregon Medical Board, *Meeting of the Board*, Oct. 2–3, 2014, http://www.oregon.gov/omb/MeetingMinutes/October%202%20-%203,%202014.pdf.

charges.[165] Dr. Ernesto Pinzon-Reyes, who gave a dying man drugs that would kill him, and then falsified the drug records, was acquitted by a jury of murder charges, and was disciplined by the Florida Board of Medicine for falsifying the records of the drugs he gave the man. His license was suspended for two years, but he was given credit for the time he had not been practicing (while charged with murdering a patient), and was free to return to practice, under probation and required to take a course in proper medical record-keeping.[166]

Dr. Lawrence Egbert, the Medical Director of the Final Exit Network, finally lost his license to practice in Maryland in December 2014 at the age of 87, several years after his acquittals in three separate nationally covered criminal trials in Georgia, Minnesota, and Arizona for assisting suicide, and after personally assisting six residents of Maryland to die.[167] Interestingly, although assisted suicide is illegal in Maryland, the Board of Medicine went out of its way to note that none of the six people Dr. Egbert assisted to die were terminally ill, and that Dr. Egbert did not follow the laws of Vermont, Oregon, or Washington in screening the people he assisted for psychological issues (indeed, it specifically noted that three of the six had depression, and for one of them, depression was the only condition that she had).[168]

There are, I think, separate reasons for the failure to discipline doctors and the failure to criminally prosecute them when they take part in assisted suicide or, in fact, cause the death of their patients. The failure to subject doctors to professional discipline by licensing boards is probably not related to anything more significant than the fact that medical boards rarely seriously discipline doctors for anything except drug addiction, mental health problems, conviction of a crime, sexual relations or assault on a patient, and certain kinds of wrongful prescription of medication.[169] There is no particular

---

[165] Joe Rojas-Burke, *Doctor Won't Be Charged in Death*, Register-Guard [Corvallis], Dec. 11, 1997, https://news.google.com/newspapers?nid=1310&dat=19971211&id=PU1WAAAAIBAJ&sjid=7-sDAAAAIBAJ&pg=4799,2544818&hl=en.

[166] State of Florida Board of Med., Dep't of Health v. Ernesto Pinzon-Reyes, Final Order, Dec. 9, 1997. This document is available by going to the Florida Board of Medicine website's licensing section, http://flboardofmedicine.gov/licensing/ clicking on "Lookup Verify a License" and verifying the license of Ernesto Pinzon-Reyes. Then click on "Link to Discipline" and the decision of the Board will appear.

[167] *In re* Lawrence D. Egbert, Case No. 2011-0870, Maryland State Board of Physicians, Dec. 12, 2014, http://www.mbp.state.md.us/BPQAPP/orders/D1604912.124.pdf.

[168] *Id.*

[169] See Peter Eisler & Barbara Hansen, *Thousands of Doctors Practicing Despite Errors, Misconduct*, USA Today, Aug. 20, 2013, http://www.usatoday.com/story/news/ nation/2013/08/20/doctors-licenses-medical-boards/2655513/; Lena H. Sun, *Report: State Boards Don't Always Discipline Doctors Sanctioned by Hospitals*, Washington Post, Mar. 16, 2011, http://www.washingtonpost.com/wp-dyn/ content/article/2011/03/16/AR2011031605966.html; David Wahlberg, *Some Doctors Not Disciplined, Even Following Large Malpractice Settlements* [second in a three-part special investigation, *Doctor Discipline*], Wis. St. J., Jan. 28, 2013, http://

reason that participating in assisted suicide would rise above the myriad of other offenses that are overlooked by medical disciplinary boards, unless, as in Dr. Egbert's and Dr. Kevorkian's cases, there is national press about the subject. The kind of conduct that spurs action on the part of licensing boards includes carving one's initials on the abdomen of your C-section patient[170] and leaving a patient anaesthetized on an operating room table with an incision in his back to go cash a check.[171] Helping a patient who wanted to die rarely receives publicity or becomes the subject of a disciplinary complaint, unless it is also the subject of criminal investigation.

The paucity of criminal prosecutions may also be due to the infrequency of reporting, but also sympathy with the defendant, or a realistic assessment of the likelihood of conviction. This has long been true of socially controversial practices engaged in by doctors: despite laws criminalizing abortions, relatively few criminal prosecutions of abortionists took place, and those usually happened only when the woman died. Even in those cases, juries often refused to convict.[172]

One of the most interesting legal developments related to assisted suicide is that as society becomes more accepting of state-regulated physician-assisted suicide for terminally ill people, it has also begun to enforce social boundaries of the emerging consensus on what constitutes "acceptable" assisted suicide. Thus, there has been an increase in criminal prosecution of members of the Final Exit Network, perhaps because the organization publicly advocates a broader scope for assisted suicide than has been legalized thus far,[173] but also, I would argue, because their assistance is not cloaked in

---

host.madison.com/news/local/health_med_fit/some-doctors-not-disciplined-even-following-large-malpractice-settlements/article_a330511e-68a2-11e2-9ecf-001a4bcf887a.html; William Heisel & Mayrav Saar, *Doctors Without Discipline: How Doctors Can Hurt Patients and Get Away With It*, Orange County Register, Apr. 7, 2002, https://groups.google.com/forum/#!topic/alt.society.conservatism/2tJu0w1B7-Q; Rosemary Gibson & Janardan Prasad Singh, Wall of Silence: The Untold Story of the Medical Mistakes That Kill and Injure Millions of Americans (2003).

[170] Dr. Alan Zarkin, sentenced to probation and prohibited from practicing medicine for five years, Paul Jung, Peter M. Lurie, & Sidney M. Wolfe, *U.S. Physicians Disciplined for Criminal Activity*, 16 Health Matrix J.L. Med. 335 (2006), http://www.citizen.org/Page.aspx?pid=696. The article goes on to note that "A large number of physicians convicted of crimes find employment within the federal government."

[171] *Surgeon Who Left an Operation to Run an Errand Is Suspended*, N. Y. Times, Aug. 9, 2002, http://www.nytimes.com/2002/08/09/us/surgeon-who-left-an-operation-to-run-an-errand-is-suspended.html.

[172] Leslie J. Reagan, When Abortion Was a Crime: Women, Medicine and Law in the United States, 1867–1973, 116 (1997).

[173] Although the organization is public, Final Exit members take a great deal of trouble to hide their involvement with the deaths of their clients. In this respect,

any medical framework. In other words, even States that formally prohibit assisted suicide are beginning to act on implicit assumptions that "appropriate" assisted suicide is exclusively the province of the medical profession. Whatever the reason, the result is that doctors who carry out sub rosa assisted suicides on extremely ill patients are rarely prosecuted, while Final Exit members are increasingly subject to publicized trials.[174]

Conclusion

The tension between the imperative to save lives and the mandate to respect patient autonomy is an ongoing issue in areas as diverse as honoring the DNR orders and advance directives of suicidal people to determining when it is appropriate to criminally prosecute and discipline medical professionals who take part in ending the lives of their patients and others. These tensions are only going to increase as more states legalize assisted suicide while concurrently mandating the involuntary detention of people who are suicidal, supposedly because of mental illness. The next chapter looks at the epicenter of irrational policy and law about suicide: the conflicting messages that we convey to mental health professionals and that they, in turn, convey to their patients, such that fears of liability, on the one hand, and involuntary detention, on the other, distort and undermine the care and healing of people who want to die. In Chapter 7 we will also discuss the voluntary cessation of eating and drinking by both terminally ill and nonterminally ill patients, and how doctors should respond in each situation.

My recommendations in this chapter are simple. As much as possible, patient autonomy in the context of an authentic doctor–patient relationship should be preserved. If possible, doctors should not be gatekeepers of suicide, but healers and counselors. This could be accomplished by providing hospice patients with a card that would enable them to obtain lethal medications (after a fifteen-day waiting period) with careful instructions on utilization and appropriate warnings.

If doctors are involved, and suicide that is medically assisted is legalized, it should apply only to people whose treating physicians, physician's assistants, and nurse practitioners agree to supply them with lethal prescriptions. Doctors should not be in the business of supplying lethal medication prescriptions to patients whom they encounter solely for that purpose.

Final Exit could not be more different from Kevorkian, who publicized every assisted death.

[174] Because these "exit guides," as Final Exit Network calls them, all seem to be retired senior citizens, often wearing Hawaiian shirts and Birkenstocks at their trials, the media coverage of the proceedings reads rather oddly. See Chapter 10 for an extensive discussion of one such trial.

But still, I think the hospice card approach is the best one of all. Patients who use medical marijuana have registration cards that enable them to obtain a drug that is otherwise illegal. Why not patients in hospice? It embodies a better assurance that the patient really does have a terminal illness than the concurrence of two Compassion & Choices doctors, and the determination that the individual is competent can be an ongoing process carried out by people who are intimately familiar with the individual's day-to-day medical and mental changes. The person's physician would not be involved in a painful professional conflict; certifying a terminal illness so that the patient can enter hospice is done all the time. And the individual wouldn't have to ask permission from two doctors to make decisions about life that are private, momentous, and personal.

6

Mental Health Professionals and Suicide

I have been smart enough to talk my way out of that when they want to civilly commit me. You sit down, you shut up and you don't act out. You explain you understand their concerns and you apologize for having been so upset. I understand the police officer is doing his duty. As long as you're incredibly reasonable, they will eventually go away. Everyone is entitled to a moment of emotional outburst, but you have to check yourself pretty fast.

—Carrie Stoker[1]

We do have terminal illnesses in psychiatry just like we do in every other medical profession, and I think we have to recognize some patients are going to kill themselves despite our best efforts. [We need to] try to avoid taking on all the responsibility of that . . . We can only do so much, and I think accepting our limits is a very important aspect.

—Dr. Glenn Gabbard[2]

I don't take medications, I weaned myself off, I don't want to be on pills. I know that meds are available and I don't want meds to be my crutch. When I act out, "Oh, are you taking your meds? Because you are acting out." No, I am crazy anyway. Winter is a very hard time for me. If I can live authentic to myself, I can be as real as I was meant to be. People lived with mental illness before drug companies existed and managed their life. I have my faith

---

[1] Interview with Carrie Stoker (Dec. 17, 2013).

[2] Claire Ginther, *Psychotherapy Strategies and the Chronically Suicidal Patient*, PSYCHIATRIC TIMES, July 1, 1999, www.psychiatrictimes.com/articles/psychotherapy-strategies-and-chronically-suicidal-patient.

and that has changed my entire life. When I get super anxious or panicky, when I get the runaway hamster in my head, I get on my knees and pray, give me the strength to get through this.

—Jenn Hurtado[3]

Every time they put me in places and cut out that part of my life, that made it a thousand times worse. You're too at risk, in their efforts to keep me safe they made me a thousand times more dangerous because they took away any chance at meaning and outside positive feedback. It took me a decade to tell myself that I had any value.

—Lynne Legere[4]

You go to the ER and you are sobbing or screaming and you sit there and then someone comes to talk to you for a few minutes and then they call the person from the psych unit, and you have to wait until they arrive, and they evaluate you, and then you wait and wait while they call your insurance company. And then this woman comes back into the room and says they want to know if you will be safe if you go home. She says, I can't tell you what to say, but if you say that you will be safe I won't be able to admit you. I said, I will not be safe, and then she left the room and I was admitted.

—Pam Nolan[5]

The economics of modern mental health care sadly reduce mental health treatment to very brief, very infrequent contacts, mainly aimed at renewing prescriptions (that may or may not be taken as prescribed.) Skill teaching is often a long and arduous task, and there is little or no place for it in the economic landscape of modern behavioral health. If managed care companies were docked lots of money for every person who dies in their care, they might take a different approach to suicide prevention.

—Dr. Joel Dvoskin[6]

[Being hospitalized] was the best thing that could have happened to me. If I hadn't wound up in the hospital, I would have wound up dead. I was thinking of jumping off something. It feels completely rational at the time.

—Abby Irving[7]

---

[3] Interview with Jenn Hurtado. Dec. 16, 2013.
[4] Interview with Lynne Legere. Dec. 16, 2013.
[5] Interview with Pam Nolan. Dec. 10, 2013.
[6] Personal communication from Joel Dvoskin to author (May 4, 2015).
[7] Interview with Abby Irving (pseudonym), Nov. 20, 2013.

Introduction

In Chapter 2, I reviewed the research that shows that at least half of all suicide attempts and suicides are not caused by serious mental illnesses such as major depression, bipolar disorder, and schizophrenia.[8] Yet one of the major assumptions in our social policy and law is that suicidality is *always* the result of mental illness. This framework diverts focus from the public health based approaches that actually work better and are less expensive.[9] Even on an individual level, it impedes adoption of evidence-based suicide prevention approaches that target suicidality rather than mental illness, which have been shown to reduce suicide attempts and emergency department (ED) visits related to suicidality.

The legalization of assisted suicide, with its implicit assumption that terminally ill people can rationally decide to kill themselves, publicly and with support, creates interesting conceptual tensions with the conflicting assumption that suicide is always a manifestation of psychiatric disability, and exposes the flaws in the equation of suicide and serious mental illness. The great conceptual chasm between the decision to hasten one's death in the context of terminal illness (socially supported suicide), and any other decision to hasten one's death (socially punished suicide) is rhetorically reflected in the efforts of advocates of physician-assisted suicide to change the name of their form of suicide to aid in dying or death with dignity. Even people who are clearly terminally ill are screened to ensure they don't want to die for the wrong reasons or in the wrong frame of mind (which would be "suicide" rather than "aid in dying").

But the principal way that disconnects in policy and law between suicide (caused by mental illness) and assisted suicide (a right of terminally ill people grounded in individual autonomy) are dealt with is to divide professional hegemony over them. Terminally ill suicidal people are the domain of the medical profession, and (if they're lucky) palliative care and hospice. People who are suicidal but not terminally ill are referred to mental health professionals, some of whom also claim jurisdiction over terminally ill people, on the grounds that medical professionals don't have the skills to identify depression or delirium in a terminally ill patient when it's staring them in the face.[10] Honest mental health professionals acknowledge that they don't do so well at identifying depression and delirium in terminally ill people either; but

---

[8] As Dr. Jon Berlin pointed out to me, anyone who wants to die in more than a passing way could surely qualify for a diagnosis of "adjustment disorder," and he's right, but "adjustment disorder" is basically a diagnosis that was constructed for insurance reimbursement purposes.

[9] See Chapter 9.

[10] Christopher J. Ryan, *Ethics, Psychiatry and End-of-Life Issues*, PSYCHIATRIC TIMES, June 8, 2010, at http://www.psychiatrictimes.com/ethics- psychiatry-and-end-life-issues.

they still insist that anyone talking about wanting to die, whether terminally ill or not, needs to talk to a mental health professional.

Many suicidal people, whether terminally ill or not, don't have a serious mental illness.[11] Yet suicidal people are routinely sent to mental health professionals, most of whom equate suicidality with serious mental illness. This leads to inevitable conflict, and not only between treater and patient. There are huge social and economic costs to conceptualizing suicide and suicide attempts as inevitably the result of untreated or inadequately treated mental illness. Research shows that, in general, mental health treatment for suicidal people does not work as well as treatment focused specifically at their suicidality.[12]

Thus, for some people who are suicidal, but have no serious mental health issues, the sudden and often unwelcome introduction to the mental health system, with its diagnoses and drugs, may feel utterly irrelevant to the life difficulties they are facing. These people are also shocked at the ease with which suicidal people can be involuntarily detained and involuntarily treated. The shock deepens if they experience ensuing difficulties with parental rights, child custody, professional licensing, employment, housing, education, and even being able to cross borders.[13] These consequences stretch out for years after a suicide attempt, even when it is immediately regretted and never repeated. The lesson that U.S. social policies and laws teach is crystal clear: if you are feeling like you wish you were dead, you'd better keep quiet about it.[14] That is, unless you want a hospital bed, or to get out of a jail cell, or to get your loved ones to take your pain seriously, in which case you should say you are suicidal whether it's true or not.[15]

For medical professionals, the death of a patient is often an emotionally difficult occasion. For mental health professionals, the suicide of a patient is seen not only as a tragedy, and a missed opportunity, but a rebuke, and, most of all, a failure.[16] It can be personally heartbreaking, but it also always

---

[11] See Chapter 2, pp. 98–104, for this argument in detail.
[12] See Chapter 9.
[13] See Chapter 8.
[14] Interview with Ann Rider, June 6, 2014.
[15] See Chapter 7, "Contingent Suicidality."
[16] H. Hendin, A. P. Haas, et al., *Factors Contributing to Therapists' Distress After the Suicide of a Patient*, 161 Am. J. Psychiatry 8, 1442–46 (2004); F. M. Wurst, I. Kunz, et al., *The Therapist's Reaction to a Patient's Suicide: Results of a Survey and Implications for Health Care Professionals' Wellbeing*, 32 Crisis 8, 99–105 (2011); J. G. Tillman, *When a Patient Commits Suicide: An Empirical Study of Psychoanalytic Clinicians*, 87 Int. J. Psychoanal. Pt. 1, 159–177 (2006); See more at J. G. Tillman, *Patient Suicide: Impact on Clinicians*, Psychiatric Times, Dec. 31, 2014, http://www.psychiatrictimes.com/special-reports/patient-suicide-impact-clinicians/page/0/2?GUID=F1BFB500-E25B-4BB8-8A7C-93CB32BEE8FB&rememberme=1&ts=13012015#sthash.DCCvKA1H.dpuf.

carries with it the shadow of liability.[17] This fear of liability leads to over-hospitalization of people who talk about being suicidal. Involuntary hospitalization can be extremely traumatic and is often ineffective for the patient. It may actually increase the chances of long-term suicide.[18]

Treating suicidality as inevitably the product of a mental disorder requiring hospitalization—involuntarily, if necessary—greatly and unnecessarily increases costs: on insurance companies, on society, and (not least of all) on people who are achingly lonely, despairing, hopeless, exhausted, and need connection, problem-solving, and help reframing perspectives rather than hospitalization and medication, which no study has ever shown reduces suicide.

Because quite a few people are, in fact, suicidal primarily as a result of serious psychiatric disability—people with schizophrenia, major depression, PTSD, or bipolar disorder—you might think it makes sense for a mental health professional to screen everyone. But when the mental health profession considers everyone who wants to die as mentally disordered by definition, there is very little screening out. Most evaluations of suicidal people by mental health professionals are simply to determine a diagnosis or diagnoses and treatment plan, almost always with medication.

Because of the stigma, possible lost liberty,[19] future discrimination,[20] and other consequences, suicidal people are often wary about being evaluated by a mental health professional. It's one of the few occasions in medicine (eating disorders and substance abuse being notable others) where the patient's central focus may be on deceiving the doctor. When my interviewees were determinedly suicidal, they clearly understood the need to lie to evaluating professionals and had no difficulty doing it. As one man I interviewed said succinctly, "[the] relationship becomes polarized because they have the power. You don't really get better, you just shine them on."[21]

To reduce the suicide rate in the United States, we need to begin with five presumptions:

1. People living in the community are legally responsible for their actions, including their suicide attempts.[22]
2. Not all people who attempt suicide have a psychiatric disability or could benefit from mental health treatment (as opposed to help or treatment focused specifically on being suicidal and the life problems underlying it).

---

[17] *Id.*

[18] See Chapters 2, 7, and 9.

[19] See Chapter 2 for a discussion of involuntary commitment of people who threaten suicide.

[20] See Chapter 8 for a discussion of discrimination on the basis of suicidality.

[21] Interview with Mark McPherson (pseudonym). August 20, 2014.

[22] This presumption would be rebuttable, as it is across the law, in individual cases involving lack of capacity such as psychoses, intoxication, or mania.

3. For most people who are suicidal, whether or not they have psychiatric disabilities, outpatient rather than inpatient help and treatment is the standard of care.
4. To save the most lives, risks must be taken such that despite the very best care and treatment, some people will commit suicide. Even if those risks are not taken, and people are institutionalized, some people will commit suicide (likely more people).
5. Perhaps most importantly, we must presume—and embody this presumption in both policy and law—that a mental health professional whose outpatient commits suicide has not failed unless he or she has acted intentionally or recklessly to cause the suicide. This is not a radical idea: indeed, it is settled law in many states.[23]

I have drafted a proposed law immunizing outpatient providers from liability for the suicide of patients unless they act intentionally or recklessly to cause the suicide (see Appendix A at the end of this book). The presumption, of course, does not apply to inpatients who commit suicide in hospital settings. Their very status of hospitalization and loss of liberty exists because of a clinical assessment of the seriousness of their suicidal risk and their inability to manage it. The hospital is getting paid for its expertise in treating the individual (although few hospitals have programs aimed specifically at suicidal people), supervising the individual, and protecting against that risk.[24] An outpatient mental health professional, on the other hand, should be expected to do what every other healthcare provider does: provide the best possible assessment and care,[25] not guarantee or be responsible for outcomes that occur outside the professional's office.

These five presumptions are necessary, as Josh Sebastian's experience[26] shows, to support the best approaches to helping people who are suicidal. These approaches require alliance with the individual, not control over him or her. They often involve risk and disengagement from intensive and absolute psychiatric oversight. However, the current culture of the mental health system, created in part by legal and social policies (but also by many mental

---

[23] Lee v. Corregedore, 925 P.2d 324 (Haw. 1996) (counselors do not have duty to prevent suicide of outpatients even if suicide is foreseeable); Truddle v. Baptist Mem'l Hosp.-DeSoto, 150 So.3d 692 (Miss. 2014) (suicide breaks chain of causation unless defendant's intentional act proximately caused an "irresistible impulse in decedent to take his or her own life"); Dux v. U.S., No. 11 C7142 (N.D. Ill. Sept. 24, 2014); Clift v. Narragansett Television, 688 A.2d 805, 810 (R.I. 1996).
[24] Jutzi-Johnson v. U.S., 263 F.3d 753 (7th Cir. 2001).
[25] DAVID JOBES & EDWIN SHNEIDMAN, MANAGING SUICIDAL RISK: A COLLABORATIVE APPROACH (2006); David Kapley, Jacob Appel, Philip Resnick, and the Group for Advancement of Psychiatry's Committee on Psychiatry and the Law, "Mental Health Innovation vs. Psychiatric Malpractice: Creating Space for 'Reasonable Innovation,'" 5 Faulkner Law Rev. 131 (2013-2014).
[26] See Chapter 1.

health professionals' profound misunderstanding of the law and how the legal system operates), discourages risk-taking with suicidal patients, including the risk of even taking these patients in the first place.

The benefits of limiting liability of mental health professionals for the suicide of their outpatients are many:

1. It will reduce existing perverse incentives for mental health professionals to cherry-pick the healthiest and least suicidal outpatients.
2. It will embody the reality that mental health professionals seeing suicidal people on an outpatient basis cannot predict (or "foresee") suicide, let alone control or prevent it.
3. It will reflect the reality that sometimes even the very best treatment cannot prevent a person from taking his or her life.
4. It will reduce existing perverse incentives to over-hospitalize, which have not been shown to prevent long-term suicide and may actually increase risk.
5. It will reduce involuntary interventions, which have drastic consequences for the individual patient, both at the time and in later life, and which may also increase suicides.
6. It will encourage patients to be more honest with mental health professionals, which in turn will improve treatment.
7. It will support the evidence-based treatment practices that are most successful, most of which necessarily take place in community settings and therefore are perceived as involving risk.
8. It will reduce anxiety and malpractice insurance bills of mental health providers and encourage them to focus on alliances with their patients.

We should be very clear that right now in most places in this country, a mental health professional who is concerned about the suicidality of his or her patient, cannot support the patient at the intensity level required, has no recourse to existing community crisis options, and cannot persuade the patient to voluntarily enter a hospital,[27] has only one option. That option involves making a phone call that often means police arriving at a person's door, unannounced,[28] day or night, breaking down the door if the person does not respond, dragging people out who do not want to go (including dragging naked people out of the shower and out to the street[29]), hauling people

---

[27] Often patients resist for the very good reason that it won't do them any good.
[28] Moore v. Wyo. Med. Ctr., 825 F. Supp. 1531 (D. Wyo. 1993); McCabe v. Life-Line Ambulance Serv., 77 F.3d 540 (1st Cir. 1996); Schorr v. Borough of Lemoyne, 265 F. Supp. 2d 488 (M.D. Pa. 2003); Sutterfield v. City of Milwaukee, 870 F. Supp. 2d 633 (E.D. Wisc. 2012), aff'd 751 F.3d 542 (7th Cir. 2014).
[29] Moore, 825 F. Supp. 1531; Kerman v. City of New York, 261 F.3d 229, 233 (2d Cir. 2001).

downstairs or upstairs,[30] even when the individual is an elderly Holocaust survivor who dies in the process.[31] The ordinary, standard process of detaining suicidal people when police are involved is to handcuff them in the back of a police car (even children). If it's an ambulance service, the person will probably be strapped down on a gurney. After this, the person is taken to an ED where the person may wait for many hours or even days (and very occasionally weeks) without any treatment, and often without much sympathy or support from ED staff who want the bed for someone they are better equipped to help. This is the remedy that our society has chosen to provide to people so lost and desolate and desperate that they don't want to live any more. You can understand why a caring mental health professional would be loath to employ it. There are other psychiatrists who sign detention papers without having ever seen or evaluated the patient—psychiatrists who would not be able to pick the person they had just involuntarily detained out of a lineup.[32]

The truth is that the very best and most skilled mental health professionals, doing their very best work, under no pressure of either time or paperwork, can neither predict nor prevent every suicide. More importantly (because the law does not actually require mental health professionals to predict or prevent every suicide), the most skilled mental health professionals doing their very best work must *necessarily* take risks that their patients will commit suicide. The journey to a life that a suicidal person considers meaningful and worthwhile must carry some risk. To increase quality of life and the absolute number of lives saved, we have to be prepared to tolerate the reality that some people will kill themselves. We cannot continue creating unnecessary misery, increasing costs, and reducing both the availability and quality of treatment to nurture the myth that all suicides are preventable. They never have been and never will be.

American culture has a peculiar and irreconcilable tension that plays out in our laws: we celebrate autonomy, but we demand to be protected from risk. Many people will say that short-term constraints on the autonomy of suicidal people are acceptable to avoid the finality of suicide. But the constraints are not short-term.[33] And—an important legal matter—they have not been shown to be effective in preventing suicide in the long run. The power to involuntarily detain and treat suicidal individuals is built into the

[30] *Life-Line Ambulance*, 77 F.3d 540; *Kerman*, 261 F.3d 229; Anderson v. Village of Forest Park, 606 N.E.2d 205 (Ill. App. 1992).
[31] *Life-Line Ambulance*, 77 F.3d 540.
[32] *Life-Line Ambulance*, 77 F.3d 540; DiGiovanni v. Pessel, 250 A.2d 756 (N.J. App. 1969); Hurley v. Towne, 156 A.2d 377 (Me. 1959); Barker v. Netcare Corp., 147 Ohio App.3d 1 (2000).
[33] As we will see in Chapter 8, once a person has a known history of hospitalization for suicide attempts, that individual's employment, education, child custody, immigration, and other rights are affected, often forever.

whole system of mental healthcare, and it constrains both individuals who are suicidal and the mental health professionals who treat them because the behavior of both is driven and distorted by avoiding risk. In the case of mental health professionals, it is the risk of liability; in the case of patients, it is the risk of involuntary interventions—loss of liberty, forced treatment—which by most accounts harm more than they help and may even increase the likelihood of suicide in the long run. Patients disclose less, and professionals intervene more, than would occur in the absence of involuntary commitment laws and liability concerns.

Thus, the fact that our laws and policies do not correspond to the realities that some suicides cannot be prevented, and that the best and most skilled suicide prevention work requires taking risks, has many consequences, and creates a number of barriers to accessing care.

For example, some people have a hard time getting any consistent, ongoing professional help. It is no secret that people who are acutely suicidal have a hard time finding any mental health professional willing to help them, and that mental health professionals will turn away clients who are suicidal because of fears of liability.[34] The help that people do get is undermined by the secrets they have to keep. Many individuals choose to keep their painful thoughts of suicide to themselves, either to obtain or maintain care from a mental health professional, or because they wish to avoid the risk of involuntary commitment and treatment.

Even if people don't keep their thoughts secret, the quality of the care that mental health professionals could provide to suicidal patients is reduced by intrusive worries about liability. Mental health professionals are more worried about liability than they need to be, and they bring some of these problems on themselves by claiming an expertise in suicide prediction and treatment that the field just does not have, and by testifying to a "standard of care" that is completely unsupported by any evidence that it works to prevent suicide. It's a counterproductive mess. This chapter examines the mess in detail and proposes solutions.

Medical and Mental Health Professionals: Contrasting Attitudes Regarding Assisted Suicide and End-of-Life Decision-Making

It is hard from the vantage point of the twenty-first century to remember that less than forty years ago, doctors hesitated to permit medical patients to refuse potentially life-saving or life-extending treatment because (at that time) to do so would conflict with the ethics of the medical profession and risk legal liability. Today, treatment refusal is publicly honored as a fundamental

---

[34] Tillman, *supra* note 16.

individual right (unless you are in prison or jail or a mental institution or have a psychiatric diagnosis or are a minor). Thirty years ago, medical professionals argued that patients were unable to understand the complexities of their illnesses or make decisions about them (sound familiar in the mental health arena?), and that physicians' professional mandate was impossible to reconcile with the principle that an individual's autonomy might be exercised through choosing to die.

Today, medical professionals are continuing to engage in a robust debate about assisted suicide. Many prominent and well-regarded physicians publicly support suicide under some circumstances[35] while being wary about assistance from private groups or as a government policy.[36] They are able to conduct this debate without much reference to the liability concerns that were prevalent in the debate about discontinuing or refusing life support in the twenty years after the *Quinlan* decision in 1976.[37] They are also relatively free to assist their patients in the manner they deem ethically appropriate without much concern about adverse consequences from their disciplinary bodies.[38] The role of the physician is increasingly evolving from the authority figure whose decisions regarding what is best for the patient constitute the last word and require compliance to the patient's partner, ally, and advocate

---

[35] SHERWIN NULAND, HOW WE DIE: REFLECTIONS ON LIFE'S FINAL CHAPTER 151 (paperback 1995) ("few would disagree that suicide would appear to be among the options that the frail elderly should consider as the days grow more difficult, at least those among them who are not barred from doing so by their personal convictions"); ATUL GAWANDE, BEING MORTAL: MEDICINE AND WHAT MATTERS IN THE END (2014).

[36] NULAND, *id.* at 157 ("depression, the periodic despondency of the chronically ill, and the death fascination of some segments of our society are not strong enough justifications for teaching people how to murder themselves, to help them do it, or to bestow a blessing on it"); compare with Ezekiel J. Emanuel, who may be changing his mind as he ages, *Why I Hope to Die at 75*, ATLANTIC MONTHLY (Oct. 2014), www.theatlantic.com/features/archive/2014/09/why-I-hope-to-die-at-75/379329/.

[37] Doctors are not sued or punished for assisting suicide even in states where it is illegal. Doctors do continue to be investigated and prosecuted when euthanasia is suspected, although convictions are rare and punishments are weak, see *supra* at pp. 264–268.

[38] When in 1991, the New York Board for Professional Medical Conduct decided that Dr. Timothy Quill had not engaged in unprofessional conduct in the wake of his article describing his prescription of pills to a patient he knew would use them to commit suicide and, furthermore, giving her instructions on how to use them in that way, it became pretty clear that doctors who assisted the suicides of patients well known to them after a deliberative period of counseling would not be subject to discipline, Lisa W. Foderaro, *New York Will Not Discipline Doctor for His Role in Suicide*, N. Y. TIMES, Aug. 17, 1991, www.nytimes.com/1991/08/17/nyregion/new-york-will-not-discipline-doctor-for-his-role-in-suicide.html. Of course, out and out euthanasia is still fair game for medical disciplinary boards.

in navigating the course of an illness or disability. A patient with a complex and terminal condition need no longer choose between aggressive treatment by a doctor or hospice, where her values and outlook and decisions are honored at the price of foregoing medical treatment. The field of palliative care has developed in medicine, and, along with geriatric medicine, is at the forefront of patient-centered care that focuses on quality of life.

Psychiatrists are much less sympathetic to the right to refuse treatment (especially the treatments they prescribe), and much more inclined to ascribe the desire to die, even among terminally ill patients, to a treatable disease. This is in part because psychiatrists see people who want to die as their exclusive professional bailiwick. As Dr. Jacob Appel observed, "[p]sychiatrists are trained to prevent suicide—an outcome widely regarded by the profession as a failure."[39] From their point of view, a desire to die is rarely the result of any rational process, but a manifestation of curable illness and treatable disability. The American Suicide Foundation's amicus brief in the *Glucksberg* and *Quill* cases asserted that "[a]lthough patients with terminal illness who seek lethal drugs from their physicians are virtually certain to have treatable, reversible mental illness, the same is not true of patients with terminal illness who decide to forego medical procedures near the end of life."[40] So there you have it: people who want to die and refuse life-sustaining treatment are mentally healthy; people who want to die and avail themselves of assisted suicide are mentally ill. It's as simple as that. Except, of course, that it's not.

A smaller number of mental health professionals even see the desire to die itself as evidence, not only of mental illness but of incompetence to make treatment decisions. It is not just suicide that they have set their faces against: Dr. Appel has astutely observed that

> [p]sychiatrists, even those who in theory favor aid in dying, have very strong biases both against "suicide" but also against any involvement in facilitating the dying process. Might be a selection effect regarding who becomes a psychiatrist. . . . [41]

---

[39] Jacob Appel, "*A Suicide Right for the Mentally Ill?*" 37 HASTINGS CENTER REP. 21 (2007), *available at* www.medscape.com/viewarticle/557817. Appel's solution to this problem—exploring "alternative mechanisms by which such patients [psychiatric patients] might obtain help in ending their lives, possibly including the use of full-time thanatologists specially trained for the act" is not one that makes sense to me, although the rest of the article is one of the best short surveys on extending assisted suicide to people with psychiatric disabilities that I have ever read.

[40] Richard E. Coleson, *The Glucksberg & Quill Amicus Curiae Briefs*, 13 Issues L. & Med. 1, 3–99 (1997), *available at* www.nightingalealliance.org/pdf/Glucksberg_Quill_Briefs.pdf; *Washington v. Glucksberg and Vacco v. Quill: An Analysis of the Amicus Curiae Briefs and the Supreme Court's Majority and Concurring Opinions*, 43 ST. LOUIS L.J. 469 (2005).

[41] Personal communication from Jacob Appel to the author (Oct. 20, 2014).

Thus, while almost 25% of Oregon psychiatrists considered it unethical to even assess the competence of terminally ill people contemplating assisted suicide,[42] only 0.4% of almost 1000 Oregon psychiatrists had ever worked with hospice patients.[43] Herbert Hendin was aghast that Timothy Quill would refer his patient to the Hemlock Society, and I don't think his attitude is anomalous among mental health professionals.[44]

It is not only that mental health professionals consider prevention of suicide their unique area of expertise in the medical profession. It is that their expertise is exercised in a uniquely personal way that precludes them from accepting a decision to die as a final and unalterable decision, as an oncologist might. For the oncologist, chemotherapy, radiation, and surgery are tools that have not succeeded. The psychiatrist's tools include medications and electroconvulsive therapy (ECT), which often do not work, or stop working; but the most fundamental part of the psychiatrist's practice is understanding, expression of empathy, interpretation—in other words, the professional himself or herself is the modality of treatment for suffering patients. A patient's rejection of treatment and decision to die is much more personal when you yourself are the treatment.

Paradoxically, despite mental health professionals' assurance that helping suicidal people is their unique specialty, many seem peculiarly unable to sit with a patient and converse at length about the patient's suicidality. As one patient told me,

> as soon as you say something that hints you might hurt yourself, you have no control over what happens to you, this completely keeps me from going to a mental health professional. We need an atmosphere in the mental health field, [where] the response could be not one of panic but of support and understanding that someone is really hurting and trying to help in whatever way the individual seeking help is willing to do. Right now I just don't see mental health professionals playing that role . . . as soon as I mention that I have attempted suicide in the past you can almost see the word lawsuit lighting up.[45]

---

[42] Linda Ganzini, G. B. Leong, et al., *Evaluation of Competence to Consent to Assisted Suicide: Views of Forensic Psychiatrists*, 157 Am. J. Psychiatry 595 (2000) (24% considered it unethical; 78% recommended a very stringent standard of competence).

[43] Mark Sullivan, Linda Ganzini, & Stuart J. Younger, *Should Psychiatrists Serve as Gatekeepers for Physician-Assisted Suicide?* 28 Hastings Center Rep. 24 (1998) (three out of seven hundred psychiatrists indicated that they had done hospice work).

[44] See also Patricia Wesley, *Dying Safely*, 8 Issues L. & Med. 467 (1993).

[45] Interview with "Colleen" (April 25, 2014).

Therapists I spoke to agreed that it was extremely helpful for a mental health professional to listen calmly to a suicidal individual while acknowledging that very few professionals were able to do this. One mental health professional who also worked on a crisis line told me

> What is most helpful is that the person that is trying to be helpful is able to sit with the person having the experience without having to immediately try to fix it. But if you are uncomfortable with what the person is saying to the point that you can't sit with it, then they [suicidal patients] have to take care of you, they have to modify what they are saying in order to satisfy you, if they say the wrong thing you may incarcerate them. I used to get calls a lot of the time from people who are cutters but they were afraid if they told their therapists they were cutting they would be hospitalized. But the crisis line was anonymous. They needed to talk about why they were doing it but they couldn't do it with their therapists because their therapists would freak out.[46]

Even if mental health professionals do not act immediately to intervene when a patient tries to talk about suicidality, many interviewees told of therapists who violated confidentiality without even notifying them or trying to talk to them about their suicidality.

> If you are a mental patient and you say, "I wish I was dead," you risk being locked up. I can't tell my counselor anything. One day I said something to him along those lines, and wasn't seriously considering it, but was just frustrated. He contacted the SRO I was living at, and they were thinking of calling the police. If he had told me that what I said was concerning him I would have said I am not really considering it, don't contact my housing. [But from the mental health professional's perspective] [i]f I am suicidal I am no longer responsible.[47]

Mental health professionals do not deny that panic and even adversarial conflict often sets in when a patient even mentions suicide. As David Jobes and Elizabeth Ballard write

> Suicide is usually a frightening prospect that we feel compelled to control or stop by any means. . . . Suicide risk in a new patient often triggers dramatic and intense power struggles surrounding the patient's autonomy and clinical control.[48]

---

[46] Interview with Stephen McCrea (Aug. 26, 2014).

[47] Interview with Steve Periard, (Aug. 25, 2014).

[48] David Jobes & Elizabeth Ballard, *The Therapist and the Suicidal Patient, in* Building a Therapeutic Relationship with a Suicidal Patient 54 (Konrad Michel & David A. Jobes eds., 2011).

Not only does a patient's announcement of suicidality stir deep discomfort and power struggles over autonomy. It can lead, as my interviews, research, and case law underscore, to a mental health professional's decision to no longer treat a patient (or "abandon" the patient, as most of my interviewees put it).[49] Given the mental health profession's claim of expertise in matters of suicide, and core commitment to combat it, it seems paradoxical to contemplate the widespread refusal of mental health professionals to accept patients who have histories of self-injury or suicide attempts.[50]

You might think that because suicide prevention is so central to mental health treatment, suicidal patients would be the ones most likely to receive the best treatment from mental health professionals. You would be wrong. Over and over again, psychiatrists and other mental health professionals don't ask about suicidality,[51] or ask in a way that discourages a full answer. Skip Simpson, an attorney whose sole practice is suicide malpractice, sees cases where suicide assessments are done at the very end of a session with the patient; another patient is waiting, and the therapist might ask, 'You aren't thinking about suicide, are you?'[52] Or the mental health professional doesn't follow up if the patient mentions it.[53] In fact, when (yet another) suicide scale was profiled on the Internet, one of the comments immediately following the article was, "This could be a great tool to assist psychiatrists in discharging high risk patients from their practices to minimize risk of wrongful death suits or being blamed when patients kill others as well as themselves."[54]

Conversely, many mental health professionals who do continue to treat suicidal patients feel like Jobes in his fourth year of caring for a chronically suicidal woman:

> I felt at my wit's end. I cared deeply for Sheila and I felt committed to her care but had also become overwhelmed and at a loss for

[49] Interview with Beth Harris (July 16, 2014) ("My old therapist said I can't treat you anymore because she didn't want the risk, I was devastated when she didn't want to see me").

[50] Personal communication from Dr. Jacob Appel (Oct. 20, 2014).

[51] D. W. Coombs, H. L. Miller, et al., *Presuicide Attempt Communications Between Parasuicides and Consulted Caregivers*, 22 SUICIDE & LIFE-THREATENING BEHAV. 3, 289–302 (1992). In a book about Skip Simpson, the only lawyer in the country whose sole practice is suicide malpractice litigation, he discusses many cases where, despite clear signs that the patient was suicidal, the mental health professional did not ask or pursue the topic. See C. C. RIESENHOOVER, THE SUICIDE LAWYERS: EXPOSING LETHAL SECRETS, viii (Kiamichi House 2004); Interview with Beth Harris, *supra* n. 49.

[52] Riesenhoover, *supra* note 51, at 118.

[53] *Id.*

[54] Comment by Barry Edwards, May 23, 2011, to Arline Kaplan, *Can a Suicide Scale Predict the Unpredictable?*, PSYCHIATRIC TIMES (May 23, 2011), www.psychiatrictimes.com/suicide/can-suicide-scale-predict-unpredictable.

what to do next. We had tried every psychotherapy approach
I could imagine. Sheila had undergone many trials on various
medications—anti-depressants, mood stabilizers, and anti-anxiety
drugs, yielding minimal results . . . But the situation remained
desperate. In truth, we both felt desperate and scared.[55]

Many mental health professionals who cannot tolerate feeling desperate and scared become angry with their patients, or fear or dislike them—
enough that there have been decades of articles on how not to hate suicidal
patients.[56] One reason for this is that the fear of liability haunts mental health
professionals who treat suicidal patients.[57] It's hard to feel unconditional
positive regard[58] for someone whose problems carry a potential of years of
expensive, shaming litigation.

In addition, suicidal patients can make a mental health professional feel
incompetent, and helpless, and the stakes are as high as they can be: life and
death. Framing the issue that way, suicidal patients can take up as much time
as the professional is willing to offer. As Jobes recounts

By our fourth year, I found myself on the phone with Sheila almost
daily . . . On the one hand, I felt like I had to do everything I could
to insure she would not take her life (which had come to mean over
functioning and burning myself out). On the other hand, I believed
that if I backed off in any way, Sheila would undoubtedly take her
own life.[59]

In the world of mental health professionals, those who treat the most
acutely suicidal patients are admired for their courage, while others either
discontinue treatment formally (this is rare), or hospitalize the patient so that
they themselves can take a break (this is more common),[60] or refuse to take
suicidal patients in the first place because they are too difficult. Imagine an
oncologist refusing a cancer patient because the cancer was too far advanced

---

[55] David A. Jobes, *Suicidal Blackmail: Ethical and Risk Management Issues in Contemporary Clinical Care, in* CASEBOOK ON ETHICALLY CHALLENGING WORK SETTINGS IN MENTAL HEALTH AND THE BEHAVIORAL SCIENCES (W. B. Johnson & Gerald P. Koocher eds., 2011).

[56] John Maltsberger & Dan H. Buie, *Countertransference Hate in the Treatment of Suicidal Patients*, 30 ARCH. GEN. PSYCHIATRY 625 (1974); Darryl Watts & Gethin Morgan, *Malignant Alienation: Dangers for Patients Who Are Hard to Like*, 164 BRIT. J. PSYCHIATRY 11 (1994).

[57] Jacob M. Appel, *"How Hard It Is That We Have to Die": Rethinking Suicide Liability for Psychiatrists*, 21 CAMBRIDGE Q. HEALTH CARE ETHICS 527 (2012).

[58] This is the mantra popularized by Carl Rogers, the famous twentieth-century humanistic psychologist.

[59] Jobes, *supra* note 55.

[60] *Id.*

or had a high chance of lethality, such as pancreatic cancer. Imagine a world in which cardiologists were considered courageous for taking on patients because they had previously had heart attacks.

On the other hand, oncologists cannot involuntarily commit patients who refuse to quit their pack-a-day cigarette habits, and cardiologists cannot force their waffle cheeseburger-eating patients to stick to arugula and halibut. If they did have those powers, their liability situations might be different. Psychiatrists are the only medical professionals who can routinely resort to involuntary treatment, and this fundamentally distorts their relationship with their patients in a number of ways.

In addition, oncologists and cardiologists are compensated for the time necessary to do their jobs right. Skip Simpson, a malpractice lawyer, agrees with me (a former civil rights lawyer) that the current health care system is structured to discourage mental health professionals from providing the care that patients need. Simpson and his partner note that "if a clinician does a good job of discovering suicidal intent, he or she may have to pay a significant price in time to handle the problem . . . even caring, compassionate clinicians are often pressured by time restraints."[61]

Even when therapists do try to listen, and try to help, people who are suicidal often feel even more alone and alienated. One of my interviewees told me

> I have experienced many doctors (but not all) who have overmedicated me. The more therapy I get, the less it helps, the more they medicate me. You find your voice when you have a rational, kind, non-judgmental listener who has been through some of the same experiences. You need to be able to give words to your own experience, not have a doctor find words for you—they tell you we have you figured out, and you are at the bottom of an abyss, and they say come on out. There is a lot of truth to pulling yourself out of a situation, you're in darkness and they think they're in light, and they are saying there are footholds, come on up. It's not too cold, not too wet, it's at least safe—they need to understand I cannot see the footholds they see. I don't know how to use the shovel to get out and it is always assumed that I do, like them, but I don't. You give up trying to explain to doctors that you were never taught how. They try, but they just don't understand. Then the anguish sets in.[62]

Mental health professionals do not enjoy having the power to involuntarily detain and treat patients. It is nothing new for medical and mental health professionals to be vested with powers that they do not want to

---

[61] Riesenhoover, *supra* note 48, at 117.
[62] Interview with Mark McPherson (Aug. 20, 2014).

exercise. When Congress passed legislation approving Social Security benefits for people with disabilities, the medical profession vehemently disclaimed
the ability to define or confirm disability.[63] Nevertheless, the new laws gave
medical professionals the sole power to determine and define disability.[64]

Later, when the Supreme Court decided that psychiatrists could predict
which murderer was most likely to kill again, it was over the official and elo-
quent protest of the American Psychiatric Association, which insisted that
its members could do no such thing and should not be asked to do so. The
Supreme Court disregarded the organization's position entirely, noting that

> The suggestion that no psychiatrist's testimony may be presented
> with respect to a defendant's future dangerousness is somewhat
> like asking us to disinvent the wheel . . . Acceptance of petitioner's
> position that expert testimony about future dangerousness
> is far too unreliable to be admissible would immediately call
> into question those other contexts in which predictions of
> future behavior are constantly made [such as involuntary civil
> commitment] . . . Third, petitioner's view mirrors the position
> expressed in the *amicus* brief of the American Psychiatric
> Association (APA). Neither petitioner nor the Association
> suggests that psychiatrists are always wrong with respect to future
> dangerousness, *only most of the time.* Yet the submission is that this
> category of testimony should be excised entirely from all trials . . .[65]
> [italics mine]

Just like Woody Allen's family in *Annie Hall,* who do not commit the
uncle who thinks he's a chicken "because they need the eggs," the Supreme
Court both needs psychiatric testimony and is fully aware of just how
uncertain, contingent, and unreliable it is: "psychiatrists disagree widely
and frequently on what constitutes mental illness."[66] As the Supreme Court
of Colorado put it, even though predicting future behavior is difficult and
controversial, "predictions of future behavior are inherent in showing that
medical intervention is mandated."[67] That medical intervention *should* be
mandated is not questioned.

---

[63] Deborah Stone, The Disabled State (1983).

[64] *Id.*

[65] Barefoot v. Estelle, 463 U.S. 880, 896, 898–99 (1983).

[66] Ake v. Oklahoma, 470 U.S. 68, 81 (1985); see also Clark v. Arizona, 548 U.S. 735
(2006) ("The controversial character of some categories of mental disease, the
potential of mental-disease evidence to mislead, and the danger of according
greater certainty to capacity evidence than experts claim for it give rise to risks. . . .
First, the diagnosis may mask vigorous debate within the psychiatric profession
about the very contours of the mental disease itself [citation omitted]".).

[67] People v. Stevens, 761 P.2d 768, 771 (Colo. 1988).

On the other hand, psychiatrists *do* assert their professional expertise in predicting suicide, regardless of official counsel to speak only in terms of risk and protective factors or probabilities. They testify at involuntary commitment hearings that a person is "dangerous to self" and against their fellow mental health professionals, asserting that a patient's suicide was "foreseeable." This happens every day even though they and we know that these predictions are impossible to make on any individual level.[68]

Because predictions are impossible to make, and the fear of patient suicide and liability frames the treatment of suicidal people, many risk-averse outpatient mental health professionals hospitalize patients who try to talk about feeling suicidal. The virtually universal consensus is that concerns about liability for suicide lead to over-hospitalization, in the sense of hospitalizing people who were never going to commit or even attempt suicide. As one highly respected emergency psychiatrist said,

> If we're talking about involuntary hospitalization for less-than-highly-acute suicidality, yes, I agree completely it's still prevalent and still a serious problem. Emergency medicine doctors and psychiatrists untrained in emergency psychiatry tend to be unreasonably risk averse, to the detriment of good care. We need a high bar for coercive hospitalization.[69]

In Massachusetts, for example, there were 75,000 admissions to psychiatric hospitals in 2012. Of these, 45,000 were involuntary admissions under the state's involuntary commitment laws.[70] Not all were for suicidality, but because so few involuntary commitments are grounded in danger to others, it's safe to assume that a substantial proportion of these involuntary admissions were because of predictions that the individual would attempt suicide. In 2011, the most recent year for which we have data, 588 people in Massachusetts committed suicide.[71] Just over half (51%) of these people had documented mental health issues, and just over a third (37%) were receiving mental health treatment at the times of their deaths. Of these, just over a

---

[68] See Chapter 9.

[69] Communication from Dr. Jon Berlin, former president of the American Association of Emergency Psychiatry and Medical Director of Milwaukee County Crisis Services to the author. June 10, 2015. Dr. Berlin also said "Recently, it appears that the pendulum may have swung too far in the other direction, and we are starting to see experienced emergency psychiatrists under-hospitalize, perhaps because of budget constraints and unrealistic expectations of excellent community services."

[70] Personal communication from Mark Larsen, Committee for Public Counsel Services, Mental Health Division, to the author. May 23, 2014.

[71] Massachusetts Department of Public Health, *Suicides and Self-Inflicted Injuries in Massachusetts: Data Summary* (Spring 2014), http://www.mass.gov/eohhs/docs/dph/injury-surveillance/suicide/suicide-update-spring2014.pdf.

third were even known to the mental health system. So, of the 45,000 involuntary detentions, about 217, which is less than one-half of 1%, committed suicide.

Concerns about liability also lead to unnecessary hospitalization of individuals the psychiatrists know quite well are not suicidal, people with "contingent suicidality" who threaten suicide to get access to a hospital bed.[72] Liability concerns also lead to overuse of involuntary detention, commitment and treatment. Psychiatry's commitment to suicide prevention does not necessarily demand an approach that recoils from any kind of risk-taking, but most thoughtful mental health professionals acknowledge that fear of liability at least shadows their decision-making. When the zone is gray or ambiguous, liability is the thumb that tips the scales toward hospitalization and involuntary commitment.

Many mental health professionals genuinely feel that they must intervene, involuntarily if necessary, even if the risk of attempted suicide is low, because the stakes are so high. This urge to force your professional skills on your clients is not necessarily the result of malice or of a domineering nature. It's understandable professional hubris. Even Stephen McCrea, a mental health professional who is deeply skeptical of the biological model of mental illness, acknowledged, "I would be very reluctant to go to assisted suicide for psychiatric disabilities because I would think that if they got the right person, namely me, or someone like me, they might have a chance."[73]

I know what he means. As an attorney, I had clients who decided to forego cases, although they had been victims of extraordinary injustice and I thought I had a good chance of winning their cases. These cases also involved high stakes: the person's liberty, custody of a child, enough money to get out of an institution and have a decent life in the community. I know attorneys who contemplated seeking guardianship for clients because the client refused generous settlement offers on grounds the attorneys considered delusional or even just short-sighted. Deep in our hearts, we understand the temptation of forcing an unwilling client to follow our professional judgment. We know more than our clients, and we mean well; we *know* our clients would be better off in the long run if they would just do what we tell them to do.

Luckily for society, attorneys don't have the power to force their services on unwilling clients. But mental health professionals do. And the power to force your expertise and professional judgment on an unwilling recipient is one side of a double-edged sword. The inevitable other edge—the one pointing toward the mental health professional—is the potential for legal liability if his or her professional judgment turns out to be wrong. The fear of liability

[72] See Chapter 7, for a discussion of contingent suicidality.
[73] Interview with Stephen McCrea (Aug. 26, 2014).

leads mental health professionals to err (and they are human) on the side of caution.

Now that the new rhetoric of mental health treatment is that "everyone can recover," mental health professionals are under even more pressure to provide the treatment than enables that recovery. A principle that was helpful in underscoring that people should never be labeled "chronically mentally ill" and that neither they nor their health care providers should give up hope obscures the reality that some people are always going to die because they cannot bear the suffering, discrimination, isolation, dependency, and endless acute recurrences of illnesses that modern mental health treatment has been unable to alleviate or ameliorate.

Paradoxically, as many have pointed out,[74] the use of involuntary interventions probably increases the rate of suicide. In the long run, the individual has to have hope that life will be worthwhile, and that hope is hard to come by when you're living on a hospital ward or congregating in the day room or doing "occupational" therapy like mending socks when you have two doctoral degrees.[75] Hope—the single most important feature of therapy for many of the people I interviewed—is modeled by trusting and supporting the patient's impulses toward life and taking the risks that accompany returning to living a normal life.

The Cost of Caring: The Case of Peter Yurkowski and Dr. James Curell

Understanding the central importance of work to the self-respect and capacity for hope of his patient was the right thing for Dr. James Curell to do. And yet, by doing so, he became embroiled in a case that has gone on for over eight years, through three trials, all of which found in his favor. He is now facing a fourth trial.[76] This case is a textbook example of the need to protect

---

[74] Jacob M. Appel, *"How Hard It Is That We Have to Die": Rethinking Suicide Liability for Psychiatrists*, 21 Cambridge Q. Health Care Ethics 527 (2012); Peter Dawson & Harriet MacMillan, Relationship Management of the Borderline Patient: From Understanding to Treatment (1993).

[75] Susan Stefan, *Beyond Residential Segregation: The Application of Olmstead to Segregated Employment Settings*, 26 Ga. St. L. Rev. 875 (2009), at n.1.

[76] For ease of reference in the following footnotes, these cases will be referred to as follows: *Yurkowski v. University of Cincinnati*, 2008 Ohio 6483 (Ct.Claims 2008) (*Yurkowski I*)(deciding immunity issue); *Yurkowski v. University of Cincinnati*, 2011 Ohio 5892 (Ct.Claims 2011) (*Yurkowski II*) (first trial); *Yurkowski v. University of Cincinnati*, 2013 Ohio 242 (Ohio App. 2013) (*Yurkowski III*) (reversing trial court for using wrong legal standard, a decision I think was an error of both law and policy, see *infra*). The case was retried by a different judge using a summary procedure, and that judge found in favor of Dr. Curell. The appellate court in *Yurkowski*

mental health professionals who are working extraordinarily hard to make difficult decisions to try to help patients who are struggling with long-term and intense desires to die.

Dr. Curell had treated Peter Yurkowski for almost five years.[77] At the time Dr. Curell accepted Yurkowski as his patient, Yurkowski had struggled for decades with depression.[78] Yurkowski had attempted suicide at the age of eighteen.[79] But Curell appreciated Yurkowski's positive strengths: Yurkowski was a national expert in pharmacology and Curell knew him professionally as a university colleague.[80] Yurkowski "traveled extensively throughout the country lecturing on pharmacology-related topics."[81] He was also married and had two children. His job and his family were major sources of meaning in his life, as well as major sources of life stress.

Dr. Curell advised his patient to ease back a little on his work to reduce his stress, and spend more time with his family.[82] Yurkowski complied, and this plan worked for three years. In June 2004, Yurkowski's depression and anxiety returned and he was hospitalized ten times in eight months for multiple suicide attempts.[83] Dr. Curell tried everything: psychotherapy, group therapy, medication, even ECT.[84] He consulted with another psychiatrist to assure himself that he wasn't missing anything diagnostically or in terms of treatment.[85]

Yurkowski's depression in 2005 was his worst. He was admitted to the hospital on February 6, 2005. On February 18, he told Dr. Curell that his wife of twenty years had notified him (while he was hospitalized for suicidality) that she was divorcing him and that he could not return home.[86] This had predictable effects on Yurkowski's mood, plunging him deeper into despair and suicidality, and Dr. Curell contemplated transferring him to a state psychiatric facility.[87]

Facing the possibility of transfer to a long-term state facility, Yurkowski appeared to improve, although Dr. Curell was still wary. A week later, at Yurkowski's urging, Dr. Curell reluctantly took a risk and granted Yurkowski a pass to leave the hospital to try to find a new place to live.[88] It

---

v. University of Cincinnati, 2015 Ohio 1511 (Ohio App. 2015) found that the summary procedure was inappropriate, and sent the case back for a fourth trial.

[77] *Yurkowski I* at ¶7.
[78] *Yurkowski II* at ¶2.
[79] *Id.*
[80] *Yurkowski II* at ¶3.
[81] *Yurkowski III* at ¶2.
[82] *Yurkowski III* at ¶4.
[83] *Id.* at ¶5.
[84] *Id.*
[85] *Id.* at ¶6.
[86] *Id.* at ¶7.
[87] *Id.* at ¶8.
[88] *Id.*

was a risk, and it worked: Yurkowski found an apartment and came back to the hospital as he had promised. Then, on March 2, Yurkowski was served with divorce papers at the hospital, and completely fell apart. [89] Dr. Curell decided that Yurkowski needed to be indefinitely confined in an institution, and began the paperwork to initiate the transfer to a state facility. As they waited for a bed to open up, Yurkowski repeatedly pled not to be sent to the state institution; he wanted to go to the apartment he had found. He seemed to improve. Curell remained skeptical, and continued with the plan of transfer to a state institution. However, the bed was still not available. Dr. Curell was well aware that to let Yurkowski go to the apartment was a high risk; he told his patient if he did this he would be "sticking his neck out" for him. On the other hand, he knew Yurkowski well, both as a patient and as a professional colleague with a national reputation in his field. For this man to be institutionalized in a state facility would be the final defeat, "so devastating to his self-esteem that he would never recover."[90] Curell decided to give Yurkowski one last chance. Aware of the risk, but believing that Yurkowski's best hope lay in attempting to put his life back together in the community, he granted his patient's wish to be discharged on March 22, 2005, on the condition that Yurkowski stay in close touch with him. Yurkowski struggled, but he complied. He saw Curell on April 4 and on April 13. He moved into his apartment, returned to work, and took his medications. On April 17, he and his soon-to-be-ex-wife celebrated his daughter's birthday together and made plans to attend an event later in the week. On April 18, almost a month after his discharge, Yurkowski killed himself by overdosing on drugs.

His wife (who had notified him that he couldn't come home while he was hospitalized and served him with divorce papers in the hospital) sued Curell. Fortunately for her, the divorce had not gone through yet, so she was still in a legal position to be able to collect any damage award for her husband's death.[91]

Of course I can't know the entire story, having never known Peter Yurkowski. It must be hellish living with an acutely suicidal man for several years, and his widow had two children to raise, so maybe she wanted them insulated from the chaos of her husband's crises. Maybe she needed the money from the lawsuit to support them. I tried to interview Yurkowski's wife, or her attorney Mitchell Allan, for over six months, but our interview dates were always canceled. I was disappointed, because I wanted to hear their side of this story. To me, this seems like a paradigmatic case of a doctor taking the right kinds of risks on behalf of a patient, and being

---

[89] *Id.* at ¶9.

[90] *Id.*

[91] Even if they had divorced, she would realistically have been able to sue as a representative of his children, who would be the surviving heirs of his estate.

punished for doing so by the very person whose actions pushed the patient over the edge.[92]

Peter Yurkowski's death was far from inevitable. He was still alive after a very long and terrible period of depression and suicidality. He had taken the initiative to successfully find himself a new apartment and gone back to work. Dr. Curell was very likely correct that for a man like Peter Yurkowski, being locked away in a long-term state psychiatric hospital would have been "devastating."

In addition, someone as determined as Yurkowski to take his own life might well have done so whether he was in the community or at the state hospital. Honest mental health professionals admit that if a person is determined to take his or her life, it's very hard to prevent that from happening. At least 10% of suicides take place in institutional settings.[93] It would have been easier for Dr. Curell to pass the buck to the state hospital staff, and certainly less risky for him personally. He took a chance on Peter Yurkowski because he cared about him in the way that you want a psychiatrist to care about a patient.

Recently, courts have finally begun to focus on this specific issue. Rather than looking at whether hospitalization would prevent suicide that day, or while the person is hospitalized, they are looking at whether hospitalization would actually provide treatment that would prevent suicide over the (reasonably) long run.[94] Sensibly pointing out that a person cannot be locked up forever, courts ask whether plaintiffs can prove that hospitalization would make suicide "unlikely" *after* discharge. That is, actually, what hospitalization is supposed to do: provide treatment for the underlying condition that lasts past the hospitalization itself. Anita Darcel Taylor[95] made it clear that hospitalization did help her, although each time her "remission" has been shorter. The point is, we should not use hospitals as a super-expensive lockup[96] to prevent people from killing themselves. Three days of involuntary detention, as

---

[92] The annals of litigation are full of plaintiffs, usually women, who leave their husbands and commence divorce proceedings and sue medical and mental health professionals when their husbands commit suicide, see, e.g., Park v. Kovachevich, 116 A.D.3d 182 (N.Y. App. Div. 1st Dept. 2014); Stepakoff v. Kantor, 393 Mass. 836 (1985); Teal v. Prasad, 772 N.W.2d 57 (Mich. App. 2009). I am not suggesting that these women have a duty to stay with their husbands to keep them alive, just that it seems ironic that they apparently expect their husband's mental health professionals to do so, and that courts' causation analysis never seems to take their actions into consideration.

[93] See Chapter 2.

[94] Rodriguez-Escobar v. Goss, 392 S.W.3d 109, 114 (Tex. 2013); Providence Health Ctr. v. Dowell, 262 S.W.3d 24 (Tex. 2008).

[95] See Chapter 1, pp. 32–33.

[96] Even the American Psychiatric Association believes that involuntary hospitalization should be "only for the purpose of providing available treatment

I proposed in Chapter 2, should be enough to stop the most impulsive people. Many people like Ms. Taylor, and a number of people I interviewed, whose suicidality is caused by psychiatric disability, go voluntarily to the hospital to get relief.

Thus, for some people—people on psychiatric wards that actually provide treatment, people whose medications aren't working, or people whose suicidality is the result of impulsive responses to time-limited situational problems—the answer may well be yes, hospitalization will help prevent suicide over the long run. For others, whose suicidality is a response to long-term, embedded problems, or medical or psychiatric difficulties that are unlikely to change, it would be much harder to prove that hospitalization would make any difference in the long run. Certainly, for Peter Yurkowski, there is no indication that his numerous hospitalizations made any difference in reducing his agonizing anxiety and depression. Kerrie Wooltorton and Josh Sebastian were hospitalized repeatedly with no change in their fundamental condition.

Another similar framework more commonly adopted by courts skeptical over suicide malpractice claims is asking the plaintiff to prove that the suicide would not have occurred "but for" the negligence of the mental health care provider.[97] Interestingly, one of the principal grounds for the negligence claim against Dr. Curell was that he should never have provided this career pharmacist with prescriptions for potentially lethal amounts of drugs when he had previously tried to commit suicide on several occasions by overdosing on drugs.

This comports with my research of hundreds of psychiatric malpractice cases involving suicide, which is that the majority of malpractice cases against outpatient psychiatrists involve prescription of medications: the medications themselves caused the suicide,[98] were the wrong medications,[99] or caused an

---

sufficiently effective to hold a realistic promise of release" (*Amicus Brief of the American Psychiatric Association, Kansas v. Crane*, http://www.psychiatry.org/File Library/Psychiatrists/Directories/Library-and-Archive/amicus-briefs/amicus-2001-Crane.pdf

[97] Wilkins v. Lamoille County Mental Health Serv., 889 A.2d 245 (Vt. 2005).

[98] Maloney v. Badman, 156 N.H. 599 (2007) (physician who prescribed Percocet and Valium not liable when patient overdosed on Percocet because he could not have foreseen suicide and there is no duty to prevent suicide of outpatient); Estate of Quackenbush v. Friedberg, 2010 Jury Verdicts LEXIS 12684 (Suffolk Aug. 13, 2010) (defendant's verdict in case alleging negligent prescription of imipramine led to suicide); Misitano v. Ghaffar, 1 Mass. L. Rep. 405 (Mass. Super. Dec. 20, 1993) (plaintiff alleges thoracic surgeon's long-term prescription of amitriptyline caused suicide; court rules defendant entitled to see plaintiff's psychiatric records); Whittle v. U.S., 669 F. Supp. 501 (D.D.C. 1989) (combination of antidepressant and barbiturates was the direct cause of patient's death).

[99] Uhlar-Tinney v. Massa, 2008 Jury Verdicts LEXIS 38790 (Mass. Nov. 13, 2008) (defendant's verdict when teenager committed suicide two weeks after

adverse reaction to which the patient had not been alerted through informed consent.[100] or the professional prescribed too many different medications;[101] prescribed them over the telephone without seeing the patient;[102] prescribed medications that interacted with each other or with alcohol;[103] or prescribed them in too large a quantity,[104] which permitted the patient to down handfuls of the pills in a suicide attempt;[105] or the provider abruptly discontinued

---

hospital discharge; plaintiffs claimed prescription of the wrong medication, misdiagnosis, and failure to warn regarding medication).

[100] Mazella v. Beals, 122 A.D.3d 1358 (A.D. Sup. Ct. 4th Dept. 2014), see also John O'Brien, *Widow of Former Henniger High School Coach Joe Mazella Wins 1.5 million in Lawsuit over His Suicide*, Syracuse Post-Standard, Nov. 21, 2012, http://www.syracuse.com/news/index.ssf/2012/11/widow_of_henninger_high_coach.html.

[101] Sherrod v. Nash General Hosp., 500 S.E.2d 708 (N.C. 1998).

[102] Edwards v. Tardif, 240 Conn. 610 (1997); Gaido v. Weiser, 558 A.2d 845, 115 N.J. 310 (N.J. 1989); *Mazella*, 122 A.D.3d 1358; see O'Brien, *supra* note 82; Granicz v. Chirillo, 147 So.3d 544 (Fla. App. 2014) (patient tells doctor's nurse that she has been having trouble sleeping and crying easily, which she attributes to Effexor and has ceased taking Effexor; doctor changes her prescription to Lexapro and leaves prescription and free sample for her without scheduling an appointment; patient hangs herself the next day).

[103] Quigley v. Michigan, 2011 W.L. 3027809 (E.D. Mich. July 25, 2011) (prescription of two antidepressants); Carney v. Tranfaglia, 57 Mass. App. 664 (2003) (affirming jury verdict in favor of psychiatrist who prescribed nine separate medications, including Percocet, Ambien, and Dalmane to patient who was known to be substance abuser); Estate of Luck v. Albeck, 2011 Mass. Super. LEXIS 103 (Mass. Super. May 17, 2011) (summary judgment in favor of psychiatrist who prescribed eight different psychotropic drugs in nine months when patient committed suicide by combining alcohol with drugs he had obtained illegally); White v. Lawrence, 975 S.W.2d 525, 530 (Tenn. 1998) (doctor liable for providing wife with Antabuse to covertly provide to patient who was alcoholic); Estate of Behn v. Tufo, 1997 Jury Verdicts LEXIS 71843 (Middlesex Cty. Dist. Ct. Apr. 16, 1997) ($1,153,000 jury award in case where patient with long history of alcohol and drug abuse was prescribed Pamelor, Amantadine, Mellaril, and Tranxene and committed suicide with Pamelor overdose); *Whittle*, 669 F. Supp. 501 (combination of antidepressant and barbiturates was the direct cause of patient's death).

[104] Watkins v. U.S., 589 F.2d 214 (5th Cir. 1979) (doctor liable for prescribing seven weeks' worth of Valium to patient without investigating his past medical history; patient proceeded to crash his car into plaintiff's car).

[105] Patton v. Thompson, 958 So.2d 303 (Ala. 2006); Kockelman v. Segal, 61 Cal. App. 4th 491 (Cal. App. 1998); *Edwards*, 240 Conn. 610 (300 Tofranil); Vinchiarello v. Kathuria, 558 A.2d 262 (Ct. App. 1989); Hobart v. Shin, 705 N.E.2d 907, 910 (Ill. 1998) (student swallows 224 doxepin pills after asking psychiatrist for larger amount because of the increased cost of filling small prescriptions frequently; jury verdict in favor of psychiatrist upheld on appeal); Sweet v. Sheehan, 932 So.2d 365 (Fla. App. 2006).

medications without warning of possible effects[106] or failed to warn of potential side effects of medication.[107]

The *Yurkowski* case was appealed after the first trial on a specific legal question: "What is the appropriate standard of care to apply to a malpractice case against a mental health professional whose patient kills himself or herself?" The Ohio Supreme Court had previously held—in a case called *Littleton*—that plaintiffs had to prove more than simply a breach of the standard of care to prove that a mental health professional was negligent in discharging a hospitalized patient who subsequently injured another person.[108] The *Littleton* court gave four reasons for making it more difficult for plaintiffs to recover damages against mental health professionals for discharging patients who subsequently hurt other people. These reasons were: 1) the inability of psychiatrists to predict violence; 2) the absence of standards to measure a psychiatrist's judgment of the likelihood of future violence; 3) that liability in such cases would predictably result in "a massive confinement of all patients who display even a remote possibility of violent behavior"; and 4) the fact that the Legislature had immunized psychiatrists from liability in civil commitment decisions if they made their decisions in good faith.[109]

In light of these facts, the Ohio Supreme Court ruled in *Littleton* that a mental health professional could only be liable for the discharge of a subsequently violent patient if he or she failed to exercise professional judgment: to do a "thorough evaluation," weigh the competing interests in devising a treatment plan, and make the decision in good faith. This formulation echoed the standard adopted in New York State.[110] Under the professional judgment standard, Dr. Curell would have no worries about liability, and, indeed, the Court of Claims (*Yurkowski II*) entered summary judgment in his favor: the plaintiffs could not take the case to trial because they had not shown that they had evidence that might lead a reasonable jury to rule in their favor.

Yet the Ohio appellate court in *Yurkowski III*, in a decision that makes no legal or policy sense, distinguished between the discharge of an individual with potential for violence to others, and the discharge of a suicidal individual, making it *harder* to successfully sue a mental health professional for the discharge of an individual who subsequently injured and killed others, and *easier* to sue a mental health professional who discharges a person who subsequently kills himself or herself. This decision makes no sense in light of the four *Littleton* factors: it is even harder to predict which individual will

---

[106] Stormont-Vail Healthcare v. Cutter, 178 P.3d 35 (Kan. App. 2007) (abruptly taking patient off Paxil).

[107] Callahan v. Jellinek, 83 Mass. App. 664 (2003) (affirming jury verdict, which found defendant negligently failed to inform decedent of potential side effects of her medication, but that this was not the cause of her death).

[108] Littleton v. Good Samaritan Hosp. & Health Ctr., 39 Ohio St. 3d 86 (1988).

[109] *Yurkowski III*, ¶21.

[110] See *infra* at n. 139.

commit suicide than to predict which individual will be violent in the future; there are no standards that successfully predict when a patient will commit suicide, and both the likelihood of massive hospitalization and legislative immunity arguments have identical force with regard to suicidal patients. In addition, as a society, I think we want mental health professionals to be more careful about assuming risk in discharging patients when the risk involves injury to third parties, than taking risk in the discharge of a man such as Yurkowski, who was never alleged to present a danger to anyone but himself.

The rationale given by the Ohio appellate court was that there were no "standards" in the psychiatric profession relating to duties to third parties, while there were "standards" relating to duties to patients. But this is just hogwash. First of all, there are standards relating to duties to third parties in Ohio law that apply to all mental health professionals,[111] who are required by this statute to weigh the interests of third parties against the interests of their patients. There are even more stringent regulations relating to third-party protection applicable to Ohio mental health professionals working for the state.[112] The American Psychiatric Association's ethical standards include one that permits revealing confidential information provided by the patient if there is a "significant risk of danger."[113]

And in fact, the whole discussion of standards and their absence is a red herring. The absence of professional standards took up one sentence of the decision in *Littleton*: the difficulties of predicting dangerousness and devising a treatment plan, and the patient's right to confidentiality and freedom from unnecessary confinement was the major focus of the parties' arguments and the court's analysis in *Littleton*, and all of those factors were equally or more true in the *Yurkowski* case.

But equally importantly, a decision making it more difficult to sue a mental health professional because there are no governing standards of care in his or her profession sets up all the wrong incentives for the profession. What kinds of incentives are created when a failure to formulate professional standards reduces chances of liability?

Most important of all, the patient's interest in autonomy and confidentiality, cited by the *Littleton* court as a major reason to insulate mental health professionals from liability for discharge decisions, is stronger when the only person at risk from the discharge decision is the patient himself or herself, and the patient is asking to be discharged. In cases of violence toward others, the patient's autonomy interests need to be

---

[111] Ohio Rev. Code 23-05-51.
[112] Ohio Admin. Code 5122-3-12 (2011) ("Duty to protect").
[113] American Psychiatric Association, Principles of Medical Ethics, with Annotations Especially Applicable to Psychiatry, sec. 4, comment 8; sec. 8 (2013) (recognizing that there may be conflicts in psychiatrists' obligations to the community and to the patient).

balanced against those of third parties; in cases of competent but suicidal patients (like Josh Sebastian), the doctor's decisions do not place absent third parties at risk.

Dr. Curell says frankly that the way he practices psychiatry has changed. He gives patients much smaller amounts of drugs at a time, and that may be all to the good. He still sees suicidal patients, which is a testament to his integrity and courage, but it must be the case that the years and years of litigation over Peter Yurkowski have changed his practice, and not necessarily to the benefit of future patients.

Liability of Mental Health Professionals: Myths and Realities

> The fear of being sued probably has more widespread and deleterious effects on clinicians than actual lawsuits.[114]

Very few psychiatrists are sued for malpractice,[115] and even fewer psychologists, social workers,[116] and nurses. Nevertheless, psychiatrists worry (even perseverate, in some cases) about the risk of liability.[117] This clearly undermines the effectiveness of the care they deliver and may even increase the risk of their being sued.[118]

There are many steps on the way to a lawsuit. First, the plaintiff has to make the decision that he or she wants to sue. Medical and mental health professionals who genuinely care about their patients and don't worry about being sued generally don't get sued. In fact, even when there are bad outcomes, patient often insist that certain medical professionals—the ones

---

[114] Bruce Bongar & Ronald Stolberg, *Risk Management with the Suicidal Patient*, NATIONAL REGISTER OF HEALTH SERVICE PSYCHOLOGISTS (2009), http://e-psychologist.org/index.iml?mdl=exam/show_article.mdl&Material_ID=100.

[115] Anupam B. Jena, Seth Seabury, Darius Lakdawalla, & Amitabh Chandra, *Malpractice Risk According to Physician Specialty*, 365 NEW ENG. J. MED. 629 (Aug. 2011), *available at* www.nejm.org/doi/full/10.1056/NEJMsa1012370 (psychiatrists lowest on the list of physician specialties in terms of risk of being sued, ranging from 19.6% a year in neurosurgery to 2.6% a year in psychiatry).

[116] FREDERIC G. REAMER, RISK MANAGEMENT IN SOCIAL WORK: PREVENTING PROFESSIONAL MALPRACTICE (2015).

[117] Phyllis Coleman & Ronald Shellow, *Suicide: Unpredictable and Unavoidable: Proposed Guidelines Provide Rational Test for Physician's Liability*, 71 NEB. L. REV. 643 (1992).

[118] Doug Mossman, *Defensive Medicine: Can It Increase Your Malpractice Risk?* 8 CURRENT PSYCHIATRY (Dec. 1, 2009), http://www.currentpsychiatry.com/index.php?id=31597&type=98&tx_ttnews%5Btt_news%5D=178248&cHash=da03e20e36; SUSAN STEFAN, DEPARTMENT TREATMENT OF THE PSYCHIATRIC PATIENT: POLICY ISSUES AND LEGAL REQUIREMENTS (2006).

they felt cared about them--be explicitly excluded from lawsuits.[119] Medical and mental health professionals who associate being sued with having made a professional mistake are missing the total picture. Patients sue doctors they don't like or trust, doctors they feel have treated them badly on an interpersonal as well as medical level: "Not all medical liability suits are prompted by medical errors. Patients often cite interpersonal aspects of care, such as poor communication or feeling rushed, as central to the decision to initiate litigation."[120]

In the case of suicide, of course, the patient is no longer around. But the principles remain the same: if the family feels that the mental health professional didn't care about his or her patient,[121] or doesn't care about them, or both,[122] they are more likely to contemplate litigation. Although it seems hard to believe, some therapists don't even go to their patients' funerals after a suicide, not because they worry about hurting the family's feelings, but because they are concerned it would somehow amount to a confession of liability.[123] It is not surprising that a therapist who is focusing on his or her own potential liability when making decisions about attending a patient's funeral may be a candidate for a notice and summons. Not surprisingly, research shows that therapists who are distant and limit their contact with surviving families are more likely to be sued than those who reach out to the surviving family,

---

[119] Theodore J. Clarke, *Avoiding a Lawsuit: Lessons from the Never-Sued*, AAOS Now, Oct. 2011, http://www.aaos.org/news/aaosnow/oct11/managing3.asp ("I did an anterior/posterior lumbar fusion and my patient, a beautiful, loving grandmother, unfortunately woke up blind. She sued the anesthesiologist, the general surgeon, and the hospital. She told her attorney that she would never sue me because I was always looking out for her. I still think about her a lot.").

[120] TEXAS MEDICAL LIABILITY TRUST, 10 THINGS THAT GET PHYSICIANS SUED: 2010–2011 (2010), http://resources.tmlt.org/PDFs/ten-things-that-get-physicians-sued.pdf.

[121] See Estate of Haar v. Ulwelling, 141 N.M. 252, 154 P.3d 67, 69, n.18 (N.M. App. 2007) (patient reports to his girlfriend that "Dr. Ulwelling doesn't give a shit" about him).

[122] Campbell v. Kelly, 2012 N.Y. Slip Op. 32525 (N.Y. Sup. Ct. N.Y. Cty. Sept. 28, 2012) (specifically citing doctor's failure to return frantic phone calls from wife on the day that husband went missing and shot himself as stating a claim for malpractice, despite the fact that even if the doctor had returned the wife's phone calls there would have been nothing the doctor could have done at that point).

[123] Stacy Freedenthal, *Should Therapists Attend the Funeral of a Client Who Dies by Suicide?* SPEAKING OF SUICIDE, Aug. 7, 2013, http://www.speakingofsuicide.com/2013/08/07/funeral-after-client-suicide/ (although 44% of families would want therapist to attend, and 22% specifically asked therapists to attend, only between 18% and 33% of therapists attend the funerals of clients who have committed suicide).

talking to them, sharing their grief, and trying to help them understand what happened.[124]

Suicide is an area where the fear of litigation invades the therapeutic alliance like a tumor, casting an adversarial shadow over what should be a joint collaboration for the benefit of the patient. With the suicidal patient, as with other patients, the "best overall risk management strategy remains a sensitive and caring therapeutic alliance within the context of the best possible clinical care."[125] The research of Dr. Charles Lidz and his colleagues has demonstrated,[126] and my interviews confirmed, that even when suicidal patients disagreed with a professional's decisions, their primary focus was on the professional's *motivations*: actions taken out of perceived caring for the patient were excused, even if they weren't helpful, while a provider whose actions or failure to act was perceived as arising from self-interest or indifference were deeply resented. This was true in the case of either actions or omissions: involuntary interventions or failure to respond. For example, one woman told me

> I said, I am killing myself, and none of them asked the hard
> questions. Every time I said I was suicidal, no one asked me any
> of the hard questions . . . I thought they didn't care, I just want to
> go away, I just want to be gone. I wanted them to ask me, no one
> ever asked me. I told them I was suicidal for three months straight,
> I said this is not my chronic suicidality that you listen to all the
> time, this is acute suicidal, this needs to end, I am bad for people,
> before I get grandkids and harm them, I harm other people just
> by existing because of my pain. I told my therapist I am saying
> goodbye to you now. My therapist said call your case manager at 6
> o'clock. I said I will never see you again, she didn't call the police.
> That would have meant I existed and someone cared.[127]

Another woman deeply resented being involuntarily hospitalized, but the underlying feeling was identical—the providers simply did not want to deal with her pain.

> When people say they are suicidal, that stops the conversation.
> They immediately go into crisis mode. Let's pack her off to the next

---

[124] Vanessa L. McGann, Nina Gutin, & John R. Jordan, *Guidelines for Postvention Care with Survivor Families after the Suicide of a Client, in* GRIEF AFTER SUICIDE: UNDERSTANDING THE CONSEQUENCES AND CARING FOR SURVIVORS (John R. Jordan & John L. McIntosh eds., 2011).

[125] Bongar & Stolberg, *supra* note 114.

[126] Charles W. Lidz, Edward P. Mulvey, et al., *Factual Sources of Psychiatric Patients' Perceptions of Coercion in the Hospital Admission Process*, 155 AM J. PSYCHIATRY 1254 (1998).

[127] Interview with Beth Harris. Ms. Harris did call her case manager. Interview, July 16, 2014.

level of care, because I am not equipped to deal with this. Why
can't they say, this must be a terrible feeling, what do you mean by
saying you feel suicidal?[128]

My surveys, interviews, and experiences has made one thing clear: suicidal
people desperately want the freedom to talk about being suicidal and to receive
a compassionate and appropriate response, without being judged as difficult,
burdensome, or weak, and without having to be afraid of being involuntarily
detained or losing complete control of their lives. They are willing to negotiate for this freedom to speak: "I have told my therapist I was suicidal. But
she and I have come to an agreement that unless I am planning to go out in
the next ten minutes, that I am allowed to have my feelings, and allowed to
express them."[129] Although the people I interviewed had made many suicide
attempts and had ample contact with doctors, psychiatrists, therapists, and
psychologists, much of it negative, not one of the people I interviewed ever
even contemplated suing a mental health professional.

Furthermore, mental health professionals who fear liability do not understand the screening function performed by lawyers, who receive hundreds of
complaints against mental health professionals for every one that they take.
Skip Simpson, whose practice includes the entire country, turns down more
than eighty percent of the people who ask him to take their cases.[130] Clyde
Bergstresser, a leading plaintiff's malpractice lawyer in Massachusetts, says
the most frequent complaints he receives are "bad therapy or wrong diagnosis leading to wrong treatment. We reject essentially all of these."[131] He rarely
takes suicide cases, because "they are tough cases to win."[132] The cases that
lawyers love—those involving therapists having sex with patients—are filed
more often, not because having sex with a patient is the most common error
made by a mental health professional, but because those are the cases most
likely to succeed.

Reading over literally hundreds and hundreds of cases and summaries
of cases,[133] I was struck by the disparity between the kind of liability that
mental health professionals fear and the actions for which mental health professionals are actually sued in a suicide case. For example, psychiatrists who
see patients on an outpatient basis usually think that liability revolves around
failing to institutionalize a patient who later kills himself or herself. The fact

---

[128] Interview with Beckie Child. Aug. 30, 2012.

[129] *Id.*

[130] Personal communication from Skip Simpson to the author. Feb. 8, 2014, confirmed Nov. 6, 2015.

[131] Personal communication from Clyde Bergstresser to the author (Mar. 27, 2014).

[132] *Id.*

[133] When a case is tried to a jury, or settled, it is not "reported" in the way that a
judge's written decisions are reported. However, attorneys on one or both sides
write up the case for a data base of jury verdicts.

of the matter, as court cases repeat ad nauseam, is that mental health professionals are not sued for their decisions or the outcomes of their decisions, but for the process (or lack of process) by which the decision is made.[134] This decision-making process must be clearly documented. And, as I mentioned earlier, even if you look at malpractice cases in terms of decisions, it is not hospitalization decisions (whether admission or discharge), but medication decisions, that predominate.[135]

Perhaps this reflects the changing role of psychiatrists. One psychiatrist once told me bitterly that his professional function has devolved to "a prescription pad with legs." More patients are being seen by social workers, psychologists, or other counselors for therapy, while psychiatrists, who are expensive, are seen for very brief visits for medication. Thus, one reason that psychiatrists give patients prescriptions for several months' worth of medications is that they only see them once every several months, and for fifteen minutes of "medication management" at that.[136] In fact, psychiatry as a profession has sued the insurance industry on several occasions for refusing to reimburse a psychiatrist for psychotherapy provided in the same visit as medical and medication management, even though the insurance company charges the patient two separate copayments for each service.[137] Insurance companies have, as a matter of settled policy, made it very difficult for patients to receive long term therapy from psychiatrists (or anyone else) over a long period of time; the attorney general of New York has sued and settled a number of cases with major insurance companies involving parity of benefits for mental health treatment.

Because insurance companies have forced the division of mental health treatment's two basic functions—therapy and medication—between two individuals, they should either pay for the combined functions in one visit or pay for the psychiatrist and therapist to consult with each other as necessary

---

[134] Sheron v. Lutheran Med. Ctr., 18 P.3d 796, 801 (Colo. App. 2000) ("defendants argue that ... plaintiff's case was premised on the alleged negligence in discharging Sheron from the hospital. This argument mischaracterizes plaintiff's claims. Rather than focusing on the discharge itself, plaintiff more specifically alleged that defendants breached their duty to perform an adequate mental status examination and risk assessment").

[135] The decision to have sex with a patient leads more often to professional discipline and loss of licensure than to malpractice litigation, but when the decision to have sex with patient is followed by the patient's suicide, it's a good bet that litigation looms in the professional's future.

[136] Davisson v. Nicholson, 310 S.W.3d 543, 547 (Tex. App. 2010) (therapist and clinic continued to provide Adderall prescriptions over a five-year period despite only seeing patient two to three times); *Mazella*, 122 A.D.3d 1358 (psychiatrist continued to prescribe medications despite not seeing the patient for ten years).

[137] American Psychiatric Association v. Anthem Health Plans, No. 3-13-cv-00494-JBA (2013). Judge Arterton dismissed this case in 2014.

over medication. Fifteen minutes every few months is simply not enough for a psychiatrist to have an adequate understanding of the patient's current situation and condition to prescribe appropriate medications. Psychiatrists are on the liability hook if a patient commits suicide using the drugs they prescribed; they should be reimbursed for the process of receiving the information necessary to make those judgments. Lack of coordination among care providers is one of the leading causes of medical errors in the country, in psychiatry as well as in medicine. Policymakers and legislators need to be pressing insurance companies to reimburse for coordination, and requiring these companies to do so as necessary for reasonable care of the patient.

Psychiatric Malpractice and the Suicidal Patient: Distinctions Between Medical Malpractice and Psychiatric Malpractice

In some states, such as New York, and Ohio in the case of a patient who harmed others, plaintiffs have a more difficult burden to prove psychiatric malpractice than medical malpractice. In New York, courts hold that as long as psychiatrists apply their professional medical judgment, they cannot be found liable, regardless of the outcome,[138] and liability only attaches to decisions "without proper medical foundation." The classic formulation of this standard is

> prediction of the future course of a mental illness is a professional judgment of high responsibility and in some instances it involves a measure of calculated risk. If a liability were imposed on the physician or the State each time the prediction of future course of mental disease was wrong, few releases would ever be made and the hope of recovery and rehabilitations of a vast number of patients would be impeded and frustrated.[139]

This standard is not a free pass: it does require a careful examination of the patient, contemplation of various forms of treatment, and a reasoned choice among those forms of treatment.[140]

---

[138] Thomas v. Reddy, 86 A.D.3d 602 (N.Y. App. 2d Dept. 2011); Derney v. Terk, 42 A.D.3rd 335, 336 (N.Y. App. 1st Div. 2007); *Kovachevich*, 116 A.D.3d 182, at 190–91.

[139] Centeno v. City of New York, 369 N.Y.S.2d 710 (N.Y. App. 1975) (dismissing malpractice action when patient was discharged and later committed suicide).

[140] O'Sullivan v. Presbyterian Hosp., 634 N.Y.S.2d 101 (N.Y. App. Div. 1995) (hospital and doctor negligently diagnosed and treated severely depressed man who subsequently committed suicide; although mere errors in judgment do not give rise to liability, failure to conform to professional standards of conduct would support malpractice claim).

The Alabama Supreme Court has noted the self-evident truth that "a medical malpractice action based on a patient's suicide is different from a general medical malpractice action because in the former the patient's death is at his own hands."[141] This makes issues of causation much more difficult to prove, in part because of the long-standing tort doctrine that an intentional act such as suicide breaks the chain of causation from the original negligence.[142]

Another critical distinction is that in most medical interactions, the patient can be supposed to share the doctor's goal of making the patient better, but that some suicidal patients only want to mislead the doctors.[143] As I state below, mental health professionals should not be liable for relying on the self-reports of their outpatients.

The Distinction Between Liability for Inpatient Suicide and Outpatient Suicide

Many (but not all) state courts distinguish between liability for inpatient suicide and outpatient suicide. This is phrased in many different ways. Although generally each individual is legally responsible for his or her own actions and has no duty to control the actions of anyone else,[144] courts have held that mental health professionals do have both the ability and responsibility to control psychiatric inpatients.[145] Some courts point to the fact of custody—jail, prison, or a hospital or psychiatric facility[146]—as creating the responsibility. Others hold that people who are hospitalized for psychiatric reasons by definition cannot fulfill their normal responsibilities to care for themselves, and that hospitals have held themselves out as being able to protect people in these situations.[147]

---

[141] *Patton*, 958 So.2d 303, at 312.
[142] See Chapter 1, pp. 22–23, for detailed discussion of this doctrine, which continues to be raised in suicide malpractice cases, see *Huddle* (Miss. 2014).
[143] People's Bank of Bloomington v. Damera, 581 N.E.2d 426, 429 (Ill. App. 1991); *Wilkins*, 889 A.2d 245.
[144] Lenoci v. Leonard, 21 A.3d 694 (Vt. 2011) (eighteen-year-old girl does not have the legal duty to prevent the suicide of her fifteen-year-old friend).
[145] MacNamara v. Honeyman, 406 Mass. 43 (1989) (duty to keep hospitalized suicidal patient on one-to-one when boyfriend notified staff that she had made suicide attempt the day before her death and she had prior suicide attempts).
[146] See, e.g., DeMontiney v. Desert Care Manor Convalescent Ctr., 695 P.2d 255 (Ariz. 1985) (specific duty of care placed on "institutions" to avoid suicide), applied in Cohen v. Maricopa County, 228 Ariz. 53 (Ariz. App. 2011) (no duty of care to boy released from involuntary inpatient treatment who committed suicide the day after crisis evaluation determined he did not need further inpatient treatment).
[147] Maunz v. Perales, 76 P.3d 1027, 1033 (Kan. 2003); Tomfohr v. Mayo Found., 450 N.W.2d 121, 125 (Minn. 1990) (holding on the facts of that case that the mentally ill patient admitted to locked hospital ward for suicidal ideations "lacked the capacity to be responsible for his own well-being"); Gregoire v. City of Oak Harbor, 244 P.3d 924, 937 (Wash. 2010).

In contrast, people who live in a community are assumed to take responsibility for their own lives.[148] They are not, and cannot be, shadowed by their mental health professionals.[149] Courts recognize and understand that, as a practical matter, mental health professionals are not in a position to control their patient's lives in the community. Thus in some states, courts hold as a matter of law that mental health professionals cannot be held legally responsible for the suicides of their outpatients.[150] In other states, courts decline to create such a hard and fast rule, often over strong dissents,[151] finding that this kind of exclusion from liability is a legislative responsibility.[152] An exception arises when there is a special relationship between the two parties, such as parents and their children; in some cases, therapists are held to have such a "special relationship" with their patients.

There *should* be a major distinction between the duties of hospitals and mental health professionals toward a patient who is hospitalized and toward an outpatient. The assumptions about the severity of the patient's condition, and his or her ability to manage it with help, inherent in being hospitalized, especially involuntary hospitalization, the degree of control over the patient, and the very reason for hospitalization of a suicidal patient—often explicitly "to keep the patient safe"—counsel in favor of imposing reasonable duties on professionals and hospitals to take measures that will protect patients in their custody without unduly interfering with treatment.[153] At the same time, there are different ways of keeping patients safe, which we will discuss next. When the measures taken to enhance patient safety interfere with treatment and recovery, then they must be balanced with those goals and some risks taken to increase the chances that the patient can function safely on discharge.

---

[148] *Mulhern v. Catholic Health Initiatives*, 799 N.W.2d 104 (Iowa 2011); *Maunz*, 76 P.3d 1027, 276 Kan. 313.

[149] Farwell v. Un, 902 F.2d 282, 288 (4th Cir. 1990) (rejecting plaintiff's contention that doctor should have followed up to ensure that man who promised he would check himself into a hospital had actually done so); *Estate of Haar*, 141 N.M. App. 252.

[150] For example, Iowa, *Mulhern*, 799 N.W.2d 104; Mississippi *Truddle*, 150 So.3d 692 (*en banc*) (distinguishing cases involving patients in hospital custody from outpatients and holding that there cannot be liability as a matter of law where there is no control over the person); New Hampshire, *Maloney*, 156 N.H. 599; New Mexico, *Estate of Haar*, 141 N.M. App. 252; Weitz v. Lovelace Health System, 214 F.3d 1175, 1181 (10th Cir. 2000) (predicting New Mexico state courts would adopt such a distinction); and in North Carolina, Muse v. Charter Hosp., 452 SE2d 589 (N.C. App. 1995) (duty exists in inpatient case where hospital discharged patient because his insurance coverage had expired).

[151] *White*, 975 S.W.2d 525, at 530–31.

[152] Peterson v. Reeves, 727 S.E.2d 171 (Ga. App. 2012).

[153] Some measures, such as ensuring a safe physical environment, or maintaining the patient on one to one observation, can be taken without detriment to the patient. Others, such as removing clothing or personal possessions, can have

As I recommend below, I agree with states finding that mental health professionals cannot be held liable for the suicides of their outpatients, if the assertion is that a professional who was providing regular care and treatment focused on the patient's stated complaints was negligent in failing to involuntarily detain a competent patient. If a therapist is conscientiously trying to help a suicidal patient, there should be no duty to involuntarily commit a patient except in the extremely rare case that the patient is clearly incompetent.[154] Professionals should not be liable for the suicides of people who are going to work, like Elizabeth von Linden,[155] or to school like Kathryn Hobart.[156] It is admittedly more difficult when mental health professionals prescribe medications that themselves cause or increase the likelihood of suicidality.[157] However, a mental health professional who has diligently engaged in a true process of informed consent should be immune from liability, unless drugs known to be dangerous in combination with alcohol and certain drugs were prescribed to patients known to be active alcohol and drug abusers (see below). In most states, courts permit juries to apportion responsibility or liability between the professional and the patient, especially patients seen on an outpatient basis. This is the legal recognition of an extremely important clinical concept: that of sharing risk.

Patient Responsibility for Suicide: Sharing Risk

Contributory or Comparative Fault or Responsibility

One of the most frequent defenses asserted against a claim of negligence on the part of a hospital or mental health professional is that the patient was "contributorily" or "comparatively" negligent in killing himself or herself.[158] This language makes no sense. It is not necessarily illogical or problematic to hold the patient responsible for his or her purposeful and competent act, or perhaps even for an incompetent act if the incompetence was caused by the individual's willful act, such as ingesting a substantial amount of drugs or alcohol.[159] But whatever a person is doing when he or she attempts suicide,

adverse consequences and are discussed at p. 426. *DeMontiney,* 144 Ariz. 6, 695 P.2d 255 (1985).
[154] See Chapter 1 for detailed discussion about the rarity of incompetence among suicidal people.
[155] *Mulhern,* 799 N.W.2d 104.
[156] *Hobart,* 705 N.E.2d 907.
[157] See Chapter 7.
[158] *Hobart,* n. 156 ; *MacNamara,* 406 Mass. 43 (1989) (no comparative negligence when patient is hospitalized; duty to keep hospitalized suicidal patient on one-to-one when boyfriend notified staff that she had made suicide attempt the day before her death and she had prior suicide attempts).
[159] People v. Chaffey, 25 Cal. App. 4th 352 (Cal. App. 1994) (woman who takes 120 Xanax to kill herself can be convicted of driving under the influence of an

it's very rarely the result of negligence,[160] and framing the issue in those terms seems, as a legal matter, to completely misapprehend what is going on. It may be a mistake or a tragedy, but it is intentional.[161]

On the other hand, if the problem with talking about comparative or contributory negligence is that suicide basically isn't "negligent" unless it's accidental, the most common alternative language used by courts is "comparative fault."[162] There are jury instructions that state "the defendant must prove . . . that [name of person who committed suicide] was at fault in the taking of her own life."[163] While this usage correctly recognizes suicide as a voluntary and intentional act, it is unhelpful (to say the least) to talk about "fault" in the context of suicide. Worse than "comparative negligence," this kind of language reinforces the notion of suicide as a character flaw or weakness for which a person can be blamed in a court of law. Some courts use both "fault" and "negligence" language at the same time.[164]

I prefer the question to be phrased "comparative responsibility." Another way that courts have framed this issue is to ask whether the suicidal person has been relieved of the legal duty that all adults have under law: the "duty of self-care."[165] Many courts have held that hospitalized patients are relieved of this legal duty because the reason for hospitalization was precisely because the patient had lost the ability to care for himself or herself.[166] In the community,

---

    intoxicating substance because her ingestion was voluntary); People v. Jacob, 117 A.D.3d 1077 (N.Y. App. 2d Dept. 2014) (defendant who took sixty Xanax to commit suicide convicted of driving under the influence and other crimes; any error in admitting suicide notes into evidence was harmless).

[160] I once heard the story of a patient who was angry with ward staff for ignoring her, and, in conversation with a fellow patient, decided to "attempt suicide" by hanging herself; the plan was that her fellow patient would alert staff in the nick of time, and thereafter they would not ignore her. At the appointed hour, the fellow patient was distracted and forgot to tell staff. If this story is true, it might constitute a rare example of negligent suicide, although, under the law, it would be an accident, since there was never suicidal intent.

[161] The Supreme Court of Iowa disagrees, finding that the essence of negligence is "reasonable care" and that a "reasonably careful person would not hang herself." *Mulhern*, 799 N.W.2d 104, at 114. With all due respect, this leaves no room for intentional behavior. A reasonably careful person would probably also not murder another person, but that doesn't keep murder from being charged as an intentional act.

[162] *Champagne*, 513 N.W.2d, at 79 ("Comparison of fault between a suicide victim and a defendant, who has a duty of medical care toward that victim, is generally for the trier of fact.").

[163] *Mulhern*, 799 N.W.2d 104, at 110.

[164] *Lutheran Med. Ctr.*, 18 P.3d 796, at 801 ("[W]e hold that a patient who is treated by health care providers for suicidal ideations, and who later commits suicide, may be found comparatively negligent or at fault. . . ."); *Maunz*, 76 P.3d 1027, 1033.

[165] *Gregoire*, 244 P.3d 924, 937.

[166] Cowan v. Doering, 545 A.2d 159 (N.J. 1988); *Tomfohr*, 450 N.W.2d 121.

however, unless a person is obviously completely incompetent,[167] there is a "duty of self-care" which is balanced against the duty of mental health professionals.[168] The vast majority of states permit (correctly) the assessment of comparative responsibility as between therapists and patients.[169]

This is important, not only for the doctors and therapists, but for society to correctly understand the nature of suicidality. To be in enormous pain does not deprive a person of competence, or agency, or responsibility. In fact, it is precisely the feeling of responsibility—to children, parents, brothers, pets, and employers—that keeps suicidal people alive. To accept a legal doctrine that portrayed suicidal people as lacking all responsibility for their actions and choices would, in the long run, be a terrible thing for the people themselves, because it would support denying them agency and choice in their lives.

The Legal and Clinical Folly of "Contracting for Safety"

The so-called safety contract is an excellent example of a practice with no known clinical effectiveness in preventing suicide, that has the potential to short-circuit a thorough suicide assessment, and is certainly of no value whatsoever in any legal sense.[170] It may be of negative value in making an argument to a jury in a subsequent malpractice case, because even nonclinically trained people might question the value of making a contract to stay alive with a person known to be suicidal where the parties are in immensely unequal positions of power, there is no consideration,[171] and there is no way to enforce the contract in case it is breached (or, to put it more concisely, the jury might not understand the "incongruity between legal and clinical concepts of contract").[172]

---

[167] The courts have different ways of phrasing this: "completely devoid of reason," *Hobart v. Shinn* 705 N.E.2d 907; 185 Ill. 2d, at 290 (1998).

[168] *Mulhern,* 799 N.W.2d 104.

[169] *Id.; Hobart,* 705 N.E.2d 907.

[170] Michael Craig Miller, Douglas G. Jacobs, & Thomas Gutheil, *Talisman or Taboo: The Controversy of the Suicide-Prevention Contract,* 6 HARV. REV. PSYCHIATRY 78 (1998); E. J. Stanford, R. R. Goetz, & J. D. Bloom, *The No-Harm Contract in the Emergency Assessment of Suicidal Risk,* 55 J. CLIN. PSYCHIATRY 344 (1994); Robert I. Simon, *The Suicide Prevention Contract: Clinical, Legal and Risk-Management Issues,* 27 J. AM. ACAD. PSYCH. & LAW 445 (1999); PATRICIA W. IYER, ed., NURSING MALPRACTICE 364 (2d ed. 2001).

[171] "Consideration" is the legal term for a required element of a contract: the value or benefit that a party receives in exchange for giving up something of value to him or her. In the case of a "contract for safety" the suicidal person is not receiving anything of benefit from the other party. Staying alive is only valuable if he or she considers it valuable, but by definition, genuinely suicidal people don't perceive this as a benefit.

[172] Miller et al., *supra* note 170.

Breach of Duty

One of the extremely odd things about malpractice cases involving suicide is that they hardly ever actually look at what kind of treatment the mental health professional was providing to the suicidal patient, with the single enormous exception of medications. Yet even though there are evidence-based and research-supported treatment methods, such as dialectical behavior therapy (DBT) (which helped some of my interviewees enormously), cognitive behavior therapy (CBT) (which helped other interviewees very much), as well as promising new approaches, including the CAMS model[173] and peer support, and no one ever sues a mental health professional for failing to treat a suicidal patient with specific evidence-based suicide-related therapies. As a policy matter, there has to be a way to shift mental health services for suicidal people into some more helpful framework. One suggestion I have is to free outpatient therapists from the fear of liability for taking risks with their patients, which would permit them to have longer and more difficult conversations about suicide and to take risks and try innovative forms of treatment. Another is to force insurance companies to reimburse for conversations between therapists and psychiatrists, if the insurers have set up structures that divide the functions of therapy and medication.

If legislatures don't want to pass those kinds of laws, another idea would be to start suing mental health professionals for not focusing on providing existing evidence-based treatments for suicidality, such as CBT or DBT. There is research showing these treatments work better than "treatment as usual"[174] and people can be trained to provide these treatments. Why are insurance companies paying for involuntary, ineffective treatments when we have approaches that have been successful? Because insurance companies reimburse by diagnosis, and "wanting to die" is not a diagnosis. If people who want to die want to get help, they have to get a diagnosis of some kind, even if it doesn't fit. Once they are diagnosed, they get the treatment for that diagnosis, even if it doesn't help. And so it goes.

What Can and Should Be Expected of a Mental Health Professional?

We need to free talented and caring mental health professionals to do the good and innovative work that they can do. Most of the praise that my interviewees had for mental health professionals who helped them involved people

---

[173] CAMS stands for Collaborative Assessment and Management of Suicidality. See Chapter 9 for more detailed descriptions of each of these methods.
[174] See Chapter 9.

doing something different: taking risks, sharing their own history,[175] and helping out with practical problems.[176]

Mental Health Professionals Should Be Willing to Talk About Suicidality with Their Patients, Including but *Never* Limited to Assessment

People who are struggling to find a reason to stay alive don't want to be "assessed." They don't want to be asked endlessly if they have a plan, if they have the means, if they will contract for safety. They want to talk with someone who cares: about hope, about solving the problems that seem insoluble, about how to get through the night.

Mental Health Professionals Should Take into Account a Person's History of Substance Abuse When Prescribing Medication

Many things surprised me when I was researching this book. One of them was the number of suicide malpractice cases that involved individuals with prior histories of substance abuse and the rather carefree way that doctors who knew or should have known these histories prescribed substantial amounts of drugs that could be fatal when taken with alcohol or drugs of abuse.[177]

Mental health professionals and doctors rarely lose these cases (they rarely lose any malpractice case). Sometimes it is difficult to even tell whether the death was actually a suicide or an accidental overdose by a person with a chaotic and turbulent life. Sometimes the doctor prevailed because someone else's irresponsible prescriptions, rather than the doctor's own irresponsible prescriptions, had been used for the final overdose. Sometimes it was impossible to tell whose drugs had been used, the ones prescribed by the doctor or the ones obtained by less conventional means.

---

[175] Research shows that such self-disclosure can be helpful to patients, Erica Goode, "Therapists Redraw Line on Self-disclosure, New York Times, Jan. 1, 2002, http://www.nytimes.com/2002/01/01/health/therapists-redraw-line-on-self-disclosure.html?pagewanted=all; Edmund Howe, "Should Psychiatrists Self-Disclose?"8 Innov. Clin. Neurosci. 14 (2011).

[176] Interview with T.R. ("the hospital helped me find traveler's aid and helped me get to Indiana with my daughter, and a nurse at the hospital took her own time, she wasn't on the clock and took me down to the bus station. Stuff like that makes me sad because I haven't had a whole lot of people be nice to me so I don't know how to react."). Oct. 7, 2014.

[177] Paradise v. Estate of Vaziri, No. 30775 (Mich. App. Aug. 8, 2013) (*per curiam* unpublished) (man with prior history of substance abuse and abusing prescription medication goes to prior prescribing physician two days after discharge from involuntary hospitalization and obtains ninety Xanax pills; autopsy also notes presence of methadone, amphetamine, alprazolam, citalopram, and quetiapine in his blood).

Courts tend to be sympathetic to doctors and indifferent to patients in these scenarios, but I don't think they should be. Too many of these cases involve doctors who haven't seen the patient in years, or have never seen the patient at all,[178] prescribing drugs that could be dangerous or misused to people with a more-than-average likelihood of misusing them. Doctors who engage in these practices should not be immune from malpractice liability for the suicides of their patients. Providing prescription medications to patients you rarely see is the opposite of a doctor–patient relationship: they are not the result of caring, thoughtful reflection about a patient's problems. Maybe they are a way of getting rid of someone who just wants the drugs without taking the trouble to get to know them; maybe it's all the insurance company will pay for, but it's too potentially dangerous to patients to immunize doctors who do this from malpractice liability.

It is absolutely the case that some of these patients are difficult, abusive, and get thrown out of practices. Many of the people I interviewed recalled their substance-abusing days as harrowing and inextricably intertwined with chaotic and violent childhoods. It is hard to work with people who have these trauma histories; it takes dedication, compassion, humility, and understanding, and sometimes with all of that people still kill themselves. The therapists who try hard to actually work with people who have been damaged and scarred by trauma and who struggle with depression and PTSD should be insulated from liability if the person commits suicide. The doctor who just writes prescriptions to a person he or she might not be able to pick out of a lineup, or who writes multiple prescriptions for powerful drugs to a patient he knows or should know has an alcohol or substance abuse problem should not benefit from any kind of liability protection.

Mental Health Professionals Should Ask Questions About the Availability of Guns

It is increasingly considered part of the standard of care for a patient who may be suicidal to ask about the presence of guns in the house,[179] and courts have supported the requirement that parents or spouses must be told to remove guns in the house.[180] Even the infamous "Docs v. Glocks" case, in which the Eleventh Circuit Court supported a Florida law forbidding medical professionals from unnecessarily asking about the presence of guns in a household,[181]

---

[178] Schmidt v. Klinman & Ahlawat, No. 05C2134 (N.D. Ill. Dec. 2, 2005) (suing doctors who prescribed Xanax and Ultram through an Internet service without physical examination; plaintiff moves to preclude defendants from introducing evidence these drugs were used in a suicide attempt).

[179] Robert I. Simon, *Gun Safety Management with Patients at Risk for Suicide*, 37 SUICIDE & LIFE-THREATENING BEHAV. 518 (2007).

[180] Randall v. Benton, 147 N.H. 786 (2002); *Maunz*, 76 P.3d 1027.

[181] Wollschlaeger v. Florida, 760 F.3d 1195 (11th Cir. 2014).

explicitly recognized that "good medical care clearly requires inquiry . . . in the case of a suicidal patient."[182]

I had initially thought that the relevant question was whether or not there were guns in the house, until I was admonished by various interviewees about regionally appropriate questions. Justin Mikel, an interviewee who lives in North Carolina, said, "In Avery County you don't say, 'Do you have a gun?' You say, 'How many guns do you have?'"[183] My stepdaughter, a New Hampshire emergency medical technician, told me the relevant question would be, "Are your guns loaded?"

Of course, even if asking about guns or other lethal means at a person's house is part of the standard of care, a plaintiff would have to prove that breach of the standard—failure to ask—proximately caused the individual's suicide, which would require family members to testify that they would have acted to remove or secure the weapons. It seems very odd, but families who know their children or siblings or parents are seriously suicidal often do nothing to secure their weapons.[184]

Warning and advising family or whoever will be present with a suicidal person about access to lethal means of self-destruction should be part of any careful and individualized discharge planning. The mental health professional is certainly not a guarantor of safety, but an adviser and counselor to help remind an often stunned family about what they should attend to in the days ahead.

What Should Not Be Expected of a Mental Health Professional

Courts Recognize That Mental Health Professionals Cannot Involuntarily Detain a Patient Who Does Not Meet the Commitment Standard

One of the more successful defenses raised by mental health professionals is that they cannot simply involuntarily detain people willy-nilly: in every state there is a statute that strictly prescribes the standards for involuntary detention.[185] If a defendant mental health professional testifies credibly that the behavior and presentation of an individual who later committed suicide could not have supported involuntary commitment, courts frequently dismiss cases on summary judgment or even reverse jury verdicts against them.[186] Mental health professionals should be aware of clinical recommendations against hospitalizing contingent and chronically suicidal individuals as well,[187] and should document when those considerations enter into their decisionmaking.

---

182 *Id.* at 1216.
183 Interview with Justin Mikel. Dec. 1, 2013.
184 See Chapter 9.
185 See Chapter 2.
186 *Rodriguez-Escobar*, 392 S.W.3rd 109.
187 See Chapter 7.

Mental Health Professionals Should Not Be Held Responsible When Patients Lie to Them

Case law reflects that patients deliberately lie about their suicidality all the time.[188] It's understandable that patients will be less than candid with someone who has the power to lock them up, but while a skilled mental health professional is perceptive, the relationship is primarily supportive. To be constantly on the lookout for lies risks transforming a therapy session into an adversarial interrogation. Courts have consistently rejected arguments that mental health professionals have a duty to ferret out deception in their patients.[189]

At the same time, suicidality is often an impulsive act, and patients aren't necessarily lying when they report that they are not suicidal, at the time they report it. In Peter Yurkowski's case, after telling Dr. Curell he was safe in the community, he had an evening with his wife and children that reminded him of all that he had lost. He might not have been deliberately deceiving the doctor when he reported being safe; circumstances change.

This can be—and has been—captured as a matter of legal doctrine in various ways. It can be captured as a duty, or shared responsibility with the mental health professional. The patient's responsibility is to be honest with treating professionals, or to seek help when things are going south, or, put another way, a patient "has a duty to cooperate with a treating physician."[190] A patient who is able to has "a duty to respond accurately to questions and tell the truth."[191] So in states with shared responsibility (contributory "fault" or "negligence"), a patient's lying about his or her suicidality should negate liability.

Thus, acting on a reasonable belief of a patient's reassurances should negate negligence, unless the actions would be negligent if the patient were not suicidal. For example, you can believe that a patient with a history of substance abuse or alcoholism is not suicidal and still negligently prescribe medications, which when combined with alcohol or drugs the patient would be likely to take, would be dangerous to ingest.

Sources of Hospital and Institutional Liability for Suicide

Hospitals are distinctly different from mental health professionals, especially outpatient treaters, because hospitals, by definition, have the patient there

---

[188] *Hobart*, 705 N.E.2d 907; *Wilkins*, 889 A.2d 245; *Paradiso v. Estate of Vaziri* (unpublished); *Maunz*, 76 P.3d 1027.

[189] *Teal*, 772 N.W.2d 57, at 60 (rejecting argument that "defendants . . . should have recognized that Teal's increasingly positive outlook on life . . . was an act").

[190] Elbaor v. Smith, 845 S.W.2d 240, 245 (Tex. App. 1993).

[191] Axelrad v. Jackson, 142 S.W.3rd 418, 424 (Tex. App. 2004) (gathering cases).

twenty-four hours a day, and sometimes against his or her will. The custodial responsibility for the individual means the hospital's obligations are considerably broader than those of the individual mental health professional.

For state hospitals, involuntary deprivation of liberty creates a constitutional obligation to keep the person safe, free from unreasonable bodily restraint, and (more controversially) provide the kind of treatment that might enable the individual to be released.[192] The individual also has, under some court decisions, the right not to have his or her condition deteriorate in the hospital setting. [193] Furthermore, because the individual is not free, his or her living space must be reasonably safe and the hospital must do a reasonable job of keeping tabs on the patient's whereabouts.

Unobservant "Patient Observation"

These two requirements form the core of many lawsuits against hospitals related to the suicides of hospital patients. If one of the main points of hospitalization is to keep an eye on someone considered very likely to harm him or herself (which is the common understanding of the reason for hospitalization, as opposed to providing the kind of treatment that makes a person want to live), then a first step is to know where the person is and what he or she is up to.

"Fifteen minute checks" and Other Fictions of Inpatient Life

A clear example of the breakdown between policy and practice is the number of suicides and attempted suicides committed while the patient is on fifteen-minute checks or even one-to-one observation.[194] As anyone who has spent any time in psychiatric facilities will tell you, lots of things come up on a ward, and fifteen-minute checks often do not take place every fifteen minutes. Then matters are infinitely worsened (from a liability perspective) by the

---

[192] *Youngberg v. Romeo*, 457 U.S. 307 (1982), *see* Susan Stefan, "Leaving Civil Rights to the 'Experts': From Deference to Abdication under the Professional Judgment Standard," 102 Yale L.J. 639 (1992).

[193] Three justices concurred in the Youngberg decision but further opined that the patient's constitutional rights included the right to treatment necessary to preserve basic skills with which he or she entered the facility, 457 U.S. at 327. This was adopted by several circuits, *Society for Good Will to Retarded Children v. Cuomo*, 737 F.2d 1239 (2nd Cir. 1984).

[194] Stefano Esposito, *$4.2 Million Verdict for Lawyer Who Attempted Suicide in Psych Ward*, CHICAGO SUN-TIMES, May 7, 2015, http://chicago.suntimes.com/news/7/71/587415/4-2-million-verdict-lawyer-attempted-suicide-psych-ward ("Staff were supposed to check on Sandler every 15 minutes but failed to do so. A nurse discovered Sandler in a pool of his own blood in the early morning hours of Aug. 7, four hours after he began stabbing himself").

aide or nurse writing in the records that the checks did take place, including one case where a series of fifteen-minute patient checks were documented for several hours after the patient was dead.[195] In another case, a nurse testified to having observed the patient alive at 9:43 p.m., while the nurse who was supposed to do fifteen-minute checks testified that at 9:45 p.m. the patient was dead, hanged by a bedsheet from a door.[196] In a rare case where nurses were found liable for malpractice, a woman on fifteen-minute checks for suicidality managed to pry both her eyes out during the thirty minutes in which she was left alone.[197]

The majority of inpatient suicides on psychiatric wards are actually committed when the patient is supposed to be on fifteen-minute checks. In at least one notorious case, nurses and doctors faced criminal charges for forging records indicating a patient had been checked every fifteen minutes when, in fact, she had been dead for several hours.[198] I have personally witnessed staff at the end of a shift initialing a list of fifteen-minute check sheets for patients they were supposed to be watching.

Group Activities Outside the Hospital

Like patient clothing, group activities off the hospital grounds present a different and more nuanced picture than the negligent failure to perform fifteen-minute checks, because trips to the community are beneficial, sometimes eagerly anticipated by patients as the only way to get off a dull unit with the television set blaring in the day hall, and offer some diluted form of community reintegration. No matter how many staff members are sent on these outings, there will never be sufficient staff to thwart a patient determined to kill himself or herself by, for example, saying "I have to vomit" and, when the car pulls over, jumping out suddenly and jumping

[195] NEW YORK CITY DEPARTMENT OF INVESTIGATION, DOI's INVESTIGATION INTO THE CIRCUMSTANCES SURROUNDING THE DEATH OF ESMIN GREEN (June 2009), http://www.nyc.gov/html/doi/downloads/pdf/pr_esmingreen_finalrpt.pdf. In this case doctors were also shown to have falsely documented medical and psychiatric evaluations of the woman. None of this false documentation would have been exposed if the woman had not died, on videotape.

[196] Graham v. Northwestern Mem'l Hosp., 2012 Ill. App. 102609 (Feb. 3, 2012).

[197] Bernadette & John French v. Med. Ctr. of Delaware d/b/a/ Wilmington Hosp., (D. De. 1994). The verdict exceeded a million dollars. This case was cited in IYER, *supra* note 170, at 365.

[198] John Marzulli, *Kings County Hospital Doctors, Nurses, Facing Charges in Esmin Green Death-by-Neglect Case*, N. Y. DAILY NEWS, June 19, 2009, http://www.nydailynews.com/news/crime/kings-county-hospital-doctors-nurses-facing-charges-esmin-green-death-by-neglect-case-article-1.375055 (noting that a nurse named Gonzalo admitted making three false entries in Green's chart over a forty-five-minute period of time stating that Green was fine).

off a bridge.[199] There are endless permutations to these kinds of events, and unless all patients are always unreasonably limited and constrained, there will always be some risk.

Patient Passes and Grounds Privileges

A variation on inadequate observation occurs when patients are taken out in groups to smoke or to events and staff fails to keep tabs on a patient who wanders away and kills himself or herself,[200] or when a patient is given grounds privileges on the campus of the hospital and uses the opportunity to commit suicide.[201]

A different situation is presented by the issue of a patient granted a pass to leave the facility who kills himself or herself. This was a risk taken (successfully) by Dr. Curell when he released Peter Yurkowski to find an apartment in the community. The fact that Yurkowski succeeded in doing so and came back to the hospital unharmed, could and should have been one reason why Curell took the risk a week later to discharge Yurkowski to the apartment he had located.

Some patients do kill themselves on passes from the hospital.[202] If staff members made a professional assessment of the patient's readiness to go out on pass, the fact that they were mistaken should not, in the absence of other evidence, lead to a finding of liability. Passes are a reasonable way of assessing a patient's readiness for discharge, and, like group activities, are a necessary and worthwhile risk for the benefit of all patients.

Wandering Away and Elopement

Suicide by an eloping patient, whether from a hospital, ED, or other custodial setting, is qualitatively different from patient suicide as a result of a

[199] Bramlette v. Charter Med. Columbia, 393 S.E.2d 914 (S.C. 1990).
[200] Balzarini v. Faulkner Hosp., 2009 Jury Verdicts LEXIS 425348 (defense verdict in case where woman with previous suicide attempt jumped off a garage while walking with a group and was injured; roommate claimed woman had said she was suicidal and roommate relayed to family who told hospital but there was no record of this in her file; because the woman had no ID bracelet when she jumped, she was admitted to hospital for medical care as Jane Doe and family only found out because a family friend worked at the hospital; hospital said woman had denied suicidality, used her privileges responsibly, and suicide attempt was not foreseeable and admitted lack of ID bracelet unrelated to her injuries).
[201] Morra v. Harrop, 791 A.2d 472 (R.I. 2002).
[202] Foster v. Charter Med. Corp., 601 So.2d 435 (Ala. 1992); Ryan J. Foley, *Iowa Hospital to Pay $250k, Apologize in Patient's Suicide*, WASH. TIMES, Jan. 14, 2015, http://www.washingtontimes.com/news/2015/jan/14/u-iowa-hospital-to-pay-250k-apologize-in-patients-/.

pass or grounds privileges. In the latter case, a decision was considered and made that the benefits to the patient of increasing autonomy and responsibility and opportunities outweighed the risk of suicide. Elopement, obviously, is not the result of any professional decision, and ought to be preventable. Nevertheless, hospitals have avoided liability even in cases of elopement by thoughtful and individualized decision-making, for example, the decision not to notify police about an eloped patient because of that patient's extreme fear of police and the likelihood of escalation.[203] I think that these are the kinds of individualized professional judgments that should protect facilities and their staff from liability.

Transfer and Transportation

It surprised me how many suicides took place in the context of transporting an individual from one place to the other,[204] often because no beds were available in the sending facility. My guess is that this is a particularly high-risk situation because it is a set of transitions between individuals who don't work together as a matter of routine, and people may be confused about how much information about the patient to convey to the transportation personnel. Or it may be because the patient is confused and uncertain about what is happening next, and more agitated and anxious. Or it could be the proximity to highways and bridges. But all too often, as the patient is being received into the vehicle, or discharged from it, the patient leaps out and runs away.

---

[203] Demers v. Khreim, 2011 M.A. Jury Verdicts Rev. LEXIS 108 (Jan. 13, 2011) (verdict for defendant in case where hospital failed to notify police after patient eloped because staff made professional judgment that, given the patient's intense fear of police, it would destroy the therapeutic alliance, and plaintiffs had specifically instructed defendant not to call police).

[204] *Hillman v. Berkshire Med. Ctr.*, 2012 MA JAS Pub LEXIS 1 (Hampden Cty Dist. Ct. Jan. 2012)(settlement of $20,000 when patient was being transferred by ambulance because there were no beds at defendant's facility and patient leaped out of the ambulance and was found dead in the Hoosic River nine days later); Dumas v. Adirondack Med. Ctr., 89 A.D.3d 1184 (N.Y. App. 3rd Dept. 2011) (suicidal person strapped into ambulance with standard safety belt across waist and ankles freed herself and jumped to her death from the ambulance); Dimilla v. Fairfield, 2010 Jury Verdicts LEXIS 33866 (Plymouth Sup. Ct., Feb. 10, 2010) (suicidal patient needed inpatient bed but no bed was available; defendant employee of less secure facility took patient there, where he escaped and ran in front of a truck; defendant psychiatrist who initially evaluated the patient and signed a blank discharge order and transfer papers was held not liable, but emergency physicians who permitted patient to be taken to less secure facility were not authorized to make this decision); *1,000,000+ Jury Verdict in Gross Negligence EMT/Wrongful Death Ambulance Case*, JACKSON WILSON LAW FIRM (July 25, 2013), http://jacksonandwilson.com/negligent-ambulance-wrongful-death/

Environmental Hazards

Among the most tragic cases are those involving suicides in hospitals that have not taken elementary precautions to cover exposed pipes or install breakaway shower rods. Environmental hazards can be addressed without impinging on patients' dignity or depriving them of any further liberty. There are ample resources and firms with expertise in making environments safe without making them institutionally repellent. Because this is such an important issue in suicide prevention, it is discussed in detail (along with the huge number of cases generated by suicides resulting from available means in hospitals) in Chapter 9.

Suicidal People in the Emergency Department

A number of cases involve people who commit suicide, either in the ED, upon eloping from the ED, or after being discharged from the ED.[205] Unsurprisingly, the liability picture in the first two situations is quite different from the third. The fact situations in the elopement and ED suicide cases tend to reflect deep structural, systemic problems with the hospital. For example, in one case, a patient who was experiencing cardiac problems after a suicide attempt was placed in a gurney in the hall of an ED for forty-eight hours awaiting a bed on the medical floor. He left the ED and hanged himself from a tree right outside the hospital entrance.[206]

Bringing suicidal people to the ED is not a great idea. Very few people I have interviewed have ever said the ED experience was helpful in any way, and ED staff have neither the environment, the training, nor the time to handle psychiatric crises. At most EDs, psychiatric patients usually comprise less than 10%—on the national average about 4%—of all the patients seen.[207] Emergency physicians are not psychiatric experts, and, unlike most of the defendant mental health professionals we have been discussing, probably have never even seen the individual before. They have far less time to undertake a comprehensive suicide risk assessment. They don't have a great atmosphere to establish a therapeutic alliance. This is particularly true of people who are brought in involuntarily.

Nevertheless, EDs see hundreds of thousands of suicidal people every year. One of the most urgent policy reforms that I advocate—in fact, I wrote an entire book about it—is to get psychiatric crises out of EDs and into

---

[205] *Wilkins,* 889 A.2d 245; *Providence Health Ctr.,* 262 S.W.3d 24; *White,* 975 S.W.2d 525; *Tolton v. Biodyne,* 48 F.3d. 937 (6th Cir.1995); Plante v. Charlotte Hungerford Hosp., 12 A.3d 885 (Conn. 2011); Carroll v. Paddock, 764 N.E2d 1118 (Ill. 2002); *Lutheran Med. Ctr.,* 18 P.3d 796, 801.

[206] Ruiz v. XYZ Hosp., 1997 Fl. Jury Verdicts Rev. 512 (Apr. 1997).

[207] See Stefan, *supra* note 118, for more than you would ever want to know about emergency departments and psychiatric patients.

community crisis evaluation, peer crisis respite, home visits, and wrap-around, and other less expensive and traumatic alternatives.[208]

Conclusion

Our supposed culture of autonomy in this country is in great tension with an increasing aversion to risk, with results as varied as rooting elderly people out of homes they have lived in for decades[209] to spiraling costs in health care caused by unnecessary medical tests, to taking off our shoes in airports, to detaining people in EDs for hours and even days without comfort or conversation when they are desolate and miserable and want to die.

If my recommendations from Chapter 2 are adopted, mental health professionals will only be able to detain individuals who are threatening suicide for three days to assess their competence and deter impulsive or drug- or alcohol-driven suicides. Mental health professionals will not be able to involuntarily commit based on suicidality alone, and therefore will not be subject to liability for failure to involuntarily commit a patient. In addition, states can also adopt the tort immunity statute I have written (see Appendix A) to free mental health professionals from the current counterproductive incentives that characterize our policy and legal framework relating to suicide.

---

[208] *Id.*
[209] GAWANDE, *supra* note 31, at 80–104.

7

Types of Suicide

"Suicidality is a symptom, but it is a symptom of many different things."

—Anonymous[1]

For me suicidal stuff had to do with big global stuff. Does it matter that I am alive? Am I making an impact? Is it ever going to matter? I made a sandcastle and the waves are going to come and wash it away. It's a spiritual challenge, it's about meaning. Most depressed suicidal people usually have (1) been massively traumatized; or (2) have this existential depression, they don't understand why they fit into this crazy-ass world. There is a cultural disconnect between what people really need and what they are expected to do in this culture, and that is kind of painful on an ongoing basis—the world is not working for me, if I decide I don't like capitalism, what am I supposed to do, how am I going to survive?

—Stephen McCrea[2]

My attempt was eight years ago this month . . . mine is a genetic disease. I suffer from depression, anxiety, I have some self-esteem issues. I don't do well with change. . . . My decision was not planned out, it was a snap decision. My parents were getting divorced, I was living alone, I was in a relationship with a guy who was very bad for me. I kept sinking deeper and deeper into this black hole. . . . I was thinking, can a car take me out, I had this pain, it's hard to describe, I was in such despair. I didn't want to

---

[1] Interview with Anonymous (Dec. 19, 2014).
[2] Interview with Stephen McCrea (Aug. 22, 2014).

be here anymore. I just popped handfuls of Tylenol in my mouth. I thought I wasn't going to wake up.

Lex Wortley[3]

Introduction

One hundred and fifty years ago, Emil Durkheim proposed four major categories of suicide: egoistic, anomic, altruistic, and fatalistic.[4] Today, suicide is understood to be more like cancer: a hundred or more different conditions grouped under one insufficient, stigmatized and frightening word. As with cancer, there are few generalizations that are universally applicable. Edwin Shneidman, the recognized dean of the study of suicide, insisted repeatedly that

> [s]uicide is not a disease. It is not like a stomachache or a headache or some special physiological state. Each suicide is sui generis. Its reasons, like the mind itself, cannot be categorized. Clinical labels are specious, and to build a profession on them is to put a skyscraper on sandy soil.[5]

The most important policy implication of this assertion is that we must cease making generalizations about "suicide prevention" and "suicidal people" and start paying much more attention to context. This is already happening: we understand that suicide in veterans needs to be addressed differently than suicide among college students or prisoners or people with terminal illness. It seems obvious that different people in different situations are suicidal for different reasons (which itself underscores the limited utility of a strictly biological model connecting suicide to depression or some other form of serious mental illness).

There are many ways to illustrate this central truth. One is as follows:[6]

> The suicide rate in the United States is 12.6/100,000 (2012),[7] 1.6% of all deaths.

---

[3] Interview with Lex Wortley (Feb. 25, 2014).
[4] EMIL DURKHEIM, LE SUICIDE (1897) (egoistic, anomic, altruistic, and fatalistic).
[5] Thomas Curwen, *Psychache*, June 3, 2001, www.cartercenter.org/health/mental_health/archive/documents/psychache_curwen.html
[6] I have found statistics about suicide to be remarkably inconsistent, even as between agencies of the Executive Branch, let alone comparing World Health Organization (WHO) statistics about a nation's suicide rate with the internal statistics of that country.
[7] S. L. Murphy, K. D. Kochanek, J. Xu, & M. Heron, *Deaths: Final Data for 2012*, 63 NATIONAL VITAL STATISTICS REPORTS 9 (Aug. 31, 2015), *available at* http://www.cdc.gov/nchs/data/nvsr63/nvsr63_09.pdf. This is the 2012 suicide rate

The suicide rate for adults in the United States between the ages of forty-five and sixty-four is 19.1/100,000 (2013).[8]

The suicide rate for blacks in the United States is 5.4/100,000 (2013).[9]

The suicide rate for Hispanics in the United States is 5.2/100,000 (2011).

The suicide rate for Native Americans/Alaskan natives is 10.6/100,000 (2011).

The suicide rate for non-Hispanic whites is 14.49/100,000 (13.88 in 100,000 age-adjusted) (2011).[10]

The suicide rate in Wyoming is 29.6/100,000 (2012).[11]

The suicide rate in Washington, D.C., is 5.7/100,000 (2012).[12]

The suicide rate in Oregon is 17.1/100,000 (2010).[13]

The assisted-suicide rate in Oregon is 2.19/100,000 (2013).[14]

The suicide rate in the United States for people living in the United States but born outside the United States is 6.7/100,000 (2011).

The suicide rate in the United States for people living in the United States and born here is 13.4/100,000 (2011).

The suicide rate for men in the world is 15.0/100,000 (2013).[15]

---

per 100,000 for all races and all sexes in the United States, depending on which federal government statistics you rely on, see Healthy People 2020, *Suicides (MHMD-1)*, Suicides Peo https://www.healthypeople.gov/2020/leading-health-indicators/2020-lhi-topics/Mental-Health/data#MHMD-1 or J. L. McIntosh & C. W. Drapeau (for the American Association of Suicidology, *U.S.A. Suicide: 2011 Official Final Data* (2014), www.suicidology.org/Portals/14/docs/Resources/FactSheets/2011OverallData.pdf, which is based on the Centers for Disease Control and Prevention, *Injury Prevention & Control: Data & Statistics (WISQARS)* [Web-based Injury Statistics Query and Reporting System], www.cdc.gov/injury/wisqars/index.html (accessed June 17, 2014).

[8] American Foundation for Suicide Prevention, *Facts and Figures* (2015), https://www.afsp.org/understanding-suicide/facts-and-figures.

[9] *Id.*

[10] K. D. Kochanek, S. L. Murphy, J. Xu, Deaths: Final Data for 2011, 63 NATIONAL VITAL STATISTICS REPORTS 3 (July 27, 2015), available at http://www.cdc.gov/nchs/data/nvsr/nvsr63/nvsr63_03.pdf.

[11] Centers for Disease Control and Prevention, *QuickStats: Age-Adjusted Suicide Rates, by State—United States, 2012*, MORBIDITY & MORTALITY W'KLY REP., available at http://www.cdc.gov/mmwr/preview/mmwrhtml/mm6345a10.htm.

[12] *Id.* at 10.

[13] OREGON PUBLIC HEALTH DIVISION, CENTER FOR PREVENTION AND HEALTH PROMOTION, INJURY AND VIOLENCE PREVENTION PROGRAM, SUICIDES IN OREGON: TRENDS AND RISK FACTORS—2012 REPORT (Nov. 2012), www.oregon.gov/oha/amh/CSAC%20Meeting%20Shedule/Suicide-in-Oregon-Report.pdf.

[14] OREGON DEPARTMENT OF HEALTH, OREGON'S DEATH WITH DIGNITY ACT—2013, http://public.health.oregon.gov/ProviderPartnerResources/EvaluationResearch/DeathwithDignityAct/Documents/year16.pdf.

[15] World Health Organization, *Global Health Observatory (GHO) Data* (2015), www.who.int/gho/mental_health/en/.

The suicide rate for men in the United States is 19.4/100,000.

The suicide rate for all men in Washington, D.C., is 7.2/100,000 (2011).

The suicide rate for white men in the United States is 22.99/100,000 (2011).[16]

The suicide rate for men older than the age of seventy-five is 36/100,000.

The suicide rate in Wyoming for men between the ages of eighty and eighty-four is 44/100,000 (2008–2012).[17]

The suicide rate for women in the United States is 5.2/100,000(2012).[18]

The suicide rate for women veterans is 28.7/100,000.[19]

The suicide rate for black women is 1.9/100,000.

The suicide rate for state prisoners is 15/100,000.

The suicide rate for police is about 17/100,000.[20]

The suicide rate for prisoners in jail is 43/100,000 (2011).[21]

The suicide rate for patients in hospitals is 100–400/100,000 admissions.[22]

---

[16] Kochanek et al., *supra* note 10.

[17] WYOMING DEPARTMENT OF HEALTH, PREVENTING SUICIDE IN WYOMING: 2014–2016 STATE SUICIDE PREVENTION PLAN 8 (July 2014), http://www.sprc.org/sites/sprc.org/files/WDH%20Suicide%20Prevention%202014-2016%20FINAL.pdf.

[18] World Health Organization, *Mental Health: Age-Standardized Suicide Rates (per 100,000 Population): 2012*, http://gamapserver.who.int/gho/interactive_charts/mental_health/suicide_rates/atlas.html.

[19] Alan Zarembo, "Suicide Rate of Female Veterans is Called 'Staggering,'" Los Angeles Times, June 8, 2015, www.latimes.com/nation/la-na-female-veteran-suicide-20150608-story.html#page=1. Although this report cited "new" government research, the fact is that female veterans were killing themselves at precisely this rate almost ten years previously, see Statement of Kara Zivin, Ph.D, Research Scientist, Dr. Kara Zivin's Testimony to the House Veteran's Affairs Committee on Dec. 12, 2007, citing the exact same figure for female veterans' suicides. In her statement, however, depressed *male* veterans' suicides were reported to be 89.5/100,000. http://www.va.gov/OCA/testimony/hvac/071212KZ.asp. By the time of the 2015 report, male suicide rates had been reduced to 32.1/100,000, but women veterans' rates remained exactly the same, still "staggering" after all these years.

[20] www.badgeoflife.com/currentmyths.php (listing police suicides as between 14-17/100,000. In fact the rate may be higher as both police and the authorities tend to underestimate police suicides. See Katherine W. Ellison, Stress and the Police Officer 57 (2nd Ed. 2004).

[21] U.S. Department of Justice, Office of Justice Programs, *Mortality in Local Jails and State Prisons, 2000–2011* (Bureau of Justice Statistics, Statistical Tables NCJ 242186, Aug. 2013), www.bjs.gov/content/pub/pdf/mljsp0011.pdf.

[22] Yi-Lung Chen, Dong-Sheng Tzeng, Ting-Sheng Cheng et al, "Sentinel Events and Predictors of Suicide Among Inpatients at Psychiatric Hospitals," 11 Annals of General Psychiatry (2012) (collecting research articles) http://www.annals-general-psychiatry.com/content/11/1/4

The suicide rate on college campuses is 7.5/100,000.[23]

The suicide rate for Massachusetts Institute of Technology (MIT) undergraduates in the past five years is 12.6/100,000.[24]

The suicide rate for Harvard undergraduates in the last decade is 11.6/100,000.[25]

The suicide rate at Worcester Polytechnic Institute in the last decade is 1/100,000.[26]

It seems fairly elementary that trying to prevent suicide among jail inmates requires a different understanding of cause and context and different policy solutions than trying to prevent suicide among men older than the age of seventy-five, and yet another set of policies and programs would be needed to address suicidality among MIT students.

Thus, rather than talk about Durkheimian categories, or even *Diagnostic and Statistical Manual of Mental Disorders* (DSM) diagnoses, I think it is more useful to look at different kinds of suicides in terms that will be helpful to legislators, judges, and policymakers. People whose killings by police are labeled "suicide by cop" present different policy dilemmas than the suicidality of college and graduate students. People who are drunk and impulsive present different policy issues than people who have decided to starve themselves to death.

I will spend this chapter looking at suicide in a variety of contexts and the policy responses and laws that might be most helpful in each one.

Slow Suicide: Voluntarily Stopping Eating and Drinking

"They just don't want us to kill ourselves fast. They don't care if we kill ourselves slowly."

—Beckie Child[27]

I am six feet and one inch and weigh one hundred and fifty three pounds. Its to the point where i cannot wear white shirts anymore because people comment on the fact that they can see my rib cage.

---

[23] M.M. Silverman, P.M. Meyer, F. Sloane et. al. "The Big Ten Student Suicide Study: a 10-Year Study of Suicides on Midwestern University Campuses," 27 Suicide and Life-Threatening Behavior 285 (1997).

[24] Matt Rochelau, *Suicide Rate at MIT Higher Than National Average*, BOSTON GLOBE, Mar. 17, 2015, https://www.bostonglobe.com/metro/2015/03/16/suicide-rate-mit-higher-than-national-average/1aGWr7lRjiEyhoD1WIT78I/story.html

[25] *Id.*

[26] *Id.*

[27] Interview with Beckie Child. August 30, 2012.

I abuse my adderall to aid this and no one takes notice. Not even my psychiatrist who knows all of my problems, she doesn't care as long as she receives her paycheck. And as i was sitting in the front of my mid-sized suburban home chain smoking my Marlboro cigarettes, tonight, i realized this was my way out. This is it. My slow suicide. And by writing this I only hope that people don't feel the way i do. I desperately want the world to go on. I care in that sense. I want everything to be perfect and happy[28]

—Posted by "Anorexic Male" June 8, 2007

"A prolonged period of self-abusive, harmful behavior, which may result in suicide completion."

—Definition of "slow suicide"[29]

Just as physicians have long been assisting their patients to die, many older people, especially those with terminal illnesses, have long been accelerating their own deaths through either starvation or refusing hydration or both for as long as anyone can remember.[30] When physician-assisted suicide began to be discussed, some suggested voluntary starvation and dehydration as an alternative to resolve the active–passive dilemma created by physician-assisted suicide.[31] For example, Dr. Ira Byock, a leader in palliative care medicine, stated that while he would never participate in physician-assisted suicide because it would constitute "collusion in the patient's belief that their situation is hopeless and their existence beyond conceivable value,"[32] he would "share with the patient the information that he or she already has the ability to exert control over the timing death [sic]."[33] Byock acknowledges that this ethical line is a very fine one indeed, but insists that there is a line because the physician is not being asked to actively assist in speeding up the dying process: "While it may require information, the decision obviates the need for doctors, nurses and society to participate."[34]

---

[28] http://ehealthforum.com/health/topic95657.html

[29] The Free Dictionary, Medical Dictionary, s.v. *Slow Suicide*, http://medical-dictionary.thefreedictionary.com/Slow+Suicide.

[30] DAVID F. MARTIN, FACING DEATH: THEME AND VARIATIONS 81 (2006).

[31] J. L. Bernat, B. Gert, R. P. Mogielnicki, *Patient Refusal of Hydration and Nutrition: An Alternative to Physician-Assisted Suicide or Voluntary Active Euthanasia*, 153 ARCH. INTERN. MED. 24 (1993) at 2723.

[32] Ira Byock, *Patient Refusal of Nutrition and Hydration: Walking the Ever Finer Line*, AM. J. HOSPICE & PALLIATIVE CARE, 8–13 (March/Apr. 1995), www.dyingwell.org/prnh.htm.

[33] *Id.*

[34] *Id.*

Perhaps as a result, voluntarily ceasing to eat and drink sits more easily with medical health professionals[35] (if not mental health professionals).
A survey of Oregon hospice nurses whose patients chose to end their lives by
refusing food and fluids showed that this happened a lot (more than twice
as many people chose to die this way than by assisted suicide, although that
option was available to them as residents of Oregon) and that significantly
fewer patients who chose to end their lives by starvation were subjected to
psychiatric evaluation than patients who requested assisted suicide (9% vs.
45%).[36] Just under 3% of the nurses (3 out of 102) thought that allowing a
hospice patient to die this way was unethical, even though 12% of the nurses
thought the patient's decision to die by voluntary starvation or dehydration
was influenced by a mental disorder such as depression.

There may be good reasons for this difference in attitude toward voluntary cessation of nutrition and hydration. By definition, a process that takes
a longer period of time is usually subject to reconsideration and discussion;
because it is less impulsive, it seems more rational. But, despite the decision
of an Australian and a British court to the contrary, it *is* suicide.[37] It is worth
considering that Elizabeth Bouvia and Kerrie Wooltorton were essentially
asking their respective hospitals for the same thing: comfort care and non-
intervention as they died. Bouvia and Woolterton were, of course, younger
and not terminally ill. And Elizabeth Bouvia wanted to die by starvation and
dehydration—a slow death—on a psychiatric ward while Wooltorton had
pursued a much quicker method in a general hospital. But length of time cannot be the distinguishing variable between voluntary cessation of nutrition

---

[35] In recounting the suicide of his best friend by refusing to eat, Martin says, "His
fasting relieved everyone, especially his doctor, from any kind of recrimination"
(Martin, *supra* note 30, at 81). In recounting his mother's death from voluntary
stopping eating and drinking (VSED), Mark Silk notes that she first asked for
and received the permission of her internist. Mark Silk, *My Mother's Physician-
Assisted Suicide*, RELIGION NEWS SERVICE, Oct. 31, 2014, http://marksilk.reli-
gionnews.com/2014/10/31/mothers-physician-assisted-suicide/.

[36] Linda Ganzini, Elizabeth R. Goy, et al., *Nurses' Experience with Hospice
Patients Who Refuse Food and Fluids to Hasten Death*, 349 NEW ENG. J. MED.
359 (2003), *available at* www.nejm.org/doi/full/10.1056/NEJMsa035086.

[37] The Australian court "accepted the distinction . . . between suicide and an individual merely speeding 'the natural and inevitable part of life known as death'
by refusing food and water," while the British Coroner refused to enter a verdict
of suicide, stating, "There is no dispute in my mind that her death was brought
about somewhat prematurely by refusing food," and found the cause of death to be
"starvation and MS [multiple sclerosis]"; despite the use of the passive voice, a person intentionally taking steps to shorten her life has always been understood to be
suicide and would clearly have been considered as such if the individuals in question did not have serious disabilities and illnesses. See Thaddeus Mason Pope &
Amanda West, *Legal Briefing: Voluntarily Stopping Eating and Drinking*, 25 J. Clin.
Ethics 68, 73 (2014) (quoting from H. Ltd. v. J. [2010] SASC 176 P 5 (Austl.) at 56).

and hydration and assisted suicide, because physician-assisted suicide, with its fifteen-day waiting period, takes longer than voluntary dehydration, and is comparably long to voluntary starvation.

Not all health professionals are supportive about slow death: some hospice staff respond to a patient's intentions to cease nutrition and hydration by involuntarily committing them for a psychiatric evaluation.[38] These patients, like so many patients before them, "quickly learn what *not* to say to hospice staff."[39] But many hospices are more understanding. A recent obituary noted that a man "died in hospice care after he had stopped eating because of depression."[40] In one case, after a man with amyotrophic lateral sclerosis (ALS) in hospice announced that he would forego food to hasten his death, the hospice honored his decision but required him to reiterate it by regularly and consistently offering him food and fluids.[41]

And yet, the decision to forego food and water does raise difficult legal and moral questions. Cases involving when to force-feed people refusing food in nursing homes have arisen for decades.[42] In at least two cases involving patients in nursing homes, the nursing home petitioned a court to force-feed competent patients who had decided to stop eating. Those petitions were denied. Presumably the nursing homes chose to try to force-feed their patients because federal law makes it difficult for nursing homes to summarily evict their patients.

Assisted living facilities, which are far less regulated than nursing homes, not only don't have as difficult a time evicting residents who have decided to voluntarily starve themselves; they are sometimes obligated to do so by state regulations. In response to these regulations, many facilities insert a clause in their contracts that the resident may be evicted if his or her "health has deteriorated to the point where the facility can no longer take responsibility for him."[43] When an older couple, the Rudolphs, informed the staff of the assisted living facility where they lived in New Mexico that they had made the decision to forego eating and drinking, the facility responded by telling them they had one day to pack up and get out despite a contractual provision

---

[38] Judith Schwarz, *Death by Voluntary Dehydration: Suicide or the Right to Refuse a Life-Prolonging Measure?* 17 WIDENER L. REV. 351, 358, (2011), at n.31.

[39] *Id.*

[40] Daniel E. Slotnik, *Mario Cooper; Sought Help for Minorities with AIDS*, BOSTON GLOBE, June 5, 2015, at B-8.

[41] Pope & West, *supra* note 37, at 72.

[42] David Armon, *Judge Grants Old Man Right to Starve to Death*, BRYAN TIMES, Feb. 3, 1984, https://news.google.com/newspapers?nid=799&dat=19840203&id=T6ZTAAAAIBAJ&sjid=7YcDAAAAIBAJ&pg=6514,2840048&hl=en.

[43] Robert G. Schwemm & Michael Allen, *For the Rest of Their Lives: Seniors and the Fair Housing Act*, 90 IOWA L. REV. 138 (2004), available at http://www.fhco.org/pdfs/ltc_rest_of_their_lives.pdf, quoting LAWRENCE A. FROLIK, RESIDENCE OPTIONS FOR OLDER AND DISABLED CLIENTS (2008).

requiring thirty days' notice.[44] When the couple and their son protested their right to stay, a facility administrator called 911 and reported that both elderly people were attempting suicide. The emergency medical technicians (EMTs) could not decide whether to take the Rudolphs to the hospital, since they were emphatically refusing to go, and called for a consult with a doctor at the University of New Mexico's emergency medicine department. The doctor showed up at the Rudolph's apartment.[45] After lengthy separate discussion with each of them, the doctor told the EMTs they could leave without the Rudolphs,[46] and the EMTs departed, no doubt heaving sighs of relief at not having to strong-arm two struggling elderly people into their ambulance.

The law around this event is murky. The Fair Housing Act, which applies to assisted living facilities such as the one where the Rudolphs resided,[47] prohibits discrimination on the basis of disability. Thus, under the Fair Housing Act, the facility could not evict the Rudolphs because they were "incapable of living independently," but depending on the state laws regulating the facility, the facility might be in violation of licensing requirements if it failed to take action regarding a resident's attempted suicide.[48] Regardless of how that issue is ultimately settled, the status of wanting to die as *per se* indicative of a disability is extremely questionable.[49] Each state regulates assisted living facilities differently, and each assisted living facility has different contractual provisions.

Since the events surrounding the Rudolphs' eviction, Compassion & Choices has publicized "voluntarily stopping eating and drinking" (VSED) as an option and is seeking to add contractual language to assisted living facility contracts to ensure that residents' competent choices will be honored. It is not clear that changing the contractual language will solve the problem (if it is a problem). The responsibility of these quasi-care facilities toward

---

[44] Paula Span, *Deciding to Die, Then Shown the Door*, N. Y. Times, Aug. 24, 2011, http://newoldage.blogs.nytimes.com/2011/08/24/deciding-to-die-then-shown-the-door/. It's not clear to me why the Rudolphs felt the need to tell staff of their decision, as opposed to quietly wasting away in their apartment.

[45] For many people, the fact that a consulting doctor would travel to the Rudolphs' apartment at the request of the EMTs is the most astonishing feature of this story.

[46] *Id.*

[47] See Schwemm & Allen, *supra* note 43, at 136–37.

[48] For more than you will ever want to know about New York's regulation of assisted living facilities, see Boykin v. 1 Prospect Park ALF, LLC, No. 12-CV-6243, Memorandum and Order on Background of Assisted Living Industry in Preparation for Argument on Motion for Summary Judgment and Class Action, (E.D.N.Y. Aug. 8, 2013), http://www.leagle.com/decision/In%20FDCO%20 20130809B50. For a more manageable discussion of this issue, see Schwemm & Allen, *id.* at 186, predicting a "gathering storm" of litigation over these conflicts between federal and state law.

[49] See Chapters 2 and 8 for extensive discussions of this issue.

their residents is governed by state law and regulations, which vary considerably from state to state,[50] and the contract between the resident and the facility. Although states vary considerably in their regulations of assisted living facilities, practically every state has a regulatory requirement that could be interpreted to ban a person engaging in VSED, whether the regulations ban residents who are "a threat to himself or others" (California), "totally bed-ridden" with limited chance of improvement, or totally bed-ridden for a specified number of days (Colorado and Delaware), or the ubiquitous "needs are greater than the facility is licensed to provide" (Arizona, Arkansas, and others).[51] In most cases, residents with medical needs as great as those of a starving person would be transferred to hospitals, hospice, or nursing homes; what happens when a resident refuses those transfers also depends on state regulations and law.

A *Hastings Center Report* article raises a different issue: the problem of a person whose competently executed an advance directive indicated that she wanted to refuse nutrition and hydration should she become debilitated with Alzheimer's disease, and then, when she reached that stage, asked for food and drink.[52] Her family and caregivers were torn about what to do. This question is going to recur as boomers with advance directives age.[53] In line with my previously expressed philosophy[54] that the decision to end one's life must not only be made but implemented by the person himself or herself, I would strongly support giving the woman the food and drink she wanted. As Rebecca Dresser would argue, the self that she is now may simply be different than the self who imagined the experience of Alzheimer's disease. The person she is now cares more about being hungry than being demented, and furthermore, the person she is now could not begin to understand the decision to deprive her of food and drink. A British Columbia court ruled (correctly, in my opinion) that if a person with an advance directive refusing food and water in the case of dementia voluntarily chewed and swallowed food placed on her tongue, that voluntary action constituted consent to the feeding that overrode the prior refusal.[55]

[50] KARL POLZER (FOR THE NATIONAL CENTER FOR ASSISTED LIVING), ASSISTED LIVING STATE REGULATORY REVIEW: 2011 (Mar. 2011), at http://www.ahcancal.org/ncal/resources/documents/2011assistedlivingregulatoryreview.pdf.
[51] *Id.*
[52] *Case Study: A Fading Decision* (May-June 2014), HASTINGS CENTER REP., http://onlinelibrary.wiley.com/doi/10.1002/hast.309/epdf.
[53] Paula Span, *Complexities of Choosing an Endgame for Dementia*, N. Y. TIMES, Jan. 19, 2015, http://www.nytimes.com/2015/01/20/health/complexities-of-choosing-an-end-game-for-dementia.html?action=click&contentCollection=Opinion&module=MostEmailed&version=Full&region=Marginalia&src=me&pgtype=article&_r=0.
[54] See Chapter 2.
[55] Bentley v. Maplewood Seniors Care Soc'http://www.courts.gov.bc.ca/jdb-txt/CA/15/00/2015BCCA0091cor1.htm

As I made clear in Chapter 5, force-feeding a nonconsenting competent individual who is not in government custody is a battery and should never happen. There is, however, an enormous moral, ethical, and legal difference between the decision of competent individuals to refuse food, such as the Rudolphs, and advance directives in the case of Alzheimer's disease or dementia that leave the dirty work to others of starving a person who, now demented, wants to eat. Third-party implementation of earlier decisions, including advance directives, to refuse food and drink should be considered revoked by a person's willingness to eat, even if the person is of questionable competence. I understand that it could be argued that this is no different from disconnecting a ventilator from a person who is no longer competent, and, as I wrote in Chapter 2, I don't necessarily disagree. I just wish we could have a system where a conscious person who wishes to have the ventilator disconnected presses a button or pulls the plug to disconnect his or her own ventilator.

The well-known public radio personality Diane Rehm's husband John, who was in severely deteriorated condition because of Parkinson's disease, asked his doctor to help him die. His doctor refused, not because he thought it was medically contraindicated, but because it was illegal in Maryland. John Rehm ceased drinking and died nine days later.[56] Diane Rehm is bitter that her husband had to die this way, although apparently he was given sufficient morphine that he did not suffer.[57] Perhaps it is because he could not choose the hour and moment of his death so that his wife could be with him—she left briefly and he died while she was gone. In that sense, physician-assisted suicide may add a benefit beyond the painlessness and brevity of VSED: like Caesarean section birth, it can be scheduled. It also involves the participation of a doctor, which, Ira Byock notwithstanding, people seem to affirmatively want. Diane Rehm said, "I will hopefully one day, with the help of a kind physician, be able to end my life when I choose."[58] This underscores another fact about VSED: unlike physician-assisted suicide in America, it is not limited to terminally ill people. VSED has also been used by people who are not terminally ill, including many elderly people[59] or people with chronic and debilitating conditions.

The hallmark of slow suicide is that it takes at least some time and deliberation, in the case of starvation or dehydration, and that it leaves room for

---

[56] Maggie Fox, *Diane Rehm: My Husband's Slow, Deliberate Death Was Unnecessary*, (NBC News, July 8, 2014), at http://www.nbcnews.com/health/health-news/diane-rehm-my-husbands-slow-deliberate-death-was-unnecessary-n150096.

[57] *Id.*

[58] *Id.*

[59] David Eddy, *A Conversation with My Mother*, 272 J. AM. MED. ASS'N 179; Jane Gross, *What an End-of-Life Adviser Could Have Told Me*, NEW OLD AGE BLOG (Dec. 15, 2008), http://newoldage.blogs.nytimes.com/2008/12/15/what-an-end-of-life-advisor-could-have-told-me/?_r=0

the participation and persuasion of others. There is time to determine both the consistency and rationality of the person's desire to die. This cuts both ways: the obduracy and consistency of an individual's decision to die, in the presence (and sometimes over the opposition) of loved ones, can bring home to family just how much a person is suffering, and how little they can do, despite their love, to ameliorate it.

Non-Suicide

Chronic Suicidality

Although it may seem similar, in that they both involve an apparently consistent desire to die over a long period of time, death by starvation or dehydration is almost the opposite of chronic suicidality, a condition well known to both clinicians[60] and the people who experience it.[61] Chronically suicidal people are suicidal over a period of years, and sometimes decades. The most thorough description of chronic suicidality is contained in a recently published book: "patients who threaten suicide in all seasons . . . and from time to time make serious suicide attempts."[62] Another article describes these individuals as "never not suicidal."[63] Another helpful description is that they are "stably unstable."[64]

But "most chronically suicidal patients do *not* end their lives by suicide."[65] This is not because of inpatient hospitalization: "[h]ospitalization tends to be ineffective and unhelpful for chronically suicidal patients."[66] One of the nation's leading experts on suicide told hospitals that "outpatient treatment may be more beneficial than hospitalization" in cases that fit the following criteria: "Patient has chronic suicidal ideation and/or self-injury without prior medically serious attempts, if a safe and supportive living situation is available and outpatient psychiatric care is ongoing."[67] The American Psychiatric Association's *Practice Guidelines on Assessing and Treating Suicidal Patients*

---

[60] Joel Paris, Half in Love with Death: Managing the Chronically Suicidal Patient (2006); American Psychiatric Association, Practice Guidelines for the Treatment of Patients with Borderline Personality Disorder 68 (2001); American Psychiatric Association, Practice Guidelines for the Assessment and Treatment of Patients with Suicidal Behaviors 53–54 (2010).

[61] Andrew Solomon, The Noonday Demon: An Atlas of Depression (2001).

[62] Joel Paris, Half in Love with Death (paperback 2007).

[63] Thomas Gutheil & Diane Schetky, *A Date with Death: Management of Time Based and Contingent Suicidal Intent*, 155 Am. J. Psychiatry 1502 (Nov. 1998).

[64] Dix v. U.S. (N.D. Ill. 2014).

[65] Paris, supra note 63, at xv.

[66] Paris, *supra* note 63, at xiii, n.8.

[67] Douglas Jacobs (for Screening for Mental Health), A Resource Guide for Implementing the Joint Commission on Accreditation

underscores that "hospitalization, by itself, is not a treatment"[68] for suicidality, but rather a venue for receiving treatment. The *Guidelines* add that

[l]ess intensive treatment [than hospitalization] may be more appropriate if suicidal ideation or attempts are part of a chronic, repetitive cycle and the patient is aware of the chronicity. For such patients, suicidal ideation may be a characteristic response to disappointment or a way to cope with psychological distress. If the patient has a history of suicidal ideation without suicidal intent and an ongoing doctor–patient relationship, the benefits of continued treatment outside the hospital may outweigh the possible detrimental effects of hospitalization [*sic*] even in the presence of serious psychiatric symptoms.[69]

Again, the *Guidelines* note "the risk of suicide outside the hospital must be balanced against the potentially detrimental risks of hospitalization."[70] Other experts feel even more strongly that chronic suicidality should not be responded to with hospitalization, even when there have been attempts, or without the protective factors mentioned earlier. There are a number of reasons for this.

Dr. Paris proposes that chronic suicidality actually serves a protective function, in that patients who remind themselves that the option of suicide always exists retain some control over their lives and may have the strength to continue because the option of respite from pain is still there.[71] Many of my interviews, as well as first-person accounts, confirm this:

I only felt suicidal when I felt trapped. I kept thinking, I'll wait two weeks more. . . ... I started standing on subway platforms and think how this would solve my anxiety and that my family would be relieved. This went on for a year. I kept thinking, I'll just wait another two weeks and see what happens.[72]

OF HEALTHCARE ORGANIZATIONS (JCAHO): 2007 PATIENT SAFETY GOALS ON SUICIDE (Jan. 2, 2007), *available at* http://www.aha.org/content/00-10/JCAHOSafetyGoals2007.pdfMentalHealthScreening.org.

[68] AMERICAN PSYCHIATRIC ASSOCIATION, THE AMERICAN PSYCHIATRIC ASSOCIATION PRACTICE GUIDELINES FOR THE ASSESSMENT AND TREATMENT OF PATIENTS WITH SUICIDAL BEHAVIORS 31 (2006).

[69] *Id.* at 32.

[70] *Id.* at 43.

[71] This view, expressed at length in HALF IN LOVE WITH DEATH and Dr. Paris' other publications, is echoed by the distinguished writer Andrew Solomon: "Knowing that if I get through this minute I can always kill myself in the next one makes it possible to get through this minute without being utterly overwhelmed. Suicide may be a symptom of depression; it is also a mitigating factor. The thought of suicide makes it possible to get through depression" (SOLOMON, *supra* note 61, at 283).

[72] Interview with C.L. Sept. 29, 2012.

Or, as Andrew Solomon noted,

> Nietzsche once said that the thought of suicide keeps many men alive
> in the darkest part of the night. . . . Knowing that if I get through this
> minute I can always kill myself in the next one makes it possible to
> get through this minute without being utterly overwhelmed.[73]

In addition, because chronic suicidality is ongoing and unremitting,
reacting to it with inpatient hospitalization will disrupt any possibility of
engagement, investment, and therapy in the community, as well as integration in employment and social circles, which might be the underlying key
to continued survival.[74] Research shows that "suicidality in BPD [border-
line personality disorder] remits when patients attain meaningful work and
establish a network of relationships,"[75] which is impossible if the patient is
cycling in and out of the hospital. In addition, Drs. Dawson and MacMillan
believe that hospitalization necessarily involves imposing control and creates
power struggles which the patient inevitably loses, adding to his or her feelings of powerlessness and despair and anger and increasing the chances of
suicide over the long term.[76]

One of the major reasons for this new understanding that the best
approach to chronic suicidality may not be hospitalization is the understanding that people who are chronically suicidal often are diagnosed with personality disorders, rather than major depression,[77] and that their treatment must
be guided by understanding of the dynamics related to the difference in these
diagnoses.[78] Thus, the chronicity, as opposed to the acuity, of the risk, as well
as the nature of the underlying disorder, are generally recognized by suicide
scholars (many of whom also have patients in clinical practice) as being key
factors in determining the appropriateness of hospitalization.

Courts have also accepted the testimony of psychiatric expert witnesses
that it is the standard of care "to treat chronically suicidal patients who are in
remission (not acutely suicidal) both inside or outside of a hospital environment, and that chronically suicidal patients who are in remission cannot be
locked up indefinitely."[79]

In sum, there is a consensus that a statement of suicidal intention or ideation is assessed differently in a patient who has been making that statement

---

[73] SOLOMON, *supra* note 61, at 283.
[74] PARIS, *supra* note 62.
[75] *Id.*
[76] DAVID DAWSON & HARRIET MACMILLAN, RELATIONSHIP MANAGEMENT OF
THE BORDERLINE PATIENT: FROM UNDERSTANDING TO TREATMENT (1993).
[77] PARIS, at xvi–xvii, n.73.
[78] DOUG JACOBS & HUBERT BROWN, EDS., SUICIDE: UNDERSTANDING AND RESPONDING
(1989); ROBERT I. SIMON & ROBERT HALES, EDS., THE AMERICAN PSYCHIATRIC
ASSOCIATION'S TEXTBOOK OF SUICIDE ASSESSMENT AND MANAGEMENT (2006).
[79] Bates v. Denney, 563 So.2d 298, 302 (La. App. 1990).

The case law has ample discussion of people who are contingently sui-cidal, although it does not use that term. The somewhat misleading term "malingering" is applied to men who say they are suicidal for secondary gain,[97] while women are often called "manipulative." In fact, the two situa-tions may be quite different: often the men are seeking some external benefit (escape from arrest or jail, shelter and food), while the women are seeking reassurance that they are loved, attention to their pain, and to be taken seri-ously. It is clear that there are mental health difficulties and needs in both cases, and those needs should be taken seriously. This can be done without giving in to whatever demand is being made using the threat of suicide as leverage, and with respect and compassion.[98]

The most important social and legal policy issue about contingent sui-cidality is that fear of liability is completely driving a clinical decision that results in the inappropriate use of extremely scarce resources. When added to the number of individuals from the criminal justice system occupying civil hospital beds because they were sent for evaluation or treatment by judges who don't stop to think about the implications of their actions for the civil population needing those beds,[99] people who mactually have an urgent need for a hospital bed for a few days because of dangerous reactions to medica-tions, or a severe psychotic break, are being crowded out. Then the public is inundated with reports of the scarcity of institutional beds, when the prob-lem is not so much scarcity as misuse.

There needs to be much more recognition of the phenomenon of contin-gent suicidality by policymakers and courts, and an explicit acknowledgment that the standard of care in response to presentation of contingent suicidality is not hospitalization, but rather to attempt to address the issues underlying the demand for a hospital bed. Many states currently provide psychiatrists and emergency department doctors with immunity from suit for decisions not to admit a patient, but doctors remain wary and concerned about denying a bed to someone who is outright saying that he or she will commit suicide if a bed is not forthcoming. If any given state were to undertake an evalua-tion of how many emergency department gurneys and inpatient civil beds on any given day were being used by people who were contingently suicidal, or referred from the criminal justice system, it would likely translate to a more than adequate number of civil hospital beds to meet any perceived shortage of inpatient psychiatric beds.

---

[97] State v. Sharkey, 821 S.W.2d 544, 545 (Mo. App. 1991) ("he subsequently admit-ted to doctors that he faked his 'depression' and suicide intentions in order to have food and a place to stay").

[98] See Jon Berlin, n. 97.

[99] Joseph Bloom, Brinda Krishnan, & Christopher Lockey, *The Majority of Inpatient Psychiatric Beds Should Not Be Appropriated by the Forensic System*, 36 J. AM. ACAD. PSYCH & LAW 438 (Dec. 2008), http://www.jaapl.org/content/36/4/438.full.

Furthermore, when judges order people from the criminal justice system into civil hospital beds—whether for evaluation of competence to stand trial; as an alternative to incarceration; because an individual has entered a plea of not guilty by reason of insanity to spitting, cursing, or urinating in the streets;[100] or as a result of "mental health court" adjudications—the legislature should require the judge to first consider all available community alternatives. If the person must be held in a secure facility, the criminal justice system should bear the cost of those beds or build its own forensic facilities (the problem with the latter option is that those facilities, with not much in the way of a constituent base, are often brutal at worst and inadequate at best).

One-Time Suicidality

Occasionally (but not rarely) as I conducted my interviews and research, I ran across people who had had one highly uncharacteristic suicide attempt, resolved the situation, and never looked back. These people either had adverse reactions to medicine, or a highly unusual personal situation, or some as yet unexplained biological storm system passed through. While shaken, they experienced their suicidality as profoundly alien to their fundamental identity. They were always glad and relieved to have survived and sometimes rather naively astonished at the social reverberations of the suicide attempt in their lives, oftens for many years afterwards.

In this way, they could not be more different from people who are chronically suicidal, and the majority of the people I interviewed. Talking with them made me think that while it may be true that the best predictor of future suicide is past suicide attempts, that this perhaps should be specifically expressed in the plural form. There should be a way for clinicians to understand that there is this category of atypical suicide attempters whose single suicide attempt actually tells us nothing whatsoever about who they are today.

Ironically, the subcategory of people who experienced suicidality as a reaction to medication includes a relatively substantial number of people whose suicides were, allegedly, the results of a group of psychiatric medications known as selective serotonin reuptake inhibitors (SSRIs), such as Lexapro[101] (including an eighty-one-year-old man caring for a seriously ill

---

[100] People spend ten years or more in state hospitals as a result of pleading not guilty by reason of insanity to misdemeanors such as these, see VIRGINIA STATE CRIME COMMISSION, REPORT OF THE VIRGINIA STATE CRIME COMMISSION: SJR 381: NOT GUILTY BY REASON OF INSANITY: A BILL REFERRAL STUDY TO THE SENATE RULES COMMITTEE AND THE GENERAL ASSEMBLY OF VIRGINIA 4 (May 2002), http://leg2.state.va.us/dls/h&sdocs.nsf/By+Year/RD312004/$file/RD31.PDF. This was also true at state hospitals in Florida in the decade that I lived and worked there.

[101] Bennett v. Forest Lab., Case No. 2:06-cv-72-FtM-38DNF, (M.D. Fla. Apr. 9, 2015) (denying defendant's motion to exclude expert testimony of Dr. George

wife who had never before had any suicidality),[102] Effexor,[103] and, especially, Paxil[104] and Prozac.[105]

A fascinating story of the impact of litigation on social policy and cultural beliefs, and on the difference between legal ethics and morality, involves the successful efforts of Eli Lilly to control the public perception of Prozac through controlling the outcome of one of the first cases to go to trial alleging that Prozac caused violence and suicidality.[106] Joseph Wesbecker had started taking Prozac in August 1988, and shot up his former workplace in September 1989. Most Prozac plaintiffs involved mildly depressed and functional people who committed suicide very shortly after starting Prozac. Because Wesbecker had a documented history of mental illness and anger issues, and had been taking Prozac for over a year at the time he mowed down twenty people, killing eight, this case, *Fentress v. Eli Lilly*, was "one of the weakest cases against

S. Glass that Lexapro was a significant contributing factor to plaintiff decedent's "violent death by suicide"); Muzichuk v. Forest Lab., No. 1:07-CV-16, (N.D. W. Va. Jan. 16, 2015) (granting defendant's motion for summary judgment on the basis that its warning about increased suicidality was adequate and that plaintiff's decedent read it); In re Celexa & Lexapro Prod. Liab. Litig., 927 F. Supp. 2d 758 (W.D. Mo. 2013).

[102] Cross v. Forest Lab., No. 1:05-cv-00170-MPM-SSA (N.D. Miss. Apr. 6, 2015) (granting defendant's motion for summary judgment on the basis that drug manufacturers only have a duty to warn physicians, not patients, and insufficient evidence that an adequate warning would have caused physician to change his behavior).

[103] Giles v. Wyeth, 556 F.3d 596 (7th Cir. 2009) (forty-six-year-old man who was injured on the job and laid off visited doctor and complained of tiredness and inability to sleep, was prescribed Effexor, took the medication, and committed suicide two days later).

[104] Estate of Tobin *ex rel* Tobin v. SmithKline, 164 F. Supp. 2d 1278 (D. Wyo. 2001) ($8 million verdict upon a finding that Paxil can cause small population of vulnerable people to become suicidal or homicidal). After this case, pharmaceutical companies spent a lot more money fighting plaintiffs' experts, and in the process developed the law on admissibility of expert testimony under the Supreme Court cases in Daubert v. Merrell-Dow, 509 U.S. 579 (1993) and Kumho Tire v. Carmichael, 526 U.S. 137 (1999)).

[105] Winkler v. Eli Lilly, 101 F.3d 1196, 1198 (7th Cir. 1996) (hundreds of families have sued Eli Lilly for suicides or homicides allegedly caused by ingestion of Prozac). Blanchard v. Eli Lilly, 207 F. Supp. 2d 308 (D. Vt. 2002) (explaining the theory and law of expert testimony regarding causation of suicide and homicide by selective serotonin reuptake inhibitors (SSRIs) in detail and finding for defendants based on specific facts of this case, i.e., plaintiff's expert's testimony was admissible that Prozac could cause suicide or homicide, but insufficient evidence that it did so in this case).

[106] Nicholas Varchaver, *Lilly's Phantom Verdict*, 17 AM. LAW. (Sept. 1995).

Lilly."[107]At the time that this case was tried, there were hundreds of cases in the pipeline; Paul Smith was the lead plaintiff's attorney for many of them. He had done the research and the discovery, understood the science and the law, and *Fentress* was the first of many cases to come.

Eli Lilly, which had made almost $2 billion a year from sales of Prozac at the time, had a lot to lose, and they were determined to use *Fentress* to their benefit. When Judge John Potter ruled—after more than a day of oral argument during the trial—that Smith could introduce damning evidence in the case, which was that British regulators had linked the medication (called "Oraflex" in Britain) with thirty-two deaths, and Eli Lilly had pled guilty to twenty-five misdemeanor counts for failing to inform the U.S. Food and Drug Administration (FDA) of some of these deaths when they applied for approval to market Prozac in the United States, Lilly's lawyers got together with Smith. Despite having won the evidentiary ruling, Smith agreed not to introduce the evidence. In return, Lilly agreed to pay a staggeringly high amount to his clients, regardless of the jury's decision. Both sides agreed not to appeal whatever decision the jury reached. This was all done in secret. But when Smith did not introduce the evidence he had worked so hard to get admitted, Judge Potter called the lawyers into his chambers and asked them specifically if a deal had been reached. On the record, the lawyers denied making any deal. The trial went on, and to all appearances it was hard fought: 47 days, 75 witnesses, and 411 exhibits.[108] But the damning Oraflex evidence was not introduced, and the jury found in favor of Eli Lilly. The nation's headlines trumpeted that allegations that Prozac was dangerous had been rejected by a jury. Paul Smith withdrew from all the other cases he was litigating against Eli Lilly.

None of this would have come to light, except for two events. One of the plaintiffs, Andrew Pointer, ended up in divorce proceedings, and in the division of marital assets, the fact came up that he had received a substantial sum (his own lawyer said, "It boggles the mind") in the *Fentress* case. But wait: didn't plaintiffs *lose* that case? Upon learning of this, the judge, a man of old-fashioned integrity, scheduled a hearing to discuss whether he should change the records of the official outcome of the case from "dismissed with prejudice" to "dismissed with prejudice as settled." He also asked lawyers for Lilly to produce some documents related to the case. He did not try to discipline or punish the lawyers who had misled him. But lawyers on both sides united to oppose him, and together, the erstwhile adversaries went to court to stop Judge Potter from changing the verdict. They said that the time to change the records had elapsed, and Judge Potter no longer had jurisdiction of the case. They won at the Court of Appeals level, but the Kentucky

[107] Jeff Swiatek, "Lilly's Legal Strategy Disarmed Prozac Lawyers," Indianapolis Star, April 22, 2000, http://www.antidepressantsfacts.com/2000-04-22-StarNews-Lilly-tactics.htm
[108] Potter v. Eli Lilly, 926 S.W.2d 449, 451 (Ky. 1996).

Supreme Court reversed, ruling in favor of Potter and finding that "in this case, there was serious lack of candor with the trial court, and there may have been deception, bad faith conduct, abuse of the judicial process, or perhaps even fraud."[109]

With this victory in hand, Judge Potter asked the State Deputy Attorney General to investigate, giving her power to subpoena documents and interview witnesses under oath.[110] She discovered that there had indeed been an agreement to settle the case, including settling all of Smith's cases and paying half his expenses. Once again, Judge Potter scheduled a hearing. But it never happened. Eli Lilly showed up, stipulated that the case had been settled, and agreed to changing the notation in the records, then argued that it no longer needed to produce any documents or answer any questions. Judge Potter recused himself from the case, saying the attention should be on "what's under the log, not the person trying to roll it over." The appellate court held private hearings, and not much attention was paid. Three years after the *Fentress* trial, cases against Eli Lilly about Prozac's effects had dropped dramatically, and Prozac's reputation was generally good.[111] Eli Lilly's marketing slogan at the time was, "Knowledge is powerful medicine."

Confidential settlements about matters affecting public health and safety are common. Paul Smith was acting for his clients, who benefited enormously from his agreements with Eli Lilly, and many legal ethicists would argue he did nothing wrong as long as these kinds of confidential settlements are legal. Senator Kohl of Wisconsin has repeatedly introduced federal legislation to ban confidential settlements (the "Sunshine in Litigation" Act), and you can guess how far it's gotten. However, Florida has a state "Sunshine in Litigation Act" that prohibits court orders or contracts (a private settlement is a contract) that have "the effect of concealing a public hazard."[112] The South Carolina federal court prohibits sealed settlements entered by the court entirely.[113] (This would have had no effect in the *Fentress* case, where the agreements were out of court.) On the other hand, Texas has a fairly robust court rule, prohibiting sealing of records "that have a probably adverse effect upon the general public health and safety," and this includes settlements and discovery not filed with the court.[114] The State of California has hesitantly suggested that confidentiality agreements about elder abuse in nursing homes are "disfavored."[115]

---

[109] *Id.* at 454.
[110] Richard Zitrin & Carol M. Langford, *Hide and Secrets in Louisville, in* THE MORAL COMPASS OF THE AMERICAN LAWYER (Ballantine Books 1999).
[111] Jeff Swiatek at n. 109.
[112] FLA. STAT. § 69.081.
[113] S.C. LOCAL RULE 5.03.
[114] TEX. REV. CIV. PROC. 76(a).
[115] 2003 Cal. Stat. ch. 242 (Elder Abuse and Adult Dependent Civil Protection Act).

If drugs and medications are causing people to become suicidal, that's something that should not be concealed in confidential settlements. Lawyers will make the best agreements for their clients until it becomes illegal to do so. This is particularly important because it is hardly only SSRIs that have been discovered to cause suicidality. Medicine for acne, psoriasis, and many other conditions appear to substantially increase people's suicidality.[116]

Accidental Deaths and "Accidental Deaths"

It is very well known that for a number of reasons, people who commit suicide often try to make it look like an accident. For the most part, it's the stigma of suicide; they don't want to hurt their families, or they have religious reasons. And finally, perhaps of less importance to the people themselves but of indubitable significance to an important sector of the American financial system, they want their families to collect insurance benefits.

This propensity to disguise suicide as an accident is particularly well known to companies that sell life insurance policies, many of which have riders that either prevent payouts for suicide, permit them only after a period of years, or—even if they permit payouts for suicide—are at pains to show that a death was not accidental, because coverage for accidents is often under double indemnity clauses that would mean a substantially higher payout.

Over the years, there have been thousands of fascinating insurance cases involving suicide. The most common, of course, is the question of whether a given death was accidental or a suicide, which resulted in a substantial number of decisions by the U.S. Supreme Court in the early days of insurance law.[117] The law has always had a presumption against suicide, so that the burden of proof is on the insurance company to show that any death is a suicide. In cases where the beneficiary is claiming double indemnity for an accident, however, the burden is generally on the beneficiary to show that the death was accidental rather than natural.[118]

This presumption against suicide has been carried to comical (unless you are the insurance company) lengths in some cases: one court decided that a man found dead on the floor of his garage, with his face one to three feet from his car's exhaust pipe, with the engine running, and the garage door closed,

---

[116] Gardner Harris, *F.D.A. Requiring Suicide Studies in Drug Trials*, N. Y. TIMES, Jan. 24, 2008, http://www.nytimes.com/2008/01/24/washington/24fda.html?pagewanted=2&_r=0.

[117] See Chapter 1.

[118] For an excellent article on different states' interpretations of suicide exclusions and burdens of proof, see Gary Schuman, *Suicide and the Life Insurance Contract: Was the Insured Sane or Insane? That Is the Question—or Is It?* 28 TORT & INS. L. J. 745 (1993).

may just have decided to attach his new license plates to the car.[119] A man who drove his car into a tree and left a suicide note was deemed not to have committed suicide when experts disagreed about whether the note was in his writing and two investigating officers testified it was extremely hard to drive a car into a tree.[120] Yet another case involved a man who stuffed rags under the doors and into the window cracks, turned on all the gas in the stove in his kitchen, and sat down to nurse a bottle of spirits and await his end. Half a bottle of vodka later he fell asleep, woke up groggy, and reached over to light a cigarette, and died from the burns sustained in the immediate explosion.[121] A jury found that he had not committed suicide. The judge granted the life insurance company's motion for a new trial.[122]

But there are other questions. Suppose a person intends to commit suicide, changes his or her mind, but it is too late? A number of cases involve a person intending to die by inhalation of carbon monoxide who are found, not in the car, nor even in the garage, but collapsed in the house, having evidently had a change of heart? Too late, say the majority of courts; as one court said, "Such a change in intent might make a difference to a man's immortal soul, but not to his beneficiary."[123]

In another ruling that underscores the law's struggle to deal with suicide in a rational way, a court found (in a tort case rather than an insurance case) that while the presumption against suicide is absolutely settled law, there is no corresponding presumption against *attempted* suicide.[124] This case involved a man who sued the New York City Transit Authority for injuries when he was hit by a subway train. He claimed he was bumped or pushed onto the tracks; the defendant claimed he tried to kill himself (in which case he would not be able to recover, see Chapter 9). The highest court of New York rejected his argument that since there was a legal presumption against suicide, there should be a legal presumption against attempted suicide, on the somewhat shaky ground that the presumption against suicide simply redresses an evidentiary imbalance (the dead party is not available to testify that it was an accident) rather than what virtually every other court decision declares it to be: a fundamental acknowledgment that most people don't want to die.

[119] Noll v. John Hancock Mutual Life Ins. Co., 66 Wash. 2d 540, 543, 403 P.2d 898 (Wash. 1965).
[120] Mass. Indem. Co. & Life Ins. v. Morrison, 745 S.W.2d 461 (Tex. App. 1988).
[121] White v. Aetna Life Ins. Co., 198 Cal. App. 2d 370, 374 (Cal. App. 1961).
[122] *Id.* at 376. The appellate court affirmed the grant of a new trial. However, in a different case with similar facts, the court ruled that the injuries were accidental, rather than self-inflicted, because she had not intended to commit suicide by means of fire or explosion, Comfort v. Continental Casualty Co., 34 N.W. 2d 588, 590 (Iowa 1948).
[123] Chepke v. Lutheran Bhd., 660 N.E.2d 477, 480 (Ohio App. 1995). See also Tedrow v. Standard Life Ins. Co., 558 N.W.2d 195, 198 (Iowa 1997).
[124] Rinaldo v. New York City Transit Auth., 39 N.Y.2d 285, 287 (N.Y. 1976).

Courts do not consider it an accident to die of an unintentional overdose of illegal drugs[125] or in a car crash while drunk.[126] On the other hand, it *is* an accident to die of an overdose of many, many legal prescription drugs.[127] Although dying while engaging in autoerotic asphyxiation is acknowledged not to be suicide, since the individual had no intention of dying, it is also generally not considered an accident.[128]

Hunger Strikes and Participation in Political Protests

(See Chapter 5)

Third-Party Participation in Suicide

Assisting Suicide, Mercy Killing, and Murder

Virtually every state criminalizes assisting suicide.[129] In the United States (unlike Germany, Switzerland, Uruguay, and Colombia)[130] there is usually no distinction between so-called mercy killing and murder.[131] However, some

---

[125] Whiteside v. New York Life Ins. Co., 503 P.2d 1107 (Wash. App. 1972).

[126] Eckelberry v. Reliastar Life Ins. Co., 4689 F.3d 340, 344 (4th Cir. 2006).

[127] Actor Heath Ledger died from combining oxycodone, hydrocodone, Restoril, Xanax, Valium, and an over-the-counter antihistamine, and his death was ruled accidental. Sewell Chen, *Heath Ledger's Death Is Ruled an Accident*, N. Y. Times City Room Blog, Feb. 6, 2008, cityroom.blogs.nytimes.com/2008/02/06/heath-ledgers-death-is-ruled-an-accident/. Nevertheless, his insurance company initially refused to pay on a policy Ledger purchased seven months previously, intimating that his death was a suicide; his estate eventually reached a settlement with the insurance company, *Settlement Reached on Heath Ledger's Life Insurance*, Reuters, Jan. 29, 2009 at http://www.reuters.com/article/2009/01/29/us-ledger-idUSTRE50S60220090129#MHSIyDLfgCv7SDvy.97.

[128] Runge v. Metro. Life Ins. Co., 537 F.2d 1157 (4th Cir. 1976); Sigler v. Mutual Benefit Life Ins. Co., 506 F. Supp. 542, 543 (S.D. Iowa), *aff'd* 663 F.3d 49 (8th Cir. 1981), but see Conn. Gen. Life Ins. Co. v. Tommie, 619 S.W.2d 199 (Tex. App. 1976) (death held accidental).

[129] But with vastly different penalties, from felony (California, Cal. Penal Code § 10.401), second-degree felony (Florida, Fla. Stat. Ann. § 782.08), Class B felony (Missouri, Mo. Rev. Stat. Ann. § 5 65.023.1, which denominates assisted suicide as voluntary manslaughter, which under common law required the defendant to be provoked, five to fifteen years), Class D felony (Tennessee, Tenn. Code Ann. § 39-13-216 with two to twelve years imprisonment and a fine up to $5000); to a court order to cease and desist from assisting suicide (Ohio, Ohio Rev. Code § 3795.02 and Va. Code Ann. § 8.01-622.1). In Ohio, there may also be professional discipline, and in Virginia civil liability.

[130] See Chapter 4.

[131] People v. Cleaves, 280 Cal. Rptr. 146 (1991); however, see N.Y. Penal Law § 125.25(1)(b), in which assisting another person to commit suicide is an

prosecutors will not bring any criminal prosecution for third-party involvement in the death of an apparently consenting individual who is terminally ill[132] or greatly physically disabled. Others will.[133] Still others arrest the family member, or even bring charges and then subsequently drop them.[134] When prosecutors do bring cases, juries and even judges distort the law to achieve what they believe to be a just result.

Murder is classically known to jurisprudence as a crime where motive makes no difference. There is no official mitigation in the law for "mercy killing," and generally no exception to the rule that an individual may not consent to his or her death.[135] The legal term for this is that such a consent is "void," unrecognized by the law. This is a good thing, since obviously acceptance of consent as a defense would create certain unsavory incentives—what various professional fields, including insurance and law, call a "moral hazard."

The case used to make these points to law students in their textbooks is often *People v. Roberts*,[136] a very old case from the Michigan Supreme Court that stood as good law in Michigan until it was partially overturned in 1994 in the *Kevorkian* case. Roberts mixed up a poisonous concoction in a glass and put it at the bedside of his wife, who was bed-ridden with multiple sclerosis. There was apparently no dispute that she herself asked him to do it, reached for and took the glass, and drank from it and died. Suicide was not a crime in Michigan, but nevertheless, Roberts was convicted of murder, a verdict upheld by the Michigan Supreme Court, which noted that providing

---

affirmative defense to a charge of second-degree murder and will mitigate the charge to manslaughter. Myers v. Schneiderman, No. 151162/2015, Defendant's Memorandum in Support of Motion to Dismiss, filed Apr. 14, 2015, at 4, http://endoflifechoicesny.org/wp-content/uploads/2015/05/2015-04-14-Mem.ofLawinSupp.ofMotiontoDismiss.pdf.

[132] Sydney P. Freedberg, *Murder or Mercy?* ST. PETERSBURG TIMES, Jan. 31, 1999, http://www.sptimes.com/News/13199/State/Murder_or_mercy.html (Florida prosecutors rarely prosecute "mercy killings").

[133] *Id.*, quoting John Young, an assistant district attorney in Jefferson Parish, Louisiana, who put a sixty-one-year-old man who shot his ailing father behind bars for life, "I worry we're expanding the boundaries of what is an acceptable killing."

[134] *Mancini* case, Chelsea Zimmerman, *Charges Dropped Against Man Killing Father in Assisted Suicide*, LIFENEWS.COM, Dec. 12, 2011, http://www.lifenews.com/2011/12/12/charges-dropped-against-man-killing-father-in-assisted-suicide/; *Missouri Drops an Assisted Suicide Case*, N. Y. TIMES, Dec. 27, 1996, http://www.nytimes.com/1996/12/27/us/missouri-drops-an-assisted-suicide-case.html; Tony Perry, *Husband Won't be Charged in Wife's Suicide*, L. A. TIMES, Aug. 23, 2012, http://articles.latimes.com/2012/aug/23/local/la-me-assisted-suicide-20120823.

[135] In Montana, since *Baxter v. State*, consent is a defense to criminal charges of assisting suicide if brought against a physician who provided a competent, terminally ill individual with a prescription for a lethal dose of medicine, see Chapter 3 for a discussion at length.

[136] People v. Roberts, 178 N.W. 690 (1920).

an individual with poison with intent that the person die from drinking it was classic first-degree murder, and that this was precisely what Roberts had done. These days, supplying the means by which another person commits suicide, such as a gun, is charged as assisted suicide.

Yet of course, motive makes a huge difference in the outcome of a murder trial. Self-defense is a justification for murder, as is the defense of others. Necessity is an excuse. Motive and context are recognized in the law in a number of ways as reducing a murder charge. Being provoked beyond endurance mitigates murder to voluntary manslaughter, because it is believed the individual had reasonable grounds for temporarily losing his capacity for self-control (e.g., by finding his wife in bed with another man, or being tormented by his girlfriend for being too chicken to kill her,[137] but never, ever being called racial slurs[138]) mitigates murder to voluntary manslaughter.

For people who assist another to commit suicide, the Model Penal Code considers a person who aids or incites a successful suicide to be guilty of a second-degree felony, while a person with the same intentions and efforts to assist suicide whose efforts do not succeed can only be charged with a misdemeanor. In punishing the latter instance, the Model Penal Code recognizes a crime of attempted assisted suicide, which many states do not.

People who get charged with the crime of assisting suicide are predominantly family members,[139] with a few friends[140] and

---

[137] People v. Borcher, 325 P.2d 97 (Cal. 1958).

[138] State v. Crisantos, 508 A.2d 167 (N.J. 1986) (defendant called "Mexican shit" and "motherfucker").

[139] *Acquittal in Aided Suicide*, N. Y. TIMES, (Feb. 15, 1992), at A-10, *available at* www.nytimes.com/1992/02/15/us/acquittal-in-aided-suicide.html (man hands his chronically ill mother a loaded gun, which she uses to kill herself a few minutes later); *Willard Skellie Allegedly Helped Wife Commit Suicide: Kathie Skellie Found Dead in Upstate New York*, HUFFINGTON POST, Dec. 18, 2012, http://www.huffingtonpost.com/2012/12/18/willard-skellie-helped-wife-commit-suicide_n_2324614.html; Chris Kelly, *Prosecuting Woman in Dad's Death Is Wrong Choice*, [SCRANTON] TIMES-TRIBUNE, Aug. 25, 2013, http://m.thetimes-tribune.com/opinion/editorials-columns/christopher-j-kelly/chris-kelly-prosecuting-woman-in-dad-s-death-is-wrong-choice-1.1541398 (on Feb. 11, 2014, a judge dismissed the case); Frank Bruni, *Fatal Mercies*, N. Y. TIMES, Aug. 11, 2013, www.nytimes.com/08/11/2013/opinion/sunday/bruni-fatal-mercies.html?ref=assistedsuicide; Tony Perry, "Assisted Suicide or a Show of Love"? Los Angeles Times May 16, 2012, http://articles.latimes.com/2012/may/16/local/la-me-assisted-suicide-20120516/2. Lodi (California woman convicted of assisting her brother, a stroke victim, to commit suicide was sentenced to community service); San Diego man arrested (but ultimately not charged) for assisted suicide because he watched his wife kill herself and didn't try to stop her, www.articles/latimes.com/2012/aug/23/local/la-me-assested-suicide-20120823

[140] Fister v. Allstate Life Ins. Co., 1998 U.S. App. LEXIS 31613 (4th Cir. Dec. 18, 1998) (friend–employee shoots and kills woman when her suicide attempt fails;

lovers[141] thrown in for good measure. Generally aiding suicide involves procuring the gun, or showing the person how to use it, or both.

One problem with family members, as illustrated by the case of George E. Delury,[142] is that they do not limit themselves to assisting suicide, but rather engage in what can only be described as murder under the law: the intentional, deliberate, and premeditated killing of another human being.[143] After initially telling police that his wife, who had been ailing with multiple sclerosis, died after drinking a lethal mixture he prepared for her, Delury admitted that he had suffocated her with a plastic bag.[144] It's a little unnerving how often the people who do the killing are fathers,[145] husbands,[146]

---

pleads guilty to voluntary manslaughter and is sentenced to five years); *People v. Cleaves*, 280 Cal. Rptr. 146 (second-degree murder conviction for killing a friend with AIDS; state conceded friend had begged Cleaves to do so); William Yardley, *Connecticut Man, 74, Gets Probation for His Role in a Friend's Suicide*, N. Y. TIMES, Apr. 8, 2005, http://www.nytimes.com/2005/04/08/nyregion/08litchfield.html?_r=0; Steve Chawkins, *Prosecutors Going Easier on Assisted Suicide Among Elderly*, L. A. TIMES, Jan. 20, 2013, http://articles.latimes.com/2013/jan/20/local/la-me-suicide-assist-20130120 (referring to case where friend helped man commit suicide and received probation); Joseph Ax, *New Murder Trial for N.Y. Man Who Claimed He Assisted Suicide*, REUTERS, Oct. 3, 2013, http://news.yahoo.com/murder-trial-   n-y-man-claimed-assisted-suicide-230608484.html (friend claims he assisted in suicide by holding a knife in place against a steering wheel while his friend repeatedly stabbed himself; appellate court held he was entitled to a jury instruction on assisted suicide).

[141] Bettina Boxall, *Judge Refuses to Drop Charges in Assisted Suicide*, L. A. TIMES, Apr. 9, 1996, http://articles.latimes.com/1996-04-09/local/me-56493_1_physician-assisted-suicide.

[142] Susan Cheever, *"An Act of Mercy?"* N. Y. TIMES ON THE WEB BOOKS, July 20, 1997, https://www.nytimes.com/books/97/07/20/reviews/970720.cheever.html.

[143] John Wise, *Ohio Man, Gets 6 Years in Wife's "Mercy Killing,"* www.cbsnews.com/news/john-wise-ohio-man-gets-6-years-in-wifes-mercy-killing/ see also Tony Perry, *Assisted Suicide or a Show of Love*, L. A. TIMES, May 16, 2012, http://articles.latimes.com/2012/may/16/local/la-me-assisted-suicide-20120516 (Thomas May charged with the murder of wife Hazel, who had amyotrophic lateral sclerosis (ALS) after sitting with her in a running car. He hoped to die with her but survived, and committed suicide with a fatal overdose of pills before the trial).

[144] Cheever, *supra* note 145.

[145] *Griffiths v. State*, 548 So.2d 244 (Fla. App. 1989) (rejecting defense's argument that severely disabled three-year-old daughter was already "brain-dead" when her father shot her in her hospital bed).

[146] Chawkins, *supra* note 142 (elderly man found driving around with his wife's body in the back seat with a plastic bag cinched around her neck pleads guilty to assisted suicide and is sentenced to two days in jail and three years' probation); *State v. Sexson*, 869 P.2d 301, 303 (N.M. App. 1994) (after man gets out of prison for murdering his first wife, he and second wife agree to a suicide pact, but "[v]ictim's

boyfriends,[147] brothers,[148] nephews,[149] and sons,[150] killing wives, girlfriends, mothers, and children, including wives and children who are not terminally ill but disabled.[151] Sometimes, of course, mothers kill their disabled children,[152] and daughters kill their disabled mothers[153] or grandmothers.[154] One of the basic themes of this book is that there is an enormous difference between giving someone a lethal prescription and injecting them with it, as there is an enormous difference between preparing a deadly mixture that your wife can choose to drink and suffocating her with a plastic bag. We cannot lose sight of the plain distinction between suicide and homicide, in whatever arena it arises (e.g., "suicide by cop" is homicide; however justified, it is not suicide).[155]

Yet it's also unnerving how rarely juries convict these individuals, and how often judges give extraordinarily lenient sentences[156] or even praise them from the bench. Faced with cases where a defendant is charged with murder for outright killing a terminally ill family member, juries have found the defendant not guilty by reason of insanity, with an accompanying postscript that the defendant is no longer mentally ill, leading to the defendant's discharge: "resorting to reasons of insanity for acquittal in mercy killing cases is a common tactic."[157] In fact, one reason that some disability organizations oppose the "right to die" is that in some of these cases, the family member was not terminally ill—indeed, not ill in any sense of the word, but rather severely disabled, and neither consulted nor consenting to the act of "mercy".[158]

---

ability to breathe after being shot 'freaked out' defendant, and as a result, he was unable to kill himself"); People v. Williams, 638 N.E.2d 345 (Ill. App. 1994); Gilbert v. State, 487 So.2d 1185 (Fla. App. 1986); see also Cheever, *supra* note 139.

[147] Boyle v. Ivanhoe, 214 S.W. 3d 250 (Ark. 2005).

[148] Zygmaniak v. Kawasaki, 330 A.2d 56 (N.J. Sup. 1974).

[149] William Kay v. Fairview Riverside Hosp., 531 N.W. 2d 513 (Minn. App. 1995).

[150] Edinburgh v. State, 896 P.2d 1176 (Okla. App. 1995) (stepson shoots terminally ill stepfather, does not prevail on argument that he should have been prosecuted as assisting a suicide); State v. Forrest, 362 SE2d 252 (N.C. 1987); Hislop v. State, 64 S.W. 3d 544 (Tex. App. 2001).

[151] GUIDO CALABRESI & PHILLIP BOBBIT, TRAGIC CHOICES 57–64 (1978).

[152] Sean Gardiner, *Mercy Killing Defense to Be Tested*, WALL ST. J., Aug. 11, 2011, http://www.wsj.com/articles/SB1000142405311190414060457649617227275084 8 (mother kills her disabled son because she believes she will lose custody to biological father who will sexually abuse son).

[153] People v. Stuart, 67 Cal. Rptr. 3d 129 (Cal. App. 2007).

[154] State v. Smith, 522 S.E. 2d 321 (N.C. App. 1999).

[155] See infra at pp. 362–370.

[156] See n. 142. *supra* and n. 160 *infra*.

[157] Daniel C. Maguire, *Death, Legal and Illegal*, ATLANTIC MONTHLY, Feb. 1974, www.theatlantic.com/past/docs/issues/95sep/abortion/mag.htm (recounting at least five such cases); see *Zygmaniak v. Kawasaki*, 330 A.2d 56.

[158] Maguire, *id.* (noting insanity defense for man who killed his "crippled adult daughter who was spastic, mute and had been hospitalized all her life"), although

The case of Louis Repouille in 1947 is an excellent example.[159] His application to become a citizen of the United States hit a snag: there was a requirement that he show himself to be of "good moral character" during the five years prior to his petition, but four years previously he had been convicted of manslaughter for chloroforming his thirteen-year-old son.[160] The difficult question before the appellate court was whether this offense should bear on his moral character. The judges in this case were among the most illustrious that have ever graced the bench in the United States: Learned Hand, Augustus Hand, and Jerome Frank. This is how Learned Hand, in a time shortly after Nazi Germany, described the man's situation:

> His reason for this tragic deed was that the child suffered from
> birth from a brain injury which destined him to be an idiot and a
> physical monstrosity malformed in all four limbs. The child was
> blind, mute and deformed. He had to be fed; the movement of his
> bowels and bladder were involuntary, and his entire life was spent
> in a small crib.[161]

The man had four other children and a wife to support and the thirteen-year-old was a burden. Repouille was charged with manslaughter in the first degree for a crime that was obviously murder. The jury reduced the charge to manslaughter in the second degree (the crime of nondeliberate killing, a finding characterized by the appellate court as "utterly absurd") and implored the judge for "utmost clemency."[162] The judge hastened to comply: Repouille was given a stayed sentence and placed on probation.

Despite finding the provocation to euthanasia "overwhelming" and comparing Repouille implicitly to abolitionists who had ignored the law to follow their conscience,[163] the majority upheld the denial of his petition for citizenship. The only reason they did so was that Repouille had the burden of proof, and they couldn't say whether his act was relevant to good moral character:

> [F]or we all know that there are great numbers of people of the
> most unimpeachable virtue, who think it morally justifiable to put
> an end to a life so inexorably destined to be a burden to others,
> and—so far as any possible interest of its own is concerned—
> condemned to a brutish existence, lower indeed than all but the
> lowest forms of sentient life.[164]

---

this is an old article, the practice has not ceased; see ANDREW SOLOMON, NOT FAR FROM THE TREE: PARENTS, CHILDREN, AND THE SEARCH FOR IDENTITY (2012).
[159] Repouille v. U.S., 165 F.2d 152 (2d Cir. 1947).
[160] Id.
[161] Id.
[162] Id. at 153.
[163] Id.
[164] Id.

On the other hand, they noted (without citation) that a man who had recently killed his disabled child in Massachusetts had been sentenced to life imprisonment[165] and surmised that "only a minority of virtuous persons" would support euthanasia "while it remains in private hands." They noted pointedly that he had only to reapply for citizenship and the five-year period would have run.

Courts are more divided in their response to friends who kill, allegedly at the request of the dead individual. For some reason, courts seem to find it more plausible and forgivable when a family member kills another family member than when a person is killed by a friend. Some courts find that this constitutes murder and do not even let the jury consider an instruction on assisted suicide.[166] Others convict the friend, but mete out extremely light sentences.[167]

Whatever the dangers of permitting physicians who were previously unknown to an individual to participate in assisted suicide under regimes requiring reporting and consultation with a second doctor, and there are many,[168] they pale in comparison to the potential for abuse in framing a family member's active killing of another family member as "assisted suicide." Sometimes these murders, as in the case of Repouille, are the result of caregiver fatigue,[169] or aging, or the caregiver being diagnosed with an illness him- or herself. As a social policy/law matter, sympathy for caregivers would be far better expressed with respite programs, subsidies for adult day-care programs, expanding insurance coverage for home health and personal care assistants, and any number of other measures, rather than simply ordering probation when a caregiver finally snaps and kills a disabled or terminally ill family member.

---

[165] This was John F. Noxon, a wealthy Pittsfield, Massachusetts attorney who had electrocuted his six-month-old son who had Down syndrome and lied about it to police. Originally sentenced to death and commuted to a life sentence, he ultimately served only six years. The facts of this case are discussed (for reasons that are not clear to me) on a website entitled 'Celebrate Boston', http://www.celebrateboston.com/crime/noxon-mercy-killing.htm, which, to its credit, recognizes that what was called a 'mercy killing' in 1943 would be called 'genocide' today.

[166] State v. Goulding, 799 N.W. 2d 412 (S.D. 2011); State v. Cobb, 625 P.2d 1133 (Kan. 1981).

[167] Yardley, *supra* note 136 (seventy-year-old man convicted of second-degree manslaughter for helping his friend to die; although crime carries a ten-year sentence, defendant given "accelerated probation," a remedy created specifically for his case).

[168] See Chapter 5.

[169] In many criminal cases involving family members, the one doing the killing describes being overwhelmed or overburdened, see Freedberg, *supra* note 128, and *State v. Goulding*, 799 N.W. 2d 412.

Suicide, Third-Party Involvement, and the First Amendment

Occasionally, members of organizations publicly devoted to assisting people to commit suicide are also criminally prosecuted. Members of the Final Exit Network (FEN) have been criminally prosecuted in Arizona,[170] Georgia,[171] and Minnesota[172] (the latter case involved the death of a woman who had suffered from chronic pain for more than ten years). The prosecutions of FEN members have resulted in making First Amendment law, with defendants successfully challenging criminal prohibitions on "intentionally advising and encouraging" suicide as violative of their free speech rights.

In the Minnesota case, the trial court judge had attended the premiere of a Tony Kushner[173] play entitled *"An Intelligent Homosexual's Guide to Capitalism and Socialism with a Key to the Scriptures"* in which a father gathers his family to inform them that he has decided to commit suicide, and the family argues about whether to respect those wishes or try to institutionalize him. In the play, a friend of the father's explains—in graphic detail—how to commit suicide. The judge asked the state prosecutors whether Kushner could be criminally prosecuted for assisting suicide. No, said the prosecutors, because Kushner wasn't targeting the information at a known person contemplating suicide, as FEN members were. FEN derided this argument as legalizing information given to many, while criminalizing information given to one. The Minnesota courts ultimately sided with FEN, throwing out both the prohibition on "advising" and "encouraging" suicide as violative of the defendants' first amendment rights. Conduct amounting to assisting suicide could still be criminalized, which FEN had never questioned.

At the same time as the FEN members' prosecution, the case of a former nurse named William Melchert-Dinkel was also wending its way through the Minnesota courts.[174] Melchert-Dinkel posed as an empathetic female nurse on the Internet, claiming he was also depressed and suicidal. He encouraged suicidal people to follow through with their plans, giving them precise instructions and at least ten times pretending to join them in a suicide

---

[170] See Chapter 10 for an extended discussion of the case of Jana van Voorhis.

[171] See Chapter 3. The criminal law under which the members were prosecuted was thrown out by the Georgia Supreme Court as violative of the First Amendment because it criminalized protected speech as well as assisting suicide; the Georgia legislature speedily passed a new law.

[172] Minnesota v. Final Exit Network, Nos.A13-0563, A13-0564, A13-0565 (Minn. App. Sept. 30, 2013) http://mn.gov/lawlib/archive/ctapun/1309/opa130563-093013.pdfv.

[173] Author of ANGELS IN AMERICA: A GAY FANTASIA ON NATIONAL THEMES (1993), among other plays.

[174] State v. Melchert-Dinkel, 816 N.W.2d 703 (Minn.App.2012)(*Dinkel I*), rev'd by State v. Melchert-Dinkel, 844 N.W. 2d 13 (Minn. 2014).

pact. He also asked to watch them commit suicide via webcam. He tried to persuade a young woman who wanted to jump off a bridge to hang herself instead so he could watch. He was convicted of assisting the suicide of one man, and attempting to assist the suicide of the young woman (the charge was reduced to attempt to assist suicide because she jumped off the bridge against his advice). An appellate court in Minnesota upheld all parts of his conviction, including the "encouraging and advising" suicide charges, around the same time that the FEN appellate court ruled that these provisions of the law violated the First Amendment. The Minnesota Supreme Court took the Melchert-Dinkel case and passed on the FEN case.

The Minnesota Supreme Court held that criminalizing "advising" and "encouraging" suicide was unconstitutionally broad. Since those were the grounds on which Melchert-Dinkel was convicted, the case was returned to the trial court to reconsider. The trial court reinstated the conviction, finding that a person could "assist" suicide by speech alone, if that speech consisted of intentionally instructing a specific individual on how to commit suicide. Melchert-Dinkel was sentenced to three years in prison but was given probation that included six months in jail.[175] At the same time, he appealed his conviction.[176] By the time this book is published, the Court of Appeals (and perhaps the Minnesota Supreme Court) will have ruled again.

Mellchert-Dinkel seems obviously more creepy than the FEN exit guides, and not only because he (honestly if rather foolishly) told police that he undertook his activities "for the thrill of the chase"[177] or because he initially blamed his daughters for the Internet messages.[178] When you think about it, though, it's hard to pinpoint why Melchert-Dinkel should be more criminally responsible than the FEN guides: the argument that he "assisted" the suicides of people who were thousands of miles away is much more tenuous than in the case of the FEN exit guides, who were right there handing out helium canisters and bags. Is it just because of the deception, the fake suicide pacts and the lying about being female and wanting to commit suicide himself? Is it because he sought people out, while FEN waits to be contacted? But FEN is out there on the Internet very publicly as well. Is it because he wanted to watch? FEN exit guides watch as well. One of Melchert-Dinkel's victims had a long-term and painful medical condition. The legal issue looks pretty much identical, and FEN filed a friend-of-the-court brief supporting Melchert-Dinkel's First Amendment argument. Interestingly, a state police association

---

[175] Amy Forliti, "William Melchert-Dinkel Sentencing: Former Nurse Tried to Assist Canadian's Suicide," Huffington Post (Canada), Oct. 15, 2014, http://www.huffingtonpost.ca/2014/10/15/william-melchert-dinkel_n_5989372.html

[176] AP, "Appeals Court Considers Minnesota Assisting Suicide Case," Oct. 9, 2015, http://www.nujournal.com/page/content.detail/id/945755/Appeals-court-considers-Minnesota-assisting-suicide-case.html?isap=1&nav=5031

[177] Id.

[178] Dinkel I at p. 13.

also filed a friend of the court brief, supporting the state and noting that liberalizing assisted suicide laws would make their jobs more dangerous.[179]

One of the interesting distinctions between FEN and Melchert-Dinkel is that their more personal approach is labor-intensive, while Melchert-Dinkel could, theoretically, encourage as many people to kill themselves as he could reach on the Internet. The Internet has raised other first amendment issues in the area of suicide, including cyberbullying, which we will take up next.

Suicides, Bullied Children, and the First Amendment

First Amendment issues also arise in cases involving the question of whether cyberbullying that causes a child, teen, or young adult to commit suicide should trigger criminal responsibility.[180] Criminal charges against the perpetrators of cyberbullying are generally either not brought, or dismissed by judges, no matter how cruel and brutal the messages. For example, after Lori Drew, the neighbor of thirteen-year-old Megan Meier, created a fake MySpace boy named "Josh Adams" to befriend the girl, and then had "Josh" turn on her inexplicably, posting "You are a bad person and everyone hates you" and "the world would be a better place without you,"[181] the girl, Megan Meier, hanged herself. The county prosecutor declined to press charges, although Missouri criminalizes negligently causing the death of another as second-degree involuntary manslaughter.[182]

The law, however, is filled with surprises, and imagine Ms. Drew's surprise when she found herself indicted for a crime in the Central District of California. The federal government charged her with violating the Computer Fraud and Abuse Act (CFAA)[183] because she accessed the servers of MySpace (guess where they are located!) and exceeded authorized access on the MySpace account to obtain information used to further a tortious act (intentionally inflicting emotional distress on Megan Meier). Drew went to trial and was acquitted of felony violation of the Act (i.e., she did not exceed

---

[179] David Chanen, *Case of Former Minnesota Nurse Convicted of Urging Suicides Sent Back to Lower Court*, Star Tribune, Mar. 19, 2014, http://www.startribune.com/local/west/251116591.html.

[180] Stephanie Slifer, *Cops: Mass Girl, 18, Encouraged Boy to Take His Life* (CBS News, Feb. 27, 2015), http://www.cbsnews.com/news/cops-massachusetts-girl-18-encouraged-boy-to-take-his-life/ (Michelle Carter charged with involuntary manslaughter for repeatedly urging boy to kill himself, including telling him to get back in the car where he was inhaling carbon monoxide when he got out and said he didn't want to leave his family).

[181] The neighbor, Lori Drew, claimed her temporary employee sent the final messages, but acknowledged having started the fake identity in order to humiliate Megan Meier.

[182] Mo. Stat. § 565.024.

[183] 18 U.S.C. §1030 (West 2014).

authorized use of the MySpace account to intentionally commit the tort of intentional infliction of emotional distress). The jury convicted her of the misdemeanor violation of the Act (she did intentionally exceed the authorized use of MySpace because she violated the MySpace contractual terms of use when she made up an individual who did not exist and used "his" account to provide information known to be false or misleading, to harass another person, and that was "potentially offensive" and "promoted hatred . . . against an individual.")[184]

There is no doubt that Drew violated the terms of use of MySpace, but the judge vacated her criminal misdemeanor conviction on "void for vagueness" grounds. To summarize a dense and scholarly ten pages or so, which thoroughly covered the meaning of "intentionally" (vs. "knowingly"), "access a computer," and "without authorization," none of us ever click on "Terms and Conditions" when we sign up for stuff on the Internet, and to convert any violation of these "terms and conditions" (set by the service provider, not the government) into a crime (even if only a misdemeanor) would "convert a multitude of otherwise innocent Internet users into misdemeanant criminals"[185] (including people who lie about their age, weight, or attractiveness on Match.com.).[186] The sweep of the statute is so broad that the police and prosecutors could easily unfairly enforce it.[187]

The CFAA is a federal statute. However, the suicides of many children as a result of Internet bullying have given rise to many, many state statutes, most of them named after the child in question[188] (e.g., the Megan Meier Cyberbullying Prevention Act, the Jessica Logan Act[189])). Missouri quickly began prosecuting cyberbullying under the Megan Meier law. The highest court in the state of New York recently struck down the Albany County cyberbullying law as violative of the First Amendment,[190] because it criminalized any communication done with "intent to annoy, threaten, abuse,

---

[184] U.S. v. Drew, Case No. 2:08-cr-00582-GW (M.D. Ca., Aug. 28, 2009) at *7. Opinion available at 259 F.R.D. 449 (C.D. Ca. 2009) or at http://www.dmlp. org/sites/citmedialaw.org/files/2009-08-28-Opinion%20on%20Drew%27s%20 Rule%2029%28c%29%20Motion_0.pdf.

[185] *Id.* at 29.

[186] *Id.*

[187] *Id.* at 31–32.

[188] Vermont's Bully Prevention Law, Act 117 (2004), was prompted by the suicide of Ryan Halligan but is not named after him. In Canada, legislation after the suicide of Amanda Todd was not named after her, and in fact her mother, who had supported legislation to curtail cyberbullying, expressed concern that the proposed legislation went too far in violating Canadians' right to privacy. CTV News Staff, "Anti-cyberbullying bill could harm privacy rights, Amanda Todd's mother warns," May 13, 2014, http://www.ctvnews.ca/canada/anti-cyberbullying-bill-could-harm-privacy-rights-amanda-todd-s-mother-warns-1.1819653

[189] Ohio H.B. 116, https://stateimpact.npr.org/ohio/tag/hb-116/

[190] People v. Marquan M., 24 N.Y. 3d 1 (2014).

taunt, intimidate, torment, humiliate, or otherwise inflict significant emotional harm on another person." The New York court said prohibitions of pure speech were prohibited unless they qualified as "fighting words, true threats, incitement, obscenity, child pornography, fraud, defamation, or statements integral to criminal conduct."[191] A later court found that the communications "Go kill yourself bitch," "You're not worth the air to take the jump bitch," and "I can have you handled" did not meet those standards.[192]

As in the *Drew, Marquan,* and *Meier* cases, most legal cases against bullies accused of crimes in the wake of the suicides of their victims amount to very little. In the most famous case—the Tyler Clementi suicide after secretly filmed sexually explicitly videos were posted on Twitter[193]—the twenty days of jail time was a result of a plea deal. Although there was a great deal of publicity about the prosecution of the teens associated with the suicide of Phoebe Prince, who took her own life in 2010, those cases also ended in plea agreements with punishments of probation and community service.

In one case, after twelve-year-old Rebecca Sedwick killed herself after a long campaign taunting her on Facebook, including "Drink bleach and die," and the fourteen-year-old arrested in connection with her death posted on Facebook, "Yes, I bullied Rebecca and she killed herself, but I don't give a __ ___,"[194] the State Attorney declined to prosecute. In fact, the fourteen-year-old girl's family sued the Sheriff of Polk County because he had named their daughter in a press conference.[195] Meanwhile, the family of Rebecca Sedwick filed their own lawsuit against the Polk County School system, accusing of insufficiently protecting their daughter from bullying.[196] Their lawsuit is highly unlikely to succeed: almost every court to consider the matter has held that schools have no affirmative constitutional duty to protect children from their vicious and rapacious fellow students,[197] and are immune from

---

[191] *Id.* at 7.

[192] People v. Orr, 2015 Slip Op. 50568 (U.) (Crim. Ct. N.Y. Cty. Apr. 22, 2015).

[193] Kelly Ebbels, *Tragic End for a True Talent,* NORTHJERSEY.COM, Oct. 1, 2010, www.northjersey.com/news/tragic-end-for-a-true-talent-1.920406?page=all.

[194] Steve Almasy, Kim Segal and John Couwels, "Sheriff: Taunting Post Leads to Arrests in Rebecca Sedwick Bullying Death," CNN Oct 16, 2013, http://www.cnn.com/2013/10/15/justice/rebecca-sedwick-bullying-death-arrests/

[195] Chris Collette, *Family of Girl Arrested in Bully Case to Sue Sheriff* (WTSP TV), Sept. 18, 2014, http://www.wtsp.com/story/news/local/2014/09/18/polk-sheriff-rebecca-sedwick-lawsuit/15819351/.

[196] *Id.*

[197] Moore v. Chilton County Board of Educ., No. 2:12-cv-424-WKW (M.D. Ala. Mar. 27, 2013) (overweight girl with disease that made her bowlegged was pushed, mocked, had her pants and underwear stripped down, was locked in a janitor's closet, jumped from bridge to her death, did not state a constitutional claim against the school because school's failure to intervene did not shock

most state tort suits. When a student suicide receives a great deal of publicity, school districts sometimes settle rather than fight them.[198]

More recently, Michelle Carter, a Massachusetts teen, was charged with involuntary manslaughter for encouraging a friend to commit suicide, to the point of rebuking him when he changed his mind and telling him to go back and do it[199] (with friends like this, who needs ...). This is a very different issue than the one of relentless bullying driving an individual to suicide, which involves cruel and thoughtless people contributing to but not necessarily intending to cause the resultant suicidality. The charges against Michelle Carter and others like her,[200] generally denominated as manslaughter, do not allege that the defendant had anything to do with causing the suicidality, but rather with deliberately encouraging an already suicidal individual to commit the act, thus showing either intention or recklessness as to the person's suicide. Knowing a person is suicidal, and urging that individual forward, makes the suicide much more foreseeable than subjecting the person to weeks and months of torment, and therefore more serious as a matter of criminal law. Morally, I don't think you have much to choose from here.

There are all sorts of interesting and complex legal and public policy questions raised by these cases. First of all, almost all of the cases involve children, teens, and young adults—on both sides. Lori Drew, who created the fake "Josh Adams," was one of the very few adult defendants. Second, in many cases the bullying is perpetrated by a group of children or teens, who egg each other on in tormenting the victim. Third, in most cases, unlike the

---

the conscience); Sutherlin v. Indep. School Dist., No. 40 Nowata County, No. 12-cv-636-JED-PJC (N.D. Okla. May 13, 2013) (school officials watched student being beaten up and failed to intervene, called student "crazy" in front of other students, who followed suit, did not shock the conscience); Estate of Asher Brown v. Cypress Fairbanks Indep. School Dist., 863 F. Supp. 2d 632 (S.D. Tex. 2012) (no constitutional duty to protect student from "private violence" by other students; no duty to enforce school's own antibullying policy).

[198] Associated Press, *Phoebe Prince School Bullying Lawsuit: Massachusetts Case Settled for $225,000*, HUFFINGTON POST, Dec. 28, 2011, http://www.huffingtonpost.com/2011/12/28/phoebe-prince-bullying-la_n_1172755.html.

[199] Michael E. Miller, "Michelle Carter Can Face Manslaughter Charge for Allegedly Encouraging Boyfriend's Suicide, Judge Rules," Washington Post, Sept. 24, 2015, https://www.washingtonpost.com/news/morning-mix/wp/2015/09/24/michelle-carter-can-face-manslaughter-charge-for-allegedly-encouraging-boyfriends-suicide-judge-rules/; Jim Hand, *Lawyer: Plainville Teen "Bewildered" Over Involuntary Manslaughter Charges in Friend's Suicide Death*, SUN CHRONICLE, Apr. 23, 2015, http://www.thesunchronicle.com/news/local_news/lawyer-plainville-teen-bewildered-over-involuntary-manslaughter-charges-in-friend/article_ba5a8a3e-e9d9-11e4-b645-e7549f97c906.html.

[200] See People v. Duffy, 79 N.Y. 2d 611 (N.Y. 1992) (person who urged a suicidal man to commit suicide and handed him a loaded gun could be charged with manslaughter when the man committed suicide).

Tyler Clementi case, these are not single events, the norm for our concept of crime, but take weeks or months of building, unceasing cruelty (thus leading to the criminal analogy to stalking, which is unsatisfactory for a variety of reasons). Fourth, the courts have sometimes appeared to draw a distinction between "pure speech" and activities such as the filming of Tyler Clementi. Fifth, in most cases, it appears that the goal is to torment the victim; the goal is not necessarily to drive him or her to suicide. The Michelle Carter case, in which the defendant allegedly specifically egged on a suicidal individual when he seemed to be hesitating in his intent, actually presents a very different legal issue than most cyberbullying. In the criminal law, "intent"— desiring a specific outcome—is very different from "recklessness"—knowing that it is possible and being indifferent to that outcome. These mental states, in turn, have an effect on the analysis of causation: did the bullying "cause" the suicide? Did Michelle Carter's alleged insistence that Conrad Roy go through with his suicide make her more culpable than Lori Drew? When a person intends for his or her actions to lead to a particular outcome, and they do, we are more likely to conclude that the person caused the outcome. On the other hand, bullying is ubiquitous,[201] but only rarely does the victim commit suicide.

I agree that children and adolescents must be protected from bullying. I think there must be a different policy and legal standard applied to the abuse and harassment that adults are expected to bear as part of an imperfect life, and what children should be expected to endure. Children *are* different from adults, and the reason we have to stop them from killing themselves[202] is the same reason they must be better protected from bullying: underdeveloped impulse control and the lack of experience to put both their own suffering and the despicable and ignorant losers who bully them in perspective.

Nowhere is there is a wider gap between the urgent command of the heart that something must be done and the painstaking and tedious work of implementing a remedy than in the case of bullying of children. Most states now have laws addressing the issue,[203] requiring, as James Maguire says, "carving out a meaningfully determinate concept of bullying from the wilderness of adolescent cruelty."[204] They do this in a climate where teens who are punished (quite mildly) for having websites that cruelly ridiculed another

---

[201] James Maguire, *"Everyone Does It to Everyone": An Epidemic of Bullying and the Legislation of Transgression in American Schools*, 16 NEW CRIM. L. REV. 413 (2012).

[202] See Chapter 1 (arguing that most adults are competent to make the decision to die, but that children are not, and excluding minors from the argument); Chapter 2 (arguing that adults should generally not be involuntarily committed on the basis of suicidality, but excluding children from the argument).

[203] Thirty-three states as of 2012, see Maguire, *supra* note 204.

[204] *Id.*

student, file lawsuits with the support of their parents for interference with their First Amendment rights.[205]

These laws are based on wildly different assumptions about the nature of the problem and its remedies. Some laws, and the publicity that accompanied their passage, treat the bullies who drove children to suicide as aberrant and evil individuals, who have to be punished to send a message that their behavior was intolerable.[206] Some laws hold parents responsible. I myself want to thrash bullies, or their parents, or both. But the bullies are children and young adults, too, with their own set of problems and pain: indifferent and conflicted families[207] and a higher than average suicide rate.[208] Should we treat bullying children and adolescents as responsible agents, punishable under the criminal law, but their victims as insufficiently responsible agents to make decisions about suicide?[209]

Other states pass laws prohibiting bullying based on certain protected characteristics, such as disability, race, or gender. Indeed, a stunning proportion of cases brought in the aftermath of student suicides are brought as disability discrimination cases under Section 504 of the Rehabilitation Act. A study of more than 600,000 students in more than 16,000 schools showed that 40% of those who were bullied attributed at least some of it to their gender, race, ethnicity, religion, physical or mental disability, and—especially—actual or perceived sexual orientation.[210] While constitutional claims against

[205] Kowalski v. Berkeley County Schools, 652 F.3d 565, 569 (4th Cir. 2011) (the school's position was upheld by the Court of Appeals. The student in question was suspended for ten days, not allowed to attend school events in which she was not a participant for ninety days, and forbidden from crowning the next "Charm Queen"—she herself having been chosen as "Charm Queen" the year prior).

[206] FLA. STAT. ANN. § 1006.147(3); OHIO REV. CODE § 3313.666.

[207] Sheryl A. Hemphill and Jessica E. Heerde, "Adolescent Predictors of Young Adult Cyberbullying Perpetration and Victimization Among Australian Youth," 55 Journal of Adolescent Health 580 (2014).

[208] Dorothy L. Espelage and Melissa K. Holt, "Suicidal Ideation and School Bullying Experiences After Controlling for Depression and Dellinquency," 53 Journal of Adolescent Health 527 (2013), http://www.ncdsv.org/images/JAH_Suicidal-ideation-and-school-bullying_7-2013.pdf; I.W. Borowsky, A.W. Taliaferro, and B.J. McMorris, "Suicidal Thinking and Behavior Among Youth Involved in Verbal and Social Bullying: Risks and Protective Factors," 53 Journal of Adolescent Health s4 (2013), *J Adolesc Health.* 2013 Jul;53(1 Suppl):S4–12. doi: 10.1016/j.jadohealth.2012.10.280.

[209] Walsh v. Tehachapi Unified School Dist., 827 F. Supp. 2d 1107, 1120 (E.D. Cal. 2011) (stating that if the alleged failure of defendants to remedy two years of severe sexual orientation based harassment when the student was eleven to thirteen years of age caused a mental condition that made him unable to understand the nature of his act or control his conduct, his suicide was not an "independent" act breaking the chain of causation).

[210] Dorothy L. Espelage, *Why Are Bully Prevention Programs Failing in U.S. Schools?* 10 J. CURRICULUM & PEDAGOGY 121 (2013).

school districts are virtually impossible to win, disability and gender discrimination claims, with a marginally easier standard of proof, are sometimes successful. When the harassment is based on a protected category, such as gender or disability, the school can be liable if responsible school officials knew of harassment that was so "severe, pervasive, and objectively offensive" that it deprived the student of access to education, and the school officials were deliberately indifferent to it.[211]

Massachusetts and other states have taken a more systemic approach to bullying, assigning to schools the responsibility for controlling bullying. Massachusetts passed a law after Phoebe Prince killed herself that addresses bullying as a structural problem to be solved by schools. This mandate (a word that seems to be used only in the cases where the law does not come with any funding, as was the case with the Massachusetts law) required schools to have bullying prevention plans, including restrictions on the use of technology to harass another student, and to ensure teachers were trained to recognize bullying. It is not clear that most of the standard anti-bullying programs are effective;[212] some of them may even increase bullying.[213]

Suicide Pacts

The tolerance and understanding shown by courts and juries to family members who directly kill a sick or disabled family member, even by shooting the person, evaporates completely if a person claims to have been part of a suicide pact who ends up surviving, even if he or she made valiant and multiple attempts to complete the deed.[214] While some courts have held that survivors of suicide pacts cannot be charged with any crime at all,[215] most courts are extremely suspicious of survivors of suicide pacts, intimating that survival "g[ives] rise to a presumption ... that the participant may have entered the pact in less than good faith."[216]

Courts have struggled with whether to conceptualize a "bad-faith" survivor of a suicide pact as a murderer, or guilty of manslaughter, or an aider or

---

[211] Davis v. Monroe County, 526 U.S. 629, 645–46 (1999).

[212] Espelage, *supra* note 196.

[213] Seokjin Jeong & Byung Hun Lee, *A Multilevel Examination of Peer Victimization and Bullying Prevention in School*, 203 J. CRIMINOLOGY (2013), http://www.hindawi.com/journals/jcrim/2013/735397/.

[214] Kirchner v. State, No. 08-11-00368-CR (8th Dist. Tex., May 16, 2014) (unpublished case) (son sentenced to twenty-nine years for murdering his mother when both attempted to die in a suicide pact of carbon monoxide poisoning; upon finding he had survived, son attempted to hang himself).

[215] These cases come from states where assisting suicide is not a crime, e.g., State v. Sage, 31 Ohio St. 3d 173, 178 (1987).

[216] S.W. Brenner, *Undue Influence in the Criminal Law: A Proposed Analysis of the Criminal Offense of "Causing Suicide,"* 47 ALB. L. REV. 62, at 85–86 (1982).

abettor of suicide. In most cases, the survivor of a suicide pact is charged with murder.[217] In one case, two teenagers entered a suicide pact and drove off a cliff. The driver survived. Had the passenger survived, he might at most have been charged with assisting suicide, but the driver was the direct agent of the death of the passenger, and under a standard application of the law, would be guilty of first-degree murder.[218] In this case, the California Supreme Court opted for the less drastic crime of aiding and abetting a suicide.

Another paradox of the law is that while suicide in the singular is often considered the result of insanity, the survivor of a suicide pact is almost never treated as insane by courts.[219] Indeed, in very few of the criminal cases is the defendant subjected to psychiatric evaluation at all.

It boils down to this: if you are part of a suicide pact, you had better follow through and make good on your promises.[220] All the talk about destigmatizing suicide, or that it's a result of a mental illness and should be treated and not punished, the temporary insanity excuses and the whole medical model vanishes in a kind of time-machine puff, because while the person who survives his or her own individual suicide attempt is generally seen as needing treatment, the person who survives suicide pact is regarded with a judicially jaundiced eye as a probable suicide malingerer.

Unlike Japan, American suicide pact partners tend to know each other and act in pairs. Also unlike Japan, many are elderly couples or teenagers. But individuals do not need to ever have met for one to be charged with assisting suicide. As we saw with William Melchert-Dinkel, the Internet has raised all kinds of possibilities unforeseen a few decades ago: encouraging suicide, inciting suicide, and even assisting suicide by sending poison to an individual in another country knowing he planned to take it to kill himself.[221]

When a defendant deliberately causes someone to commit suicide, the notion that the individual behaved independently and voluntarily is erased, and the defendant is generally found guilty of some form of homicide. While it is true that in many cases, the court concludes that the defendant's act drove the victim mad, and the suicide resulted from that inability to control

---

[217] Williams v. State, 53 So.3d 734 (Miss. 2010); Nordstrom v. State, No. 03-12-00012-CR (Tex. App. 3d Dist., May 12, 2014); Perry, *supra* note 140.

[218] *In re* Joseph G., 34 Cal. 3d 429, 667 P.2d 1176 (1983). Implicit in these cases is the intention of the dead individual to also have committed suicide. See also Patterson v. Gomez, 223 F.3d 959 (9th Cir. 2000).

[219] This is true of both the suicide pact where each person is in charge of his or her own self-destruction and the murder–suicide pact where one person kills another and is supposed to then kill himself (in murder–suicide pacts, the murderer is usually a man).

[220] Unless you are elderly, in which case you will often get more of a break.

[221] Scott Dolan, *Windham Man Denies Mailing Cyanide Used in Suicide*, Portland Press Herald, Nov. 14, 2014, http://www.pressherald.com/2014/11/05/maine-man-arrested-in-fatal-poisoning-of-man-in-england/.

conduct,[222] courts have also found the defendant guilty if a criminal act led to a "sane" suicide, for example in the case of a man who deliberately starved himself to death several years after being shot and rendered severely disabled.[223]

The punishment of the law is supposed to be the same whether someone assists, encourages, persuades, or coerces another to commit suicide, but it seems to me that these verbs describe very different situations. For example, when a husband taunts his drunk, emotionally disturbed, and suicidal wife and helps her to obtain and fire a loaded gun,[224] it seems qualitatively different from the boyfriend who, when asked by his drunk and suicidal girlfriend (she had lost custody of her children) to explain how to load a gun, not only showed her but also loaded it and placed it near her.[225]

Duty to Prevent Another from Suicide

Under U.S. law, no one has a duty to prevent anyone else's suicide unless that person is in your custody and control and/or you have a "special" relationship with that person. There is no duty for pastoral counselors,[226] landlords, bartenders, friends,[227] and, especially schools,[228] which don't have a duty to prevent someone from committing suicide, even if they had a pretty good idea it might happen. The Hawaii Supreme Court has held that counselors don't have a duty to prevent suicide.[229] The absence of duty to prevent suicide has also been used to bar liability when a security company hired, trained, and provided a gun to Mr. Bailey, who had a history of mental illness, including several hospitalizations and a diagnosis of bipolar disorder with psychotic features. He used the weapon he had been provided to kill himself a month after he was hired. The Court of Appeals for the District of Columbia Circuit held that the "special relationship" exception did not apply, when the security company had neither physical custody nor specialized training in mental health, and that Bailey's suicide was a deliberate, intentional, intervening act.[230]

---

[222] Stephenson v. State, 205 Ind. 141, 179 N.E. 633 (1932).
[223] People v. Velez, 159 Misc.2d 38 (N.Y.Sup.Ct. Bronx Cty 1993).
[224] Persampieri v. Commonwealth, 175 N.E. 2d 387, 390 (Mass. 1961) (husband guilty of manslaughter).
[225] State v. Marti, 290 N.W. 2d 570, 579 (Iowa 1980).
[226] Nally v. Grace Community Church, 47 Cal. 3d 278 (Cal. 1988).
[227] Lenoci v. Leonard, 21 A.3d 694 (Vt. 2011) (eighteen-year-old friend did not have duty to prevent suicide of fifteen-year-old when she took fifteen-year-old to party where she drank and slept with a man not her boyfriend and took her life in remorse).
[228] Mikell v. School Admin. Unit No. 33, 972 A.2d 1050 (N.H. 2009); Walsh v. Tehachapi Unified School Dist., No. 1:11-cv-01489-LJO-JCT (E.D. Cal. 2014), see generally pp. 358–359, supra.
[229] Lee v. Corregedore, 925 P.2d 324 (Haw. 1996).
[230] Rollins v. Wackenhut Serv., 703 F.3d 122 (D.C. Circ. 2012).

Virtually the only people outside medical and mental health professionals who may have some kind of affirmative duty around suicide are the police. When the Ninth Circuit asked the California Supreme Court[231] "whether sheriff's deputies owe a duty of care to a suicidal person when preparing, approaching, and performing a welfare check," the California Supreme Court substantially rephrased the question as whether "liability can arise from tactical conduct and decisions employed by law enforcement officers preceding the use of deadly force,"[232] and, unsurprisingly, phrased that way, affirmed that the police had a duty to refrain from unreasonable use of deadly force. In other words, police don't have to affirmatively keep a suicidal person in the community alive, but when they shoot that person dead, they should (at the very least) have acted reasonably.

Suicide by Cop

"The more I think about it, police should be required to make reasonable accommodations before shooting *anybody*."

Dr. Joel Dvoskin, commenting on *Sheehan*, a case raising the issue of whether police should have accommodated a mentally ill woman prior to shooting her

This book is about the irrationality of social policy and law in the realm of suicide, and rarely is that irrationality so clearly reflected as the fact that the first responders in many cases involving suicidal people are the police. When people are suicidal, if they or their family or friends call 911 for help, they will likely be connected to the police.[233] School officials who think a student is suicidal call the police.[234] Even suicide hotlines, if they are convinced the person may be imminently suicidal, call the police.

This sometimes results in armed police coming in cars with sirens flashing. Even when they approach more quietly, police cannot, by their own rules, back away from an encounter without at least making contact with the subject, and often the very last thing a frightened, desperate person who is already at the end of his or her rope wants is a chat with a uniformed police officer. This stalemate almost never ends well. If the person does not want to talk or let police into the house, they may push in anyway, or they may call for backup. This situation may evolve into the police surrounding the house

---

[231] In our federal–state court system, federal courts, faced with an important question of state law as yet unresolved by the state's courts, can "certify" a question to the highest court of that state.

[232] Hayes v. County of San Diego, 57 Cal. 4th 622, 626, 305 P.3 252 (Cal. 2013).

[233] Mercado v. City of Orlando, 407 F.3d 1152, 1154 (11th Cir. 2005).

[234] Bruce v. Guernsey, 777 F.3d 872, 874 (7th Cir. 2015); Shuay'B Greenaway et al. v. County of Nassau, No. 11-CV-2024 (WFK) (AKT), (E.D.N.Y. Mar. 31, 2015).

for hours, and sometimes days.[235] They may break down the door to get to a suicidal person. If the person doesn't want to come along, he or she may be dragged out, however elderly or undressed they happen to be.[236] People very often are killed in the first few minutes of these encounters, episodes which are often erroneously called "suicide by cop" (see below).

It is perfectly clear that police kill a lot of people with psychiatric disabilities: for three years in a row, every single person killed by San Francisco police had a mental illness.[237] Even if the individual opens the door and lets the police in, if the police decide to take the person to an emergency department for evaluation, police protocol will almost inevitably require that the person be placed in handcuffs. This includes children in most parts of the country. It includes people up to the age of ninety-seven. This may be the first time the person has ever been in handcuffs, or in a police car. And this is a person who was feeling powerless, friendless, and miserable in the first place.

I would like to be clear at the outset here. I am not (except in certain individual cases) blaming the police. They are the fall guys here. Like emergency departments, they have to respond, especially if there is any indication that a weapon might be involved and public safety threatened. Like emergency departments, they are trained to respond in a certain way, which is great for most of their job but is the worst possible way to respond to a suicidal person. They probably didn't choose to be police officers because they wanted to help convince people that life was worthwhile, or because they had a knack for therapeutic engagement.

Police are routinely placed in impossible situations. Towns and cities may be unwilling to fund crisis services, or, when they do, crisis workers who are supposedly trained to help people in crisis (hence the job title) may insist that uniformed police accompany them if someone is suicidal. When police are notified that an unstable individual has access to weapons, they are trained

---

[235] Heckensweiler v.McLaughlin, 515 F. Supp. 2d 707, 712-13 (E.D. Pa. 2007) (between 3:30 p.m. on Sept. 15, and the morning of Sept. 16, 2004, police engaged in a "military-style showdown," surrounded the house of a suicidal man, cut off electricity, played loud music, told him over a megaphone that he was "all talk," and fired "hundreds of canisters of pepper spray" into his home); Kris Mohandie, J. Reid Meloy, & Peter I. Collins, *Suicide by Cop Among Officer-Involved Shooting Cases*, 54 J. FORENSIC SCI. 2, 456 (2009), http://www.researchgate.net/profile/John_Meloy/publication/24018739_Suicide_by_Cop_Among_Officer-Involved_Shooting_Cases/links/0912f50a68d944e6fc000000.pdf (officers surrounded a suicidal person's house for nine days).

[236] McCabe v. Life-Line Ambulance Serv., 77 F.3d 540 (1st Cir. 1996) (elderly Holocaust victim); Moore v. Wyo. Med. Ctr., 825 F. Supp. 1531 (D. Wyo. 1993) (dragged out of house from shower); Kerman v. City of New York, 261 F.3d 229 (2d Cir. 2001); Anaya v. Crossroads Managed Care Sys., 195 F.3d 584 (10th Cir. 1999).

[237] AlexEmslie and Rachael Bale, *infra* at n. 270.

to not stop until the threat is eliminated, and in the case of people who are desperate and despairing, the threat is sometimes eliminated by eliminating the person. A man named Sam Cochrane who worked for the Memphis Police Department has saved many lives by developing an intensive training for police in dealing with people with psychiatric disabilities called "crisis intervention training (CIT)," but CIT has been implemented unevenly—San Francisco had a hard time even getting police to sign up—and in many situations a better alternative would be to leave police out of suicide altogether.

Nor do I blame frightened and desperate family members for calling 911. They are afraid of what is going on with their (usually) child and don't know what to do or how to help. This is a book about policy and law, and it's up to the larger communities—commissioners of police, mayors, governors, and state legislatures—to fix this so that people stop dying. By the time the family calls 911 and the police arrive, it's too late to prevent (at the very least) trauma and humiliation.

At the outset, I want to raise a specific objection to the phrase "suicide by cop." We don't call euthanasia "suicide by doc" and I think that's a good thing. There are many reasons that "suicide by cop" is inappropriate. The most important one is that the word "suicide" should never be used to describe a killing by another person, whether it's a mercy killing or seppuku or euthanasia, or a killing by someone acting in what he or she genuinely believes to be self-defense. Particularly in the case of ending someone's life, we need to keep boundaries clear.[238] Killing someone in self-defense may indeed be unavoidable, but that doesn't convert the action somehow into the other person's suicide.[239]

---

[238] This is also true of another suggested term, "suicide by proxy." Courts agree that when someone kills someone else, it's not "suicide" in all sorts of cases, see Fister v. Allstate Ins., 783 A.2d 194 (Md. 2001) (a suicidal person who persuades a friend to kill her has not committed suicide, explicitly overruling lower court that had used "suicide by cop" analogy to hold that such a situation constituted suicide). In some ways, these boundaries were blurred early because many important right to refuse treatment decisions, from *Quinlan* to *Cruzan*, involved third-party decisions that someone else would not have wanted to live. One of the most important aspects of the *Cruzan* decision is the explicit recognition that there is an enormous and important distinction between decisions made and actions undertaken by a specific individual that result in his or her own death, and decisions made and undertaken by someone else to end that person's life. I think people with disabilities are largely overestimating the risk to disabled people posed by assisted suicide, but I think they are absolutely right to worry about euthanasia, treatment refusal, and do not resuscitate (DNR) orders agreed to by a guardian on behalf of a disabled person.

[239] All instances of "suicide by cop" in Los Angeles between 1987 and 1997 were correctly ruled by the coroner as "homicides" rather than "suicides," H. Range Hutson, Deirdre Anglin, John Yarborough, & Kimberly Hardaway, *Suicide by Cop*, 32 ANN. EMERG. MED. 665 (1998).

One alternative that has been suggested by Vivian B. Lord is "victim-precipitated homicide."[240] It is accurate to use the word "homicide" ("the killing of one human being by another"), but "victim-precipitated" has some ugly associations: "they asked for it."[241] The public thinks that is literally true, but on many occasions, it is simply not accurate. In most cases that I have reviewed, as well as in the research literature, it is relatively rare for an individual to decide in advance to kill himself (at least 90% of these cases involve men) and deliberately set up a situation in which the person lures a cop to do the deed.[242] There are exceptions, of course, but most cases reflect absolutely the opposite: people who are terrified of the police, situations that escalate out of control very quickly that could have been prevented, and that the person who was killed did not plan or deliberately provoke. There is a massive disconnect between police training and protocols and what people who are in the grip of intense emotions need, but calling these situations "victim-precipitated" does not do justice to the discretion available to the police officer to have behaved differently, and the skill, courage, and professionalism of officers who do behave differently.[243]

Another proposed term is "law enforcement officer assisted suicide,"[244] which I don't think captures the nature of the interaction between the law enforcement officer and the suicidal person. These are traumatizing events with many consequences for the police officers involved, always investigated and often litigated, and while the use of the phrase "suicide by cop" is correctly seen by police officers as trivializing and derogatory,[245] I think "law enforcement officer-assisted suicide" would seem even creepier.

No one likes "suicide by cop," but it is nevertheless part of the lexicon and a popularly understood term. Therefore, it is important to define it as accurately and narrowly as possible. As I define it, "suicide by cop" means a suicidal person who purposely and with intent to be killed provokes a police

---

[240] The title of the book is equally off-putting: VIVIAN B. LORD, SUICIDE BY COP: INDUCING OFFICERS TO SHOOT: PRACTICAL DIRECTION FOR RECOGNITION, RESOLUTION AND RECOVERY (2004) (2d ed. 2015). The words "de-escalation," "slow down," and "CIT" appear nowhere in the first edition of this book. When an individual is killed by a police officer, Lord considers that "successful" for the individual.

[241] By this logic, Emmett Till was a victim-precipitated homicide.

[242] When they do, it's often because they don't have easy access to guns, see Julia Dahl, *How to Stop Suicide by Cop*, PACIFIC STANDARD, Feb. 21, 2011, *available at* www.psmag.com/health-and-behavior/how-to-stop-suicide-by-cop-27758.

[243] See Sullivan v. State, 898 So.2d 105 (Fla. App. 2005) (man charges at two armed police officers with knife and they do not fire; he drops it at the last minute, within five to fifteen feet of one police officer).

[244] Hutson et al., *supra* note 239.

[245] Suicide by Cop: Averting the Crisis (2009). http://www.medicine.virginia.edu/community-service/services/ciag/programs/preparedness/conferences/suicide-by-cop-averting-the-crisis.html

encounter in which the police officer is placed in the position of reasonably believing he or she must fatally shoot the individual to save his or her own life or the life of others.

My definition of true "suicide by cop" corresponds to James Drylie's definition, that a person must "voluntarily enter into a confrontation with the police, communicate suicidal intent, and act in a threatening manner toward the police,"[246] or with the first of Homant and Kennedy's three definitions: "Direct Confrontations, in which suicidal subjects initiated attacks on police."[247] Using this definition, suicide by cop (SBC) happens[248]—often the person asks or demands or begs the police officer to shoot him—but this describes far fewer than half of police encounters called "suicide by cop." For example, in the definitive study by Mohandie and colleagues,[249] only 16% of the so-called SBC situations were deliberate and planned; 82% of individuals had not intended to die the day they were shot by police. In Homant and Kennedy's study, only 30% of the events were "Direct Confrontations" and (logically) only 30% were planned. Almost three-quarters of the individuals killed by police had no intention when they began the day to end the day dead. These situations are tragedies involving interactions between individuals who are each, in different ways, pushed to the breaking point.

Like many others, I disagree strongly with Homant and Kennedy's second definition of "suicide by cop": "Disturbed Interventions, in which potentially suicidal subjects *took advantage of police interventions* to attempt SBC."[250] As Mohandie and colleagues point out, without apparent irony, "The paradox among SBC cases is that unplanned, acute suicidality becomes, within moments, a resolute intentionality to be killed by the police once the engagement begins."[251] Far from taking advantage of police interventions to force the police to kill them, cases show these people locking doors or barricading them[252] (which are broken down by the police with battering rams),[253]

---

[246] JOHN M. VIOLANTI & JAMES DRYLIE, COPICIDE: CONCEPTS, CASES AND CONTROVERSIES OF SUICIDE BY COP (2008); see also Hutson et al., *supra* note 239 (defining suicide by cop as "an incident in which a suicidal individual intentionally engages in life-threatening and criminal behavior with a lethal weapon or what appears to be a lethal weapon toward law enforcement officers or civilians to specifically provoke officers to shoot the suicidal individual in self-defense or to protect civilians").

[247] Robert J. Hormant & Daniel B. Kennedy, *Suicide by Police: A Proposed Typology of Law Enforcement Officer-Assisted Suicide*, 23 Policing: Int. J. POLICE STRATEGIES & MGMT. 339 (2000); Mohandie et al., *supra* note 235.

[248] See, e.g., *Hummell v. Rivera*, (D.N.M. 2013).

[249] Mohandie et al., *supra* note 235.

[250] *Id.* (italics mine).

[251] Mohandie et al., *supra* n. 235.

[252] *Russo v. City of Cincinnati*, 953 F.2d 1036 (6th Cir. 1992).

[253] *Stewart v. City of Prairie Village, Kan.*, 904 F. Supp. 2d 1143 (D. Kan. 2012); *Linbrugger v. Abercia*, 363 F.3d 537 (5th Cir. 2004).

hiding in bathrooms[254] and basements, or behind bushes in their own backyards,[255] refusing to come out and confront the police who are throwing blinding grenades into their houses[256] or cutting off their electricity.[257] These are the majority of police killings of suicidal people.

Homant and Kennedy's third scenario, when a perpetrator caught in a crime acts in a provocative and reckless way, often because of drugs or alcohol in his or her system, doesn't correspond to any but the broadest definitions of suicide, the ones that include an enormous swath of reckless behavior where the risk of death was both foreseeable and, in complex ways, part of the motivation of undertaking the conduct. A lot of behavior while drunk or high might fall in this category, but I don't think it's properly understood as suicidal. To use the language of the law, suicide requires the mental state of "intent," and these situations are the very essence of "recklessness." Many people speak of leaving their deaths up to fate, acting out the ambivalence that characterizes many suicidal people. Cases involving this kind of situation read so differently from the other situations we have just considered[258] that I don't even think this category is properly included.

The most common situation called "suicide by cop" is a complete misnomer applied when a police officer, called to the scene by onlookers or family concerned about a person's explicit or implicit suicidality, kills an individual who had taken no steps whatsoever to initiate contact with police and was not in the process of committing any crime except, perhaps, trespass on land.[259] These situations are almost always the result of rapid escalations in which the police (whose arrival is often a total surprise to the suicidal person[260]) engage in tactics—pointing guns, yelling orders, unleashing barking dogs,[261] that increase the pressure on and overwhelm an individual already at the breaking point. The police themselves are far from calm or controlled

---

[254] Molchon v. Tyler, 546 S.E. 2d 691 (Va. 2001); Furtado v. Law, No. 4D09-3223 (4th Dist.Ct.Appeal Fla Feb. 2, 2011).

[255] Adams v. City of Fremont, 80 Cal. Rptr. 2d 196 (1999).

[256] Meckensweiler v. McLaughlin, 515 F. Supp. 2d 707, 712–13 (E.D. Pa. 2007).

[257] *Id.*

[258] Compare, e.g., *Boyd v. City & County of San Francisco*, 576 F.3d 938 (9th Cir. 2009) (man is killed by police after assaulting two women at gunpoint and leading police on a high speed chase).

[259] There are cases where homeowners are horrified to find a stranger in their house, and understandably call the police, who have a duty to respond. This is not what I mean by trespass.

[260] Linbrugger v. Abercia, 363 F.3d 537 (5th Cir. 2004).

[261] Adams v. City of Fremont, 80 Cal. Rptr. 2d 196, 68 Cal. App. 4th 243 (1998).

in these situations. The mean number of rounds fired by police in these incidents is sixteen. The range is 0^{262} to $614.^{263}$

A clear protocol should be in place to deal with situations such as Dustin Wernli's in Tucson. If a veteran with PTSD like Wernli calls 911 to say "he was feeling suicidal and wanted to be shot by a police officer,"[264] the police department should not obligingly send over six armed police officers to shoot him within fifteen minutes. When Susan Stuckey, known to the police to have a psychiatric disability, called 911 and asked "that the police bring her cigarettes and that the police should be armed because she wanted police to kill her, she would give them a reason to kill her, and she was going to commit suicide by cop,"[265] it wasn't necessarily the right thing to do to send "fifteen or more police officers"[266] to her apartment. One of the clearest situations in which the Rolling Stones' principle that "you can't always get what you want" should be adhered to is when someone calls 911 to explicitly ask for suicide by cop.[267]

Often when families call police for assistance with a person who is suicidal, that person is killed or injured within minutes of police arrival.[268] In one major study, 29% of police encounters were over within the first ten minutes, and 41% within the first fifteen minutes.[269] The mode in that study was ten minutes for men and two minutes for women. Other times there are "stakeouts" that take hours, if not days, and escalate the situation unbearably for the suicidal person. Police throw "flash-bang" grenades into the house.[270]

---

[262] Sometimes people kill themselves during encounters with police.

[263] Mohandie et al., *supra* note 235; *Russo*, 953 F.2d 1036 (by the time he died, man had been tasered four times and shot with twenty-two bullets; the last round of bullets was fired after he had dropped crumpled in a stairwell).

[264] Veronica M. Cruz, *Suicidal Man Shot by Tucson Police Dies*, ARIZONA DAILY STAR, Jan. 17, 2013, http://tucson.com/news/local/crime/suicidal-man-shot-by-tucson-police-dies/article_f0467aae-6056-11e2-abd5-001a4bcf887a.html.

[265] *Stewart*, 904 F. Supp. 2d 1143.

[266] *Id.*

[267] See also Hainze v. Richards, 207 F.3d 795 (5th Cir. 2000) (aunt calls police to tell them her nephew says he wants to commit "suicide by cop" and three armed deputies were dispatched in a marked police car; upon first encountering Hainze one police officer immediately drew his weapon).

[268] *Id.* (20 seconds between police arrival and shooting of Hainze); Nelson v. County of Wright, 162 F.3d 986 (8th Cir. 1998) (unarmed person beaten on the head with nightstick and shot in his bedroom within three minutes of police arrival); Clem v. Corbeau, 284 F.3d 543 (4th Cir. 2002) (plaintiff was pepper sprayed and shot three times "within a short time" after police arrival); Allen v. Muskogee, 119 F.3d 837 (10th Cir. 1998) (shooting took place within 90 seconds of police arrival on scene).

[269] Mohandie et al., *supra* note 235, at 458; Hutson et al., *supra* note 239 (70% of shootings take place within first thirty minutes).

[270] Alex Emslie & Rachel Bale, *More Than Half of Those Killed by San Francisco Police Are Mentally Ill* (KQED, Sept. 30, 2014), http://blogs.kqed.org/newsfix/2014/

Sometimes a person with a psychiatric disability is more or less minding his or her own business at home, asleep, or in the shower,[271] but his or her so-called helping professionals are worried, and so they call the police. They should know better.

Although the numbers are not clear, and depend very much on definitions, it is clear that many suicidal people are killed every year by police, and many of these deaths result in heart-breaking litigation, a way for parents and loved ones who feel endlessly guilty because they called the police to absolve themselves, or avenge their children, or to make the world a better place by having better training for police officers.

The litigation is heart-breaking in part because during the course of it, the family relives and relives the circumstances of the person's death, and because at the end of it all, the police usually win. There are a number of potential claims under the U.S. Constitution: unreasonable seizure under the Fourth Amendment, deprivation of the substantive due process right to life under the Fourteenth Amendment, or failure to train under the Fourteenth Amendment. There are also claims for discrimination brought under the Americans with Disabilities Act and Section 504 of the Rehabilitation Act.

In cases that solely involve suicidality (not where family members or friends fear for their own safety or the safety of others), we need to reframe the issue as primarily one for crisis intervention, rather than police. This does not require a new three-digit number: a 911 operator receiving a call about a suicidal person could connect immediately to 24/7 crisis response services, who can take more time on the telephone to ask questions that should be explored prior to taking any action. Perhaps these calls should be connected to suicide hotlines, where people are trained to listen and have vast experience in this specific issue. Even when police have policies requiring that the most basic information be obtained prior to response to a call regarding suicidality, this policy is often ignored.[272]

Those crisis workers would have to be confident and sufficiently trained to not involve the police themselves. Police should have clear and distinct protocols about when to respond, and when to refer the call to entities better equipped to respond. And they should have training and assistance to deal with "mixed" situations where a person may be psychotic, threatening,

---

09/30/half-of-those-killed-by-san-francisco-police-are-mentally-ill/?utm_source=Facebook&utm_medium=Social&utm_campaign=FBKQED4123 (recounting the story of Errol Chang, who was eventually killed by the police after his mother called because she was worried about her son's deteriorating psychiatric state, which took the form of thinking people were trying to assassinate him. Having armed police pointing automatic weapons at him didn't help).

[271] *Moore*, 825 F. Supp. 1531.

[272] *Shuay'B Greenaway*, No. 11-CV-2024 (Nassau County policy required inquiry about specific mental health condition, background, and behavior before interacting with individual, but this was not done).

and suicidal. The CIT units can be effective when they hew to the original Memphis model, but there is not much out there stopping any police department from calling any unit its "CIT" unit without much fidelity to Sam Cochrane's original conception.

Conclusion

Although there are many different kinds of suicidality and suicide requiring different policy and law responses, I have tried to emphasize some overarching themes in this chapter, which echo the themes of earlier chapters.

First, we should draw a very bright and explicit line between a person's own actions in ending his or her life, and those of a third party. Euthanasia, "mercy killing" by relatives, and "suicide by cop" are all shorthand words for homicide, and we should never, ever forget it.[273] One reason that I am opposed to rhetorical devices like "aid in dying" is because they blur the line between suicide and homicide. It has been observed countless times that people who are suicidal are very often profoundly ambivalent: the insertion of a euthanizing doctor or an armed cop or a caretaker with complex motivations into this mix diminishes the chance that the person will ultimately decide in favor of life because the decision is, in a very concrete way, taken out of his or her hands. Protections for autonomy in decisions about suicide are important, but any extension of these protections to third parties should, as in the *Cruzan* case, rightly command heightened scrutiny—extremely heightened scrutiny. If there is a right to die, it is the classic example of a right that should not be exercised by proxy.

A second theme of this book is to slow things down and keep talking. This applies to police, to holding off on involuntary detention and hospitalization of chronically suicidal and contingently suicidal people, and to avoiding immediate coercive interventions with people who state that they wish to cease eating and drinking. Voluntary cessation of eating and drinking as a method permits a degree of conversation that most other suicide methods preclude. Thus, providers err when they act to force-feed or evict or involuntarily commit people who communicate the intention of foregoing food and even hydration. It is enormously important to free people to talk about feeling suicidal without catastrophic consequences. People who are chronically suicidal use the possibility of suicide as a kind of reassurance to get through hard times, and the nation's most experienced clinicians do not believe that

---

[273] For example, as one writer pointed out in a somewhat different context, the death of Jesus, although easily avoidable by Jesus' making different decisions, should not be characterized as "empire assisted suicide" (Christian Piatt, *Was Jesus' Death an Act of "Empire-Assisted Suicide"?* HUFFINGTON POST, Nov. 13, 2014, http://www.huffingtonpost.com/christian-piatt/was-jesus-death-an-act-of_b_6153660.html).

hospitalization is necessarily an appropriate response when people are suicidal in an ongoing way. If people who are chronically suicidal are going to substitute a more constructive framework, they are going to have to be able to talk about their feelings without the hammer of hospitalization being held over their heads.

A third theme of this book, highlighted in this chapter, is the importance of a public health approach. While some people have suicidality etched into their identity by trauma, and others are the unwitting victims of medication reactions or a life crisis that feels impossible to handle, there is almost always a *reason* for being suicidal. Assuming that suicidality is a symptom of mental illness that can be medicated away, or that the solution is to fix the person, short-circuits the attempt to resolve underlying systemic issues, like cyber bullying. For example, reduction of the rate of suicide among women veterans, or people in jail, or members of the Navajo tribe, may require a structural approach. Certainly, police shootings of suicidal people requires such an approach, and blaming individuals solves little if any of the underlying issues. In the next chapter, we will look at how employers and universities do better by approaching suicide as a community issue, and worse by approaching it as the problem of aberrant individuals.

8

Discrimination on the Basis of Suicidality

Fear about professional and social repercussions is the only reason.
Not being considered as a candidate for a job even though I am
qualified because information about suicide is known about me.
          "Kara,"[1] (explaining why she wished to be anonymous)

I was afraid [of giving talks about suicide prevention citing her
personal experience] because I wondered whether my job is going
to be at stake. I went to my principal and told the principal, I am
going to come out about this, what if parents find out and say they
don't want me teaching their kids? Am I going to be in danger of
losing my job? I have been given this opportunity to try to help
others, and I want to use it.

—Lex Wortley[2]

Introduction

There is no doubt whatsoever that people who are known to have attempted
suicide suffer adverse consequences, socially and professionally. Most
people are unaware of just how far this discrimination reaches: decisions
about where you live, what kind of employment you can have, whether
you can be licensed to pursue a profession, whether you can keep custody of your children, or even keep visiting them,[3] whether you can go
back to your dorm or your college or even attend off-campus college

---

[1] Interview with Kara (pseudonym) (Jan. 11, 2015).
[2] Interview with Lex Wortley (Feb. 25, 2014).
[3] *In re* David D., 28 Cal. App. 4th 941 (Cal. App. 1994).

events.[4] Discrimination on the basis of suicidality can be hazardous to your health: if a person is known to be suicidal, medical symptoms are interpreted through a psychiatric lens, which may mean missing an important medical condition, with resulting complications and even death.[5]

As a society, we are torn between conflicting narratives about suicide, including whether, when, and how much it should be stigmatized and punished. Police officers and members of the military who attempt suicide are subject to punishment.[6] We are still uncertain what, if anything, a suicide attempt means about a person. The law reflects our confusion. This confusion begins with the question of whether discrimination on the basis of suicidality is or should be illegal.

Employment

In the workplace, people who are known to have thought about suicide or attempted suicide are fired,[7] even when their doctors say they are fine to

---

[4] Lyons v. Marist College, N. 7:2009cv02290 (S.D.N.Y. filed Mar. 12, 2009), complaint *available at* The Law Office of Karen Bower, https://thelawofficeofkaren-bower.wordpress.com/home/court-cases/.

[5] For a comprehensive and illuminating discussion of the medical issues which can be misdiagnosed as psychiatric issues, see William Matteson, "Missing the Diagnosis: The Hidden Medical Causes of Mental Disorders," a continuing education lecture, June 26, 2015, http://www.continuingedcourses.net/active/courses/course067.php

[6] In several cases, female police officers who attempted suicide were charged with disciplinary infractions, see Stokes v. City of Montgomery, Civil Action No. 2:07cv686-WHA (WO) (M.D. Ala. Sept. 25, 2008) (charged with violating the rule that an officer must remain fit for duty); Perkins v. Silverstein, 939 F.2d 463, 467 (7th Cir. 1991) (female police officer who attempted suicide was charged with violating Rule 15.20, which prohibited police officers from "engaging in any activities, on or off duty, 'which indicate instability of character or personality' and 'give the appearance of impropriety.'"). In another case, when an employee attempted suicide with a gun, his employer was stunned that he was released after four days in the hospital and was "not in jail." *Lizotte v. Dakotah Bank*, 677 F. Supp. 2d 1155, 1166 (D.N.D. 2010) (although the facts of the case reflect that when his sister tried to take the gun away from him, he told her to 'let go unless you want to go first,' there is no indication from the employer's testimony that he knew about this or was referring to it). Almost one hundred years ago, the U.S. Supreme Court asserted confidently that "it cannot be doubted that the State may prohibit and punish self-maiming and attempts at suicide," N. Y. Cent. R.R. Co. v. White, 243 U.S. 188, 207 (1917).

[7] Velger v. Cawley, 525 F.2d 334 (2d Cir. 1975) (information about suicide attempt would necessarily stigmatize man seeking work as police officer), *rev'd on other grounds sub nom* Codd v. Velger, 429 U.S. 624 (1977) (*per curiam*) (as a probationary employee plaintiff only had right to hearing if he claimed report of suicide attempt was false).

return to work,[8] even when the employers' doctors say they are fine to return to work,[9] and even when they have been exemplary employees.[10] They are denied security clearances, and therefore cannot obtain or maintain certain jobs.[11] Their licenses to practice law and medicine are made contingent on indefinite and nonconfidential therapy.

Both the Americans with Disabilities Act (ADA) and Section 504 of the Rehabilitation Act[12] prohibit discrimination based on disability. A "disability" is defined as a "physical or mental impairment that substantially limits one or more major life activities."[13] Many "life activities" are considered "major" under the ADA; the most relevant one in connection with suicidality is "caring for self."[14]

I have spent much of this book arguing that suicidality is not necessarily caused by or an indication of mental illness, nor does it necessarily impair a person's ability to function. Therefore, I strongly believe that suicidality, by itself, is insufficient to constitute a disability under federal law. Even people who are so suicidal that they are substantially limited in the major life activity of caring for themselves would not necessarily be disabled under the law unless their desire to die was a symptom of a "physical or mental impairment." Wanting to die, by itself, does not mean that a person has a physical or mental impairment under Section 504 or the ADA. Thus, a person whose suicidality is caused by major depression or bipolar disorder is likely to be found to be disabled, as long as he or she is also substantially limited in one or more major life activities. Having a diagnosis of a psychiatric condition is also insufficient by itself, because a person may have a psychiatric diagnosis and not be substantially limited in any major life activity. In fact, at least one court has held that a doctor's work clearance demonstrates that the person is not disabled,[15] a magnificent demonstration of precisely the kind of

---

[8] Wolski v. City of Erie, 773 F. Supp. 2d 577 (W.D. Pa. 2011); Chandler v. Specialty Tires of Am., 283 F.3d 818 (6th Cir. 2002) (state antidiscrimination law); Spades v. City of Walnut Ridge, 186 F.3d 897 (8th Cir. 1999); *Lizotte*, 677 F. Supp. 2d 1155; *Stokes*, Civil Action No. 2:07cv686-WHA(WO); EEOC v. Amego, 110 F.3d 135 (1st Cir. 1997); Doe v. Region 13 Mental Health-Mental Retardation Comm'n, 704 F.2d 1402 (5th Cir. 1983); *Peters v. Baldwin-Union Free School Dist.*, 320 F.3d 164 (2d Cir. 2003).

[9] *Stokes*, Civil Action No. 2:07cv686-WHA (WO), at n.5; *Wolski*, 773 F. Supp. 2d 577, at n.5.

[10] *Chandler*, 283 F.3d 818 (6th Cir. 2002); *Doe v. Region 13*, 704 F.2d 1402.

[11] Blazy v. Tenet, 979 F.Supp. 10, 21 (D.D.C. 1997).

[12] 29 U.S.C.A. § 794a (2014). Section 504 prohibits discrimination on the basis of disability by all entities receiving federal funds.

[13] 42 U.S.C.A. § 12102(1).

[14] 42 U.S.C.A. § 12102(2)(a).

[15] *Stokes*, Civil Action No. 2:07cv686-WHA (WO).

stereotypes the law was intended to prohibit, since many disabled people go to work every day.

However, a person who is suicidal but not mentally ill is protected by both Section 504 and the ADA if an employer *regards* the person as being mentally ill (having a physical or mental impairment) and acts adversely toward the person based on that perception.[16] Thus, a person who joked about being suicidal at work and suffered adverse employment consequences argued successfully that her employer perceived her as mentally ill and substantially limited in the major life activity of caring for herself,[17] even though she was not.[18] The law also protects a person who currently has no disability from discrimination based on his or her record of disability.[19] Thus, a person who is discriminated against because of a history of hospitalizations and suicide attempts related to a psychiatric disability also falls into the category of "person with a disability" even if that individual is not currently disabled.

Whether suicidality, by itself, suffices to constitute disability under the ADA or Section 504 doesn't often arise as a legal issue. This is because people whose failed suicide attempts come to the attention of an employer are usually hospitalized, and once they are hospitalized, they inevitably end up with a diagnosis that constitutes a mental impairment. For the most part, defendants tend to concede that an employee who attempted suicide is disabled under Section 504 and the ADA.[20]

This is because both Section 504 and the ADA also require that an employee be "qualified" for the job,[21] which is defined as "able to perform the essential elements of the job, with or without reasonable accommodations." Employers, especially those involved with public safety, such as police and fire departments, or with vulnerable populations or access to medications, such as mental health workers or pharmacists, tend to argue that a person who has attempted suicide cannot, by definition, be "qualified" for his or her job.[22] But this is clearly not true, by itself. If a doctor clears the person to

---

[16] 42 U.S.C.A. § 12102(2)(C).

[17] *Peters*, 320 F.3d 164; *Stokes*, Civil Action No. 2:07cv686-WHA (WO), at n.11. Before the Americans with Disabilities Amendments Act of 2008 (ADAA) took effect in 2009, plaintiffs had to prove that the employer both perceived them as having an impairment and also perceived that the impairment substantially limited them in one or more major life activities. Since 2009, plaintiffs must only prove that the employer perceived them as having a physical or mental impairment and acted adversely toward them based on that perception. Of course, both before and after the ADAA, plaintiffs must show that they are qualified for the job in question.

[18] *Chandler*, 283 F.3d 818, at n.7 (interpreting Tennessee antidiscrimination law).

[19] 42 U.S.C.A. § 12102(2)(B).

[20] *EEOC*, 110 F.3d 135; *Doe v. Region 13* 704 F.2d 1402, 1408, see n. 8.

[21] 42 U.S.C. § 12111(8), 29 C.F.R. 1630.2(m).

[22] *Wolski*, 773 F. Supp. 2d 577; *Stokes*, Civil Action No. 2:07cv686-WHA (WO); *EEOC*, 110 F.3d 135, at n.14, *Doe v. Region 13*, 704 F.2d 1402.

return to work, courts tend to assume that the person is qualified for the job, in the absence of evidence to the contrary.

Even if an employee can prove all the elements of her discrimination claim, employers also often use the "direct threat" affirmative defense in cases involving suicidality.[23] An affirmative defense means that the employer concedes that it discriminated on the basis of disability, but can establish that it had an excuse recognized by law to do so. The affirmative defense of "direct threat" permits an employer to discriminate on the basis of disability if the disability causes a "direct threat" to the person[24] or to others that cannot be remediated by a reasonable accommodation.[25] For example, refusing to hire a blind school bus driver is clearly discrimination on the basis of disability, but an employer could argue either that the disabled person could not prove that he or she was qualified for the job, or that the applicant would have posed a "direct threat" to others that could not be remediated by a reasonable accommodation. Because suicide endangers the person attempting it, you might think the direct threat defense would be automatically applied to all cases involving suicidality, but the employer must meet a very high bar to prove "direct threat"—the focus is on the employee's "present ability to safely perform the essential functions of the job," requiring an "individualized and reasonable medical assessment . . . based on the most current medical knowledge and/or on the best available objective evidence."[26] The danger must be "a significant risk of substantial harm," that cannot be remedied by a reasonable accommodation.

The "direct threat" analysis is an individualized one, even (or especially) in cases where the outcome may seem obvious. Mary Wolski was a firefighter in Erie, Pennsylvania, who attempted suicide by lighting a fire in her bathtub. She survived, and was fired, even though her psychiatrist cleared her to return to work. Although this may seem like a slam-dunk for the City, it was not. [27]

First, the City lost its motion for summary judgment, because it had not performed an individualized assessment of Wolski, and therefore it had not

---

[23] In cases where the essential element of the job involves safety, a number of circuits have held that plaintiff bears the burden of proof of showing she can perform the job safely, *EEOC*, 110 F.3d 135; LaChance v. Duffy's Draft House, 146 F.3d 832, 836–37 (11th Cir. 1998).

[24] The language of the Americans with Disabilities Act (ADA) limits "direct threat" to a direct threat to others, but the Equal Opportunity Employment Commission (EEOC), the agency in charge of implementing the law against employment discrimination, has interpreted this language to include direct threat to self, 29 C.F.R. 1630.15(b)(2), and the U.S. Supreme Court has upheld this interpretation. Chevron, U.S.A. v. Echazabal, 536 U.S. 73 (2002).

[25] 42 U.S.C. § 12113.

[26] 29 C.F.R. § 1630.2(r).

[27] *Wolski*, 773 F. Supp. 2d 577.

rebutted her evidence (the report from her treating physician) that she was qualified to return to work. In addition, representatives of the City of Erie testified that even if she had never set the fire, she would not have been permitted to be a firefighter if she was taking psychiatric medication because that made her "not completely stable." Although Erie was entitled to fire Wolski for misconduct,[28] Wolski argued that this was a pretext for discrimination, and that the City of Erie "had an unexamined and generalized fear that an employee who attempts suicide automatically poses a direct threat," and a number of comments by her employer supported this position.

The court found that there was a substantial question to be decided by a jury whether the employer had fired her for misconduct (her acts in the past) or because of its concerns about her mental health going forward. At trial, a jury decided in Wolski's favor.[29]

Part of the discrimination against people who have contemplated or attempted suicide arises from this very fact: the assumption that a suicide attempt tells us anything about the person going forward. It really doesn't. Many (not all) people who attempt suicide are relieved to be alive. A number of my interviewees believed they must have survived for a reason, and felt a renewed energy and purpose in life. In the aftermath of their suicide attempts, and going forward, they were less suicidal than they had ever been:

> I just popped handfuls of Tylenol in my mouth. I thought I wasn't going to wake up. I woke up the next morning and I thought oh, crap, I am not dead. Then it hit me, maybe I am alive for a reason. I wasn't supposed to die. I had this suddenly clear feeling. I am not dead, what does that mean? Maybe I need some help. I realized right then and there, I am supposed to be living.[30]

Some of my interviewees made it their mission to try to give others hope and to prevent suicide:

> I started working at a prison in July ... I want to be the angel that I always prayed for, I want to be the angel they may be praying for ... the hurt and suffering in my life had a purpose. I share my story that the labels other people put on you are not life sentences.[31]

---

[28] She was initially arrested for arson, but the City declined to pursue criminal charges.

[29] After a series of complicated post-trial motions, which resulted in vacating the jury's verdict, the City settled with Wolski for $350,000 and reinstatement. Lisa Thompson, *Erie Firefighter Wolski Wins Reinstatement*, GoErie.com, Nov. 8, 2013, http://www.goerie.com/article/20131108/NEWS02/311089889/erie-firefighter-wolski-wins-reinstatement-350000-2013-11-08-19-24#.

[30] Interview with Lex Wortley, *supra* note 2.

[31] Interview with Jenn Hurtado (Dec. 16, 2013).

This is also true of the people who survive jumping from the Golden Gate Bridge, several of whom travel the country delivering suicide prevention messages.[32] Therefore, despite the reflexive reactions of many employers, an individual's suicide attempt actually tells you very little about his or her state of mind and approach to the world going forward. If they were qualified before, they may well be qualified now, and they would certainly not necessarily meet the threshold for "direct threat."

The importance of ascertaining, on an individualized basis, an employee's present fitness to continue to work justifies in some instances an employer's requirement for the employee to have a mental health evaluation. The ADA prohibits requiring medical examinations of employees[33] unless the employer's concerns are "job-related and consistent with business necessity."[34] This means the employer must have a "reasonable basis" or "significant evidence" to conclude that the employee "is unable to perform the functions of her job" or presents "a direct threat to her own safety of the safety of others."[35] Although "job-related and consistent with business necessity" is a difficult and searching standard to meet in some cases,[36] courts run the gamut on the leeway they provide employers in demanding that an employee with an apparent emotional disturbance undergo a psychological exam. In

---

[32] However, I think this proves less than most people do, because by definition, only people who profoundly regretted their suicide attempt and desperately wanted to live *would* survive; it takes not only a huge amount of luck, but considerable effort, to survive a jump from the Golden Gate Bridge. The people who want to die, and even the people who are ambivalent, just won't make the effort to fight the current and the cold and make their way toward rescue.

[33] The rules are somewhat different for job applicants, who may be required to undergo job-related medical examinations *after* a contingent offer of employment and *only* if the policy is generally applied to all individuals contingently hired for the job. EEOC, *Enforcement Guidance: Disability-Related Inquiries and Medical Examinations of Employees Under the Americans with Disabilities Act (ADA)*, http://www.eeoc.gov/policy/docs/guidance-inquiries.html

[34] 42 U.S.C. 12112(d)(4)(a). See also EEOC, *Enforcement Guidance: Disability-Related Inquiries and Medical Examinations of Employees Under the Americans with Disabilities Act (ADA)*, n. 33. This is one of the few provisions in the ADA that most courts have held protects all employees; an employee need not prove that he or she is disabled in order to sue the employer for making an inappropriate inquiry or examination into his or her disability status. See, e.g., Owusu-Ansah v. Coca-Cola, 715 F.3d 1306 (11th Cir. 2013), Kroll v. White Lake Ambulance Auth., 691 F.3d 809, 816 (6th Cir. 2012); Thomas v. Corwin, 483 F.3d 516, 527 (8th Cir. 2007); Conroy v. N. Y. St. Dep't Corr. Serv., 333 F.3d 88, 94 (2d Cir. 2002); Roe v. Cheyenne Mountain Conference Resort, 124 F.3d 1221, 1229 (10th Cir. 1997).

[35] Kroll v. White Lake Ambulance Auth., 763 F.3d 619 (6th Cir. 2014); Brownfield v. City of Yakima, 612 F.3d 1140 (9th Cir. 2010).

[36] Bates v. UPS, 511 F.3d 974 (9th Cir. 2007) (*en banc*).

some professions (e.g., police[37] or firefighter[38]), this might make sense,[39] if you believe in the efficacy of psychological evaluations.[40] In others, it might make less sense. For example, a customer service representative who banged a fist on the table and said, "Someone's going to pay for this,"[41] was required to undergo a psychological evaluation. Nevertheless, the Eleventh Circuit upheld the employer's decision, holding that the evaluation was job-related because "an employee's ability to handle reasonable necessary stress is an essential function of any position."[42]

It is crystal clear that refusing to submit to a psychological evaluation constitutes a nondiscriminatory reason to be terminated.[43] Likewise, employers may require a note from an employee's doctor that he or she is fit to return to work after a medical leave of absence, and may even legally require the employee to submit to an evaluation by their own treatment professionals.

There are limits to these evaluations, however. The employer cannot evaluate for or ask for any information beyond that which relates to fitness for the duties of the job. There is a conflict in the circuits as to whether an employer may demand to know the employee's diagnosis as a condition of time off work or as a condition of returning to work.[44] Ordering an employee to go to psychological counseling has been held to be the same as ordering the employee to have a psychological evaluation, for purposes of the ADA:[45] the employer cannot do it unless it is job-related and consistent with business necessity.

---

[37] Watson v. City of Miami Beach, 177 F.3d 932, 935 (11th Cir. 1999) (police officer can be required to have a psychological exam if he or she is "mildly paranoid, hostile, or oppositional").

[38] Coffman v. Indianapolis Fire Dep't, 578 F.3d 559 (7th Cir. 2009) (firefighter acting "withdrawn" and "defensive" sufficient to order psychological evaluation, given the nature of the job).

[39] *Conroy*, 333 F.3d 88, 99 (noting that what constitutes an inquiry "consistent with business necessity" will vary depending on the nature of the job).

[40] Most of the examinations are either personal interviews by mental health professionals, which have been shown to have no better than chance ability to predict dangerousness, see, e.g., W. M. Grove, D. H. Zald, B.S. Lebow, *et. al. Clinical vs. Mechanical Predication: A Meta-Analysis*, 12 PSYCHOL. ASSESSMENT 19 (2000); Christopher Slobogin, Proving the Unprovable: The Role of Law, Science and Speculation in Adjudicating Culpability and Dangerousness (2007).

[41] *Owusu-Ansah*, 715 F.3d 1306.

[42] *Id.*

[43] Sullivan v. River Valley School Dist., 197 F.3d 804 (6th Cir. 1999); Williams v. Motorola, 303 F.3d 1284 (11th Cir. 2002).

[44] *Conroy*, 333 F.3d 88 (ADA violation to ask for diagnosis); Pa. State Troopers Ass'n v. Miller, 621 F. Supp. 2d 246 (M.D. Pa. 2008) (same), *contra* Lee v. City of Columbus, 636 F.3d 245 (6th Cir. 2011).

[45] *Kroll*, 691 F.3d 809.

Even my interviewees who were angry or ambivalent about having survived were still alive when they talked to me. The truth of the matter is that hundreds of thousands, if not millions, of people, struggle through life with a profound ambivalence about being alive: they sometimes wish they were dead, but they aren't going to kill themselves. These people are not "direct threats" in any imminent sense, they are just human beings. If they were not qualified to do their jobs, hundreds of thousands of jobs in our economy would not get done.

The problem with suicidality is similar to the problem with being gay thirty years ago: massively more people are suicidal than we imagine, and the images we have of suicidal people don't correspond to the reality because no one feels free to be open and talk about it. If employers contemplating an employee's suicidality only knew how many of their neighbors, teachers, ministers, coworkers, and sports heroes had been suicidal, perhaps they would feel more comfortable and less frightened and could make better employment decisions.

Many of my interviewees, like the employees in the discrimination cases, were extremely good at their jobs. For some, the job conditions caused or exacerbated their suicidality; for others, the job itself provided some degree of suicide prevention:

> I did manage to drag myself to work most of the time. I do a lot
> better when I am working, I am around people and I am not
> isolated, and I have to at least go through the motions like I do feel
> good and sometimes going through the motions is the main thing
> you can do.[46]

There is little doubt that despite all the public health and public relations efforts, employers are still profoundly uneasy and even angry when they learn an employee has attempted suicide. One employer who fired an exemplary employee after a suicide attempt off the job premises contended that it was not discriminating on the basis of disability: the employee was fired because her suicide attempt reflected irresponsibility, not because the employer thought she was mentally ill.[47] The court ruled that the employer could not prevail simply by asserting this; the plaintiff was entitled to a jury trial on whether she had been perceived as disabled by the employer.[48] After a bank employee went to a cemetery with a gun to kill himself, and threatened his sister when she tried to take the gun away from him, his employer was "blown away" that he was discharged from a psychiatric unit in four days, rather than being in jail.[49]

The Equal Employment Opportunity Commission (EEOC) is concerned enough about this issue to have addressed it specifically and at some length

---

[46] Interview with Martha Brock (May 9, 2014).

[47] *Chandler*, 283 F.3d 818, at n.8.

[48] *Id.*

[49] *Lizotte*, 677 F. Supp. 2d 1155.

in its *Enforcement Guidance on the Americans with Disabilities Act and Psychiatric Disabilities*:

> 35. Does an individual who has attempted suicide pose a direct threat when s/he seeks to return to work?
>
> No, in most circumstances. As with other questions of direct threat, an employer must base its determination on an individualized assessment of the person's ability to safely perform job functions when s/he returns to work. Attempting suicide does not mean that an individual poses an imminent risk of harm to him/herself when s/he returns to work. In analyzing direct threat (including the likelihood and imminence of any potential harm), the employer must seek reasonable medical judgments relying on the most current medical knowledge and/or the best available factual evidence concerning the employee.
>
>> Example: An employee with a known psychiatric disability was hospitalized for two suicide attempts, which occurred within several weeks of each other. When the employee asked to return to work, the employer allowed him to return pending an evaluation of medical reports to determine his ability to safely perform his job. The individual's therapist and psychiatrist both submitted documentation stating that he could safely perform all of his job functions. Moreover, the employee performed his job safely after his return, without reasonable accommodation. The employer, however, terminated the individual's employment after evaluating the doctor's and therapist's reports, without citing any contradictory medical or factual evidence concerning the employee's recovery. Without more evidence, this employer cannot support its determination that this individual poses a direct threat.[50]

There are obviously very different kinds of situations associated with people who are suicidal in employment contexts. In some cases, the working conditions, management styles, imminent layoffs, or work discipline themselves cause employees to consider and attempt suicide.[51] Some people are driven to suicide or suicide attempts by bullying or harassment at work:

> In [large Southern city], I had a boss who was trying to get rid of me and trying to terrorize me and make me quit, and instead

---

[50] EEOC, *Enforcement Guidance on the Americans with Disabilities Act and Psychiatric Disabilities*, Mar. 25, 1997, http://www.eeoc.gov/policy/docs/psych.html.

[51] CNN Wire Staff, *Microsoft Probes Mass Suicide Threat at China Plant*, (CNN, Jan. 12, 2012), http://www.cnn.com/2012/01/11/world/asia/china-microsoft-factory/

of quitting I kind of fell apart. I screwed her over in the process because she couldn't fill my position when I was on disability leave. I am an epidemiologist, working for a city health department, it was a physician who did this.[52]

Another interviewee who had an exemplary record at work told me how a combination of her boss's personal style and trying to resolve unethical behavior at work resulted in her suicide attempt:

With the boss, a couple of things she used to say that used to get under my skin were "I think of you like a daughter." And she knew . . . my mother was an alcoholic; my boss was an alcoholic as well. It was like working for my mother. Perhaps that's why it was so difficult to handle for me. Seven other people left . . . I thought how the heck am I going to get out of this. I didn't see any other option. I didn't see any other way . . . I raised red flags . . . early on because there were some things I was seeing that my boss was doing, we were getting into ethical and legal gray areas. It's worker's comp and there are very set laws that you have to abide by. We were walking a thin line between what was legal and what wasn't. I notified people, I directly talked to her, I went through the grievance process. Everyone said you have to just deal with it. I started developing more migraines. I had migraines before but they started getting worse. In July I went on leave to try a new medication to get them under control. My boss started getting mad because I had been taking time off because of my migraines. I returned after two weeks, she was saying you're not doing your job right, you haven't been the same since you came back. The last day I was there, she blew up at me, yelled at me, "You have been a nightmare since you've come back." . . . I . . . thought I cannot imagine going back to that place. Quitting in my brain was a sign of weakness. I thought I can't quit, so I gotta think of something else. You gotta take yourself out of the equation physically, and maybe then they'll get the message that something's wrong. It was a split second decision, I was very upset, I will take a bunch of pills, I took seven Klonopin. That didn't work, so I started cutting

---

(the article notes that after a spate of suicides in 2010, the subcontractor said it was improving workers' lives, including "calling in Buddhist monks to offer spiritual consolation"); Angelique Chrisafis, *France Telecom Executive Resigns After Employee Suicide Tally Rises to Twenty-Four*, THE GUARDIAN, Oct. 5, 2009, www.theguardian.com/business/2009/oct/05/telecoms-france; see also Susan Stefan, *You'd Have to Be Crazy to Work Here*, 31 LOYOLA L. REV.795 (1998). Individuals serving in combat in the military are an example of employment where the conditions of employment are directly related to employees' suicidality.

[52] Interview with Abby Irving (pseudonym). Nov. 20, 2013.

my wrists. Then I thought this isn't going to work. So I wrapped a
cord around my neck, in an attempt to strangle myself.[53]

In cases where the employment conditions are responsible for the suicidality
of the employees, there is a higher chance that the individual will attempt or
commit suicide on the job premises.[54] Even employers who are aware of harsh
or bullying conditions and the employee's fragility will very rarely be held
responsible in tort if the employee commits suicide,[55] nor are they likely to be
found liable for discriminating against an employee by failing to take steps to
improve the work environment.[56]

Then there are people who perform their jobs in exemplary fashion and
attempt suicide off-duty for personal reasons entirely unrelated to the job;[57]
in some cases, the employer never finds out.

There are several ways an employer can approach the issue of employees
attempting suicide. The most common is to frame the issue as employee-
specific. This can involve blaming and firing the employee, which, in the
absence of individualized assessment or any attempt at accommodation, is
probably illegal for any job.

It can involve taking a more benevolent approach of offering leave, mental health services, or job-accommodation. Cara Anna, nationally known
journalist and advocate for individuals who have attempted suicide, cites her
own experience as an example of the best possible individual approach an
employer could take:

> Part of what led to my first attempt in China was my fear that
> admitting "weakness" would get me fired. Foreign correspondents
> can't have problems. But after telling an editor about my attempt,
> I found that my employer didn't panic. They asked that I come
> back to the U.S. so they could get a look at me and they asked me
> to come back to work at their headquarters in New York as soon
> as I felt like it, which was in days, if I remember correctly. The
> human resources department assisted me with any insurance

---

[53] Interview with Chelsea Andrus. Dec. 14, 2013.

[54] In 2008, 251 people killed themselves at work in the United States, out of 5071
total deaths at work, Andrew Clark, *Big Increase in US Suicides at Work*, The
Guardian, Aug. 21, 2009, www.theguardian.com/business/2009/aug/21/
us-suicide-work-office.

[55] See, e.g., Olson v. Barrett, Case No. 6:13-cv-1886-Orl-40KRS (M.D. Fla., Mar.
20, 2015) (Sprint not liable for suicide of woman bullied at work and terminated
despite a promise they would meet with her first); Jones v. Cate, No. 2:12-cv-2181
TLN CKD (E.D. Ca., Mar. 27, 2015) (employer not liable for prison guard's suicide when guard was relentlessly abused after complaining about inmate mis-
treatment because he did not commit suicide from an "uncontrollable impulse").

[56] Stefan, *supra* note 51.

[57] *Doe v. Region 13*, 704 F.2d 1402, at n. 8; *Chandler*, 283 F.3d 818, at n.8.

arrangements and questions, which included staying in touch with my therapist and psychiatrist for updates on whether and when I was well enough to go back overseas. After my second attempt in China about two years later, my employer arranged for me to go on medical leave for a few months. Again, they stayed in touch with my therapist and psychiatrist. Their help in dealing with any insurance issues was especially good, as that kind of wrangling is pretty much the last thing someone needs when trying to get well.

No one recoiled. People expressed concern in the best way they knew how, which came off as concern about any health issue. That was appreciated.

In short, if employers can treat people with calm and respect and help make the logistics of getting care as smooth as possible, that would be super.[58]

This approach is also strategically a smart course for the employer to follow. Staying in touch with the individual's therapist and psychiatrist gives the employer an up-to-the-minute perspective on the employee's readiness to return to work, as does offering her the opportunity to return to work as soon as possible. Ensuring that the insurance benefits that the employer pays for are provided seamlessly and promptly is a good way to ensure that the insurance company is providing value for money. The accommodations of working in New York, and medical leave, would probably be required by law: providing them voluntarily and proactively earns the loyalty and gratitude of the employee. But ultimately, what most reflects a caring rather than just a canny employer is the respect, the calmness, the failure to recoil, the continued employment in a challenging job after two suicide attempts.

Either the punitive or the supportive approach, however, assumes that the cause of the suicide attempt resides primarily with the employee, and the response must be centered on the employee. Another approach entirely is to create a suicide-prevention culture in the work environment. This makes sense, especially with larger employers and more stressful jobs. The United States Air Force reduced its suicide rate from 15.8 in 100,000 to 3.5 in 100,000 through a comprehensive suicide prevention program that is one of the few such plans in the country. The description of its program is fascinating,[59] though in some ways disheartening: After presenting a compelling case for funding nonclinical prevention workers who could talk to service members without creating paper records,[60] we find that the additional workers recommended were not funded; nor was a less extensive pilot project involving

---

[58] Personal communication from Cara Anna to the author.

[59] The Air Force Suicide Prevention Program, www.dmna.ny.gov/suicideprevention/AFPAM44-160.pdf.

[60] *Id* at 15.

preventive workers funded.[61] The modest goal of dedicating 5% of all mental health activities to prevention was never achieved. [62] However, the Air Force has apparently succeeded at least in part on destigmatizing suicide enough that a number of active duty officers and enlisted men have been public about their stories, and these stories celebrate victories, not of the medical model and drugs, but of intensive individualized therapy (which sounds a lot like cognitive behavioral therapy[63]):

> [Colonel Robert Swanson had attempted suicide twice when he began meeting] with a psychiatrist almost daily for six months for intense therapy sessions designed to put him back on the path to a healthy state of being.
>
> "I read your file; you're really good at telling us everything we want to hear," his psychiatrist told him. "I've seen your IQ and you're smarter than I am. Nothing I'm going to do, or say, is going to get through to you, until you are willing to take a chance, and let me try to help you."
>
> Only when he was ready to accept his psychiatrist's advice did he start to heal—and the healing came almost immediately.
>
> "We got rid of the anti-depressants," Swanson said. "I hated them, and they really interfered with me making real progress."
>
> His psychiatrist taught him how to look at the world realistically; how to examine different events in his life, sort through his reactions to these events and figure out what is normal behavior and what emotions are distorted.[64]

While the ADA absolutely prohibits a prospective employer from asking about medical conditions, or a history of medical conditions, or requiring the release of medical records, a more complicated form of discrimination exists that the law has not adequately addressed. Because the police are so often (and sometimes so inappropriately) involved in interactions with people who are suicidal, there may be police records that a prospective employer *can* check: if the police make a welfare check, or take a person to the emergency department, for example. One survey respondent wrote,

> I've been blocked from a volunteer job doing clerical work because a background check showed I had had welfare checks from police because even though my medical records are not available the

---

[61] *Id* at 16.
[62] *Id.*
[63] Cognitive behavioral therapy is discussed at length in Chapter 9.
[64] Matthew McGovern, *Airman Reveals Tough Past to Help Others Face Future*, HEALTH.MIL, Mar. 31, 2014, at http://www.health.mil/Reference-Center/Articles/2014/03/31/Airman-Reveals-Tough-Past-to-Help-Others-Face-Future.

police records show this information. A prospective employer will have access to these records as well. This is discrimination.

The respondent is absolutely correct, but it is not a form of discrimination that advocates have been able to get the courts to recognize. In the most extreme example of this, police pickups on involuntary detention orders for mental health purposes were recorded by New York State Police using an "Arrest Report" form; in the box labeled "Charge," they wrote "mentally ill person."[65] This process was upheld as not discriminatory, because, technically, what happens when people are transported to a hospital *is* an arrest, just not a criminal one.[66]

One of the central contentions of this book is that while this society claims to care about suicide prevention, its policies and laws demonstrate otherwise. The profound resistance to understanding that suicide can best be prevented by structural reforms—gun control, suicide barriers at the Golden Gate Bridge, programs such as the U.S. Air Force pursued—comes from a deeply embedded social assumption and cultural value that the responsibility for suicide prevention rests squarely and solely on the individual him- or herself. We can believe that and act on it as a society if we want to, but we should never say in the same breath that we are dedicated to suicide prevention.

Institutions of Higher Education and Suicidal Students: Putting the "Loco" back in *In Loco Parentis*

Many of my interviewees first became seriously suicidal when they went to college. Then and now, college is not a great place to experience your first serious breakdown. If you want to see examples of how fear of liability has twisted practices to be as unhelpful and irrational as possible, look no farther than the mind-boggling policies of universities toward suicidal students. Like mental health professionals and police, universities and colleges are trapped in an untenable tension between their professed philosophies—the liberal arts model of letting students learn and grow and bloom in an atmosphere of autonomy and independence—and the expectation of parents that their children will be protected from harm, including self-harm. Employers complain about excessive governmental regulation, but educational institutions are also subject to an accumulation of acronyms: ADA, FERPA, and HIPAA, to name the most relevant in the context of suicide. Tort liability always lurks as a background (or sometimes foreground) possibility.

---

[65] Disability Advocates v. McMahon, 279 F. Supp. 2d 158, 161 (N.D. N.Y. 2003), *aff'd* 124 Fed. App'x 674 (2d Cir. 2005).
[66] *Id.*

In general, academic courage and empathy do not prevail. As the Book of Proverbs might have said, students come and go, but the Office of University Counsel abides. Despite being places where the diversity of students' experience should be explored and supported, colleges and universities have some of the most stigmatizing attitudes about suicidality and psychiatric disabilities, just as they once did about homosexuality, another behavior for which students used to be disciplined and expelled in shame.[67] Colleges and universities still expel transgender students, not just obscure Christian colleges, but large mainstream universities like the University of Pittsburgh.[68]

Let's get specific about how universities have behaved with regard to students who they suspect might be suicidal.

When Jordan Nott was a freshman at George Washington University, one of his closest friends committed suicide. Nott was trying to break through a locked door when his friend, who was to have been his roommate sophomore year, jumped out a window. Almost immediately after Nott came back for his sophomore year, another student committed suicide. Nott became depressed and suicidal himself and sought help from George Washington University Hospital. Within a day and a half of seeking help, he received a letter from the university, telling him that his "endangering behavior" violated the Code of Student Conduct and that he faced suspension and expulsion from the school unless he withdrew and deferred the charges while he got treatment.[69] The same year (2004), a Hunter College student who called 911 after swallowing pills in a suicide attempt returned to her college dorm after being hospitalized, only to find that the locks had been changed in her absence.[70]

Many students who seek help for being suicidal are told they have violated Codes of Student Conduct.[71] If they are hospitalized, they are told upon

---

[67] These practices have not ended completely, as the Department of Education has granted Title IX exemptions to Christian colleges and universities, which permit them to expel gay and transgender students, see Scott Jaschik, *The Right to Expel*, INSIDE HIGHER ED, July 25, 2014, https://www.insidehighered.com/news/2014/07/25/2-christian-colleges-win-title-ix-exemptions-give-them-right-expel-transgender.

[68] Johnston v. University of Pittsburgh, Case 3:13-cv-00213-KRG (W.D. Pa. Mar. 31, 2015) (finding that discrimination on the basis of transgender status is not unlawful under either Title IX of the Civil Rights Act or the equal protection clause of the Constitution).

[69] Susan Kinzie, *GW Suit Prompts Questions of Liability*, WASHINGTON POST, Mar. 10, 2006, http://www.washingtonpost.com/wp-dyn/content/article/2006/03/09/AR2006030902550.html.

[70] Doe v. Hunter College, No. 04-CV-6740 (shs), Second Amended Complaint, filed Sept. 2005, see https://thelawofficeofkarenbower.files.wordpress.com/2011/10/doe-v-hunter-second-amended-complaint-final.pdf.

[71] *Lyons*, N. 7:2009cv02290; Katie J.M. Baker, *How Colleges Flunk Mental Health*, NEWSWEEK, Feb. 11, 2014, http://www.newsweek.com/2014/02/14/how-colleges-flunk-mental-health-245492.html (student who sought help after cutting herself received a letter saying she had violated housing policy and that she

discharge that they cannot return to their dorm rooms,[72] or come back to find the locks changed without notice on their dorm rooms.[73] One student was handed a notice of eviction from her dorm as she was getting into an ambulance.[74] Some are told they are completely banned from campus.[75] Until recently, a student was better off sexually assaulting a fellow classmate than admitting to being suicidal, in terms of the chance of being allowed to stay in school and graduate.[76]

Since some universities may have student populations of more than 50,000 students,[77] keeping track of each and every one is impossible.[78] According to an administrative staff member at one large Boston university, larger schools don't even know if a student is on campus at all, or attending

---

had three days to schedule a meeting. "'I broke down after reading the letter,' Shireen recalls. 'I already felt so bad and now I was getting in trouble for it.'"). See also Paul Appelbaum, *'Depressed? Get Out!' Dealing with Suicidal Students on College Campuses*, 57 PSYCHIATRIC SERVICES 914 (2006).

[72] Letter of the Office of Civil Rights to Princeton University, Department of Education, Complaint No. 02-12-2155 (Jan. 18, 2013); Christina Cantero, *Western Michigan University Revises Policy Related to Students Showing Suicidal Tendencies*, MICHIGAN LIVE, Dec. 29, 2013, http://www.mlive.com/news/kalamazoo/index.ssf/2013/12/western_michigan_university_re_15.html ("'I asked [university officials where] am I supposed to go?' said Peebles during the Oct. 4 interview. 'I was crying.'").

[73] *Doe v. Hunter College*, No. 04-CV-6740, at n.65.

[74] Department of Justice Settlement with Quinnipiac University, www.ada.gov/quinnipiac_sa.htm.

[75] Office of Civil Rights to Princeton University, *supra* note 72, at n.67.

[76] Okezie Nwoka, *Letter to the Brown Community on the Death of Michael Dawkins*, '12/'13.5, http://issuu.com/okezienwka/docs/letter_to_the_brown_community_-_11-/1.

[77] Arizona State University had an enrollment of 76,711 in the fall of 2013, https://facts.asu.edu/Pages/Default.aspx; Ohio State had an enrollment of 57,466 in 2013, Ohio State University, *Statistical Summary*, www.osu.edu/osutoday/stuinfo.php; University of Michigan had just less than 44,000, University of Michigan, Office of Registrar, *Total Enrollment Overview*, www.ro.umich.edu/report/14enrollmentsummary.pdf

[78] In one case, a student from another college called the Health Center at Virginia Polytechnic Institute (VPI) to tell them that his friend Daniel Kim was suicidal and had a gun. Kim was reportedly suicidal because VPI students compared him to Seung-Hui Cho, who had killed 27 students. At a meeting called to address this, university staff realized that the university had more than one "Daniel Kim" enrolled, including two who lived off campus, and they had to be very careful to determine the correct student, Kim v. Commonwealth of Virginia, No. CL-2009-2011-0017445 Jury Verdicts LEXIS 214256 (Va. Cir. Ct., Nov. 16, 2011). The student committed suicide a month later. The Commonwealth settled this case for $250,000, with $100,000 being given to a scholarship in Kim's memory.

classes; professors may take roll in seminars and smaller classes, but it's hard to do in large classes and even harder to force an unwilling professor to take class attendance.[79] The only way a large university can know if a student is having difficulties is if the student reaches out for help. But students understand that college and university mental health services are instrumental in forcing students off campus and are reluctant to reach out for help when it means imperiling their own academic careers, including scholarships and student loans.

These students are not wrong to be cautious. When a suicidal student does come to the attention of a university, the reflexive response has often been to force the student to take a medical leave,[80] sometimes even forbidding the student from returning to his or her dorm (even to pick up belongings prior to taking the forced leave);[81] to prohibit the student from returning without a doctor's note; and sometimes (as with employers) to prohibit the student from returning even when the doctor says everything is perfectly all right.[82] Some colleges and universities do not do this: Barnard does not place students on involuntary medical leave, although it will place them on involuntary academic leave if justified.[83] However, students do complain that Barnard, like other colleges, will press strongly on a student to take a "voluntary" leave. The University of Illinois requires students to have four sessions with a counselor, and "rarely advocates taking time off from school."[84] As a comparison, in twenty-five years, one student at the University of Illinois was required to leave; in one year at Cornell, more than one hundred students were "pushed" to take medical leave.[85]

Involuntary medical leave can have far-reaching consequences on student scholarships, student loans, student majors and ability to complete a degree course, student internships, and, especially, on the student's perception of him- or herself. As one student said:

> I was really shocked and hurt . . . I didn't understand why I couldn't go back to my room to get my stuff. Why was I considered such a danger when the hospital was letting me out? I felt kind of stupid

[79] Interview with Anne DeNoto, Aug. 28, 2014, Boston, MA.
[80] Rachel Williams, *We Just Can't Have You Here*, YALE DAILY NEWS, Jan. 24, 2014, http://yaledailynews.com/weekend/2014/01/24/we-just-cant-have-you-here.
[81] *Id.* See also Settlement with Quinnipiac University, *supra* note 71; Office of Civil Rights to Princeton University, *supra* note 72; Cantero, *supra* note 72.
[82] Katie J.M. Baker at n.71.
[83] Abby Abrams, *Absent, Alone, Apart: Examining the Effect of Columbia's Medical Withdrawal and Readmission Policies*, COLUMBIA SPECTATOR, Mar. 4, 2015, http://features.columbiaspectator.com/eye/2015/03/04/absent-alone-apart/.
[84] Julia Rawe & Kathleen Kingsbury, *When Colleges Go on Suicide Watch*, TIME MAGAZINE, July 8, 2006, *available at* https://www.jedfoundation.org/press-room/news-archive/when-colleges-go-on-suicide-watch.
[85] *Id.*

and kind of like a failure. I felt like I had just ruined my entire life in one day.[86]

In sum, students confirm that universities' reactions to a student's suicidality can make the student's life far more miserable than the suicidality itself. As Attorney Karen Bower, whose practice is centered on representing college and university students with psychiatric disabilities, reports:

> Here's how it plays out. You go and get help at the Counseling Center. They do a quick assessment. Many of those students do stay on campus. But if they send the student to the hospital, that information is shared with Student Affairs. They tell the student, "You can go voluntarily," and hint that if the student doesn't go that way, they will put the student on involuntary leave, call the police, and the police will handcuff you. They tell the student if there is an involuntary leave it will show up on the transcript and make it harder to get back in. Kids are given this option while they are sitting there, so they feel coerced to take voluntary leave.[87]

The hypersensitivity of universities to liability for student suicide is generally traced to litigation after the suicide of Elizabeth Shin at MIT.[88] Prior to the *Shin* case, courts had virtually uniformly held that colleges and universities had no affirmative duty to prevent a student's suicide, because the student was not sufficiently within university custody and control to impose such a duty on educational institutions.[89] So-called special relationships giving rise to affirmative duties had been found in the case of facilities with complete control—such as psychiatric hospitals[90]—but courts had explicitly ruled across the country that institutions of higher education had no legal duty to prevent student suicides and could not be sued if a student killed himself or herself.[91] Universities certainly kicked students out when they became aware of self-harming behavior, but in the absence of much in the way of mental health services, they often simply didn't know about mental

[86] Kathleen Megan, *Quinnipiac Agrees to Settlement in Case of Depressed Student Placed on Mandatory Leave*, HARTFORD COURANT, Jan. 13, 2015, http://www.courant.com/news/connecticut/hc-quinnipiac-settles-ada-case-0113-2-20150112-story.html.

[87] Interview with Karen Bower, March 18, 2015.

[88] See Shin v. Massachusetts Institute of Technology [MIT], Super. Ct. Civil Action No. 02-0403, http://tech.mit.edu/V125/N30/shin-decision.pdf; for the reaction of colleges and universities, see Eric Hoover, *Judge Rules Suicide Suit Against MIT Can Proceed*, 51 J. HIGHER EDUC. 49 (Aug. 12, 2005); Marcella Bombardieri, *Lawsuit Allowed in MIT Suicide*, BOSTON GLOBE, July 30, 2005, at B-1.

[89] Bogust v. Iverson, 10 Wisc. 2d 129 (1960); Jain v. State of Iowa, 617 N.W. 2d 273 (Iowa 2000).

[90] See Chapter 6.

[91] *Jain v. Iowa*, 617 N.W. 2d 273.

health crises except through failing grades and/or when the student threatened suicide to school authorities.[92]

Prior to the *Shin* case, in *Schieszler v. Ferrum College*,[93] college officials were repeatedly notified by a student's former girlfriend that he had sent her notes threatening to hang himself in the student dorms where he lived. On investigation, campus security and the dorm resident assistant saw the student had self-inflicted bruises. They told the Dean of Student Affairs, who asked the student to sign a statement that he would not hurt himself—the famously untenable "contracts" that are so futile.[94] Campus police prohibited his girlfriend from checking on him. The court in *Schieszler* held that there was a jury issue on the question of whether the college had a special relationship with Schieszler that would create a duty to protect him.[95]

In stark contrast to the do-nothing staff at Ferrum College, Shin's suicidality had been the focus of a great deal of concern and continual assistance by the staff at MIT, including her dorm housemaster, the Dean of Counseling and Support Services, as well as two faculty members, a teaching assistant, a social worker, and two MIT psychiatrists.[96] The school arranged for her to be hospitalized twice, and in March and early April of 2000, Shin met virtually every day with an MIT staff member. On April 10, two students told the house master that Shin had said she planned to kill herself, and the housemaster followed up. Shin made vague threats ("you won't have to worry about me anymore"),[97] and the housemaster brought up the situation at a meeting, where an appointment at a counseling center was made for Shin for the next day. A call to inform her of this appointment went to voicemail. Shin lit herself on fire that night, and her parents disconnected life support four days later.

MIT had also settled a few other student suicide cases for amounts in the millions at the time of the Shin case. However, neither *Schieszler* nor those prior cases generated the national publicity accorded to *Shin*. There were many unusual aspects to the Shin case—perhaps because her parents insisted they had a right to know what was going on with their daughter, raising privacy issues, perhaps because they sued for more than $27 million, perhaps because Ms. Shin was alleged to have burned herself to

---

[92] Tedeschi v. Wagner College, 49 N.Y.2d 652 (N.Y. 1980) (after student tore up her blue book during a final exam and was advised by the professor that this meant she flunked the course, she called him repeatedly beginning at 4 a.m. threatening suicide).

[93] *Schieszler*, 236 F. Supp. 2d 602 (W.D. Va. 2002).

[94] See Chapter 6.

[95] See note 93, *supra*.

[96] Shin v. Massachusetts Institute of Technology, 2005 Mass.Super.LEXIS 333 (Mass.Super. June 27, 2005); Heather Moore, "University Liability When Students Commit Suicide: Expanding the Scope of the Special Relationship," 40 Ind. Law Rev. 423, 432-34 (2007).

[97] 2005 Mass.Super.LEXIS at *13.

death.[98] There are many little known aspects of the Shin case: for example, that her emotional condition deteriorated severely after being prescribed psychotropic medications. But the most ominous, from the point of view of universities, was the Massachusetts' lower court's finding that (essentially because MIT had gone to great lengths to help Ms. Shin) a "special relationship" existed between the university and Shin which might create a duty on the university's part to protect her from killing herself.

This is yet another example of counterproductive laws and policies. If MIT had been utterly clueless about Shin's suicidality, it could not have been held liable, because her suicide would have been unforeseeable. Under current law, the more involved the university became in trying to help Shin, the greater "notice" they had of her difficulties, the more "foreseeable" her eventual suicide[99] and the more likely the law was to impose a duty on them.[100] If Ms. Shin had been kicked out and sent back to her parents the instant she started having problems, the university's legal duties to her under the special relationship doctrine would have ceased. This single fact has guided university policymakers like the North Star, leading to mandatory withdrawal policies, and has created untold misery for students, who can be charged with disciplinary infractions and even threatened with criminal prosecution if they attempt suicide,[101] or if they try to stay on campus after being told to leave. Some are barred from off-campus events held by their college[102] and others are banned even from places in the university that are open to the general public.[103] Fear of liability drives many of these policies and practices.

Yet mandatory withdrawal policies have kept students from seeking help, and may have even resulted in increasing student suicides.[104] For many

---

[98] There was apparently some evidence that she never intended to commit suicide and that her death was accidental.

[99] As we saw in Chapters 2 and 6, individual suicides are never truly foreseeable.

[100] See Heather Moore, note 96 at 437, ("The good news for universities is that a court is unlikely to find that a suicide is foreseeable if the student does not give any warning or make public threats").

[101] Jordan Nott sued George Washington University when it placed him on involuntary suspension, prohibited him from going on campus, and charged him with a disciplinary infraction for exhibiting "endangering behavior" after he checked himself into a hospital because he was thinking about suicide. The letter he received from George Washington University threatened him with "suspension, expulsion, or criminal charges" for trespassing if he were to set foot on the campus again, see Juhi Kaveeshar, *Kicking the Rock and the Hard Place to the Curb: An Alternative and Integrated Approach to Suicidal Students in Higher Education*, 57 EMORY L.J. 651, 654 (2008).

[102] *Lyons*, N. 7:2009cv02290, at n.66.

[103] Office of Civil Rights to Princeton University, *supra* note 72.

[104] Rachel Siegal & Vivian Wang, *Student Death Raises Questions on Withdrawal Policies*, YALE DAILY NEWS, Jan. 29, 2015, http://yaledailynews.com/blog/2015/01/29/student-death-raises-questions-on-withdrawal-policies/. A student

students, the routine of their classes and the community of their friends provides support they need to stay alive,[105] and the economic consequences to loans and scholarships sometimes means that the students cannot come back even if the university permits it. One student's suicide note, posted on Facebook, read:

> Dear Yale: I loved being here. I only wish I could've had some time. I needed time to work things out and to wait for new medication to kick in, but I couldn't do it in school, and I couldn't bear the thought of having to leave for a full year, or of leaving and never being readmitted.[106]

This student was an Asian-American. For minority students who are already feeling uncertain and desperate, being forced to leave a university they often worked very hard for years to attend may be the final blow, especially when loans and scholarships depend on the student's continuing presence in school. A moving and angry eulogy by a Brown University student for a fellow student named Michael Dawkins, who was African-American, minced no words about students' understanding of the reason for these mandatory leave policies:

> Michael, while studying at Brown, was told to take medical leave due to reasons concerning his mental health. . . . he, like so many Brown students, was told to go away. Because when a student who is dealing with the difficulties of a mental health condition is told "You must take a medical leave," in their ears they tend to hear, "Go, go away."
> . . . This is not unique to Michael, nor is it specific to his case. Brown has done this to several other students across the spectrum of mental health conditions. There have been other students who needed help, students who were dealing with mental health conditions for the first time, and all that was afforded them was a dismissal. They, like Michael, were told to go away: to leave all their friends, to not see their professors, to discontinue academic engagement at Brown, to go away . . .
> So, like Michael, you go away because you realize that Brown has the legal right to remove you from its premises if it considers you a liability, a threat to the smooth functioning of the university and its

---

at Brown University blamed its mandatory leave policy for the suicide of fellow student Michael Dawkins, who committed suicide while on mandatory leave. An MIT freshman on leave committed suicide, Tech Staff, "After Second Freshman's Death, Some Professors Lighten Students' Workload," The Tech Online Edition, March 15, 2015, http://tech.mit.edu/V135/N7/tournant.html

[105] *Id.* See also Williams, *supra* note 80.
[106] Siegal and Wang, note 104.

activities. Even if you have no history of being violent or disruptive on campus, you are removed—quarantined. You are isolated, isolated at a time in your life when you need as much love as the world can give, as your friends can give, as Brown can give . . .
All the while you receive phone calls asking you to donate money to help fund the university's projects . . . no Brown administrator has called to see if you are faring well . . .

Michael was a musical prodigy. Michael articulated a mental health concern. Michael was told to go away.

Many people might say, "Brown cannot afford the liability of having unstable students on campus. I say, "Unstable people are of every kind and are everywhere, known and unknown." People might say, "They have to go away; they are too unstable to read and learn and take classes." To them I say, "Most medical leave students spend their time either working or taking classes elsewhere. Their brains still work, their intelligence is still intact." People might say, "Brown cannot afford what you are suggesting." I say, "Brown's wealth is greater than the GDP of several countries . . ." People might say, "Brown is the happiest school in the United States." To them I answer seldom a word.[107]

Mandatory leave policies following suicide attempts or even mentioning suicide[108] are among the most counterproductive university policies toward suicidal students; they are also illegal under the ADA and Section 504 of the Rehabilitation Act (see the following).

Another response that university counseling centers increasingly adopt, as the demand for their services swells and the budget for their staffs shrink,[109] is to insist that students be hospitalized when they seek assistance from university counseling centers for suicidal thoughts. These hospitalizations are frequently experienced by students as extremely aversive[110] and unhelpful. The insistence on hospitalization is part of a larger strategy to limit university-based counseling appointments, refer the student out swiftly to possibly unaffordable outside providers, and limit mental health and counseling centers to prescribing an ever more expansive panoply of prescriptions for medications. As one former Harvard law student wrote me:

---

[107] Nwoka, *supra* note 76.
[108] Kaveeshar, *supra* note 101 (the Jordan Nott case).
[109] David J. Drum, Chris Brownson, Adryon Burton Denmark, & Shanna E. Smith, *New Data on the Nature of Suicidal Crises in College Students: Shifting the Paradigm*, 40 PROF. PSYCHOL. RES. & PRAC. 213 (2009) ("most campus counseling centers are facing an increasing demand for services with no corresponding increase in resources").
[110] See Mahoney v. Allegheny College, No. AD 892-2003 (Pa. Ct. Common Pleas, Dec. 22, 2005).

I went in because I was having trouble with stress from school and also dealing with a break up. I really felt like I just needed someone to say "I hear you, and this is difficult stuff." I was processed by a psychiatrist who pretty quickly pushed medication. She said that I should, at the very least, be taking a sleeping pill because if I couldn't sleep I wasn't going to be able to address the issues. I think I talked her out of the antidepressants but took the sleeping pill scrip (and I can't remember if I ever took any). I was pretty firm that I was looking for someone to talk to, not for meds. At that point I was referred to a licensed social worker who was great, and was able to get in with a cognitive behavioral therapy group, which I found very helpful. It has admittedly been more than a decade since this happened, so my recollection is not as clear as it was at the time, but I do remember feeling like they thought I needed to medicate first before any talk therapy would be helpful, and feeling like I had to convince them otherwise.[111]

According to other interviews, things have not changed. Indeed, Harvard is being sued for the death of John B. Edwards III, who committed suicide after being seen by Harvard University Health Services once, diagnosed with attention deficit hyperactivity disorder and given a prescription for Adderall (which is an amphetamine), and two drugs for depression, Prozac and Wellbutrin.[112] Edwards was already taking Accutane, a powerful antiacne medication. [113] In 1998, Roche, the manufacturer of Accutane, added a warning that it might cause psychiatric disorders in the wake of more than 500 formal adverse reaction reports related to suicide from national and international agencies.[114] Roche withdrew the drug from the market in 2009, two years after Edwards' suicide (it is still available in generic form).[115]

For a while after *Shin*, it seemed that universities had come up with a good strategy to avoid negligence liability in the case of suicidal students: require them to leave, automatically,[116] and prohibit them from coming back until a

---

[111] Personal communication from A.C. to the author (Jan. 2015).

[112] Alan Schwarz, *Harvard Student's Suicide as a Case Study*, N.Y. TIMES, Apr. 30, 2013, http://www.nytimes.com/2013/05/01/us/harvard-suit-highlights-adhd-medication-problems.html?_r=0; Danielle J. Kolin, *Family Sues Harvard Over Son's Suicide*, HARVARD CRIMSON, Dec. 4, 2009, http://www.thecrimson.com/article/2009/12/4/edwards-harvard-suicide-lawsuit/.

[113] Schwarz, at note 112.

[114] *What Is Accutane? Its Uses and Interactions*, DRUG WATCH (last modified, Sept. 29, 2014), http://www.drugwatch.com/accutane/.

[115] *Id.*

[116] See the extremely well written story of Williams, *supra* note 80 (when Williams protested her involuntary withdrawal, pointing out that "school was my stimulation, my passion, and my reason for getting up in the morning," the psychiatrist conceded that "we don't necessarily think you'll be safer at home. But we

physician cleared them to return (and often not even then). Ironically, these policies were implemented and enforced by the school's mental health staff and disability offices: the very people that suicidal students might expect would be on their side.

But then students and student advocates began protesting these enforced withdrawals,[117] and they and their advocates came up with a legal claim to back them up: contending that to require automatic withdrawal of suicidal students was to discriminate against students with psychiatric disabilities under the ADA and Section 504 of the Rehabilitation Act. The first student to challenge a mandatory withdrawal as discriminatory was Jordan Nott, but others have followed.[118]

Universities have long claimed to exclude students as a means of protecting them, but the ADA in fact defines discrimination to include "overprotective rules and policies"[119] and "exclusionary qualification standards and criteria."[120] In order to understand the evolution of legal theory about these claims, it helps to understand three facts: first, Title II of the ADA (which applies to state colleges and universities) and Title III of the ADA (which applies to private universities) must be interpreted in the same way as Section 504 of the Rehabilitation Act[121] (which applies to both private and state colleges and universities that receive federal funds). However, complaints under the ADA are handled by the Department of Justice, and complaints under Section 504 of the Rehabilitation Act are handled by the Department of Education. Although the two agencies are supposed to be interpreting the law in the same way, some differences in their respective approaches are significant enough that individuals contemplating filing a discrimination complaint would be well advised to understand those distinctions in making their choice about where to file. These are discussed in more detail next.

---

just can't have you here." The 291 comments after the story contain many individuals' confirmation that the same thing happened to them, with the same cast of characters.).

[117] At Columbia, students formed a task force, see Emma Bogler, *Student Task Force to Examine Leave of Absence Policy*, COLUMBIA SPECTATOR, Mar. 24, 2014, http://columbiaspectator.com/news/2014/03/24/student-task-force-examine-leave-absence-policy. At Yale, a robust discussion has followed Williams' column, *supra* note 80.

[118] Settlement with Quinnipiac University, *supra* note 74; Letter to Bluffton University, Department of Education Complaint 15-04-2042 (Dec. 22, 2001); Office of Civil Rights, Department of Education, Letter to Western Michigan University.

[119] 42 U.S.C. 12101(a)(5).

[120] *Id.*

[121] 29 U.S.C. § 794, prohibiting discrimination on the basis of disability by any entity receiving federal funds. In the case of educational institutions, complaints are investigated by the Department of Education.

Students are both articulate and voluble about what they need.[122] First and foremost, they want clarity and transparency about policies and procedures regarding both departure and readmission that are shrouded in vague terms and substantial discretion. Students want both clarity and flexibility, because some policies are clear, but harsh. Until 2015, Yale's policy was that all leaves of absence had to be arranged within two weeks of the beginning of the semester, or that only one leave of absence would generally be permitted.[123] Columbia's Arts and Sciences graduate school forbids a student from taking medical leave during the first year, and requires that a student on leave must see a Columbia psychologist, even if the student has gone home to the Midwest,[124] and many colleges refuse to guarantee dormitory space to a student returning from medical leave. In those cases, students hope for accommodations, some form of reassurance that they will not be effectively punished for having taken a medical leave.

Students want decent mental health services, that they are not afraid to use,[125] without having to wait a month (Yale)[126] or three weeks (Columbia) for an initial appointment. Every student health service caps psychotherapy visits, at eight or twelve; having more therapists, or at least group therapy or peer support groups, has been shown to be effective. Colleges and universities naturally triage when they have scarce resources, so that in a mental health emergency students generally get seen quickly, but the students who could have benefited from earlier intervention and counseling are left to deteriorate in isolation until their condition qualifies them for a quicker appointment. Some colleges and universities openly state that the expectations of students and their parents for more timely and consistent mental health services are unrealistic. One compared it to expecting the University Health Services to treat cancer;[127] another said that they were expected to have superior resources than what was available in the community, and this

---

[122] See, e.g., Bogler, *supra* note 117; Wilfred Chan & Sarah Ngo, *How We're Doing*, Columbia Spectator, Dec. 1, 2011, http://columbiaspectator.com/eye/2011/12/01/how-were-doing; Nwoka, *supra* note 76.

[123] Under student pressure in the wake of the suicide of a Yale student, these policies are changing, see following.

[124] Bogler, *supra* note 117.

[125] Megan, *supra* note 86 (the student is quoted as saying, "They [students] shouldn't be discouraged to get help if they need it. I don't want them to be fearful of expressing themselves, to be able to get the help they need. This shouldn't happen to any other student").

[126] Andrew Giambrone, *Overwhelmed: Why Students Are Unhappy with Yale's System of Mental Health Care*, Yale News Weekend, Jan. 17, 2014, http://yale-dailynews.com/blog/2014/01/17/overwhelmed-why-students-are-unhappy-with-yales-system-of-mental-health-care-2/

[127] Baker, *supra* note 71.

was unfair.[128] Perhaps so, but with demand rising, many universities maintain level funding for mental health services, or even cut their budgets.

In addition, changing attitudes about mental health issues does not cost money. When a student cut herself, she was told that she was putting her entire high rise dormitory in danger, including students she didn't know, because "she might well start running around the halls, threatening her floormates with a knife."[129] Permitting students to stay who want to stay enrolled in school does not cost money. Letting students come back on campus to see their friends does not cost money. The most important request that students make is to be treated individually, with respect and compassion, and to be heard. Some students want to stay and continue with their courses, perhaps with a lighter load. Some students want a voluntary leave of absence, with no consequence to school-based scholarships or loans. Schools may come up with some form of enrollment status for these students since federal and private loan agreements require students to be enrolled in school. In some cases these requirements specify that the student must be enrolled full time. If universities were allied with their students, they could work jointly to solve these problems.

Instead, an adversarial attitude has grown up between students and some institutions of higher education, although U.S. college and university students have not yet been asked, as is the case with some of their Chinese counterparts, to sign a waiver of liability for the university if they commit suicide while a student.[130] Although most students are far too stressed and feel too confused and powerless to take action when they are excluded from colleges and universities, some have filed complaints, with either the Office of Civil Rights (OCR) of the Department of Education or with the Department of Justice's Disability Rights Division, or lawsuits in federal court. While settlements by the Departments of Education and Justice do not carry the force of law, they are often read and parsed by individuals seeking to understand how the agencies charged with enforcing the law understand its requirements.

The Department of Education, which was the principal enforcer of anti-discrimination provisions against colleges and universities in this area for many years, long held that mandatory withdrawal, without any individualized determination by a mental health professional, violated a student's right to be free from discrimination on the basis of perceived disability.[131] However,

---

[128] *Id.*

[129] *Id.*

[130] Brittany Kern, Abstract, *Balancing Prevention and Liability: The Use of Waiver to Limit University Liability for Student Suicide* (Aug. 8, 2014), http://ssrn.com/abstract=2478038, discusses the potential uses of waivers and whether they would survive challenges as being against public policy or unconscionable.

[131] Letter to Bluffton University, Complaint 15-04-2042; Letter to Guilford College, Complaint 11-02-2003 (Mar. 6, 2003).

until 2010, OCR also recognized that colleges and universities could avail themselves of the so-called direct threat defense if it was found to apply through individualized investigation and contemporary medical assessment.

Both the ADA and Section 504 permit a defendant to discriminate against an individual with a disability if the disability causes an individual to be a "direct threat": a significant risk to the health and safety of others that cannot be resolved by reasonable modifications of policies, practices, or procedures, or by the provision of auxiliary aids and services.[132] For example, an individual who is uncontrollably contagious with tuberculosis and refuses treatment may be quarantined;[133] although the quarantine is discrimination based on the student's disability, it is justified because the student is a "direct threat to the health and safety of others" and, in the absence of his or her willingness to accept treatment, there is no way to alleviate that threat short of quarantine.[134] The EEOC, which regulates employment discrimination, has (with the blessing of the Supreme Court[135]) expanded the statutory language of the ADA to include "threat to self" under "direct threat." For many years, the OCR of the Department of Education interpreted "direct threat" in a similar way, despite an absence of authority to extend the interpretation to Titles II and III of the ADA or to Section 504 of the Rehabilitation Act.[136]

However, in 2010, the Department of Justice specifically adopted regulations that also permitted the direct threat defense in state colleges and universities only when a disabled individual is a direct threat to others, a more faithful reflection of the language of the ADA itself. Around this time, the OCR of the Department of Education ceased to use "direct threat to self" language in analyzing whether the student had been subject to discrimination; when it uses "direct threat" language at all, it refers only to threats to others. Instead, it began to focus primarily on the question of whether students with psychiatric disabilities were treated differently than other, nondisabled, students.[137]

---

[132] 28 C.F.R. 35.104, 35.139 (Title II).
[133] City of Newark v. J.S., 652 A.2d 265 (N.J. Super. 1993).
[134] Id.
[135] Chevron, 536 U.S. 73.
[136] Title II of the ADA, which covers state colleges and universities, never had any direct threat language in either the statute or the regulations, and Title III, which covers private universities and colleges, had limited direct threat to "others." The Supreme Court's ruling on direct threat in both Nassau County v. Arline 480 U.S. 273 (1987) and Bragdon v. Abbott, 524 U.S. 624 (1998) involved only risks to the health and safety of others.
[137] This is known as "disparate treatment" and is illegal under antidiscrimination law. The "direct threat to self" was always intended solely as a defense, but in practice, the Department of Education blended the direct threat inquiry into the investigation as a whole.

The Department of Education's change in focus has not meant that colleges and universities may take no action in response to students' suicidality, or even necessarily that universities and colleges must change their practices of kicking students out of dorms and out of school. The *process* and the *language* must change. This is clear from the Department of Education's decisions in cases involving State University of New York (SUNY)-Purchase,[138] Mount Holyoke,[139] Georgetown,[140] and especially, the most recent decision in a nationally publicized case involving a Princeton freshman, who has subsequently brought suit in federal court.

The SUNY-Purchase, Mount Holyoke, and Georgetown cases underscored that a student who was suicidal could be summarily kicked out of school and forced to withdraw under the school's disciplinary code, as long as the code was (ostensibly) applied equally to all students, the decision was based on individualized assessment of the student's conduct and consultation with appropriate medical and mental health personnel, and provisions were made to permit the student some form of due process and appeal. Mandatory withdrawal following a suicide attempt, with no individualized inquiry or consultation with mental health professionals, continues to be discriminatory,[141] as it always has been. But it was the Princeton case that brought the issue of universities' treatment of suicidal students to national attention.

The student, known as W.P., attempted suicide by taking an overdose of pills, but immediately changed his mind, vomited up the pills, and went to Princeton's Counseling and Psychological Center for help. He was hospitalized for three days, found to be suitable for discharge, and explicitly *not* to be a danger to himself or others. By then, however, the university had called his mother and informed her he was banned from his dorm and classes. At a meeting the day after he was discharged, university staff pressured the student to "voluntarily" withdraw for a year, and agree to not set foot on campus for three months. Under coercive pressure, he agreed, later arguing he was given no choice. At this point, university officials had not spoken to or consulted with any of his treaters at the hospital or his own mental health treaters.

The next day, W.P. registered with Princeton as a student with a disability and requested accommodations, asking that his classes be taped or

---

[138] Office of Civil Rights, Department of Education, Letter to Purchase College, State University of New York, Complaint No. 02-10-2181 (Jan. 14, 2011).

[139] Office of Civil Rights, Department of Education, Letter to Mount Holyoke College, Complaint No. 01-08-2024 (July 18, 2008), http://www.bazelon.org/LinkClick.aspx?fileticket=abfhk9Tupko%3d&tabid=313

[140] Office of Civil Rights, Department of Education, Letter to Georgetown University, Complaint No. 11-11-2044 (Oct. 13, 2011).

[141] See Office of Civil Rights, Department of Education, Letter to Spring Arbor University, (Dec. 16, 2010); Office of Civil Rights Letter to Western Michigan University, *supra* note 118.

transcribed. The university never responded. He asked to take a reduced course load, to live off campus, and/or to take a leave of less than a year. Princeton refused this request, claiming that to fulfill it would be a "fundamental alteration" of a Princeton education.[142] Although Princeton denies that they have a blanket policy forcing withdrawals in the case of attempted suicide, the letter W.P. received was virtually identical to a letter received by another student the previous year who was also forced to withdraw after a suicide attempt.

In the face of these basically undisputed facts, the Department of Education found that Princeton had not discriminated against W.P.[143] First, his withdrawal was required pursuant to Princeton's Conduct Code, which applies to all students, and which permits the university to "summarily bar" any student "in circumstances seriously affecting the health or well-being of a student, or where physical safety is seriously threatened," as long as the student receives a "reasonably prompt review process." This language applies to all students, regardless of disability. Similarly, although much less credibly, the Department of Education found that his year-long withdrawal was not discriminatory, despite the fact that Princeton's involuntary withdrawal policy was a "direct threat to self" policy in all but the specific language: a student could be "involuntarily withdrawn" if his or her behavior posed "a serious and imminent health or safety risk to him/herself or others," including "anorexia, serious substance abuse, life-threatening behavior, repeat psychotic episodes, etc." Again, the Department of Education found that this was a policy of "general applicability," a finding reminiscent of Anatole France's observation that the law, in its majestic equality, forbids the rich as well as the poor to sleep under bridges. The Department of Education made much of the fact that Princeton had given the student a hearing, and considered the information of the student's medical providers, who said he could return to school. However, as the student contended, the outcome was predetermined from the beginning.

Nowhere in the Department of Education's current philosophy is any consideration of whether the university considered making reasonable modifications to its policies and procedures. Nor does it give any weight to the student's own opinions about what would serve him best. On appeal, with W.P. represented by the nationally known Bazelon Center for Mental Health Law, the Department of Education affirmed its findings on W.P.'s withdrawal but reopened the question of whether Princeton's readmission requirements were discriminatory.

---

[142] Princeton University, as a private university, is a public accommodation and as such must make "reasonable modifications in its policies, practices or procedures" unless those modifications would fundamentally alter the nature of its "goods, services, facilities, privileges, advantages or accommodations." 28 C.F.R. §36.302(a).
[143] Office of Civil Rights to Princeton University, *supra* note 72.

The readmission requirements made no pretense of applying equally to disabled and nondisabled students alike. If W.P. wanted to be readmitted, he was required to follow all the university's treatment recommendations, undergo a readmission evaluation at the health center, and follow any recommendations for ongoing treatment. In addition, he had to "demonstrate an increased ability to handle safely the stresses that arise from studying" at Princeton. This is a far, far cry from conditions on returning to employment, including police,[144] which basically amount to a note from the individual's doctor that the person is able to go back to work, sometimes with the concurrence of the employer's doctor. [145] Although it agreed to reconsider whether these conditions were discriminatory, OCR closed its complaint when W.P. filed suit in federal court.[146]

However, the Department of Justice has begun to take an interest in the issue of mandatory withdrawals, and it has a different approach. The Department of Justice's settlement of a student's complaint against Quinnipiac University offers revealing insights into the different approaches of the two agencies.

In the Quinnipiac case, a young woman went to the university's counseling center because she wanted to talk to someone about feeling depressed. The next thing she knew, an ambulance had been called and she was handed a letter telling her she could not return to the university or her dorm room. The university, in addition to unilaterally banning her from campus, kept her tuition money for that semester and refused to give it back. This may sound unbelievable, but this is, in fact, what happens on college and university campuses with some regularity.[147] The Department of Justice, in concert with the Office of Protection and Advocacy in Connecticut, filed

---

[144] *Lee*, 636 F.3d 245, 248; Sams v. City of Chicago, No. 13 CV 7625 (N.D. Ill. Nov. 25, 2014).

[145] Rodriguez v. School Board of Hillsborough County, (M.D. Fla. 2014) (custodian who said she had thought about suicide placed on summary leave of absence, despite being cleared to return to work by treating mental health professional and one other, employer wanted fitness for duty exam performed by their own doctor, but eventually waived the requirement).

[146] W.P. v. Anita McLean et al., No. 3:14-cv-01893-JAP-TJB (D.N.J. complaint filed March 26, 2014).

[147] A student who simply went for free information about sexually transmitted diseases at Georgia State University's Health Center was asked to leave after clinicians discovered he was diagnosed with schizophrenia. That student obtained counsel, R. Robin McDonald, *Schizophrenic Student Fights GSU Dorm Ouster*, DAILY REPORT, Feb. 6, 2015, http://www.dailyreportonline.com/id=1202717313061/Schizophrenic-Student-Fights-GSU-Dorm-Ouster?slret urn=20151010161020. Counsel obtained a favorable ruling regarding the university's actions, see R.W. v. State of Georgia, Case 1:13-cv-02115-LMM (N.D. Ga., Feb. 27, 2015) (denying state's motion for summary judgment).

a complaint against Quinnipiac. The settlement garnered the student compensation for her emotional distress, and also reimbursed a student loan she had been forced to pay back after being withdrawn, an issue that is given too little attention. But most importantly, the Department of Justice found that the university had violated the law by failing to consider modifications of its mandatory leave policy, for example, permitting the student to live off campus and complete her coursework by attending classes in person or online—the very accommodations requested by W.P. in the Princeton case. Deirdre Daly, with the Department of Justice, stated the obvious when she said, "Quinnipiac removed this student from the university at a very vulnerable time in her life, and saddled her with a large student loan payment." U.S. Attorney Daly said, "Instead of removing students from school, educational institutions must be equipped to manage and educate students who recognize, disclose and are treating their mental health disabilities."[148] Acting Assistant Attorney General Vanita Gupta summarized the law: "universities like Quinnipiac cannot apply blanket policies that result in unnecessary exclusion of students with disabilities if reasonable modifications would permit continued participation; in many cases, such modifications can be as simple as allowing a student to complete coursework on a modified schedule."[149]

Unnecessary exclusion is, in fact, the very heart of the issue. Universities must become comfortable with educating a broader spectrum of students. In 1963, Ed Roberts became the first person with a severe disability to attend Berkeley. He had to sue to be admitted, and his arrival was headline news in the campus newspaper: "Helpless cripple attends classes at UC."[150] He and other disabled students who were admitted in his wake were housed in Cowell Hospital, the Berkeley Infirmary.[151] Lex Frieden, a disability rights advocate who uses a wheelchair, was refused admission by Oral Roberts University in 1968 because "my presence in a wheelchair would be an imposition on other students."[152] The progress we have made in the last fifty years is that now students with disabilities are admitted to universities to struggle

---

[148] Press Release, U.S. Department of Justice, Justice Department Settles Americans with Disabilities Act Case with Quinnipiac University (Jan. 14, 2015), http://www.justice.gov/usao/ct/Press2015/20150112.html.
[149] Megan, *supra* note 86.
[150] Susan O'Hara, *The Disability Rights and Independent Living Movement*, 55 BENE LEGERE (2000), http://vm136.lib.berkeley.edu/give/bene-legere/bene55/disability.html; Ed Roberts became not only a revered icon of disability rights, but ran the Department of Rehabilitation for Governor Jerry Brown.
[151] DORIS ZAMES FLEISCHER & FRIEDA ZAMES, THE DISABILITY RIGHTS MOVEMENT: FROM CHARITY TO CONFRONTATION 38.
[152] *Id.* at 43. Frieden was accepted by the University of Tulsa, which made certain that its program was accessible to him, long before it was forced by law to do so.

with inaccessible campuses and dorms[153] and with class schedules, registration, and coursework on Internet applications that cannot be used by blind students.[154] It is a little ironic to contemplate the U.S. Air Force launching a program to help its suicidal members while U.S. universities are banning students from campus who seek help at the university counseling center. The fact of the matter is that some universities, as entities, do not actually behave as though they care about the sources of individual students' suicidality and what they can do to help (or at least not hurt), including what policy changes might improve the situation. The changes that are being made are brought about through litigation, student pressure, and outside influence of groups such as the Jed Foundation[155] and the Bazelon Center for Mental Health Law.

The Department of Justice has correctly focused on ending exclusion and on the university's obligations to modify its practices so that students who are suicidal can receive the help they need to continue getting the education that will end up making an enormous difference in their lives, and in their ability to contribute to society.

What to make of this difference? Perhaps the Department of Education is "captured" by its academic constituents, as it deals with them more frequently. Another and more charitable way to say the same thing is that perhaps the Department of Education is more aware of the difficulties universities face. Reading the complaints filed by two different Columbia University graduate students reveals a study in contrasting approaches to students: in one case, how much energy members of the university staff spent trying to help a struggling student,[156] and how they were obstructed at every turn by inflexible university policies; on the other, how unforgivably rude behavior was treated as a medical rather than a disciplinary issue.[157] In both cases, the university arranged for a student to be involuntarily committed, an outcome that could probably have been avoided.

Colleges and universities with enormous student bodies are floundering between the rock of tort liability if they keep and attempt to help students

---

[153] Vivian Wang, *Students in Wheelchairs Find Campuses Inaccessible*, YALE DAILY NEWS, Feb. 24, 2015, http://yaledailynews.com/blog/2015/02/24/wheelchair-accessibility-leaves-much-to-be-desired/.

[154] www.ada.gov/louisiana-tech.htm; for eighteen other universities sued for inaccessible course registration and other materials, see Laura Carlson, *Higher Ed Accessibility Lawsuits, Complaints, and Settlements*, http://www.d.umn.edu/~lcarlson/atteam/lawsuits.html.

[155] The Jed Foundation (www.jedfoundation.org) is the leading nonprofit voice dedicated to improving the emotional health of college students.

[156] Milonopoulos v. Trustees of Columbia University, complaint found at http://www.scribd.com/doc/238376253/Milonopoulos-v-Columbia-lawsuit, see paragraphs 13-31, 33-44.

[157] Kate McDonough, "Student Sues Columbia University for Involuntary Hospitalization," Salon, Feb. 3, 2013, http://www.salon.com/2013/02/03/student_sues_columbia_university_for_involuntary_hospitalization/

struggling with suicidality, and the hard place of discrimination liability if they make those students take leaves of absence. Once again, tort law distorts incentives for institutions of higher education to do the right thing, which is to try to help students by providing them with the care and assistance the students themselves believe they need rather than seeing the suicidal student as a potential liability.

One recent tort case shows that these concerns can be harmonized.[158] The claims in this case are a perfect illustration of the expectations that parents have of colleges and universities: the parents claimed that the university breached its "duty of care" by failing to prevent the suicide; that it had a duty to notify the parents about their son's problems; that the university should have involuntarily committed their son and/or should have required him to take a leave of absence; and that it breached a contractual duty to provide him with mental health services.[159] These are all problematic expectations for parents to have, especially in light of the facts of the case.

The facts of the case show that the student had a long-standing and continuous relationship with an extraordinarily involved counselor at the university, who saw him many times per semester, responded to his emails at 9:30 p.m., altered her schedule to see him, and consulted with doctors when she was concerned about him. She implored him to talk to his parents or give her permission to do so, and his response was vehemently negative, and invoked the trust that he had in the confidentiality of their relationship. She also tried to persuade the student to accept hospitalization (he had agreed to hospitalization his first year and resolved never to go back to "that terrible mental ward"), or take time off. She didn't force him to do anything, and he kept coming back, kept emailing her, kept talking to her. Like Dr. Curell, she appeared to genuinely care for her patient (or "client," as she is a counselor). He saw a university doctor for medication, and the university made arrangements for continuity over the summer. He had plans for the future: he wanted to go to law school. The triggering stress that finally pushed him to kill himself was that his former girlfriend, whom he still loved, began dating a member of his fraternity. Universities cannot prevent heartbreak and loss, and the court declined to create a new duty of care.

However, the court hastened to remind the university that the finding it had no duty of care in these circumstances

> is not an invitation to avoid action. We believe the "University"
> has a responsibility to adopt prevention programs and protocols
> regarding students' self-inflicted injury and suicide that address
> risk management from a humanistic and therapeutic as compared

---

[158] *Mahoney*, No. AD 892-2003 (order on motion for summary judgment). The portion of the case that remained for trial was decided by the jury in favor of the defendants in three hours.

[159] *Id.* at 2.

to just a liability or risk avoiding perspective. In our view, the likelihood of a liability determination (even where a duty is established) is remote, when the issue of proximate causation (to be liable, the university's act/omissions would have to be shown to be substantial) is considered. By way of illustration, even as to the issue of the lesser duty of notification of parents/others, there is always the possibility that such may make matters worse and increase the pressure on the student to commit the act. Rather than create an ill-defined duty of due care, the University and mental health community have a more realistic duty to make strides toward prevention.[160]

What duties do colleges and universities have toward their students? This issue is being raised in many different areas: campus sexual assault and other student safety issues, including hazing, alcohol, and safety from outside attack; medical care and general attention to health, including the mental health, of students; regulation of speech through codes of student conduct, and accommodation of physical, psychiatric and learning disabilities.

Universities cannot be guarantors of either physical or mental health, and they cannot be held to the duty to prevent a student's suicide. This is particularly true if the student lives off-campus. However, if universities offer health services for non-emergent conditions (and they all do), they should offer decent, confidential mental health services, not just a few pills to make it through exams or an immediate call to 911. Because of issues raised by student demand for these services, parent demands for information about their children, and liability fears, it may be better all around for colleges and universities to give all students vouchers for a specific number of completely confidential mental health sessions by independent community providers located convenient to the university but unconnected with it. (I recognize this would be easier to do in urban universities than rural ones). Doing this would relieve universities of many of the dilemmas that we have discussed. I completely recognize and anticipate that a market of sorts would be created in the vouchers, so that students who needed more than the set number of sessions might negotiate with students who were never going to use their vouchers at all. While people might object that this would interfere with students' confidentiality, everything I have read and heard leads me to the conclusion that students would rather their friends know about their mental health problems than university officials. The university could focus on students with academic or conduct problems, and communicate with the local mental health service provider only if the student gave permission. The mental health service provider would not have the conflicts of interest associated with being employed by the university.

---

[160] *Id.* at 25.

The vexing question of communication with parents would likewise diminish substantially.

There should be no "duty" to notify parents of an adult student. Everyone who knows a person who committed suicide wonders what they could have done differently, and heartbroken parents more than anyone else. Parents have to feel that if they had known what was happening with their child, they could have prevented the suicide. The fact that this is usually not true doesn't matter; parents' bitterness and rage at not being notified leads to many a lawsuit. But fear of liability must not prevent a college or university from putting the student first. Student privacy is not absolute: the Department of Education has interpreted the Family Educational Rights and Privacy Act (FERPA) to permit notification in a health or safety emergency, but does not require it. [161]

The most important thing that universities can do is to change their policies of exclusion: forcing students to take leaves of absence, barring or placing unreasonable conditions upon their return. Under pressure from their students, alumni, and the press, some universities are changing their policies. In the spring of 2015, Yale agreed to most of the recommendations made by a panel it had appointed to look into policies impacting students seeking to take time off for "medical, personal or other reasons."[162] It agreed to changes "allowing students more time to declare a leave of absence instead of outright withdrawing" (meaning fifteen days instead of ten in the fall semester, and sixteen days instead of ten in the spring); to change the name of the process of going back from "readmission" to "reinstatement," and to provide financial aid for the two college courses it requires withdrawn students to take to prove they are ready to come back to Yale.[163] Even these changes do not reflect an ideal policy, and certainly there is ample room for improvement. But it is heartening that they came about because of an intra-university process led by students; it is enormously important to keep talking about these issues.

Discrimination and Institutionalization

Many students who tell a college or university official that they are feeling suicidal end up hospitalized that day, with no inquiry into whether it is really needed. The same thing happened to at least some of my interviewees when they revealed their suicidality at work, although older people may be more guarded and less impulsive about revealing their inner lives than students.

---

[161] U.S. Department of Education, Law and Guidance, Disclosure of Information from Education Records to Parents of Post-Secondary Students, June 7, 2007, http://www2.ed.gov/policy/gen/guid/fpco/hottopics/ht-parents-postsecstudents.html

[162] Melissa Korn & Angela Chen, *Yale Alters Leave Policy Amid Protest Over Student Suicide*, WALL ST. J., Apr. 29, 2015.

[163] *Id.*

These hospitalizations, in turn, are often pivotal points in decisions about student withdrawal or employee termination.

I argued in Chapter 2 that it is unconstitutional to involuntarily commit an individual for talking about suicide, including suicidal threats, in the absence of corroborating conduct. In Chapter 9, we will look at the most effective treatment approaches to help suicidal people, and they are all community-based treatments. In this section, I argue that it may violate the ADA to institutionalize people unnecessarily for suicidality, when the services that would help them are available in the community (and especially when they are not available in the hospital).

This is because the ADA contains an "integration mandate:" the requirement that when public entities offer mental health and other services to people, they must offer them in the most integrated setting appropriate to the individual's needs. When Congress passed the ADA, it explicitly found that "historically, society has tended to isolate and segregate people with disabilities."[164] This isolation and segregation is a form of discrimination for disabled people just as it is for racial and ethnic minorities. Congress found that discrimination persisted in such critical areas as health care and institutionalization.[165] The Department of Justice's regulations for state and local governments[166] require that if they provide services to disabled people, those services must be provided in the most integrated setting appropriate to their needs.[167]

An "integrated" setting in the disability context is one that enables individuals with disabilities to interact with nondisabled individuals to the greatest extent possible. In other words, if hospitalization is unnecessary for suicidal people to receive the help that they need, institutionalization for suicidality constitutes discrimination on the basis of disability or perceived disability under the ADA. Nor can a state only offer needed services in a segregated setting, that is, force people to be institutionalized to receive the services they need.[168]

The Supreme Court affirmed this understanding in 1999 in the case of *Olmstead v. L.C.*[169] This case involved two women whose treatment professionals acknowledged did not need to be institutionalized, but who nevertheless

---

[164] 42 U.S.C. § 12101(a)(2).

[165] 42 U.S.C. § 12101(a)(3).

[166] Congress empowered the Department of Justice to write implementing regulations for the ADA, 42 U.S.C. §12134 (2014).

[167] 28 C.F.R. 35.130(d).

[168] See Department of Justice, *Questions and Answers on the ADA's Integration Mandate and Olmstead Enforcement*, http://www.ada.gov/olmstead/q&a_olmstead.htm#_ftn6 (Question 8: "Do the ADA and Olmstead require a state to provide services in the community to individuals with disabilities when it would otherwise provide such services in institutions? A: Yes.").

[169] 527 U.S. 581 (1999).

remained hospitalized. The Supreme Court held that if the women were able to live in the community, then the State had to place them in the community, unless to do so would fundamentally alter the state's mental health services (e.g., if the women were on an effectively functioning waiting list for community services, with people being discharged at a reasonable pace, the Court would not require the State to jump people to the front of a line just because they were plaintiffs in a lawsuit).

Since then, courts across the country have held that *Olmstead* applies both to people who are institutionalized and people who are at risk of being institutionalized because they are being denied the services necessary to keep them out of institutions.[170] People who repeatedly cycle in and out of emergency departments and hospitalizations because of suicidality, and who are not receiving the evidence-based services that have been shown to specifically help suicidal people in the community, remain at risk of institutionalization as long as they don't receive those services.

People who are suicidal are sometimes, but not always, disabled under the ADA. They are almost invariably regarded as being disabled. They may also have a record of disability that qualifies them for coverage. They are "qualified" for state-provided community services if they are clients of the state mental health system, or receiving services from the state, for example, are institutionalized in a state facility or a state-contracted private facility, are on Medicaid, or receiving other state-provided or subsidized care for suicidality. They are discriminated against if they are forced to receive these services in an unnecessarily segregated environment, that is, an institutional setting.

A state policy that prohibited people who had attempted suicide from accessing certain kinds of community services, or from receiving an advantage or benefit offered by the state would almost certainly violate the ADA as a blanket policy based on perceived disability. I have argued at great length elsewhere in this book[171] that people who are thinking about dying, or who want to die, or who are talking about dying, or even threatening suicide, should not be automatically institutionalized, especially not involuntarily. As discussed in Chapter 7 and elsewhere in this book, this is particularly true of people who are chronically suicidal, people who are contingently suicidal, people with diagnoses of personality disorder, and people who have trauma histories. My argument in Chapter 2 was based on constitutional law: that our fundamental right to liberty precludes total deprivation of that liberty unless it is necessary to serve a compelling state interest that cannot be served in a less restrictive way. My argument here is based on antidiscrimination law: the prohibition of unnecessary isolation and segregation based on disability,

---

[170] Fischer v. Oklahoma Health Auth., 335 F.3d 1175 (10th Cir. 2003); M.R. v. Dreyfus, 663 F.3d 1100 (9th Cir. 2011).

[171] See Chapter 2.

or what is regarded as disability. The constitutional argument merely precludes the state from involuntary institutionalization, but the ADA's integration mandate underscores that when a state chooses to provide treatment, it must provide it in the most integrated setting appropriate for the individual. The best reasons for a person to stay alive are not found on the wards of a psychiatric hospital, and the approaches that work to reduce suicide—dialectical behavior therapy (DBT), cognitive behavioral therapy (CBT), collaborative assessment and management of suicidality (CAMS), and peer support—are overwhelmingly community based.

Conclusion

Our silence about suicide translates into misunderstandings and stereotypes, as well as (perhaps even more potently) fear of liability. This combination causes people who are already wondering if they want to be alive to be involuntarily hospitalized, which then can lead to being kicked out of school, and their dormitories, fired from work, and losing custody of their children. Discrimination and loss in turn amplify the suicidality.[172]

The statistics are clear. Literally millions of people have suicidal thoughts, and for young adults in their first few years of independence, whether at school or in their first jobs, transitioning stresses and the difficulties of meeting an entirely different set of expectations are completely predictable. Some small proportion of young adults and other people in difficult transitions are, unfortunately but predictably, going to feel suicidal.

Employers, and, even more, colleges and universities, can compound and exacerbate these difficulties enormously, or they can provide support and assistance. Despite the fact that universities are paid enormous sums of money each year to educate students they have chosen to accept, they do a terrible job of providing support for suicidal students, having preferred for some time to try to persuade or force students to leave campus. Employers, for the most part, probably do better than universities in supporting employees who are suicidal. Ironically, universities' inferior track record probably is related to the fact that they *are* seen as owing the students some affirmative quantum of care and services, whereas employers are simply expected not to discriminate against their employees. The greater obligations of universities lead to greater worries about potential liability, which in turn has generally

---

[172] Ann P. Haas, Phillip L. Rodgers, Jody L. Herman, *Suicide Attempts Among Transgender and Gender-Nonconforming Adults*, AMERICAN FOUNDATION FOR SUICIDE PREVENTION/WILLIAMS INSTITUTE (Jan. 2014), http://williamsinstitute. law.ucla.edu/wp-content/uploads/AFSP-Williams-Suicide-Report-Final.pdf (finding that 50% to 59% of transgender individuals in the study who had been the subjects of discrimination or harassment at work had attempted suicide).

led to worse, not better, policies. On the other hand, it has also led to a far larger array of support services, peer services, groups, and mental health services on campus—still inadequate to meet the need, but vastly increased from the pre-*Shin* days.

It's the same old story: autonomy versus protection from risk, with anti-discrimination law championing the former value, and tort law underpinning the latter. What is desperately needed are unified national standards that colleges and universities could follow: basic numbers for mental health services and basic protections for students to discuss what they are going through without fearing being banned and shunned by one of the major sources of their identities. Some efforts have been made in the direction of national standards, but we haven't approached consensus yet.

Colleges and universities, like places of employment, could clearly benefit from a public health prevention approach, an idea that has been advocated for many years.[173] School policies should address issues relating to medical leave, loans, confidentiality, housing, visas for international students, and readmission. Cultural sensitivity is a major issue, especially with burgeoning populations of international students, and should include sensitivity to the enormous stresses faced by students from low-income families, for whom time off may be literally unaffordable. These policies should, at a minimum, understand that for many students, remaining on campus is a protective factor. For most (not all) students, staying on campus sustains their identities, keeps them in a structured environment, with friends, and does not increase stress by requiring them to move and deal with student loans and scholarships and finding new mental health professionals at a time when they are experiencing profound struggles. These students are not isolated anomalies. They are a substantial part of the student body, and colleges and universities must reframe their understanding and policies to recognize this reality.

---

[173] Drum et al., *supra* note 109.

9

Prevention and Treatment: Policy and Legal Barriers

Help . . . must attend to people's "careers" as suicidal people over time, either consistently or episodically . . . help aimed at achieving immediate safety teaches no skills. Staying alive requires myriad skills, way beyond the obvious skills needed to attain shelter and safety and food. It takes skills to endure the endless bullshit that each of us has to endure as a person. If you make a list of all of the trauma and heartbreaks and fears that each of us must learn to deal with, it is literally impossible to find anyone who hasn't been traumatized at some point in their life. Whether it is criminal victimization (property, assault, or sex), death of a loved one, sickness, sickness of a loved one, poverty, wealth, obesity, anorexia, unemployment, underemployment, bullying, treachery, loss of a love relationship, death of a pet, or a thousand other things, it takes skills to get through the day. If a person is seriously and persistently suicidal, and crisis services do nothing more than keep them alive for a few days, they may have done nothing to prevent the person's ultimate suicide.

—Dr. Joel Dvoskin[1]

It's a pretty big distortion to think we can design any kind of intervention system that is going to automatically prevent people from killing themselves. But why not do the thing that is going to make the person feel better?

—Stephen McCrea[2]

---

[1] Personal communication from Joel Dvoskin to the author (June 17, 2015).
[2] Interview with Stephen McCrea (Aug. 22, 2014).

Instead of saying "You feel suicidal, let's stop it," they should say, "What does it mean?" Therapists shouldn't say "I have answers," but "I'm with you while you work out your answers."

—Laura Delano

Introduction

Despite millions and millions of dollars poured into suicide research and prevention,[3] the national rate of suicide has remained essentially unchanged for the last two decades.[4] Many current suicide prevention efforts are fundamentally misguided and unhelpful to people who are suicidal. The federal government gives states millions of suicide prevention dollars, and then does not hold them accountable for any results in reducing suicide. Take a look at random state suicide prevention strategic plans—most of them are on the Internet.[5] They follow an extremely predictable format: data on suicide, findings about stigma and lack of public understanding, something about "vision" and "principles," and "action" steps that involve "promoting," "encouraging," "recognizing," or "facilitating" various unimpeachably benign goals. Montana is a good example of a state whose suicide prevention

---

[3] The National Institutes of Health (NIH) estimates it will spend $66 million solely on suicide and suicide prevention research in fiscal year 2016, NIH, Estimates of Funding for Various Research, Condition, and Disease Categories (RCDC) (Feb. 5, 2015), http://report.nih.gov/categorical_spending.aspx; the Clay Hunt Suicide Prevention for American Veterans Act alone authorizes an additional $24 million targeted at veterans. Martin Matishak, *Obama Signs Military Suicide Prevention Bill into Law*, The Hill, Feb. 12, 2015, http://thehill.com/policy/defense/232659-obama-signs-military-suicide-prevention-bill-into-law.

[4] Thomas R. Insel, The Research Prioritization Task Force Report (National Institute of Mental Health, Feb. 26, 2014) at slide 3 (suicide rates have not changed over the past two decades), *available at* http://www.google.com/url?sa=t&rct=j&q=&esrc=s&source=web&cd=7&ved=0CFIQFjAG&url=http://www.afsp.org/content/download/11050/193412/file/AFSP%202-26%20TI%20Suicide%20Prevention-final.pptx&ei=cUx5U9TtBpWTqAa2roKgDg&usg=AFQjCNGYgY2GVVp3gpAqeAyoU_wAMZSlLQ&bvm=bv.66917471,d.b2k.

[5] See, just as an example, Massachusetts' state suicide prevention plan for 2009, Massachusetts Coalition for Suicide Prevention (MCSP), Massachusetts Department of Public Health, & Massachusetts Department of Mental Health, Massachusetts Strategic Plan for Suicide Prevention (Sept. 2009), http://www.mass.gov/eohhs/docs/dph/com-health/injury/suicide-strategic-plan.pdf. Compare it to Connecticut's 2005 plan, Connecticut Department of Public Health, Connecticut Comprehensive Suicide Prevention Plan (2005), http://www.ct.gov/dph/lib/dph/publications/family_health/suicide_prevention_plan[1].pdf.

plan is one of the best in the country: it has excellent and comprehensive data, a public health approach, far more concrete proposals than many plans, and can point to specific goals and accomplishments over time.[6] Despite this, Montana has consistently been in the top five states in terms of its suicide rate, and since its Suicide Prevention plan has been in effect, its suicide rate has increased.[7] There's a possible reason for this: despite the fact that 75% of its youth suicide deaths and 63% of adult suicide deaths are from firearms,[8] Montana continues to have among the most permissive gun laws in the country.[9] Montana's goal in the area of suicide prevention related to firearms is to "encourage and promote the safe storage and protection of firearms from high-risk populations through the use of gunlocks and other gun safety measures."[10] I am not saying that it would be politically feasible to do any more than this with regard to guns in Montana, or that Montana has not done a lot within the range of political feasibility in funding worthwhile, specific initiatives.[11] I *am* saying that states receiving suicide prevention dollars (like many federal to state transfers) are not held accountable for actually accomplishing any reduction in their suicide rates.

Meanwhile, business continues as usual in all the states. Access to guns proliferates. Suicidal people continue to be treated in ways that are unsupported by any evidentiary basis, and may actually be harmful, damaging, and ineffective. Coercive and involuntary "treatment" in inpatient settings leads that list. While I understand and acknowledge the political difficulty of curbing access to firearms, the expensive and unnecessary institutionalization of suicidal people in environments such as hospitals, prisons, and jails, when the more effective approaches are community-based, is costing us money, incalculable pain, and people's lives. It can and should be addressed.

---

[6] Montana Strategic Suicide Prevention Plan (2015), http://www.sprc.org/sites/sprc.org/files/State%20Suicide%20Plan-2015_0.pdf

[7] *Id.* at pp. 13–14.

[8] *Id.* at p. 18.

[9] MONT. STAT. ANN. § 45-8-301. Montana has a preemption law that precludes local municipalities from enacting stricter gun control. A child of fourteen can buy a gun in Montana without any waiting period (as long as he or she is not intoxicated or under the influence of a controlled substance). There is no registration, license, or permit requirement, except for machine guns, which must be registered and kept on the owner's property.

[10] Montana Strategic Suicide Prevention Plan, at n. 6, p. 55.

[11] In Gallatin and Park Counties, for example, when police receive calls about people in emotional or psychiatric crisis, they have the option of calling two peers—people with a great deal of experience and training in such crises—to handle the situation. See JIM HAJNY [EXECUTIVE DIRECTOR], MONTANA'S PEER NETWORK, PEER SUPPORT AND MOBILE CRISIS OUTREACH PROJECT, JAN. 2014– JUNE 2015. The project has saved the counties and state money by diverting emergency department and inpatient bed usage and will be renewed. For more information, contact Jim Hajny at jim@mtpeernetwork.org.

The effectiveness of other efforts receiving federal funding is controversial: the seemingly endless catalog of questionnaires and checklists to determine suicidality,[12] which research repeatedly shows to be ineffective. Our society currently spends millions of dollars on suicide prevention and research, much of it in an unending quest for the holy grail of a suicide assessment instrument that would enable evaluators to predict which suicidal people will actually attempt or complete the act.[13] A comparable amount of money has *not* been spent ensuring people will have access to existing treatments and interventions already known to be effective.

In addition to the sheer difficulty of devising a short questionnaire to predict suicide, the task itself seems misguided, for two basic reasons. The first is that preventing a person from dying is laudable but insufficient. You could do it by putting someone in a cage, but that would miss the point. Suicide prevention is like everything else in our medical system: we don't focus on it until the suicide is imminent or attempted, which is expensive and leaves a lot of people pretty miserable for a pretty long time.

The majority of our suicide prevention resources seem concentrated on identifying a potential suicide and restraining that person, rather than preventing the buildup of desperation or healing the underlying wounds. Emergency department visits and inpatient units are more expensive than hotlines, but even hotlines are focused on keeping a person alive in the moment, rather than looking to what might help the person find meaning and purpose in his or her life over the long term.

The kind of suicide prevention I advocate in this chapter, focused on more than the bare fact of keeping a person unwillingly alive, is not the kind of fuzzy and aspirational plan produced by most states in exchange for federal dollars. It involves a public health style, community-based approach such as that advocated by Montana and employed by the Air Force,[14] including serious work on preventing access to means of suicide, and a concerted effort to force hospitals to address environmental risks. It calls for requiring providers to be trained in a number of evidence-based treatment approaches that focus on the suicidality itself, rather than treating the suicidal person as mentally

---

[12] Some of the better known of these include the Columbia Suicide Safety Rating Scale (C-SSRS), the Suicide Assessment Five-Step Evaluation and Triage (SAFE-T), the Suicide Behaviors Questionnaire-Revised (SBQ-R), explained at the Substance Abuse and Mental Health Services Administration's Screening Tools website, http://www.integration.samhsa.gov/clinical-practice/screening-tools#suicide. Others include the Suicidal Ideation Questionnaire (SIQ), Tool for the Assessment of Suicidal Risk—Adolescent (TASR-A), the Scale for Suicidal Ideation (SSI), and the Beck Hopelessness Scale.

[13] See Chapter 2.

[14] This is one of the few suicide prevention programs that has been shown to work. Kerry Knox, Steven Pflanz, Gerald W. Talcott, et al., *The U.S. Air Force Suicide Prevention Program: Implications for Public Health Policy*, 100 AM. J. PUB. HEALTH 2457 (2010). See also extended discussion in Chapter 8.

ill. It involves stepped-up funding for a number of innovative peer support programs,[15] including peer groups specifically for people who are struggling with suicidality, and peer crisis respite. It also requires wading into the weeds to make diversion from police and emergency departments real.

In order for all of this to happen, the framework of our understanding of suicidality must change. As I underscored in Chapter 7, there are many different kinds of suicidality, and they cannot all be treated the same. Nevertheless, understanding the roots of much (not all) suicidality are not in mental illness but in trauma, transitions, or both, is a good first start. We need to understand that for many people, suicidality starts in childhood. My extensive interviews confirmed this over and over again in heartbreaking ways. People told me they had first wanted to die at the age of eight, or ten. Case law and news articles reflect situations where six-year-olds and fourth-graders commit suicide.[16] This does *not* mean more screening and labeling and pharmaceuticals for our already over-screened, over-labeled, and over-drugged children. It does mean focusing hard on bullying,[17] and increasing in-home family support programs. It also means that we have to recognize that all the heavy lifting cannot be done by government programs. We need adults paying attention and providing kindness, support, and understanding—school teachers, guidance counselors, neighbors, Little League coaches, babysitters, rabbis and pastors, and anyone who suspects something may not be quite right with a child. It takes a while to build a trusting relationship, and we hurry around our lives with little enough time to spare for our own families, but there are seven- and eight-year-olds out there right now who wish every day that they were dead.

---

[15] "Peer" is a term that has been developed to refer to individuals who use their personal experience of the mental health system and mental health conditions to help others in similar situations, see, e.g., Larry Davidson, *Peer Support Among Persons with Severe Mental Illness: A Review of Evidence and Experience*, 11 WORLD PSYCHIATRY 123 (2012). There are a few peer-run groups for suicidal people, which are sort of a suicidal person's Alcoholics Anonymous (AA) without the religion, see *infra* at pp. 455–463.

[16] Estate of Lance v. Lewinsville Indep. School, 743 F.3d 982 (5th Cir. 2014) (granting summary judgment to the school and finding that it had not displayed deliberate indifference to bullying of a special-needs child); see also Moore v. Chilton County Board of Educ., 936 F. Supp. 2d 1300 (2013); Associated Press, *Case Closed on Hanging Death of 6-Year-Old* (KARE-TV, Minneapolis-St. Paul, Minn., Jan. 15, 2015), http://www.kare11.com/story/news/crime/2015/01/15/case-closed-on-hanging-death-of-6-year-old-kendrea-johnson/21817087/ ; Michael E. Young, *What Would Lead a Child to Suicide?* DALLAS MORNING NEWS, Feb. 8, 2010 (nine-year-old boy commits suicide in his elementary school restroom), http://webmedia.newseum.org/newseum-multimedia/tfp_archive/2010-02-08/pdf/TX_DMN.pdf.

[17] See Chapter 7 for an in-depth discussion of this issue and the legal and policy difficulties it raises.

There certainly is suicidality that is caused by psychiatric disabilities and mental illness, and plenty of room in my model for mental health professionals, but we need to change what we expect from them, and they need to change their approach. It is not the responsibility of a mental health professionals to save a suicidal person's life; it is up to a mental health professional to provide the support, skills, and assistance a person may need to save his or her own life. We need to reduce liability concerns by passing immunity statutes and by greatly curtailing the ability of mental health professionals to involuntarily commit suicidal people. The law must allow a minimal detention to account for competence assessments, detoxification, and to deter impulsive suicides, but ultimately the person has to be given hope for a better life, and it is the rare hospital psychiatry ward that provides this service. That kind of work, providing connections with the community, is better done by peer groups than mental health professionals.

Prevention means focusing on skills training that currently exists and has been shown over and over again to work better than traditional therapy. Whether in the form of cognitive behavioral therapy (CBT), dialectical behavior therapy (DBT), or the Collaborative Assessment and Management of Suicidality (CAMS), there are manuals for this sort of stuff. It's less expensive than the cycle of emergency department to hospital to step down to community to emergency department again; and it helps people get on with their lives. For some people whose suicidality is clearly related to depression or schizophrenia or bipolar disorder, then by all means treat those—but still, try the CBT, DBT, or CAMS.

Prevention means ensuring that people who are suicidal do not automatically lose access to education,[18] employment opportunities,[19] or their children,[20] which only exacerbates suicidality. We need policies to ensure people are not punished and derailed from pursuing their goals because sometimes things get difficult and overwhelming. This translates to very specific social and mental health policies and programs, from ensuring continuity of care when people find a person or program that actually helps, to funding peer support programs that work, to inquiring in far greater detail about childhood violence and trauma. These specific recommendations are discussed in the following sections.

In a broader way, we need as a society to consciously understand the link between losing a job, being evicted, being subjected to domestic violence,

---

[18] A Yale student recently killed herself, leaving a note that she was afraid of seeking help because she would not be allowed to return to Yale, Rachel Siegel & Vivian Wang, *Student Death Raises Questions on Withdrawal Policies*, YALE DAILY NEWS, Jan. 29, 2015. For extensive discussion of college and university policies regarding students who are suicidal, see Chapter 8, pp. 386–401.

[19] See Chapter 8.

[20] See this chapter, *infra* at pp. 457–450.

and suicide,[21] in the same way that we now viscerally understand the link between school bullying and suicide. We don't suggest to kids who are being bullied that they are overreacting, or that they take medications so that they won't be suicidal, we try to stop the bullying. A lot of people are suicidal because they don't see a way out of a life that is objectively miserable and pretty hopeless. As the Montana Suicide Prevention plan notes (to its credit) in discussing suicide among Native Americans:

> ... historical trauma is a risk factor for suicide. Historical trauma includes forced relocations, the removal of children who were sent to boarding schools, the prohibition of the practice of language and cultural traditions, and the outlawing of traditional religious practices. Today's American Indian youth are experiencing a new type of historical trauma in the form of poverty, substance abuse, violence, loss of language, and disconnect from their culture.[22]

One of the reasons that evidence-based forms of suicide prevention work is that they take seriously a person's understanding of the crises that are pushing him or her to the edge,[23] and work to provide the skills and hope to adapt, overcome, or transcend the specific problems underlying the crises, rather than diagnosing a despairing person with a mental illness and then treating the illness as the cause of the suicidality.

Thus, if we pay attention to causes, and the skills people need to cope with genuinely harrowing traumas, we can save lives. We can save lives in ways that are far more effective, cheaper, and less emotionally devastating than hours of involuntary detention in an overcrowded emergency department or psychiatric ward. These well-known methods—from more attention to access to lethal means, to family support and violence reduction efforts, to recognizing the value of peer support and ensuring the availability of CBT, DBT, CAMS, and other evidence-based treatments focusing on suicidality— would save thousands of lives at a fraction of the cost we incur today, yet are implemented sporadically and often only after decades of determined effort. Peer efforts can work at a fraction of the cost of hospitalization, but with

---

[21] Katherine A. Fowler, R. Matthew Gladden, Kevin J. Vagi, Jamar Barnes, & Leroy Frazier, *Increase in Suicides Associated with Home Eviction and Foreclosure During the US Housing Crisis: Findings from 16 National Violent Death Reporting System States, 2005–2010*, 105 AM. J. PUB. HEALTH 2, 311–16 (Feb. 2015).

[22] Montana Suicide Prevention Plan, n. 6 at p. 32.

[23] One man who was prevented from jumping off the Golden Gate Bridge had a child born 2 ½ months premature, could not pay the child's medical bills, and had lost his job. Aaron Kinney, "Golden Gate Bridge Suicides: 'Guardian' and Would-be Jumper Discuss Near-Death Experiences," San Jose Mercury News, April 21, 2015, http://www.mercurynews.com/san-mateo-county-times/ci_28681900/chp-officer-shares-experience-guardian-golden-gate-bridge. Other people kill themselves because they are destitute and cannot pay their bills, see *infra* at n. 119.

even the smallest government grants come bureaucratic requirements that just don't make sense in the peer context.

This chapter is about the best methods of suicide prevention: the ones that do the least damage, are the most effective, the least expensive, and leave people not only alive but wanting to live. The first section looks at prevention through creating barriers to the means of suicide: guns, bridges, and other such methods.[24] The second section looks at evidence-based suicide treatments, which are all (not coincidentally) community-based. The third section looks at what people who made serious attempts at suicide say worked to keep them alive and compares that to our current policies, practices and laws.

We can do this if we care enough. Unfortunately, much of the evidence of our policies and our laws points to the conclusion that as a society, we really don't care very much at all. You may not be surprised to learn that we ignore, obstruct, and thwart the simplest and least expensive solutions, the ones that work in the moment, and the ones that work long term. I make specific recommendations on how we can alter our policies, laws, and practices to correspond more closely to effective suicide prevention.

The Public Health Approach and Limiting Access to Means

It may seem paradoxical, but even if individual suicides cannot be predicted, the suicide rate as a whole can be reduced. This has been shown repeatedly around the world with public health measures aimed at reducing access to lethal means and taking the most rudimentary and inexpensive precautions to reduce opportunities in places where people who are suicidal might be most likely to be found: the Golden Gate Bridge, psychiatric hospital wards, and Veterans Administration (VA) hospitals.

In the United States, this primarily means figuring out a way to reduce suicide by guns, without undermining the legal rights of the vast number of people who aren't suicidal to own guns. Banning guns to prevent suicide is like locking up people who talk about suicide to prevent suicide: the ratio of many thousands of people suffering from significant restrictions to the single person who might benefit from those restrictions just doesn't make sense (and, I would argue, is unconstitutional in both situations). But there are some kinds of things that society can do to reduce suicide deaths from guns—which make up almost half the suicide deaths in this country.

Restricting access to means takes other forms in specific locations and venues. Despite the fact that the Golden Gate Bridge is the most popular place in the United States to commit suicide (and among the most popular places

---

[24] Policies to curtail irresponsible prescriptions of medications are discussed in Chapter 6.

in the world),[25] it took seventy-five years of unrelenting grass-roots effort just to get the Golden Gate Bridge, Highway and Transportation District,[26] its governing body, to agree to erect a suicide barrier at the Golden Gate Bridge. Despite the fact that hospitals pay out millions of dollars in damage awards, they continually fail to undertake the most routine and fixable environmental alterations (breakaway shower rods or towel racks, unbreakable glass, light fixtures embedded in the ceiling). Hospitals will strip a woman naked to search her for means of self-harm and then, after traumatizing her, place her in a room with an exposed overhead pipe. It makes you wonder whether society really cares that much about preventing suicide.

As we saw in the last chapter, suicide, like cancer, presents in such different ways that only the grossest of generalizations unite the term. However, like cancer, with its incredible variations, there are a few generalizations about prevention that do seem to cut across the different kinds of suicide. Just as reducing obesity and fat intake reduces the likelihood of many different cancers, restricting access to culturally popular lethal means of suicide appears to reduce suicide.[27] In England, changing from coal gas to natural gas in stoves reduced the suicide rate by 30% and it has not risen since.[28] In Denmark, restrictions on the availability of barbiturates and reducing the carbon monoxide content of household gas was associated with a suicide reduction rate of more than 50%.[29] In the Developing World, restricting access to insecticides and pesticides has had similar success.

It seems counterintuitive that suicidal people, thwarted of one method, will abandon their suicide attempts rather than try a different method, but (with exceptions of course) that seems to be a truism across societies. Like Frank Sinatra, suicidal people are not only drawn to the idea of dying; in many cases they want to do it "their way." For a majority of people, one suicide attempt is all that they will ever make; 93% of people who attempt suicide do not die by suicide.[30]

---

[25] Carol Pogash, *Suicides Mounting, Golden Gate Looks to Add a Safety Net,* N. Y. TIMES, Mar. 26, 2014. See pp. 421–23 *infra* for a more extensive discussion of policy and law issues related to the Golden Gate Bridge.

[26] Hereafter referred to as "The Golden Gate Bridge District."

[27] Marco Sarchiapone, et al., *Controlling Access to Suicide Means,* 8 INT. J. ENVIRON. RES. PUB. HEALTH 4550 (2011).

[28] Scott Anderson, *The Urge to End It All,* N. Y. TIMES MAG. (2008).

[29] Merete Nordentoft, Ping Qin, Karin Helwig-Larsen, & Knud Juel, *Restrictions in Means for Suicide: An Effective Tool in Preventing Suicide: The Danish Experience,* 37 SUICIDE & LIFE-THREATENING BEHAV. 688 (2007) (abstract available online at http://onlinelibrary.wiley.com/doi/10.1521/suli.2007.37.6.688/abstract).

[30] David Owens, Judith Horrocks, & Allan House, *Fatal and Non-Fatal Repetition of Self-Harm,* 181 BRIT. J. PSYCHIATRY 193 (2002). Of course, this is one of those tricky statistics, because that 7% figure is still way, way higher than the risk of suicide in the population of people who have never made an attempt. The policy conundrums posed by the extremely low incidence of suicide are a central theme of this book.

Bridges

Like bullets (and unlike most pills), there is very little time between the suicidal act and death when a person jumps from a bridge. No time to call for
help, no life-saving vomiting. Basically, preventing bridge jumping is the
only way to prevent death from bridge jumping.[31]

The Golden Gate Bridge presents a classic example of one of the themes
of this book: often policymakers don't behave as though they want to adopt
policies and changes that actually would prevent suicide. There is no doubt
that the Golden Gate Bridge is a suicide magnet. As of 2003, more than 1200
people had committed suicide there, making it the prime suicide location
in the United States,[32] akin to the Aokigahara Forest in Japan.[33] One of the
oddest things about suicide, and especially suicide magnets, is that it is quite
clear that the vast majority of people prevented from committing suicide at
a particular place (like the Golden Gate Bridge) or in a particular way (like
sticking their heads in the oven) will not simply go somewhere else or try
another method.[34] In fact, a man who was prevented from jumping off the
Golden Gate Bridge in the precise spot that he picked to do so refused to
jump off on the other side of the bridge.[35] Furthermore, once thwarted from
jumping off a bridge, very few people come back and try to jump again.[36]

---

[31] It is well known that very few people survive jumps from the Golden Gate
Bridge, but this is also true of smaller bridges. Of twenty-nine people who
jumped off much smaller bridges in Ithaca between 1990 and 2010, only
two survived, Ginsburg v. City of Ithaca, 839 F. Supp. 2d 537, 540 (N.D. N.Y.
2012). All eighteen people who jumped from the George Washington Bridge
in 2014 died, Brendan O'Connor, *New York Woman Jumps to Her Death
from George Washington Bridge*, GAWKER, Apr. 9, 2015, http://gawker.com/
new-york-woman-jumps-to-her-death-from-george-washingto-1698784611.

[32] Imrie v. Golden Gate Bridge Highway & Transp. Dist., 282 F. Supp. 2d 1145
(N.D. Ca. 2003).

[33] In 2010, 247 people attempted suicide in the Aokigahara Forest, and 54 succeeded,
Rob Gilhooly, *Inside Japan's Suicide Forest*, JAPAN TIMES, June 26, 2011, http://
www.japantimes.co.jp/life/2011/06/26/general/inside-japans-suicide-forest/#.
VkOAvLerS70, while 32 people died at the Golden Gate Bridge in that year. Justin
Berton, *Golden Gate Bridge Suicides Totaled 32 Last Year*, SF GATE, Jan. 5, 2011.

[34] R. L. Seiden, *Where Are They Now?: A Followup of Suicide Attempters from the
Golden Gate Bridge*, 8 SUICIDE & LIFE-THREATENING BEHAV. 203 (1978) (fol-
lowing up 515 people who attempted suicide at the Golden Gate Bridge and
finding only 7 had subsequently returned to jump off the bridge, and only 6%
committed suicide); Kinsey Kiriakos & Sam Brock, *Reality Check: Will Golden
Gate Suicide Barrier Reduce Number of Jumping Suicides in the Bay Area?* (NBC
Bay Area, Sept. 18, 2014), http://www.nbcbayarea.com/news/local/Reducing-
Suicides-at-the-Golden-Gate-Bridge-and-Beyond-275831931.html.

[35] JOHN BATESON, THE FINAL LEAP: SUICIDE ON THE GOLDEN GATE BRIDGE 200 (2012).

[36] Ginsburg v. City of Ithaca, 5 F. Supp. 3d 243, 251–52 (N.D. N.Y. 2014). A young
woman named Sarah Birnbaum is the only person known to have come back and
jumped a second time from the Golden Gate Bridge, *The State: Second Leap from
Bridge Feared*, L. A. TIMES, Feb. 4, 1988, http://articles.latimes.com/1988-02-04/

Thus, almost every person who commits suicide at the Golden Gate Bridge would not die elsewhere, and the means of preventing these suicides has long been clear, available, and affordable.[37]

The Golden Gate Bridge's "safety" railings are three and a half feet high.[38] Toddlers and children have been thrown over the edge, followed by their mother or father.[39] It is literally true that some people who are too afraid to scale the railings and jump from the edge get a running start and hurdle the railings. The California Department of Transportation's minimum acceptable height for railings on a pedestrian bridge is forty-two inches.[40]

Public pressure and policy are the only ways to accomplish a barrier, because the law has provided no assistance at all. When private individuals whose family members have jumped to their deaths tried to force the Golden Gate Bridge District to install some kind of barrier by suing them, the courts insisted that the individuals who jumped off the bridge were autonomous and responsible agents who brought about their own deaths.[41] While I endorse the premise to a substantial extent with competent adults, the Golden Gate Bridge District made this argument in the case of a fourteen-year-old girl who paid $150 to a taxi driver to take her to the Golden Gate Bridge.[42] It's also hard to see how this fits with other cases, where the law permits people who get drunk, dress in black clothing, and walk late at night on a bridge with low railings to recover damages, because it's foreseeable that such people will fall over low railings on a bridge.[43] I just don't see how courts can stubbornly insist that government entities have no responsibility to do anything to reduce the completely foreseeable likelihood that people will jump from the Golden Gate Bridge, because it's their own autonomous decision to commit suicide, while daily locking up Californians for even mentioning that they are thinking about killing themselves. I don't think the latter should happen, but if it does, it seems as though the courts shouldn't play the autonomy card when it comes to children jumping off the Golden Gate Bridge.

Another set of claims against the Golden Gate Bridge Highway and Transportation District relating to suicide charged that it maintained a

---

news/mn-40474_1_golden-gate-bridge. Apparently Birnbaum was disappointed over not being accepted by Stanford University, and unhappy with the University of California, Los Angeles (UCLA).

[37] Much of the material in this section is taken from Bateson's well-researched and exhaustive treatment of this subject, Bateson, *supra* note 35.

[38] *Imrie*, 282 F. Supp. 2d 1145 (fourteen-year-old girl).

[39] Bateson, *supra* note 35.

[40] California Department of Transportation, "Bridge Rails and Barriers: A Reference Guide for Transportation Projects in the Coastal Zone", p.25, www.dot.ca.gov/hq/LandArch/barrier_aesthetics/Caltrans_Bridge_Rails_and_Barriers.pdf

[41] Milligan v. Golden Gate Bridge Highway & Transp. Dist., 15 Cal. Rptr. 3d 25 (Cal. App. 2004); see also Nelson v. Mass. Port Auth., 55 Mass. App. 433 (Mass. App. 2002) (to similar effect regarding the Tobin Bridge in Boston).

[42] *Imrie*, 282 F. Supp. 2d 1145.

[43] See, e.g., Cay v. State DOTD, 631 So.2d 393 (La. 1994).

dangerous condition of public property under state law by failing to install a safety barrier.[44] These claims were dismissed because in committing suicide, the plaintiff's daughter was not using the bridge for its proper purpose. The Bridge even suggested that the mother of the girl who committed suicide was at fault. Finally, the doctrine of government immunity was successfully asserted to combat the plaintiffs' claims.

These results are not inevitable. In the last few years, courts have begun to be more hospitable to claims that when suicides are a foreseeable consequence of failing to create barriers on certain bridges, the entities responsible for maintaining those bridges may be found liable, especially if the bridge has been used before by people committing suicide.[45]

Of course, when government entities do try to behave in a responsible way to prevent suicides on bridges, they may find themselves defendants in litigation brought by people who want to preserve the aesthetics of the bridge.[46]

Hospital Environments of Care

Of people who successfully commit suicide, between 5% and 10% do it in hospital settings.[47] Of these, a third were on fifteen-minute checks.[48] The single most effective method of suicide prevention in hospitals is to remove ligature points.[49] Often, the simplest environmental steps that might prevent this—collapsible shower rails or door hooks, shatterproof glass, tamper-resistant light fixtures, and so forth—are ignored by facilities that claim to be acting to keep a person safe, despite the fact that models of how to do this are free and available on the Internet. The VA has an excellent environment of care checklist for hospitals that is available on the Internet.[50]

Few hospitals are as egregious as Benjamin Rush Psychiatric Center in Syracuse, which placed Joel Kerker, who had just made a suicide attempt, in a

---

[44] *Milligan*, 15 Cal. Rptr. 3d 25.

[45] *Ginsburg*, 5 F. Supp. 3d 243.

[46] Nat'l Trust for Historic Preservation v. Dole, 828 F.2d 776 (D.C. Cir. 1987) (after thirty-seven suicides, government decides to construct barriers on Duke Ellington Bridge; in administrative law decision against entity seeking to preserve the bridge, court finds that suicide barriers do not have a "transportation purpose" and therefore regulatory requirements relating to construction for transportation purposes in public parks do not apply).

[47] American Psychiatric Association, *Practice Guidelines for the Assessment and Treatment of Patients with Suicidal Behaviors* 160 AM. J. PSYCHIATRY 1 (2003) (just under 5%); James L. Knoll IV, *Inpatient Suicide: Identifying Vulnerability in the Hospital Setting*, PSYCHIATRIC TIMES, May 22, 2012, http://www.psychiatrictimes.com/suicide/inpatient-suicide-identifying-vulnerability-hospital-setting (6%).

[48] James L. Knoll IV, *Id.*

[49] Insel, *supra* note 4, at slide 12.

[50] See U.S. Department of Veterans Affairs, *Mental Health Environment of Care Checklist* (June 1, 2015), http://www.patientsafety.va.gov/professionals/onthe-job/mentalhealth.asp.

room with exposed overhead sprinkler pipes.[51] When he (inevitably) attempted to hang himself from the exposed sprinkler pipes, the hospital did not attempt to cover them up. Indeed, the hospital did not even move Joel Kerker out of the room. The next time he tried to hang himself from the sprinkler pipes, he suffered severe brain damage.[52] In another case involving exposed sprinkler pipes, the award was almost $2 million, perhaps in part because the hospital attempted to evade responsibility for the death by blaming the patient.[53]

I cannot count the number of cases I have read or been involved with where an emergency department or locked psychiatric unit is violently intrusive with psychiatric patients—stripping them of their clothing, restraining them to beds—while maintaining an environment filled with sharp objects, protrusions, and opportunities for hanging and suffocation. Psychiatric hospitals—even when warned by advocates and human rights officers—do not take the most rudimentary precautions to cover or remove sharp objects or extrusions from which patients can hang themselves.

It's not for lack of being successfully sued. As noted in the following, there are dozens of million-dollar damage suits against private hospitals, where hospitals entrusted with the care of suicidal patients did not fix the most obvious environmental hazards. State facilities often benefit from governmental immunity, which I argue should be modified. Liability creates incentives, and the law should be drafted to create the right incentives. Thus, immunity should be retained for professional decisions (so-called discretionary functions in tort law), such as the decision to take a patient off security precautions,[54] but it should be removed for suicides resulting from clearly preventable environmental hazards in state facilities.[55] Texas law has an odd version of this distinction

---

[51] Kerker by Kerker v. Hurwitz, 163 A.D. 2d 859, 558 N.Y.S. 2d 388, 390 (N.Y. Sup. Ct. App. 4th Dept. 1990).

[52] *Id.*

[53] Inyang v. Arbour Hosp. & Orvin, 2007 Jury Verdicts LEXIS 45598 (Suffolk County Dist. Ct., Sept. 26, 2007) ($1,848,000 verdict against hospital and doctor when suicidal woman hangs herself from exposed sprinkler with her nightgown; hospital claims she created the opening around the sprinkler even though there is no residue under her fingernails, no debris on the floor; defendant doctor did not order fifteen-minute checks and claimed she thought fifteen-minute checks were nursing policy because she was new at the hospital).

[54] McNesby v. New Jersey, 231 N.J. Super. 568 (1989) (immunizing state department of health and human services for hospital professionals' decision to take patient off suicide precautions and put him on open psychiatric unit after eleven days; patient set himself on fire); *Ex parte* Kozlovski, No. 1140317 (Ala. Apr. 24, 2015) (immunity for doctor who discharged patient who subsequently eloped from group home and was hit by a car); Dallas County Mental Health & Mental Retardation v. Bossley, 968 S.W.2d 339 (Tex. 1998) (immunity when patient discharged to group home dashed out temporarily open door and was killed by oncoming car); Johnson v. Patel, 2008 Ohio 596 (Ohio App. 2008) (immunity for doctors who discharged patient who hanged himself immediately upon arriving home).

[55] Jensen v. Augusta Mental Health Institute, 574 A.2d 885 (Me. 1990) (immunity when patient hanged himself from ceiling pipe with bed sheet).

that leads to bizarre and convoluted legal arguments: it waives state immunity only when the tort involves the use or condition of state property. Thus, for example, a patient who fell out of a bed not equipped with side rails could sue the state (the claim involved the use or condition of the bed),[56] while the family of a suicidal patient who escaped from a facility by pushing aside a staff member could not[57] (if the lock on the door hadn't worked, or been insufficient, the family might have been able to bring the claim).

Removing environmental hazards does *not* mean taking away bed sheets and making patients wear paper clothes. It means common-sense attention to things such as hooks, handles, bars and rails, breakable glass and sharp metal corners. In addition to exposed pipes,[58] people in hospitals hang and strangle themselves using doors[59] and doorstops[60] and bed sheets,[61] and commit suicide using plastic utensils.[62] They also jump out of windows[63] and suffocate themselves with plastic bags.[64]

---

[56] Overton Mem'l Hosp. v. McGuire, 518 S.W.2d 528 (Tex. 1975).

[57] *Dallas County Mental Health & Mental Retardation*, 968 S.W.2d 339.

[58] *Id.*

[59] Alison Leigh Cowan, *Suit Over a Woman's Suicide at an Elite Private Hospital*, N. Y. Times, Nov. 22, 2007, http://www.nytimes.com/2007/11/23/nyregion/23psych.html (librarian hanged herself with black Spandex pants using a door); Graham v. Northwest Memorial Hosp., 2012 Ill. App. 102609 (Feb. 3, 2012).

[60] Dodd v. Sparks Reg'l Med. Ctr., 204 S.W.3d 579 (Ark. App. 2005) (verdict for hospital when patient hanged herself by tying sheet to doorstop; plaintiff did not establish standard of care).

[61] *Graham*, 2012 Ill. App. 102609; Kennedy v. Schafer, 71 F.3d 292 (8th Cir. 1995).

[62] Acerbo v. State of New York, 2011 N.Y. Slip Op. 51498(u), No. 113869 (N.Y. Ct. Claims, June 17, 2011) (plastic knives from state hospital cafeteria).

[63] Honey v. Barnes Hosp., 708 S.W.2d 686 (Mo. App. 1986); Guaranty Nat'l Ins. Co. v. North River Ins. Co., 909 F.2d 133 (5th Cir. 1990) (patient was supposed to be sent to a secure unit, but all the beds were taken; she was put on an insecure unit where she jumped out a window); Cowan v. Doering, 545 A.2d 159 (N.J. 1988); Humana of Kentucky v. Akers, 1990 W.L. 186449 (Ky. 1990) (reversing a jury verdict of $942,744 because judge based charge on hospital's obligation under state regulations rather than under negligence); Jennings v. Lee, 2008 MA JAS Pub. LEXIS 651 (Apr. 18, 2008) (verdict for defendants in case where psychiatric patient jumped out window that was not impact resistant; defendants successfully claimed patient was not suicidal during evaluation); Ribotto v. Kaufmann, 14 Mass. L. Rep. 366, 2002 Mass. Super. LEXIS 48 (Jan. 24, 2002) (chief of psychiatry at hospital not liable when stroke patient jumped from fourth-floor window and hospital did not have seclusion room on medical floor for mentally disturbed medical patients; maintenance of a safe environment was not responsibility of psychiatry but up to hospital maintenance and architects hired to design new psychiatry ward); Lannon v. Bauer, 2009 Jury Verdicts LEXIS 266653 (Aug. 26, 2005) (case dismissed on claim of failure to medicate plaintiff's decedent who fell from hospital window).

[64] Cole v. Fromm, 94 F.3d 254 (7th Cir. 1996).

To some extent, these different methods of suicide raise different issues. Exposed pipes can be hidden from view, and hooks and shower rails and towel racks can be replaced with breakaway hooks and rails and racks, without sacrificing patient dignity. Windows can be made of unbreakable material without humiliating a person. But people should have bed sheets to sleep with, and towels to use after showers. And people should definitely be allowed to wear their own clothing.

Patient Clothing and Personal Effects

Making the environment safer using devices such as breakaway shower rods is uncontroversial. There is nothing personally humiliating about recessed fixtures and different kinds of doorknobs. Taking away shoelaces and belts is one thing: plenty of shoes come without shoelaces, and robes and pants don't need to have belts.[65] But clothing of any kind can be used to commit suicide: a patient whose street clothes were taken away hanged himself with his pajamas in a seclusion room.[66] That is why in many places, patients used to be (or still are) given flimsy and extremely thin paper "johnnies," which heighten the fear and insecurity of women with histories of sexual abuse, and feel flimsy and degrading regardless of whether you have ever been sexually assaulted. They are really very close to having people milling around with strangers stark naked, and they send a message: we don't trust you at all. There are well-known alternatives to forcing people to dress in paper: keeping an eye on people thought to be suicidal and (gasp!) working with them intensively to reduce suicidality and help them cope. Some hospitals have relaxation rooms, or the staff members go on walks with patients.

In terms of policies, and taking risks, letting people wear clothes that make them feel safe trumps whatever relief hospital administrators and staff might feel from making people wear paper gowns. There is no point in taking away people's clothing when they can just as easily use their bed sheets or towels to hang themselves.[67]

---

[65] Estate of Jane Doe v. Defendant Hosp. 2013 MA Jury Verdicts Rev. LEXIS 70 (Feb. 7, 2013) (settlement for $1.7 million in case of drug-addicted suicidal woman admitted to hospital and given terrycloth robe with removable tie, which she used to attempt to hang herself; she suffered severe brain injury and died two years later; plaintiff claimed that both giving her the robe and then not conducting sufficient safety checks constituted negligence).

[66] Dunnam v. Ovbiagele, 814 So.2d 232 (Ala. 2001).

[67] *Dodd*, 204 S.W.3d 579 (verdict for hospital when patient hanged herself by tying sheet to doorstop; plaintiff did not establish standard of care); DeMontiney v. Desert Manor Convalescent Ctr. Inc., 144 Ariz. 6, 695 P.2d 255 (1985) (juvenile hung himself with bed sheet from exposed overhead pipe).

Gun Control and Suicide

When I told my husband I was writing about limiting access to guns as one of the best ways to reduce suicide rates, he rolled his eyes and said, "Why bother?" I know the current legal, social, and political landscape for this kind of proposal is pretty bleak, thanks to Supreme Court interpretations of the Second Amendment to limit the power of states to restrict individuals' access to firearms.[68] I know the Eleventh Circuit recently upheld a Florida statute forbidding physicians from asking patients about the presence of guns in their houses unless it is relevant to the patient's medical care[69] (the so-called Docs v. Glocks case). I know that if the murder of twenty first-graders, six school staff members, and the shooter's mother prior to his own suicide cannot move the nation to meaningful restrictions on access to guns, a pathetic little argument that half the country's suicides are caused by guns has no chance.

There is actually a fairly strong argument against global gun control proposals as a means of reducing suicide. It's basically the same as my argument that you can't involuntarily commit people for thinking about suicide or planning suicide. Millions of people think about suicide, talk about suicide, and plan suicide, just as millions of people own guns, and only the tiniest fraction of those millions ever attempts or commits suicide. Between one-third and one-half of American households report owning guns.[70] That's about 120 million households. If you took away everyone's guns, you would prevent one gun-related suicide for every 3000 households that own a gun. Alcohol certainly causes a lot more misery and death than guns (although the interaction between alcohol and guns is pretty damn lethal), but vastly more people (including me) drink responsibly. Prohibition didn't work, and neither would banning guns.

Negligent Storage of Guns: Children

But we don't have to take people's guns away from them, just enforce the kind of responsible ownership precautions that many gun owners advocate and practice anyway. My guess is that most gun owners actually don't object to pediatricians asking parents of little children about whether they have guns in their houses and how they are kept.[71] The majority of gun owners, I think,

---

[68] District of Columbia v. Heller, 554 U.S. 570 (2008).

[69] Wollschlaeger v. Governor of Florida, 760 F.3d 1195 (11th Cir. 2014). The court held that one instance in which such inquiry was clearly relevant involved suicidal patients.

[70] Both the Pew Research Center and the Gallup Poll say 37% as of 2013, Drew Desilver, *A Minority of Americans Own Guns, but Just How Many Is Unclear*, PEW RESEARCH CENTER FACT TANK, June 4, 2014, http://www.pewresearch.org/fact-tank/2013/06/04/a-minority-of-americans-own-guns-but-just-how-many-is-unclear/.

[71] More than 50% of the 41,149 deaths from suicide in 2013 (21,175 to be exact) were caused by a firearm, Centers for Disease Control and Prevention, *Suicide and*

would be shocked by the facts and result in *State v. Bauer.*[72] A nine-year-old child stayed at his mother's boyfriend's house, which was littered with guns, took one to school, and shot a classmate. When "[t]he police searched the [boyfriend's] house . . . [they] found a loaded handgun next to the computer, a loaded shotgun in the downstairs bedroom, an unloaded handgun in Bauer's car's glove compartment, and ammunition in a dresser drawer."[73] This was not counting the gun the child had taken. Bauer hadn't even realized one of his guns was missing when the police came to call. In the death of the classmate, Bauer was charged with third-degree assault, a minor crime: that he caused injury to another by criminally negligent behavior. It seems to fit, but the Washington Supreme Court dismissed the charge, finding the defendant's "decision to keep loaded weapons around the house is not, in itself, a crime in this state."[74] Criminal charges against parents whose children kill themselves or others when their small children find and use guns are rarely sustained.[75]

I think stringent laws on child access to guns (called "child access prevention" or "CAP") is a first step on which many can agree,[76] from the

---

Self-Inflicted Injury, CDC/NATIONAL CENTER FOR HEALTH STATISTICS (Sept. 30, 2015), http://www.cdc.gov/nchs/fastats/suicide.htm. This statistic has held true since we started keeping records, Centers for Disease Control and Prevention, *Leading Causes of Death Reports, National and Regional, 1999–2013,* WISQARS, http://webappa.cdc.gov/sasweb/ncipc/leadcaus10_us.html, accessed Oct. 2, 2012 (fatal injury data, 2009 and 2010; 2010: 50.5% of suicide deaths from firearms; 2009: 50.8% of suicide deaths resulting from firearm use; 2008: 50.6%). For an in-depth account of suicide rate differences by age, groups, and sex, as well as strategies and preventions for suicide in the United States, see U.S. DEPARTMENT OF HEALTH & HUMAN SERVICES, NATIONAL STRATEGY FOR SUICIDE PREVENTION: GOALS AND OBJECTIVES FOR ACTION: A REPORT OF THE U.S. SURGEON GENERAL AND THE NATIONAL ALLIANCE FOR SUICIDE PREVENTION (Sept. 2012), *available at* www.surgeongeneral.gov/library/reports/national-strategy-suicide-prevention/index.html. In 2013, there were 11,208 homicides by firearm, Centers for Disease Control and Prevention, *Assault or Homicide,* CDC/NATIONAL CENTER FOR HEALTH STATISTICS (Feb. 6, 2015), http://www.cdc.gov/nchs/fastats/homicide.htm. If you add in accidental deaths, the total deaths in 2013 from firearms rises to 33,363. Centers for Disease Control and Prevention, *All Injuries,* CDC/NATIONAL CENTER FOR HEALTH STATISTICS (Sept. 30, 2015), www.cdc.gov/nchs/fastats/injury.htm.

[72] 295 P.3d 1227 (Wash. App. 2013), *rev'd* 329 P.3d 67 (Wash. 2014).

[73] *Id.* at 1230.

[74] State v. Bauer, 329 P.3d 67 (Wash. 2014). See also State v. Ayers, 478 N.W. 2d 606 (Iowa 1991) (no criminal liability in girl's death when defendant illegally sells gun to minor who accidentally kills his girlfriend a few days later).

[75] State v. Smith, No. 2014-KA-0213 (La. App. 4th Cir. Dec. 17, 2014) (quashing felony murder charge against mother who left her five-year-old child alone and the child found a loaded gun and shot herself).

[76] Sejal H. Patel, *Kids and Gun Safety,* AMERICAN BAR ASSOCIATION, LITIGATION SECTION, CHILDREN'S RIGHTS LITIGATION (Aug. 10, 2014), https://apps.

National Rifle Association (NRA) to the American Bar Association.[77] As of 2013, some form of CAP law has been adopted in at least half of the states, including some in the South and some very red states.[78] Some states make it a crime to store firearms in a manner that can easily be accessed by children,[79] while others make it a crime only if the child gains access to the gun and uses it to cause harm.[80] In Florida, after it adopted a CAP felony law, unintentional firearm deaths declined by 51%.[81] Research shows that four practices reduce suicide, accidental deaths, and injuries of children and teenagers from firearms: keeping guns in locked storage or with an extrinsic lock, keeping guns unloaded, storing ammunition separately from guns, and storing ammunition in a locked location (homicide and deliberate assaults were not included in the research).[82] A recent analysis examining the impact of eighteen CAP laws found an 8.3% decrease in suicides among youth aged

---

americanbar.org/litigation/committees/childrights/content/articles/ spring2014-0414-kids-gun-safety.html (reporting that 75% of Americans believe that children's parents should be charged with a crime if they fail to prevent a child from having access to a gun used to shoot someone).

[77] *Id.*; see, e.g., Commonwealth v. McGowan, 464 Mass. 232 (M.A. 2013).

[78] Thus, not only California (Cal. Penal Code § 25000–25225, Cal. Civil Code § 1714.3), but also Florida (Fla. Stat. Ann. § 790.174); not only Connecticut (Conn. Gen. Stat. Ann. 53a-217a), but also Kentucky (Ky. Rev. Stat. Ann. 527.110); not only Maryland (Md. Code Ann. Crim. Law § 4-104), but also New Hampshire (N.H. Rev. Stat. Ann. 650-C.1); not only New Jersey (N.J. Stat. Ann. § 2C:58–15) (also requiring that any store selling guns post warning about CAP law), but also North Carolina (N.C.G.S. 14-315.1) (crime to not secure weapons in premises shared with a minor); not only Rhode Island (R.I. Gen. Laws § 11-47-60.1), but also Utah (§§ 76-10-509(1)-(2), -09.4, -509.5) (crime for parents or guardian to allow minor to handle a gun without consent or supervision), not only Massachusetts (Mass. Gen. Laws 140 § 131L) but also Texas (Tex. Penal Code Ann. § 46.13). For a complete list, see Law Center to Prevent Gun Violence, Child Access Prevention Policy Summary (Aug. 1, 2013), smartgunlaws.org/child-access-prevention-policy-summary/#identification_35_5958; D. W. Webster, J. S. Vernick, A. M. Zeoli, & J. A. Manganello, *Association Between Youth-Focused Firearm Laws and Youth Suicide*, 292 J. Am. Med. Assoc. 5, 594–601 (2004); J. Birchmayer & D. Hemenway, *Suicide and Firearm Violence: Are Youth Disproportionately Affected?* 31 Suicide & Life-Threatening Behav. 303 (2001); D. C. Grossman, B. A. Mueller, C. Riedy, et al., *Gun Storage Practices and Risk of Youth Suicide and Unintentional Firearm Injuries*, 293 J. Am. Med. Assoc. 707 (2005).

[79] For example, Massachusetts, California, Minnesota, and the District of Columbia, see Patel, *supra* note 76.

[80] For example, Florida and North Carolina.

[81] Daniel W. Webster & Marc Starnes, *Reexamining the Association between Child Access Prevention Gun Laws and Unintentional Shooting Deaths of Children*, 106 Pediatrics 1466 (2000).

[82] Grossman et al., *supra* note 78.

fourteen to seventeen.[83] In one study, adolescent suicide was four times as likely to occur in homes with a loaded, unlocked firearm as in homes where guns were stored unloaded and locked.[84]

CAP laws do not impose in the way of difficulty or inconvenience. In 2005, in legislation known as the "Protection of Lawful Commerce in Arms Act," Congress prohibited lawsuits in federal and state courts against manufacturers of properly functioning firearms.[85] As part of that statute, the law required gun dealers and manufacturers to provide a secure storage or safety device with each pistol sold. The law also immunized gun owners who used them from liability for death or injury caused by an unauthorized third party's use of the gun if the secure storage or safety device was used.[86]

This law was quite a substantial departure for conservatives who usually advocate a limited federal government and robust states' rights, since it restricts states' rights to formulate both tort laws and gun regulations, traditional areas of state autonomy. People who are somewhat conversant with our federal–state legal system might react to this law with some jurisprudential version of "Yikes! Is that constitutional?" However, attempts to challenge the law as a violation of separation of powers and overreaching federal regulation of the states have failed.[87]

State CAP laws, however, are also very likely constitutional, even under the Supreme Court's recent rulings in *District of Columbia v. Heller*[88] and *McDonald v. City of Chicago*.[89] In 2008, the Supreme Court, in a 5–4 opinion, struck down the District of Columbia's prohibition on owning handguns. The Court also struck down the requirement that anyone who did lawfully

---

[83] Webster et al., *supra* note 78.

[84] See e.g., J. H. Sloan, F. P. Rivara, D. T. Reay, et al., *Firearm Regulations and Rates of Suicide. A Comparison of Two Metropolitan Areas*, 322 New Eng. J. Med. 369–73 (1990); J. Bickmayer & D. Hemenway, *Suicide and Firearm Prevalence: Are Youth Disproportionately Affected?* 31 SUICIDE & LIFE-THREATENING BEHAV. 3, 303–10 (2001); M. Miller, D. Azrael, & D. Hemenway, *Firearm Availability and Suicide, Homicide, and Unintentional Firearm Deaths Among Women*, 79 J. URBAN HEALTH 1, 26–38 (2002).

[85] 15 U.S.C. 7901 *et seq.*

[86] 18 U.S.C. 922(z)(1).

[87] See, e.g., Ileto v. Glock, Inc., 565 F.3d 1126 (9th Cir. 2009) (rejecting separation of powers, due process, equal protection, and takings challenges); City of New York v. Beretta U.S.A., Corp., 524 F.3d 384 (2d Cir. 2008) (rejecting First and Tenth Amendment challenges as well as separation of powers challenge); Estate of Charlot v. Bushmaster Firearms, Inc., 628 F. Supp. 2d 174 (D.D.C. 2009) (rejecting separation of powers challenge); Estate of Kim v. Coxe, 295 P.3d 380 (Ala. 2013) (rejecting separation of powers challenge); Adames v. Sheahan, 909 N.E.2d 742 (Ill. 2009) (rejecting Tenth Amendment challenge).

[88] 554 U.S. 570 (2008).

[89] 561 U.S. 742 (2010).

own a gun must keep it disassembled and unloaded, or secured by a trigger lock.[90] The Court pointed out that its opinion should not be read to undermine prohibitions on unusual weapons, carrying concealed weapons, gun ownership by felons and people with mental illness, or carrying guns in sensitive places such as schools. Significantly, the Court noted that its holding did not "suggest the invalidity of laws regulating the storage of firearms to prevent accidents." In 2010, the Court both confirmed *Heller* and reiterated that it did not doom all efforts at gun control, once again citing limitations on gun ownership of "the mentally ill" and on carrying guns in sensitive places like schools.[91] In states where CAP laws have been challenged as violating Second Amendment rights, they have uniformly been upheld.[92]

In addition, nothing about either the Protection of Lawful Commerce in Arms Act or any of the Supreme Court's decisions interpreting the Constitution forecloses findings of liability when children are harmed by negligently stored guns, although of course, it comes too late to save the child.[93]

Negligent Storage of Guns: Adults

What about adults? Should someone be liable, either criminally or civilly, if an adult third party takes a negligently stored gun and uses it to commit suicide? Certainly access to guns is correlated with suicide rates, whether by children or adults. Careful review of the research reveals a significant association between rates of suicide and access to guns, including levels of household firearm ownership. Scholars have consistently found empirical evidence linking the presence of firearms to risk of suicide. In Wyoming, the state with the highest suicide rate (29.6 in 100,000), almost two-thirds of suicides are completed with a gun.[94] In Massachusetts, a state with a lower suicide rate (9.4 in 100,000) and strict gun control laws, 29% of men and 8% of women used a gun to commit suicide in 2012.[95]

---

[90] Some courts have interpreted this to apply only to occasions when the gun is under the defendant's control, Commonwealth v. Reyes, 464 Mass. 245 (2013).

[91] McDonald v. City of Chicago, 130 S.Ct. 3020 (2010).

[92] See, e.g., *Commonwealth v. McGowan,* 464 Mass. 232.

[93] Kuhns v. Brugger, 390 Pa. 331 (Pa. 1957) (grandfather held liable for leaving loaded gun in dresser drawer in his bedroom; grandson accidentally shot friend).

[94] Wyoming Department of Health, Preventing Suicide in Wyoming: 2014–2016 State Suicide Prevention Plan 8 (July 2014), http://www.sprc.org/sites/sprc.org/files/WDH%20Suicide%20Prevention%202014-2016%20FINAL.pdf.

[95] Massachusetts Department of Public Health, Injury Surveillance Program, Suicides and Self-Inflicted Injuries in Massachusetts: Data Summary 3 (Winter 2015), http://www.mass.gov/eohhs/docs/dph/injury-surveillance/suicide/suicide-update-winter-2015.pdf.

The rationale underlying these findings is that suicidal acts are generally impulsive,[96] that suicidal crises are typically self-limiting and caused by immediate stressors, and that guns are lethal methods of attempting suicide in comparison to other measures. A recent 2008 assessment of the research finds that there are at least a dozen U.S. case-controlled studies in the peer-review literature that have found that a gun in the home is associated with an increased risk of suicide.[97] The increase in suicide risk is typically two to ten times that in homes without guns, depending on the sample population.[98] Moreover, the association between gun ownership and suicide risk is primarily caused by a large increase in the risk of suicide by firearm that is not counterbalanced by a reduced risk of nonfirearm suicide. Equally important, the increased risk of suicide is not explained by increased suicidal ideation, suicide attempts, or psychopathological characteristics among members of the gun-owning households.[99] Many of the case control studies suggested that the high risk of suicide applied not only to gun owners, but to their family members living in the home, and the manner in which the guns were stored impacted suicide rates.

In their literature analysis, Miller and Hemenway also review ecological studies covering multiple regions in the United States, finding a link between the prevalence of gun ownership and rates of suicide,[100] and conclude that

---

[96] One study found that 24% of people who made near-lethal suicide attempts took less than five minutes between the decision to kill themselves and the actual attempt while 70% took less than one hour. See O. R. Simon, A. C. Swann, K. E. Powell, L. B. Potter, M. J. Kresnow, P. W. O'Carroll, *Characteristics of Impulsive Suicide Attempts and Attempters*, 32 SUICIDE LIFE THREAT BEHAV. 49–49 (Suppl., 2001).

[97] M. Miller & D. Hemenway, *Guns and Suicide in the United States*, 359 NEW ENG. J. MED. 989 1 (2008).

[98] See e.g., D. A. Brent, J. A. Perper, G. Moritz, et al., *Firearms and Adolescent Suicide: A Community Case-Control Study*, 147 J. AM. ACAD. CHILD ADOLESC. PSYCHIATRY 10, 1066–71 (1993); A. L. Kellermann, F. P. Rivara, G. Somes, et al., Suicide in the Home in Relation to Gun Ownership, 327 NEW ENG. J. MED. 467–72 (1992); D. J. Wiebe, *Homicide and Suicide Risks Associated with Firearms in the Home: A National Case Control Study*, 41 ANN. EMERG. MED. 771–82 (2003).

[99] In an earlier study performed by the authors, in which they found that between 1981 and 2002 changes in household firearm ownership over time were associated with significant changes in suicide rates, the authors note that one critique of case control studies is that these studies do not adequately control for the possibility that members of gun-owning households are inherently more suicidal than members of non-gun-owning households, that some people purchase handguns for the purpose of committing suicide, and that the association may be confounded by differential recall bias of firearm ownership and comorbid conditions. See M. Miller, D. Azrael, L. Hepburn, D. Hemenway, & S. J. Lippmann, *The Association Between Changes in Household Firearm Ownership and Rates of Suicide in the United States, 1981–2002*, 12 INJ. PREV. 3, 178–82 (2006).

[100] See e.g., Sloan et al. *supra* note 84; Bickmayer and Hemenway *supra* note 84; Miller et al. *supra* note 84.

states with higher rates of gun ownership had higher rates of firearm suicide and overall suicides.[101] Similarly, a study conducted by Dahlberg and colleagues found that persons with guns in the home were more likely to have died from suicide committed with a firearm than from one committed by a different method.[102] The authors tested for whether having a firearm in the home increases the risk of violent death in the home and whether the risk varies by storage practice, gun type, or number of guns in the home. They found that regardless of storage practices, gun type or number of guns, the presence of a gun in the home increases the chance that a suicide will be committed with a firearm rather than by any other means.[103]

Nevertheless, most state courts, including courts in states with CAP laws, refuse to find a duty to store guns safely in the home. For example, the highest court in Maine found no duty in the case of parents who kept a loaded gun in the kitchen even after their adult daughter, whom they knew to be very suicidal, came to stay with them.[104] In Illinois, an appellate court refused to find that a man had a duty to secure guns in his house when his brother, who had just been discharged from the hospital for being suicidal, came to stay with him, holding that the latter's suicide using the gun was "unforeseeable", because he had no mental health training.[105]

In any event, the adult most likely to use a gun in the house to commit suicide is the gun's owner or someone entitled to have access. The issue of owner liability for negligent storage of a gun usually arises when a third party uses the gun to harm someone else.[106] Courts seldom find any negligence in these cases. Andrew McClurg has called this "the Second Amendment right

---

[101] M. Miller, S. J. Lippmann, D. Azrael, & D. Hemenway, *Household Firearm Ownership and Rates of Suicide Across the 50 United States*, 62 J. TRAUMA 1029–35 (2007).

[102] L. L. Dahlberg, R. M. Ikeda, M. J. Kresnow, *Guns in the Home and Risk of a Violent Death in the Home: Findings from a National Study*, 160 AM. J. EPIDEMIOL. 929–36 (2004).

[103] *Id.*

[104] Estate of Cummings v. Davie, 40 A.3d 971 (Me. 2012). Admittedly, the facts in this case were compelling: the daughter was suicidal because of her abuse by her husband, and one reason for keeping the gun loaded was in case her husband came to the house, as he threatened he would.

[105] Chalhoub v. Dixon, 788 N.E.2d 164, 167–68, 338 Ill. App. 3d 535, 539–40 (2003). This case was cited favorably by the Illinois Supreme Court in holding that a building management company that had pressured and coerced a family to move out, despite the fact that they had a rental contract, to the point of starting demolition around them, could not be held liable for the father's suicide (Turcios v. the DeBruler Co., Ill., May 21, 2015).

[106] Bridges v. Parrish, 742 S.E.2d 794 (N.C. 2013).

to be negligent."[107] Occasionally, however, courts will find a householder negligent if he or she knew that someone with "a history of mental instability"
will have access to the weapons.[108]

Pesticides and Poisons

Although in the United States, guns are used more often than any other
method, the most frequently used method of suicide across the world is pesticide.[109] The World Health Organization has spent significant resources on
successful programs to reduce access to pesticides and poisons in Developing
World countries, where they are the primary means of suicide.[110] Recent
research in the United States has linked pesticides to suicide risk,[111] possibly
because of their effect on the nervous system, so that pesticides are not only
used to commit suicide, they may create the desire to commit suicide in the
first place. Since a number of class actions relating to exposure to chemi-
cals mention that the people exposed suffered from "headaches . . . nervous-
ness" and other "psychological injuries,"[112] the relationship between pesticide
exposure and suicide seems to be an interesting one to pursue in research;
currently, there is little legal action in this area.

The law in the United States relating to suicide prevention and access
to poisons revolves around the extent to which regulatory agencies can take
protective measures based on the surmise that people will not follow directions and/or ignore precautionary labels. For example, several decades ago,
the government attempted to ban phosphorus paste for use in the home as a

---

[107] Andrew Jay McClurg, "The Second Amendment Right to be Negligent," 68
Florida Law Rev. __ (*forthcoming* 2016), available on the Internet at http://
papers.ssrn.com/sol3/papers.cfm?abstract_id=2584588##
[108] Jupin v. Kask, 447 Mass. 141 (2006); Volpe v. Gallagher, 821 A.2d 699 (R.I. 2003);
Delaney v. Reynolds, 63 Mass. App. 239, 245 (2005) (it should have been foreseeable
to police officer defendant that his depressed, alcoholic, drug-addicted girlfriend
whose recent changes in medication had increased her feelings of depression, isolation, and fatigue might use his unsecured, loaded gun to try to kill herself), but
see Blevins v. Hartman, 2013 Ohio 3297 (Ohio App. July 18, 2013).
[109] Justin Worland, *Pesticide Poisoning Is the Leading Method of Suicide*, TIME,
Sept. 4, 2014, http://time.com/3270766/pesticide-poisoning-is-the-leading-
method-of-suicide/.
[110] WORLD HEALTH ORGANIZATION, GUNS, KNIVES AND PESTICIDES: REDUCING
ACCESS TO LETHAL MEANS (2009), www.who.int/mental_health/prevention/
suicide/vip_pesticides.pdf.
[111] Brian Bienkowski, *High Rates of Suicide, Depression, Linked to Farmers' Use
of Pesticides*, SCI. AM., Oct. 6, 2014, http://www.scientificamerican.com/article/
high-rates-of-suicide-depression-linked-to-farmers-use-of-pesticides/ (farmers using organochlorine pesticides 90% more likely to be diagnosed with
depression than those who hadn't).
[112] Sterling v. Velsicol Chem. Corp., 855 F.2d 1188, 1201–1202 (6th Cir. 1988).

roach and rodent killer because it had caused so many deaths, both from suicide and accidental ingestion.[113] The paste was covered with huge and vivid
admonitions to keep it away from children, but as the government representative said, "the general public is incapable of handling these things and
following directions."[114] The court held in favor of the paste company, finding that in balancing the harms caused by poison, the law must presume
that people read and follow warnings, at least those as easy to understand as
"Keep Out of the Reach of Children."

Other countries have not been so sanguine. Suicides fell by 11% after
South Korea banned the pesticide most commonly used to commit suicide,
which was the first year that the rate of suicide declined.[115] As one psychiatrist
involved with suicide prevention in South Korea pointed out, "we still have
bridges and charcoal briquettes."[116] A man who had almost committed suicide using pesticide said he was happy to be alive, but pointed out that young
and old suffered from unemployment and "quick economic development,"
and added, "I hope the government will care more about people's health."[117]

Carbon Monoxide: Car Exhaust, Charcoal Grills, and Other Means

Using car exhaust to commit suicide is an example of the success of a prevention of access to means of suicide approach, even though the regulations that
accomplished it were not principally focused on preventing suicide, but rather
saving the environment. People do not commit suicide nearly as often using
cars and carbon monoxide as they used to, in part because the Clean Air Act,
passed in 1970, required cars to conform to environmental emission standards that reduced the amount of carbon monoxide emissions from cars. The
introduction of the catalytic converter accomplished this, as well as providing
the unexpected benefit of reducing suicide through inhaling car fumes.

An attempt to highlight this achievement backfired (as it were) when
Hyundai created an ad showing a man trying to commit suicide in a
Hyundai car and being thwarted because its emissions are 100% water-
based; Hyundai apologized and withdrew the ad.[118] However, people still do

[113] Stearns Elec. Paste Co. v. EPA, 461 F.2d 293 (7th Cir. 1972).

[114] *Id.* at 297.

[115] Ju-Min Park, *Pesticide Ban Cuts South Korea's High Suicide Rate—A Bit*,
REUTERS, Sept. 30, 2013, http://www.reuters.com/article/2013/09/30/us-korea-
suicide-idUSBRE98T05R20130930.

[116] *Id.*

[117] *Id.*

[118] Alastair Jamieson, *Car Maker Hyundai Apologizes for Commercial Showing
Attempted Suicide* (NBC News, Apr. 25, 2013), http://worldnews.nbcnews.com/_
news/2013/04/25/17913878-car-maker-hyundai-apologizes-for-commercial-
showing-attempted-suicide?lite.

try to—and succeed in—to killing themselves using carbon monoxide.[119] A poverty-stricken couple in Ohio, after their attempts to raise $1000 on line to pay their electricity, gas and water bills drew no response at all, dragged two charcoal grills inside their house, put out their two cats and a note on the door warning anyone who might enter to beware of carbon monoxide, and killed themselves by inhaling the fumes from the grills.[120]

Subways and Trains

The introduction of trains to this country heralded any number of health and social consequences, including the first known cases of whiplash, called "railway spine." The understanding that technological and industrial accidents caused psychological consequences also first began with railroad crashes. The recognition in tort that a defendant responsible for an industrial accident could be liable in negligence for the suicide of a person as a result of that accident began to be popularized with the advent of trains, although the Supreme Court reined it in before it did too much economic damage to the railroad industry. The case in which this happened, *Scheffer v. Railroad Company*,[121] described Charles Scheffer's claim in language that can only make the modern reader of cell phone and car rental insurance contracts weep at the deterioration of legal language:

> Whereby said sleeping-car was rent, broken, torn, and shattered, and by means whereof the said Charles Scheffer was cut, bruised, maimed, and disfigured, wounded, lamed, and injured about his head, face, neck, back, and spine, and by reason whereof the said Charles Scheffer became and was sick, sore, lame, and disordered in mind and body, and in his brain and spine, and by means whereof phantasms, illusions, and forebodings of unendurable evils to come upon him, the said Charles Scheffer, were produced and caused upon the brain and mind of him, the said Charles Scheffer, which disease, so produced as aforesaid, baffled all medical skill, and continued constantly to disturb, harass, annoy, and prostrate the nervous system of him, the said Charles Scheffer, to wit, from the seventh day of December, A.D. 1874, to the eighth day of August, 1875, when said phantasms, illusions, and forebodings, produced as aforesaid, overcame and prostrated all his reasoning

---

[119] Jerry Hunt, the musician, committed suicide using carbon monoxide, see "How to Kill Yourself Using the Inhalation of Carbon Monoxide Gas," http://www.jerryhunt.org/kill.htm

[120] Dean Narciso, "Despondent Couple Found Dead in their Bellefontaine Home," Columbus Dispatch, April 15, 2015, http://www.dispatch.com/content/stories/local/2015/04/15/co-deaths.html

[121] Scheffer v. R.R. Co., 105 U.S. 249 (1882).

powers, and induced him, the said Charles Scheffer, to take his life
in an effort to avoid said phantasms, illusions, and forebodings,
which he then and there did, whereby and by means of the careless,
unskilful, and negligent acts of the said defendant aforesaid, the
said Charles Scheffer, to wit, on the eighth day of August, 1875, lost
his life and died, leaving him surviving a wife and children.[122]

Unmoved by this vivid rhetoric, the Court held that Scheffer's suicide was
not caused by the railroad accident, but rather constituted an intervening
independent act that broke the chain of causation between the railroad's negligence and Scheffer's death.

Since then, there have remained a number of legal issues related to suicides and railroads or (more often) subways. While the *Scheffer* case looked
at whether injuries from a railroad accident can be imputed to have *caused*
someone's suicide, there is a different question regarding the level of care the
railroad or subway has to exercise to *prevent* suicide. For example, to this day,
railroad tracks run right by the grounds of the Montana State psychiatric
hospital at Warm Springs, and trains still run on them (in fact, the tracks are
being improved as this goes to press). No fence separates the hospital from
the train tracks. At least one patient has thrown himself in front of the train
that passes so conveniently by, although that was long ago.[123] The Montana
State Hospital's "Hazardous Condition Reporting Policy"[124] accurately notes
that these tracks are "in fact hazardous" but since this condition "cannot be
remedied,"[125] "reasonable measures will be taken to mitigate the potential for
risk."[126] The railroad tracks are grouped together in this category with "the
fishing pond."[127]

If people sit or lie on train tracks, and get hit by the train, does the estate
have an action against the operator of the train for negligence if there is proof
the operator could have stopped the train in time? What if a subway operator
was using marijuana and cocaine?[128] Courts have been very unsympathetic
to these claims. Even when a jury found that a subway operator acted negligently in failing to stop the subway train, perhaps had drugs on board, and
had the last clear chance to prevent the death of a woman on the tracks, the

---

[122] *Id.*
[123] *Patient Killed by Train Near State Hospital,* [Helena, Montana] Independent Record, June 20, 1962, at 2, http://www.newspapers.com/newspage/35785679/.
[124] Montana State Hospital Policy and Procedure, *Hazardous Condition Reporting Policy* (Policy No. SF-06, May 15, 2014), http://www.dphhs.mt.gov/Portals/85/amdd/documents/msh/volumeii/safety/hazardreporting.pdf.
[125] Presumably because no funding has been forthcoming from the legislature to do so.
[126] *Supra* note 124 at V-G.
[127] *Id.*
[128] Johnson v. Metro. Area Transit Auth., 883 F.2d 125 (D.C. Cir. 1989).

highest court in the District of Columbia found that the "last clear chance" tort doctrine did not apply in the case of suicide, where an individual does more than act in reckless disregard of his or her own safety, but actually "purposely invited the harm that resulted."[129]

Prevention versus Treatment: The Policy Conundrum

The current model of suicide prevention is not working, in part because it is focused too specifically: too much on the individual instead of the environment, too much on preventing the moment of self-destruction rather than what led up to that moment. The public health model is cheaper and more effective than the medical model, in both fiscal and emotional terms. It doesn't come with the same fears of liability. And yet, one of the most difficult barriers to public health community-based prevention approaches is that they don't fit well with modern outcome- and evidence-based analysis and budgeting. As the Air Force report candidly acknowledged in discussing the failure of the Air Force to fund more prevention services:

> The existing manpower standard was based on "bean count"—one patient equaled one bean. "X" number of beans equaled one FTE. Prevention activity does not lend itself to bean counting . . . [130]

The kind of community prevention activity the Air Force was proposing focused on people *before* they became patients, working with them in the natural community to try to resolve problems before they got worse. It's harder with those approaches to pinpoint cause and effect, which people might eventually have been driven to suicide, which method worked to prevent that outcome. The pool of beneficiaries is larger and not as obviously in dire need. Also, many of these community approaches don't require people with a lot of letters after their names; paradoxically, this makes them more difficult to fund because as a society, we are enamored with approaches involving credentialed mental health professionals, even if they have never been able to show they are effective in preventing suicide either.

In today's budget-strapped times, this paradox of focusing on suicide only at the very last minute is reflected in many other arenas. State mental health agencies only provide intensive services to people who are seriously incapacitated by their conditions. One person who responded to my survey

---

[129] Washington Metro. Area Transit Auth. v. Johnson, 726 A.2d 172, 175 (D.C. 1999). Yes, it's the same case as in the last footnote, still dragging along after ten years. See also Rinaldo v. New York City Transit Auth., 39 N.Y.2d 285, 288 (N.Y. 1976) (approving an instruction that would not permit jury to apply last clear chance doctrine if it determined man jumped on the tracks in a suicide attempt).

[130] "The Air Force Suicide Prevention Program," (Doc. AF-PAM 44-160) April 2001, p. 16, http://dmna.ny.gov/r3sp/suicide/AFPAM44-160.pdf

endorsed the concept that assistance to suicidal people should be provided earlier in no uncertain terms: help should be provided after "the first attempt/ SI thoughts/actions or disclosure, NOT after the person becomes 'eligible' for ACT [Assertive Community Treatment] team services or wraparound. Those types of 'resource control'-based policies are asinine and extremely stigmatizing. 'Oh . . . now I'm SICK ENOUGH for your stupid service??' "[131]

These are obviously important policy issues: how far "up river" should suicide prevention programs go? Many of the most innovative approaches, by definition, do not have sufficient research behind them to demonstrate that they work. In other cases, models that work spectacularly well in one place because of the fierce commitment and leadership of particular individuals may not be transferable. In the following section, I describe models of individual treatment that have been shown to work and are transferable.

Evidence-Based Suicide Treatments

The Air Force approach discussed in Chapter 8 is a community-based public health approach. This kind of foundation is absolutely crucial to any suicide prevention effort. At the individual level, every provider of mental health services should be proficient in at least one of a number of evidence-based approaches to treating suicidal individuals, such as DBT[132] or CBT. All of the following approaches discussed, from the first focused effort by the father of suicidology, Dr. Edwin Shneidman, to the most recent frameworks developed by the AESCHI group,[133] including the promising screening and treatment approach, CAMS,[134] have several things in common.

First, they are relatively indifferent to psychiatric diagnoses, and reject the premise that psychiatric diagnosis serves as the framework to treatment,[135] preferring to focus on the individual him- or herself, and that

---

[131] Survey Response No. 196.

[132] Dialectic behavior therapy is a modular, principle-driven multidiagnostic behavior treatment developed by Dr. Marcia Linehan that has been shown to reduce suicide attempts, inpatient hospitalizations, and emergency department visits for suicidality, see infra at pp. 442–44.

[133] CONRAD MICHEL & DAVID JOBES, BUILDING A THERAPEUTIC ALLIANCE WITH THE SUICIDAL PATIENT (2011).

[134] See DAVID JOBES, MANAGING SUICIDAL RISK: A COLLABORATIVE APPROACH (2006).

[135] Marjan Ghahramanlou-Holloway, Laura L. Neely, & Jennifer Tucker, *A Cognitive-Behavioral Strategy for Preventing Suicide*, 13 CURRENT PSYCHIATRY 18 (2014) (CBT theory is that "suicide mode" occurs independently of psychiatric diagnoses and must be targeted directly); Aeschi Working Group, *Problems in Clinical Practice: The Usual Clinical Practice*, MEETING THE SUICIDAL PERSON: THE THERAPEUTIC APPROACH TO THE SUICIDAL PATIENT: NEW PERSPECTIVES FOR HEALTH PROFESSIONALS, http:// www.aeschiconference.unibe.ch/usual_clinical_practice.htm; KONRAD MICHEL,

person's unique story.[136] These therapies focus on the patient's narrative of his or her own suicidality.

Second, unlike traditional psychotherapy, these are specific models, using explicit forms that are taught through manuals. This makes it easier to ensure fidelity to the model, to test its effectiveness, to replicate the model, and to train others to use it.

Third, they are all focused on problem solving in one way or another, and on teaching skills of coping and problem solving to the patient. As Dr. Marsha M. Linehan notes, suicide is a solution for the patient and a problem for the therapist, and treatment must target solving whatever problem or problems is driving the suicidality. This focus directly derives from Dr. Edwin Shneidman's approach to reducing what he called "psych-ache." Many of the people I interviewed confirmed the validity of this approach:

> A key thing people are missing when they talk about suicide prevention, a lot of people talk about asking the right questions, persuade them to go to a hospital or seek therapy. If someone is in that kind of state, they need a human connection with someone who cares about them. The most neglected part of this conversation is that they often need practical help with some real life problem. I was having a very bad night and I had basically said to two of my closest friends that I was going to kill myself. They knew what was going on, they knew I was freaking out, and they spent about seven hours helping me come up with a brilliant safety plan, a plan that met my basic needs for housing, safety, medical care.[137]

Fourth, unlike Dr. Herbert Hendin's approach,[138] these approaches are based on the premise that the therapist and patient share the responsibility, and the risks, in treatment. Unlike Dr. Hendin, they advocate an informed consent process with a highly suicidal patient that explicitly shares with the patient the risks that the treatment will not work.[139] These are collaborative approaches are aimed at empowering people and increasing their feelings of agency.

Fifth, they are all insistently noncoercive and almost completely community-based. Being safe in a hospital doesn't really generalize to being safe

---

THE SUICIDAL PATIENT AND THE AESCHI PHILOSOPHY (May 30, 2013), http://www.aeschiconference.unibe.ch/Aeschi%20Introduction.pdf.

[136] Id. EDWIN SHNEIDMAN, THE SUICIDAL MIND (1998).
[137] Interview with "Colleen" (Apr. 29, 2014).
[138] See Chapter 5.
[139] David Rudd, Gregory Brown, Thomas Joyner, Kelly Cukrowicz, David Jobes, & Morton Silverman, *The Realities of Risk, the Nature of Hope, and the Role of Science: A Response to Cook and Van de Creek*, 46 PSYCHOTHERAPY RES. PRAC. & TRAINING 474, 475 (2009).

in the patient's everyday life in the world. This is because there is no research showing that spending time in the hospital reduces suicidality, and there is some research suggesting hospitalization may increase suicidality.

Sixth, they are generally quite skeptical of medication, or at least not focused on medication, as a treatment for suicidal people. They are not necessarily antimedication, especially in very specific situations (e.g., escalating agitated anxiety), but they certainly do not see it as a major component of treating a suicidal patient—rather, they try to decrease patients' medications.

There are differences in these therapies: DBT requires therapist outreach and telephone contact with the patient, which is not necessarily the case with the other therapies. DBT is group-based, which CAMS is not. DBT also has an explicit focus on irreverence. DBT is team-based.

But studies show all of these therapies work better than traditional psychotherapy, or psychotherapy and medication, at reducing suicidal ideation, suicide attempts, hospitalization, and emergency department visits.

All of these treatments have completely transcended the model of decades ago, which understood suicidal people as incompetent and mentally ill (and yet emphasized "no-suicide contracts"); focused on inpatient hospitalization, sometimes for lengthy periods and medication (usually for depression or anxiety); and basically ignored immediate life stresses except to provide hospitalization as a "milieu" therapy that offered temporary relief from those stresses. In the past, there was no effort to discover whether any of these interventions—medication, hospitalization, mental health treatment— actually worked. No one seemed to care that suicide rates were not falling.

Cognitive Behavioral Therapy and Cognitive Behavioral Therapy for Suicide Prevention

> "I have a CBT therapist as well which I have been doing for about thirteen years. It helps to hear your issues in a different context and see your life through a different filter, because a lot of things get distorted and it's hard to keep reality and distortion apart."[140]

CBT was developed by Dr. Aaron Beck as a short-term therapy focused on reframing the way an individual conceptualizes his or her problems, and approaches them. Although CBT has been used to treat everything from PTSD to insomnia,[141] it has also been specifically shown to reduce suicide attempts compared to "treatment as usual" ("TAU" to researchers).[142] In addition, a specific intervention for adolescents who had attempted suicide within the last 90 days (cognitive behavioral therapy for suicide prevention

---

[140] Interview with Abby Irving (pseudonym) (Nov. 20, 2013).

[141] Ghahramanlou-Holloway et al., *supra* note 135.

[142] Gregory Brown, Thomas Ten Have, Gregg R. Henriques, et al., *Cognitive Therapy for the Prevention of Suicide Attempts: A Randomized Controlled Trial*, 294 J. Am. Med. Ass'n 563 (2005).

[CBT-SP]) was developed from the CBT framework by Drs. Barbara Stanley and Gregory Brown. While CBT is generally a ten-session approach, the suicide prevention version for adolescents has twelve sessions, and a twelve session follow-up.

Both CBT and CBT-SP focus specifically on changing the framework with which the patient views his or her life and the decisions that need to be made. It focuses on automatic thoughts ("there's no point in trying," "what's the use"), conditional assumptions ("if I don't get into this college, my life is ruined"), and core beliefs ("I am unlovable", "I am bad"). Challenging these frameworks and formulations, and teaching a different way of approaching these situations, is at the core of CBT. It is easy to see how it can be applied to suicidal people: Shneidman argued that suicidality involved a pathological narrowing of focus, which he called "constriction," that allowed the suicidal person to see only two choices: cessation of life, or an unbearable or unendurably painful situation.

These therapies also provide education about preventing relapses into suicidality.

Dialectic Behavioral Therapy

"DBT helped me a lot. They should have DBT in middle school."[143]

Dr. Marsha M. Linehan's dialectic behavioral therapy was first developed explicitly as therapy for people with the highest suicide risk, but it has been expanded to cover people who are more moderately suicidal. Dr. Linehan developed this therapy because her patients experienced CBT as critical, and too focused on expecting them to change. Yet she found that if she simply provided warmth and support, her patient's outcomes remained unchanged. Thus, "dialectical" behavior therapy was born: a synthesis of the change-oriented skills training of CBT with more traditional empathy, acceptance and support.

Like CBT, DBT focuses on problem-solving strategies. In traditional DBT, this includes a skills-building component, individual therapy, and group therapy. [144] This therapy has been shown to be better (in the sense of reducing visits to ERs, hospitalizations, suicide attempts, and non-suicidal self injury) than standard therapy for psychiatric conditions delivered by

---

[143] Interview with Beth Harris (July 15, 2014).
[144] Marsha M. Linehan, Kathryn E. Korslund, Melanie S. Harned, Robert J. Gallop, et al., "Dialectical Behavior Therapy for High Suicide-Risk in Individuals with Borderline Personality Disorder: A Randomized Clinical Trial and Component Analysis," *JAMA Psychiatry* doi:10.1001/jamapsychiatry.2014.3039, published on line March 25, 2015, https://www.nami.org/getattachment/Blogs/NAMI-Blog/April-2015/test/Linehan-et-al-DBT-for-High-Suicide-Risk-in-Individuals-with-BPD.pdf

experts.[145] As Linehan describes her therapy, it is to create a life worth living when suicide feels like the only option. The first step is to motivate the patient: many people who don't want to die, but also don't want to change the behaviors that lead them to be suicidal, end up succeeding in DBT where other programs have failed.

In cases of patients who are not chronically psychotic and not substance abusers, DBT therapists prefer significant reduction of psychiatric medication. Part of the structure of DBT is to get a second opinion on the medications the patient is taking, and to ensure that the individual is not receiving too large a quantity of potentially lethal medication. Dr. Linehan notes that many patients who are seriously suicidal regularly receive prescriptions for medications that they can easily use to kill themselves.[146] DBT is also consciously community-based. Although some DBT programs are delivered in institutional settings, its skills components are best practiced in the community.

DBT begins with an assessment called the Linehan Risk Assessment and Management Protocol (L-RAMP). There are a number of standard components of this protocol: long-term risk assessment in the first session, and then at the beginning of every treatment session, the therapist asks about suicidality, wish to escape, and wish to quit treatment. Every week the therapist evaluates for hospitalization, and documents why the patient was not hospitalized. Studies of patients who had already attempted suicide show that compared to expert psychotherapists in Seattle, nominated by the mental health professional community, DBT reduced suicide attempts by 50%, emergency department visits for 53%, and inpatient hospitalizations by 73%. These 50% reductions held true over time.

DBT helps many people, but it is not for everyone. Like CBT-SP, it works best with people who are smart and highly motivated (although Dr. Linehan acknowledges that part of the job of the DBT team is to help the individual with motivation). Both approaches require a fair amount of reading and writing, understanding acronyms and relatively complex concepts, and involve commitment to the program as well as substantial "homework."

Dr. Linehan gave hope to thousands of suicidal people around the world when she revealed that she developed her treatment in the wake of her own suffering and suicidality, and the inability of a mental health system which hospitalized and restrained her to provide the kind of help she needed. People

---

[145] See (really do see; it's an outstanding power point presentation) David A. Jobes, Marsha Linehan, & Diana Cortez Yanez, *Principles of Effective Suicide Care: Evidence-Based Treatments*, NATIONAL ACTION ALLIANCE FOR SUICIDE PREVENTION, Feb. 10, 2015, http://zerosuicide.sprc.org/sites/zerosuicide. actionallianceforsuicideprevention.org/files/Principles%20of%20Effective%20 Suicide%20Care%202-10-15%20slides.pdf.

[146] See Chapter 6.

like Marsha Linehan and Steve Miccio, [147] once-suicidal people who developed effective alternatives to a system that served them poorly, are reminders of the need to listen to people who have first-hand experiences of wanting and attempting to die, and what they need to help them live.

Collaborative Assessment and Management of Suicidality

This is yet another suicide-specific approach, developed by Dr. David Jobes, and involves the professional sitting side by side with the individual, while the individual him- or herself fills out an assessment form (Suicide Status Form, or SSF) that is both quantitative and qualitative. For example, the form includes a "Reasons for Wanting to Live" section and a "Reasons for Wanting to Die" section, as well as a sentence completion component ("What I find most painful is …"). Thus, the form itself is a detailed assessment and treatment plan, prepared in collaboration between the patient and the professional.

The treatment focuses on "suicidal drivers," as identified by the patient. "Drivers" is a word for the problems that need to be solved or addressed to reduce suicidality. A stabilization plan is developed to help the patient get through the hardest times. The research shows that CAMS reduces suicidal ideation, and research is currently underway looking at whether it reduces suicide attempts, emergency department visits, and hospitalizations. The State of Oklahoma has started adopting CAMS for its state mental health system.

Dr. Jobes, who is a longtime expert in treating people with suicidality, strongly supports keeping most suicidal people out of the hospital, and using suicide-specific interventions rather than targeting mental disorders, which relegate suicidality to symptom status. He has extensive personal experience treating suicidal individuals, and has worked nationally and internationally to spread the word about his own treatment approaches and those of others such as Dr. Aaron Beck and Dr. Marsha Linehan.

Nondemand Caring Follow-up Contact

Nondemand caring follow-up contact is, along with hotlines and warm lines, a "brief intervention" and one of the simplest of suicide prevention methods. It just means following up after a suicidal individual has visited the emergency department, either by visiting, calling on the telephone, email, or letter, to see how the person is doing.[148] The term "nondemand" is used

---

[147] Mr. Miccio's peer programs are discussed below at p. 457, *infra*.

[148] J. A. Motto & A. G. Bostrum, *A Randomized Controlled Trial of Postcrisis Suicide Prevention*, 52 PSYCHIATRIC SERV. 828 (2001).

to indicate that nothing is asked for or required of the individual—it's just a letter (or email or phone call) saying some version of the following: "It's been some time since you were at the hospital, and we hope things are going well for you. If you want to get in touch with us, please feel free to do that—we hope you do."

Although findings are somewhat mixed, it appears that this simple outreach may reduce the suicide rate. And it's so easy to do. Just reaching out for a little extra connection beyond the hurried and sometimes traumatic emergency department visit with a caring message—what does that tell us about what suicidal people need?

Embracing Life: Stories of People Who Are No Longer Suicidal

"I want my life to be an example, not a waste."

Michelle Sese-Khalid[149]

But now I am afraid I know too much to kill myself
Though I would still like to jump off a high bridge
At midnight, or paddle a kayak out to sea
Until I turn into a speck, or wear a necktie made of knotted rope
But people would squirm, it would hurt them in some way . . .

Tony Hoagland, *Suicide Song*[150]

Suicide leaves loved ones shocked and surprised in a deep and fundamental way. What is equally shocking and surprising, but in a joyful way, and receives far less attention, is the transformation of some suicidal people from being mired in an endless cycle of attempts and hospitalizations into leading fulfilled and meaningful lives (although they may still be intermittently suicidal). Staff who see someone sobbing or screaming or threatening in the emergency department for the tenth time in less than a year, or people lining up for paper cups of medications in the day hall, or clustered outside the group home waiting for the van or smoking, never get to see the very same person graduating from law school or getting a doctorate, working, raising children, and celebrating life. Service providers for suicidal people often only see people on their very worst days, and would benefit enormously from meeting their patients again in other contexts.

---

[149] Interview with Michelle Sese-Khalid (Feb. 13, 2015).

[150] Tony Hoagland, *Suicide Song*, in What Narcissism Means to Me. Copyright ©2003 by Tony Hoagland. Reprinted with the permission of The Permissions Co., Inc. on behalf of Graywolf Press, Minneapolis, Minnesota, www.graywolfpress.org.

It's hard sometimes to really grasp how incredibly mutable people can be. This is true in tragic ways—sunny and successful people end up filthy, incoherent, and suicidal. But it is also true in miraculous and joyful ways. I interviewed and read the stories of many people who years ago would have been labeled "chronically mentally ill"—people with literally hundreds of hospitalizations for self-injury and suicide attempts, people who lived in grubby group homes or dealing drugs on the street, who now had careers and babies and—even for those who remain on disability—lives filled with purpose and even happiness. That isn't to say their lives aren't complex, and often difficult, as all our lives are, but they are glad to be alive. Just as the people who die are almost impossible to predict, the people who rise from the ashes of their misery are very hard to predict too.

They include people who were jailed or living in group homes who now work in difficult and demanding jobs,[151] people whose combination of addiction and suicidality could have been lethal but who now are stunning inspirations who lead others in a mission of hope.[152] I spoke to people who had been homeless, people with repeated hospitalizations who now have master's and nursing and doctoral degrees.[153] I also interviewed mental health professionals and read articles about seemingly intractable patients who responded to treatment methods that departed from the norm, and who now live meaningful and productive lives. Jobes' patient, described in Chapter 6, is now happily married with a challenging job in the healthcare sector. I wanted to know what these people had to tell us. Because that's the goal, isn't it? As Edwin Shneidman wrote, "One can live a long, unhappy life with depression."[154] We don't just want suicidal people to survive, restrained and detained in hospitals, or living marginal lives on the street or in group homes, or even in their own homes, numb and going through the motions. We want our—and their—lives to be worth living.

What commonalities characterize the lives of people who have come through very rough periods and are doing very well now? And what law and policy changes might make it easier to get there?

---

[151] Interview with Leah Harris (June 2, 2014); interview with C.L. (Sept. 29, 2012); interview with Steve Periard, Aug. 25, 2014.

[152] Talking to Laura Delano, Mark McPherson (pseudonym), Jenn Hurtado, Anne Rider, Justin Mikel, Cheryl Sharp, Cara Anna, Steve Periard, Sean Donovan, Wyatt Ferrarra, "Colleen," Lynn Legere, Michelle Sese-Khalid, and many, many other people left me humbled and amazed at how people who had suffered so much loss and rejection could give back kindness and caring.

[153] Beckie Child, Eduardo Vega, and De Quincy Lezine; see DEQUINCY LEZINE & DAVID BRENT, EIGHT STORIES UP (2008) and Mental Health Association of San Francisco, *Directors & Senior Staff*, http://mentalhealthsf.org/about-us/staff/.

[154] Edwin S. Shneidman, Suicide as Psychache: A Clinical Approach to Self-Destructive Behavior 54 (1993).

Connections with Children and Grandchildren

Children and grandchildren are at the top of the list of people who talk about joy and fulfillment (although they are also the source of a great deal of stress and worry and aggravation.) As one interviewee told me,

> [When I had a baby was] when I started having feelings. I was determined that I was going to take care of this child and that she would never go through what I went through. I was very attentive. At each age that she was I re-experienced what had happened to me, I was able to do the right thing by her and cry and cry. I knew how it was supposed to be, and grieved not having had it. Take my daughter out of the picture and I am back to I have no purpose, no meaning, I am not grounded, I am not here. When my daughter wasn't around I was lost.[155]

A number of my women interviewees kept themselves going for their children's sake. One disclosed thoughts of hurting her child; she gave the child to her sister to raise, which broke her heart. Being responsible for a child is clearly a suicide deterrent for the women I spoke to who had children.

There are serious public policy implications in this finding. It would take all the pages allotted for this book to list every court case where a parent (usually a woman) loses her children or has her parental rights terminated because of suicidality and its consequences. Often, those children represent the woman's best reason to stay alive. Most of the people I spoke to were mothers and most of them seem to have done a pretty decent job, despite a lot of problems. Some of them had a substantial amount of help taking care of their children,[156] but for others, help was sporadic or nonexistent.

This is obviously a difficult and complex policy issue. Many of my interviewees also had chaotic childhoods, and traced their suicidality pretty clearly to parents or relatives who were emotionally, physically or sexually abusive, often because of substance abuse addiction, but also sometimes because of psychiatric disabilities. However, there seems to be little doubt that the current child welfare system does not differentiate very well between parents who, despite their difficulties, are loving and struggling to do the right thing, and parents who are fundamentally damaging their children. The child welfare system is permeated with discrimination against parents with psychiatric disabilities, or even just diagnoses of psychiatric disability without significant functional consequences.[157] One appellate court drew

---

[155] Harris, *supra* note 143.

[156] Sese-Khalid, *supra* note 149.

[157] NATIONAL COUNCIL ON "DISABILITY, ROCKING THE CRADLE: ENSURING THE RIGHTS OF PARENTS WITH DISABILITIES AND THEIR CHILDREN" (2012), http://www.ncd.gov/publications/2012/Sep272012/.

attention to this in a decision that could serve as a wake-up call for everyone involved in these difficult cases:

> Finally, we are troubled by the State's apparent heavy reliance on the labels "depression," "social anxiety" and "mental health problems." A label can encompass a wide spectrum of effects and is not, standing alone, reliably indicative of a person's level of functionality. We hold a diagnosis of depression, anxiety, a personality disorder or even schizophrenia does not automatically render a parent unfit. Rather, it is the actual conduct and behavior of the parent that is determinative on the question of fitness, not the label associated with such conduct or behavior. Consequently, our analysis has intentionally focused solely on the conduct of respondent, not any particular label.
>
> The use of such labels without *directly* linking them to specific conduct or behavior reinforces an unfair and incorrect conclusion that individuals suffering from mental illness cannot successfully parent. We believe the practical effect of this misapprehension is that many mentally ill individuals fail to seek treatment due to the fear of being labeled and stigmatized.
>
> Respondent, in the instant case, exhibited actual conduct that warranted a finding that she was dispositionally unfit. She did seek help on her own (going to the hospital) and she should be commended for making that brave choice. She also voiced a willingness to do whatever is necessary to secure A.T.'s return to her. If she successfully completes her tasks, she may be restored to fitness even while retaining the labels.
>
> The Act "recognizes, both implicitly and explicitly, that it covers people who are failing at their parental responsibilities but who should be given assistance in the development of proper skills and adequate information to provide the non-injurious environment to which their children are statutorily entitled." *In re O.S.*, 364 Ill. App. 3d 628, 635 (2006). It is for these reasons, that we hope to see the distinction between labels and actual conduct/behavior more clearly illustrated in future filings with this court and the trial courts of this district.[158]

While most state statutes do provide that parents must be given services to enable them to meet their responsibility for their children, in a number of states, mental disability remains a basis for terminating parental rights without providing statutorily required reunification services. Thus, if a parent falls into a category called "aggravating circumstances," the state need not provide reunification services. These aggravating circumstances include

---

[158] *In re* A.T. No. 3-14-0372 (Ill. App. 3d Dist. Jan. 3, 2015).

a diagnosis of mental illness, right up there with a parent having killed, tortured, or sexually abused another child.[159]

So it may not be a surprise that state departments of family services do not serve the needs of parents with psychiatric disabilities very well.[160] (In fact, the "conduct" to which the court referred in the preceding quote included the mother telling a police officer that she would rather drown her child than have him in the care of the Department of Child and Family Services).[161] Despite the fact that many parents in the child welfare system have disability issues, child welfare workers do not receive training on how to best assist both parents and their children, and programs are not structured to be accessible to those parents. Parents who are otherwise adequate and loving parents are at risk of losing their children if they make a suicide attempt, or sometimes even if they report being suicidal to the wrong person (often the mental health professional who is supposed to be helping them.)

As I have written at some length, the structure of the child welfare system in most states is ripe for a systemic disability discrimination claim under the Americans with Disabilities Act (ADA) and Section 504 of the Rehabilitation Act.[162] Recently, the Department of Justice and the Department of Health and Human Services' Office of Civil Rights, in a rare joint investigation, found that the Massachusetts Department of Children and Families (DCF) violated the rights of a mother with a mental disability by removing her child. She lived with her parents who wanted to and were able to help her take care of her child; her mother had quit her job to help take care of the child full time. Experts evaluated the mentally disabled mother as a person who would be a "loving, caring, conscientious mother,"[163] and the parents' home as having everything the child would need. When the Department of Justice interviewed DCF staff, one of them said that he reached his conclusions about a person's abilities to parent based on "intuition" and that "you get a vibe whether they're going to be able to do it or not."[164] And this is Massachusetts. There are model statutes that could be adopted to protect the

[159] ALASKA STAT. § 47.10.086(c)(5); ARIZ. REV. STAT. § 8-846(B)(1)(b); CAL. WELF. INST. CODE § 361.5(b)(2); KY. REV. STAT. ANN. § 610.127(6); UTAH CODE ANN. § 78A-6-312(22)(a).

[160] NATIONAL COUNCIL ON DISABILITY, *supra* note 157; Jennifer Mathis, *Keeping Families Together: Preserving the Rights of Parents with Disabilities*, 46 CLEARINGHOUSE REV. J. POVERTY L. & POL'Y 517 (Mar./Apr. 2013).

[161] *In re A.T.* No. 3-14-0372, at n.126.

[162] Susan Stefan, *Accommodating Families: Using the Americans with Disabilities Act to Keep Families Together*, 2 ST. LOUIS U. J. HEALTH L. & POL'Y 135 (2008).

[163] Joint Letter from the Department of Justice and the Department of Health and Human Services to the Massachusetts Department of Children and Families (Jan. 15, 2015), http://www.ada.gov/ma_docf_lof.pdf.

[164] *Id.*

right of parents with disabilities[165] without unnecessarily taking risks with their children.

It should be underscored that while almost every person I interviewed mentioned relationships—children, parents, spouses and beloved friends, grandchildren, and often beloved dogs—as a reason they were glad to be alive, they also said virtually unanimously that it is not helpful to invoke these relationships at the time the person is acutely suicidal. Doing so was experienced as blaming ("How could you be so selfish?") or appealing to shame and guilt. A powerful combination of tunnel vision and the belief that loved ones would be better off if the person was dead is the reality that many seriously suicidal people experience. The joy of human connection is the reason they are glad to be alive now, but it is not a potent lure to life when people are engulfed in despair.

Connections with Other Family and Friends

Parents, spouses, brothers, sisters, and friends who were loving and support-ive, nonjudgmental, and didn't give up on the person came in a close second. Many people cited parents and loved ones who trusted their accounts of what they needed to get better over the warnings of mental health professionals and took them out of hospitals and group homes.[166] It was clear to me from these stories that this support lasted over a long, long time, and in some cases continues to this day:

> I had a best friend who was just vital. I would have killed myself
> if it weren't for her. I tended to make friends with people who had
> therapy degrees. She just listened and gave support and didn't
> judge me. She said it was hard for her because I would call her out
> of the mental hospital. She kept up with me; I wasn't much of a
> friend to her at the time. But even so, she kept up with me.[167]

Nor was the support of friends limited to phone calls. In the case of one woman who had one break once in her life that no one understands to this day

> A friend stayed with me. She said, I'll stay with you, and she
> stayed for days on end, and finally she said, I'll have to go back
> and take care of my kids. . . . My neighbors walked with me,
> brought me food, totally took care of me, she'd come over and
> we'd talked [when she was hospitalized] my friends came every

---

single day, brought food, played cards. People really did surround me and take care of me.[168]

Doing these interviews and reading people's stories confirmed to me one truth, which is that saving a suicidal person's life requires a lot of time over an extended period, and a lot of patience. Not super-sophisticated medical technology, or gene testing, or monoclonal antibodies, just human connection and patient, caring perseverance. This is almost a cliché, except that our laws and policies including but not limited to: insurance reimbursement practices, family and medical leave policies, expectations of clinicians, continuity of care, teacher-student ratios, visiting policies at hospitals and institutions, availability of peer support and personal care assistants (PCAs),[169] time limits on suicide hotline calls[170] (which makes some sense when you realize there are so many calls to suicide hotlines that people get put on hold,[171] but still ...), undermine rather than maximize supportive and nurturing human contact over an extended period of time. Insurance companies, despite parity laws, are known for trying all sorts of gimmicks to reduce use of mental health services, including requiring preauthorization for behavioral health visits,[172] charging higher copayments, and starting to pressure mental health professionals for more documentation after eight or ten or twelve visits.[173] Since insurance regulators don't

---

[168] Anonymous (1), *supra* note 166.

[169] See pp. 455–63 for discussion of peer support and Chapter 10 for discussion of PCAs.

[170] One hotline had a limit of twenty minutes per call, one call per shift, see Askreddit, *What Is It Like Working/Volunteering for a Suicide Prevention Hotline?* (Dec. 4, 2013), http://www.reddit.com/r/AskReddit/comments/1s2jx8/serious_suicide_ hotline_operators_of_reddit_what/; another line had a thirty-minute maximum, Lipstick Alley, *I Had To Call a Suicide Hotline Last Night* (Oct. 13, 2010), http://www. lipstickalley.com/showthread.php/259824-I-Had-To-Call-A-Suicide-Hotline-Last-Night/page3 ("they can only talk thirty minutes or less, I think; they tried to rush me off the line after they got me to say I wouldn't hurt myself tonight").

[171] Josh Sanburn, *Inside the National Suicide Hotline: Preventing the Next Tragedy*, Time, Sept. 13, 2013, http://healthland.time.com/2013/09/13/inside-the-national-suicide-hotline-counselors-work-to-prevent-the-next-casualty/3/.

[172] *A.G. Schneidermann Announces Settlement with ValueOptions to End Wrongful Denial of Mental Health and Substance Abuse Treatment Services*, [New York State Attorney General], Mar. 5, 2015, http://www.ag.ny.gov/press-release/ ag-schneiderman-announces-settlement-valueoptions-end-wrongful-denial-mental-health.

[173] National Alliance for the Mentally Ill, "A Long Road Ahead: Achieving True Parity in Mental Health and Substance Use Care," (April 2015), http://www. nami.org/parityreport

seem up to policing these companies, attorneys general, especially in New York, have started to step in.[174]

Connection with Pets

A striking number of suicidal people, including a growing number of veterans, refer with deep gratitude to their dogs. Interviewing people and reading the accounts of people who are or were suicidal brings home one basic truth: for a lot of people, dogs help a lot.[175] For returning veterans with PTSD from Iraq and Afghanistan, service dogs help a lot.[176] Dogs help prevent suicide simply by caring about their people, but several people told me that when they attempted suicide, their dogs actively sought help from others, barking and howling and whining until rescuers investigated.[177]

Unfortunately, many places resist permitting animals, including service animals, even those with spotless behavior and health records. These practices are based more on culture and habit than on any kind of rationality: for example, in one case, an emergency department permitted a woman with severe medical problems to have her service dog with her in the emergency room, but when the emergency department staff decided that her pain was being caused by psychiatric medications that needed to be adjusted, the psychiatric unit upstairs refused to admit her dog (from whom she had never been separated). The judge ordered the unit to admit the dog.[178] Dogs really help a substantial number of people who are suicidal, and this should be taken into account in developing visiting policies and therapeutic programs at hospitals and residential settings, and in interpreting rules and laws.

For example, although having service animals is a protected right under both the ADA and the Fair Housing Amendments Act, the federal government has an interagency conflict about the scope of the right. The

---

[174] "A.G. Schneiderman Announces Settlement with Excellus Health Plan to End Wrongful Denial of Mental Health and Addiction [sic]: Unprecedented Enforcement of Mental Health Parity Laws Leads to Fifth Settlement by Attorney General Schneiderman," Press Release, New York State Attorney General, March 15, 2015, http://www.ag.ny.gov/press-release/ag-schneiderman-announces-settlement-excellus-health-plan-end-wrongful-denial-mental

[175] Becky Chung, *The Veteran and the Labradoodle: How a Service Dog Helped a TedActive Attendee Step Back into the World*, TEDBLOG, Sept. 4, 2014, http://blog.ted.com/the-veteran-and-the-labradoodle/; Tessa Glaze, *The Ultimate Barrier: For All Those Who Never Made It Back*, in OUR ENCOUNTERS WITH SUICIDE (2013) 109 (Alec Grant, Judith Haire, Fran Biley, & Brendan Stone eds.) (recounting the comfort she derived from Sammy the basset hound puppy, and that the first time suicidal thoughts entered her head were when Sammy died).

[176] Chung, *supra* note 175.

[177] Interview with Carolyn Noble (Aug. 29, 2014).

[178] Tamara v. El Camino Hosp., 964 F. Supp.2d 1077 (N.D. Ca. 2013).

Department of Housing and Urban Development, in charge of interpreting the Fair Housing Act, says that psychiatric service animals are service animals under the Act; whereas the Department of Justice, in charge of interpreting the ADA, says they are not. This is just folly on the part of the Department of Justice, which has generally been excellent on disability issues under the Obama administration.

It is true that people without disabilities relentlessly abuse the law permitting service animals, and show their disrespect and thick-headedness by clothing their hare-brained and ill-behaved little pets in cute service vests while parading them in places where only service animals are allowed. I have been incensed about this just like many other people, because it devalues disability rights and embodies a kind of self-centered and self-indulgent obliviousness that cries out to be punished. It should be very clear that the law does not permit people, disabled or not, to be accompanied by smelly[179] or badly behaved animals, whether they call them service animals or not.

Spirituality and Spiritual Support

The mental health profession and suicide prevention initiatives tend to give quite short shrift to spirituality. Both state and private psychiatric hospitals do little to nurture people's spiritual side. At Worcester Hospital and Recovery Center, a brand new hospital in Massachusetts, there is a gorgeous chapel and two full-time chaplains. The chapel is open for an hour a day during the week, and locked the rest of the time. Non-denominational services are held on Sundays.

Yet for many of my interviewees, people from backgrounds of chaos and violence and abuse, spirituality was truly the only source of salvation.[180] The answer of spirituality manifested itself in very different forms. As Jenn Hurtado recounts

> I wrote a suicide note, prayed one last time—I said to God, do you have a purpose for any of this, if so, you need to show up, you have 30 days to show up—3 weeks to the day later [her mother called to tell her about a free training program for psychiatric nurses] . . . There were 600 applicants for this program, I went for 2 interviews, the program paid for everything. My family helped me take care of my son, I stopped using substances and graduated with a 4.0. . . . God gave me my life back.[181]

---

[179] Roe v. Providence Health System-Oregon, 655 F. Supp.2d 1164 (D. Or. 2009).
[180] Interview with Jenn Hurtado (Dec. 16, 2013); interview with Mark McPherson (pseudonym) (Aug. 20, 2014); interview with Steve Periard (Aug. 25, 2014).
[181] Hurtado, *supra* note 180.

Jenn Hurtado follows the Celebrate Recovery program,[182] developed by Pastor Rick Warren, whose own son committed suicide. Like the programs described earlier in this chapter, it is manualized. There is a *Leader's Guide*, four *Participant's Guides*, a *Recovery Journal*, and the Bible. The program takes place through groups, and is guided by principles that are somewhat akin to Alcohol Anonymous (AA) principles, although much more explicitly aligned with religion. It is forward-looking and emphasizes personal responsibility (which is very closely related to personal agency and control). Interestingly, many conservative Christians consider that it owes too much to psychology, and not enough to the Bible, even though every principle is anchored by verses from the New Testament.

A substantial percentage of the men I spoke to were former substance abusers who had recovered through evangelical Christianity and sometimes AA or Narcotics Anonymous (NA). They felt very strongly that their faith was at the heart of their recovery, and (not coincidentally, I think) felt quite alienated from the traditional mental health system.

Marsha Linehan forthrightly acknowledges that DBT, the therapeutic model she invented, which has turned out to be one of the most effective suicide prevention methodologies around (see "Dialectical Behavioral Therapy, *supra* at pp. 442–444), is based in part on Zen: she calls it "a behavioral translation of Zen."[183] One of my interviewees combined Chinese medicine practices with mindfulness meditation to combat suicidal feelings.

But trying to support spirituality as a suicide prevention method runs into all sorts of difficulties. For one thing, as I have noted in earlier chapters, the mental health profession has claimed suicide as its own territory, and the mental health profession generally operates in splendid isolation from matters spiritual. It yearns to be considered a true science, a part of medicine, and feels more at home in the twenty-first century with pharmacy than philosophy. Yet comfort and solace are pastoral, not pharmaceutical, properties, and many churches provide genuine community and shelter for those in despair.[184] As Anne Lamott says, people who were suicidal can be "a resurrection story, in the wild, non-denominational sense,"[185] with the support of their faith and their communities.

---

[182] *Celebrate Recovery: A Christ-Centered Recovery Program*, www.celebraterecovery.com.

[183] Wise Counsel Interview Transcript: An Interview with Marsha Linehan, Ph.D on Dialectical Behavior Therapy, with David Van Nuys, Ph.D. http://www.rvcc-inc.org/poc/view_doc.php?type=doc&id=13825

[184] Some church teachings, of course, are at the root of people's suicidality, especially people in the LGBT community whose churches reject them or their gay parents. But very few of my interviewees blamed the church for misery associated with their sexual orientation, while a striking number of them claimed that being involved in a faith community had saved their lives.

[185] Anne Lamott, August 12, 2014, Facebook post, https://www.facebook.com/AnneLamott/posts/531917520271229

Peer Support

Peer Support Groups for People Who Are Suicidal

Many people I interviewed gave a great deal of credit to peer support in help-ing them through their struggles with suicidality.[186] In the mental health ser-vices field, "peer" is a word for people who have experience—of the mental health system, or a psychiatric diagnosis or condition, or of being suicidal. It is the equivalent of the AA or NA concept without the religious over-tones: people who can best understand and help are the people who have been there before, and survived to make it to the other side, whether the other side is sobriety or a meaningful life.

One of the most exciting innovations I have heard about in a long time are peer support groups aimed specifically at people who are suicidal.[187] The National Strategy for Suicide Prevention acknowledges that "peer support plays an important role in the treatment of mental health and substance use disorders and holds potential for helping those at risk of suicide."[188] The National Action Alliance for Suicide Prevention also emphasizes the role of peer support in suicide prevention.[189] Peer programs have been in place for quite some time,[190] but the focus on suicidality is new.

---

[186] Michelle Sese-Khalid, Leah Harris, Steve Periard, Mark McPherson (pseud-onym), Beth Harris, Colleen (pseudonym), Beckie Child, and C.L. Others strongly support peer advocacy, Cara Anna, Justin Mikel, Cheryl Sharp, Pam Nolan, Lynn Legere, Dese'Rae Stage, and Jenn Hurtado.

[187] There are, of course, both suicide attempt groups and crisis respite houses that are not specifically run by peers, and I am not trying to suggest that these are not useful. For example, the Didi Hirsch Community Mental Health Center in Los Angeles runs a group for people who have survived suicide attempts. This is not a peer group because they are led by a therapist, and, unlike many of the groups described here, people sign up for eight weeks of meeting in advance and cannot simply "drop in" (Didi Hirsch Mental Health Services, *Survivors of Suicide Attempt Support Group*, http://www.didihirsch.org/survivors-of-suicide-attempt-support-group). Any group that allows people to speak freely and without fear of involuntary detention about suicidal feelings is a great improvement over the current situation most people face.

[188] Jerry Reed, *Advancing Peer Support in Suicide Prevention*, Suicide Prevention Resource Center, Mar. 8, 2013, http://www.sprc.org/directorsblog/advancing-peer-support-suicide-prevention.

[189] National Action Alliance for Suicide Prevention: Suicide Attempt Survivors Task Force, The Way Forward: Pathways to Hope, Recovery and Wellness with Insights from Lived Experience 17 (July 2014), http://actionallianceforsuicideprevention.org/sites/actionallianceforsuicideprevention.org/files/The-Way-Forward-Final-2014-07-01.pdf.

[190] Campbell, J., "The history and philosophy of peer-run programs," In S. Clay, B. Schell, P.W. Corrigan, and R. O. Ralph (Eds.), On our own, together: Peer programs for people with mental illness. (2005).

The intense isolation and alienation of suicidality that is often exacerbated by encounters with police and emergency departments can be are diffused by peer groups where people who are suicidal can speak freely about their feelings. The peer groups and respite houses preserve people in their community rather than removing them from it as hospitalization does.

"Alternative to Suicide" Groups and the Western Massachusetts Recovery Learning Community

The Western Massachusetts Recovery Learning Community (RLC)[191] offers "Alternative to Suicide" peer support groups in four different towns in Western Massachusetts, where people who are suicidal come together and talk about their feelings and issues about wanting to end their lives.[192] These groups are not at all the same as professional-led group therapy. There is no rush to dissuade the person, just questions, such as, "What's going on?" "What's happening?" "Have you felt this way for a long time?" Good clinicians ask the same questions, but in a different context; no one in the Alternative to Suicide group has any power to involuntarily commit an individual, nor any desire to do so.

As Sean Donovan, one of the peer facilitators, describes them, "These are groups where people who feel or have ever felt suicidal can talk about these experiences without fear or judgment or coercion and we share about all aspects of our lives and being human in these spaces."[193] The groups range from small (four to five) to large (twenty), and people can just drop in.[194] There is a great deal of turnover in people's attendance at the groups.[195] When I asked how the existence of these groups was publicized, Donovan ran down a variety of ways: a public forum on suicide, with Susan Rose Blauner, a local resident and the author of *How I Stayed Alive When My Brain Was Trying to Kill Me* as a featured speaker, to see if anyone was interested in having such a group; while providing community "bridging" support on hospital psychiatric wards;[196] through the Western Massachusetts Recovery Learning

---

[191] There are five RLCs in Massachusetts, state-funded peer run centers for people with psychiatric disabilities that offer drop in centers, advocacy, and assistance to clients of the Department of Mental Health and others. Each RLC has its own individual programs, so that the Western Massachusetts Alternatives to Suicide groups are not offered at other RLCs.

[192] Western Massachusetts Recovery Learning Center, *Local Alternatives to Suicide Groups* (Nov. 11, 2015), http://www.westernmassrlc.org/alternatives-to-suicide/314-local-alternatives-to-suicide-groups.

[193] Personal communication from Sean Donovan to the author (June 26, 2015).

[194] Interview with Sean Donovan (Worcester, Massachusetts, June 2, 2015).

[195] *Id.*

[196] When inpatients in hospital psychiatric wards are about to be discharged, many hospitals in Massachusetts ask peers in the community to come talk to

Community and its website.[197] The groups are funded by the Massachusetts Department of Public Health.

I asked Donovan whether most of the people who came to the group were people in the mental health system, already clients of the Massachusetts Department of Mental Health, and he disagreed, pointing out that because Northampton is the home of Smith College, they can also see students who are suicidal who feel more comfortable coming to an off-campus group than seeking services from the college.[198]

"Live for Today" in Northern New York

Although PEOPLe, Inc.[199] has long run crisis respite houses, it has only recently started a peer support group for suicidal people called "Live for Today." Like the Alternatives to Suicide group in Western Massachusetts, anyone can drop in. It is facilitated by two peers, and its membership fluctuates. I asked Steve Miccio if anyone ever raised liability concerns about having a support group for suicidal people. He laughed. "Not so much," he said. "I try to do things intelligently."[200] Miccio acknowledges that most of the people who come to the groups are clients of the mental health system. He says when he is having conversations with people, many of the "chronically normal" will acknowledge that there was a time in their past that they were suicidal, but they will only talk about it when it is safely in the past.

There are a few other peer run support groups for people who are suicidal, for example, the Attempters Support Group of Suicide Prevention Services in Batavia, Illinois (they reserve the term "survivors" for people who have lost a loved one to suicide);[201] and peer-run suicide support groups offered by the Mental Health Association in San Francisco.[202] There is a group run

---

the individual to provide "bridging" services—connections with peers and resources in the community.

[197] The website also features a webinar on alternatives to suicide (Western Mass Recovering Learning Community, http://www.westernmassrlc.org/).

[198] See Chapter 8 for a discussion about discrimination by colleges and universities against suicidal students.

[199] Project to Empower and Organize the Psychiatrically Labeled (PEOPLe, Inc.), headquartered in Poughkeepsie, New York, has evolved into a major provider of alternative and peer services in Northern New York. Its CEO, Steve Miccio, is known nationally and internationally for his work in developing alternative service models (PEOPLe, Inc., [homepage], http://projectstoempower.org/).

[200] Interview with Steve Miccio (May 27, 2015).

[201] I attempted to get more information by contacting Stephanie as the website instructs but never received a response (Survivors of Suicide Support Group, Aurora, Ill., http://www.spsamerica.org/#!3-support-groups/cvii).

[202] Mental Health Association of San Francisco, *Support Groups/Self-Help*, http://mentalhealthsf.org/help-now/support-groups-self-help/.

by a "prosumer" (a mental health professional who has attempted suicide) at St. Michael's Hospital in Toronto, Canada.[203]

Peer-Run Crisis Respite Houses

Peer-run crisis houses are not explicitly for suicidal people, but they do see many people who are suicidal. They are a relatively older development than the support groups, and there are many more of them.[204] While different peer-run crisis centers have different rules for length of stay and when a person can return, all share in common a community location, in a regular house, with a few bedrooms for people to work through crises in nonclinical settings, and an indifference to diagnosis. They are all voluntary, unlocked, noncoercive, and run by peers, people who have some understanding of the crises they are experiencing. There are eighteen of these currently operating around the country, mostly in New England,[205] New York,[206] and the Northeast.[207] There are peer-run crisis respite houses in Georgia, Virginia, Nebraska, and Santa Cruz, California, and one is due to open soon in Wisconsin. I interviewed a number of providers of peer services for this section—Sean Donovan of Alternatives to Suicide, Wyatt Ferrera of Afiya, Miccio of Rose House and Live for Today, and Mark Nelson of Stepping Stone. I was extraordinarily impressed by their thoughtfulness and the scope of their vision.

Afiya and the Western Massachusetts Recovery Learning Community

The Western Massachusetts Recovery Learning Community also offers Afiya House, a retreat and respite house for people in crisis, including suicidal people, which has been open in Northampton, Massachusetts, since August 4, 2012. According to the website, "Afiya" is a Swahili word meaning physical, spiritual, and emotional health and wholeness.[208] Up to three people can spend one to seven days there. They are funded by the Department of Mental

---

[203] Talking with Yvonne Bergmans, Talking about Suicide, June 28, 2012 http://talkingaboutsuicide.com/2012/06/28/talking-with-yvonne-bergmans/

[204] A list of peer-operated crisis centers is available on the website of the National Empowerment Center, *Directory of Peer-Run Crisis Services*, http://www.power2u.org/peer-run-crisis-services.html.

[205] Stepping Stone in New Hampshire, Afiya in Massachusetts, Alyssum and Soteria House in Vermont (Alyssum, *Welcome*, http://www.alyssum.org/).

[206] PEOPLe, Inc. operates four houses in northern New York, and Parachute House operates in four locations in New York City.

[207] There is a crisis house in Pennsylvania and one in New Jersey, which offer support for up to ten days, Collaborative Support Programs of New Jersey, *Wellness & Recovery Initiatives*, http://www.cspnj.org/#!wellness--recovery-initiatives/c14i1.

[208] *Afiya*, WESTERN MASSACHUSETTS RECOVERY LEARNING CENTER (Nov. 11, 2015), http://www.westernmassrlc.org/afiya.

Health at a cost of $375,000 a year, and the house stays full, with a three-person waiting list that is also full at virtually all times. Although some of the people who stay there are clients of the Department of Mental Health, others are not. Priority is given to residents of Western Massachusetts, where the house is located.

A stay at Afiya is free. The person has to call ahead (no referrals from providers or family are accepted—the person has to call him- or herself) and have a fifteen- to twenty-minute conversation to see if a stay at Afiya would be a "good fit." Team Coordinator Wyatt Ferrera explained that what is meant by a "good fit," for example, while being homeless is clearly a crisis situation, Afiya is not a shelter or transitional housing space, so a person must be experiencing an emotional crisis other than homelessness and needing a place to stay in order to come to Afiya.[209] Some visitors come with thoughts or feelings of suicide.

While people at Afiya are voluntary, and are not actively violent toward others or trying to kill themselves, some people's stays "can be pretty intense," says Ferrera. "We do get people experiencing extreme distress . . . I feel passionate about being able to support folks through hearing voices, thoughts and feelings of suicide, anger and spiritual emergencies."[210] He describes behaviors that would clearly result in restraint if the individual was in an emergency department or psychiatric ward, including men who are very angry and raise their voices and throw property around. "In men, often their emotions look like anger, sadness appears as anger. It's not that men are angry per se, they just seem angry because of larger societal pressures of how masculinity is set up."[211]

This is not to say that anarchy reigns. Unlike emergency departments or psychiatric wards, Afiya always has people who are able to talk to a person going through crisis, and they maintain a balance between accepting where a person is, and requiring respect for certain rules of the house. Ferrera notes, "They need to stay with the values of the house, try to be respectful, as hard as that is. People will say it's too much to ask to hold to these values, such as respect [in a crisis]. I disagree. Violence is not something we can do. I am not willing to be hit."[212] People have been asked to leave Afiya if they are unable to follow the values and mission of the house, although every effort is made to talk to them and work with them.

As Ferrera summarizes,

> we are always willing to have difficult conversations and sit with
> our own discomfort when we have to . . . the key thing in the house
> is not to come from a fear-based place, to know that you don't

---

[209] Interview with Wyatt Ferrera, June 4, 2014, South Hadley, Massachusetts.
[210] *Id.*
[211] *Id.*
[212] *Id.*

know and to always be curious, compassionate, and willing to learn and grow. I am often just as deeply impacted by the people who stay here as they may be by us, and that's the entire point of it all, genuine human relationships.[213]

Not surprisingly, people want to return to Afiya, often. Unlike Stepping Stone, Afiya permits people to return if they are experiencing a new crisis, although "we may tell people if it feels too soon."[214]

Talking to Ferrera made me both hopeful and frustrated. I thought, this is what we can have when people don't have to worry about liability, these oases for people who may feel they cannot take another step. Places like Afiya are necessarily local, but they are also virtually inherently unreplicable on any grand scale, because the healing and listening they provide are not, and could not be, reimbursable by Medicaid. The listeners have no professional credentials, just compassion, patience, and a life experience of their own which makes it easier to relate to the person in crisis. A similar crisis house, Soteria Alaska, foundered and failed because funders kept pushing for it to change so that it could be Medicaid-reimbursable.[215] Yet if even half the people who show up at Afiya would otherwise have gone to the emergency department, and some of those people had been hospitalized, it is pretty clear that Afiya saves the state and federal government thousands of healthcare dollars.

Rose House in Northern New York

Rose House operates in four locations and has been operating in Milton, New York, since 2001. It was started by Steve Miccio, who had a terrible experience in an emergency department in 1994 and used his determination to improve the experience of people in crisis to create an entire alternative peer-run system of services. The services offered by PEOPLe, Inc.[216] include four crisis houses, a 24/7 warm line, peers in traditional emergency departments to help navigate the system, an advocate in the Partial Hospitalization program, peers going to people in their homes during crisis if that is more comfortable, and social groups (as well as the suicide support group discussed earlier). Miccio says, "We don't believe in referrals. If it's needed, we try to do it ourselves." These houses for people in crisis serve between 230 and 260 individuals a year[217] at a cost of between $250,000 and $360,000.

---

[213] *Id.*

[214] *Id.*

[215] Jim Gottstein, *Lessons from Soteria-Alaska*, MAD IN AMERICA BLOG, June 29, 2015, http://www.madinamerica.com/2015/06/lessons-from-soteria-alaska/.

[216] Not to be confused with People, Inc., a non-profit serving people with developmental disabilities.

[217] These are unduplicated, meaning that the figure does not include return visits by the same person. Interview with Steve Miccio (May 27, 2015).

Stepping Stone in New Hampshire

Stepping Stone is another peer crisis respite that has been operating for a long time. It opened its doors in Claremont, New Hampshire, in July 1995. It is open for free to anyone from New Hampshire. If people in that rural state cannot get to Stepping Stone, staff will come and pick them up from anywhere in the state, and drive them back after their stay. The house in Claremont can provide respite for two people at a time, although New Hampshire is looking to add two peer-run crisis beds in Conway and one in Keene. People who stay at Stepping Stone are expected to be able to cook for themselves, and clean up their rooms (especially before they leave). Like Afiya, the maximum stay is seven days, and like Afiya, people who stay at Stepping Stone are expected to act respectfully toward other people at the house.

Stepping Stone costs $500 a day to operate, and provides 24-hour peer support to a person in crisis. People who are suicidal can come to Stepping Stone to talk about their feelings and try to work through them. Someone who indicated that he or she was imminently about to commit suicide could not stay.

Both Stepping Stone and Afiya train staff in a model called "Intentional Peer Support," first developed by New Hampshire resident Shery Mead.[218] Like "motivational interviewing," Intentional Peer Support is a great model with an annoyingly Delphic name, but its essence boils down to mutuality and relationship: a rejection of the notion that one person provides help or services and the other person receives them—in fact, a thorough-going rejection of the notion of professional boundaries. Both people are expected to learn from and help each other; neither is seen as having a problem to be diagnosed, but rather a relationship to be developed.

One difficulty Stepping Stone has experienced is discriminatory insurance practices: when the insurance company that insured the crisis house found out what services it provided, the premiums went up astronomically. This reaction is obviously based on stereotypes rather than experience; Stepping Stone has been operating for two decades without any problems.

Policy and Legal Barriers to Full Realization of the Peer Model

Peer services have great potential to transform the way suicide help is provided to people, and a lot of room to expand. Ironically, given that many people who run these services are skeptical at best of the traditional mental health system, they are often funded by mental health agencies, and have become incorporated into the offerings of mental health agencies in ways that feel far more embedded in the mental health system than AA or NA are in any state or local substance abuse treatment agency. Because of this, depending on their location, the population of people they serve may be

---

[218] Intentional Peer Support, [homepage], www.intentionalpeersupport.org.

largely comprised of traditional clients of the mental health system rather than drawing from all suicidal people. Even if they only divert those traditional clients from emergency departments and hospitalizations, they will have accomplished transformative work. The difference in atmosphere, and the kinds of conversations, between an emergency department and a quiet house talking to someone who has all the time in the world to talk to you, speaks for itself. But they have the potential for so much more.

Wyatt Ferrera points out that Afiya House gets college students who are not part of the traditional mental health system (Smith College is located in Northampton), which, given how colleges and universities treat suicidal students,[219] may be extraordinarily important in providing respite without compromising the student's academic career. In fact, having peer respite houses for people in crisis located in college and university towns may be very good planning.

As peer services become more successful and recognized, they run the risk of being strangled and thwarted in their missions by well-meaning government regulations. For example, one of things suicidal people fear most is that revealing their feelings will lead to a one-way trip to the local emergency department and psychiatric ward. This used to be one of the great advantages of peer services: the ability to talk freely. Now Steve Periard, who works in a peer-run component of a mental health agency, laments that

> [we] aren't bound to report when someone says they are suicidal but that's going to change. I think a lot more is going to change as the NYS Office of Mental Health merges with managed care. So, yeah, I could say to the person, "If we continue this conversation I'm going to have to report it." I don't agree with that. I think most people need to talk about it. Instead, it is reported, the police come, the person is handcuffed then taken to a locked ward. I have been there so I'm not likely to endorse it.[220]

Peer groups and residences are, by their own philosophy, voluntary and unlocked. People who come generally sign a form indicating that they will not be destructive or violent. Leah Harris, a national advocate for peer services, is deeply disappointed that some peer crisis residences will not accept people who are actively and imminently suicidal, forcing them to go to emergency departments. This may be in part a result of state funding requirements, insurance practices, or both.

Peer services also tend to take relatively few people at a time, allowing them to preserve a highly personalized and individualized approach. This does not mean that the model is doomed to irrelevance, only that it must be intensely local, which is a good thing. Many local two- to five-bedroom

---

[219] See Chapter 8.
[220] Periard, *supra* note 186.

houses helping people in crisis means, by definition, adopting an intensely individual, personalized approach, which (compared to emergency departments) is not necessarily more expensive but almost certainly likely to be more effective.

So far, peer support is paid for largely out of state and local funding from public health and mental health funding. Where it has attempted to expand into Medicaid, it has run into difficulties, including requirements for credentialed staff with professional training providing supervision, which increases the costs, changes the dynamic, and introduces liability concerns where they are refreshingly absent. Without Medicaid support, the model must look to AA and NA, which may be a better way to proceed in any event.

Suicide Prevention and the Story of Michelle Sese-Khalid

One woman whose story both embodies and transcends many of the suicide prevention issues I have discussed in this chapter is Michelle Sese-Khalid. Her story reflects these themes and is also uniquely her own.[221]

Like many people I interviewed, Sese-Khalid experienced physical and sexual abuse in childhood. Her father was a police officer who "would have himself together when he went to work but he would come home and get raging drunk." When she was fifteen years old, her brother was accused of a crime, and in their small town, "people painted stuff on our garage, egged our garage, beat us up in school. I started getting messages in my locker that I needed to watch my back, that someone was going to hurt me."

During this time, two men she worked with at a fast food joint offered her a ride home when her oldest brother didn't show up to pick her up as usual. "I got raped by both of them. They left me to walk home, it was in the woods. It was around the time this local girl had been murdered in the same area where they kicked me out of the car and I had to walk home." She did not tell her family or anyone else about the rape. She just "kind of snapped ... I tried to kill myself ... I wouldn't leave the house, I didn't want to go to school." Her family let her stay home for a while, but finally her father made her go to school. "He dragged me out of the house crying. That was the quietest bus ride I ever had, no one said a word the whole way." When she arrived, she refused to get off the bus. The principal and the guidance counselor had to coax her off the bus, and at first she did all her classes in the counselor's office.

> In my senior year, the school gave me buddies so I could spend
> more time with other students. Students volunteered to sit with
> me. Spencer was one, he was gay but I was in love with him because

---

[221] Sese-Khalid, *supra* note 149.

he was so kind to me. Noelle was another, me and Noelle are still friends on Facebook, and Karen, they were my three buddies at school.

The counselor said to get involved in outside activity, so my mom and I went to adult Sunday School at church, but I got kicked out because I made the adults feel uncomfortable. I have a tendency to rock when I am nervous, so they kicked me out. So we went to a different church . . . I got the idea that church was the way I could get away from home and away from my dad, so I started lying to my parents and sneaking off to the church when no one was there. I would sit by myself and sing and play the piano. [Youth Minister] Daniel[222] would come in and say, "Why are you here?" but back then I didn't talk. [Daniel befriended her over time.] He started treating me like his little sister, taking me around with him on errands, blasting Motown on the radio. Wherever he went, I stayed in the car. Eventually I started talking . . .

I married my first husband to get away from my mom and dad. I didn't know he had an anger streak, he had gone away for Desert Storm and when he came home he had PTSD really bad, he beat me up regularly. He left me after I got in a car accident—a drunk driver hit my car and left me with physical and brain injuries . . . He left me with five kids. One had Asperger's, another was a baby, nine months old, my brain was still healing from the accident and I had a hard time talking. I put in for disability payments. A social worker came after he left and decided they needed to remove the kids and put me in a group home. I was so upset, my husband had just left, [and] I hadn't worked because I'd been with my kids. The social worker said the only way to keep my kids was to go on welfare and food stamps and get a job, so I did. But because my brain was still healing, I couldn't keep a job, I would lose the job and it would take a while to get another one and it made it hard to pay bills or pay rent, and meanwhile Social Services would accuse me of child neglect.

There was this gentleman in our community and he started to take an interest in me and my kids, he would walk my kids home from the bus stop, he went out and bought winter coats for all my kids . . . My church didn't believe in a single mother raising five kids and everyone thought it was a good idea to get remarried. We dated for four or five months, and he asked me to marry him. One of the church ladies told me God is putting this gift in your face. I am still healing from this car accident, using a cane or leaning on a baby carriage—I am not making excuses but I had the mentality

---

[222] Name changed for privacy purposes.

of a [fourth-]grader, I was still was going to speech therapy and physical therapy and cognitive therapy. So I married him[.]

Well, he wasn't what he seemed. He had unsavory friends. He didn't like it when I asked him questions. I kept asking, and one afternoon he punched me in the face. I don't remember much after that. I woke up in the psych ward, tied down, and I started screaming. A group of nurses came in and gave me a needle. I have nightmares about being in that quiet room. Even today, I have an extreme phobia of needles. Show me a needle and I start screaming and I go back to that time. While I was in the hospital my husband raped my daughter and 7 other kids in the neighborhood. The hospital released me on all these drugs—Trazodone, Effexor and Seroquel—and my husband would give me drugs with vodka to wash them down. For the next six months, I was just a zombie, I slept and stared out the window.

I don't know how long this would have gone on for, but one day the police broke into the house—they didn't knock, they came charging in with big huge guns and surrounded my kids and me and arrested my husband. The social worker came and took my kids from me and they took me down to the police department. You know how on *Law and Order* they have the witness in there and yell and yell? They really do that, they scream in your face, and they try to catch you in a lie, they made threats, they said I was going to jail for 20-life, they screamed at me for six hours and I guess at some point it became evident to them that I knew nothing. Then they threw me in a holding cell for 24 hours. It was about 50 degrees and I had on a T-shirt and shorts, there was a bright light on for 24 hours, no place to sleep, no food, no water, no human contact. I just lost my mind and started screaming and yelling. They came and put me in an orange jump suit and I talked to a judge on TV. He told them to let me go home.

I went home, and didn't come out of the house for a long, long time. Finally a member of the church coaxed me out of the house. We were driving over the Rappahannock Bridge, and the thought came to my mind that if I jumped off the bridge I could fly to my kids. The person driving the car got out of the car and ran after me and a cop who happened to be there got out of his car and the two of them caught me as I was getting ready to jump. The cop took me to the [hospital].

The hospital helped. Not the medication, not the programs. I wouldn't talk at all. It wasn't fear anymore[.] I had an extreme hatred of people[.] I wanted nothing more to do with people. I hated people so much I couldn't even acknowledge that I was a person. There was this nurse there that helped me start talking . . . she wasn't judgmental of me, nothing shocked her, nothing surprised her. I felt it was my fault that my kids and the kids in the community got hurt by my husband, that I wasn't there to protect them. I carried a lot of guilt.

The Court ordered me to move home to Dale City and join a clubhouse. It was either that or go to Western State. They wanted to keep me from isolating myself. A lady named Michelle came to the clubhouse to teach us about Wellness Recovery Action Plans [WRAP][223] and put a plan together. Part of my WRAP plan was no longer isolating, I had to talk to one person a day for five minutes. I would find someone I thought was safe and talk about my [WRAP] plan. And Daniel came back into my life. We lost contact for 14 years—he's my big brother again, he's my guardian angel. If I didn't have Daniel in my life, I would have gone into my house and not come out.

They took my kids away for three years. I had to pay for a high[-]priced lawyer, I got a disability settlement and took half the money and gave it to a very good lawyer. He told me he was going to have to bring up the past that my dad was an abuser, I didn't want that, my brothers and I had a quiet pact, but the lawyer said because you have a mental illness, if you want your kids back, I have to be able to explain it. It didn't sit too well with my family and brothers, my father disowned me and my older brothers disowned me, but I have my kids.

I work a part-time volunteer job, WRAP facilitator, inspirational speaker and singer. I wouldn't be any of that if it wasn't for Daniel. I interact with people, help people create a daily plan for living with their disability, mental or physical, [and] I use my own personal experience to help other people [feel] that there is hope, make that choice, try, when things are hopeless, try to keep that hope light on. There is someone in your life who can keep your hope light on, it can be the last person we expect, there is always someone, trust that, look forward because it can only get better.

You have to forgive, you have to let it go. I haven't forgotten the past, but I use it to benefit other people. I sit down with someone who has been a rape victim and show that I am a rape survivor, we are still here and we are not going to allow what happened to us to hold us back, we use it to make us stronger, more mature and wiser. I still have nightmares, I have to use wellness tools to deal

---

[223] Developed by Mary Ellen Copeland, a Wellness Recovery Action Plan (WRAP) is a "self-designed wellness and prevention process that anyone can use to get well, stay well, and make their life the way they want it to be." WRAP and Recovery Books, http://mentalhealthrecovery.com/wrap-is/

with that. . . . Daniel could have retired, but he's helping my kids go to college. Daniel is at our house [two to three] times a day. My kids grew up with a dad. There is nothing obligating this guy[. We] have never dated, [and] as a big brother he took on the obligation of raising my kids. When the court said I needed a legal guardian he spoke to the judge himself, and there was created an extensive power of attorney so that I didn't have to have a guardian.

Because of my WRAP, because of Daniel, because of my church, I am here. I do deal with depression, it can get really deep and very dark, I do get to the point of hopelessness, I think about suicide but I haven't followed through. I try to hold on until the next day because it's going to be better. I try to reach out to my supporters, just somebody to give me a word of encouragement.

My brain injury is progressive, it's not going to get better. I'm like 45 going on Alzheimer's. It takes a lot of tenacity to want to get up and get out, but it took a group of people who really cared. Hope didn't come overnight, or the next week or the next month. It took a long time for me to really get hope, to fight to get my kids back. There are people at church who do not like me because I have a mental illness, they don't like people with mental illness and they don't like me. I confront my anger and hurt and fear by forcing myself to be around people and care about them and try to help them. I make a point of being a greeter at church, I have to greet the good and bad, that keeps me from isolating and not wanting to be with people. I have to fight it for my kids and myself and all the people that I mentor. I say to people, I am fighting and you can fight too, we can fight together, it's not just me talking. I want my life to be an example, not a waste.

What I love about Michelle Sese-Khalid's story is its true-to-life complexity. When you think about school, police, psychiatric hospitals, and church, we see in her story the school bullies who threatened her, and the three students who sat with her to give her the courage to go to classes; the police who traumatized her, and the cop who saved her life at the Rappahannock Bridge; the church people who didn't and don't like her because of her symptoms of brain injury and psychiatric disability, and the Youth Minister, Daniel, who has stepped in to support her and her children with respect and devotion; the horror of her first psychiatric hospitalization and the nurse in the second hospitalization who got her talking and ultimately out of the hospital.

We see the interlocking abuse and violence of her childhood, and her inability to prevent the same thing from happening to her own children. We see the unhelpful response of one social service system after another, and then the transformative power of the clubhouse, the WRAP plan, and the current work she does, all products of a newer social system (not to mention the disability payments that help her survive). We see the power of individuals to contribute to saving a life. Her story reflects two equal truths: she would not be alive today without the help of many people, and her survival is the result of her own courage, tenacity, faith, and optimism.

Another facet of the complexity is that her two suicide attempts were so very different: the first the reaction of a bullied, abused, traumatized teenager to burdens of cruelty and suffering she could no longer endure, and the second, by her own account, the confused longings of a mother who had only a tenuous hold on reality: "the thought came to my mind that if I jumped off the bridge I could fly to my kids." Although most decisions to commit suicide are competent, these are two examples of situations where I believe the state should intervene, involuntarily if necessary, to stop a person from suicide: teenage suicide decisions and the kinds of emotional conditions that lead a person to think she can fly off a bridge to her children. But the hospital didn't help her; she would have been immured there forever, hating people and refusing to talk, if one individual nurse hadn't kept trying to reach out to her. Her story does not give much support for hospitalization as a treatment alternative, even for people whose connections with reality are very distorted.

Finally, Michelle Sese-Khalid's own amazing candor about the combination of anger, hurt, fear, hope, gratitude, and resilience with which she greets the circumstances of her life reflects the complexity of a person who still struggles with suicidality. She credits her faith and the church, Daniel, the WRAP plan, the lawyer who got her kids back, and acknowledges that every single day is a struggle.

Conclusion

The current framework of suicide prevention doesn't work, and statistics about suicide bear this out. Analyzing suicide as a symptom and product of mental illness, to be stopped at all costs and treated in hospitals, involuntarily if necessary, by mental health professionals is a model that works (if at all) for a minority of cases. It is expensive, inordinately stressful to suicidal individuals and mental health professionals, and, if attention were paid to the voices of people who are suicidal and who have attempted suicide, it would be abandoned as the primary framework.

We need a public health approach that focuses on addressing suicidality in the community, both directly and by reducing the kinds of exposure to trauma and violence that plant the seeds of later self-destruction. We need to be more focused on limiting access to lethal means, including being crystal clear about making sure that all states have CAP laws, record data about sales at gun shows, and strictly enforce laws about selling guns to minors (at the very least). A public health approach would minimize coercion and involuntary treatment, and offer—if not mandate--the proven skill-building and problem-solving approaches instead. We also need to be far more proactive in incorporating human and spiritual connections, from peer support to supporting people in their religious beliefs.

10

Conclusion: People with Psychiatric Diagnoses and Assisted Suicide

"If you say to me today you want to die, I'm obliged to commit you. Now there will be people who say, 'I want to die,' and I'm supposed to say, 'Okay, go die?'"[1]

—Dr. David ("Ted") George

I have known people who call 911 whenever they are lonely and in despair. They know that they have to use the S-word (suicide) in order to get the desired response. But they call because, for some of them, the police or paramedics who respond are the only people that are nice to them and talk to them and treat them with respect. And because they are in chronic despair, it should come as no surprise that sooner or later they give up and kill themselves.

—Dr. Joel Dvoskin

"Hard cases make bad law."

—Oliver Wendell Holmes, Jr.

Introduction

One of the major reasons I wrote this book was to try to conceptualize some kind of unified field theory that could harmonize U.S. policy and legal issues involving suicide, assisted and otherwise. Could there possibly be a policy

---

[1] Erin Cox, *Raven O.J. Brigance Joins Emotional Debate over "Death with Dignity" Bill*, Baltimore Sun, Mar. 10, 2015, http://www.baltimoresun.com/news/maryland/politics/bs-md-death-with-dignity-hearing-20150310-story.html#page=2.

470

and legal structure that would have worked for Josh Sebastian,[2] Ms. E.,[3] Ms. Black,[4] Anita Darcel Taylor,[5] Elizabeth Bouvia,[6] Michael Freeland,[7] Mary Maxey,[8] Peter Yurkowski,[9] Michelle Sese-Khalid,[10] and all the other people we have encountered in this book? Perhaps, but we need to examine one final story, the epitome of the hard case that Oliver Wendell Holmes Jr. said makes bad law,[11] or bad policy, anyway: the life and death of Jana van Voorhis.

The Case of Jana van Voorhis

Jana van Voorhis was lucky. She came from a wealthy and loving family, and she was attractive and bubbly and outgoing. Jana van Voorhis was also profoundly unlucky. She began talking about suicide at the age of ten, and by high school, she had been psychiatrically hospitalized. She received every treatment, every therapy, and seemingly every diagnosis under the sun. Because of her family's caring and wealth, she lived in her own apartment, with an accountant, a maid, and a gardener,[12] and lived a semblance of a normal life. She loved her nieces and nephews dearly, and she was not dangerous or violent. But it was hard for her to sustain relationships, and the years of her life became an accumulation of disappointment: jobs that she obtained through family connections that didn't work out; as she grew older, her hope for love and a family of her own ebbed away. She had brief romantic relationships with men, which inevitably were ended by the man, whom she equally inevitably continued to pursue, begging for reconsideration. One person whose stepfather had been briefly involved with van Voorhis wrote

> I first heard her name when I was ten years old. It was the early 1980s and Jana called our home repeatedly one evening, crying and threatening to commit suicide. There was a small party going on at

---

[2] See Chapter 1.
[3] See Chapter 1. Although E. was a citizen of Great Britain, the concerns her case raises apply equally in the United States.
[4] See Chapter 1.
[5] See Chapter 1.
[6] See Chapter 2.
[7] See Chapter 3.
[8] See Chapter 5.
[9] See Chapter 6.
[10] See Chapter 9.
[11] Northern Securities Company v. United States, 193 U.S. 197, 400 (Holmes, J., dissenting).
[12] I have been unable to unearth an explanation of why someone who lived in an apartment would need a gardener. The reference to the gardener is found in Paul Rubin, *Death Wish*, PHOENIX NEW TIMES, Aug. 23, 2007, www.phoenixnewtimes.com/2007-08-23/news/death-wish.

our house when she phoned, and I remember my stepfather coldly placing the receiver on the kitchen countertop and turning back to the stove to tend to a bubbling skillet of chicken cacciatore. I could hear Jana pleading on the other end of the line.[13]

The more that van Voorhis tried to establish a normal life for herself, a life that looked like the lives of people around her, the more she was rejected. The more she was rejected, the needier she became.

Her downward spiral will be achingly familiar to many people reading this book. She began calling places where the people had to take her calls and respond. She called 911 fifty-nine times between 1998 and her death in 2007.[14] She was convinced that she had numerous physical maladies, and made trip after trip after trip to the emergency department (ED), where test after test revealed no medical disease. She called the governor's office to complain that she had been misdiagnosed. She was certain that she had cancer. She had an oncologist for eleven and a half years; toward the end of her tenure as his patient she called his office ten times a week or more. He ordered tests in response to each complaint of new symptoms, and each test came back negative. Finally, when she asked to be put into hospice, he severed his relationship with her. He was an oncologist, and she did not have cancer. Her mother, who had been her support and bulwark, who had listened to her on the telephone multiple times a day for hours in a row, developed dementia in the late 1990s and died in July 2006. A month later, in a last effort to transcend the loneliness of her life, van Voorhis joined a megachurch. In January 2007, she changed her will to leave all of her considerable estate to Pastor Richard Maraj of the church, disinheriting her sister and brother.[15]

At some point around that time, she also contacted the Final Exit Network (FEN) and had an "intake interview." In March 2007, a few weeks after her doctor "fired" her as a patient, and less than a year after the death of her mother, she initialed the necessary paperwork to go through with assisted suicide. Two FEN "exit guides," Wye Hale-Rowe and Frank Langsner, came to visit her and do a rehearsal on April 11, 2007. On April 12, 2007, van Voorhis took her own life in their presence, using helium tanks and a hood to block out oxygen.

Although she had a caring sister and brother-in-law who lived locally, and talked with her "almost every day," a brother in Washington, and a psychiatrist, van Voorhis had lost within one year the only two people who took her calls multiple times a day. In order to find life worth living, van Voorhis

[13] Jaime Joyce, *Kill Me Now: The Troubled Life and Complicated Death of Jana van Voorhis*, BuzzFeed News (Dec. 27, 2013), http://www.buzzfeed.com/jaimejoyce/kill-me-now-the-troubled-life-and-complicated-death-of-jana#.wg8bm7La0.

[14] *Id.*

[15] Pastor Maraj never claimed his $650,000 inheritance. Presumably it went to van Voorhis's sister and brother. Rubin, *supra* note 12.

simply needed more attention, reassurance, and patience than humans can provide in voluntary relationships. Van Voorhis's condition is not a terminal illness, but it aptly characterizes the situation of thousands of people in this country. I have known a number of people like her in my work as a lawyer for people with psychiatric disabilities (sadly, very few came from supportive, wealthy families). What would have happened to van Voorhis if her sister had gotten wind of her plans with Final Exit? Van Voorhis knew very well what would happen: when Hale-Rowe and Langsner suggested that she involve her sister and brother-in-law in her decision to end her life, she became extremely frightened and begged them not to call: "she would just put me away [in a mental institution]," said van Voorhis, and she was probably right. It is no answer to the van Voorhises of this world to lock them up indefinitely in state psychiatric hospitals where they will get even less attention and live out their days in numb and dehumanizing safety. As one of her Final Exit guides observed:

> Maybe we have a more enlightened vision these days, because we don't blame people for wanting to die anymore. Some of them can be made much more comfortable and can enjoy living and stay around for a long time. But others really can't, and Jana was one of them. She wasn't getting better, and she could have been sent to some kind of facility and lived another 20 years—miserably.[16]

Van Voorhis had been talking about killing herself since she was ten. Everyone who knew her knew she was suicidal. She even talked about committing suicide to her next door neighbor.[17] But people had stopped taking her seriously. As her own brother said,

> She'd swallow eight Tylenol or something and then drive herself to the ER or call 911, and they'd come racing over . . . I think we all kind of realized that this was her way of getting attention rather than actually doing harm to herself.[18]

Like van Voorhis, many people threaten to kill themselves for years. They stay alive, using suicide threats as currency to get the attention and caring that they crave. But over the years, the currency gets inevitably devalued. In van Voorhis's case, ambulances no longer bothered to take her to the ED, so her sister and one of her friends and her neighbor would take her, at her insistence, and the ED would refuse to do tests. After a while, her sister and her friend wouldn't take her either.

---

[16] Rubin, *supra* note 12.
[17] *Id.* A week before her death, she also gave the neighbor a key to her condo and said, "You may be needing this soon." The neighbor thought nothing of it because van Voorhis talked about suicide so much.
[18] Joyce, *supra* note 13.

Van Voorhis was fifty-eight and no longer had anyone to call multiple times a day. She got in touch with the FEN, and told them of her numerous medical problems. Undoubtedly it was a great relief to her to finally find people who took her at her word, who believed that she had "possible breast cancer," "lesions on her liver," and ongoing lung and back pain. She initialed a letter stating that she had been diagnosed by a physician with a hopeless illness. In April, she met two Final Exit volunteers, Hale-Rowe, a seventy-nine-year-old former family therapist, and Langsner, a former college professor, who was eighty-six at the time of his trial for manslaughter.

FEN members have been criticized for not following up with a physician or involving van Voorhis's family, and their mission statement has changed since her case. It now emphasizes the word "physical": FEN assists "mentally competent adults who suffer from fatal or irreversible physical illness, from intractable physical pain, or from a constellation of chronic, progressive physical disabilities."[19] Although FEN had previously been open to assisting people with psychiatric disabilities for whom (like van Voorhis) years of treatment had failed, her case probably spelled the end of that involvement.

If van Voorhis had committed suicide using some combination of the many, many medications that she had been prescribed over the years, her death would never have caught the attention of the national media. And this, I think, is entirely appropriate. A recurring theme of this book is that third-party involvement in suicide rightly should be an occasion for careful scrutiny, whether that third party is a medical professional, a family member, or an organization like FEN.

Van Voorhis certainly had the wherewithal at her disposal to commit suicide by herself. But, like many suicidal people, she was extremely afraid of the pain associated with suicide, and, like Kerrie Wooltorton, she did not want to die alone. In fact, in an ironic refrain of her entire life, she asked the Final Exit volunteers for so much reassurance about the pain associated with her demise that Hale-Rowe finally inquired whether she was having second thoughts and did not want to die after all (thus repeating her lifelong pattern of repeated and urgent requests for reassurance leading to the threatened departure and withdrawal of support by the person in question). Van Voorhis quickly reasserted her desire to die, and Hale-Rowe and Langsner stayed.

With the Final Exit people, van Voorhis probably felt important, and taken seriously, and treated as a competent and mature person, for the first time in years, maybe ever. It's sad that her experience of being taken seriously occurred in the context of a wish to die that may or may not have been authentic. One of the most difficult parts of this case for me is that I think van Voorhis probably did not really want to die. I think she wanted unending

---

[19] Final Exit Network, *Guiding Principles and Mission*, http://www.finalexitnet-work.org/Mission.html.

reassurance, to have her medical anxieties and worries taken seriously, to be beloved and respected and listened to unstintingly. But I also think that despite all her money and her caring family, those needs were never, ever going to be met.

Even FEN was a little wary about working with van Voorhis. There was an initial "intake interview" in February with a woman named Roberta Massey, who "red-flagged" her case because the wide range of medical problems she reported (including multiple head injuries, overexposure to radiation, lesions on her liver, and probable breast cancer) strained credulity. There were follow-up calls in March, and hours spent in person in April with Langsner and Hale-Rowe.

Although Langsner had been assigned to assist three people to die before Jana van Voorhis, all three changed their minds, and that was fine by Langsner and FEN.[20] "One of the first things that we see is if someone is hospice-eligible," said Hale-Rowe. "We do want them in hospice care if possible, to give comfort to people who are dying."[21] But van Voorhis was not hospice-eligible. She didn't even have an oncologist anymore. At the suggestion of Langsner, she ordered two helium tanks and a hood, and they stayed with her while she breathed in the helium under the hood. Then they took the tanks and the hood away and disposed of them (although not the receipts, which police found). Hale-Rowe made an anonymous call to van Voorhis's sister to tell her that someone "in the church" was concerned about her, using Langsner's cell phone, which was traced by the police. As criminals, they were hopelessly inept.

Arizona had never before criminally charged anyone with the crime of assisted suicide. The law prohibits a person to "intentionally aid another in committing suicide." Van Voorhis was a person with psychiatric disabilities who had outraged and well-off relatives, and Final Exit was, as the prosecutor pointed out, an organization that publicly proclaimed itself willing to assist nonterminally ill people to commit suicide. So Arizona went all out. They charged Hale-Rowe and Langsner, as well as Dr. Lawrence Egbert, the Medical Director of Final Exit, who never met van Voorhis but issued the approval for assisting her suicide, and Massey, a "case coordinator" for Final Exit, who spoke with van Voorhis on the telephone. All were charged with conspiracy to commit manslaughter, and Langsner was charged with manslaughter. Neither Egbert nor Massey were present at Van Voorhis' death.

Hale-Rowe pled guilty to "facilitation to commit manslaughter," in exchange for testifying for the prosecution. She also agreed to sever her connection to FEN. Massey also pled guilty to lesser charges. Langsner and Egbert, both in their eighties, went to trial, wearing Birkenstocks and

---

[20] Rubin, *supra* note 12.

[21] *Id.*

Hawaiian shirts like aging hippies:[22] Egbert, in fact, does not own a cell phone or a car and used to work for Doctors Without Borders.[23]

To prove that Egbert and Langsner had "aided" van Voorhis's suicide, the prosecutors needed to show beyond a reasonable doubt that to "aid" a suicide "means to assist in the commission of the act, either by an active participation in it or in some manner advising or encouraging it"—[24] not a difficult task, especially for Langsner.

Yet after extended deliberations that included "loud arguing,"[25] the jury acquitted Egbert and deadlocked on Langsner, with seven jurors voting for acquittal on the conspiracy charge, and four for conviction on the manslaughter charge, three for acquittal, and one who could not decide.[26] A year later, Langsner pled guilty to "endangerment," with a fine of $460, a sentence of one year's probation and his record reflecting a misdemeanor (even though endangerment is a felony). Hale-Rowe received a fine of $1840, a year's probation, and was banned from any further participation in Final Exit's programs.[27]

The failure of a jury to convict either Egbert or Langsner in Van Voorhis's case—assisting the suicide of a woman who was not terminally ill but suffered from the delusion that she was—is an extreme version of the jury and judicial nullifications that are very often the result of taking assisted-suicide cases to trial.[28] As noted in Chapter 7, jurors and judges are very reluctant to convict individuals of assisting suicide.

Yet a jury did recently convict *the organization* Final Exit Network in the death of Doreen Dunn, who had suffered from chronic pain after a medical procedure went wrong.[29] Convicting an organization carries with it a fine, but

[22] Meg Baker, *Billboard Campaign Puts Right to Die Group in Spotlight* (Fox News, July 15, 2010), http://www.foxnews.com/us/2010/07/21/radical-right-die-groups-controversial-suicide-campaign/.

[23] Sanjay Gupta, *Assisted Suicide or Manslaughter* (CNN, June 23, 2012), transcript *available at* http://www.cnn.com/TRANSCRIPTS/1206/23/hcsg.01.html.

[24] Joyce, *supra* note 13.

[25] Terry Greene Sterling, *Lawrence Egbert: Suicide Doctor's Lucky Break*, Daily Beast, Apr. 22, 2011, http://www.thedailybeast.com/articles/2011/04/22/lawerence-egbert-suicide-doctor-acquitted.html; Michael Keefer, *Jury Acquits Phoenix Doctor in Assisted Suicide Case*, Arizona Republic, Apr. 21, 2011, http://archive.azcentral.com/community/ahwatukee/articles/2011/04/21/20110421phoenix-doctor-assisted-suicide-verdict.html.

[26] *Frank Langsner Pleads Guilty to Minor Offence in Assisted Suicide Case*, Assisted-Dying Blog, July 19, 2011, http://assisted-dying.org/blog/2011/07/19/frank-langsner-pleads-guilty-to-minor-offence-in-assisted-suicide-case/.

[27] Joyce, *supra* note 13.

[28] See Chapter 7.

[29] Debra Cassens Weiss, *Final Exit Network is Convicted for Assisting Suicide*, A.B.A. J., May 15 2015, http://www.abajournal.com/news/article/final_exit_network_is_convicted_for_assisting_suicide.

(obviously) no jail time. Egbert was granted immunity for testifying against his own organization,[30] thus enabling a man who makes Jack Kevorkian look like a piker (Egbert acknowledges having helped more than 300 people to die) avoid ever being convicted of any crime associated with assisting suicide. The organization plans to appeal; that decision will come down after this book is published.

FEN operates as an interesting counter-model to the increasingly accepted U.S. framework of assisted suicide, as something that is not quite medical treatment but acceptable only with the participation of an approving physician. Medical professionals serve as the gatekeepers to determine who qualifies for assisted suicide, and they provide the assistance through prescriptions of medication. Medical and mental health professionals also serve as the gatekeepers of involuntary commitment for suicidal people. I have argued in this book that doctors and mental health professionals have been entrusted with the social role of determining culturally acceptable suicide. Physicians are so deeply embedded in mainstream culture that if they are willing to participate in assisting suicide, it goes a long way toward making it socially acceptable. This is only possible because physicians have no fear of being sued for their participation in these decisions. Mental health professionals, by contrast, are the gatekeepers of involuntary treatment for suicidality, and their potential liability ensures that they continue to open those gates more widely than necessary.

But, as FEN shows, doctors need not be involved at all. The Final Exit Network was created in 2003, when the former Hemlock Society (which had changed its name to End of Life Choices and merged with Compassion in Dying) split into Compassion & Choices and the Final Exit Network.[31] The Final Exit Network, the American Medical Association, Dr. Thomas Szasz, and Professor Kevin Yuill[32] are among the strange bedfellows who criticize involving the medical profession as gatekeepers in determining acceptable candidates for suicide. Dr. Szasz and the Final Exit Network object to medical oversight because they support suicide as a human right and object to giving power to the medical profession to determine its exercise; Yuill because he believes doctors and courts should not be overseers of our most private decisions; and the American Medical Association because doctors should not be providing their patients with the means to prematurely end their lives.

---

[30] Crimesider Staff, *Right to Die Group Convicted of Assisting Minnesota Suicide* (CBS News, May 14 2015), http://www.cbsnews.com/news/right-to-die-group-convicted-of-assisting-minnesota-suicide/.

[31] It is a little difficult to get the history straight, since the Final Exit Network and Compassion & Choices tell it differently, compare http://www.finalexitnetwork.org/About-Us.html and https://www.compassionandchoices.org/who-we-are/timeline/

[32] KEVIN YUILL, ASSISTED SUICIDE: THE LIBERAL, HUMANIST CASE AGAINST LEGALISATION (2013).

Neither Autonomy nor Paternalism: A Third Way

To me, van Voorhis's story is tragic because it exposes the inadequacy of all of our existing models. I don't think the model of autonomy served her very well, although it was better than the alternative model of involuntary detention and commitment to prevent her suicide, which wouldn't have solved her problems either. I think van Voorhis's story reflects the situation of many people who are suicidal but don't really want to die. They are suicidal because they can't live with the loneliness and rejection of a society that paints enormous dependence and neediness as either character flaws or symptoms of mental illness.[33] Even people in the "helping professions" often despise the van Voorhises they see in their practices. Of course, this is not limited to the United States. Kathleen Toole Gilhooly, the woman in Ireland who was assisted in suicide by George Exoo,[34] was described by a Scottish assisted-suicide advocate who refused to help her as "very, very lonely. She didn't want to be alone."[35]

The van Voorhises of this world form a particular subset of suicidal people, the "hard cases" that Holmes says make bad law. She is not at all similar to Josh Sebastian, Cara Anna, Anita Darcel Taylor, or many of the people I interviewed, some of whom expressed impatience with the likes of van Voorhis. People who are suicidal on a daily basis like Josh Sebastian and Wyatt Ferrera, or suicidal in cycles like Anita Darcel Taylor, or just twice and not again like Cara Anna, may lead difficult lives, but what they ask for (and deserve) from society is relatively straightforward: don't treat me as though I am incompetent or have lost my considerable intelligence and talents, or as though I should be ashamed; respect my understanding of my own needs and my liberty to make decisions about my life as I see fit. What Josh Sebastian and Anita Darcel Taylor and Wyatt Ferrera and Cara Anna need is not expensive, because it is essentially about liberty and freedom from discrimination:

---

[33] A heartbreaking line in a story about a father seeking a diploma for his son who committed suicide during his freshman year in high school, the father says, "I'll be the first to tell you Jonathan did wrong. Jonathan did the worst thing he could ever do," Katheleen Conti, *A Tribute to a Son as His Classmates Graduate*, BOSTON GLOBE, June 5, 2015, at B-5; ARTHUR CAPLAN, IS MEDICAL CARE THE RIGHT PRESCRIPTION FOR CHRONIC ILLNESS? 80 (July 2014), https://www.aei.org/wp-content/uploads/2014/07/-is-medical-care-the-right-prescription-for-chronic-illness_111427350177.pdf (noting that dependence "is not an especially popular status in our culture"). In McKay v. Bergstedt, 801 P.2d 617, 632 (Nev. 1990), the Nevada Supreme Court decides that a man who sought to disconnect his ventilator had the right to do so, and was issuing its decision in spite of his death because "[h]is memory is deserving of no taint or inference relating to an act of suicide."

[34] See Chapter 4.

[35] *Fate of U.S. Minister Rests on Extradition Hearing in Irish Assisted Suicide Case*, 21 PATIENTS RIGHTS COUNCIL UPDATE 042, 3 (Nov. 2007), http://www.patientsrightscouncil.org/site/update042/.

they should not be involuntarily committed; they should not lose their jobs; they should not be discriminated against; they should be treated like other citizens. Like lesbian, gay, bisexual, and transgender (LGBT) rights, while attaining these goals may be a cultural battle, they are easy to implement if society decides it is ready to do so. If Sebastian, Taylor, Ferrera, Anna, and the substantial number of people who are like them were terminally ill, with six months to live, and residing in Oregon or Washington or Vermont or Montana or California, there should be no question that they could avail themselves of assisted suicide if they so desired.

People like Jana van Voorhis represent the hard cases where the autonomy model falters a little. Our current model of suicide prevention is especially ill-suited to these hard cases. Van Voorhis did not simply need to be left alone to lead her life as she saw fit. If only it were that easy; in fact, she more or less needed never to be left alone.

At the same time, paternalistic coercion would not have solved anything either. To believe that the tragedy in van Voorhis's case was that FEN assisted her suicide on April 12, 2007, is to fail to understand and recognize the needs that led up to the events of April 12, which were long-standing, ongoing, and (if her life's experience was any guide) realistically unlikely to change. As a society, we see preventing suicide as analogous to snatching a person out of the way of a speeding vehicle. We don't see it as walking along the road with a person who is completely lost and uncertain about his or her destination, when we don't know the destination either. It may be a long way away. The person may never get there. But the walk is a process; it's how we stay alive.

Our current model does not emphasize a long-term process. It is focused on the car bearing down on the pedestrian, focused on and in many ways rewarding (and reimbursing) crisis. A system that is focused on crisis unsurprisingly results in repeated crises: repeated trips to the ED, repeated calls to the police and crisis lines, repeated hospitalizations, repeated suicide attempts. It's like a record (am I showing my age?) or tape that is stuck playing the same jarring crisis music over and over again. You have to get past that for the music that was meant to be heard.

While people like van Voorhis are a small subset of suicidal people, they are very important for two reasons: they dominate the use of social resources such as EDs, emergency medical technicians (EMTs), oncologists, and others; and they don't really want to die. They just want more attention and reassurance than can be voluntarily sustained in most ordinary human relationships. One of the most difficult questions of the whole suicide debate is this: do we have a social obligation to meet the needs of the van Voorhises of this world, rather than cooping them up in institutions to keep them "safe" and completely miserable?

Certainly meeting the complex emotional needs of Jana van Voorhis and people like her would require intensive human resources. On the other hand, our society funds around-the-clock intensive personal care for plenty of children and adults with incredibly complex medical needs at the cost of hundreds of thousands of dollars a year.[36] For example, Eric Radaszewski was diagnosed at age thirteen with medulloblastoma, a cancer of the brain. He suffered a severe stroke the following year. He is "immobilized, catheterized, and relies on oxygen."[37] There's more:

> Eric's current medical conditions include the lack of any meaningful pituitary gland function, which makes Eric reliant on several hormonal preparations to maintain normal bodily functions. Eric is completely reliant on outside sources of hormonal support. Eric receives thyroid treatment, adrenal hormone, and a supplemental form of testosterone. Eric is reliant on supplemental forms of nutrition given via hyperalimentation to maintain normal salt balances and caloric intake. He has difficulty absorbing and utilizing things [sic] properly by mouth so he requires intravenous administration.
>
> Eric has an active seizure disorder that is treated with two different seizure medications. By virtue of Eric's disease state, Eric has a chronic immune suppressive condition that causes him to be very prone to infections, including pneumonia, urinary tract infections, and soft-tissue infections. These infections oftentimes require that Eric receive very strong antibiotic therapy through home intravenous antibiotic therapy. Eric's hormonal therapies have resulted in deformities of his bones and spinal column. Eric has trouble breathing properly and is prone to aspirating things he eats into his lungs. The spinal deformity is progressive and affects his ability to breathe, especially when he sleeps at night.
>
> Eric is globally developmentally delayed. He communicates on a simple basis, but he cannot communicate how he feels very clearly in most situations. Eric receives between 20 to 25 different medications on a daily basis, and approximately 10 other medications on an as-needed basis for things such as nausea and pain.[38]

Eric also likes drawing and painting, going to the movies, and watching videos.[39] The cost of his care at home is $20,868.19 per month, and that's only because his parents, who are aging and have serious medical issues

---

[36] Radaszewski v. Maram, 383 F.3d 599 (7th Cir. 2004) (child with stroke and brain cancer requires round-the-clock nursing costing between $180,000 and $240,000 per year); Grooms v. Maram, 563 F. Supp. 2d 840 (N.D. Ill. 2008) (child with type II glycogen storage disease requires round-the-clock nursing costing $221,760 per year); Wilborn by Wilborn v. Martin, 965 F. Supp. 2d 834 (M.D. Tenn. 2013) (child with brain anoxia needs round-the-clock medical care costing $238,320 per year).
[37] Radaszewski v. Maram, 2008 U.S. Dist. LEXIS 24923 (N.D. Ill. Mar. 26, 2008).
[38] Id.
[39] Id.

themselves, provide eight hours of the care he needs per day. That $20,868.19 per month only buys sixteen hours of skilled nursing care a day (and all the prescriptions and equipment).[40] Medicaid pays this cost.

We have decided as a society that we owe it to Eric Radaszewski to keep him alive. Do we have the same obligation to Jana van Voorhis? Because we could probably, in fact, have kept her alive with intensive peer support, "wraparound services," a personal care assistant (PCA), or all three. In very different ways, she and Radaszewski need the same thing—people paying intense attention to them in their homes. A Medicaid waiver funds states to provide thousands of people who are elderly or have serious physical disabilities with 12-24 hours a day of in-home services.[41] States provide this program for people with psychiatric disabilities far more rarely, and private insurance more rarely still.

The federal government doesn't prohibit states from using the PCA benefit for people with psychiatric disabilities. It's just that most states don't do it. Massachusetts does: I know someone in Massachusetts who has a PCA, and despite recurrent suicidality and a fairly severe psychiatric disability, she has not been hospitalized in years. I think it's likely that the provision of a PCA to this woman has saved Massachusetts a substantial amount of money over the years. I think the program may have saved this woman's life. What I know is that her quality of life has been immeasurably improved. As Lea Morin, another woman with a psychiatric disability who uses a PCA, says,

> [On] an emotional and psychological level I can't afford to be isolated. My PCA will give me rides to the clubhouse, food shopping, doctors' appointments, etc. I'm a very sociable person. I need contact. My PCA is my friend and we do things together. Sometimes we just listen to the radio together or go out for an inexpensive meal or she cooks a meal for me if I'm not feeling up to it. I also take a lot of different medications and my PCA helps me keep them organized and we always check to make sure I have enough.[42]

PCAs can meet other needs for people who have psychiatric disabilities and are suicidal: "help with hygiene and getting out of bed when severely depressed; getting support during times of feeling suicidal; being driven . . . to work or appointments; . . . help[ing] during flashback experiences, [and] reality testing if you're having frightening, suspicious or paranoid thinking."[43]

---

40 *Id.*
41 Personal care services can be offered as an optional part of a state plan under Medicaid, or through a Section 1915 waiver under Medicaid, see 42 C.F.R. 441.450.
42 Patricia Deegan, *Personal Care Attendant Services Available to People with Psychiatric Disabilities*, NATIONAL EMPOWERMENT CENTER (2013), http://www.power2u.org/articles/selfhelp/pca.html.
43 *Id.*

Let's not compare van Voorhis with Radaszewski, who had childhood cancer. Rather, let's compare her with Jeremy Wilborn.[44] Wilborn tried to commit suicide as a child and failed, and as a result suffers from extremely serious brain damage because his brain was deprived of oxygen before his life was saved. He is "unable to attend to his bodily needs and unable to communicate, except that family members interpret his facial expressions and sounds as communicating with them."[45] Wilborn receives twenty-four hours of home care seven days a week, at an annual cost of $238,320.00. If we as a society could have kept van Voorhis alive at a fraction of that cost by providing her with a PCA or peer support services or wraparound support, should we have done that?

If the answer is no, as it currently is in most states,[46] I think we should be very clear why not, and what the logical extension of our answer means in policy and legal terms. There are several possible responses to explain why people like Wilborn receive enormous social resources *after* their suicide attempts made them brain damaged and disabled, but not before. Some of them are pretty distasteful, but let's look at them all.

One of the major barriers to providing services that will actually help suicidal people is an issue I have highlighted in my previous writing[47] about accommodations for people with psychiatric disabilities: while most people don't want braille books, sign language interpreters, ramps, or (in the case of Radaszewski and Wilborn) intravenous (IV) lines for food and antibiotics, everyone wants flexible work schedules, transfers to positions where we won't be "subject to prolonged and inordinate stress [by coworkers],"[48] and a PCA to cook a meal for us if we're "not feeling up to it." The attractiveness of the service, combined with the ubiquity and imprecision of suicidality, leads to a kind of combined floodgates/moral hazard policy concern: too many people are going to say they are suicidal to get the PCA. For every Jeremy Wilborn who survives a suicide attempt with serious brain damage, there are hundreds of other kids who just die, and save us both the suicide prevention money and the bill for post-suicide intensive home care. Too many suicidal people—it's just too expensive. Too many people who would want a PCA—ditto.

So let's look at this a little more closely. The average *annual* salary of a PCA in this country is about $21,000 to $23,000 a year.[49] Estimates of

---

[44] See *Wilborn by Wilborn*, 965 F. Supp. 2d 834.

[45] *Id.* at 836.

[46] Four states currently provide PCA services to people with psychiatric disabilities through Medicaid waivers.

[47] SUSAN STEFAN, HOLLOW PROMISES (2001).

[48] Gaul v. Lucent Technologies, 134 F.3d 576, 577 (3rd Cir. 1998).

[49] *Personal Care Attendant (PCA) Salary (United States)*, PAYSCALE.COM, http://www.payscale.com/research/US/Job=Personal_Care_Attendant_(PCA)/Hourly_Rate.

psychiatric hospitalizations differ dramatically, by payer (Medicare and private insurance pay more than Medicaid) and state. The Agency for Health Care Research and Quality estimated the average hospital stay for mental health purposes would cost $6600 in 2013.[50] But in 2007, the average cost of a single hospital stay for a person with a mental health and/or substance abuse diagnosis in the State of Washington was between $21,000 and $23,000.[51] And many people only have a PCA for a few hours a day, so a given PCA can probably serve two or three people a day.

If someone is on Medicaid or Medicare, they have already qualified for a program that will provide them ED and inpatient hospital services on the basis of their poverty, age, disability, or all three. Why not provide something that is less expensive and that actually helps?[52] Why be so worried about free riders? We don't ask people to go through screening before they call hot lines or warm lines for suicidal people, and indeed, many people call who are not suicidal at all.[53] At Stepping Stone, the crisis respite centers in Claremont, New Hampshire, all services are free to New Hampshire residents.[54] Afiya, the crisis house in Western Massachusetts, is also free. They have modest waiting lists, and certainly both Massachusetts and New Hampshire could use more peer crisis houses, but the fact that they are free doesn't mean that they are overrun. PCAs could, like so many other alleged "entitlements," be subject to waiting lists and prioritization.

---

[50] Audrey J. Weiss, Marguerite L. Barrett, & Claudia A. Steiner, *Trends and Projections in Inpatient Costs and Utilization, 2003–2013* (Agency for Healthcare Res. & Quality, Healthcare Cost & Util. Project, Stat. Brief No. 175, July 2014), http://www.hcup-us.ahrq.gov/reports/statbriefs/sb175-Hospital-Cost-Utilization-Projections-2013.pdf.

[51] Washington State Institute for Public Policy, *The Costs and Frequency of Mental Health-Related Hospitalizations in Washington State Are Increasing* 5 (Doc. No. 09-04-3401, Apr. 2009), exhibit 6, http://www.wsipp.wa.gov/ReportFile/1040.

[52] PCAs have been shown to be helpful, Linda Stewart, "Personal Assistance Services for People with Psychiatric Disabilities," in World Institute on Disability, Personal Assistance Services: Political and Personal Insights in Developing a National System (1991); Patricia E. Deegan, *The Independent Living Movement and People with Psychiatric Disabilities: Taking Back Control Over Our Own Lives*, 15 PSYCHOSOCIAL REHAB. J. 3 (1992), P. J. Dautel & Lex Frieden, *Consumer Choice and Control: Personal Attendant Services and Supports in America* (Rep. of the Blue Ribbon Panel on Personal Assistance Serv., Indepen. Living Res. Utilization, 1999); D. D. Pita, M. L. Ellison, & M. Farkas, *Exploring Personal Assistance Services for People with Psychiatric Disabilities: Need, Policy and Practice*, 12 J. DISABILITY POL'Y STUD. 2 (2001).

[53] See Diane Ackerman's account of her experiences on a crisis hot line, A SLENDER THREAD: REDISCOVERING HOPE AT THE HEART OF CRISIS (1998), in which she tells of a few people who regularly call the crisis hotline in order to have someone listen to their pornographic thoughts.

[54] Stepping Stone, *About Us*, http://www.steppingstonenextstep.org/5.html.

Instead of pouring millions of research dollars into devising yet another set of five questions to figure out who's going to commit suicide, maybe we should divert that money to fund PCAs and crisis respite, paying for someone to provide a personal connection and help out another person who's floundering and desperate. It seems increasingly likely that this would be a cost-effective policy. Why not adopt it?

Maybe the reason we don't have more PCAs and crisis respite is the social assumption that being suicidal is both voluntary and somehow immoral, so we don't want to "reward" or "encourage" people for their suicidality by giving them PCAs, or wraparound services, or other desirable services. To the people who talk about "rewarding" suicidal people, I say: let's be clear who you are talking about. You may be talking about the adolescent or adult version of the children you felt so sorry for when you read about them in the paper, children with lives like this:

> Because I was raised in my grandparents' household, and because
> my grandparents always welcomed their children back into their
> home, it was a sort of revolving door situation. While my mom
> and I have always been close, she wasn't always living in our home.
> My uncle, whose presence in our home was a constant, had a
> crack problem and brought a lot of violence into my life in a lot of
> different ways, and I didn't know how to deal with it. He pulled me
> aside when I was 11 or 12, showed me a gun and bullets and said, "I
> am going to kill your grandmother, she's a waste of skin." She was
> my best friend.[55]

Or read—please read—the suicide note of the brilliant inventor and Princeton graduate student Bill Zeller, who killed himself at the age of twenty-seven after a childhood racked by sexual abuse (I would have excerpted it, but he specifically asked that if it was republished, it must be reproduced in its entirety).[56] People who think in terms of "rewarding" suicidality should think about trading lives with a person who wants to die, complete with its backstory and all its "rewards."

And when people talk about suicide being voluntary, I want them to know how hard most suicidal people try to live, all the things that they do, all the suffering that they go through, and the pain they endure to stay alive. I agree that most suicides are voluntary and competent, within the context of the person's life as he or she understands it. It is also true that ultimately the person himself or herself must make the decision to live, but that doesn't mean that people who had no control over the circumstances of rape, abuse,

---

[55] Interview with Dese'Rae Stage (Dec. 2, 2014).
[56] *Bill Zeller, Princeton Grad Student and "Brilliant" Programmer, Dies in Apparent Suicide*, DAILY PRINCETONIAN, Jan. 7, 2011, *available at* HUFFINGTON POST, http://www.huffingtonpost.com/2011/01/07/bill-zeller-dead-princeton_805689.html.

of his mental state, his liberty interest would provide no basis
for asserting a right to terminate his life with or without the
assistance of other persons. Our societal regard for the value of an
individual life, as reflected in our Federal and State Constitutions,
would never countenance an assertion of liberty over life in such
circumstances.[63]

Thus, in one swift piece of rhetoric, the court manages to both devalue the
lives of severely physically disabled people *and* the rights and degree of suffering of psychiatrically disabled ones. While people who kill themselves
because of unbearable emotional pain are "cowardly,"[64] people with severe
physical disabilities or terminal illnesses who opt for assisted suicide are
invariably "brave."[65] But Bergstedt wasn't brave. The Nevada Supreme Court
made chillingly clear that Bergstedt wanted to die because he was terrified
about the lack of social resources to help him live after his father, who was his
primary caretaker, died:

It is apparent that Kenneth's suffering resulted more from his fear
of the unknown than from any source of physical pain. After more
than two decades as a quadriplegic under the loving care of his
parents, Kenneth understandably feared for the quality of his life
after the death of his father . . . He feared that some mishap would
occur with his ventilator without anyone being present to correct
it, and that he would suffer an agonizing death as a result.[66]

Call me a pie-in-the-sky idealist, but it doesn't seem to me that the proper
response to someone who is afraid that no one will be there to help him if a
mishap occurs with his ventilator after his father dies is to support his right
to end his life by disconnecting the ventilator.[67] Isn't it possible to devise a
in-home support system for Mr. Bergstedt that has the kind of back-up to
alleviate his understandable fears? Is the only alternative disconnecting the
machine in a "vindication" of his rights or forcing him to live out his days
lying in his own waste in a nursing home?

And right there, the distinctions between the situation of people with
severe physical disabilities and people who are suicidal are overshadowed by

---

[63] *McKay v. Bergstedt*, 801 P.2d 617, 625.
[64] Elias Isquith, *Fox News' Shep Smith: Robin Williams Was "Such a Coward,"* SALON,
Aug. 12, 2014, http://www.salon.com/2014/08/12/fox_news_shep_smith_robin_
williams_was_such_a_coward/ (Smith later apologized for this remark).
[65] Matthew Balan, *NBC, CBS Praise "Brave" Brittany Maynard After Her Assisted
Suicide, Hail "Freedom of Choice,"* LIFE NEWS, Nov. 4, 2014, http://www.lifenews.
com/2014/11/04/nbc-cbs-praise-brave-brittany-maynard-after-her-assisted-
suicide-hail-freedom-of-choice/.
[66] *McKay v. Bergstedt*, at 624.
[67] He had in fact died prior to the opinion.

one great commonality. It is the reflexive social and legal response to both their situations, which is exclusion and segregation—whether in hospitals, nursing homes, or state institutions—rather than providing them the help that they need to thrive in the communities where they live. This policy response is backed up by law—reimbursements by Medicaid and Medicare and private health insurance, civil commitment law—which help funnel disabled and suicidal people out of sight, into facilities where any rational person might question the value of continued life.

This segregation results, of course, from a second commonality: the social response to suicidal people and severely disabled people. I don't like the word "stigma"—it seems to float around in a kind of accountability vacuum. I prefer "discrimination." Whether expressed as fear or stupidity or diffidence or revulsion or embarrassed averting of the gaze or profound uneasiness, it means that people who are suicidal or have attempted suicide and people with severe physical disabilities have a hard time getting an education, a job, meaningful friendships or romance, or keeping custody of their children if they do find romance: all the things that add up to social integration.

Because we are so uncomfortable in the presence of suicidal people or severely disabled people, we don't talk very much about their situations. We don't ask suicidal people or physically disabled people what their lives are like at all, or else we end up having very weird conversations, sometimes about both topics in a single conversation. John Hockenberry, a host on National Public Radio who uses a wheelchair, recalls rolling onto a plane and being greeted by a flight attendant who said to him, "I guess you are the first handicapped person I've ever met up close. Have you ever thought of killing yourself?"[68] Harriet McBryde Johnson, who was severely physically disabled, wrote that strangers would come up to her in the street and say, "If I had to live like you, I think I'd kill myself."[69] Duane French, a Washington activist whose body is almost completely paralyzed and who opposes assisted suicide, said the same thing: people's "earnest expressions of admiration that came, he said, in various forms of the same thought: 'If I were in your position, I would kill myself.'"[70]

So it's not surprising that people with severe physical disabilities, who are used to being shunted away into nursing homes, having very few options offered to them to ease their way to education and employment, and generally being discriminated against, are suspicious about the advantages of

---

[68] JOHN HOCKENBERRY, MOVING VIOLATIONS: WAR ZONES, WHEELCHAIRS AND DECLARATIONS OF INDEPENDENCE 97 (1995).

[69] Harriet McBryde Johnson, *Unspeakable Conversations*, N. Y. TIMES MAG. (Feb. 16, 2003), http://www.nytimes.com/2003/02/16/magazine/unspeakable-conversations.html?pagewanted=2. This is one of the best articles I have ever read.

[70] Daniel Bergner, *Death in the Family*, N. Y. TIMES MAG. (Dec. 2, 2007), http://www.nytimes.com/2007/12/02/magazine/02suicide-t.html?pagewanted=9&_r=1&.

legalizing assisted suicide. Some people with disabilities favor assisted suicide; the assistance is a kind of accommodation for being unable to do by one's self what others could do.[71] Others, like Carol Gill, are skeptical of the beneficence and empathy of people who imagine that the lives severely disabled people lead are an endless horror.[72]

By contrast, people with invisible wounds, amputations, and horrendous traumatic damage are rarely told how courageous and admirable they are, or even necessarily believed about their pain. They may be condemned as "attention-seeking," berated for being "oversensitive," rejected, or even punished by healthcare staff: more than one person has reported being denied local anesthetic when her self-injuries were stitched by healthcare workers who were explicitly angry at a person who would attempt suicide.[73] As Steve Periard says, "The pain is so intense you are unable to consider anything but stopping that pain. The fact that people don't understand just makes the situation worse."[74] Indeed, people who have had both medical and mental conditions report clearly that the mental conditions cause greater suffering, in part because of our social response to them:

> I had cancer when I was little, but that was different. The world
> stops when you have cancer. My anxiety and depression has
> been much more debilitating and difficult than my cancer. It's so
> much harder. You're supposed to take care of it on your own time.
> Therapy during lunch, take your pills at breakfast or dinner, and
> it's not supposed to affect the rest of the day. You're supposed to
> take care of it yourself.[75]

I don't think we should legalize assisted suicide for chronic, untreatable, unendurable pain. But if we do, it is pretty clear to me that people who have long-term psychiatric disabilities that are "refractory" to treatment would have to be included,[76] as long as every nonintrusive approach had been tried: PCAs, peer support, the problem-solving approaches of Collaborative Assessment and Management of Suicidality (CAMS), cognitive behavioral therapy (CBT), and dialectical behavior therapy (DBT), care that was trauma-informed and respectful. You can have some relatively objective boundary

[71] Andrew I. Batavia, *A Call for Civility in the Disability/Assisted Suicide Debate*, 7 PSYCHOLOGY, PUB. POL'Y & L. 728 (2001).

[72] Carol Gill, *Professionals, Disabilities and Assisted Suicide: An Examination of the Relevant Empirical Evidence and Reply to Batavia*, 6 PSYCHOLOGY, PUB. POL'Y & L. 526, 528–30 (2000).

[73] SUSAN STEFAN, EMERGENCY DEPARTMENT TREATMENT OF THE PSYCHIATRIC PATIENT: POLICY ISSUES AND LEGAL REQUIREMENTS (2006).

[74] Interview with Steve Periard (Aug. 25, 2014).

[75] Interview with Christine O'Hagan (Nov. 21, 2013).

[76] See discussion regarding Anita Darcel Taylor, Chapter 1.

like "six months to live" that includes neither Josh Sebastian or Elizabeth Bouvia. But you cannot honor Elizabeth Bouvia's subjective understanding of the quality of her life and dismiss Josh Sebastian's evaluation of a state that has existed at least as long with at least as much treatment.

I understand that if this were the case, some people would die who otherwise would not have chosen to end their lives, but I think that is the fundamental assumption of assisted suicide. If death is going to be framed as a social benefit, then people with psychiatric disabilities should not be denied the benefit on the basis of discriminatory assumptions about their competence, or that their condition is somehow less painful than people with physical disabilities. It is one of the core aspects of discrimination against people who are suicidal and people with psychiatric disabilities to assume that emotional or spiritual pain is not as bad as physical pain.

This opinion is basically shared, with a lot of ambivalence, by the people I surveyed who had attempted suicide. Both in the survey and in the interviews, I asked people who had attempted suicide the following question: "Do you support the expansion of assisted suicide to include adults with psychiatric disabilities who have tried every treatment and been unable to find anything to help their condition?" In the survey, the choices were "Yes," "No," "It depends," and "Other" with space for comments. Many people were torn, even agonized, about this issue. A plurality of people—just over 36%—supported assisted suicide for people with psychiatric disabilities for whom treatments had been unsuccessful and who wanted assistance to kill themselves, closely followed by 27.66% of people who did not. "It depends" garnered only 12%, and "Other," which permitted the responder to write in an answer, received 23.83%.

The people who answered "Yes" focused on the incredible pain that people with untreatable psychiatric disabilities endure and/or endorsed powerful philosophies of personal autonomy. Currently, the five U.S. states that permit assisted suicide focus on the futility of medical treatment (patient must have less than six months to live) rather than either the pain endured by the individual or individual autonomy and self-determination.

The futility of available treatment was a major focus of those who answered "It depends" to my question about assisted suicide for people with psychiatric disabilities. They tended to highlight the yawning abyss between what people need to stay alive and what is currently available to them:

> **My response is actually, it depends, but I wanted to clarify.
> I actually do believe a person has a right to end their life if they
> so choose. I also believe that treatment in this country is so
> backwards that we have a long way to go before the system is good
> enough to consider assisted suicide. I had to go way outside of the
> system to get what I needed and we are only beginning to explore
> true alternatives to healing. This question actually (excuse me)
> pisses me off because treatment is so limited and small minded.

**I would welcome suicide if we have no access to safe, knowledgeable care. We can only suffer for so long.

**It depends. I think the current treatments available for psychiatric challenges are inadequate and often make people feel worse. We need to move toward more humane kinds of treatments, less coercion, fewer drugs, and more support.

**The way the current system works, yes. If the system were to change where getting one on one long term counseling was actually made accessible and more programs existed that helped individuals with community and job involvement, then no.

**I think so many times folks have just not been able to access the right kind of treatment for them. I believe there is almost always hope; we as a society don't do a very good job of imparting that to others.

It is a transcendently worthwhile social goal to proclaim that all lives are worth living, and not to budge from the limitation of assisted suicide to terminal illness. But why do we insist in this country on the sanctity of life, but not on the quality of life? If people with chronic and disabling conditions cannot avail themselves of assisted suicide because we want to send them a message about the value of their lives, wouldn't that message be more credible if it was backed up with a little help—help with decent housing and healthcare, protection from violence and bullying, flexibility and accommodation through the bad times, a little personal care to soften the exhaustion of getting through the day?

This is the issue posed by the people who responded "It depends" to the question about assisted suicide for people with psychiatric disabilities: does denying assisted suicide to people who are suffering unendurable emotional pain because society is not willing to fund the kind of healthcare or personal support they need make them hostages to our desire for social change? Is it like denying terminal cancer patients the right to die because if they hung around suffering in excruciating pain it might accelerate funding for cancer research?

Or are we being paternalistic to impose our affirmation of the worth of their lives on their own, more first-hand assessment? The "Other" responses included a person who didn't support "assisted" suicide because "I support the blanket right for all adults over 18 years of age to exit this life without ANY government oversight. The only reason 'assistance' is required is because the government has prohibited easy access to the drugs that make for a peaceful death."

Conclusion

When you look at the literature put out by Compassion & Choices, it is quite clear that the principles underlying their position oppose any limitations on people's rights to make their own choices about ending their lives. In one photograph, a person holds a sign saying, "I support medical aid in dying because only I can know what's right for me . . . I have the right to die peacefully when, where, and with who I want to."[77]

This is a venerable philosophical position, most clearly associated with John Stuart Mill:[78] a person can do anything with his or her body, as long as it does not harm others. Of course, suicide does harm others, often for generations. Justice Stevens used this argument to support state laws prohibiting assisting suicide in most cases.[79] The argument that one's suicide would hurt other people has been made through time, and recently in a well-received book.[80]

When I was younger and stronger, and had less experience of life, I was a whole-hearted advocate of the Mills position, because (this is especially true in a life devoted to advocacy for people with psychiatric disabilities) all I could see was the harm done by the State in the name of coercive beneficence. As one respondent to my survey said, assisted suicide for people with psychiatric disabilities is already happening in the form of neglect and abusive treatments that lead to premature mortality rates for this population of people. I just wanted the State to leave people alone, get out of the suicide business, and let people work out their own fates for themselves. I am still against force and involuntary treatment in almost all circumstances.

But now I think the Mills autonomy and rights perspective lets the State off the hook too easily. Just leave us all alone, to struggle and flounder and

---

[77] George Brown & Tribune Media Wire, *Three File Lawsuit in California for Right to Physician-Assisted Suicide* (News 3-WREG, May 19, 2015), http://wreg.com/2015/05/19/terminally-ill-christian-mom-sues-for-right-to-die-her-way/ (the photograph is credited to Compassion & Choices).

[78] Although some have argued that Mill would not approve of suicide or assisted suicide for the same reason he would not permit voluntary slavery, that it undercut the value of life and liberty on which society is based. Susan M. Wolf, *Physician-Assisted Suicide, Abortion, and Treatment Refusal: Using Gender to Analyze the Difference*, in PHYSICIAN-ASSISTED SUICIDE 175 (Robert Weir ed., 1997).

[79] See Chapter 2.

[80] Jennifer Michael Hecht in her book STAY: A HISTORY OF SUICIDE AND THE PHILOSOPHIES AGAINST IT (2013). As noted in Chapter 2, while I have certainly known families wounded for generations by suicide, I don't like Hecht's argument, because it devalues the life of a person who is alone in the world and reinforces that person's loneliness and miserable and distorted intuition that his or her life is worthless. I have spent too much time at state institutions with people whose families completely abandoned them to the tender mercies of institutional care to believe that a person's worth is measured by the number of people who would be hurt by his or her self-destruction.

weaken and then give us access to prescription drugs so we can die, and pat yourself on the back for respecting our autonomy, while avoiding difficult questions about why so many people in our country want to end their lives in the first place. I think people like Michelle Sese-Khalid deserve better than to be left alone in their houses after they have been raped, jailed, and lost their children. Offering a painless assisted death to terminally ill people suffering from cancer because of the Love Canal, or to people suffering from radiation sickness after Hiroshima, might be a genuinely merciful thing to do. But no one would suggest that we shouldn't look into nuclear proliferation treaties and environmental regulations, reform, and oversight, to prevent the suffering in the first place.

Prison suicides often cause an inquiry into prison conditions. The suicide of children makes us look at bullying in school. People are suicidal in part because of larger systemic issues of child abuse, domestic violence, bullying, and trauma at home and overseas. They are suicidal in part because they have biological conditions that do not get the attention or care that medical conditions do. They are suicidal in part because of things that society can do nothing about: the death of a parent, the breakup of a marriage, infidelity, and terminal illness. People should have their own decisions about life and death respected, but they should get help, too—not help to die, but help to change their lives into lives worth living. For the most part, they know what they need: to stay in school, to get support taking care of their children, to be taught a new perspective to frame their problems and solve them, to get a bit of a break and some rest, and to have a community that sticks by them for the long, long haul, to have someone listen. They know what they don't need: involuntary hospitalization, getting shot by police, moralizing judgments by people who don't have a clue what they've been through, and to never be permitted to actually articulate how terribly they are feeling without having their drug dosage increased.

So, in summary, I offer my unified field theory of suicide. First, there *should* be a unified theory of suicide: there should be policies and laws that apply to everyone, not parallel tracks for society and a third rail for the folks with psychiatric disabilities, untouchable and dangerous. Second, we should all talk more about feeling suicidal. Just like LGBT issues in the past, you'd be amazed how many people around you have personal experiences relating to suicide. People didn't talk about those issues in the past because it meant a significant personal risk of discrimination, discrediting, even violence. People should talk more about being suicidal, and the current wisdom—that talking this way means that the person spoken to should immediately "seek help" from a professional qualified to deal with these extraordinary thoughts, that the baton of the uncomfortable conversation should be handed off as quickly as possible to some professional—needs to change. It wasn't so long ago that this same advice was given about homosexuality, with encouraging news about professional treatment: "After reviewing a number of psychoanalytic, group, and behavioral studies, Clippinger (1974) concluded that 'at least 40% of the homosexuals were cured and an additional 10–30% of the homosexuals were improved.'"[81]

Being suicidal, unlike homosexuality, is sometimes the symptom of a condition that should be treated, but not always. It's mostly a part of being human that people have struggled with for years. And whether or not it is a symptom of a treatable condition, people should not risk being involuntarily detained for talking about how they are feeling. They should not be involuntarily committed solely because they are suicidal, unless they don't know what they are doing or have no control over their actions. Mental health professionals should not be the gatekeepers of permissible speech about wanting to die, holding the keys to the institution if the conversation gets too uncomfortable. If they don't have the keys, they also should not have the liability. This will permit people who are thinking about dying to speak their thoughts more freely, permit mental health professionals to provide the kind of help that works, and save lives in the long run.

Conversely, a third party who actually causes the death of someone else should never have their actions characterized using the word "suicide." Doctors engage in euthanasia in other countries; it should never be legal here. Family members who kill their spouses or children or siblings should not be lauded for their mercy or compassion; they should be subject to very close investigation. Police who kill people may have had no reasonable choice, but I think we should stop using the phrase "suicide by cop."

Providing assistance to a person who is suicidal should also be illegal, except (maybe) people who are terminally ill. Even in those cases the help should come, if at all possible, in a way that does not directly involve the medical profession as gatekeepers—for example, competent people who are in hospice should have identification cards that entitle them to terminal medication without a doctor's prescription (see Chapter 5). If medical gatekeepers have to be involved, they should be people who have treated the person long enough to have knowledge of the person's character and values over time, not just a Compassion & Choices member with an M.D.

People who are chronically and incurably (but not terminally) ill should not be helped to die. If we ever get to the point where we permit that, then we must also permit people with chronic, "refractory" psychiatric disabilities to participate. But better, far better, to focus, like the title of the play, on "The How and the Why."[82]

"How" means paying a lot more attention to blocking access to means of suicide, covering up exposed pipes in psychiatric hospitals, really pushing

[81] P. Scott Richards, *The Treatment of Homosexuality: Some Historical, Contemporary and Personal Perspectives*, 19 Ass'n Mormon Couns. & Psychotherapists J. 29, 30 (1993).

[82] Sarah Treem, "The How and the Why" first performed in 2011.

child access prevention (CAP) laws, at the very least, and suing and criminally prosecuting people who leave loaded guns lying around. In the mental health field, professionals need to pay more attention to their prescription habits, especially with people who are known substance abusers or have issues with confusion. A public health approach to access to means does not mean forcing hospital patients to clothe themselves in paper johnnies or submit to strip searches; we have many, many avenues to explore without interfering with people's dignity, especially people who have been traumatized in the past.

And that past trauma leads to the more important public health question: why? Why does the person want to die? Sometimes it really is a result of a medication reaction or a symptom of a psychiatric condition. But a lot of the time it is not. It is easier for us to think about suicide as the symptom of a biological condition so that we don't have to think about traumatized children,[83] lonely old white men, kids going from their proms to war zones, transgender individuals terrified of beatings and worse, and athletes out of the spotlight whose brains are relentlessly deteriorating.

There are ways to help, at least some of these people, especially by preventing the violence, abuse, and trauma in the first place, or by looking for it and talking about it before reaching for a prescription pad and the phone number of psychiatric emergency services. One of the most important messages of this book, on an individual and policy level, is that suicidal people are not the special and exclusive province of the mental health profession: they are us, all of us, not to be exiled and segregated or treated as "sick." Anyone can listen, even to an agitated and sobbing person.

Another important message of this book, on an individual and policy level, is that helping means not needing to control the situation and the person at all costs. Mental health professionals might be able to help a lot more if our society did not, as a matter of policy and law, expect them to control, restrain, restrict, constrain—it hardly leaves time for sitting and listening. Ceding control does mean acknowledging that some people will die, as they do now. We cannot stop all suicide, even trying our very best. No one is to blame for this. No one is liable for this. It's no one's fault. I believe if we give up trying to exert total control over suicidal people, fewer people will die, because more people will be able to speak freely and have hope, fewer people will be damaged by the experience of coercion and involuntary treatment, and people will be less terrified of asking for help. As Sean Donovan, who runs a group for people who are suicidal and has been suicidal himself, says, "What we've found is that by letting go of this need to control, ultimately, whether someone lives or dies that many more people find the wisdom and strength within themselves to live, and live on their own terms."[84]

---

[83] S. R. Dube, R. F. Anda, V. J. Fellitti, et al., *Childhood Abuse, Household Dysfunction, and the Risk of Attempted Suicide Throughout the Lifespan: Findings from the Adverse Childhood Experiences Study*, 286 J. Am. Med. Ass'n 3089 (2001).

[84] Personal communication from Sean Donovan to the author (June 19, 2015).

A small minority of people—people who are drunk, or impulsive, or hearing angry commands to kill themselves—do need to be held safe, for a very short time, whether they want it or not. But for most suicidal people, the involuntary trip to the ED just confirms that life has nothing hopeful to offer. People who are desperate and despairing are looking for answers and comfort as much as they are looking for death: they may find some comfort or answers in peer crisis centers, or in spirituality, from their dogs,[85] or from music or natural beauty. Generally speaking, they won't find much comfort or answers in an ED cubicle.

As I have tried to point out in this book, these observations have implications in policy and law: from focusing on ED diversion to permitting service dogs in residences and hospitals to placing more emphasis on spirituality to understanding the connection between childhood trauma and adult suicidality. Most of all, we need to understand, as Edwin Shneidman taught us years ago, to approach suicidality as its own issue, not necessarily involving mental illness at all. I have attached sample statutes and regulations in Appendix B to get us started.

---

[85] Some would even include cats.

Appendix A: Model Statutes

MODEL STATUTE: Civil Commitment/Provider Immunity

THE STATE OF [   ]

———————————

In the Year Two Thousand and Sixteen

———————————

AN ACT PERTAINING TO IMPROVING CARE FOR PEOPLE WHO ARE SUICIDAL

Be it enacted by the Senate and House of Representatives, and by the authority of the same, as follows:

Section 1. This Act may be cited as "The Suicide Prevention and Treatment Improvement Act."

Section 2. Findings and Purpose. (a) The ___Legislature finds and declares that

(1) The willingness of mental health professionals to offer their services to suicidal individuals is deterred by the potential for liability actions against them;
(2) The willingness of suicidal individuals to seek help is deterred by the fear of involuntary hospitalization and treatment;
(3) The vast majority of individuals with suicidal ideation do not attempt or commit suicide;

(4) The scarcity and expense of inpatient beds requires that they be available for patients who truly need them;

(5) The most seriously suicidal individuals are often unable to find professionals willing to treat them;

(6) The law is unclear as to the relative responsibilities of provider and patient in cases where an individual is suicidal;

(7) As a result, insurance costs increase, treatment of suicidal people is difficult to obtain, and emergency department visits are increased;

(8) Clarifying and limiting the liability risks assumed by mental health professionals would improve the treatment provided

(b) The purpose of this Act is to promote the availability of treatment to people who are suicidal by protecting people who seek treatment for suicidality from involuntary treatment, and reducing unnecessary liability costs by clarifying the limitations on actions available in the case of suicide attempts or injuries by outpatients treated by mental health providers in the community.

Section 3. Amending Civil Commitment Law

[Insert current legislative provision relating to civil commitment for danger to self here] is amended to provide:

"Danger to self" is established by demonstrating that the person has recently inflicted serious bodily injury on himself or herself or has attempted suicide or serious self-injury and there is a reasonable probability that the conduct will be repeated if admission is not ordered.[1] Any individual who seeks help for suicidal ideation, thoughts about suicide, and urges to commit suicide is not "dangerous to self" under this subsection, provided that nothing in this provision shall limit voluntary hospitalization for suicidality.

Sec. 4. **Immunity from liability for suicide of outpatient treated in the community.** (a) A person licensed to practice medicine under the provisions of [insert relevant state licensing statute here]____, a person licensed as a psychologist under the provisions of __, or a person licensed as a social worker under the provisions of __, shall be immune from liability for civil damages to any patient or patient's estate for any personal injuries or death arising out of a suicide attempt or suicide of any non-hospitalized patient, which is alleged to result from acts or omissions in the care of such patient. The immunity in this subsection shall not apply to intentional or reckless acts or omissions [or gross, willful, or wanton negligence].

---

[1] This language is based on ARK. CODE § 20-47-207 (c)(1)(A)

MODEL STATE "ASSISTED" SUICIDE STATUTE

For States That Have or Are Considering
Assisted Suicide

THE STATE OF [   ]

_____

In the Year Two Thousand and Sixteen

_____

AN ACT PERTAINING TO DEATH WITH DIGNITY

Section 1.01 Definitions

"Adult" means any individual who is eighteen (18) years of age or older and is a resident of _____.

"Attending physician" means the physician who has primary responsibility for the care of the patient and treatment of the patient's terminal disease.

"Capable" means that in the opinion of a court or a patient's attending physician who certifies a terminal illness or of the hospice providing the patient with services, the patient has the ability to make and communicate health care decisions, including communication through sign language.

"Hospice" is defined as [insert state definition of "hospice" here]

"Pharmacy" is an entity licensed, certified, or otherwise authorized or permitted by the laws of the state to dispense medication in the ordinary course of business or practice of a profession.

"Pharmacist" is a person licensed, certified, or otherwise authorized or permitted by the laws of the state to dispense medication in the ordinary course of business or practice of pharmacy.

"Qualified person" is any capable adult accepted for hospice services, whether the person receives those services at home or in a hospice facility.

Section 1.02. Who May Initiate a Written Request for Medication

A "qualified person" shall be provided with an identification card with a photograph identifying him or her as a recipient of hospice services, the hospice from which the adult is receiving services, and contact information for the hospice. If a person is assessed by the hospice as being no longer capable, the card shall be revoked and removed from the person's possession.

Section 1.03 Form of the Written Request

(a) A qualified person may complete a written request for lethal medication, which must be signed and dated by the individual and witnessed by at least two individuals who, in the presence of the qualified patient, attest that to the best of their knowledge the patient is capable, acting voluntarily, and not being coerced to sign the request.

(b) Neither witness shall be a person who would be entitled to any portion of the estate of the qualified person upon death under any will or operation of law. At least one witness shall be an individual who is employed by the hospice. The witness who is employed by the hospice must immediately inform the hospice of the intentions of the qualified person.

Section 1.04 Responsibilities of the Hospice

(a) No more than 24 hours after any hospice employee informs the hospice of the request for medication under this act, the hospice will designate the professional most familiar with the qualified person to discuss the person's desire for the medications, alternative approaches, consequences of taking the medications, and to ensure the person remains a capable person who is making an informed choice. This conversation must take place no more than 48 hours after the hospice employee witnessed the request.

(b) The hospice may not discharge the patient as a result of the qualified person's choice to end his or her life, but may continue to discuss with the patient options for pain relief, palliative care, and voluntary cessation of nutrition and hydration.

(c) The hospice shall recommend that the qualified person's family, if any, be notified but may not require the person to do so.

(d) When the qualified person or his or her agent receives the medication, the hospice will repeat the conversation and assessment required by 1.04(a).

(e) If the hospice is aware that the person has died as a result of taking the medication, the hospice will report the fact of his or her death by taking these medications to the State Department of Health using forms to be developed by the State Department of Health.

(f) Any hospice or hospice employee whose practice conforms to the requirements of this statute cannot be held liable in any legal action arising from doing so.

Section 1.05 Responsibilities of the Pharmacy

(a) The qualified person may deliver the written request for medication personally, through an expressly identified agent, or by mail to a pharmacy. If the request is sent through an expressly identified agent, that agent will produce the hospice identification card and appropriate documentation of authority from the person. If the request is made by mail, it will include a photocopy of the person's hospice identification card, both front and back, and a statement of who will pick up the medication.

(e) Upon receipt of the written request, the pharmacy will immediately confirm with the hospice that the qualified person is enrolled and notify the hospice of the request. The pharmacist will enter the date that the request was received and take steps to ensure that the pharmacy has an appropriate supply of secobarbitol.

(f) Fifteen (15) days after the request is received by the pharmacy, the qualified person may pick up the medications or have an expressly identified agent pick up the medications. The medications will include careful instructions, approved by the State Department of Health, as to how to prepare and consume the medication, as well as written warnings on the potential risk of taking the medication and probable result of taking the medications.

(g) If the request is mailed and/or delivered and picked up by the designated agent, the agent will produce the hospice card. The pharmacist will make a copy of the card, front and back, and notify the hospice by telephone and in writing (including by email) that the agent has received the medications.

(h) The pharmacist will report the dispensing of medications to the [State] Department of Public Health, and will keep a copy of the written request for lethal medication for ten (10) years.

(i) Any pharmacist or pharmacy whose practice conforms to the requirements of this statute will not be liable for any acts arising out of doing so.

Section 1.06 Responsibilities of the Qualified Person and his or her Designated Agent

(a) The qualified person or his or her designated agent will keep the medication in a place that is secure and safe. The hospice will not be required to store or administer the medication.

(b) Any individual who without authorization of the qualified person willfully alters or forges a hospice identification card or a request for medication, or retains medication lawfully intended for a qualified person without the consent of the qualified person, shall be guilty of a felony.

Section 1.07 Responsibilities of the State

(a) The Department of Public Health will develop forms for qualified persons to request medications, for pharmacies to report these requests, and for hospices to report deaths known to be related to these requests.

(b) The Department of Public Health will annually publish the number of requests to pharmacies for lethal medications, and the number of deaths reported by hospices, as well as the number of pharmacies and hospices involved in requests and deaths.

Appendix B: Survey of People Who Have Attempted Suicide

1. EXPERIENCES WITH SUICIDE

Question 1: Could you rank the following feelings in the order in which they contributed to your attempt to commit suicide?
   A. Powerlessness or hopelessness of changing your circumstances
   B. Despair or feeling of meaninglessness
   C. Sadness or grief at a loss or anticipated loss

Question 2: How many times have you attempted suicide?
   A. Once
   B. 2–5 times
   C. More than 5 times

Question 3: After your first suicide attempt, were you hospitalized on a psychiatric unit?
   A. Yes, voluntarily
   B. Yes, involuntarily
   C. No

Question 4: If yes, please check helpful treatments.
   A. Counseling or therapy
   B. Medication

C. Hospitalization

D. Other (please specify)

Question 5: Are you glad that you did not succeed in your suicide attempt?

A. Yes

B. No

C. I am not sure/it varies

Question 6: If you answered "Yes" to Question 6 can you tell me why you are glad to be alive?

Question 7: If you could tell suicide prevention policymakers and mental health professionals three things, what would they be?

Question 8: Do you support the expansion of assisted suicide to include adults with psychiatric disabilities who have tried every treatment and have been unable to find anything to help their condition?

A. Yes

B. No

C. It depends—see below

D. Other—please specify

Question 9: Do you think involuntary commitment of suicidal people is justified?

A. Yes

B. Never

C. Only if psychotic or intoxicated or minors

D. Other (please specify)

2. FINAL RESULTS OF SURVEY[1]

Question 1

	1st choice	2nd choice	3rd choice
Powerlessness or hopelessness	56.14%	35.96%	7.89%
Despair or feeling of meaninglessness	34.50%	48.91%	16.59%
Sadness or grief at a loss or anticipated loss	9.13%	15.22%	75.65%

Question 2

Attempted once	38.03%
Attempted 2–5 times	44.44%
Attempted more than 5 times	17.52%

Question 3

Voluntarily hospitalized	21.85%
Involuntarily hospitalized	27.73%
Not hospitalized	50.42%

Question 4

Counseling or therapy helpful	66.88%
Medication helpful	46.25%
Hospitalization helpful	28.75%
Other	46.88% (Answers are discussed in the Introduction.)

Question 5

Glad first suicide attempt was unsuccessful	36.71%
Not glad first suicide attempt was unsuccessful	16.03%
I am not sure/it varies	47.26%

Question 6 (Answers are discussed in Chapter 9.)

Question 7 (Answers are discussed in the Introduction and throughout the book.)

---

[1] Total number of respondents 242.

Question 8

Support assisted suicide for people with psychiatric disabilities	36.17%
Oppose	27.66%
It depends	12.34% (Answers are discussed in Chapter 10.)
Other	23.83% (Answers are discussed in Chapter 10.)

Question 9

Involuntary commitment of suicidal people justified	19.31%
Involuntary commitment of suicidal people never justified	20.17%
Only if psychotic or intoxicated or minors	29.61%
Other	30.90%[2]

---

[2] Responses included: "Yes, but there should be a mandatory release after 3 days if the person doesn't change his/her mind and agree to voluntary commitment. The option for clinicians to deny release after a 72-hour hold and go to court for a further commitment crosses a line that terrifies me"; "In a facility that helps, not hinders. Three day stays can perpetuate the problem and run up medical costs without even identifying the problem. Last year I experienced a traumatic experience in a short-term facility and witnessed inhumane treatment of others"; "Only if the person lacks capacity in the legal sense—just as any other person presenting with a medical illness."

Table of Cases

Bibliography

Abrams, Abby, *Absent, Alone, Apart: Examining the Effect of Columbia's Medical Withdrawal and Readmission Policies*, COLUMBIA DAILY SPECTATOR, Mar. 4, 2015, *available at* http://features.columbiaspectator.com/eye/2015/03/04/absent-alone-apart/.

Aeschi Working Group, *Problems in Clinical Practice: The Usual Clinical Practice* (Meeting the Suicidal Person: The Therapeutic Approach to the Suicidal Patient: New Perspectives for Health Professionals), www.aeschiconference.unibe.ch/usual_clinical_practice.htm (last visited Nov. 13, 2015).

Alford, Suzanne M., *Is Self-Abortion a Fundamental Right?* 52 DUKE L.J. 1011 (2003).

ALVAREZ, A., THE SAVAGE GOD: A STUDY OF SUICIDE (1990).

Altman, Lawrence, *Doctor Says He Gave Patient Drug to Help Her Commit Suicide*, N. Y. TIMES, Mar. 7, 1991, *available at* http://www.nytimes.com/1991/03/07/us/doctor-says-he-gave-patient-drug-to-help-her-commit-suicide.html.

American Medical Association, *Medical Ethics Opinion 2.06—Capital Punishment* (issued July 1980, updated June 1994), www.ama-assn.org/ama/pub/physician-resources/medical-ethics/code-medical-ethics/opinion206.page.

American Medical Association, *Medical Ethics Opinion 2.211—Physician-Assisted Suicide* (issued June 1994), www.ama-assn.org/ama/pub/physician-resources/medical-ethics/code-medical-ethics/opinion2211.page.

American Medical Association, *Medical Ethics Opinion 10.015—The Patient-Physician Relationship* (issued Dec. 2001), http://www.ama-assn.org/ama/pub/physician-resources/medical-ethics/code-medical-ethics/opinion10015.page.

AMERICAN PSYCHIATRIC ASSOCIATION, PRACTICE GUIDELINES FOR THE ASSESSMENT AND TREATMENT OF PATIENTS WITH SUICIDAL BEHAVIORS (2006), *available at* www.psych.org/psych_pract/treatg/pg/suicidalbehavior_05-15-06.pdf.

American Psychiatric Association, *Practice Guidelines for the Assessment and Treatment of Patients with Suicidal Behaviors*, 160 AM. J. PSYCHIATRY 1 (2003).

AMERICAN PSYCHIATRIC ASSOCIATION, PRINCIPLES OF MEDICAL ETHICS, WITH ANNOTATIONS ESPECIALLY APPLICABLE TO PSYCHIATRY (2013).

Anderson, Scott, *The Urge to End it All*, N. Y. TIMES MAG. (July 6, 2008), available at www.nytimes.com/2008/07/06/magazine/06suicide-t.html

Angelova, Reni, *Right to Die Campaign Heats Up in Courts, CA Legislature*, COURTHOUSE NEWS SERV., May 20, 2015, available at http://www.courthousenews.com/2015/05/20/right-to-die-campaign-heats-up-in-courts-ca-legislature.htm.

Annas, George, & Joan E. Densberger, *Competence to Refuse Medical Treatment: Autonomy vs. Paternalism*, 15 TOLEDO L. REV. 561 (1984).

ANNIE HALL (United Artists 1977).

Anonymous, *A Piece of My Mind: It's Over, Debbie*, 259 JAMA 272 (1988).

Appel, Jacob, *Are We Too Afraid of Suicide?* N. Y. POST, Sept. 14, 2011, available at nypost.com/2011/09/14/are-we-too-afraid-of-suicide/

Appel, Jacob, *How Hard It Is That We Have to Die: Rethinking Suicide Liability for Psychiatrists*, 21 CAMBRIDGE Q. HEALTH CARE ETHICS 527 (Oct. 2012).

Appel, Jacob, *A Suicide Right for the Mentally Ill?* 37 HASTINGS CENTER REP. 21 (2007), *available at* http://www.thehastingscenter.org/Publications/HCR/Detail.aspx?id=814.

Appelbaum, Paul, *Assessment of Patients' Competence to Consent to Treatment*, 357 NEW ENG. J. MED. 1834 (2007).

Appelbaum, Paul, *"Depressed? Get Out!" Dealing with Suicidal Students on College Campuses*, 57 PSYCHIATRIC SERV. 914 (2006).

Appelbaum, Paul, *Judge's Guide to Mental Health Evidence* in REFERENCE MANUAL ON SCIENTIFIC EVIDENCE (3d ed. 2011).

Appelbaum, Paul, & Thomas Gutheil, *"Rotting with Their Rights On": Constitutional Theory and Drug Refusal by Psychiatric Patients*, 7 BULL. AM. ACAD. PSYCHIATRY & L. 306 (1979).

Appelbaum, Paul, & Charles W. Lidz, *Re-Evaluating the Therapeutic Misconception: A Response to Miller and Joffe*, 16 KENNEDY INST. ETHICS J. 367 (2006).

APPLEBY, MARGARET, & MARGARET CONDONIS, HEARING THE CRY: SUICIDE PREVENTION (1990).

Apter, Alan, *Why Is the Suicide Rate So High for Anorexia? How the Eating Disorder Takes Over a Patient's Life*, CHILD MIND INSTITUTE, Nov. 14, 2010, http://www.childmind.org/en/posts/ask-an-expert/2011-10-14-why-suicide-rate-so-high-anorexia.

Areheart, Bradley A., *Disability Trouble* 29 YALE L. & POL'Y REV. 347 (2011).

Arizona State University, *ASU Facts: Welcome to ASU Facts*, https://facts.asu.edu/Pages/Default.aspx (last visited 2014).

Armon, David, *Judge Grants Old Man Right to Starve to Death*, BRYAN TIMES, p. 2, Feb. 3, 1984. https://news.google.com/newspapers?nid=NtGNdKbuCngC&dat=19840203&printsec=frontpage&hl=en

Ax, Joseph, *New Murder Trial for N.Y. Man Who Claimed He Assisted Suicide*, REUTERS, Oct. 3, 2013. www.reuters.com/article/2013/10/03/us-usa-crime-assisted-idUSBRE99215O2013i003#

Bahari, Lauren, *Local Hospice Weighs In on Alternatives to Assisted Suicide*, GASTON GAZETTE, Oct. 31, 2014, *available at* http://www.gastongazette.com/news/local/local-hospice-weighs-in-on-alternatives-to-assisted-suicide-1.394852.

Baker, Katie J.M., *How Colleges Flunk Mental Health*, NEWSWEEK, Feb. 11, 2014, *available at* http://www.newsweek.com/2014/02/14/how-colleges-flunk-mental-health-245492.html.

Bania, T.C., R. Lee, & M. Clark, *Ethics Seminars: Health Care Proxies and Suicidal Patients*, 10 ACAD. EMERGENCY MED. 65 (Jan. 2003)

Bard, Bernard, & Joseph Fletcher, *The Right to Die*, ATLANTIC MONTHLY, 59–64, Apr. 1968.

Barron, Margaret, *Case Study: A Terminally Ill Suicide Patient in the ED*, FROM THE FIELD (Catholic Health Association of the United States, 2011), available at https://www.chausa.org/docs/default-source/general-files/case-study---a-terminally-ill-suicide-attempt-patient-in-the-ed-pdf.pdf?sfvrsn=0.

BATESON, JOHN, THE FINAL LEAP: SUICIDE ON THE GOLDEN GATE BRIDGE (2012).

Baughman, William, et al., *Euthanasia: Criminal, Tort, Constitutional and Legislative Considerations*, 48 NOTRE DAME L. REV. 1202 (1973).

Bazelon, Emily, *The Dawn of the Post-Clinic Abortion*, N. Y. TIMES MAG., Aug. 30, 2014, *available at* http://www.nytimes.com/2014/08/31/magazine/the-dawn-of-the-post-clinic-abortion.html?r=0.

Bergner, Daniel, *Death in the Family*, N. Y. TIMES MAG., Dec. 2, 2007, *available at* http://www.nytimes.com/2007/12/02/magazine/02suicide-t.html?pagewanted=7&_r=1.

BERNAT, JAMES, ETHICAL ISSUES IN NEUROLOGY (2d ed. 2001).

Bernat, J.L., B. Gert, & R.P. Mogielnicki, *Patient Refusal of Hydration and Nutrition: An Alternative to Physician-Assisted Suicide or Voluntary Active Euthanasia*, 153 ARCH. INTERN. MED. 408 (2000).

Beyette, Beverly, *The Reluctant Survivor: 9 Years After Helping Her Fight for the Right to Die, Elizabeth Bouvia's Friend and Lawyer Killed Himself—Leaving Her Shaken and Living the Life She Dreaded*, L. A. TIMES, Sept. 13, 1992, *available at* http://articles.latimes.com/1992-09-13/news/vw-1154_1_elizabeth-bouvia.

Bhavsar, Ayesha, *Respect and Rationality: The Challenge of Attempted Suicide*, 13 AM. J. BIOETHICS 24 (2013).

Bickmayer, J., & D. Hemenway, *Suicide and Firearm Prevalence: Are Youth Disproportionately Affected?* 31 SUICIDE & LIFE-THREATENING BEHAV. 303 (2001).

Bienkowski, Brian, *High Rates of Suicide, Depression, Linked to Farmers' Use of Pesticides*, SCI. AM., Oct. 6, 2014, *available at* http://www.scientificamerican.com/article/high-rates-of-suicide-depression-linked-to-farmers-use-of-pesticides/.

Bilefsky, Dan, *Belgium Close to Allowing Euthanasia for Ill Minors*, N. Y. TIMES, Feb. 13, 2014, www.nytimes.com/2014/02/14/world/europe/belgium-close-to-enacting-child-euthanasia-law.htm

Bingham, John, & Andy Burnham, *Living Wills Law Could Be "Revisited" After Kerrie Wooltorton Suicide Case*, TELEGRAPH (London), Oct. 4, 2009, *available at* www.telegraph.co.uk/news/health/news/6259181/Living-wills-law-could-be-revisited-after-Kerrie-Woolterton-suicide-case-Andy-Burnham.html.

Birchmayer, J., & D. Hemenway, *Suicide and Firearm Violence: Are Youth Disproportionately Affected?* 31 SUICIDE & LIFE-THREATENING BEHAV. 303 (2001).

Blackall, G.F., R.L. Volpe, & M.J. Green, *After the Suicide Attempt: Offering Patients Another Chance*, 13 AM. J. BIOETHICS 3 (2013).

BLACKSTONE, WILLIAM, COMMENTARIES ON THE LAWS OF ENGLAND, ch. 14, at 189 (8th ed. 1778).

Bloom, Joseph, Brinda Krishnan, & Christopher Lockey, *The Majority of Inpatient Psychiatric Beds Should Not Be Appropriated by the Forensic System*, 36 J. AM. ACAD. PSYCH & L. 438 (Dec. 2008).

Blume, John, *Killing the Willing: "Volunteers," Suicide and Competency*, 103 MICH. L. REV. 939, 940 (2005).

Bogler, Emma, *Student Task Force to Examine Leave of Absence Policy*, COLUMBIA SPECTATOR, Mar. 24, 2014, http://columbiaspectator.com/news/2014/03/24/student-task-force-examine-leave-absence-policy.

Bolton, J.M., et al., *Predicting Suicide Attempts with the SAD PERSONS Scale: A Longitudinal Analysis*, 73 J. CLIN. PSYCHIATRY 6, e735–41 (June 2012).

Bombardieri, Marcella, *Lawsuit Allowed in MIT Suicide*, BOSTON GLOBE, July 30, 2005, at B-1.

Bongar, Bruce, & Ronald Stolberg, *Risk Management with the Suicidal Patient*, NATIONAL REGISTER OF HEALTH SERVICE PSYCHOLOGISTS (2009), *available at* http://e-psychologist.org/index.iml?mdl=exam/show_article.mdl&Material_ID=100.

Boonstra, Heather D., & Elizabeth Nash, *A Surge of State Abortion Restrictions Puts Providers—and the Women They Serve—in the Crosshairs*, 17 GUTTMACHER POL'Y REV. 1 (2014), *available at* www.guttmacher.org/pubs/gpr/17/1/gpr170109.html.

Booth, Jenny, *DPP Defends Bringing Murder Charges Against Right-to-Die Mum Kay Gilderdale*, TIMES (London), Jan. 26, 2010, *available at* www.thetimes.co.uk/tto/news/uk/crime/article1877794.ece.

Borjupari, Priyanka, *Suicide or Protest? Hunger Strike Rivets India*, BOSTON GLOBE, Sept. 8, 2014, at A-14.

Bosshard, G., et al., *A Role for Doctors in Assisted Dying? An Analysis of Legal Regulations and Medical Professional Positions in Six European Countries*, 34 J. MED. ETHICS 28 (2008).

Boudreau, J. Donald, *Physician-Assisted Suicide and Euthanasia: Can You Even Imagine Teaching Medical Students How to End Their Patients' Lives?* 15 PERMANENTE J. 79 (2011), *available at* www.ncbi.nlm.nih.gov/pmc/articles/PMC3267569/.

Boxall, Bettina, *Judge Refuses to Drop Charges in Assisted Suicide*, L. A. TIMES, Apr. 9, 1996, *available at* http://articles.latimes.com/1996-04-09/local/me-56493_1_physician-assisted-suicide.

Bracchi, Paul, *Special Investigation: What Kind of a Country Have We Become If Doctors and Lawyers Allow a Disturbed Young Woman to Die?*, DAILY MAIL

ONLINE, Oct. 9, 2009, www.dailymail.co.uk/news/article-1219389/SPECIAL-INVESTIGATION-What-kind-country-doctors-lawyers-allow-disturbed-young-woman-die.html.

Braw, Elisabeth, *Should a Sick Child Be Allowed to Choose Death? Belgians Think So*, NEWSWEEK, Dec. 5, 2013, *available at* www.newsweek.com/should-sick-child-be-allowed-choose-death-belgians-think-so-223851.

Brent, D.A., et al., *Firearms and Adolescent Suicide: A Community Case-Control Study*, 147 J. AM. ACAD. CHILD ADOLESC. PSYCHIATRY 1066 (1993).

Brietbart, William, et al., *Neuropsychiatric Syndromes and Psychological Symptoms in Patients with Advanced Cancer*, 10 J. PAIN SYMPTOM MGMT. 131–41 (1995).

Brody, Jane, *Is Doctor-Assisted Suicide Ever an Acceptable Option?* SUN-SENTINEL (Miami), Mar. 25, 1993, *available at* http://articles.sun-sentinel.com/1993-03-25/features/9302010885_1_doctor-assisted-suicide-patient-sanctions/2.

Brown, Gregory, et al., *Cognitive Therapy for the Prevention of Suicide Attempts: A Randomized Controlled Trial*, 294 JAMA 563 (2005).

Brown, Samuel, C. Gregory Elliott, & Robert Paine, *Withdrawal of Non-Futile Life Support After Attempted Suicide*, 13 AM. J. BIOETHICS 3 (2013).

BRUCH, HILDE, THE GOLDEN CAGE: THE ENIGMA OF ANOREXIA NERVOSA (1978).

Brumberg, Joan Jacobs, *From Psychiatric Syndrome to Communicable Disease: The Case of Anorexia Nervosa*, in FRAMING DISEASE: STUDIES IN CULTURAL HISTORY 149 (Charles E. Rosenberg & Janet Golden eds., 1997).

Bruni, Frank, *Fatal Mercies*, N. Y. TIMES, Aug. 10, 2013, *available at* www.nytimes.com/2013/08/11/opinion/sunday/bruni-fatal-mercies.html

BURTON, ROBERT, THE ANATOMY OF MELANCHOLY (1621).

BYOCK, IRA, THE BEST CARE POSSIBLE (2012).

Byock, Ira, Op-Ed: *We Should Think Twice about "Death with Dignity,"* L. A. TIMES, Jan. 30, 2015, *available at* http://www.latimes.com/opinion/op-ed/la-oe-0201-byock-physician-assisted-suicide-20150201-story.html#page=1.

Byock, Ira, *Patient Refusal of Nutrition and Hydration: Walking the Ever Finer Line*, 8 AM. J. HOSPICE & PALLIATIVE CARE 13 (Mar./Apr. 1995).

Byrn, Robert, *Compulsory Lifesaving Treatment for the Competent Adult*, 44 FORDHAM L. REV. 1 (1975–76).

CALIFORNIA DEPARTMENT OF TRANSPORTATION, BRIDGE RAILS AND BARRIERS, www.dot.ca.gov/hq/LandArch/16_la_design/aesthetics/barriers/pdf/Caltrans_Bridge_Rails_and_Barriers.pdf.

California Lawmakers to Introduce New Right-to-Die Legislation, CALIFORNIA HEALTHLINE, Jan. 21, 2015, http://www.californiahealthline.org/articles/2015/1/21/calif-lawmakers-to-introduce-new-righttodie-legislation.

California Medical Association, *California Medical Association Removes Opposition to Aid in Dying Bill*, May 20, 2015, *available at* http://www.cmanet.org/news/press-detail?article=california-medical-association-removes.

Callahan, Sascha, & Christopher Ryan, *Refusing Medical Treatment After Attempted Suicide: Rethinking Capacity and Coercive Treatment in Light of the Kerrie Wooltorton Case*, 18 J. L. MED. 811 (2011).

CAMUS, ALBERT, THE MYTH OF SISYPHUS (1944).

Carlson, Laura, *Higher Ed Accessibility Lawsuits, Complaints, and Settlements*, 2015, http://www.d.umn.edu/~lcarlson/atteam/lawsuits.html.

Carney, Susanne S., et al., *Suicide over Sixty: The San Diego Study*, 42 J. Am. Geriatrics Soc'y 174 (1994).

Celebrate Recovery: A Christ-Centered Recovery Program, www.celebraterecovery.com (last visited Nov. 13, 2015).

Centers for Disease Control and Prevention, *All Injuries*, FastStats (2013), http://www.cdc.gov/nchs/fastats/homicide.htm.

Centers for Disease Control and Prevention, *Assault or Homicide* FastStats (2013), http://www.cdc.gov/nchs/fastats/homicide.htm.

Centers for Disease Control and Prevention, *Injury Prevention & Control: Data & Statistics* (Web-based Injury Statistics Query and Reporting System [WISQARS]), http://www.cdc.gov/injury/wisqars/index.html (last visited Nov. 13, 2013).

Centers for Disease Control and Prevention, *Leading Causes of Death Reports, National and Regional—2009* (WISQARS), http://webappa.cdc.gov/sasweb/ncipc/leadcaus10_us.html (last visited Nov. 13, 2013).

Centers for Disease Control and Prevention, *Leading Causes of Death Reports, National and Regional—2010* (WISQARS), http://webappa.cdc.gov/sasweb/ncipc/leadcaus10_us.html (last visited Nov. 13, 2013).

Centers for Disease Control and Prevention, *National Center for Health Statistics: 2011 United States Suicide Injury Deaths and Rates*, available at www.cdc.gov/nchs.

Centers for Disease Control and Prevention, *National Center for Health Statistics: 2012 United States Suicide Injury Deaths and Rates*, available at www.cdc.gov/nchs.

Centers for Disease Control and Prevention, *Suicide and Self-Inflicted Injury* FastStats (2013), http://www.cdc.gov/nchs/fastats/suicide.htm.

Centers for Disease Control and Prevention, *QuickStats: Age-Adjusted Suicide Rates, by State—United States*, 2012, Morbidity and Mortality Weekly Report (MMWR, Nov. 14, 2014), http://www.cdc.gov/mmwr/preview/mmwrhtml/mm6345a10.htm.

Chabot, Boudewijn, A Hastened Death by Self-Denial of Food and Drink (2008).

Charland, L.C.E., *Mental Competence and Value: The Problem of Normativity in the Assessment of Decisionmaking Capacity*, 8 Psychiatry Psychol. & L. 135 (2001).

Chin, Arthur Eugene, Katrina Hedberg, Grant K. Higginson, & David W. Fleming, Oregon's Death with Dignity Act: The First Year's Experience (Oregon Department of Health—Division of Public Health, Feb. 18, 1999), *available at* https://public.health.oregon.gov/ProviderPartnerResources/EvaluationResearch/DeathwithDignityAct/Documents/year1.pdf.

Chrisafis, Angelique, *France Telecom Executive Resigns After Employee Suicide Tally Rises to 24*, The Guardian, Oct. 5, 2009, *available at* www.theguardian.com/business/2009/oct/05/telecoms-france.

Clark, Andrew, *Big Increase in US Suicides at Work*, The Guardian, Aug. 21, 2009, *available at* www.theguardian.com/business/2009/aug/21/us-suicide-work-office.

Clarke, Theodore J., *Avoiding a Lawsuit: Lessons from the Never-Sued*, Am. Ass'n Orthopedic Surgeons (AAOS) Now, Oct. 2011, http://www.aaos.org/news/aaosnow/oct11/managing3.asp.

COELHO, PAULO, VERONIKA DECIDES TO DIE (1998).

Cohen, Brandon, *Should You Resuscitate a Suicide Patient?* MEDSCAPE, Oct. 8, 2013, www.medscape.com/viewarticle/812112.

Colbert, James, Joann Schulte, & Jonathan N. Adler, *Physician-Assisted Suicide—Polling Results,* 369 NEW ENG. J. MED. e15 (Sept. 12, 2013).

Coleman, James, *Litigating at the Speed of Light,* 16 LITIGATION 14 (1990).

Coleman, Phyllis, & Ronald Shellow, *Suicide: Unpredictable and Unavoidable: Proposed Guidelines Provide Rational Test for Physician's Liability,* 71 NEB. L. REV. 643 (1992).

COLT, GEORGE HOWE, THE ENIGMA OF SUICIDE (2006).

Compassion & Choices, https://www.compassionandchoices.org/ (last visited Nov. 13, 2015).

Conner, K.R., & P.R. Duberstein, *Predisposing and Precipitating Factors for Suicide Among Alcoholics: Empirical Review and Conceptual Integration,* 28 ALCOHOL CLIN. EXP. RES. 6S–17S (2004).

Conwell, Y. & E.D. Caine, *Rational Suicide and the Right to Die: Reality and Myth,* 325 NEW ENG. J. MED. 1100 (1991).

Cook, Renee, Philip Pan, Ross Silverman, & Stephen M. Soltys, *Do-Not-Resuscitate Orders in Suicidal Patients: Clinical, Ethical, and Legal Dilemmas,* 51 PSYCHOSOMATICS 277 (July-Aug. 2010).

Coombs, D.W., H.L. Miller, R. Alarcon, C. Herlihy, J.M. Lee, & D.P. Morrison, *Presuicide Attempt Communications Between Parasuicides and Consulted Caregivers,* 22 SUICIDE & LIFE-THREATENING BEHAV. 289 (1992).

Cormally, W. Luke, et al., *Editorial: The Final Autonomy,* 340 LANCET 976 (1992).

Cowan, Alison Leigh, *Suit over a Woman's Suicide at an Elite Private Hospital,* N. Y. TIMES, Nov. 22, 2007, *available at* http://www.nytimes.com/2007/11/23/nyregion/23psych.html.

COX, D.W., HEMLOCK'S CUP: THE STRUGGLE FOR DEATH WITH DIGNITY (1993).

Crosby, Alex, et al., *Suicidal Thoughts and Behaviors Among Adults ≥ 18 Years, U.S. 2008-2009,* CENTERS FOR DISEASE CONTROL, MORBIDITY & MORTALITY WEEKLY REP., SURVEILLANCE SUMMARIES, Oct. 21, 2011, at 60-SS13.

Crutchfield, N.J., To Succeed or Not to Succeed: How Do Political Influences, Culture, and Demographics of a State Affect the Passing of Physician Assisted Suicide Initiatives? (Dec. 19, 2008) (Ph.D. dissertation, Auburn University).

Dahlberg, L.L., R.M. Ikeda, & M.J. Kresnow, *Guns in the Home and Risk of a Violent Death in the Home: Findings from a National Study,* 160 AM. J. EPIDEMIOL. 929 (2004).

DAWSON, DAVID, & HARRIET L. MACMILLAN eds., RELATIONSHIP MANAGEMENT OF THE BORDERLINE PATIENT: FROM UNDERSTANDING TO TREATMENT (1st ed. 1993).

Death with Dignity: An Inquiry into Related Public Issues, Hearings before the Special Commission on Aging, U.S. Senate, 92d Cong. 2d Sess. Part 2. Aug. 8, 1972.

Dignitas, http://www.dignitas.ch/?lang=en (last visited Nov. 13, 2015).

DIRECTOR OF PUBLIC PROSECUTIONS, POLICY FOR PROSECUTORS IN RESPECT OF ENCOURAGING OR ASSISTING SUICIDE (Feb. 2010, updated Oct. 2014), *available at* https://www.cps.gov.uk/publications/prosecution/assisted_suicide_policy.html.

Dowbiggan, Ian, A Concise History of Euthanasia: Life, Death, God and Medicine (2005).

Dowbiggan, Ian, A Merciful End: A Review of the Euthanasia Movement in America (2003).

Draper, John, Gillian Murphy, Eduardo Vega, David W. Covington, & Richard McKeon, *Helping Callers to the National Suicide Prevention Hotline Who Are at Imminent Risk of Suicide: The Importance of Active Engagement, Active Rescue, and Collaboration between Crisis and Emergency Services*, Suicide & Life-Threatening Behav. 1, 5 (2014).

Dresser, Rebecca, *Feeding the Hunger Artists: Legal Issues in Treating Anorexia Nervosa*, Wis. L. Rev. (Mar.-Apr. 1984) 297, 328–29 (1984).

Dresser, Rebecca, *Pre-Commitment: A Misguided Strategy for Securing Death with Dignity*, 81 Tex. L. Rev. 1823 (June 2003).

Drum, Charles, Glen White, Genia Taitano, & Willi Horner-Johnson, *The Oregon Death with Dignity Act: Results of a Literature Survey and Naturalistic Inquiry*, 3 Disabil. & Health J. 3 (2010).

Drum, David J., Chris Brownson, Adryon Burton Denmark, & Shanna E. Smith, *New Data on the Nature of Suicidal Crises in College Students: Shifting the Paradigm*, 40 Prof. Psychol. Res. & Prac. 213 (2009).

Druss, Benjamin, & Harold Pincus, *Suicidal Ideation and Suicide Attempts in General Medical Illness*, 160 Arch. Intern. Med. 322 (2000).

Drylie, James, & John Violanti, Copicide: Concepts, Cases, and Controversies of Suicide by Cop (2008).

Dunn, Patrick, Bonnie Reagan, Susan W. Tolle, & Sarah Foreman, The Oregon Death with Dignity Act: A Guidebook for Health Care Professionals (2d ed. 2008).

Durkheim, Émile, Le Suicide [Suicide], (1897).

Ebbott, Kristina, *A "Good Death" Defined by Law: Comparing the Legality of Aid in Dying Around the World*, 37 Wm. Mitchell L. Rev. 170 (2010).

Eddy, David, *A Conversation with My Mother*, 272 JAMA 179 (1994).

Emanuel, Ezekiel, *Euthanasia: Historical, Ethical and Empiric Perspectives*, 154 Arch. Intern. Med. 1890 (1994).

Emmanuel, Ezekiel, *Whose Right to Die?* 279 Atlantic Monthly 73 (Mar. 1997).

Espelage, Dorothy L., *Why Are Bully Prevention Programs Failing in U.S. Schools?* 10 J. Curriculum & Pedagogy 121 (2013).

European Court of Human Rights, European Convention on Human Rights (Oct. 1, 1994), *available at* www.echr.coe.int/Documents/Convention_ENG.pdf.

European Institute of Bioethics, Euthanasia in Belgium: 10 Years On, (Apr. 2012), *available at* www.ieb-eib.org/en/pdf/20121208/dossier-euthanasia-in-Belgium-10-Years.pdf.

Euthanasia and Assisted Suicide—Euthanasia in the Netherlands, http://www.libraryindex.com/pages/573/Euthanasia-Assisted-Suicide-EUTHANASIA-IN-NETHERLANDS.html (last visited Nov. 13, 2015).

Euthanasia Research & Guidance Organization, *The Euthanasia World Directory: Website of Hemlock Society Founder Derek Humphry*, http://www.finalexit.org/ (last visited Nov. 13, 2015).

Exit, *Self-Determined Living and Dying*, http://www.exit.ch/en/ (last visited Nov. 13, 2015).

Fawcett, Jan, *Time-Related Predictors of Suicide in Major Affective Disorders*, 147 AM. J. PSYCHIATRY 1189 (1990).

FLEISCHER, DORIS ZAMES, & FRIEDA ZAMES, THE DISABILITY RIGHTS MOVEMENT: FROM CHARITY TO CONFRONTATION (2011).

Fletcher, Joseph, *Euthanasia: Our Right to Die*, 1 PASTORAL PSYCHOL. 9 (1950).

Fletcher, Joseph, *Indicators of Humanhood: A Tentative Profile of Man*, 2 HASTINGS CENTER REP. 1 (Nov. 1972).

FLETCHER, JOSEPH, MORALS AND MEDICINE (1960).

Fletcher, Joseph, *Our Right to Die*, 8 THEOLOGY TODAY 202 (1951).

Fletcher, Joseph, *The Patient's Right to Die*, HARPER'S (Oct. 1960).

Fowler, Katherine A., R. Matthew Gladden, Kevin J. Vagi, Jamar Barnes, & Leroy Frazier, *Increase in Suicides Associated with Home Eviction and Foreclosure During the US Housing Crisis: Findings from 16 National Violent Death Reporting System States, 2005–2010*, 105 AM. J. PUB. HEALTH 311 (2015).

Frei, Andreas, et al., *Assisted Suicide as Conducted by a "Right to Die" Society in Switzerland: A Descriptive Analysis of 43 Consecutive Cases*, 131 SWISS MED. WKLY. 375 (2001).

Friedman, H., & R. Kohn, *Mortality in the Suicidal Population*, 38 SUICIDE & LIFE-THREATENING BEHAV. 287 (2008).

Frierson, Robert, *Suicide Attempts by the Old and Very Old*, 152 ARCH. INTERN. MED. 141 (1991).

Ganns, Margery, & William B. Gunn Jr., *End-Stage Anorexia: Criteria for Competence to Refuse Treatment*, in APPLIED ETHICS IN MENTAL HEALTH CARE: AN INTERDISCIPLINARY READER (Dominic Sisti, Arthur L. Caplan, Hila Rimon-Greenspan, & Paul S. Appelbaum eds., 2013).

Ganzini, Linda, Elizabeth R. Goy, & Steven K. Dobscha, *Prevalence of Depression and Anxiety in Patients Requesting Physicians' Aid in Dying: A Cross-Sectional Study*, 337 BRIT. MED. J. 682 (Oct. 8, 2008).

Ganzini, Linda, et al., *Evaluation of Competence to Consent to Assisted Suicide: Views of Forensic Psychiatrists*, 157 AM. J. PSYCHIATRY 595 (2000).

Ganzini, Linda, et al., *Nurses' Experience with Hospice Patients Who Refuse Food and Fluids to Hasten Death*, 349 NEW ENG. J. MED. 359 (2003).

Gauthier, Saska, Julian Mausbach, Thomas Reisch, & Christine Barsch, *Suicide Tourism: A Pilot Study on the Swiss Phenomenon*, J. MED. ETHICS 1 (2014).

GAWANDE, ATUL, BEING MORTAL (2014).

Geppert, Cynthia M.A., *Saving Life or Respecting Autonomy: The Ethical Dilemma of DNR Orders in Patients Who Attempt Suicide*, 7 INTERNET J.L. HEALTHCARE & ETHICS 1 (2010), http://ispub.com/IJLHE/7/1/11437.

Ghahramanlou-Holloway, Marjan, Laura L. Neely, & Jennifer Tucker, *A Cognitive-Behavioral Strategy for Preventing Suicide*, 13 CURRENT PSYCHIATRY 18 (2014).

GIBSON, ROSEMARY, & JANARDAN PRASAD SINGH, WALL OF SILENCE: THE UNTOLD STORY OF THE MEDICAL MISTAKES THAT KILL AND INJURE MILLIONS OF AMERICANS (2003).

Gill, Carol, *Professionals, Disabilities and Assisted Suicide: An Examination of the Relevant Empirical Evidence and Reply to Batavia*, 6 PSYCHOL. PUB. POL'Y & L. 526 (2000).

GOLDSMITH, S.K., T.C. PELLMAR, A.M. KLEINMAN, W.E. BUNNEY, EDS., REDUCING SUICIDE: A NATIONAL IMPERATIVE (2002).

Goodman, Ellen, & Donald Beschle, *Autonomous Decisionmaking and Social Choice: Examining "the Right to Die,"* 77 KY. L.J. 319 (1988).

Goodwin, Renee D. *Is COPD Associated with Suicidal Behavior?* 45 J. PSYCHIATRIC RES. 1269 (Sept. 2011).

Green, Milton D., *Proof of Mental Incompetency and the Unexpressed Major Premise*, 53 YALE L.J. 271 (1944).

Grossman, D.C., et al., *Gun Storage Practices and Risk of Youth Suicide and Unintentional Firearm Injuries*, 293 JAMA 707 (2005).

Grove, W.M., D.H. Zald, B.S. Lebow, B.E. Snitz, & C. Nelson, *Clinical vs. Mechanical Prediction: A Meta-Analysis*, 12 PSYCHOL. ASSESSMENT 19 (2000).

Gupta, Vanita, Jocelyn Samuels, & Susan M. Pezzullo Rhodes, Joint Letter from the Department of Justice and the Department of Health and Human Services to the Massachusetts Department of Children and Families, Jan. 15, 2015, *available at* http://www.ada.gov/ma_docf_lof.pdf.

Gutheil, Thomas, *Suicide and Suit: Liability after Self-Destruction*, in SUICIDE AND CLINICAL PRACTICE (D. Jacobs ed., 1992).

Gutheil, Thomas, & Diane Schetky, *A Date with Death: Management of Time Based and Contingent Suicidal Intent*, 155 AM. J. PSYCHIATRY 1502 (Nov. 1998).

GUTKIND, LEE ed., AT THE END OF LIFE: TRUE STORIES ABOUT HOW WE DIE (2012).

Hamilton, N. Gregory, & Catherine A. Hamilton, *Competing Paradigms of Response to Assisted Suicide Requests in Oregon*, 162 AM. J. PSYCHIATRY 1060 (2005).

Harris, D., B. Richard, & P. Khanna, *Assisted Dying: The Ongoing Debate*, 82 POSTGRAD. MED. J. 479 (2006).

HAUGEN, DAVID M., & MATTHEW J. BOX, EDS., SUICIDE (2005).

Hayashi, Mike, & Toshinori Kitamura, *Euthanasia Trials in Japan: Implications for Legal and Medical Practice*, 25 INT'L J.L. & PSYCHIATRY 557 (2002).

Hebert, Philip C., & Michael A. Weingarten, *The Ethics of Forcefeeding in Anorexia Nervosa*, 144 CAN. MED. J. 141, 143 (1991).

HECHT, JENNIFER MICHAEL, STAY: A HISTORY OF SUICIDE AND THE PHILOSOPHIES AGAINST IT (2013).

Hendin, Herbert, *Assisted Suicide, Euthanasia, and Suicide Prevention: The Implications of the Dutch Experience*, 25 SUICIDE & LIFE-THREATENING BEHAV. 193 (1995).

Hendin, Herbert, *Seduced by Death: Doctors, Patients, and the Dutch Cure*, 10 ISSUES L. & MED. 123 (1994).

HENDIN, HERBERT, SUICIDE IN AMERICA (1982).

Hendin, Herbert, et al., *Factors Contributing to Therapists' Distress After the Suicide of a Patient*, 161 AM. J. PSYCHIATRY 1442 (2004).

HILLYARD, D., & J. DOMBRINK, DYING RIGHT: THE DEATH WITH DIGNITY MOVEMENT (2001).

Hjelmeland, H., G. Dieserud, K. Dyregrov, B.L. Knizek, & A.A. Leenaars, *Psychological Autopsy Studies as Diagnostic Tools: Are They Methodologically Flawed?* 36 DEATH STUD. 7, 605–26 (2012), *available at* http://dx.doi.org/10.1080/07481187.2011.584015.

Hormant, Robert, & Daniel B. Kennedy, *Suicide by Police: A Proposed Typology of Law Enforcement Officer-Assisted Suicide*, 23 POLICING: INT'L J. POLICE STRATEGIES & MGMT. 339 (2000).

Horton-Deutsch, S.L., et al., *Chronic Dyspnea and Suicide in Elderly Men*, 43 PSYCHIATRIC SERV. 1198 (1992).

HUMPHRY, DEREK, FINAL EXIT (3d ed. 2010).

Hutson, H.R., Deirdre Anglin, John Yarborough, & Kimberly Hardaway, *Suicide by Cop*, 32 ANNALS EMERG. MED. 665 (1998).

Instituto Nacional de Estadistica, Press Release: *Deaths According to Cause of Death: Year 2012*, Jan. 31, 2014, *available at* www.ine.es/en/prensa/np830_en.pdf.

Isquith, Elias, *Fox News' Shep Smith: Robin Williams Was "Such a Coward*, SALON, Aug. 12, 2014, *available at* http://www.salon.com/2014/08/12/fox_news_shep_smith_robin_williams_was_such_a_coward/.

JACOBS, DOUGLAS, SCREENING FOR MENTAL HEALTH: A RESOURCE GUIDE FOR IMPLEMENTING THE JOINT COMMISSION ON ACCREDITATION OF HEALTH CARE ORGANIZATIONS (JCAHO) 2007 PATIENT SAFETY GOALS ON SUICIDE, *available at* www.MentalHealthScreening.org.

JACOBS, DOUGLAS, & HUBERT BROWN, EDS., SUICIDE: UNDERSTANDING AND RESPONDING (1989).

JAMISON, KAY REDFIELD, NIGHT FALLS FAST: UNDERSTANDING SUICIDE (1999).

Jankowski, Jane, & Lisa Campo-Engelstein, *Suicide in the Context of Terminal Illness*, 13 AM. J. BIOETHICS 13 (2013).

JEFFREY, DAVID, PHYSICIAN ASSISTED SUICIDE VS. PALLIATIVE CARE: A TALE OF TWO CITIES (June 2007), *available at* http://www.pccef.org/articles/PCCEF_June07_posting.pdf.

Jena, Anupam B., Seth Seabury, Darius Lakdawalla, & Amitabh Chandra, *Malpractice Risk According to Physician Specialty*, 365 NEW ENG. J. MED. 629 (Aug. 2011).

JOBES, DAVID, MANAGING SUICIDAL RISK: A COLLABORATIVE APPROACH (2006).

Jobes, David, *Suicidal Blackmail: Ethical and Risk Management Issues in Contemporary Clinical Care*, in CASEBOOK ON ETHICALLY CHALLENGING WORK SETTINGS IN MENTAL HEALTH AND THE BEHAVIORAL SCIENCES (W.B. Johnson & G.B. Koocher eds., 2011).

Jobes, David, & Elizabeth Ballard, *The Therapist and the Suicidal Patient*, in BUILDING A THERAPEUTIC RELATIONSHIP WITH A SUICIDAL PATIENT (Konrad Michel & David A. Jobes eds., 2011).

JAMISON, KAY REDFIELD, NIGHT FALLS FAST: UNDERSTANDING SUICIDE (1999).

Johnson, Kathleen, *The Death Row Right to Die: Suicide or Intimate Decision?* 54 S. CAL. L. REV. 575, 592 (1981).

Johnson, Mary, *Right to Life; Fight to Die: The Elizabeth Bouvia Saga*, RAGGED EDGE (Jan./Feb. 1997; Disability Rag, 1984), http://www.broadreachtraining.com/advocacy/artbouvia.htm.

Kai, Katsunori, *Euthanasia and Death with Dignity in Japanese Law*, 27 WASEDA BULL. COMP. L. 1 (2010).

Karlinsky, H., et al., *Suicide Attempts and Resuscitation Dilemmas*, 10 GEN. HOSP. PSYCHIATRY 423 (Nov. 1988).

KATZ, JAY, THE SILENT WORLD OF DOCTOR AND PATIENT (1984).

Kellermann, A.L., et al., *Suicide in the Home in Relation to Gun Ownership*, 327 NEW ENG. J. MED. 467 (1992).

Kern, Brittany, Balancing Prevention and Liability: The Use of Waiver to Limit University Liability for Student Suicide (Michigan State University, College of Law, 2014), http://ssrn.com/abstract=2478038.

Kaveeshar, Juhi, *Kicking the Rock and the Hard Place to the Curb: An Alternative and Integrated Approach to Suicidal Students in Higher Education*, 57 EMORY L.J. 651 (2008).

Kimura, Rihito, *Death, Dying and Advance Directives in Japan: Sociocultural and Legal Point of View*, in ADVANCE DIRECTIVE AND SURROGATE DECISIONMAKING IN TRANSCULTURAL PERSPECTIVE (1998).

Kissane, D.W., D.M. Clarke, A.F. Street, *Demoralization Syndrome—A Relevant Psychiatric Diagnosis in Palliative Care*, 17 J. PALLIATIVE CARE 12 (2001).

Knoll IV, James, *Inpatient Suicide: Identifying Vulnerability in the Hospital Setting*, PSYCHIATRIC TIMES, May 22, 2012, http://www.psychiatrictimes.com/suicide/inpatient-suicide-identifying-vulnerability-hospital-setting.

Knox, Kerry, et al., *The U.S. Air Force Suicide Prevention Program: Implications for Public Health Policy*, 100 AM. J. PUB. HEALTH 2457 (2010).

Koenig, Kristi, & Angelo A. Salvucci, *Out-of-Hospital Do Not Attempt Resuscitation in the Suicidal Patient: A Special Case*, 4 ACAD. EMERG. MED. 926 (1997).

Krahn, Gloria L. *Reflections on the Debate on Disability and Aid in Dying*, 3 DISABIL. & HEALTH J. 51–5 (2010).

KUSHNER, HOWARD I. AMERICAN SUICIDE. (1991).

Larremore, Wilbur, *Suicide and the Law*, 17 HARV. L. REV. 331 (1903–04).

LEPORE, JILL, THE MANSION OF HAPPINESS: A HISTORY OF LIFE AND DEATH (2012).

Lidz, Charles, Edward P. Mulvey, Steven K. Hoge, Brenda L. Kirsch, John Monahan, Marlene Eisenberg, William Gardner, & Loren H. Roth, *Factual Sources of Psychiatric Patients' Perceptions of Coercion in the Hospital Admission Process*, 155 AM. J. PSYCHIATRY 9 (1998).

Lambert, Michael T., *Seven Year Outcomes of Patients Evaluated for Suicidality*, 53 PSYCHIATRIC SERV. 92 (2002).

Lambert, Michael T., *Suicide Risk Assessment and Management: Focus on Personality Disorders*, 16 CURR. OPIN. PSYCHIATRY 71 (2003).

Lambert, Michael T., & J. Bonner, *Characteristics and Six Month Outcome of Patients Who Use Suicide Threats to Seek Hospital Admission*, 47 PSYCHIATRIC SERV. 871 (1996).

Leidig, Michael, *Dignitas Is Investigated for Helping Healthy Woman Die*, 331 BRIT. MED. J. 1160 (2005).

Lim, Ah-Young, et al., *Clinical and Sociodemographic Correlates of Suicidality in Patients with Major Depressive Disorder from Six Asian Countries*, 14 BMC PSYCHIATRY 37 (2014).

Loggers, E.T., et al., *Implementing a Death with Dignity Program at a Comprehensive Cancer Center*, 368 NEW ENG. J. MED. 1417 (2013).

LORD, VIVIAN B., SUICIDE BY COP: INDUCING OFFICERS TO SHOOT: PRACTICAL DIRECTION FOR RECOGNITION, RESOLUTION AND RECOVERY (2004).

LUNGE, ROBIN, MARIA ROYLE, & MICHAEL SLATER, OREGON'S DEATH WITH DIGNITY LAW AND EUTHANASIA IN THE NETHERLANDS: FACTUAL DISPUTES (2004), *available at* www.leg.state.vt.us/reports/04death/death_with_dignity_report.htm.

Magnusson, Roger S., *The Sanctity of Life and the Right to Die: Social and Jurisprudential Aspects of the Euthanasia Debate in Australia and the United States*, 6 PAC. RIM L. & POL'Y J. 1 (Jan. 1997).

Maguire, James, *"Everyone Does it to Everyone": An Epidemic of Bullying and the Legislation of Transgression in American Schools*, 16 NEW CRIM. L. REV. 413 (2012).

Maltsberger, John, *Calculated Risks in the Treatment of Suicidal Patients*, 57 PSYCHIATRY 199 (1994).

Maltsberger, John, & Dan H. Buie, *Countertransference Hate in the Treatment of Suicidal Patients*, 30 ARCH. GEN. PSYCHIATRY 625 (1974).

MANNING, MICHAEL, EUTHANASIA AND PHYSICIAN-ASSISTED SUICIDE: KILLING OR CARING? (1988).

Marco, C.A., E.S. Bessman, & G.D. Kelen, *Ethical Issues of Cardiopulmonary Resuscitation: Comparison of Emergency Physician Practices from 1995 to 2007*, 16 ACAD. EMERG. MED. 270 (Mar. 2009).

Martin, Annika K., *Stick a Toothbrush Down Your Throat: An Analysis of the Potential Liability of Pro-Eating Disorder Websites*, 14 TEX. J. WOMEN & L. 151(2005).

MARTIN, F. DAVID, FACING DEATH: THEME AND VARIATIONS (2006).

MASSACHUSETTS DEPARTMENT OF PUBLIC HEALTH INJURY SURVEILLANCE PROGRAM, SUICIDES AND SELF-INFLICTED INJURIES IN MASSACHUSETTS: DATA SUMMARY (Spring 2014), *available at* http://www.mass.gov/eohhs/docs/dph/injury-surveillance/suicide/suicide-update-spring2014.pdf.

MASSACHUSETTS DEPARTMENT OF PUBLIC HEALTH, SUICIDES AND SELF-INFLICTED INJURIES IN MASSACHUSETTS: DATA SUMMARY (2015), *available at* http://www.mass.gov/eohhs/docs/dph/injury-surveillance/suicide/suicide-update-winter-2015.pdf

MATHER, INCREASE, A CALL TO THE TEMPTED: A SERMON ON THE HORRID CRIME OF SELF-MURDER (1682).

Mathews, Martha, *Suicidal Competence and the Patient's Right to Refuse Lifesaving Treatment*, 75 CAL. L. REV. 707, 754 (1987).

Mathis, Jennifer, *Keeping Families Together: Preserving the Rights of Parents with Disabilities*, 46 CLEARINGHOUSE REV. J. POVERTY L. & POL'Y 517 (Mar./Apr. 2013).

McGann, Vanessa L., Nina Gutin, & John R. Jordan, *Guidelines for Postvention Care with Survivor Families after the Suicide of a Client*, in GRIEF AFTER SUICIDE: UNDERSTANDING THE CONSEQUENCES AND CARING FOR SURVIVORS (John R. Jordan & John L. McIntosh eds., 2011).

McLeod, Adam, *A Gift Worth Dying For?: Debating the Volitional Nature of Suicide in the Law of Personal Property*, 45 IDAHO L. REV. 93 (2008).

Meier, Diane E., et al., *A National Survey of Physician-Assisted Suicide and Euthanasia in the United States*, 338 NEW ENG. J. MED. 1193 (1998).

MICHEL, CONRAD, & DAVID JOBES, EDS., BUILDING A THERAPEUTIC ALLIANCE WITH THE SUICIDAL PATIENT (2011).

MICHEL, KONRAD, THE SUICIDAL PATIENT AND THE AESCHI PHILOSOPHY (Mayo School of Continuous Professional Development, Aeschi West: Basic Principles in Working with Suicidal Adults, May 30, 2013), www.aeschiconference.unibe.ch/Aeschi%20Introduction.pdf.

Miles, Steven H., & Allison August, *Courts, Gender and "The Right to Die,"* 18 L. MED. & HEALTH CARE, 85–95 (Spring-Summer, 1990).

Miller, Daryl, *Legal Killing: The Imminent Legalization of a Physician's Affirmative Aid-in-Dying*, 34 Santa Clara L. Rev. 663 (1994).

Miller, M., D. Azrael, & D. Hemenway, *Firearm Availability and Suicide, Homicide, and Unintentional Firearm Deaths Among Women*, 79 J. Urban Health 26 (2002).

Miller, M., D. Azrael, L. Hepburn, D. Hemenway, & S.J. Lippmann, *The Association Between Changes in Household Firearm Ownership and Rates of Suicide in the United States, 1981–2002*, 12 Inj. Prev. 178 (2006).

Miller, M., & D. Hemenway, *Guns and Suicide in the United States*, 359 New Eng. J. Med. (2008).

Miller, M., S.J. Lippmann, D. Azrael, & D. Hemenway, *Household Firearm Ownership and Rates of Suicide Across the 50 United States*, 62 J. Trauma 1029 (2007).

Miller, Michael Craig, Douglas G. Jacobs, & Thomas Gutheil, *Talisman or Taboo: The Controversy of the Suicide-Prevention Contract*, 6 Harv. Rev. Psychiatry 78 (1998).

Minois, Georges, History of Suicide: Voluntary Death in Western Culture (Lydia Cochrane trans., 1999).

Mohandie, Kris, J. Reid Meloy, & Peter I. Collins, *Suicide by Cop Among Officer-Involved Shooting Cases*, 54 J. Forensic Sci. 456 (2009).

Mossman, Doug, *Defensive Medicine: Can It Increase Your Malpractice Risk?* 8 Current Psychiatry (Dec. 1, 2009).

Motto, J.A., & A.G. Bostrom, A Randomized Controlled Trial of Postcrisis Suicide Prevention, 52 Psychiatric Serv. 828 (2001).

Muehlenkamp, J.J., & P.M. Gutierrez, *Risk for Suicide Attempts Among Adolescents Who Engage in Non-Suicidal Self-Injury*, 11 Arch. Suicide Res. 69 (2007).

Najmi, Sadia, Daniel M. Wegner, Matthew K. Nock, *Thought Suppression and Self-Injurious Thoughts and Behaviors*, 45 Behav. Res. & Therapy 1957 (2007).

National Action Alliance for Suicide Prevention: Suicide Attempt Survivors Taskforce, The Way Forward: Pathways to Hope, Recovery and Wellness with Insights from Lived Experience (July 2014), *available at* http://actionallianceforsuicideprevention. org/sites/actionallianceforsuicideprevention.org/files/ The-Way-Forward-Final-2014-07-01.pdf.

National Bioethics Advisory Commission, Research Involving Persons with Mental Disorders That May Affect Decisionmaking Capacity (1998).

National Council on Disability, Rocking the Cradle: Ensuring the Rights of Parents with Disabilities and Their Children (2012), *available at* http://www.ncd.gov/publications/2012/Sep272012/.

National Institutes of Health, *Estimates of Funding for Various Research, Condition, and Disease Conditions (RCDC)*, Feb. 5, 2015, *available at* http:// report.nih.gov/categorical_spending.aspx.

New York State Task Force on Life and the Law, When Death Is Sought: Assisted Suicide and Euthanasia in the Medical Context (1994).

Nordentoft, Merete, Ping Qin, Karin Helwig-Larsen, & Knud Juel, *Restrictions in Means for Suicide: An Effective Tool in Preventing Suicide: The Danish Experience*, 37 Suicide & Life-Threatening Behav. 688 (2007).

Nuland, Sherwin, *Accidents, Suicide and Euthanasia,* in How We
    Die: Reflections on Life's Final Chapter 140–62 (1995).
Oregon Health Authority, Death with Dignity Annual
    Report (1999, 2000), *available at* https://public.health.oregon.gov/
    ProviderPartnerResources/EvaluationResearch/DeathwithDignityAct/
    Pages/ar-index.aspx.
Oregon Health Authority, Death with Dignity Annual
    Report (2008, 2009), *available at* https://public.health.oregon.gov/
    ProviderPartnerResources/EvaluationResearch/DeathwithDignityAct/
    Pages/ar-index.aspx.
Oregon Department of Health, Death with Dignity Act—2013, 2014,
    available at http://public.health.oregon.gov/ProviderPartnerResources/
    EvaluationResearch/DeathwithDignityAct/Documents/year16.pdf.
Oregon Department of Health, Death with Dignity Act—2014, 2015,
    available at https://public.health.oregon.gov/ProviderPartnerResources/
    EvaluationResearch/DeathwithDignityAct/Documents/year17.pdf.
Organisation for Economic Co-operation and Development (OECD), *Suicides,*
    in OECD Factbook 2013: Economic, Environmental and Social
    Statistics (Nov. 20, 2013), *available at* http://www.oecd-ilibrary.org/
    economics/oecd-factbook-2013_factbook-2013-en.
Oquendo, M.A., D. Currier, & J.J. Mann, Review: *Prospective Studies of Suicidal
    Behavior in Major Depressive and Bipolar Disorders: What is the Evidence for
    Predictive Risk Factors?* Acta Psychiatrica Scand. 114: 151–58 (2006).
Paris, Joel, Half in Love with Death: Managing the Chronically
    Suicidal Patient (2006).
Paris, Joel, *Managing Suicidality in Patients with Borderline Personality Disorder,*
    Psychiatric Times, July 1, 2006, http://www.psychiatrictimes.com/articles/
    managing-suicidality-patients-borderline-personality-disorder.
Parker, F.R. Jr., *Washington v. Glucksberg and Vacco v. Quill: An Analysis of the
    Amicus Curiae Briefs and the Supreme Court's Majority and Concurring
    Opinions,* 43 St. Louis L.J. 469 (1999).
Patching, J., & J. Lawler, *Understanding Women's Experiences of Developing an
    Eating Disorder and Recovering: A Life History Approach,* 16 Nurs. Inq. 10
    (2009).
Perlin, Michael L., *Everything's A Little Upside Down, As a Matter of Fact the
    Wheels Have Stopped: The Fraudulence of the Incompetency Evaluation
    Process,* 4 Houston J. Health L. & Pol'y 239 (2004).
Pettit, J.W., et al., *Thought Suppression and Suicidal Ideation: Preliminary
    Evidence in Support of a Robust Association,* 26 Depress Anxiety 758
    (2009).
Pokorny, A.D., *Prediction of Suicide in Psychiatric Patients: Report of a Prospective
    Study,* 40 Arch. Gen. Psychiatry 249 (1983).
Pokorny, A.D., *Suicide Prediction Revisited,* 23 Suicide & Life-Threatening
    Behav. 1 (1993).
Pratt, David, *Too Many Physicians: Physician-Assisted Suicide after Glucksberg/
    Quill,* 9 Alb. L.J. Sci. & Tech. 161, 203 (1999).
President's Commission for the Study of Ethical Problems in Medicine
    and Biomedical and Behavioral Research, Deciding to Forego Life-
    Sustaining Treatment (1983).

PRESIDENT'S COMMISSION FOR THE STUDY OF ETHICAL PROBLEMS IN MEDICINE AND BIOMEDICAL AND BEHAVIORAL RESEARCH, DEFINING DEATH (1981).

PRESIDENT'S COMMISSION FOR THE STUDY OF ETHICAL PROBLEMS IN MEDICINE AND BIOMEDICAL AND BEHAVIORAL SCIENCES, MAKING HEALTH CARE DECISIONS (1982).

Prokopetz, Julian J.Z., & Lisa Soleymani Lehmann, *Redefining Physicians' Role in Assisted Dying*, 367 NEW ENG. J. MED. 97 (2012).

Pugliese, J. *Don't Ask, Don't Tell: The Secret Practice of Physician-Assisted Suicide*, 44 HASTINGS L.J. 1291 (1991–92).

Quill, Timothy, *Death and Dignity: A Case of Individualized Decisionmaking*, 324 NEW ENG. J. MED. 691 (1991).

Reed, Jerry, *Advancing Peer Support in Suicide Prevention*, SUICIDE PREVENTION RESOURCE CENTER, Mar. 8, 2013, http://www.sprc.org/directorsblog/ advancing-peer-support-suicide-prevention.

Relman, Arnold S., *The Saikewicz Decision: Judges as Physicians*, 298 NEW ENG. J. MED. 508 (Mar. 2, 1978).

Rich, Ben, *Suicidality, Refractory Suffering and the Right to Choose Death*, 13 AM. J. BIOETHICS 18 (2013).

Rich, Emma, *Anorexic (Dis)connection: Managing Anorexia as an Illness and Identity*, 28 SOC. HEALTH ILLNESS 284 (2006).

RISENHOOVER, C.C., THE SUICIDE LAWYERS: EXPOSING LETHAL SECRETS (2004).

Rogers, J.R., Lewis, M.M., & Subich, L.M. *Validity of the Suicide Assessment Checklist in an Emergency Crisis Center*, 80 J. COUNS. & DEV. (2002).

Ronquillo, L., A. Minassian, G.M. Wilkie, & M.P. Wilson, *Literature-Based Recommendations for Suicide Assessments in the Emergency Department: A Review*, 43 J. EMERG. MED. 836–42 (2012).

Rudd, David, Gregory Brown, Thomas Joyner, Kelly Cukrowicz, David Jobes, & Morton Silverman, *The Realities of Risk, the Nature of Hope, and the Role of Science: A Response to Cook and Van de Creek*, 46 PSYCHOTHERAPY RES. PRAC. & TRAINING 474 (2009).

Ryan, Christopher J., *Ethics, Psychiatry and End of Life Issues*, PSYCHIATRIC TIMES, June 8, 2010, http://www.psychiatrictimes.com/ ethics-psychiatry-and-end-life-issues.

Ryan, Christopher J., & Sascha Callaghan, *Legal and Ethical Aspects of Refusing Medical Treatment after a Suicide Attempt: The Wooltorton Case in the Australian Context*, 193 MED. J. AUST. 239 (2010).

Shahtamasebi, Said, *Problems with Interpreting and Reporting Suicide Research*, 1 DYNAMICS HUM. HEALTH 4 (2014), *available at* http://journalofhealth.co.nz/ wp-content/uploads/2014/12/DHH_Said_Problems.pdf.

Sheldon, Tony, *"Existential Suffering" Not a Justification for Euthanasia*, 323 BRIT. MED. J. 7326 (2001).

SCHERER, JENNIFER M., & RITA J. SIMON, EUTHANASIA AND THE RIGHT TO DIE: A COMPARATIVE PERSPECTIVE (1999).

Schneider, CARL E., ed., LAW AT THE END OF LIFE (2000).

Schuman, Gary, *Suicide and the Life Insurance Contract: Was the Insured Sane or Insane? That Is the Question—or Is It?* 28 TORT & INS. L.J. 745 (1993).

Schwartz, D.A., D.E. Flinn, & P.F. Slawson, *Suicide in the Psychiatric Hospital*, 132 Am. J. Psych. 150 (1975).

Schwartz, D.A., D.E. Flinn, & P.F. Slawson, *Treatment of the Suicidal Character*, 28 AM. J. PSYCHOTHERAPY 194 (1979).

Schwartz, Judith, *Death by Voluntary Dehydration: Suicide or the Right to Refuse a Life-Prolonging Measure?* 17 WIDENER L. REV. 351 (2011).

Schwartz, Victor E. *Civil Liability for Causing Suicide: A Synthesis of Law and Psychiatry*, 24 VAND. L. REV. 217 (1971).

Schwemm, Robert, & Michael Allen, *Seniors and the Fair Housing Act*, 90 IOWA L. REV. 121 (2004).

Seiden, R.L. *Where Are They Now?: A Followup of Suicide Attempters from the Golden Gate Bridge*, 8 SUICIDE & LIFE-THREATENING BEHAV. 203 (1978).

SHEN X., & L. MILLET, SUICIDE IN OREGON: TRENDS AND RISK FACTORS (Oregon Health Authority, 2012), *available at* www.oregon.gov/oha/amh/CSAC%20 Meeting%20Shedule/Suicide-in-Oregon-Report.pdf.

Shneidman, Edwin, Letter to the Editor: *Rational Suicide and Psychiatric Disorder*, 326 NEW ENG. J. MED. 889 (Mar. 26, 1992), *available at* www.nejm.org/doi/full/10.1056/NEJM199203263261311.

SHNEIDMAN, EDWIN, THE SUICIDAL MIND (1998).

Shneidman, Edwin, Thomas Insel, & Michael Phillips, *Rethinking the Role of Mental Illness in Suicide*, 167 AM. J. PSYCHIATRY 731 (2010).

Simon, O.R., A.C. Swann, K.E. Powell, L.B. Potter, M.J. Kresnow, & P.W. O'Carroll, *Characteristics of Impulsive Suicide Attempts and Attempters*, 32 SUICIDE & LIFE-THREATENING BEHAV. 49 (2001).

Simon, Robert, *Imminent Suicide: The Illusion of Short-Term Prediction*, 36 SUICIDE & LIFE-THREATENING BEHAV. 296 (2006).

SIMON, ROBERT, PREVENTING PATIENT SUICIDE: CLINICAL ASSESSMENT AND MANAGEMENT (2011).

Simon, Robert, *The Suicide Prevention Contract: Clinical, Legal and Risk-Management Issues*, 27 J. AM. ACAD. PSYCHIATRY & L. 445 (1999).

SIMON, ROBERT, & ROBERT HALES, EDS., THE AMERICAN PSYCHIATRIC ASSOCIATION'S TEXTBOOK OF SUICIDE ASSESSMENT AND MANAGEMENT (2006).

SIMON, ROBERT, & ROBERT HALES, EDS., THE AMERICAN PSYCHIATRIC ASSOCIATION'S TEXTBOOK OF SUICIDE ASSESSMENT AND MANAGEMENT (2006).

Simon, Robert, James L. Levenson, & Daniel W. Shuman, *On Sound and Unsound Mind: The Role of Suicide in Tort and Insurance Litigation*, 33 J. AM. ACAD. PSYCHIATRY L. 176 (June 2005).

Sloan, J.H., et al., *Firearm Regulations and Rates of Suicide: A Comparison of Two Metropolitan Areas*, 322 NEW ENG. J. MED. 369 (1990).

Smets, Tinne, et al., *Legal Euthanasia in Belgium: Characteristics of All Reported Euthanasia Cases*, 47 MED. CARE 1 (Dec. 2009).

SOLOMON, ANDREW, FAR FROM THE TREE: PARENTS, CHILDREN, AND THE SEARCH FOR IDENTITY (2012).

SOLOMON, ANDREW, THE NOONDAY DEMON: AN ATLAS OF DEPRESSION (2007).

Solomon, Andrew, *To an Aesthete Dying Young: In Memoriam T.R.K.*, *available at* http://andrewsolomon.com/articles/to-an-aesthete-dying-young/.

Sorrentino, Renee, *Performing Capacity Evaluations: What's Expected for Your Consult*, 13 CURRENT PSYCHIATRY 41 (2014).

Sontheimer, D., *Suicide by Advance Directive?* 34 J. MED. ETHICS e-4 (Sept. 2008).

Spike, J. *Physicians' Responsibilities in the Case of Suicidal Patients: Three Case Studies*, 9 J. CLIN. ETHICS 311 (1998).

Stanford, E.J., R.R. Goetz, & J.D. Bloom, *The No-Harm Contract in the Emergency Assessment of Suicidal Risk*, 55 J. CLIN. PSYCHIATRY 344 (1994).

STAYER, AMANDA, SUICIDE BY COP: AVERTING THE CRISIS (2011).

Stefan, Susan, *Accommodating Families: Using the Americans with Disabilities Act to Keep Families Together*, 2 ST. LOUIS U. J. HEALTH L. & POL'Y 135 (2008).

Stefan, Susan, *Beyond Residential Segregation: The Application of Olmstead to Segregated Employment Settings*, 26 GEO. ST. U. L. REV. 12 (2009).

Stefan, Susan, *Dead Serious About Plaintiffs*, 85 J. A.B.A. 104(Jan. 1999).

STEFAN, SUSAN, EMERGENCY DEPARTMENT TREATMENT OF PSYCHIATRIC PATIENTS: POLICY ISSUES AND LEGAL REQUIREMENTS (2006).

Stefan, Susan, *Leaving Civil Rights to the "Experts": From Deference to Abdication Under the Professional Judgment Standard*, YALE L. REV. (1992).

Stefan, Susan, *Silencing the Different Voice*, 47 U. MIAMI L. REV. 763 (1993).

Stefan, Susan, *You'd Have to be Crazy to Work Here: Worker Stress, the Abusive Workplace, and Title I of the ADA*, 31 LOYOLA L. REV. 795 (1998).

Steinbrook, R. *Physician-Assisted Death—From Oregon to Washington State*, 359 NEW ENG. J. MED. 2513 (Dec. 11, 2008).

Steinbrook R., & Bernard Lo, *The Case of Elizabeth Bouvia: Starvation, Suicide, or Problem Patient?* 146 ARCH. INTERN. MED. 161 (1986).

Stewart, C., C. Peisah, & B. Draper, *A Test for Mental Capacity to Request Assisted Suicide*, J. MED. ETHICS (2010), available at http://www.jme.bmj.com/content/early/2010/11/21/jme.2010.037564 (2010).

Stone, Alan, *The Right to Die: New Problems for Law and Medicine and Psychiatry*, 37 EMORY L. J. 627 (1988).

Suicide Risk, NATIONAL EPILEPSY FOUNDATION, http://www.epilepsy.com/learn/impact/mortality/suicide-risk.

Sullivan, Mark, Linda Ganzini, & Stuart J. Younger, *Should Psychiatrists Serve as Gatekeepers for Physician-Assisted Suicide?* 28 HASTINGS CENTER REP. 24 (1998).

SZASZ, THOMAS, FATAL FREEDOM: THE ETHICS AND POLITICS OF SUICIDE (2002).

Tan, Jacinta, Tony Hope, Anne Stewart, & Raymond Fitzgerald, *Competence to Make Treatment Decisions in Anorexia Nervosa: Thinking Processes and Values*, 13 PHILOS. PSYCHIATRY PSYCHOL. 267 (2006).

Tay, Hywote, & David Magnus, *Suicide and the Sufficiency of Surrogate Decisionmakers*, 13 AM. J. BIOETHICS 1 (2013).

Taylor, Anita Darcel, *By My Own Hand*, BELLEVUE LITERARY REV., 117–121 (2006).

Timmerman, Stefan, *The Fifty-One Percent Rule of Suicide*, in POSTMORTEM: HOW MEDICAL EXAMINERS EXPLAIN SUSPICIOUS DEATHS (Stefan Timmerman ed., 2006).

SCOTT, JENIECE, JENNIFER MATHIS, & IRA BURNIM, SUPPORTING PARENTS WITH PSYCHIATRIC DISABILITIES: A MODEL REUNIFICATION STATUTE (U. Penn Collaborative on Community Integration), http://www.bazelon.org/LinkClick.aspx?fileticket=Kxu0I14DT-A%3d&tabid=640 (last visited Nov. 13, 2015).

U.S. Air Force, *The Air Force Suicide Prevention Program: A Description of Program Initiatives and Outcomes* (Apr. 2001), *available at* http://dmna. ny.gov/r3sp/suicide/AFPAM44-160.pdf

U.S. Census Bureau, *State & County QuickFacts: California, May 28, 2015,* *available at* http://quickfacts.census.gov/qfd/states/06000.html.

U.S. Department of Justice, U.S. Attorney's Office, District of Connecticut, Press Release: Justice Department Settles Americans with Disabilities Act Case with Quinnipiac University, Jan. 12, 2015, http://www.justice.gov/usao/ct/ Press2015/20150112.html.

U.S. Department of Justice Civil Rights Division, Press Release: Settlement Agreement Between the U.S. of America, Louisiana Tech University, and the Board of Supervisors for the University of Louisiana System under the Americans with Disabilities Act, 2013, www.ada.gov/louisiana-tech.htm.

U.S. Department of Veterans Affairs, *Public Health: Publications List by Title* (2015), http://www.publichealth.va.gov/epidemiology/publications.asp.

U.S. Equal Employment Opportunity Commission, Enforcement Guidance on Disability-Related Inquiries and Medical Examinations of Employees Under the Americans with Disabilities Act (July 27, 2000), *available at* http://www.eeoc.gov/policy/docs/guidance-inquiries.html.

U.S. Surgeon General and the National Alliance for Suicide Prevention, National Strategy for Suicide Prevention: Goals and Objectives for Action (Sept. 2012), *available at* www.surgeongeneral.gov/ library/reports/national-strategy-suicide-prevention/index.html.

Virginia State Crime Commission, *SJR 381: Not Guilty by Reason of Insanity, a Bill Referral Study to the Senate Rules Committee and the General Assembly of Virginia* (May 2002).

Watts, Darryl, & Gethin Morgan, *Malignant Alienation: Dangers for Patients Who Are Hard to Like,* 164 Brit. J. Psychiatry 11(1994).

Webb, David. Thinking about Suicide: Contemplating and Comprehending the Urge to Die (2010).

Webb, R.T., et al., *Suicide Risk in Primary Care Patients with Major Physical Diseases: A Case Control Study,* 69 Arch. Gen. Psychiatry 256 (2012).

Webster, Daniel, & Marc Starnes, *Reexamining the Association between Child Access Prevention Gun Laws and Unintentional Shooting Deaths of Children,* 106 Pediatrics 1466 (2000).

Webster, Daniel, Jon Vernick, April Zeoli, & Jennifer Manganello, *Association Between Youth-Focused Firearm Laws and Youth Suicide,* 292 JAMA 594 (2004).

Werth, James L. Jr. Rational Suicide? Implications for Mental Health Professionals (1996).

Western Mass Recovery Learning Community, *Afiya,* www.westernmassrlc.org/ afiya (last visited Nov. 13, 2015).

Whybrow, Peter, A Mood Apart: Depression, Mania and Other Afflictions of the Self (1997).

Wiebe, D.J., *Homicide and Suicide Risks Associated with Firearms in the Home: A National Case Control Study,* 41 Ann. Emerg. Med. 771 (2003).

WMA Declaration of Malta on Hunger Strikers, World Medical Association (WMA, 1991), *available at* www.wma.net/en/30publications/10policies/h31.

World Health Organization, Guns, Knives and Pesticides: Reducing Access to Lethal Means (2009), www.who.int/mental_health/prevention/suicide/vip_pesticides.pdf.

Wurst, F.M., et al., *The Therapist's Reaction to a Patient's Suicide: Results of a Survey and Implications for Health Care Professionals' Wellbeing*, 32 Crisis 99 (2011).

Wolf, Susan M. *Gender, Feminism, and Death*, in Feminism and Bioethics: Beyond Reproduction (Susan M. Wolf ed., 1996).

Yuill, Kevin, Assisted Suicide: The Liberal, Humanist Case Against Legalization (2013).

Index